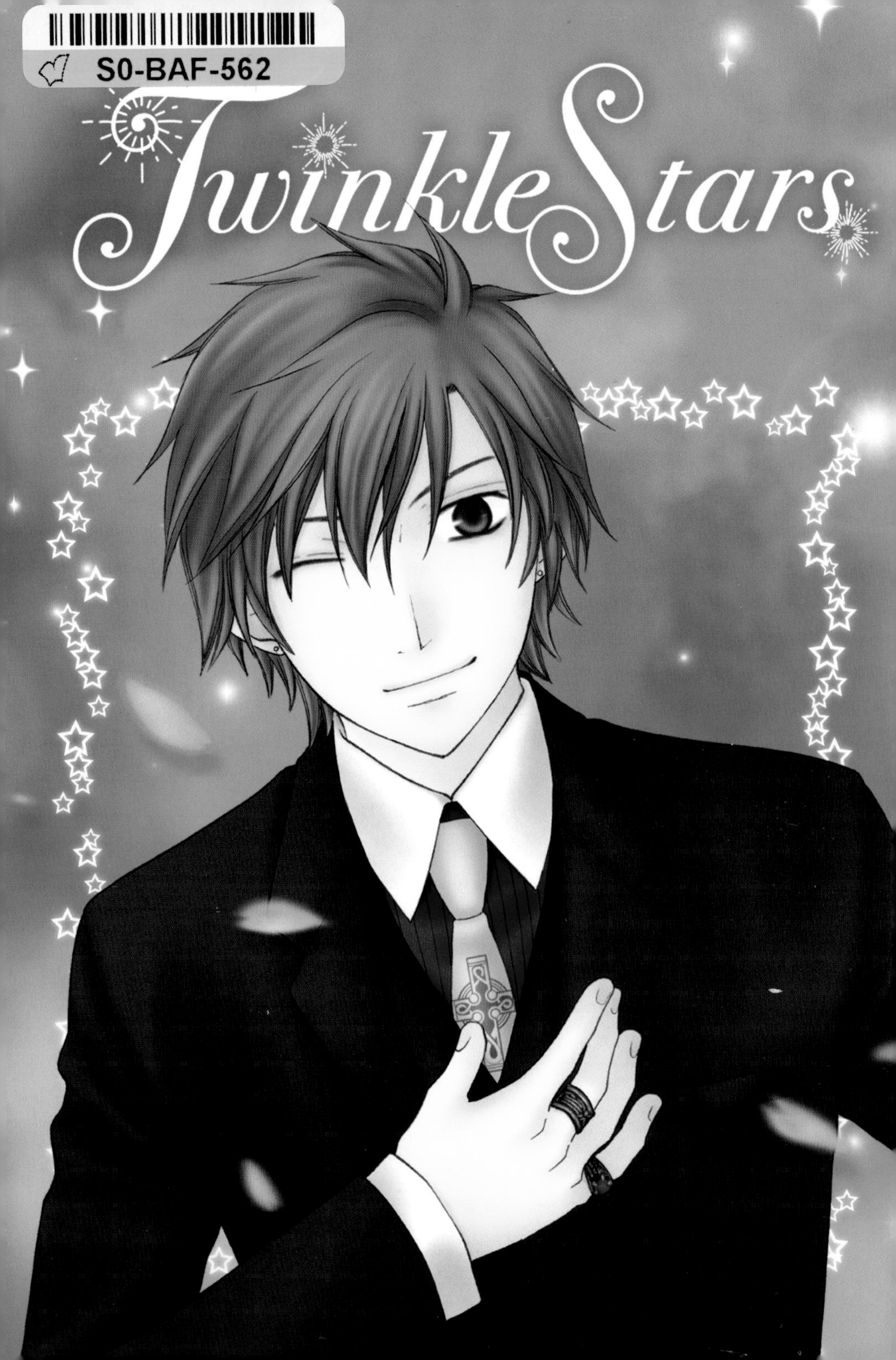
Twinkle Stars

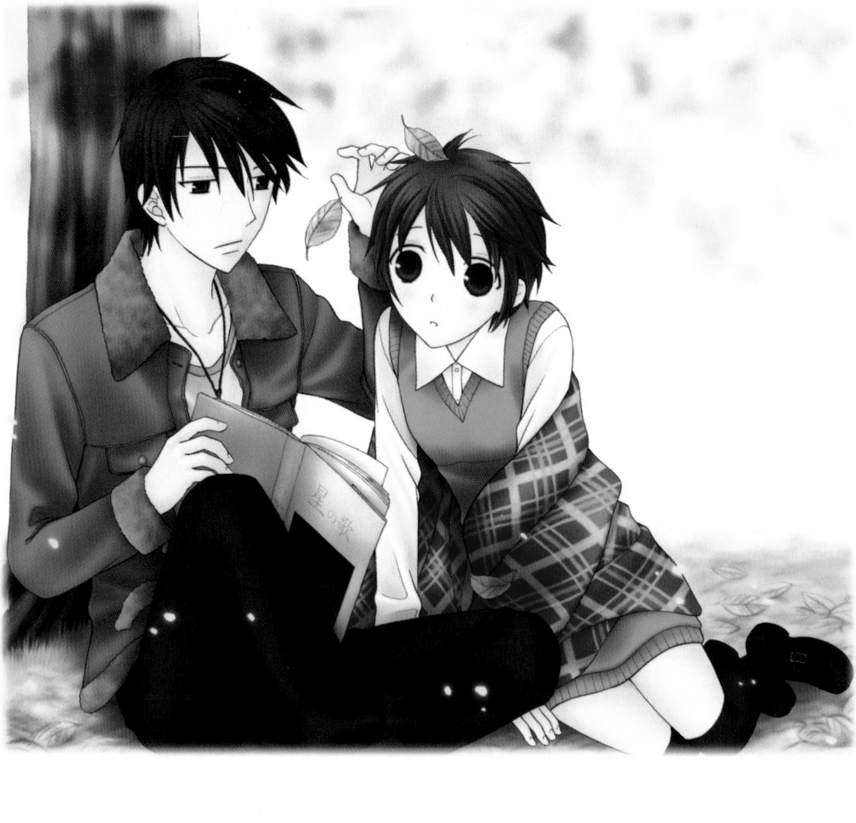
星の歌

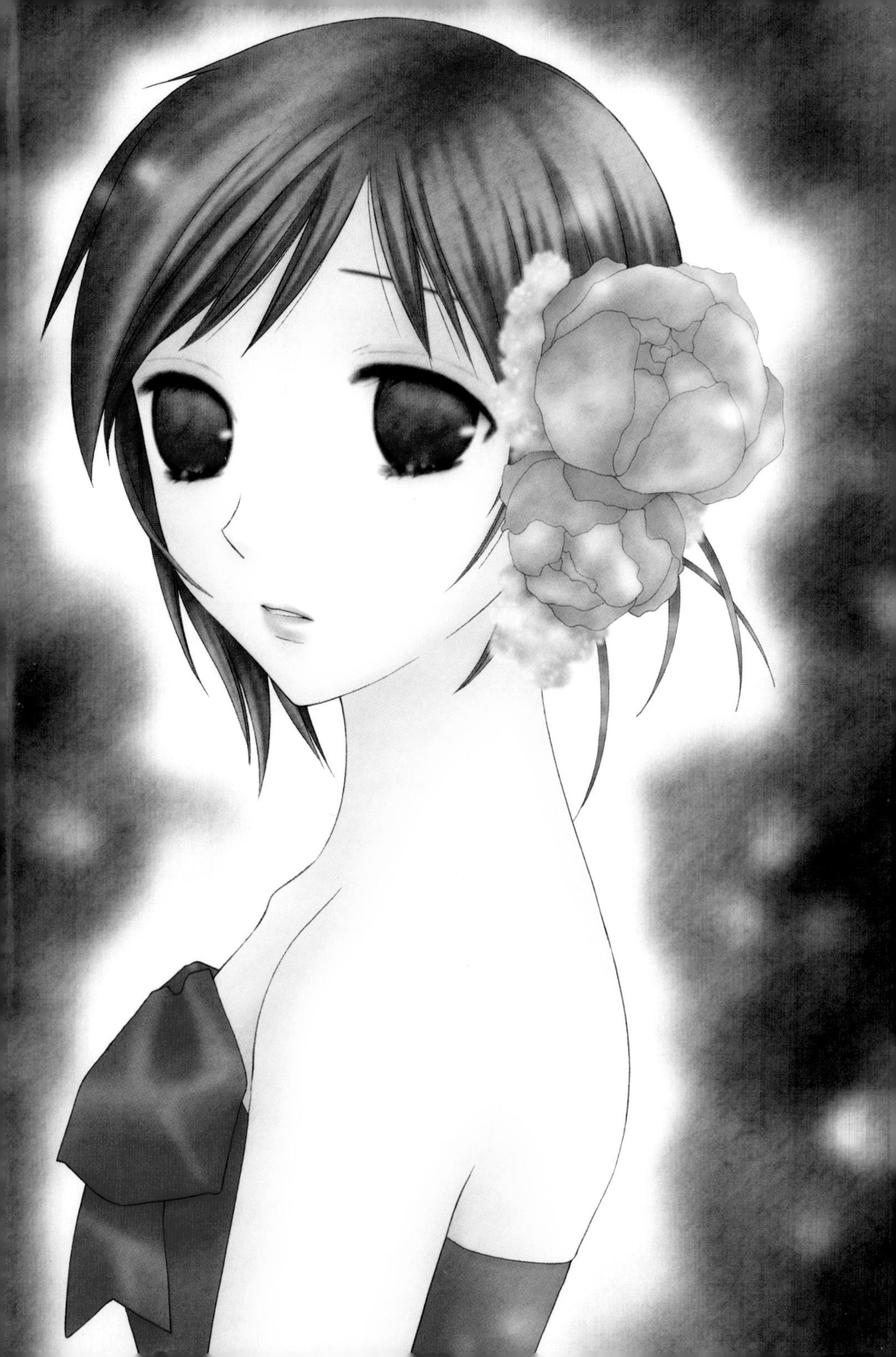

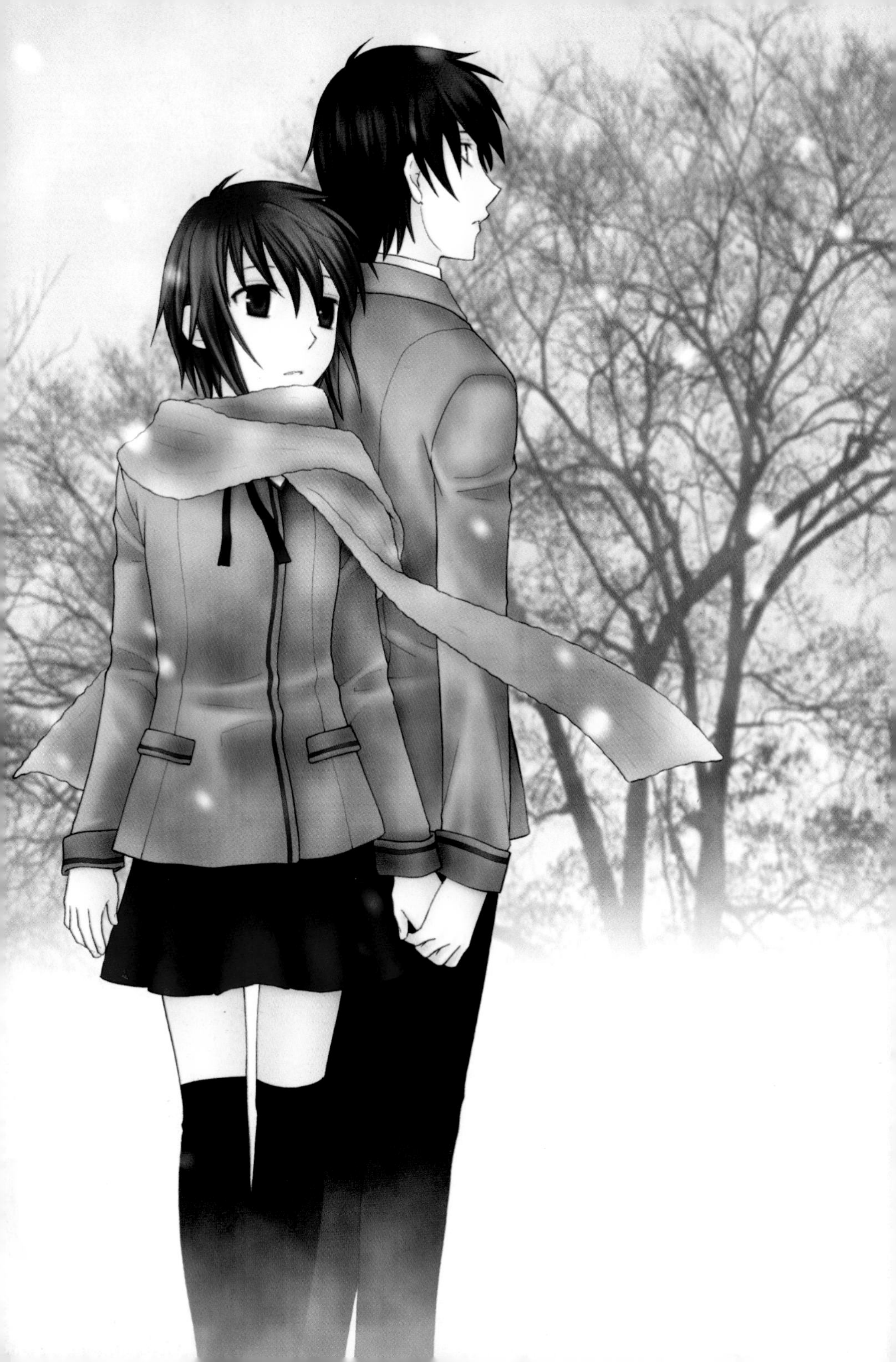

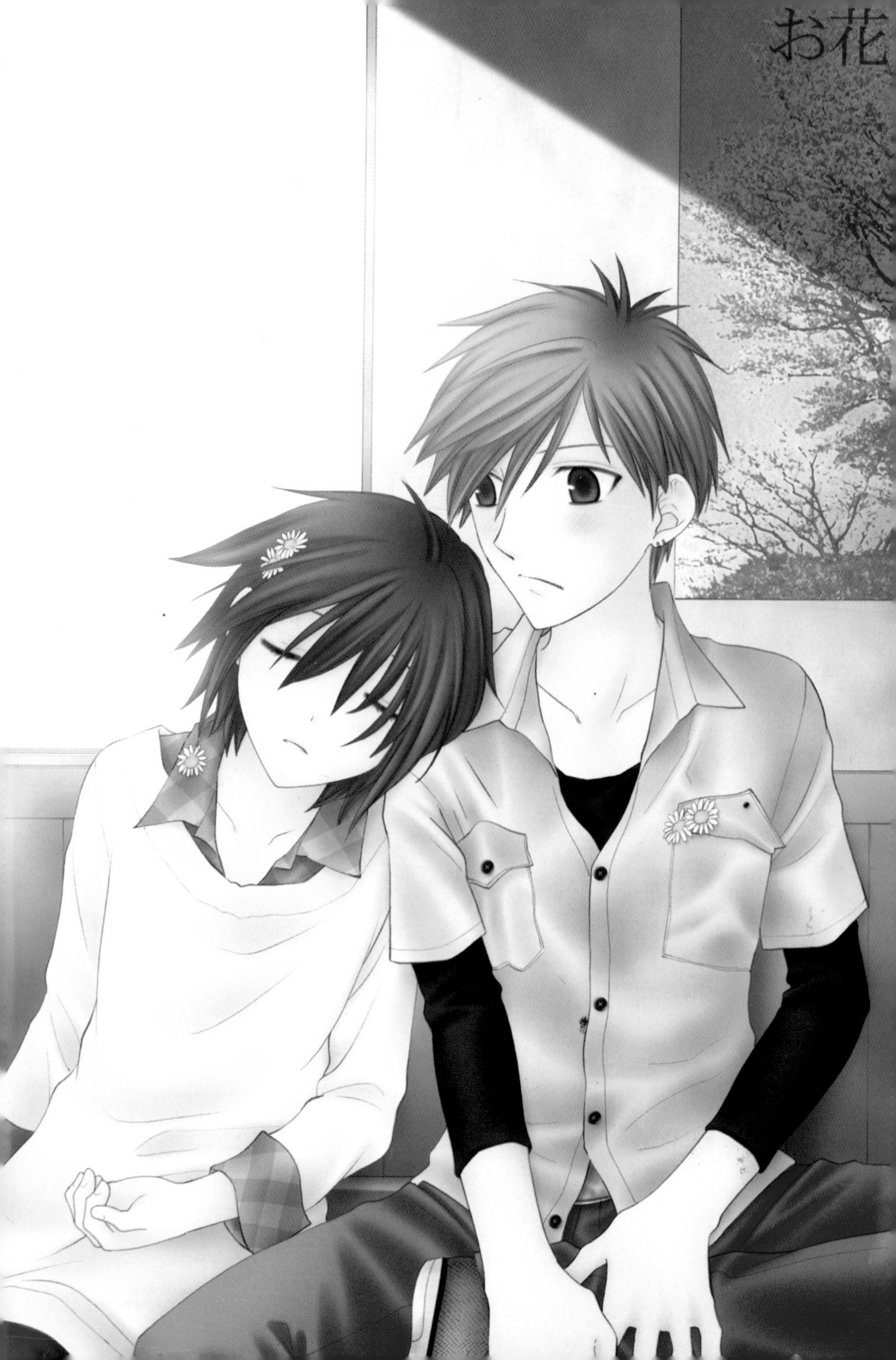
お花

Twinkle Stars

Volume 3

NATSUKI TAKAYA

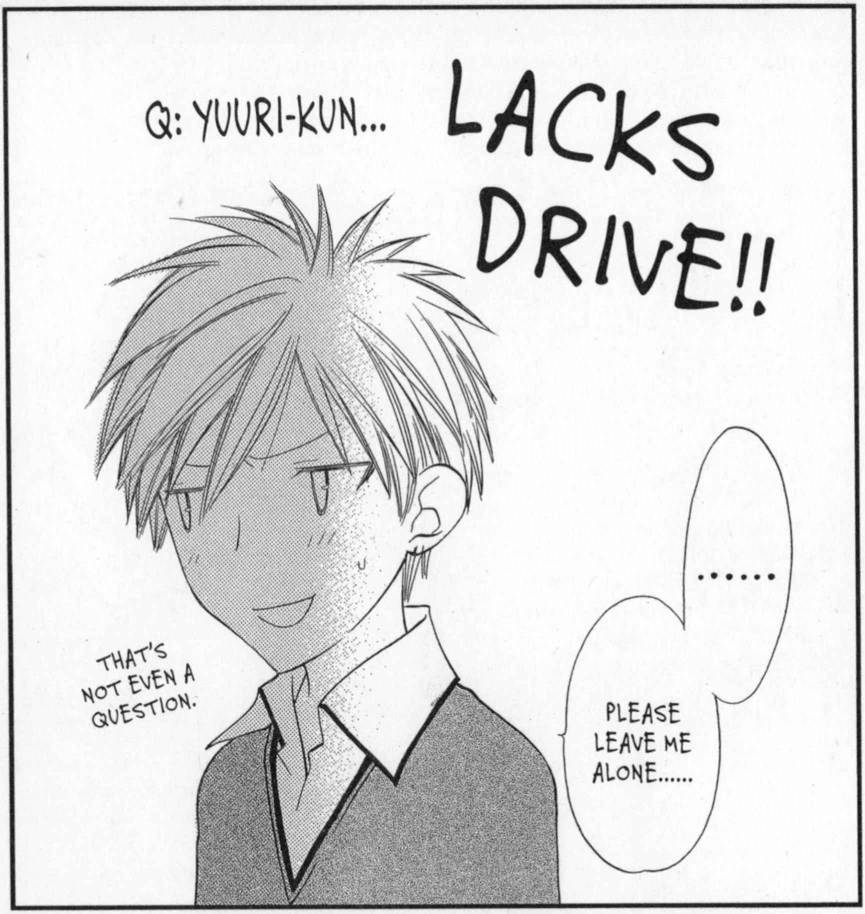
Q: YUURI-KUN... LACKS DRIVE!!
......
PLEASE LEAVE ME ALONE......
THAT'S NOT EVEN A QUESTION.

STORY & CHARACTER INTRODUCTION

STORY

▶Third-year high school student Sakuya Shiina lives with her cousin Kanade in a rural town by the sea. On her birthday, she encounters Chihiro, a mysterious boy who shows up at the house to celebrate with Kanade.

▶Sakuya can't stop thinking about his kind words to her, as well as his sad smile. She starts searching for Chihiro so she can see him and talk to him once more.

▶Finally, Sakuya is briefly reunited with Chihiro, but unlike their first meeting, Chihiro treats her coldly for some reason. In the end, he leaves after flatly rejecting her. Sakuya then realizes for the first time that she's fallen in love with Chihiro...

▶Sakuya is depressed, but thanks to the kindness of Hijiri, Yuuri, and Kanade, she's finally about to get over Chihiro when he suddenly transfers into her school!!

▶Sakuya's awkward relationship with Chihiro, who treats everyone but her nicely, continues. Everything changes when he saves her at the club information session. Sakuya uses this as an opportunity to get Chihiro to join the Star Appreciation Club (or "S.A.C." for short).

▶Chihiro gradually becomes kinder to her, and while Sakuya is overjoyed, she's also unsure how to interpret this kindness.

CHARACTERS

CHIHIRO AOI

Mysterious teen Sakuya met on her birthday; suddenly transfers into Sakuya's class; is mean to Sakuya exclusively for some reason

SAKUYA SHIINA

The main character; a third-year high school student who loves stars; lives with Kanade, her legal guardian; realizes she is in love with Chihiro after he rejects her...

KANADE

Lives with Sakuya as her foster parent; a deeply flawed individual; blunt and foulmouthed but is occasionally kind to Sakuya

Happy just to be around him and spend time with him, Sakuya hasn't even considered letting Chihiro know how she feels.

▶Meanwhile, Yuuri is fed up with Chihiro, who, in his view, seems to understand Sakuya a little too well. As events unfold, Yuuri realizes that he's in love with Sakuya.

▶The day of the club's summer camp arrives, and its members are still sorting out their feelings! Hoping to get even a little closer to Chihiro, Sakuya makes plans with him to go see the fireworks. Chihiro agrees, but with a hint of loneliness in his eyes...?

Who is Chihiro really thinking about ...?

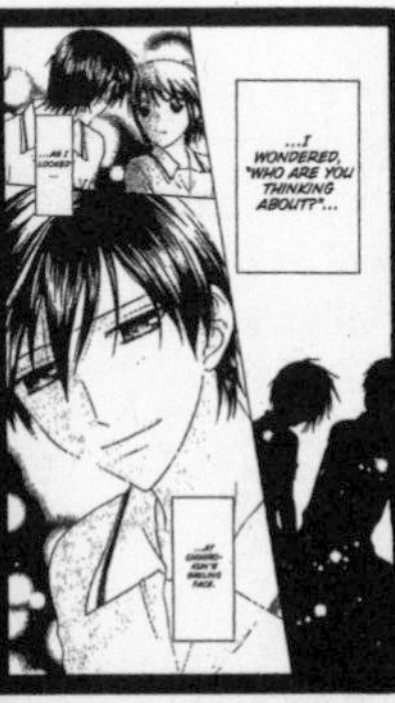
...I WONDERED, "WHO ARE YOU THINKING ABOUT?"...

Yuuri comes to terms with his feelings for Sakuya ...?

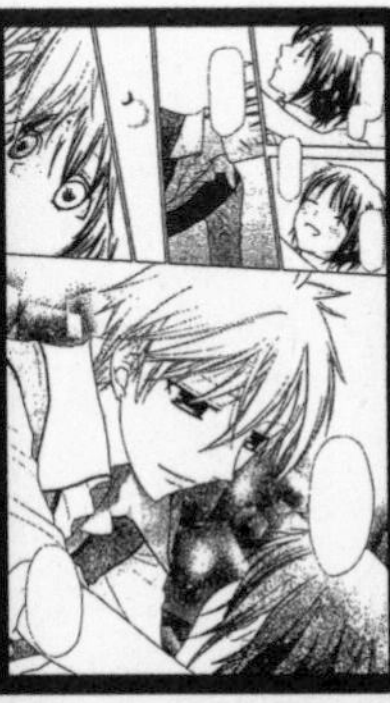

Little by little, the relationship among the three begins to change.

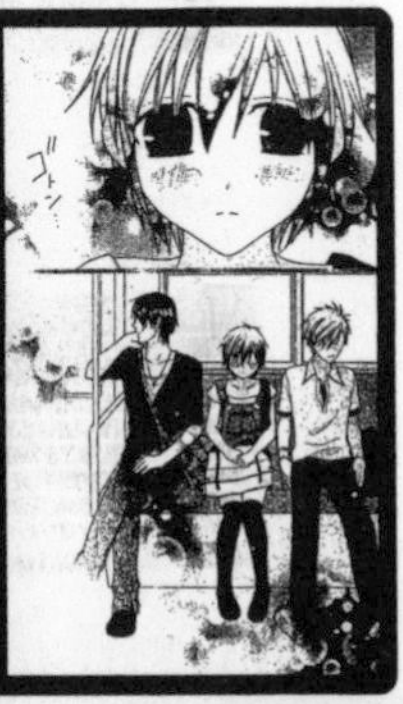

★

SHIZUKA KUTANI

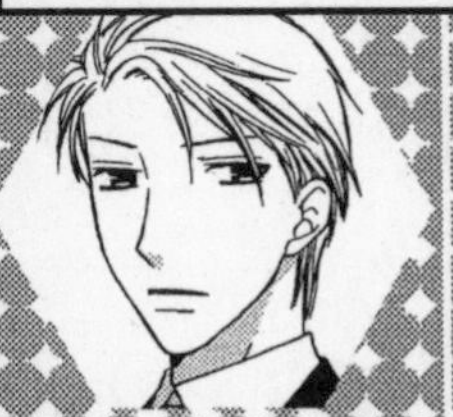

Sakuya's homeroom teacher and faculty adviser of the Star Appreciation Club

Sakuya's classmate and close friend; popular class clown; has feelings for Sakuya

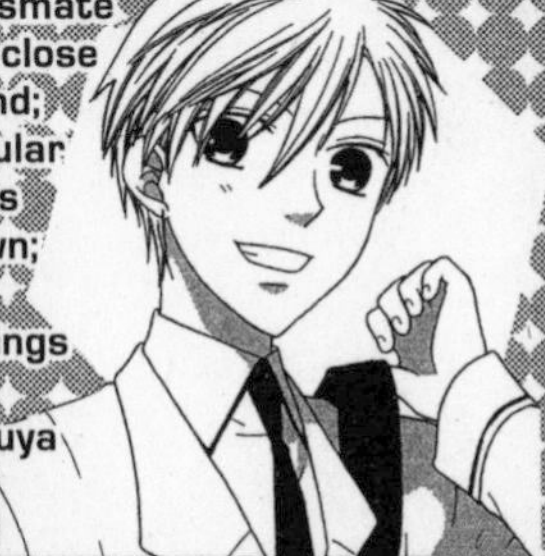

YUURI MURAKAMI

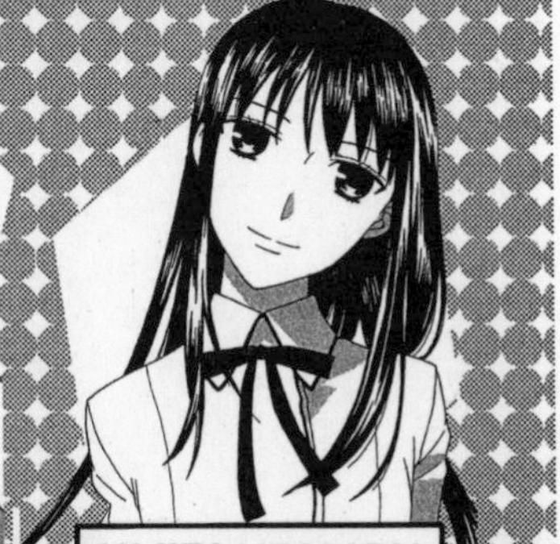

HIJIRI HONJOU

Sakuya's classmate and best friend; beautiful but has a sharp tongue; has a huge soft spot for Sakuya

Servant of the Honjou family; Hijiri's protector; extremely indulgent toward Hijiri

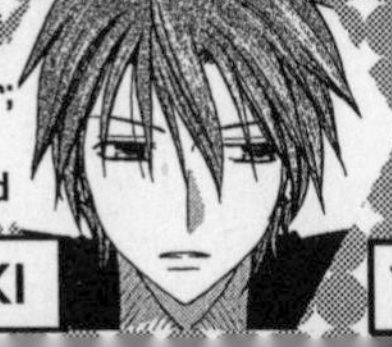

SAKI

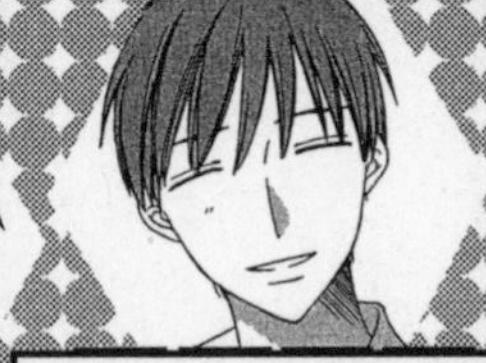

YUUTO MURAKAMI

Runs the family liquor store where Sakuya works; Yuuri's big brother

Twinkle Stars

3

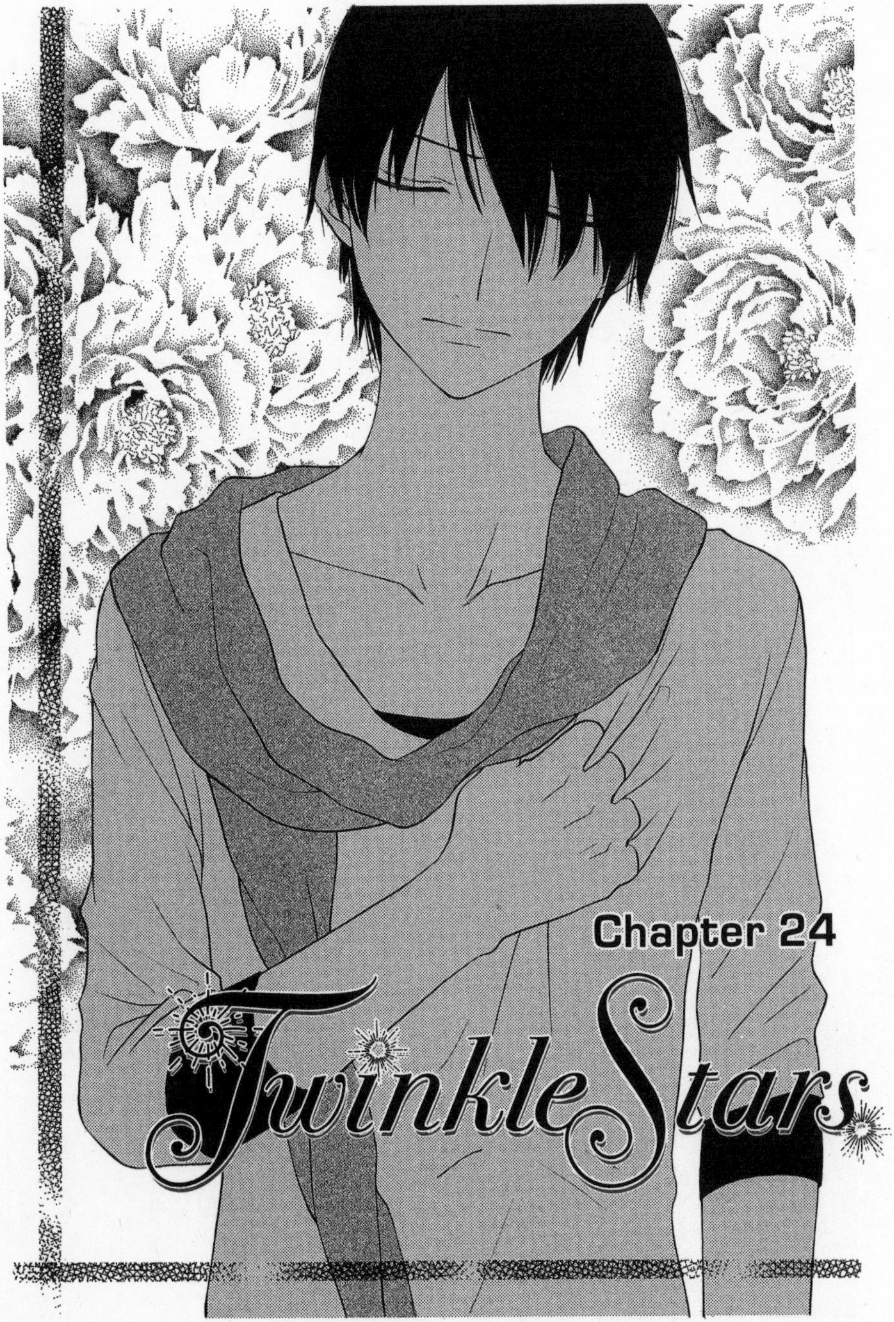
Chapter 24
Twinkle Stars

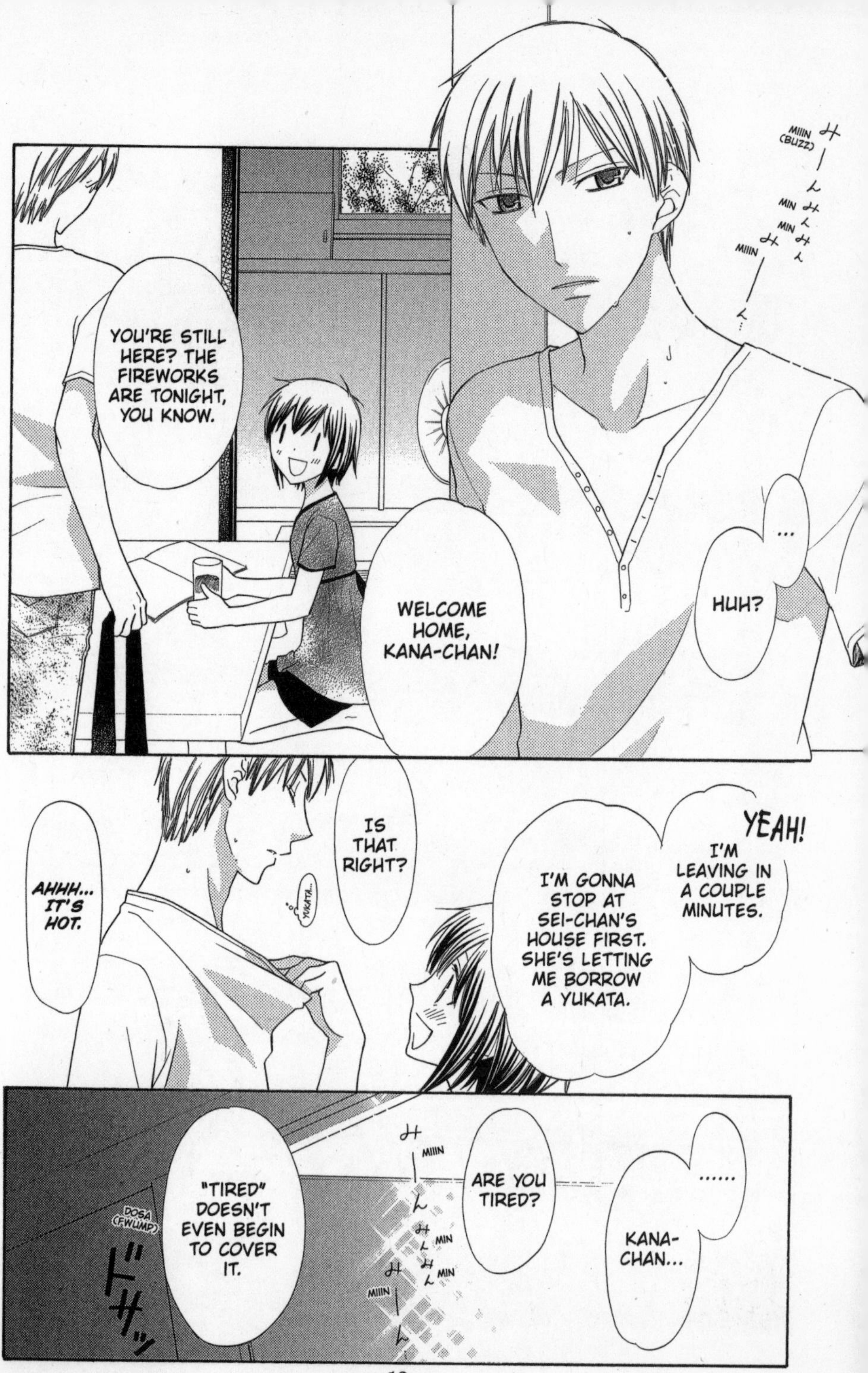
MIIIN (BUZZ)
MIN
MIN
MIIIN
...
HUH?
WELCOME HOME, KANA-CHAN!
YOU'RE STILL HERE? THE FIREWORKS ARE TONIGHT, YOU KNOW.
YEAH! I'M LEAVING IN A COUPLE MINUTES.
I'M GONNA STOP AT SEI-CHAN'S HOUSE FIRST. SHE'S LETTING ME BORROW A YUKATA.
IS THAT RIGHT?
YUKATA...
AHHH... IT'S HOT.
......
KANA-CHAN...
ARE YOU TIRED?
MIIIN
MIN
MIN
MIIIN
"TIRED" DOESN'T EVEN BEGIN TO COVER IT.
DOSA (FWUMP)

Twinkle Stars

Nice to meet you and hello.
I'm Takaya.
This is Volume 5 of Twinkle Stars.
This is the only sidebar of the volume. It's a serious story, so I wanted to avoid distracting from it as much as possible...
If there are sidebar fans out there, my apologies.

And now, Volume 5 begins.

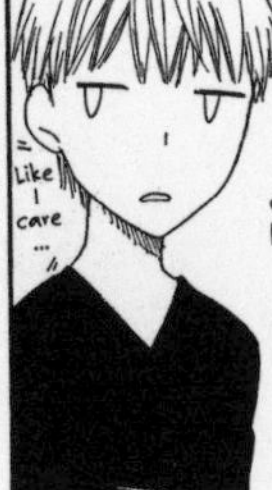

Like I care...
Kanade-chan is on the cover, but he barely appears in this volume.

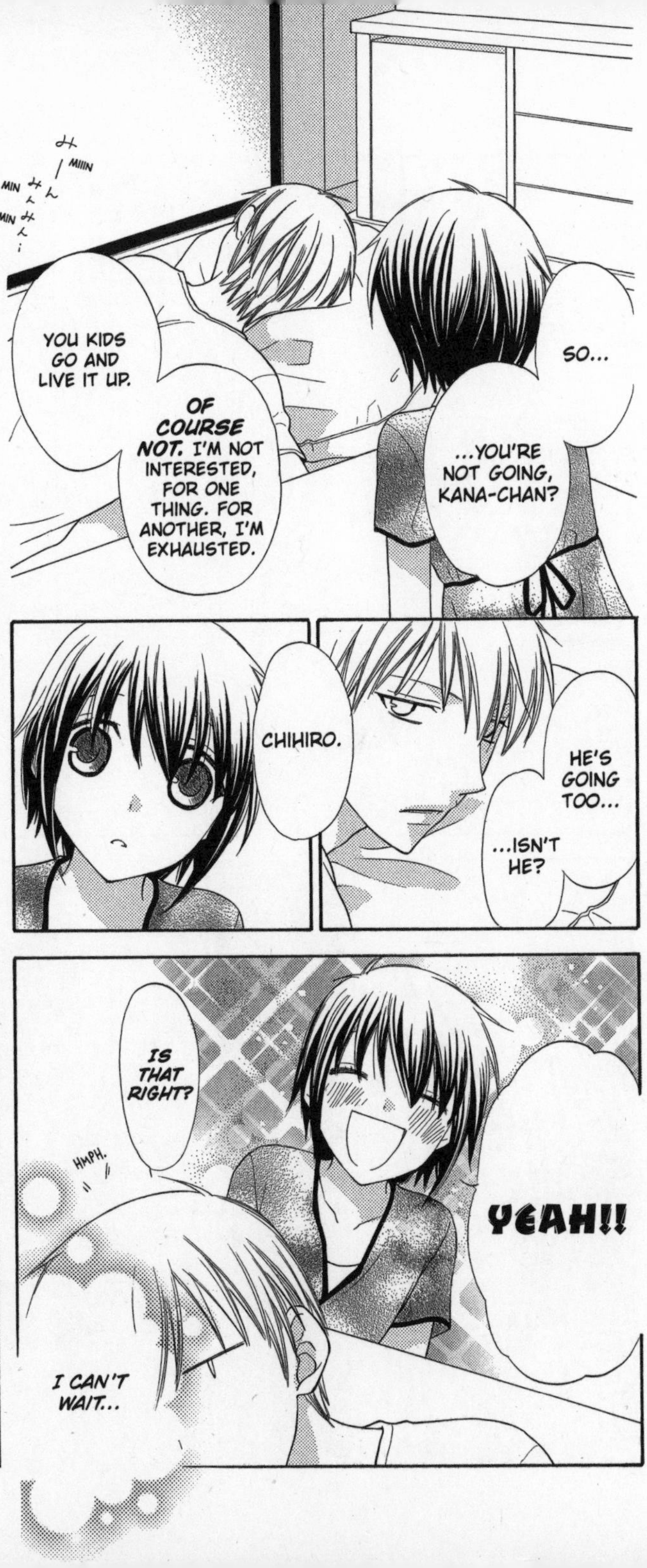

MIIIN
MIN
MIN
SO...
...YOU'RE NOT GOING, KANA-CHAN?
OF COURSE NOT. I'M NOT INTERESTED, FOR ONE THING. FOR ANOTHER, I'M EXHAUSTED.
YOU KIDS GO AND LIVE IT UP.
CHIHIRO.
HE'S GOING TOO...
...ISN'T HE?
YEAH!!
IS THAT RIGHT?
HMPH.
I CAN'T WAIT...

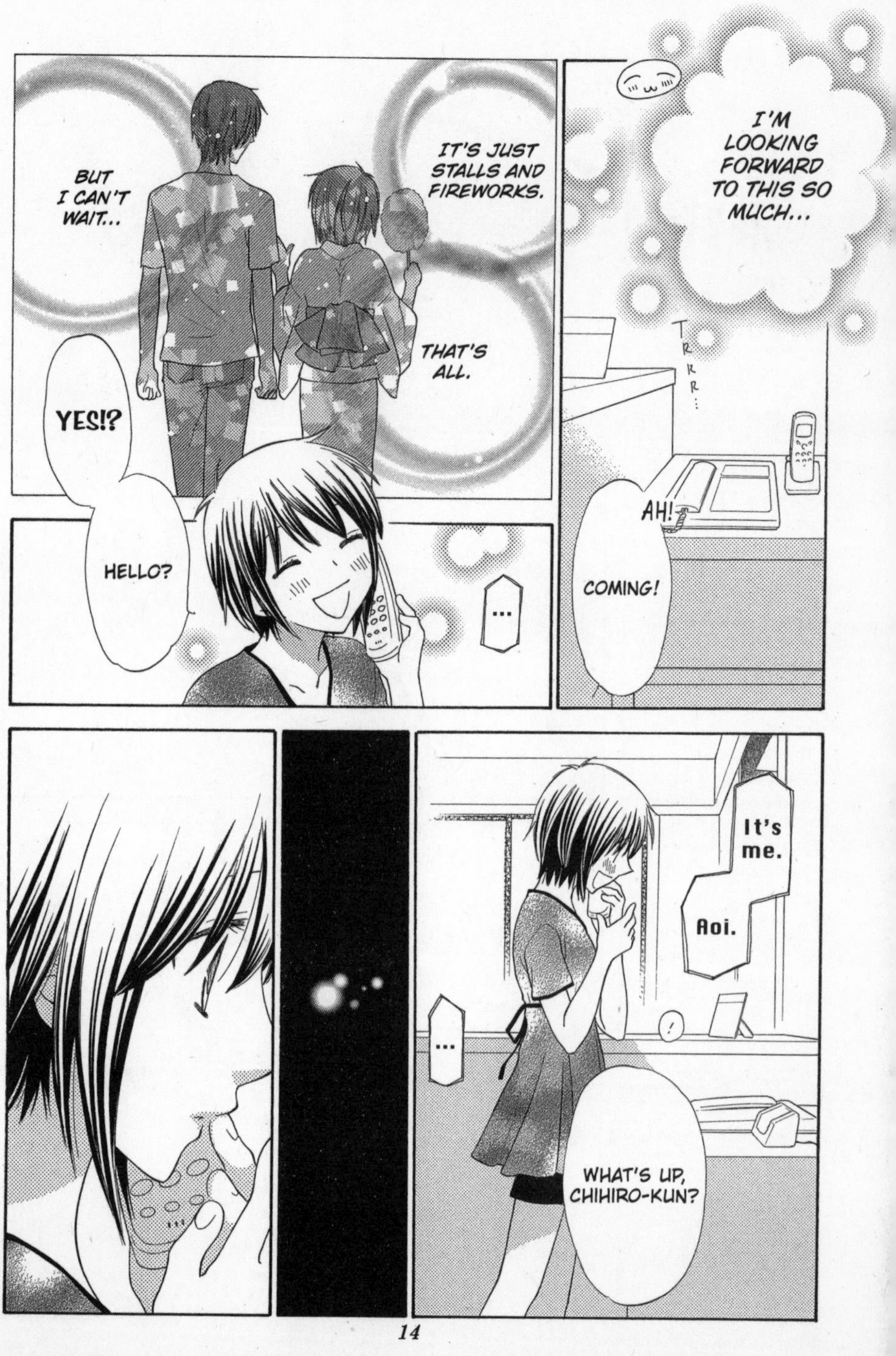

I'M LOOKING FORWARD TO THIS SO MUCH...
TRRR...
AH!
COMING!
IT'S JUST STALLS AND FIREWORKS.
BUT I CAN'T WAIT...
THAT'S ALL.
YES!?
...
HELLO?
It's me.
Aoi.
!
...
WHAT'S UP, CHIHIRO-KUN?

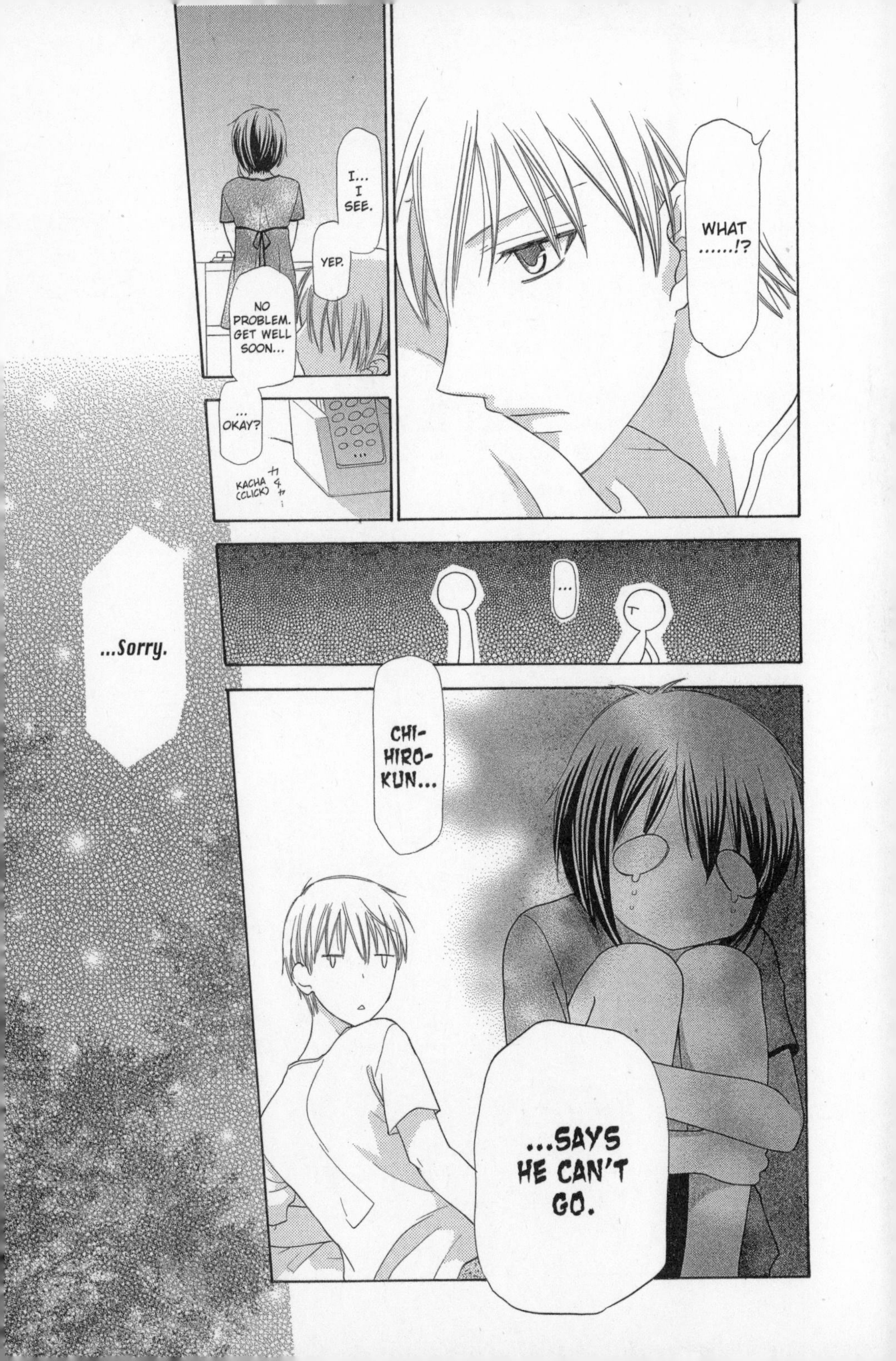
WHAT ......!?
I... I SEE.
YEP.
NO PROBLEM. GET WELL SOON...
... OKAY?
...
KACHA (CLICK)
...
...Sorry.
CHI-HIRO-KUN...
...SAYS HE CAN'T GO.

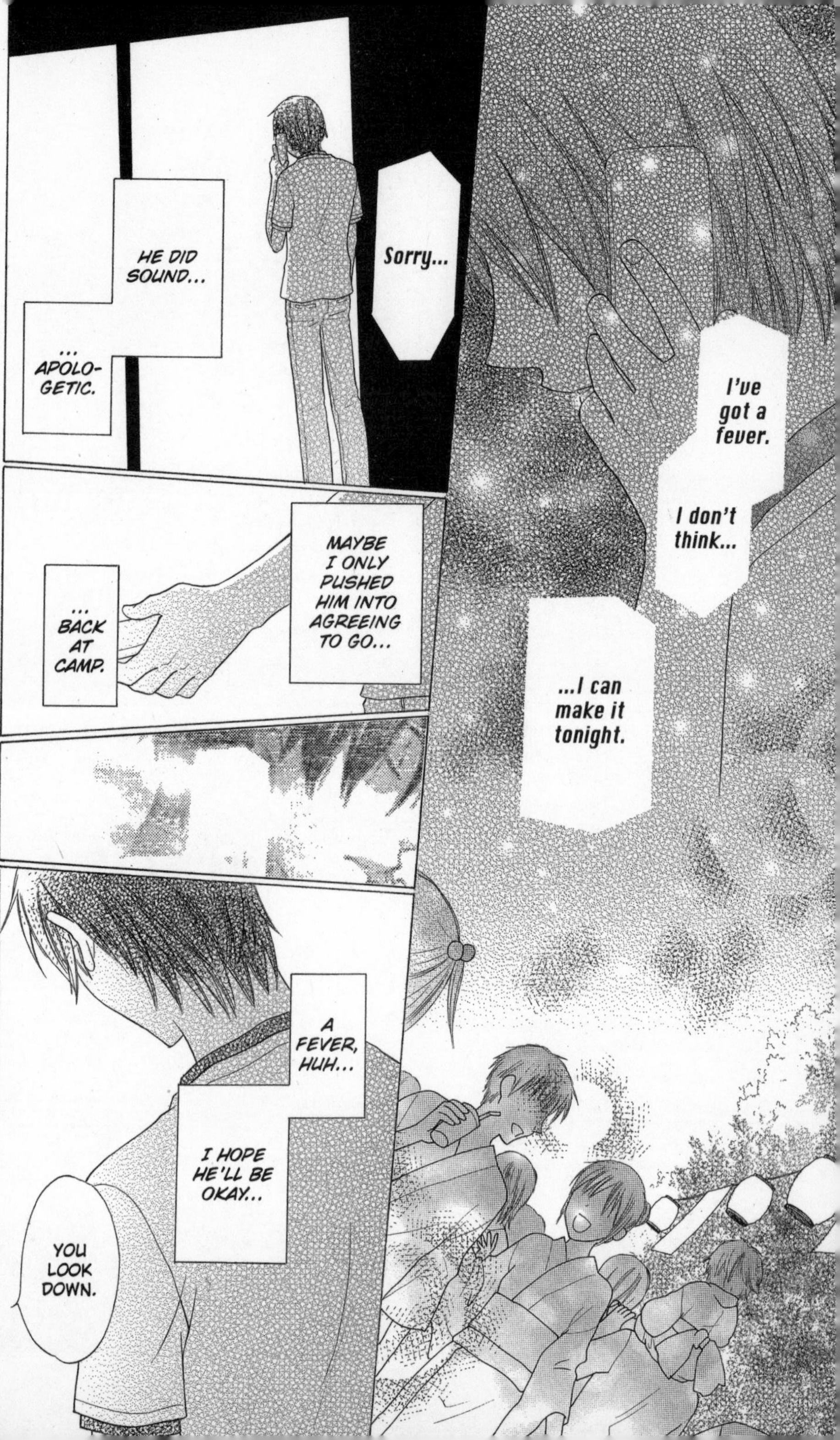
I've got a fever.
I don't think...
...I can make it tonight.
Sorry...
HE DID SOUND...
...APOLOGETIC.
MAYBE I ONLY PUSHED HIM INTO AGREEING TO GO...
...BACK AT CAMP.
A FEVER, HUH...
I HOPE HE'LL BE OKAY...
YOU LOOK DOWN.

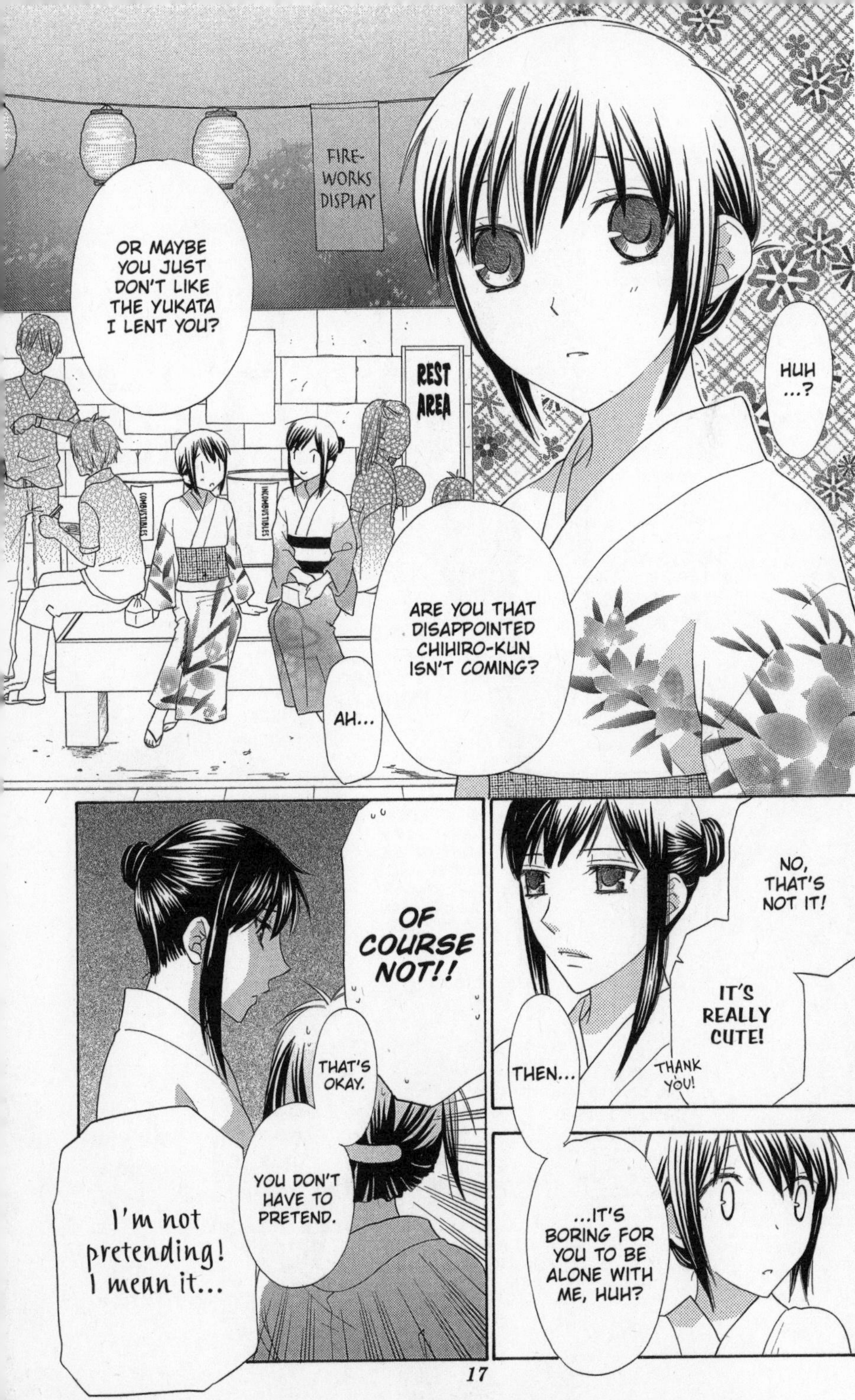
HUH ...?
ARE YOU THAT DISAPPOINTED CHIHIRO-KUN ISN'T COMING?
AH...
OR MAYBE YOU JUST DON'T LIKE THE YUKATA I LENT YOU?
FIRE-WORKS DISPLAY
REST AREA
INCOMBUSTIBLES
COMBUSTIBLES
NO, THAT'S NOT IT!
IT'S REALLY CUTE!
THANK YOU!
THEN...
...IT'S BORING FOR YOU TO BE ALONE WITH ME, HUH?
OF COURSE NOT!!
THAT'S OKAY.
YOU DON'T HAVE TO PRETEND.
I'm not pretending! I mean it...

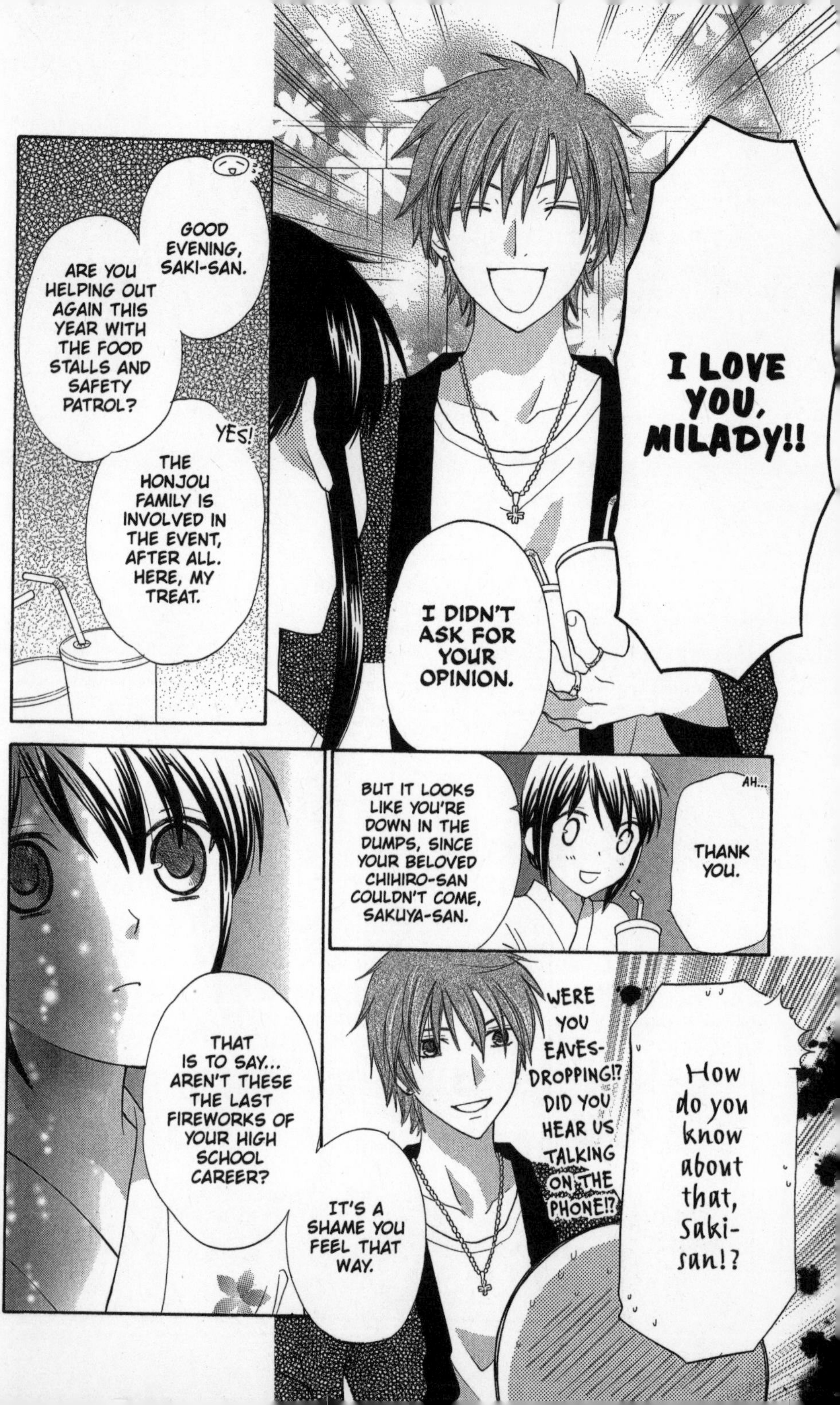
I LOVE YOU, MILADY!!
I DIDN'T ASK FOR YOUR OPINION.
GOOD EVENING, SAKI-SAN.
ARE YOU HELPING OUT AGAIN THIS YEAR WITH THE FOOD STALLS AND SAFETY PATROL?
YES!
THE HONJOU FAMILY IS INVOLVED IN THE EVENT, AFTER ALL. HERE, MY TREAT.
AH...
THANK YOU.
BUT IT LOOKS LIKE YOU'RE DOWN IN THE DUMPS, SINCE YOUR BELOVED CHIHIRO-SAN COULDN'T COME, SAKUYA-SAN.
How do you know about that, Saki-san!?
WERE YOU EAVES-DROPPING!? DID YOU HEAR US TALKING ON THE PHONE!?
THAT IS TO SAY... AREN'T THESE THE LAST FIREWORKS OF YOUR HIGH SCHOOL CAREER?
IT'S A SHAME YOU FEEL THAT WAY.

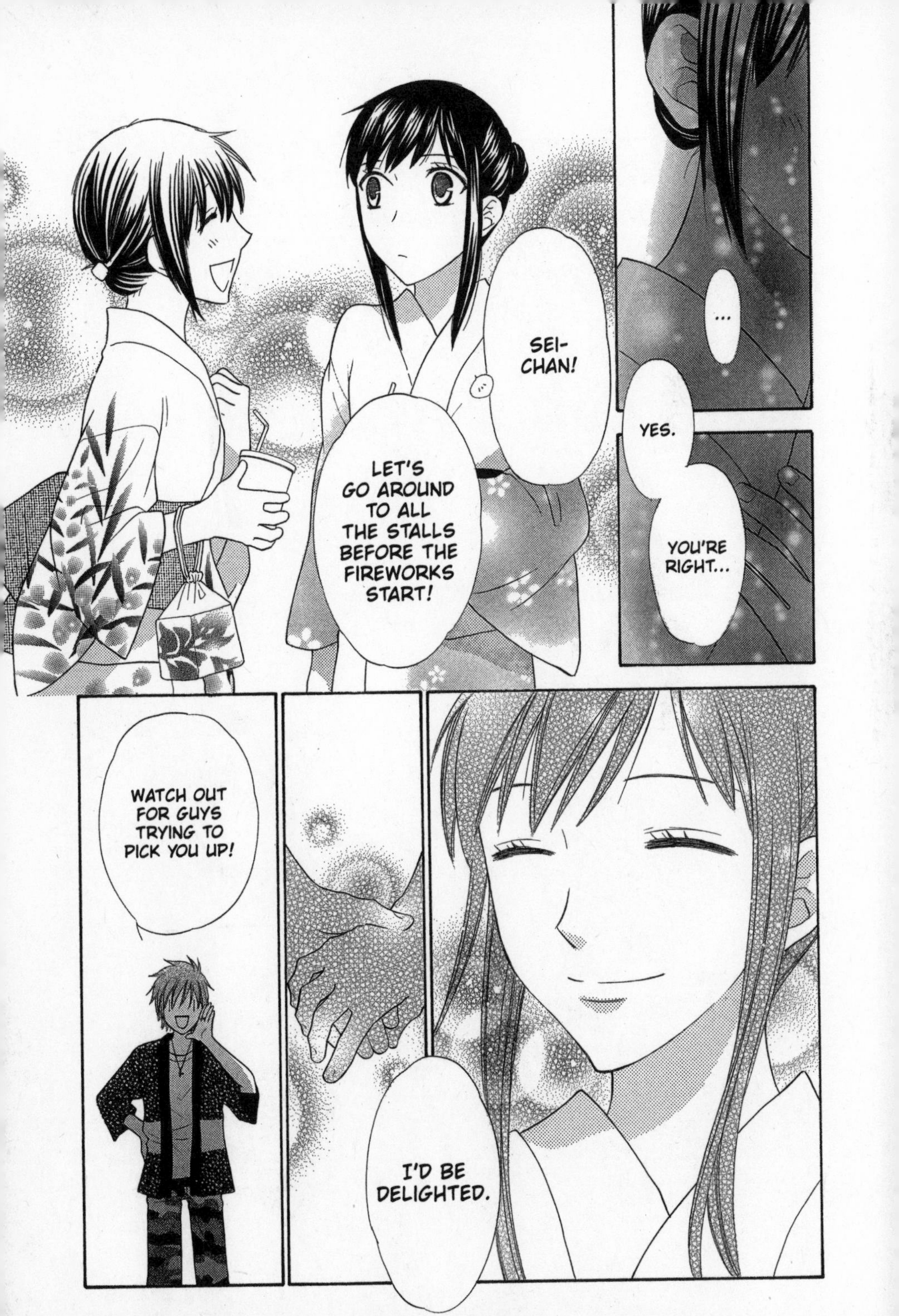
...
YES.
YOU'RE RIGHT...
SEI-CHAN!
LET'S GO AROUND TO ALL THE STALLS BEFORE THE FIREWORKS START!
I'D BE DELIGHTED.
WATCH OUT FOR GUYS TRYING TO PICK YOU UP!

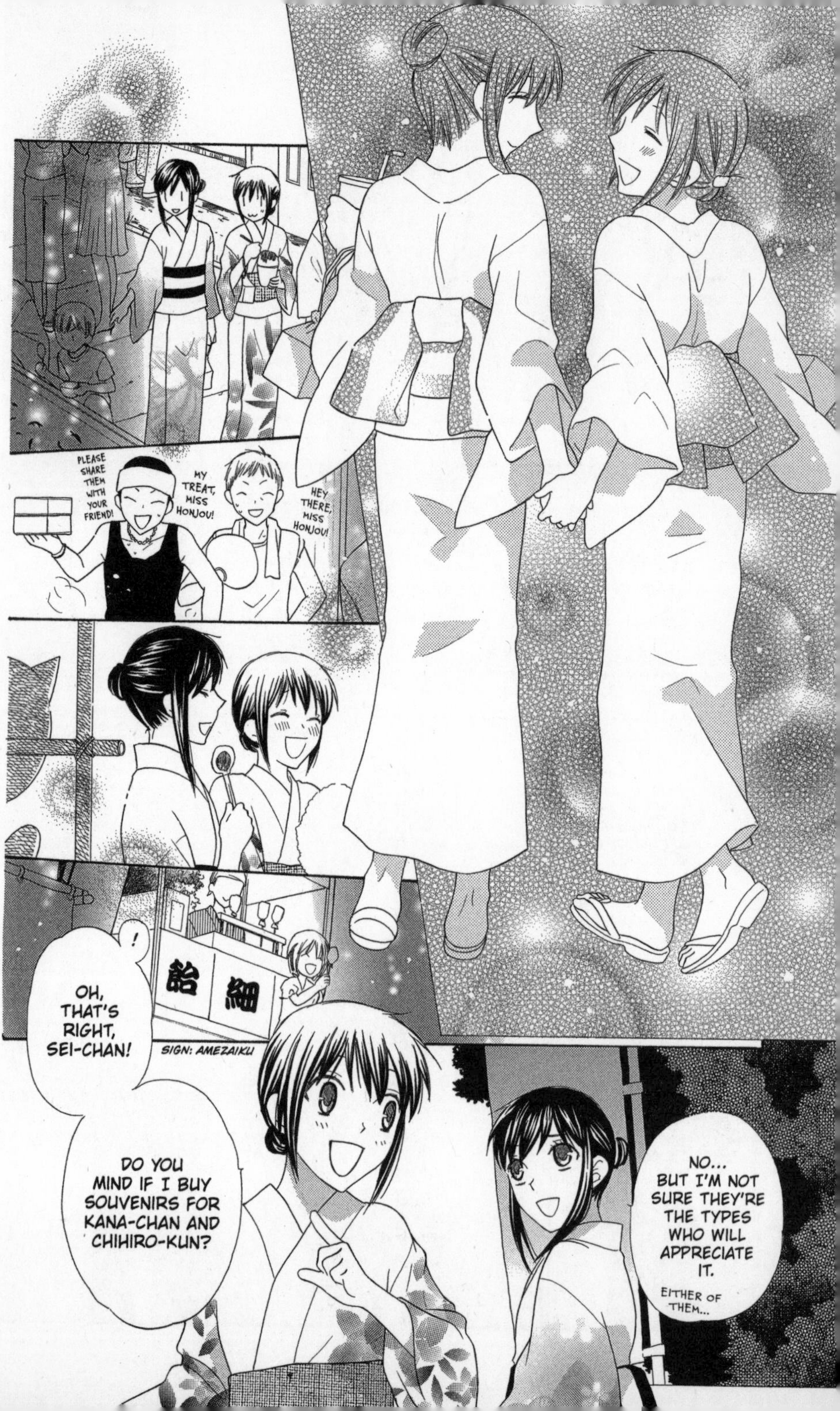
HEY, THERE, MISS HONJOU!
MY TREAT, MISS HONJOU!
PLEASE SHARE THEM WITH YOUR FRIEND!
!
OH, THAT'S RIGHT, SEI-CHAN!
SIGN: AMEZAIKU
DO YOU MIND IF I BUY SOUVENIRS FOR KANA-CHAN AND CHIHIRO-KUN?
NO... BUT I'M NOT SURE THEY'RE THE TYPES WHO WILL APPRECIATE IT.
EITHER OF THEM...

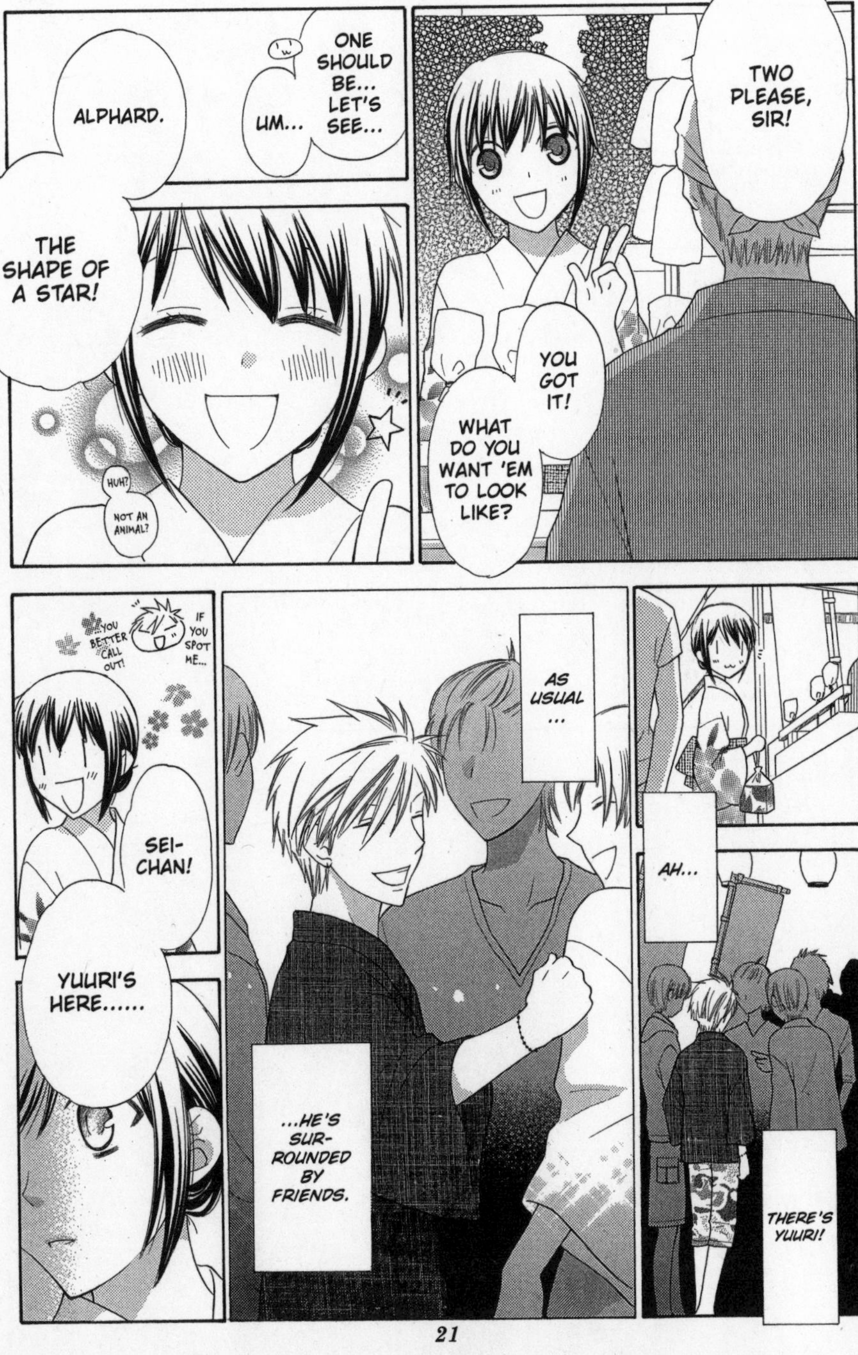
TWO PLEASE, SIR!
YOU GOT IT!
WHAT DO YOU WANT 'EM TO LOOK LIKE?
ONE SHOULD BE... LET'S SEE...
UM...
ALPHARD.
THE SHAPE OF A STAR!
HUH?
NOT AN ANIMAL?
AH...
THERE'S YUURI!
AS USUAL...
...HE'S SUR-ROUNDED BY FRIENDS.
IF YOU SPOT ME...
YOU BETTER CALL OUT!
SEI-CHAN!
YUURI'S HERE......

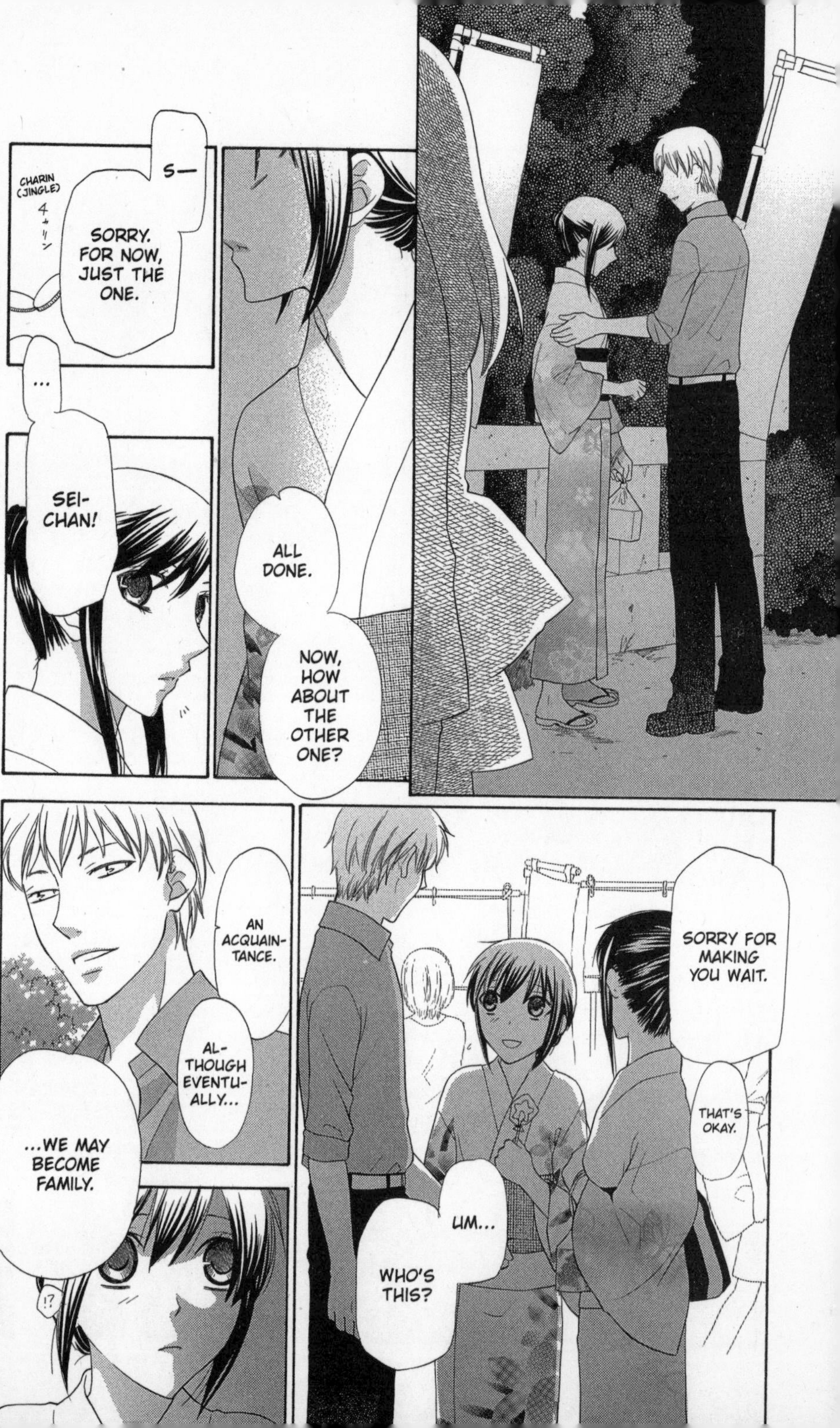
ALL DONE.
NOW, HOW ABOUT THE OTHER ONE?
S—
CHARIN (JINGLE)
SORRY. FOR NOW, JUST THE ONE.
...
SEI-CHAN!
SORRY FOR MAKING YOU WAIT.
THAT'S OKAY.
UM...
WHO'S THIS?
AN ACQUAINTANCE.
ALTHOUGH EVENTUALLY...
...WE MAY BECOME FAMILY.
!?

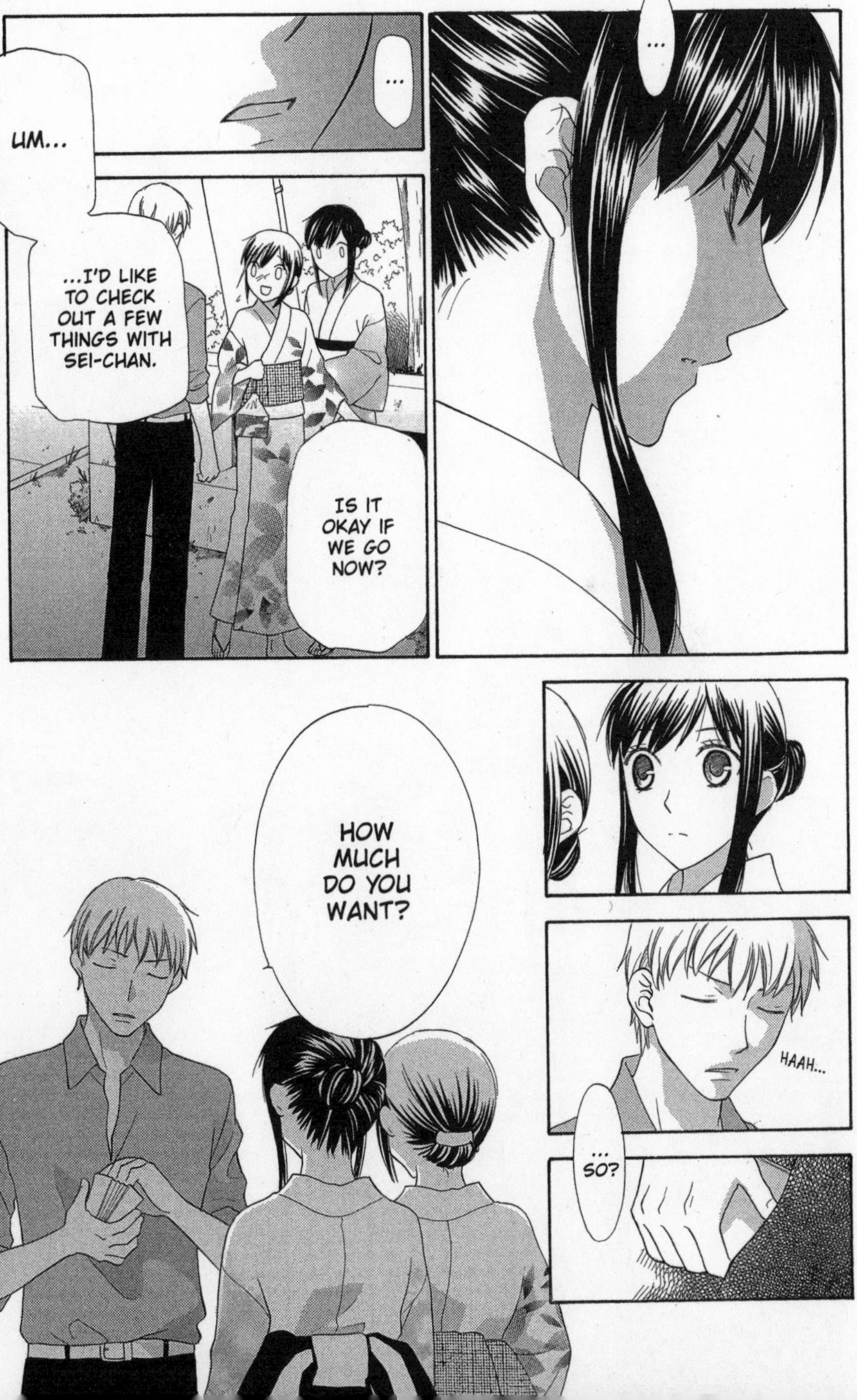
...
...
UM...
...I'D LIKE TO CHECK OUT A FEW THINGS WITH SEI-CHAN.
IS IT OKAY IF WE GO NOW?
HAAH...
...SO?
HOW MUCH DO YOU WANT?

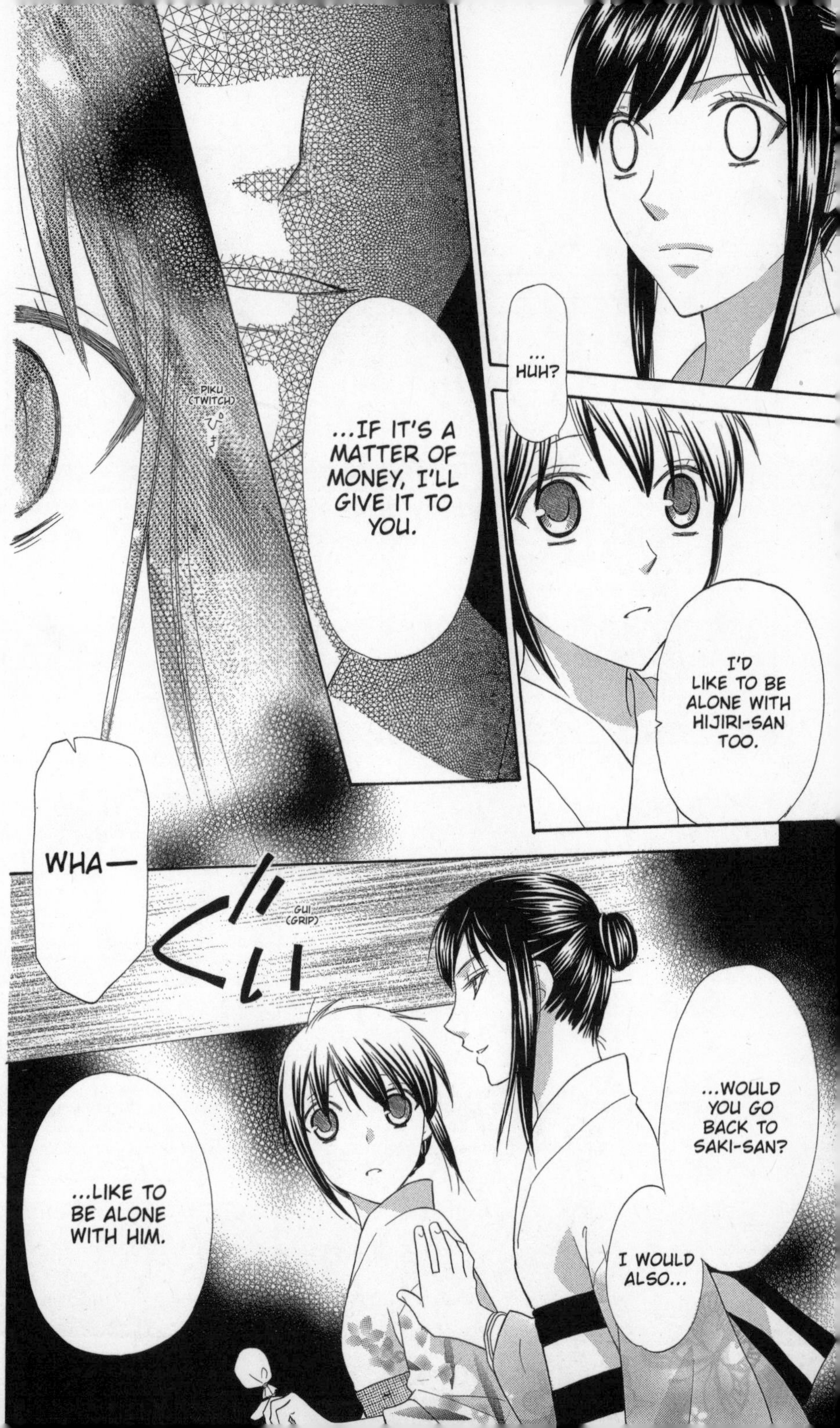
...HUH?
I'D LIKE TO BE ALONE WITH HIJIRI-SAN TOO.
...IF IT'S A MATTER OF MONEY, I'LL GIVE IT TO YOU.
PIKU (TWITCH)
WHA—
GUI (GRIP)
...WOULD YOU GO BACK TO SAKI-SAN?
I WOULD ALSO...
...LIKE TO BE ALONE WITH HIM.

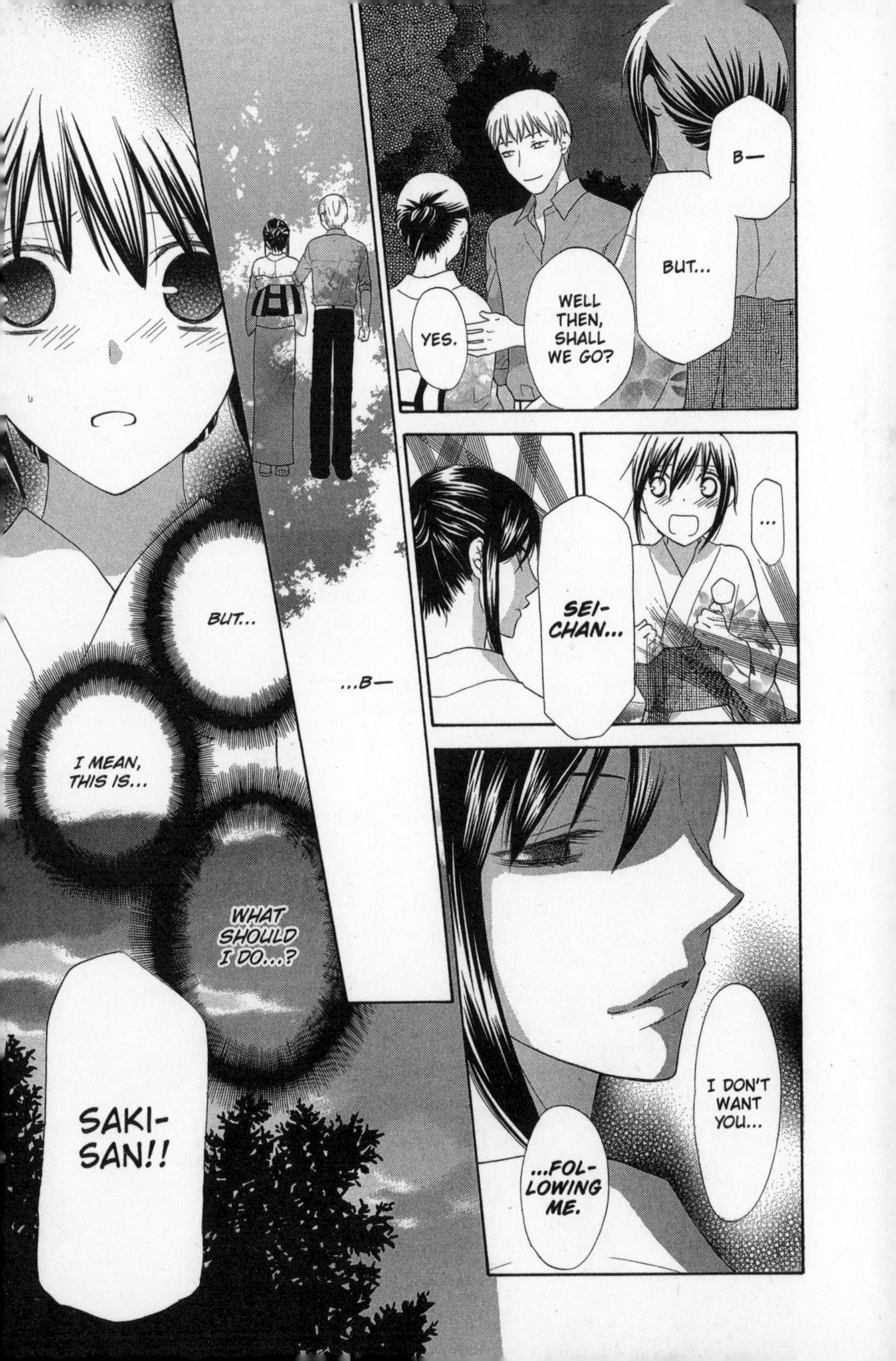
B—
BUT...
WELL THEN, SHALL WE GO?
YES.
...
SEI-CHAN...
I DON'T WANT YOU...
...FOL-LOWING ME.
...B—
BUT...
I MEAN, THIS IS...
WHAT SHOULD I DO...?
SAKI-SAN!!

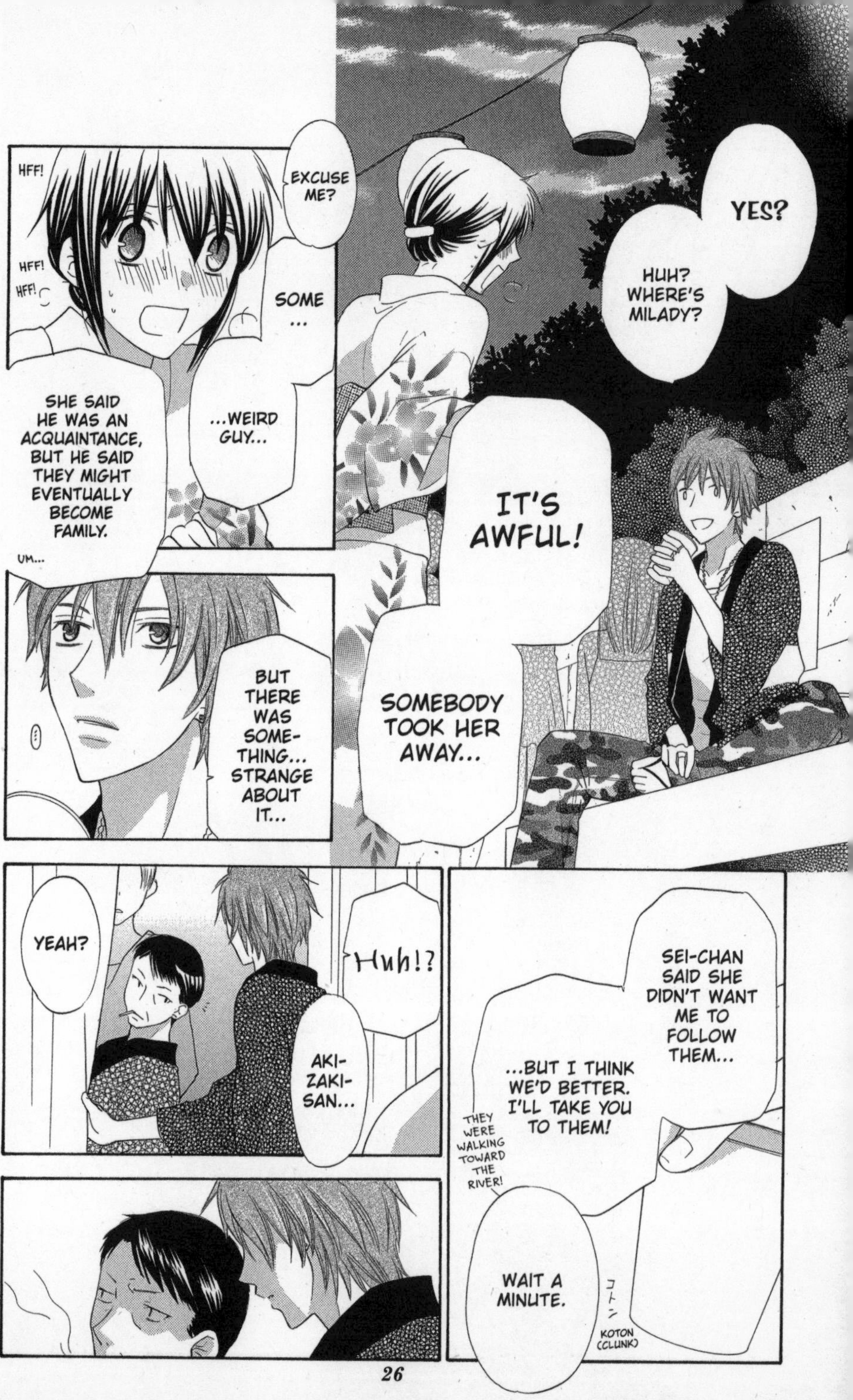

YES?
HUH? WHERE'S MILADY?
IT'S AWFUL!
SOMEBODY TOOK HER AWAY...
EXCUSE ME?
HFF!
HFF!
HFF!
SOME...
...WEIRD GUY...
SHE SAID HE WAS AN ACQUAINTANCE, BUT HE SAID THEY MIGHT EVENTUALLY BECOME FAMILY.
UM...
BUT THERE WAS SOME-THING... STRANGE ABOUT IT...
SEI-CHAN SAID SHE DIDN'T WANT ME TO FOLLOW THEM...
...BUT I THINK WE'D BETTER. I'LL TAKE YOU TO THEM!
THEY WERE WALKING TOWARD THE RIVER!
WAIT A MINUTE.
コトン
KOTON (CLUNK)
Huh!?
YEAH?
AKI-ZAKI-SAN...

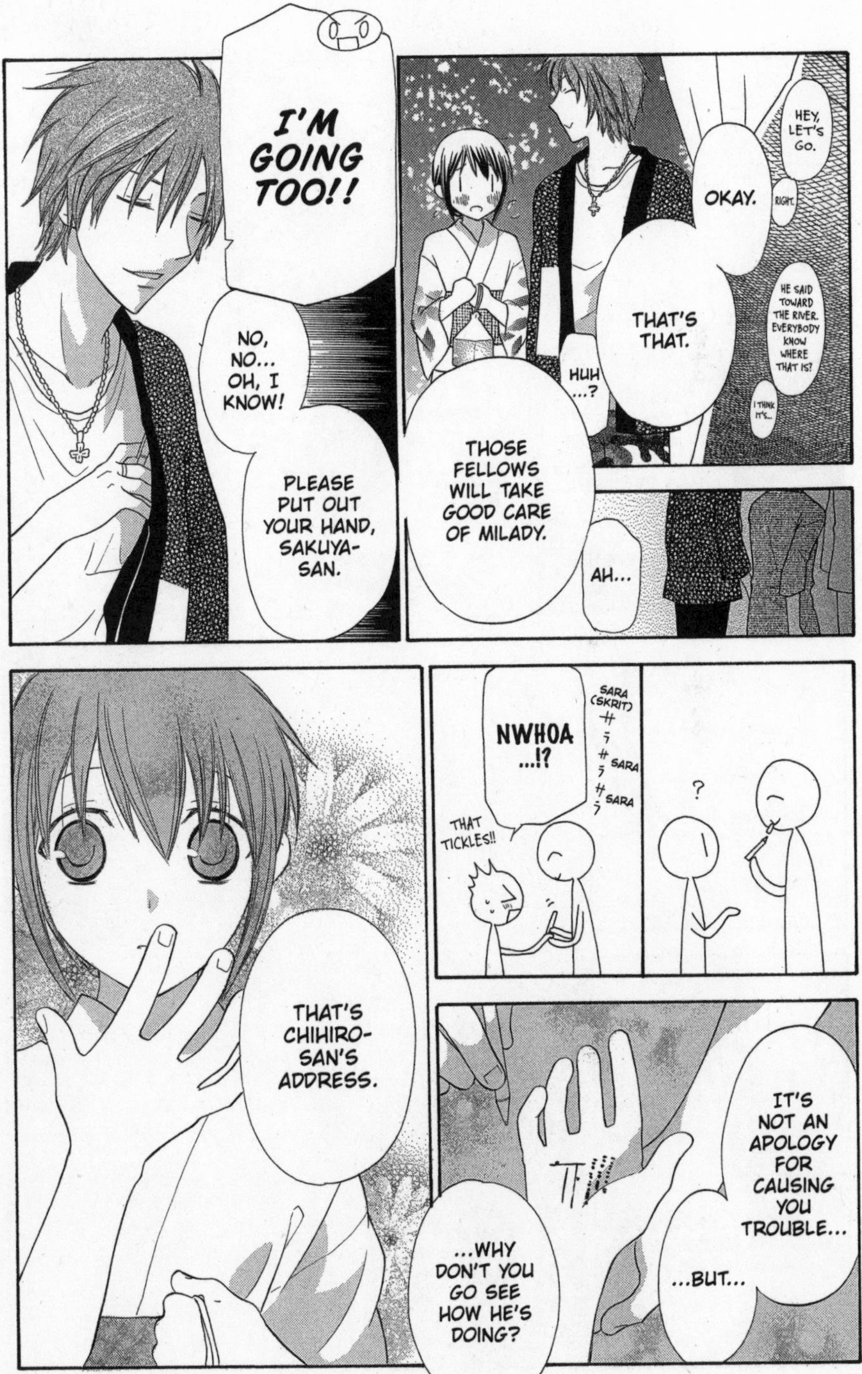
HEY, LET'S GO.
RIGHT.
OKAY.
HE SAID TOWARD THE RIVER. EVERYBODY KNOW WHERE THAT IS?
I THINK IT'S...
THAT'S THAT.
HUH...?
THOSE FELLOWS WILL TAKE GOOD CARE OF MILADY.
AH...
I'M GOING TOO!!
NO, NO... OH, I KNOW!
PLEASE PUT OUT YOUR HAND, SAKUYA-SAN.
?
SARA (SKRIT) SARA SARA
NWHOA ...!?
THAT TICKLES!!
IT'S NOT AN APOLOGY FOR CAUSING YOU TROUBLE...
...BUT...
...WHY DON'T YOU GO SEE HOW HE'S DOING?
THAT'S CHIHIRO-SAN'S ADDRESS.

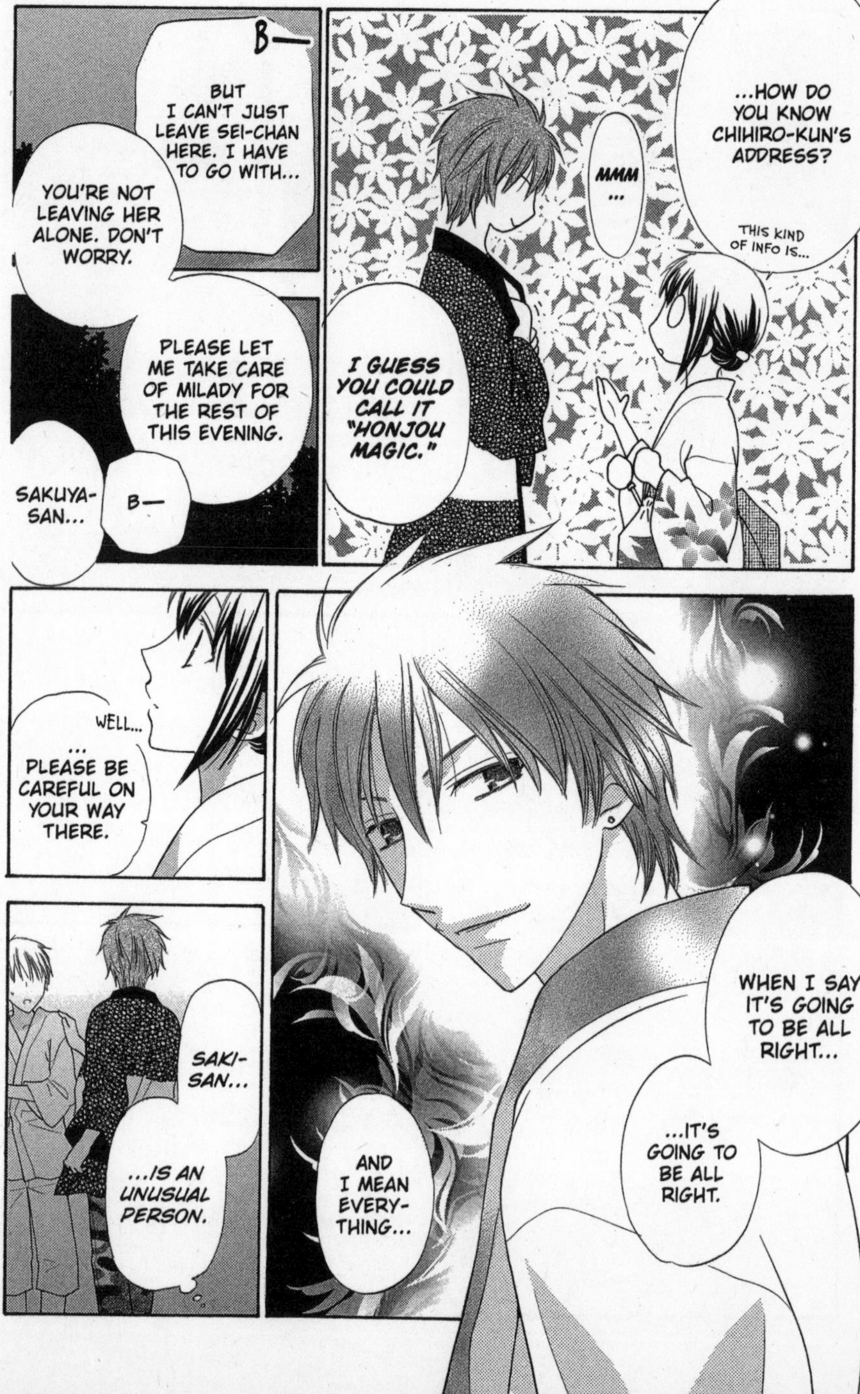
...HOW DO YOU KNOW CHIHIRO-KUN'S ADDRESS?
THIS KIND OF INFO IS...
MMM...
I GUESS YOU COULD CALL IT "HONJOU MAGIC."
B—
BUT I CAN'T JUST LEAVE SEI-CHAN HERE. I HAVE TO GO WITH...
YOU'RE NOT LEAVING HER ALONE. DON'T WORRY.
PLEASE LET ME TAKE CARE OF MILADY FOR THE REST OF THIS EVENING.
B—
SAKUYA-SAN...
WHEN I SAY IT'S GOING TO BE ALL RIGHT...
...IT'S GOING TO BE ALL RIGHT.
AND I MEAN EVERYTHING...
WELL...
...PLEASE BE CAREFUL ON YOUR WAY THERE.
SAKI-SAN...
...IS AN UNUSUAL PERSON.

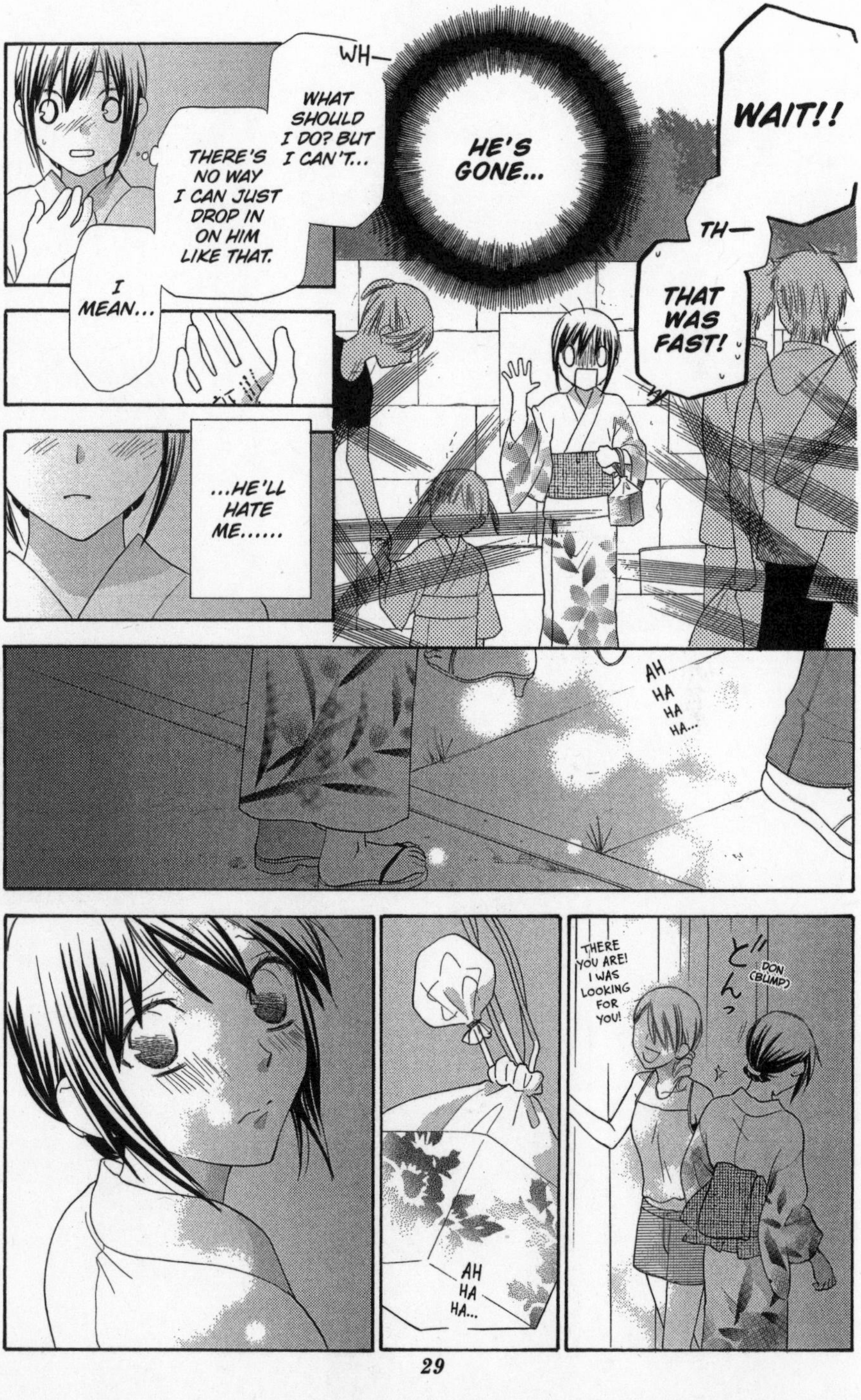
WAIT!!
HE'S GONE...
TH—
THAT WAS FAST!
WH—
WHAT SHOULD I DO? BUT I CAN'T...
THERE'S NO WAY I CAN JUST DROP IN ON HIM LIKE THAT.
I MEAN...
...HE'LL HATE ME......
AH HA HA HA...
どんっ
DON (BUMP)
THERE YOU ARE! I WAS LOOKING FOR YOU!
AH HA HA...

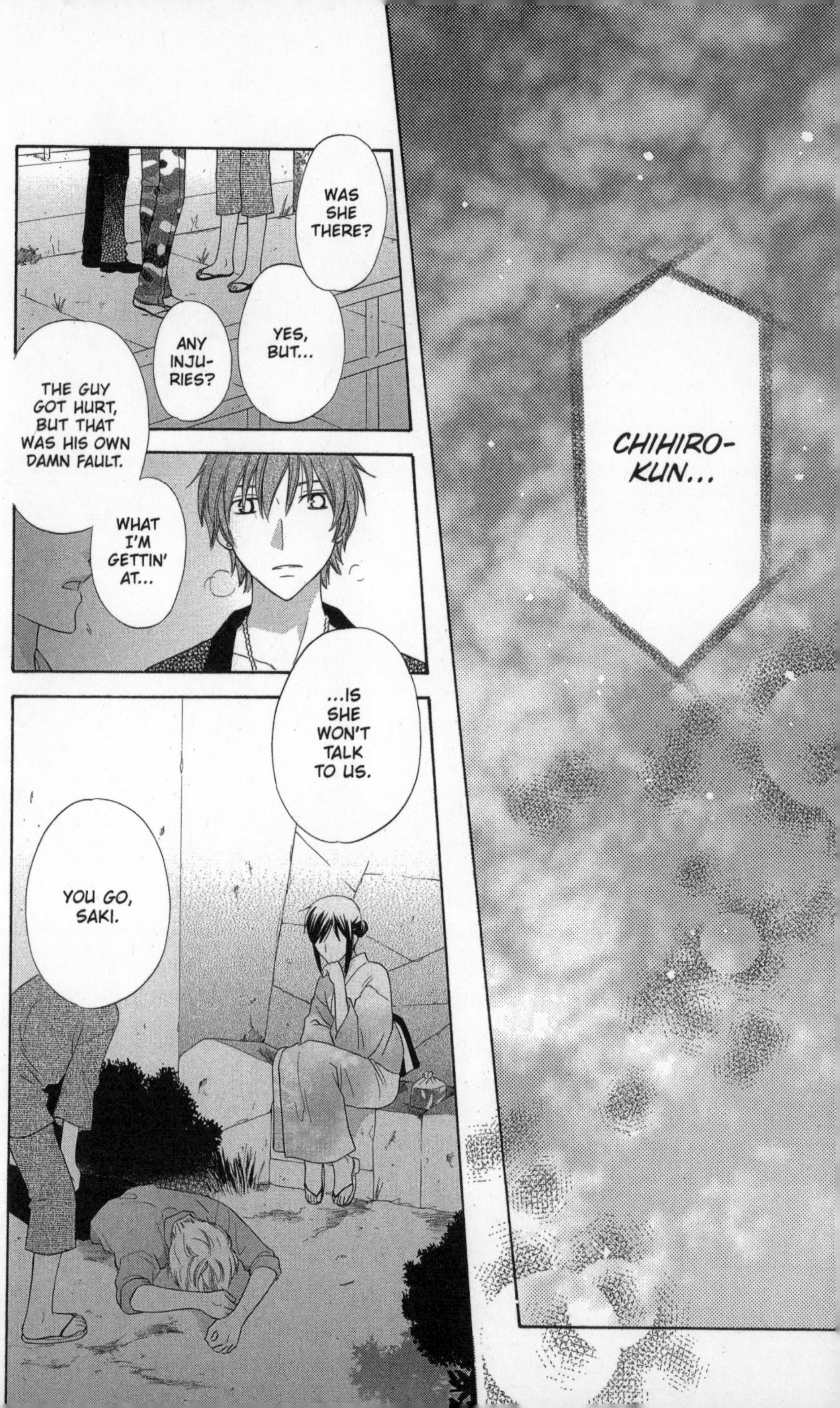
CHIHIRO-KUN...
WAS SHE THERE?
YES, BUT...
ANY INJURIES?
THE GUY GOT HURT, BUT THAT WAS HIS OWN DAMN FAULT.
WHAT I'M GETTIN' AT...
...IS SHE WON'T TALK TO US.
YOU GO, SAKI.

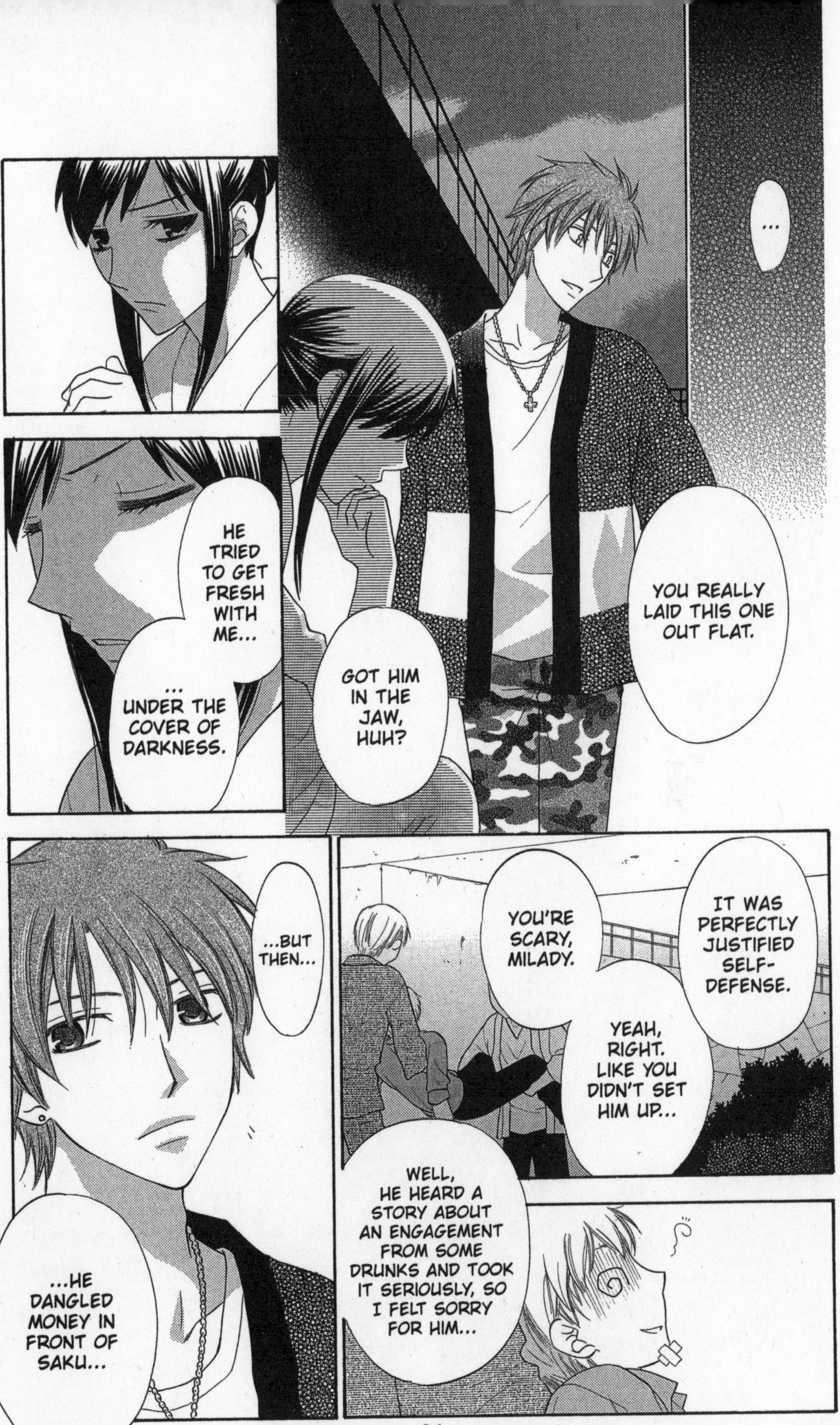
...
YOU REALLY LAID THIS ONE OUT FLAT.
GOT HIM IN THE JAW, HUH?
HE TRIED TO GET FRESH WITH ME...
...UNDER THE COVER OF DARKNESS.
IT WAS PERFECTLY JUSTIFIED SELF-DEFENSE.
YOU'RE SCARY, MILADY.
YEAH, RIGHT. LIKE YOU DIDN'T SET HIM UP...
WELL, HE HEARD A STORY ABOUT AN ENGAGEMENT FROM SOME DRUNKS AND TOOK IT SERIOUSLY, SO I FELT SORRY FOR HIM...
...BUT THEN...
...HE DANGLED MONEY IN FRONT OF SAKU...

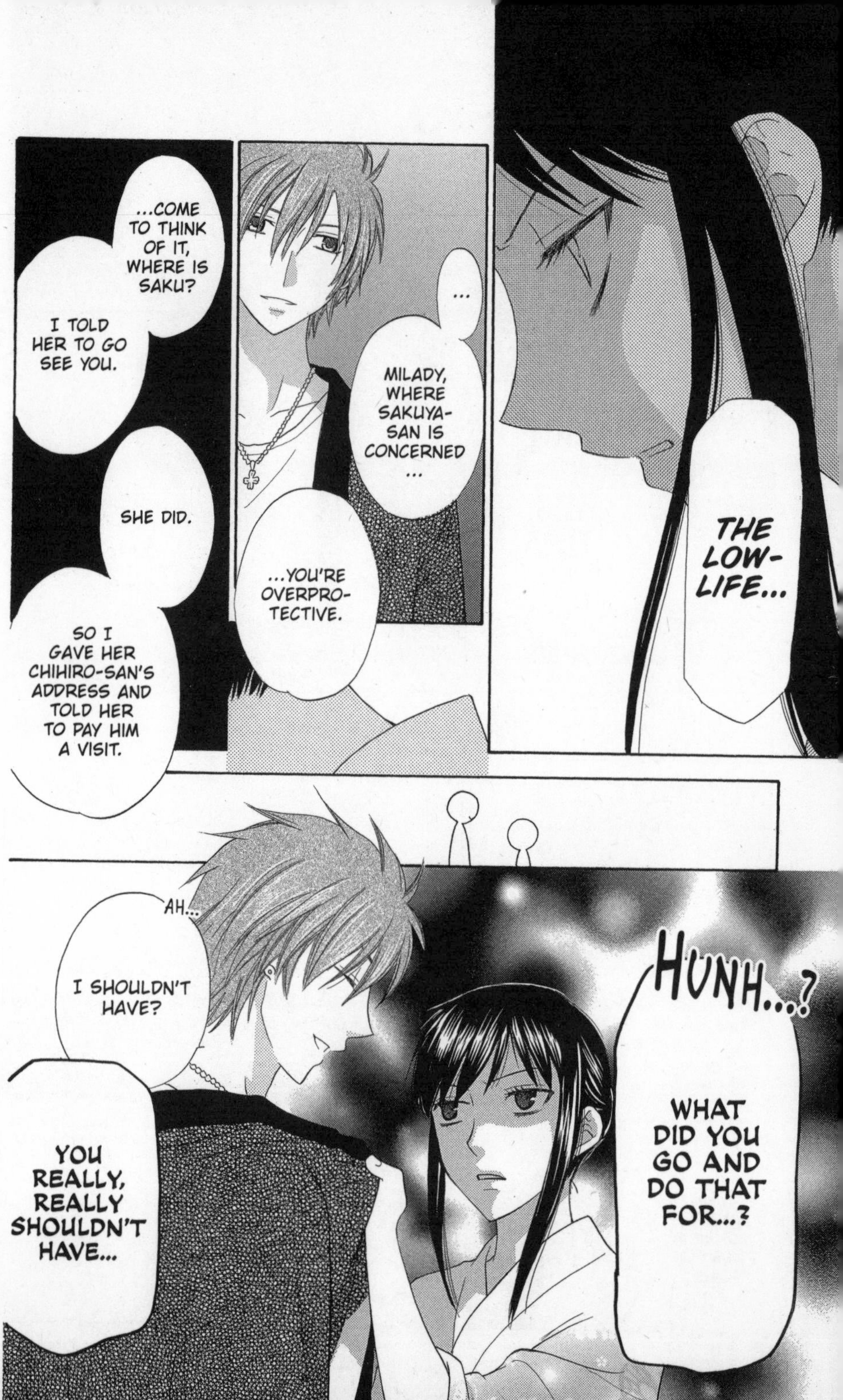
THE LOW-LIFE...
...
MILADY, WHERE SAKUYA-SAN IS CONCERNED...
...YOU'RE OVERPROTECTIVE.
...COME TO THINK OF IT, WHERE IS SAKU?
I TOLD HER TO GO SEE YOU.
SHE DID.
SO I GAVE HER CHIHIRO-SAN'S ADDRESS AND TOLD HER TO PAY HIM A VISIT.
HUNH...?
WHAT DID YOU GO AND DO THAT FOR...?
AH...
I SHOULDN'T HAVE?
YOU REALLY, REALLY SHOULDN'T HAVE...

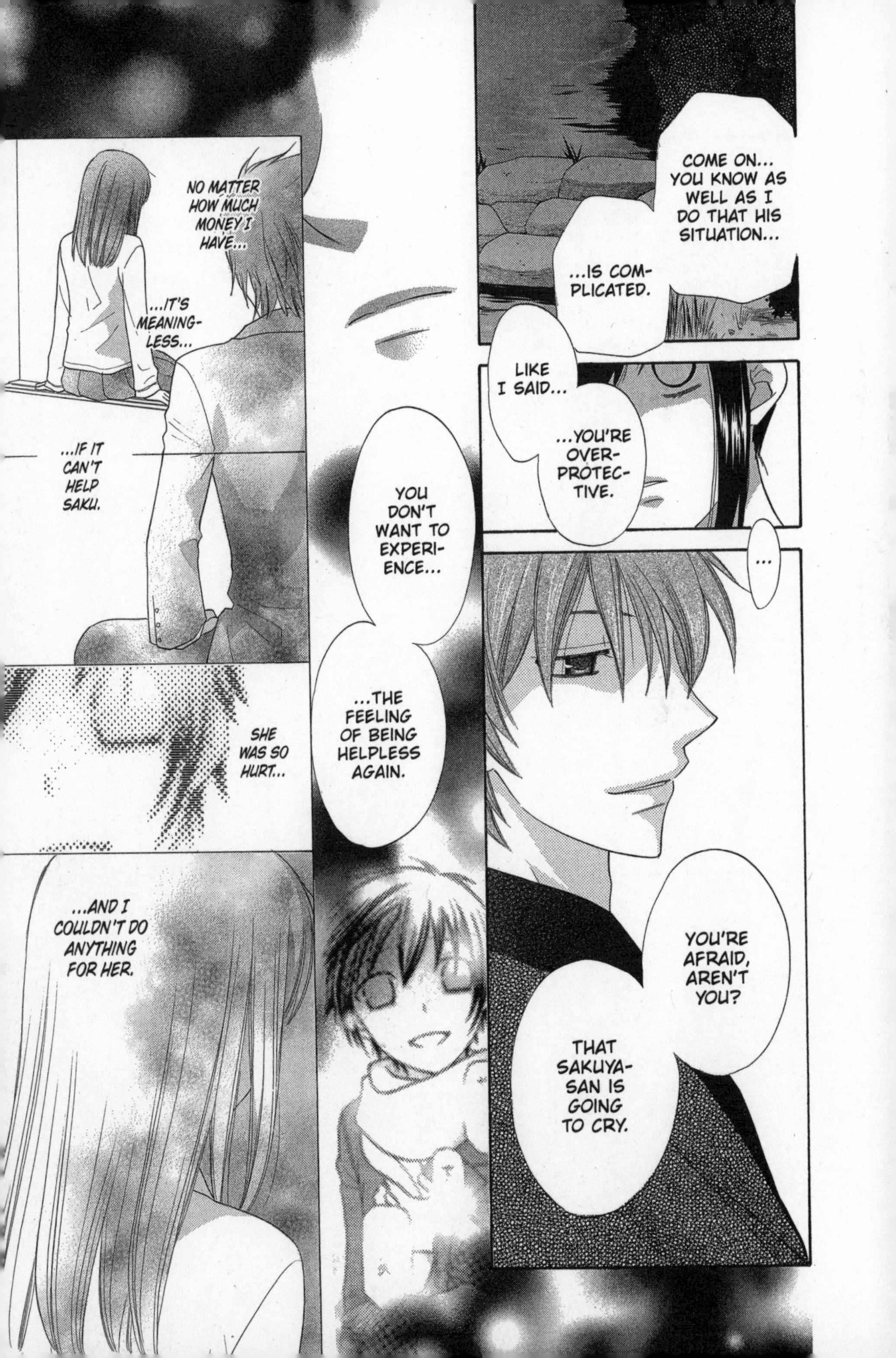
COME ON... YOU KNOW AS WELL AS I DO THAT HIS SITUATION...
...IS COMPLICATED.
LIKE I SAID...
...YOU'RE OVERPROTECTIVE.
...
YOU'RE AFRAID, AREN'T YOU?
THAT SAKUYA-SAN IS GOING TO CRY.
YOU DON'T WANT TO EXPERIENCE...
...THE FEELING OF BEING HELPLESS AGAIN.
NO MATTER HOW MUCH MONEY I HAVE...
...IT'S MEANINGLESS...
...IF IT CAN'T HELP SAKU.
SHE WAS SO HURT...
...AND I COULDN'T DO ANYTHING FOR HER.

DON'T TALK LIKE YOU KNOW HOW I FEEL.

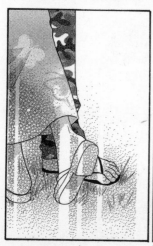

...

BUT...

...I DO KNOW HOW YOU FEEL.

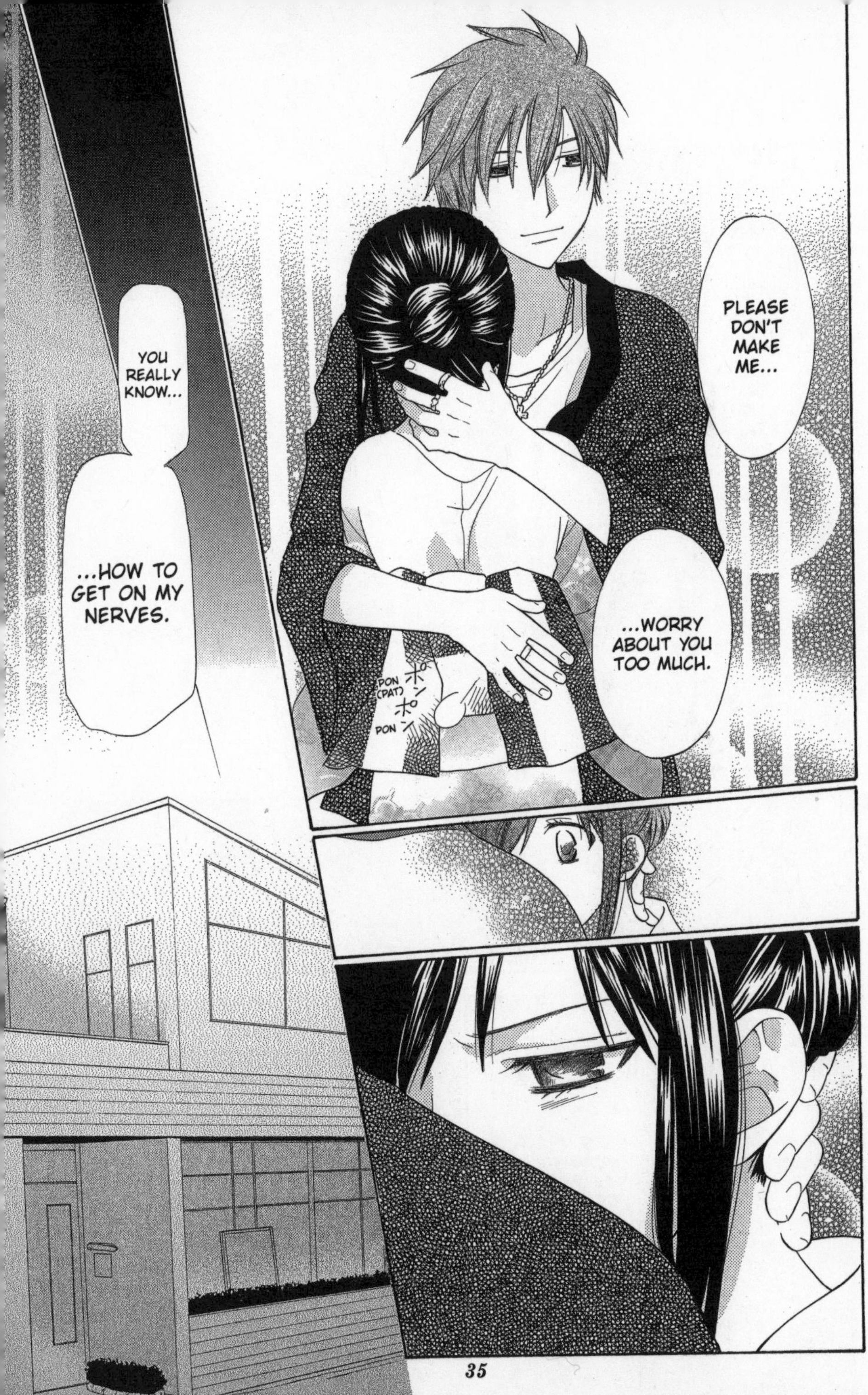
PLEASE DON'T MAKE ME...
...WORRY ABOUT YOU TOO MUCH.
ポン PON (PAT)
ポン PON
YOU REALLY KNOW...
...HOW TO GET ON MY NERVES.

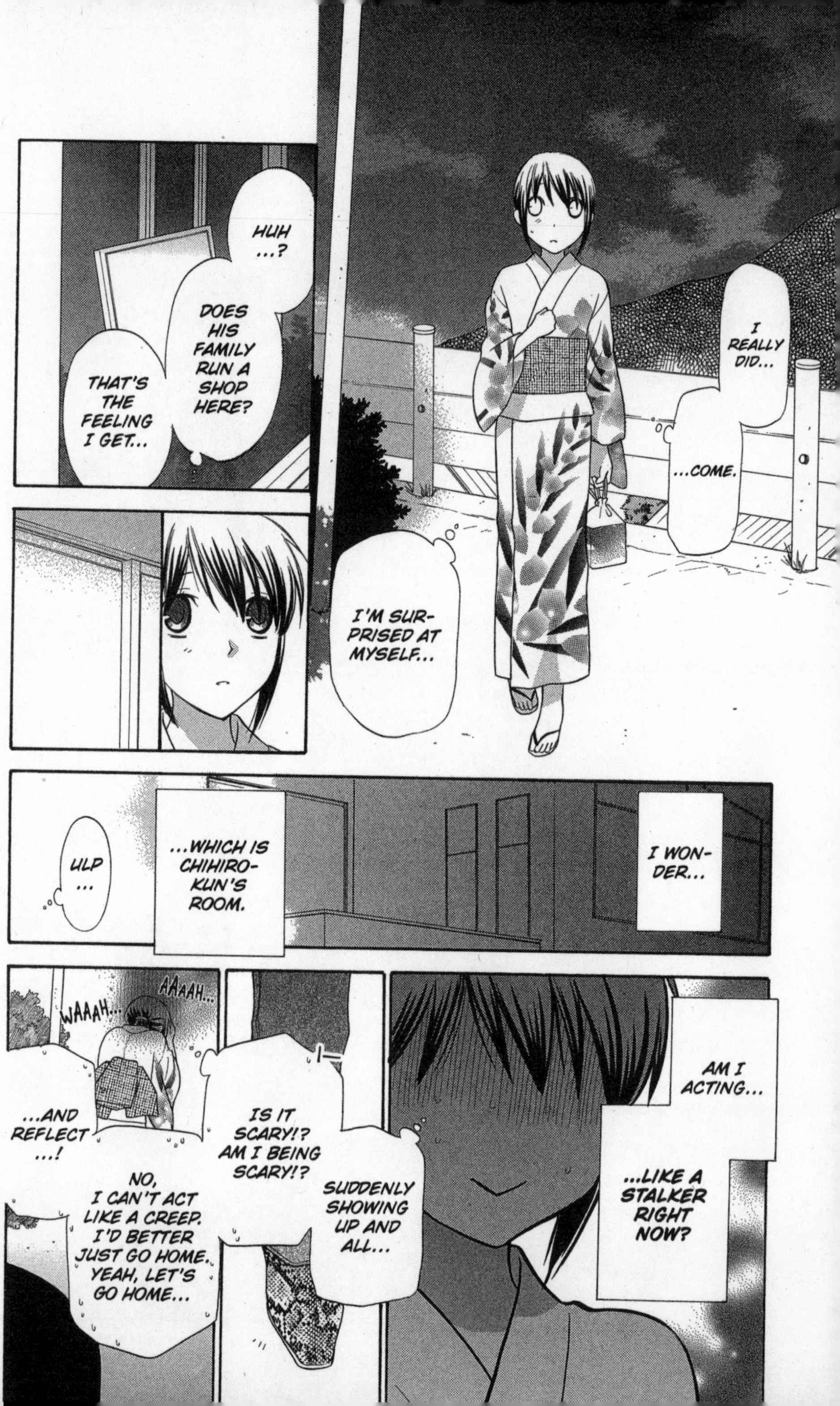
I REALLY DID...
...COME.
I'M SURPRISED AT MYSELF...
HUH...?
DOES HIS FAMILY RUN A SHOP HERE?
THAT'S THE FEELING I GET...
I WONDER...
...WHICH IS CHIHIRO-KUN'S ROOM.
ULP...
AM I ACTING...
...LIKE A STALKER RIGHT NOW?
IS IT SCARY!? AM I BEING SCARY!?
SUDDENLY SHOWING UP AND ALL...
AAAAH...
WAAAH...
...AND REFLECT...!
NO, I CAN'T ACT LIKE A CREEP. I'D BETTER JUST GO HOME. YEAH, LET'S GO HOME...

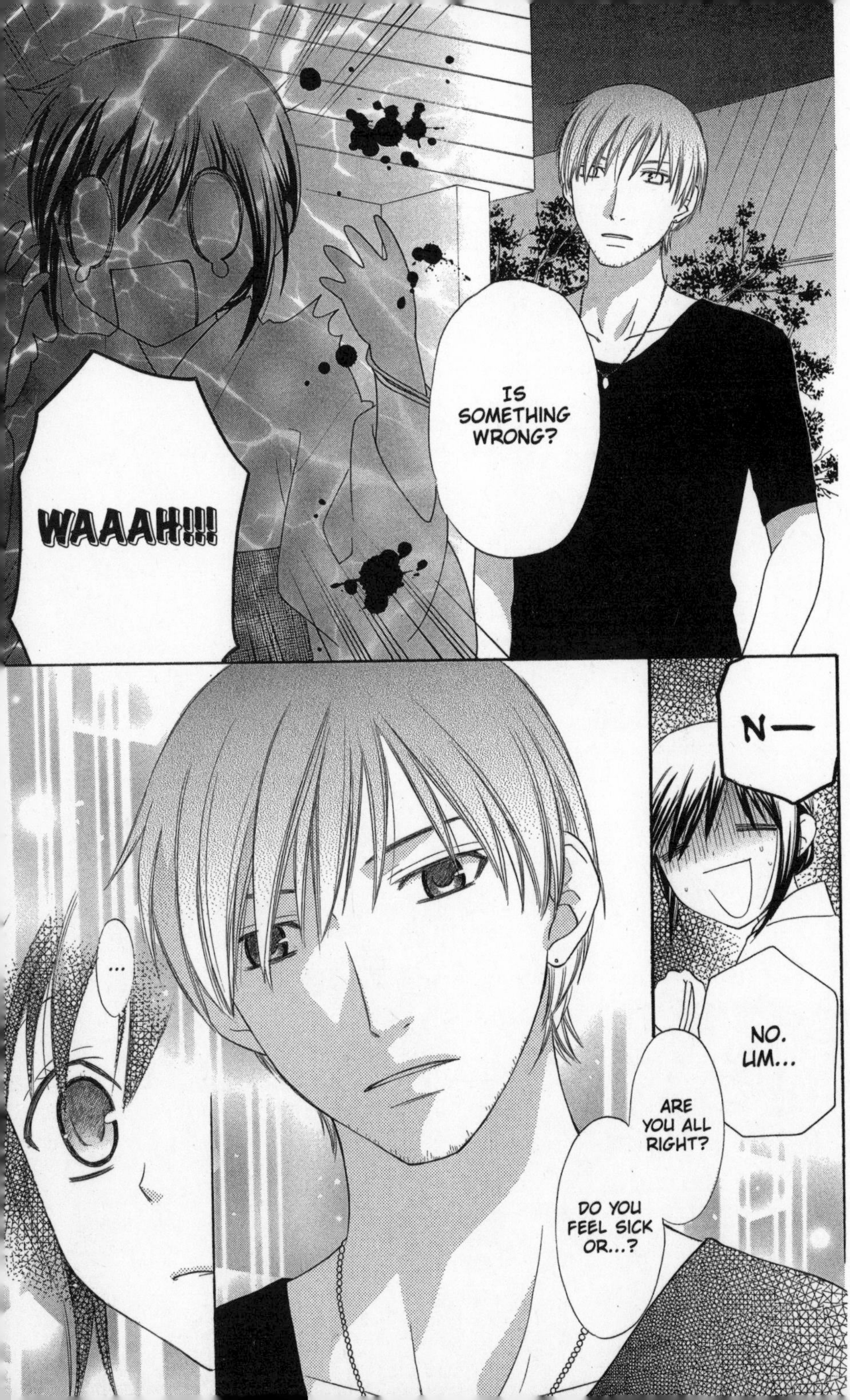
IS SOMETHING WRONG?
WAAAH!!!
N—
NO. UM...
...
ARE YOU ALL RIGHT?
DO YOU FEEL SICK OR...?

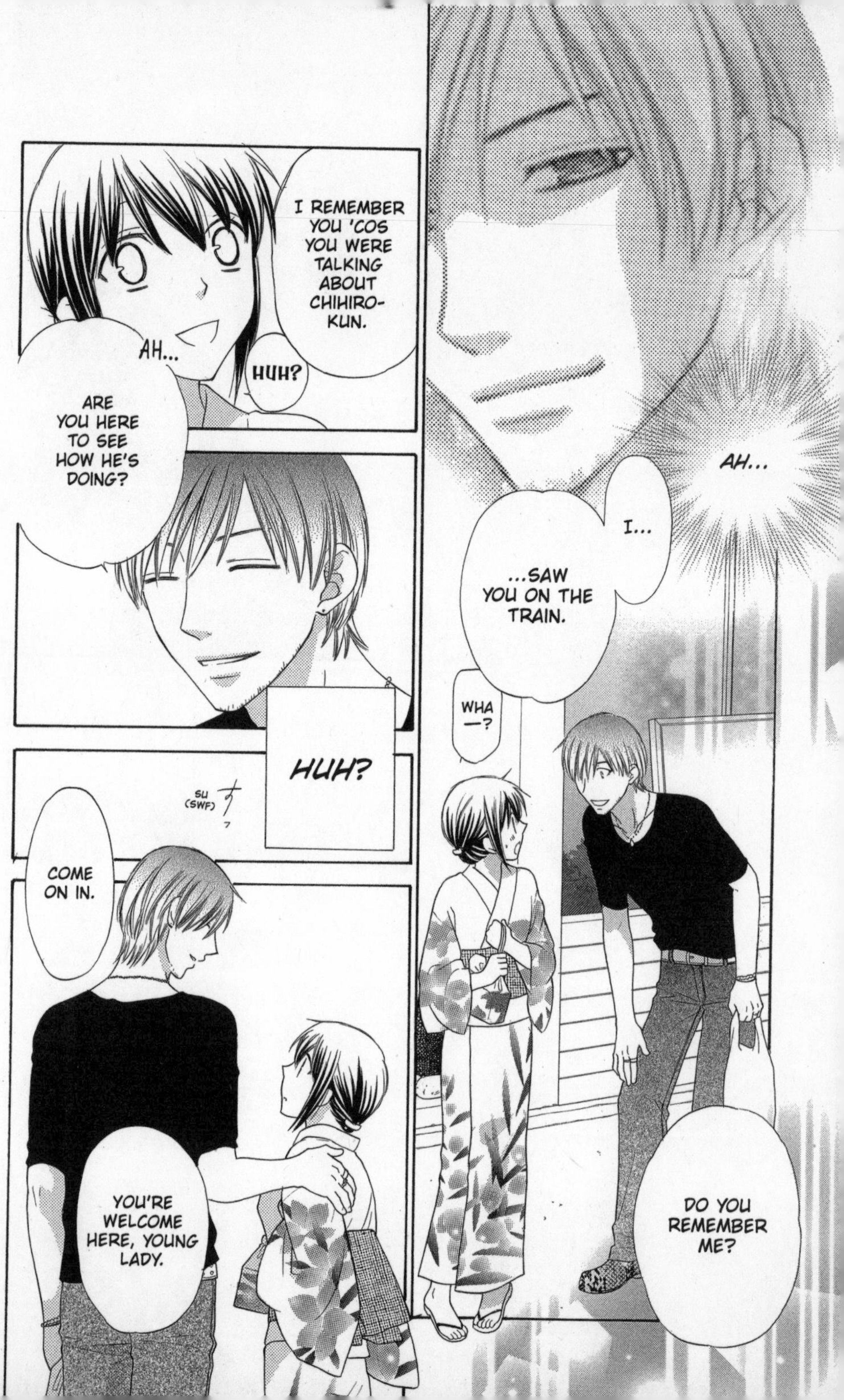
AH...
I...
...SAW YOU ON THE TRAIN.
WHA—?
DO YOU REMEMBER ME?
I REMEMBER YOU 'COS YOU WERE TALKING ABOUT CHIHIRO-KUN.
HUH?
AH...
ARE YOU HERE TO SEE HOW HE'S DOING?
HUH?
SU (SWF)
COME ON IN.
YOU'RE WELCOME HERE, YOUNG LADY.

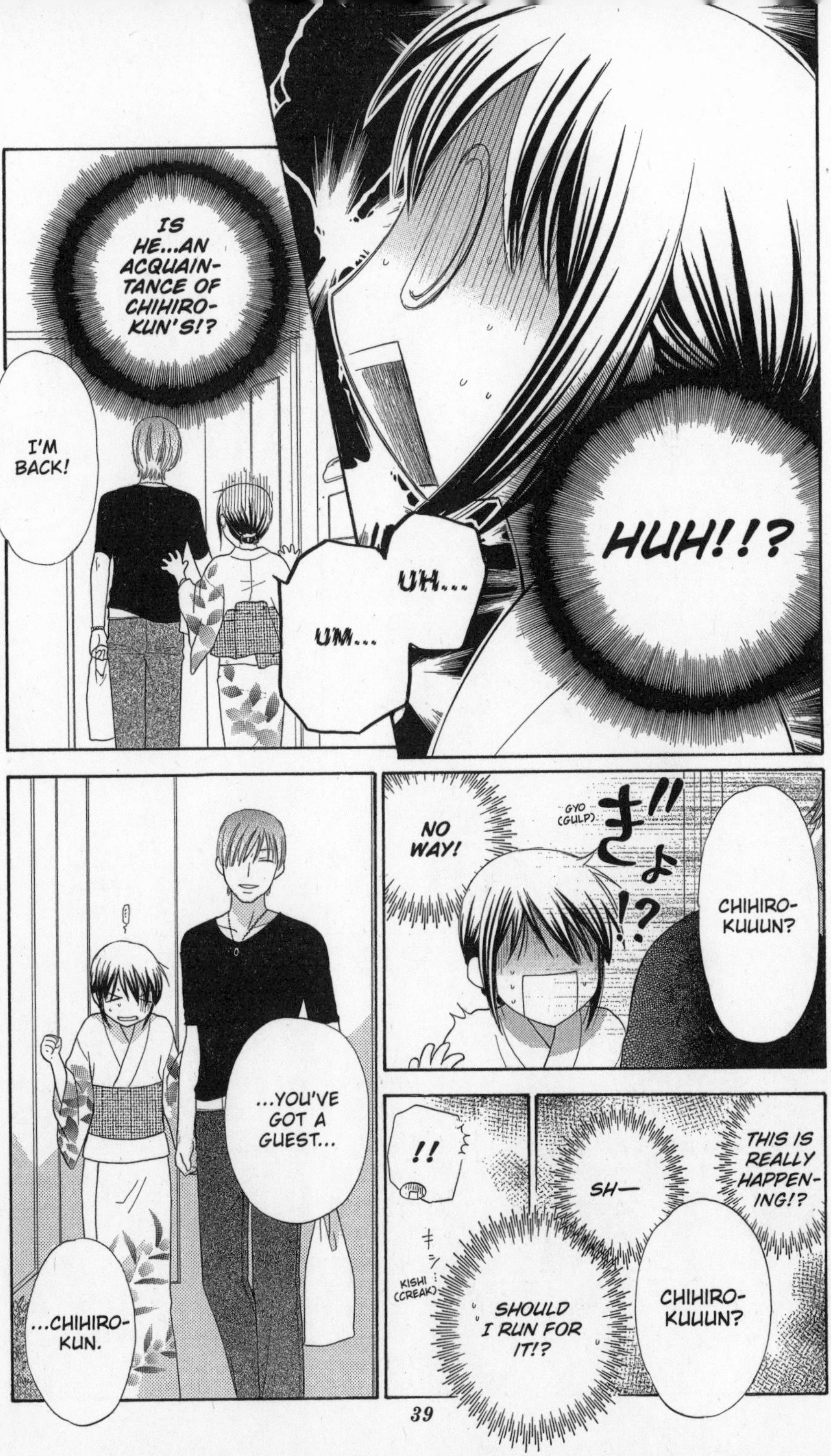
HUH!!?
UH... UM...
IS HE...AN ACQUAINTANCE OF CHIHIRO-KUN'S!?
I'M BACK!
CHIHIRO-KUUUN?
GYO (GULP)
NO WAY!
THIS IS REALLY HAPPENING!?
SH—
CHIHIRO-KUUUN?
SHOULD I RUN FOR IT!?
KISHI (CREAK)
!!
...YOU'VE GOT A GUEST...
...CHIHIRO-KUN.

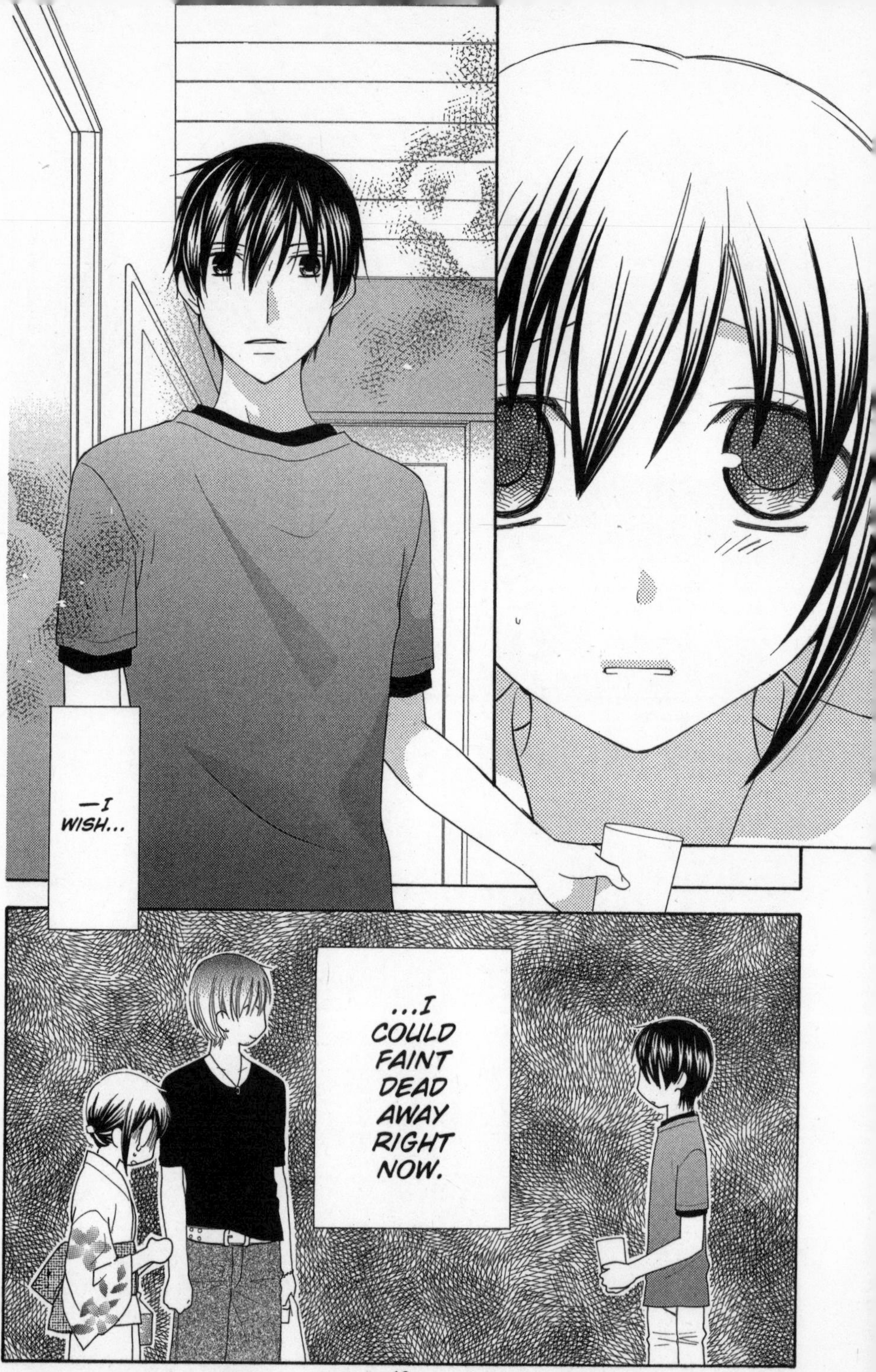
—I WISH...
...I COULD FAINT DEAD AWAY RIGHT NOW.

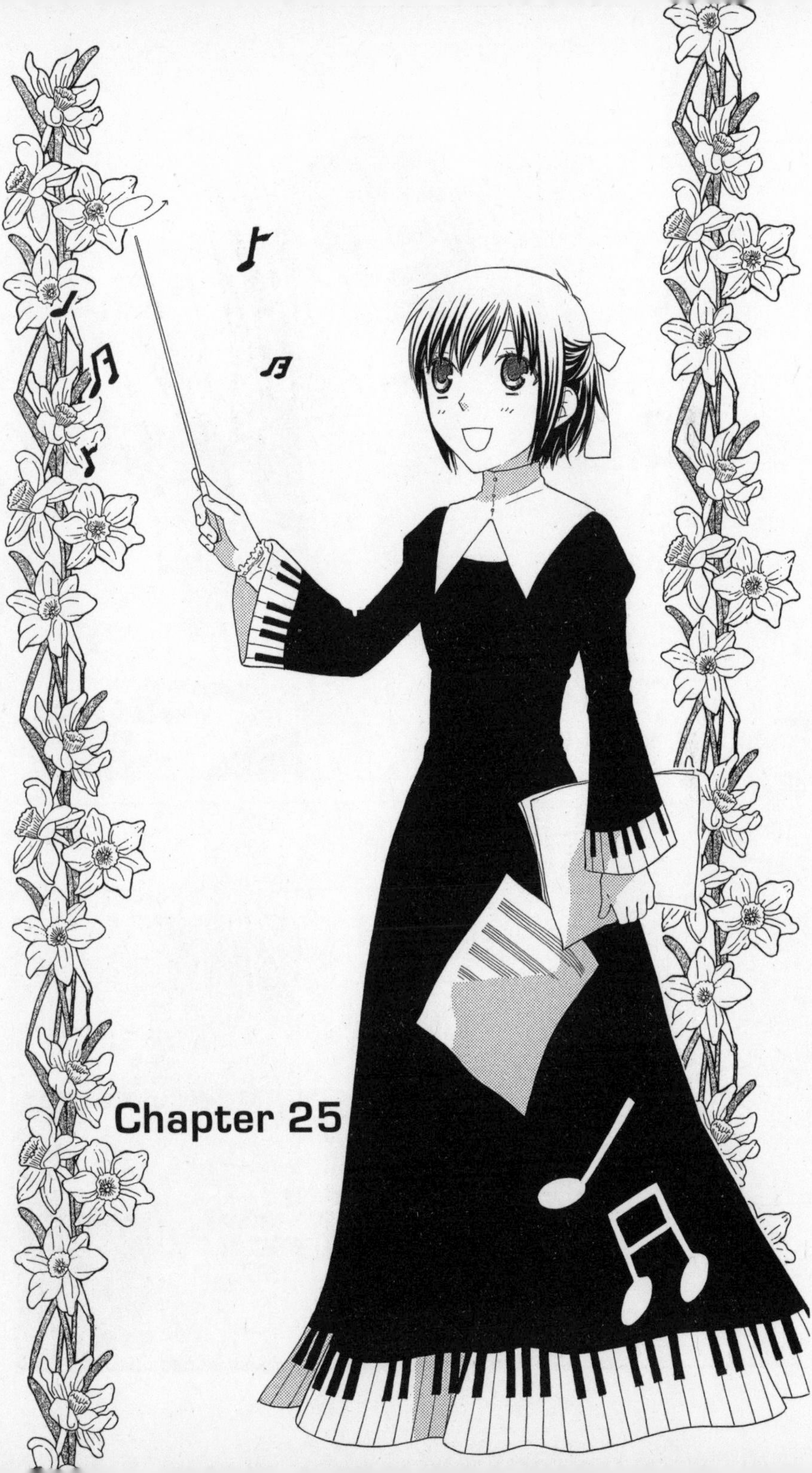
Chapter 25

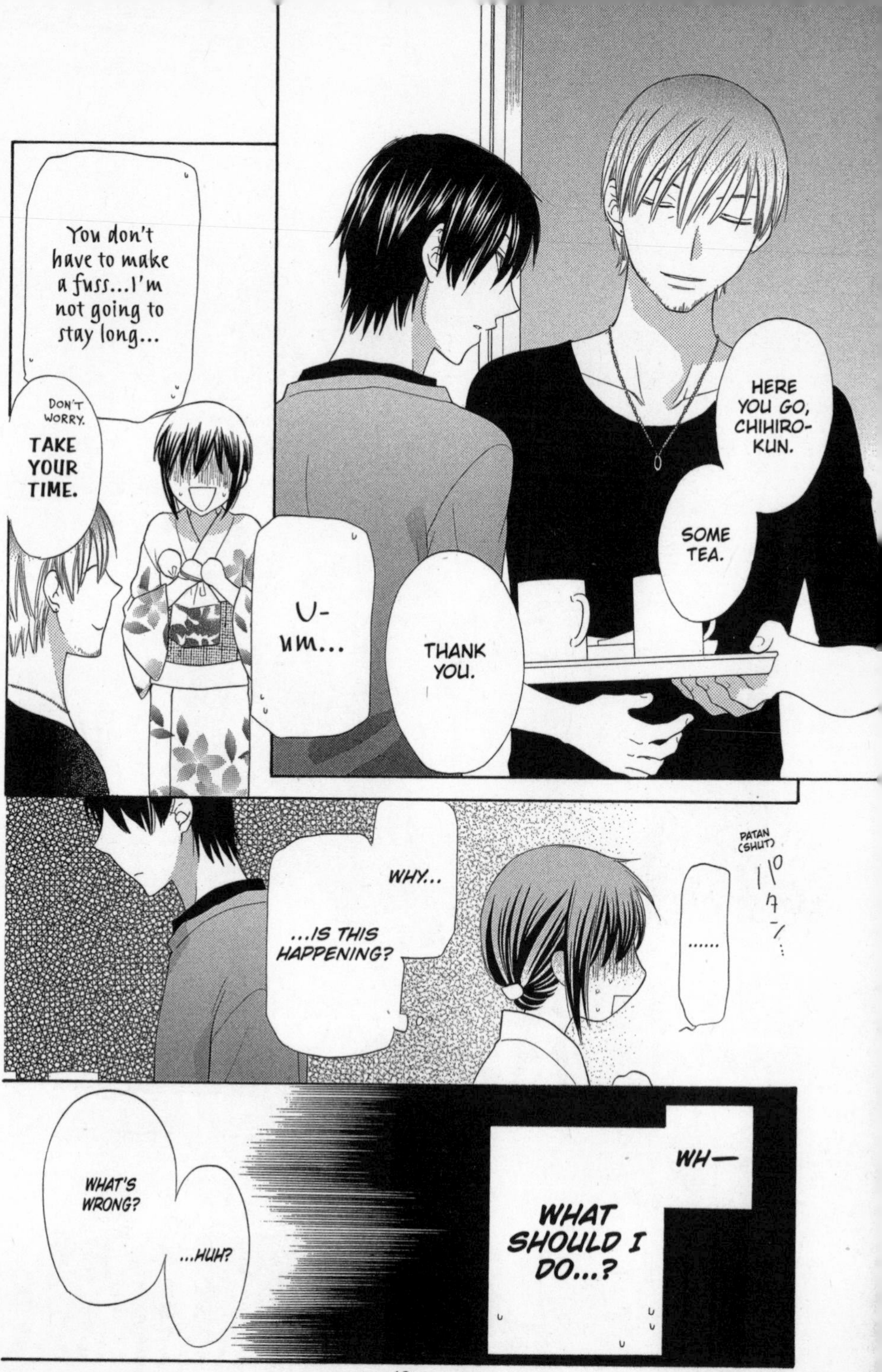
HERE YOU GO, CHIHIRO-KUN.
SOME TEA.
THANK YOU.
U-um...
You don't have to make a fuss...I'm not going to stay long...
DON'T WORRY. TAKE YOUR TIME.
PATAN (SHUT)
......
WHY...
...IS THIS HAPPENING?
WH—
WHAT SHOULD I DO...?
WHAT'S WRONG?
...HUH?

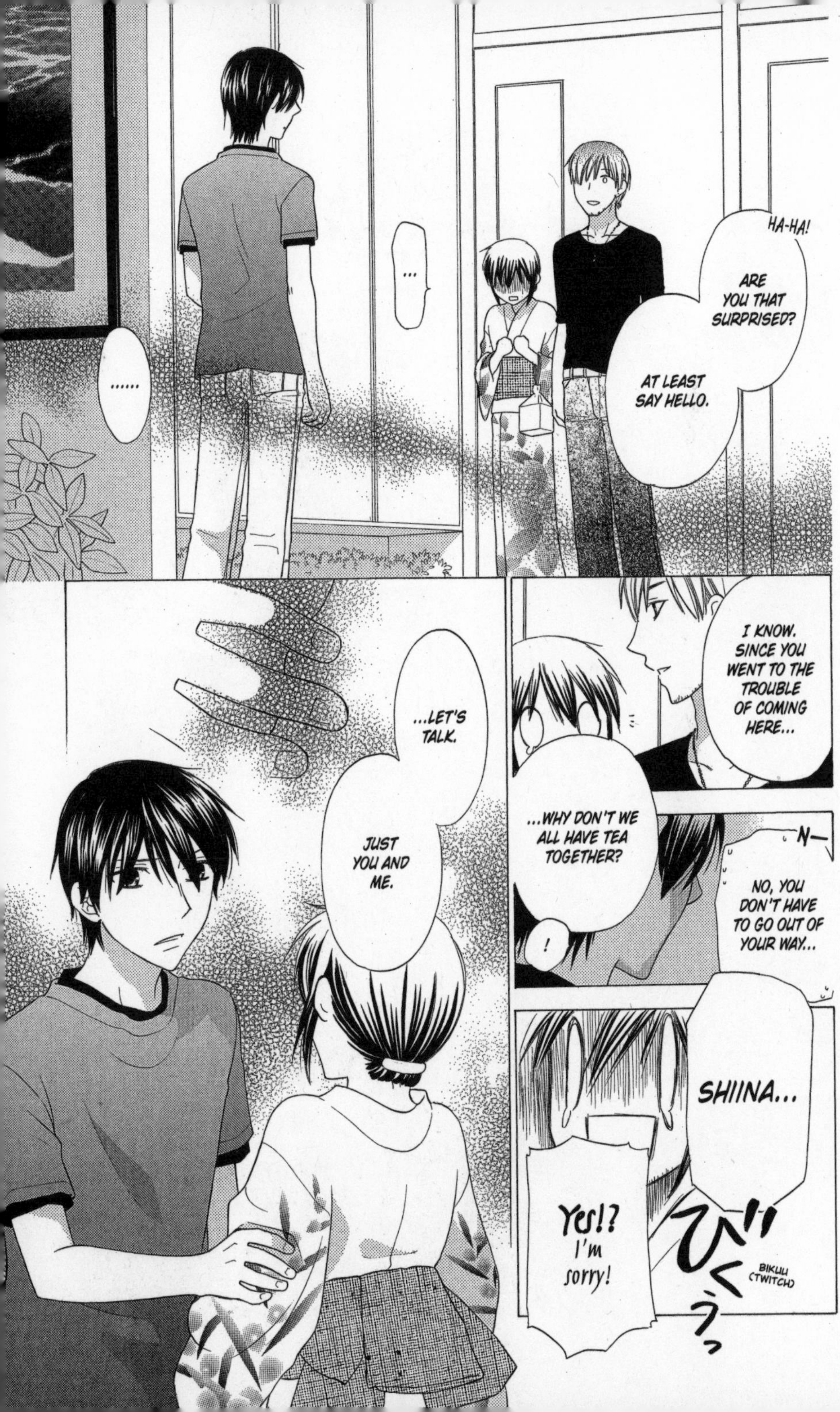
HA-HA!
ARE YOU THAT SURPRISED?
AT LEAST SAY HELLO.
...
......
I KNOW. SINCE YOU WENT TO THE TROUBLE OF COMING HERE...
...WHY DON'T WE ALL HAVE TEA TOGETHER?
N—
NO, YOU DON'T HAVE TO GO OUT OF YOUR WAY...
!
SHIINA...
Yes!? I'm sorry!
BIKUU (TWITCH)
...LET'S TALK.
JUST YOU AND ME.

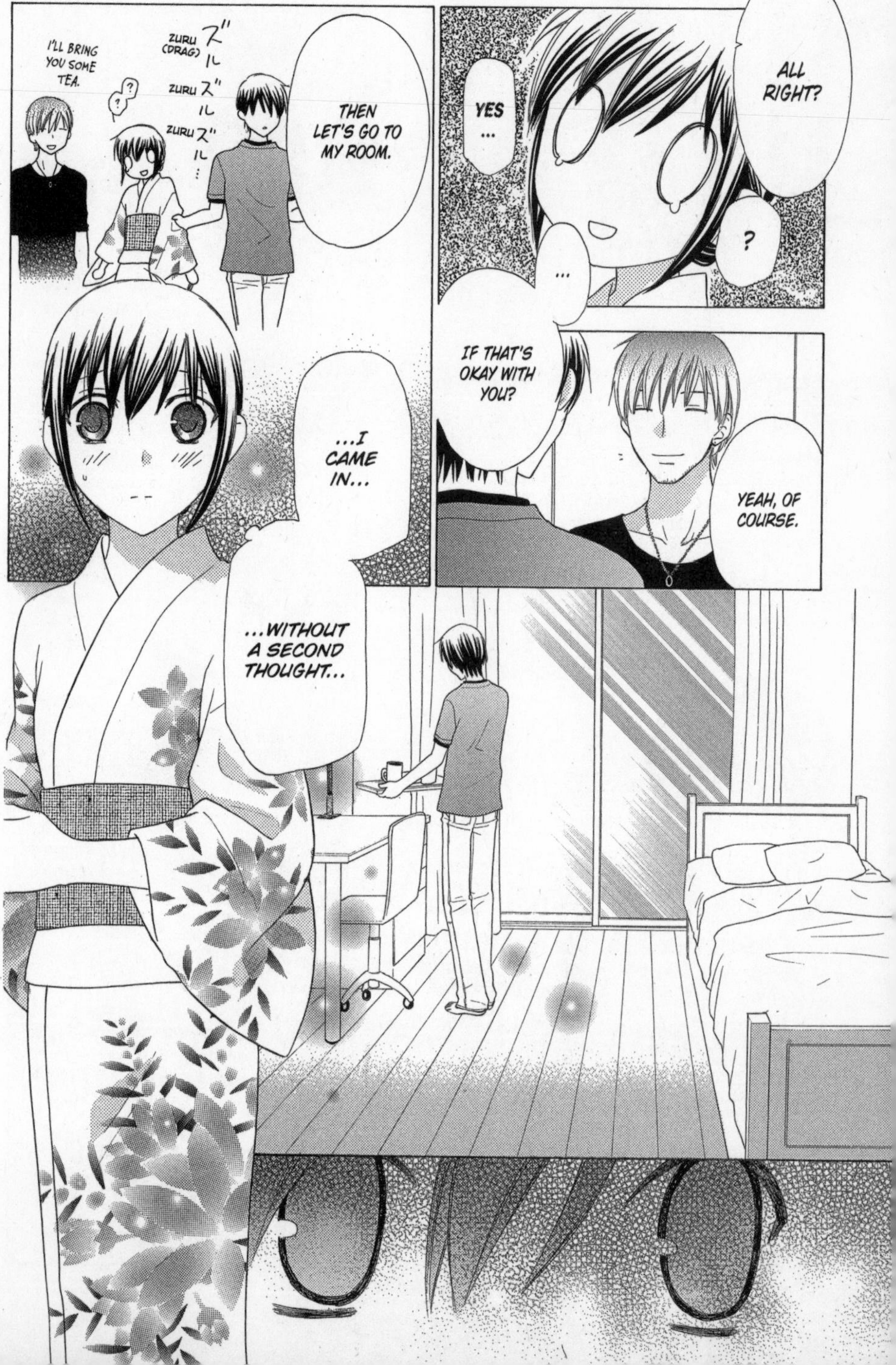
ALL RIGHT?
YES...
?
...
THEN LET'S GO TO MY ROOM.
ズルズルズル...
ZURU (DRAG) ZURU ZURU
??
I'LL BRING YOU SOME TEA.
IF THAT'S OKAY WITH YOU?
YEAH, OF COURSE.
...I CAME IN...
...WITHOUT A SECOND THOUGHT...

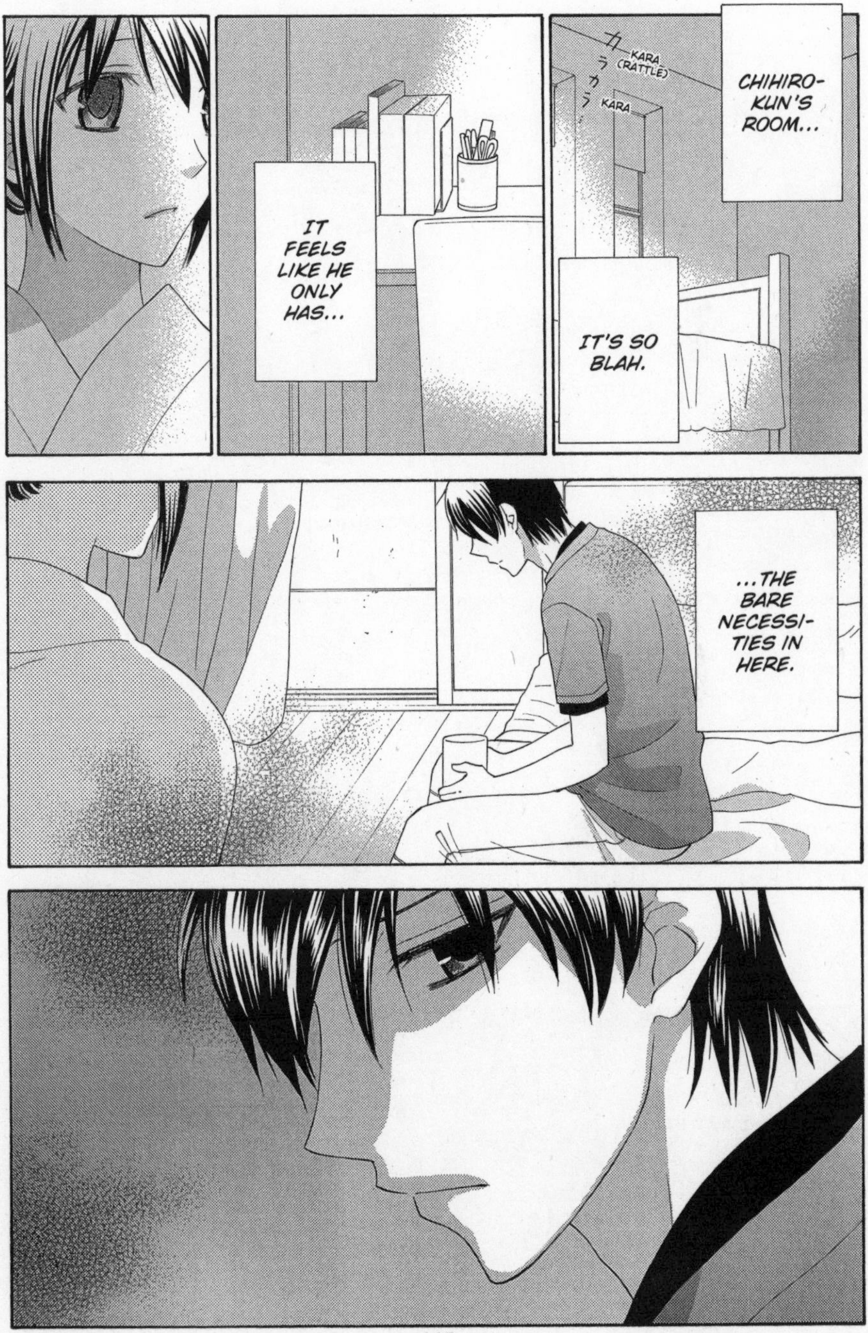
CHIHIRO-KUN'S ROOM...
カラカラ
KARA (RATTLE)
KARA
IT'S SO BLAH.
IT FEELS LIKE HE ONLY HAS...
...THE BARE NECESSITIES IN HERE.

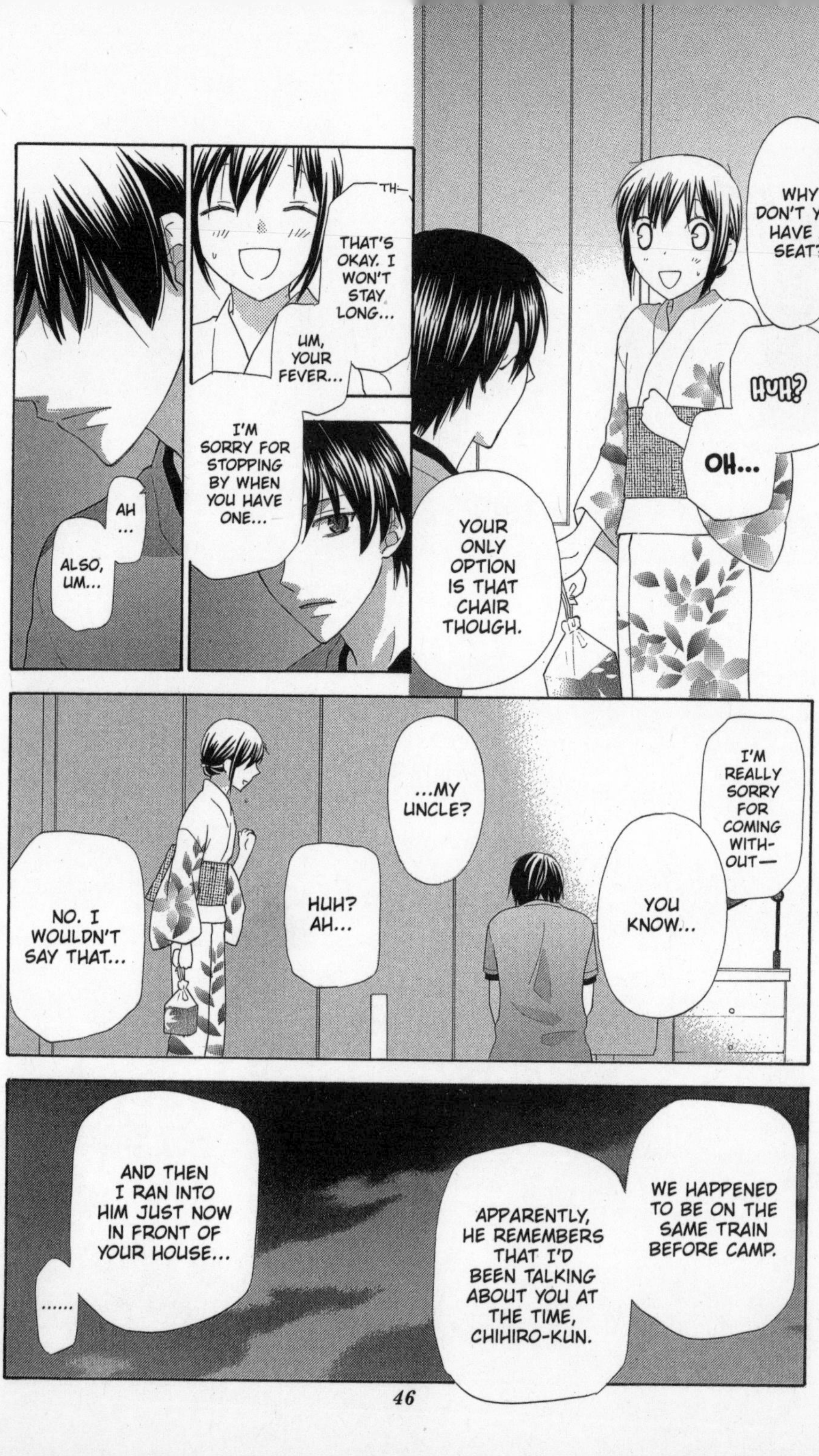
WHY DON'T YOU HAVE A SEAT?
HUH?
OH...
YOUR ONLY OPTION IS THAT CHAIR THOUGH.
TH—
THAT'S OKAY. I WON'T STAY LONG...
UM, YOUR FEVER...
I'M SORRY FOR STOPPING BY WHEN YOU HAVE ONE...
AH...
ALSO, UM...
I'M REALLY SORRY FOR COMING WITH-OUT—
YOU KNOW...
...MY UNCLE?
HUH? AH...
NO. I WOULDN'T SAY THAT...
WE HAPPENED TO BE ON THE SAME TRAIN BEFORE CAMP.
APPARENTLY, HE REMEMBERS THAT I'D BEEN TALKING ABOUT YOU AT THE TIME, CHIHIRO-KUN.
AND THEN I RAN INTO HIM JUST NOW IN FRONT OF YOUR HOUSE...
......

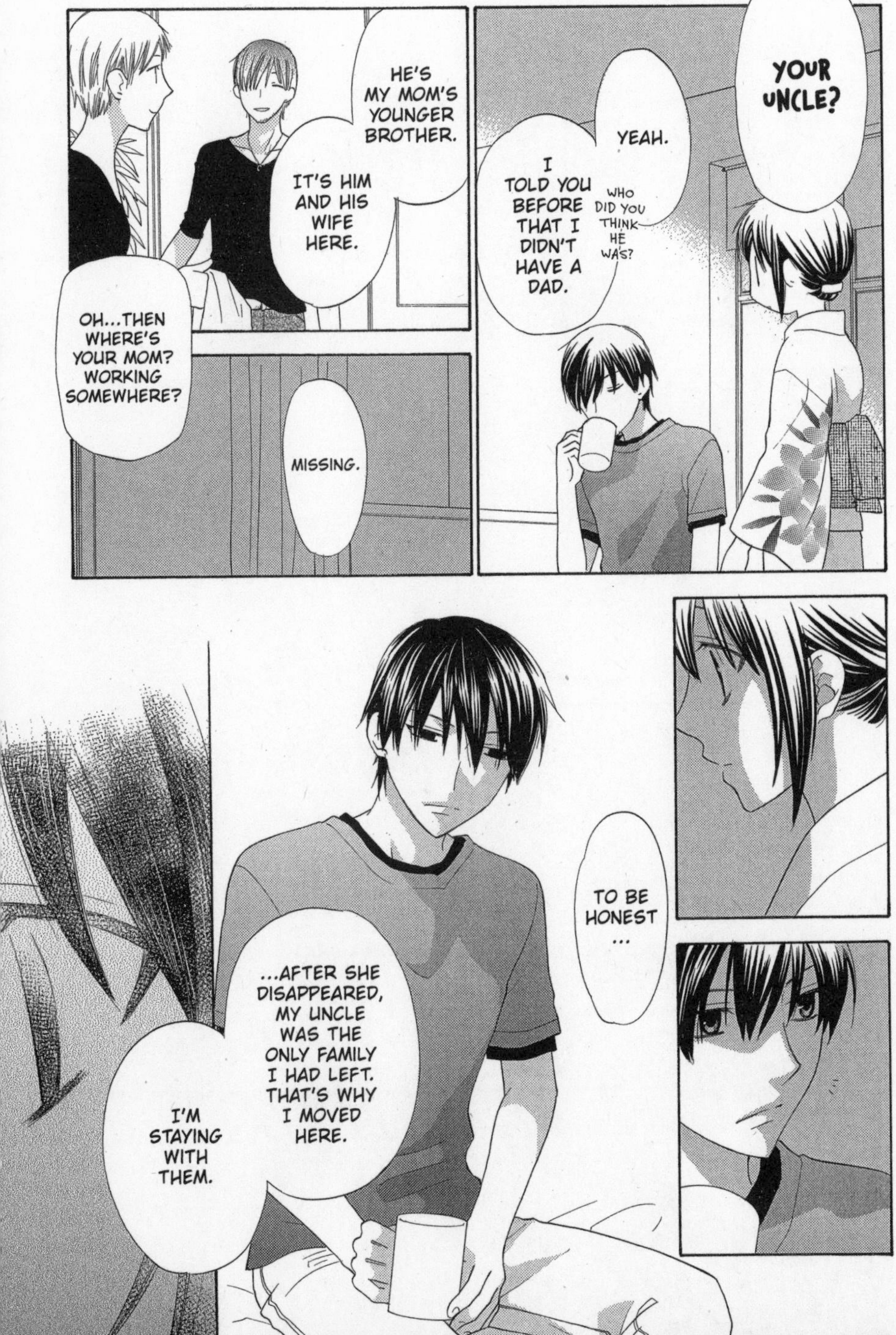
YOUR UNCLE?
YEAH.
I TOLD YOU BEFORE THAT I DIDN'T HAVE A DAD.
WHO DID YOU THINK HE WAS?
HE'S MY MOM'S YOUNGER BROTHER.
IT'S HIM AND HIS WIFE HERE.
OH...THEN WHERE'S YOUR MOM? WORKING SOMEWHERE?
MISSING.
TO BE HONEST...
...AFTER SHE DISAPPEARED, MY UNCLE WAS THE ONLY FAMILY I HAD LEFT. THAT'S WHY I MOVED HERE.
I'M STAYING WITH THEM.

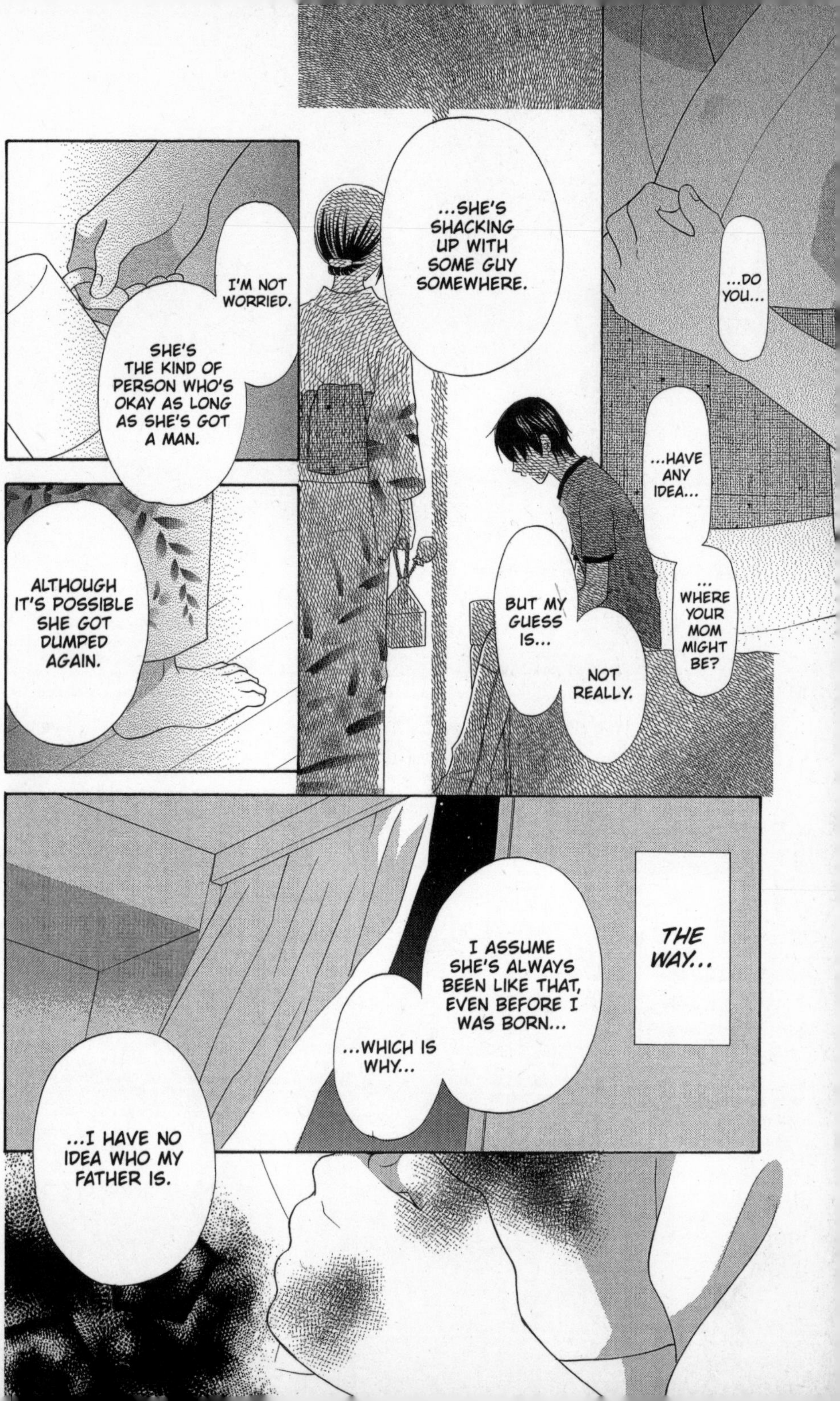
...DO YOU...
...HAVE ANY IDEA...
...WHERE YOUR MOM MIGHT BE?
NOT REALLY.
BUT MY GUESS IS...
...SHE'S SHACKING UP WITH SOME GUY SOMEWHERE.
I'M NOT WORRIED.
SHE'S THE KIND OF PERSON WHO'S OKAY AS LONG AS SHE'S GOT A MAN.
ALTHOUGH IT'S POSSIBLE SHE GOT DUMPED AGAIN.
THE WAY...
I ASSUME SHE'S ALWAYS BEEN LIKE THAT, EVEN BEFORE I WAS BORN...
...WHICH IS WHY...
...I HAVE NO IDEA WHO MY FATHER IS.

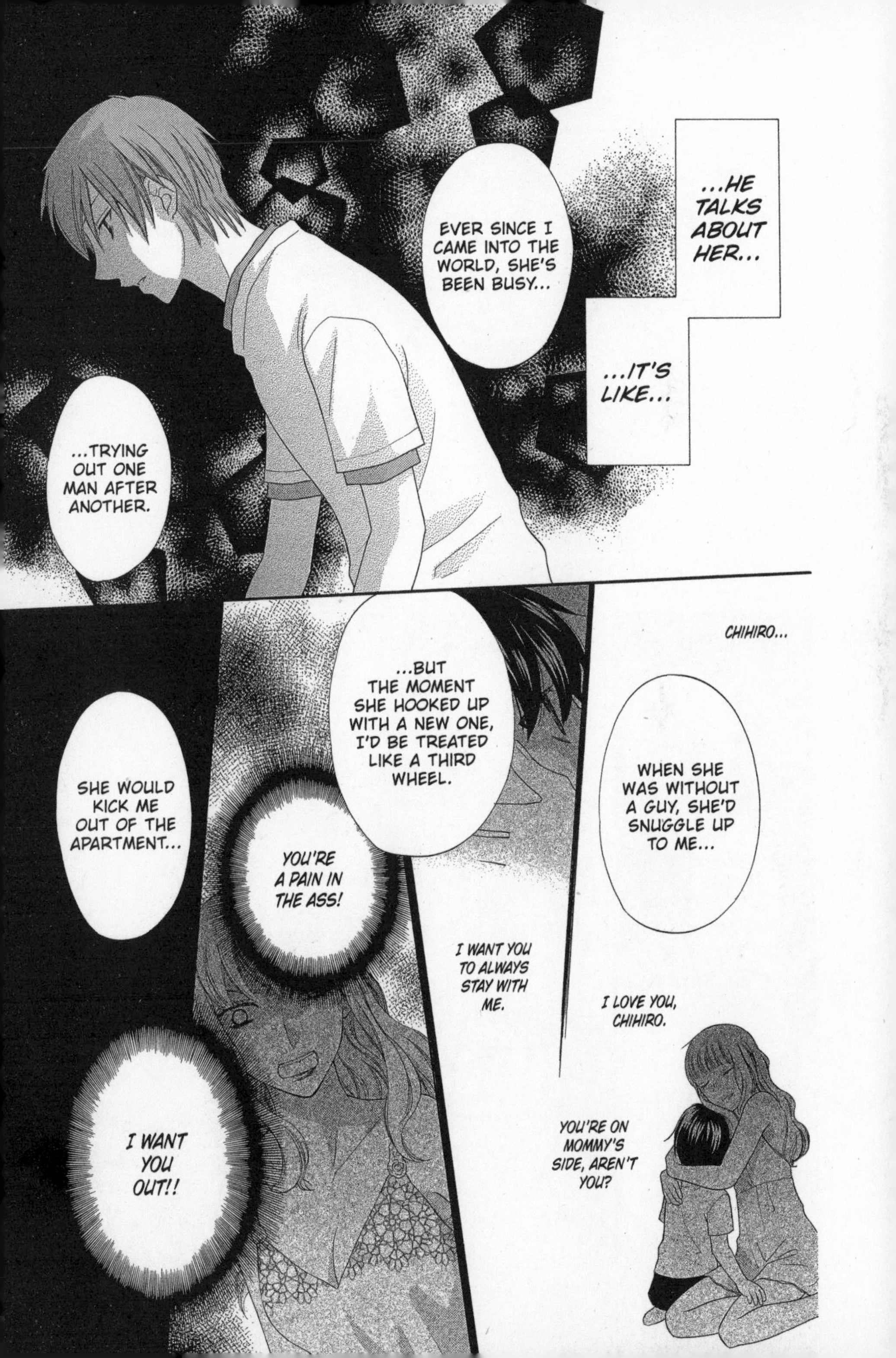
...HE TALKS ABOUT HER...
...IT'S LIKE...
EVER SINCE I CAME INTO THE WORLD, SHE'S BEEN BUSY...
...TRYING OUT ONE MAN AFTER ANOTHER.
CHIHIRO...
WHEN SHE WAS WITHOUT A GUY, SHE'D SNUGGLE UP TO ME...
I LOVE YOU, CHIHIRO.
I WANT YOU TO ALWAYS STAY WITH ME.
YOU'RE ON MOMMY'S SIDE, AREN'T YOU?
...BUT THE MOMENT SHE HOOKED UP WITH A NEW ONE, I'D BE TREATED LIKE A THIRD WHEEL.
SHE WOULD KICK ME OUT OF THE APARTMENT...
YOU'RE A PAIN IN THE ASS!
I WANT YOU OUT!!

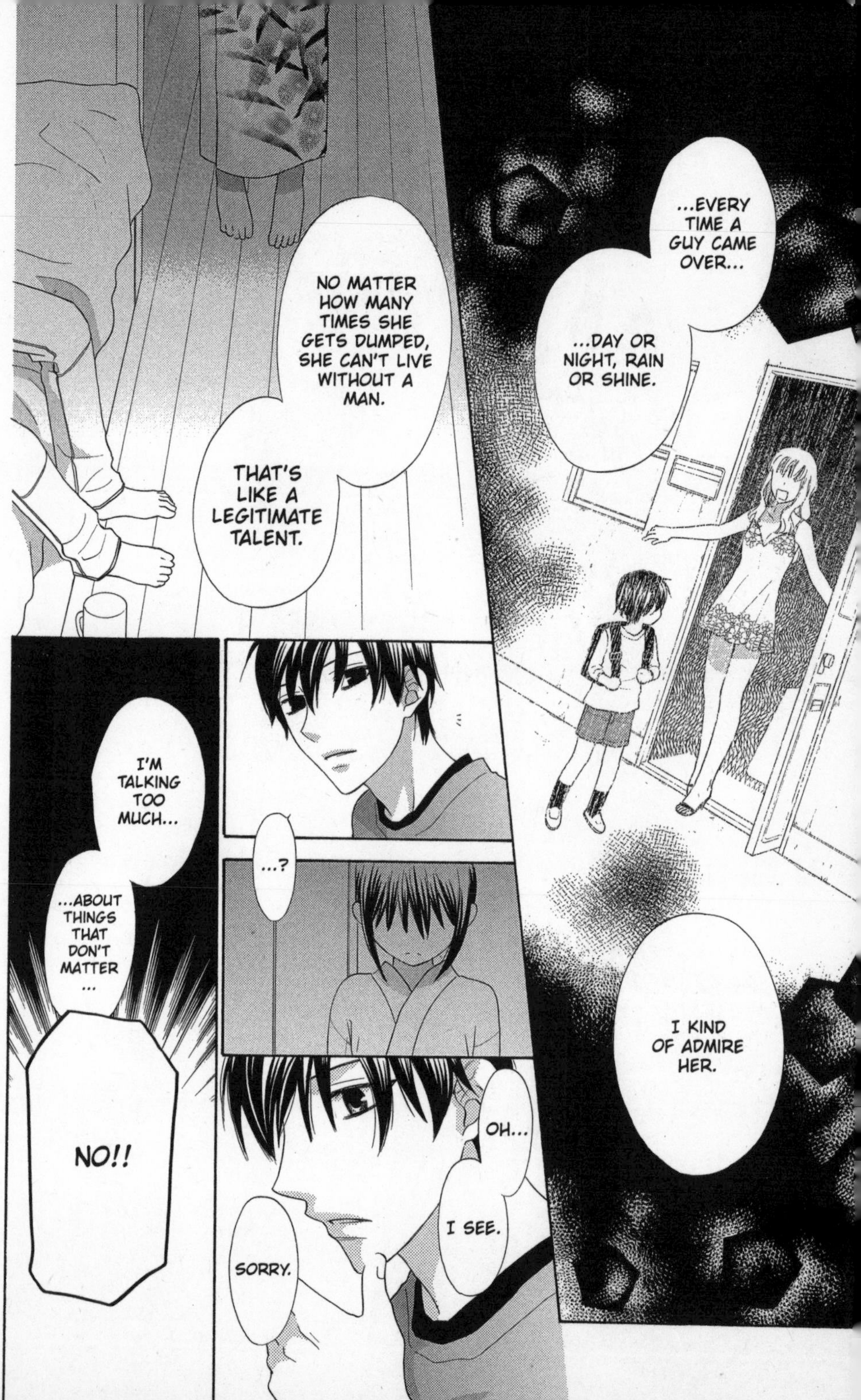
...EVERY TIME A GUY CAME OVER...
...DAY OR NIGHT, RAIN OR SHINE.
I KIND OF ADMIRE HER.
NO MATTER HOW MANY TIMES SHE GETS DUMPED, SHE CAN'T LIVE WITHOUT A MAN.
THAT'S LIKE A LEGITIMATE TALENT.
...?
I'M TALKING TOO MUCH...
...ABOUT THINGS THAT DON'T MATTER...
NO!!
OH...
I SEE.
SORRY.

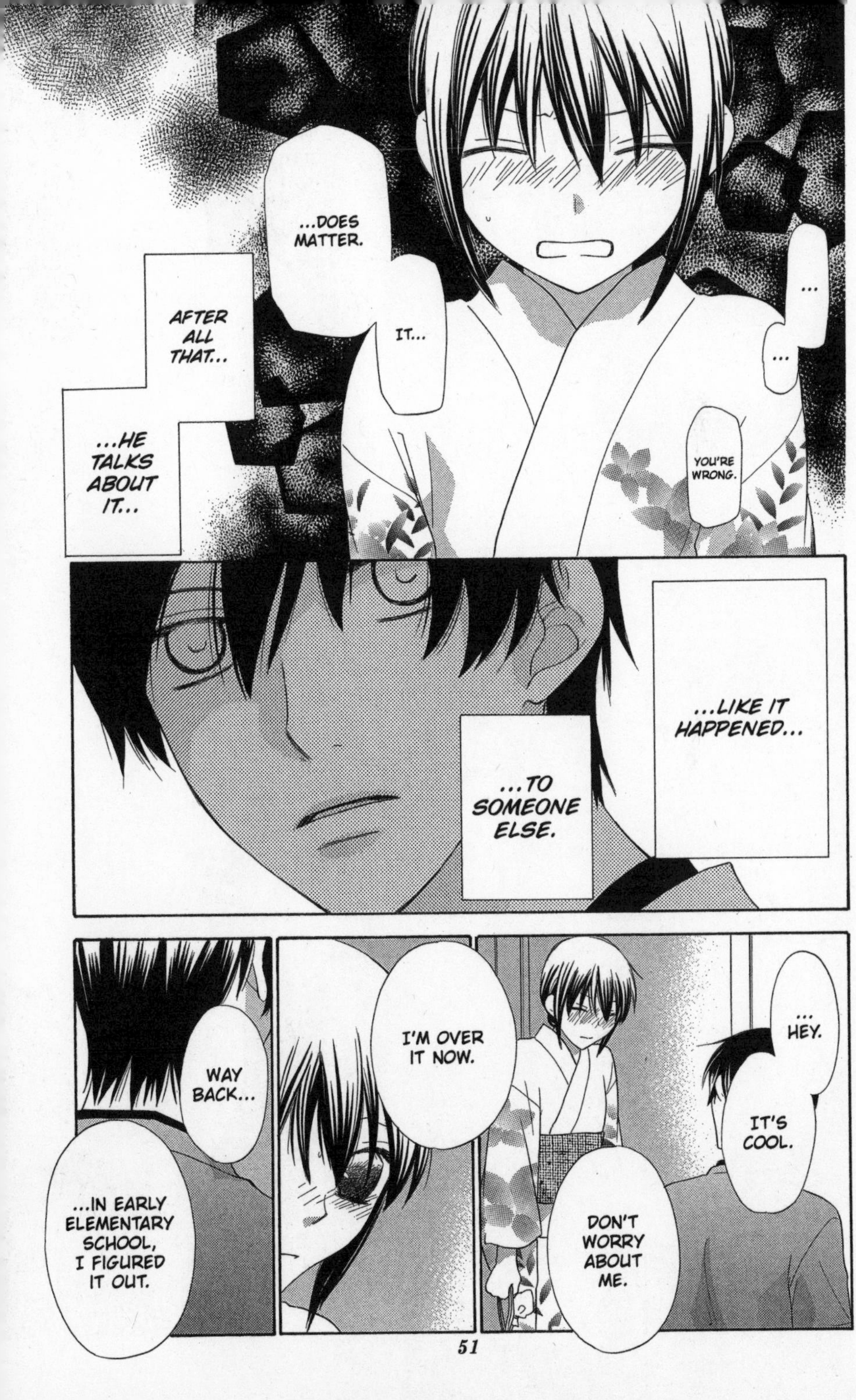
...
...
YOU'RE WRONG.
IT...
...DOES MATTER.
AFTER ALL THAT...
...HE TALKS ABOUT IT...
...LIKE IT HAPPENED...
...TO SOMEONE ELSE.
... HEY.
IT'S COOL.
DON'T WORRY ABOUT ME.
I'M OVER IT NOW.
WAY BACK...
...IN EARLY ELEMENTARY SCHOOL, I FIGURED IT OUT.

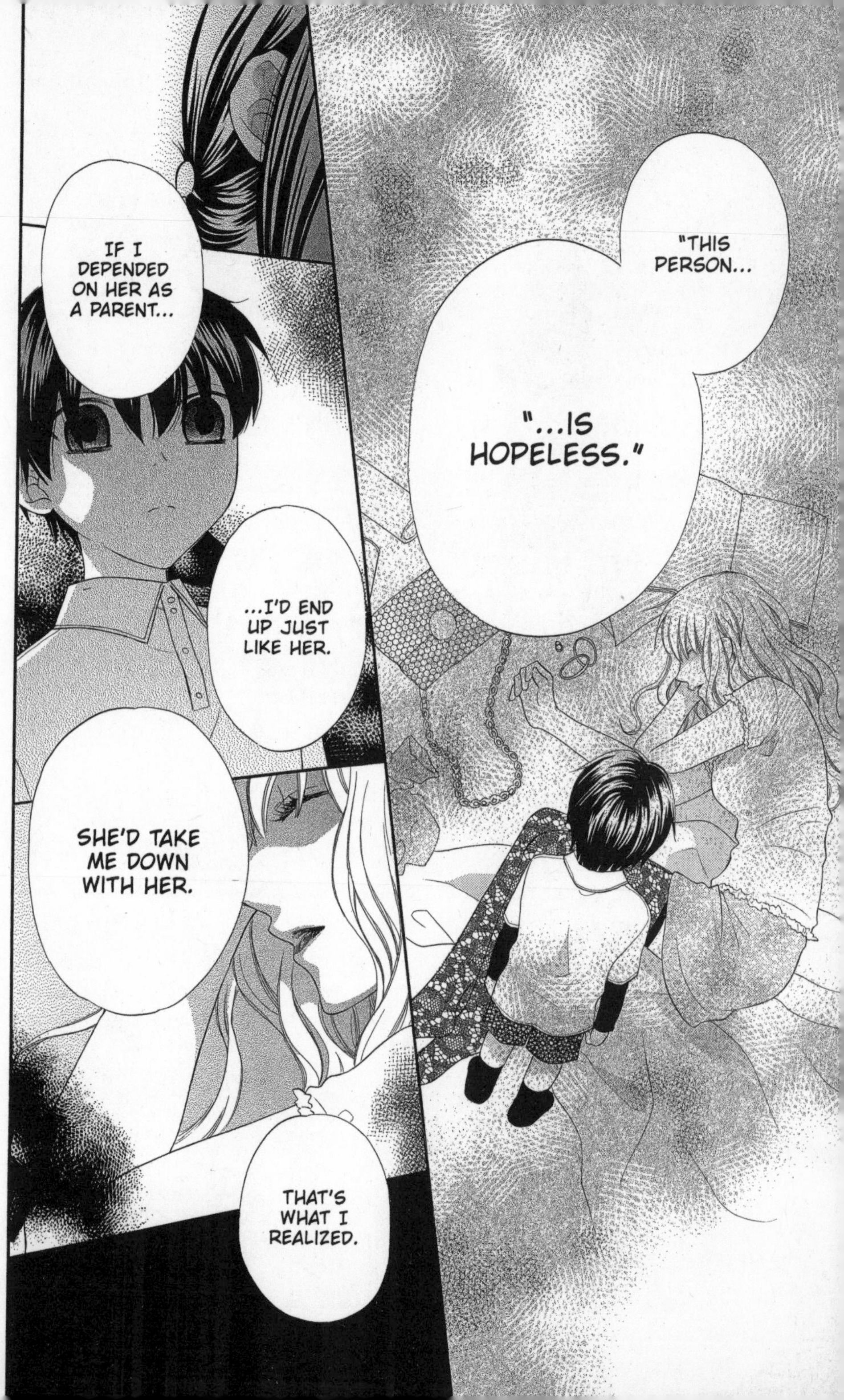
"THIS PERSON...
"...IS HOPELESS."
IF I DEPENDED ON HER AS A PARENT...
...I'D END UP JUST LIKE HER.
SHE'D TAKE ME DOWN WITH HER.
THAT'S WHAT I REALIZED.

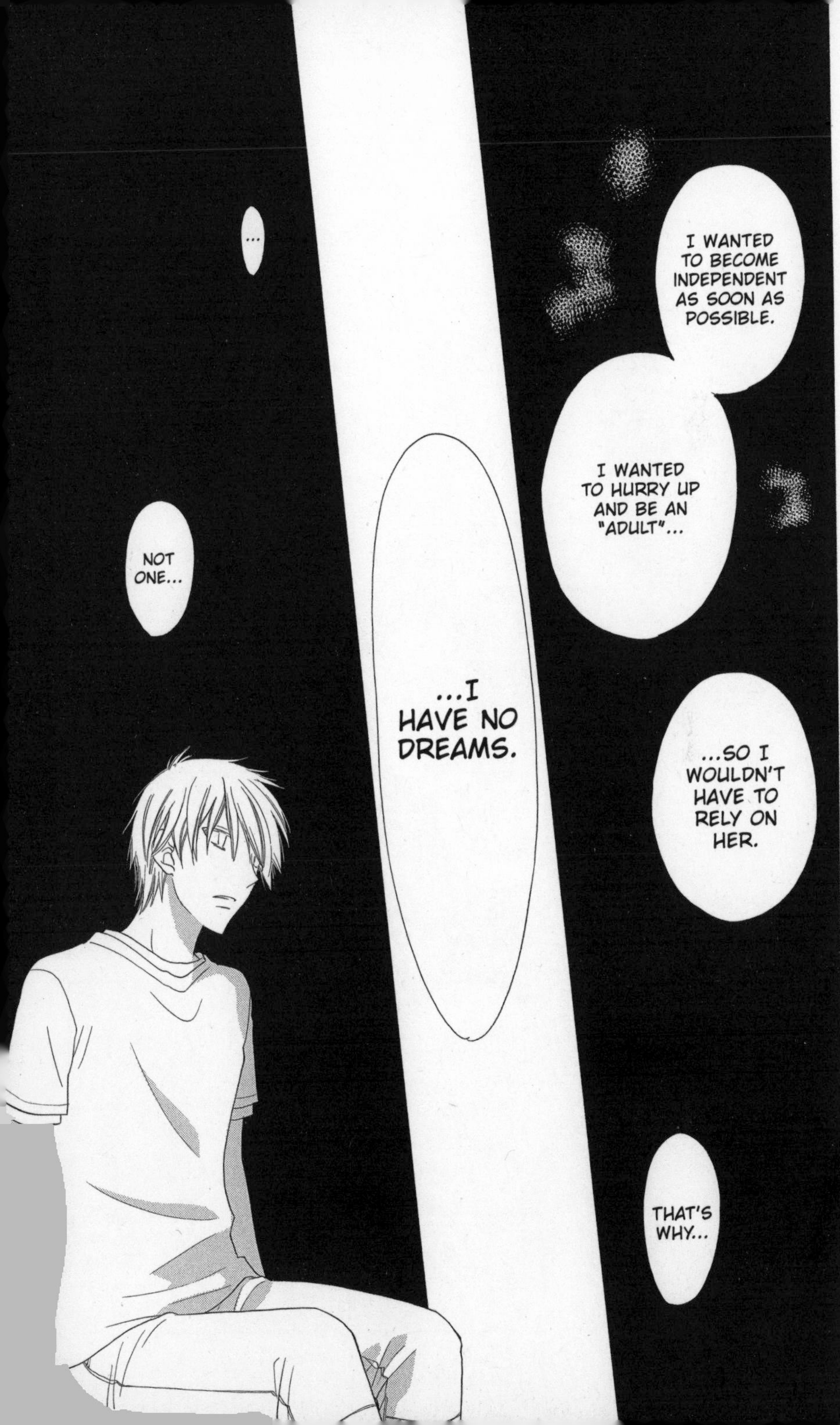
I WANTED TO BECOME INDEPENDENT AS SOON AS POSSIBLE.
I WANTED TO HURRY UP AND BE AN "ADULT"...
...SO I WOULDN'T HAVE TO RELY ON HER.
THAT'S WHY...
...I HAVE NO DREAMS.
...
NOT ONE...

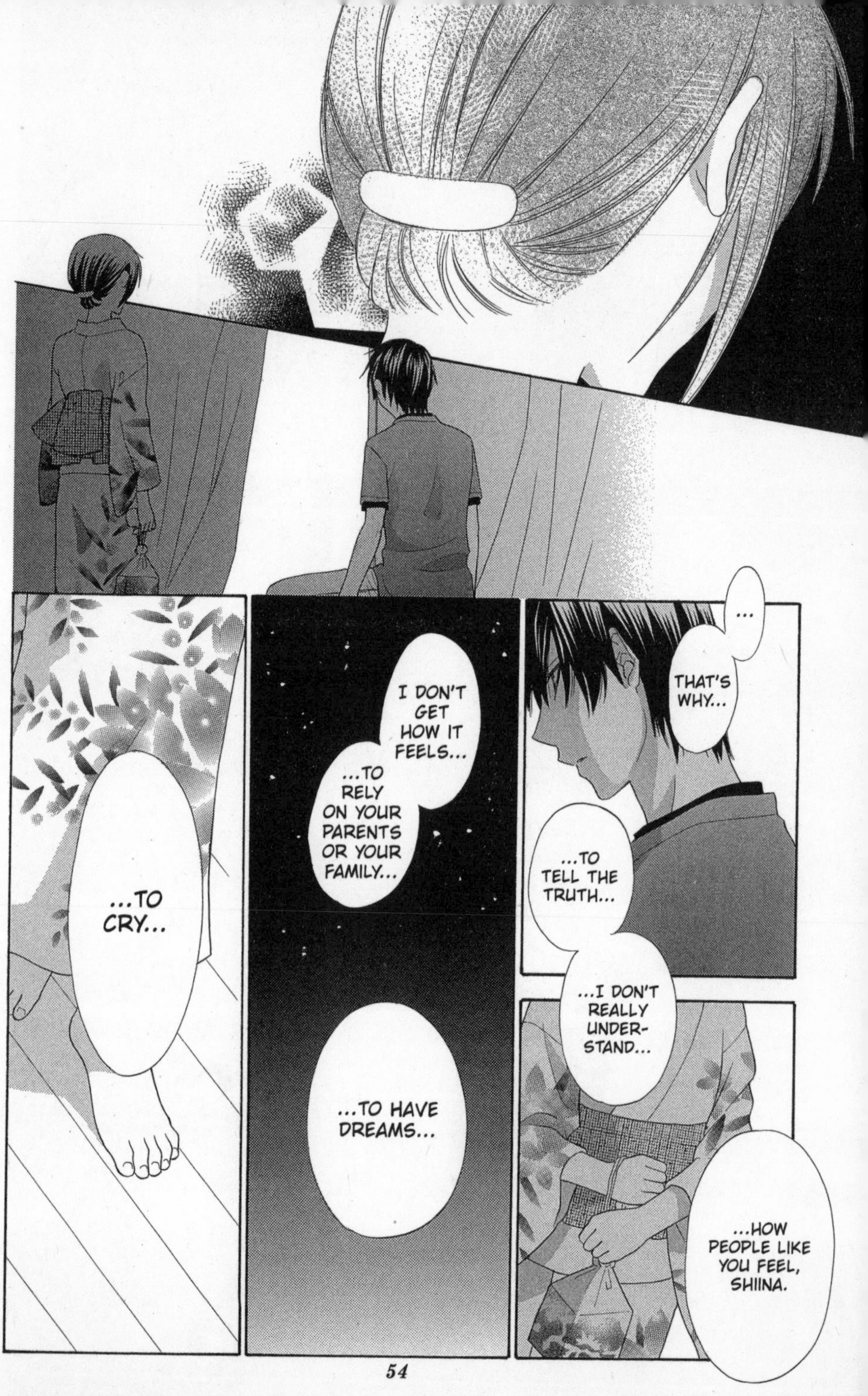
...
THAT'S WHY...
...TO TELL THE TRUTH...
...I DON'T REALLY UNDER-STAND...
...HOW PEOPLE LIKE YOU FEEL, SHIINA.
I DON'T GET HOW IT FEELS...
...TO RELY ON YOUR PARENTS OR YOUR FAMILY...
...TO HAVE DREAMS...
...TO CRY...

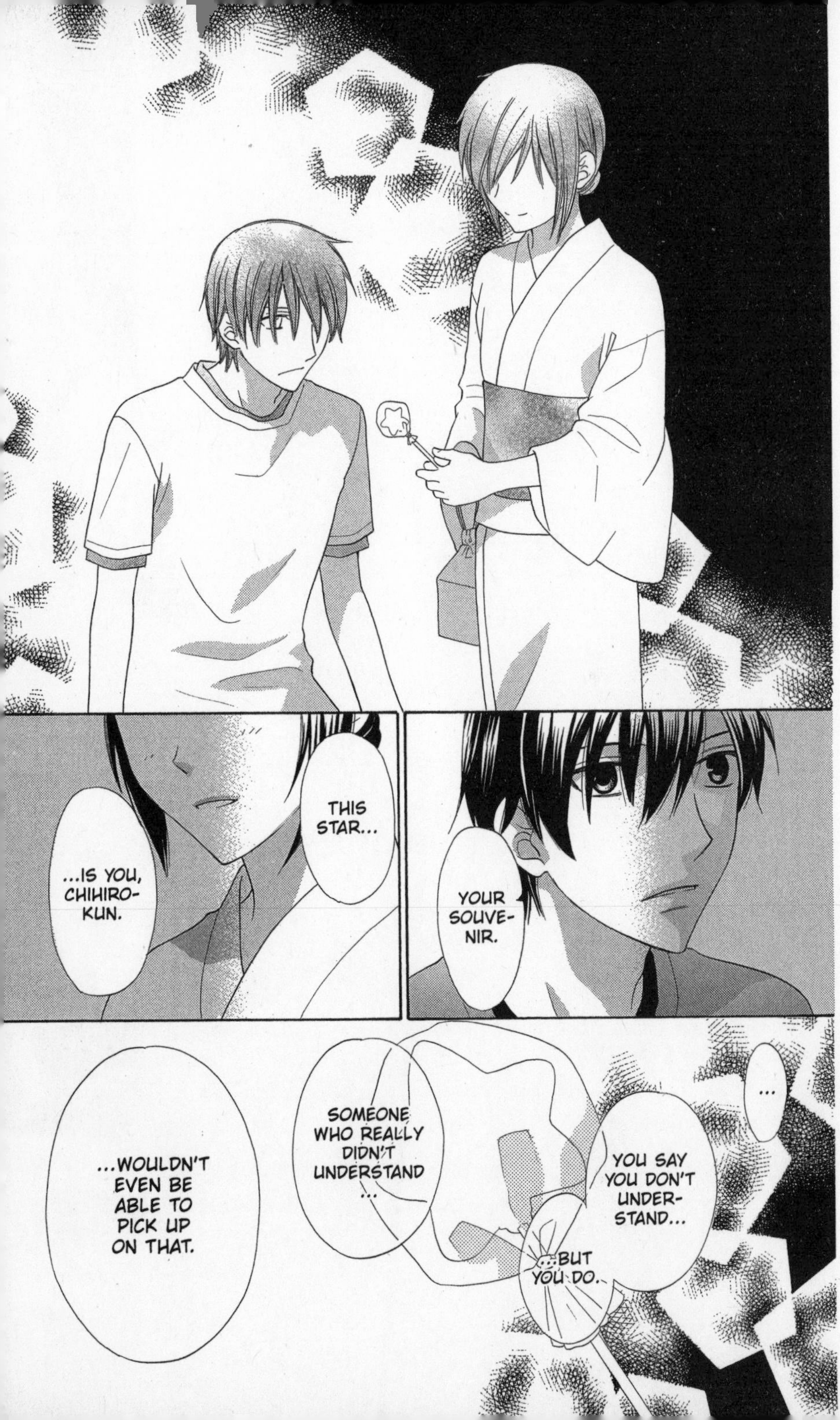
YOUR SOUVENIR.
THIS STAR...
...IS YOU, CHIHIRO-KUN.
...
YOU SAY YOU DON'T UNDERSTAND...
...BUT YOU DO.
SOMEONE WHO REALLY DIDN'T UNDERSTAND...
...WOULDN'T EVEN BE ABLE TO PICK UP ON THAT.

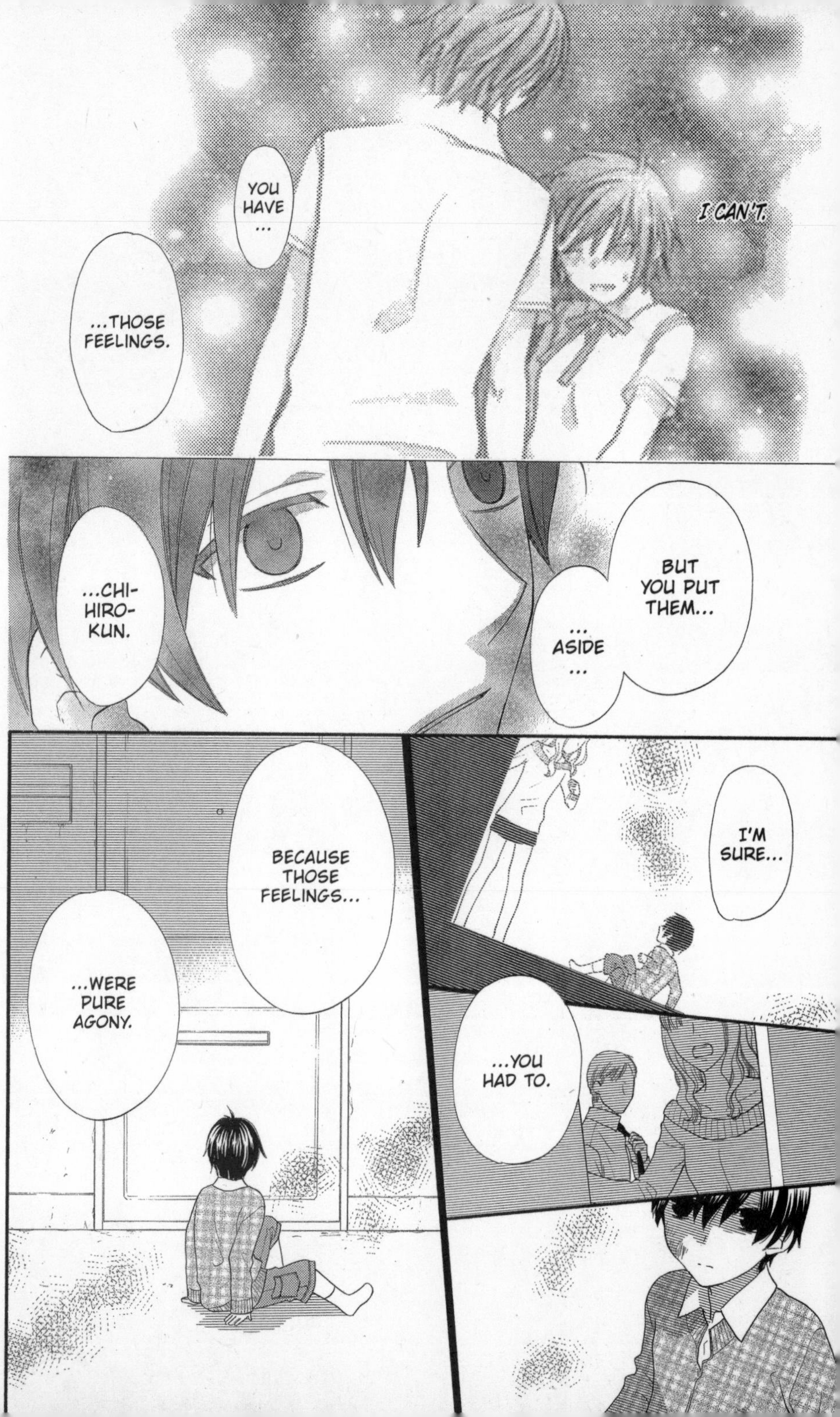
I CAN'T.
YOU HAVE ...
...THOSE FEELINGS.
BUT YOU PUT THEM...
...ASIDE...
...CHI-HIRO-KUN.
I'M SURE...
...YOU HAD TO.
BECAUSE THOSE FEELINGS...
...WERE PURE AGONY.

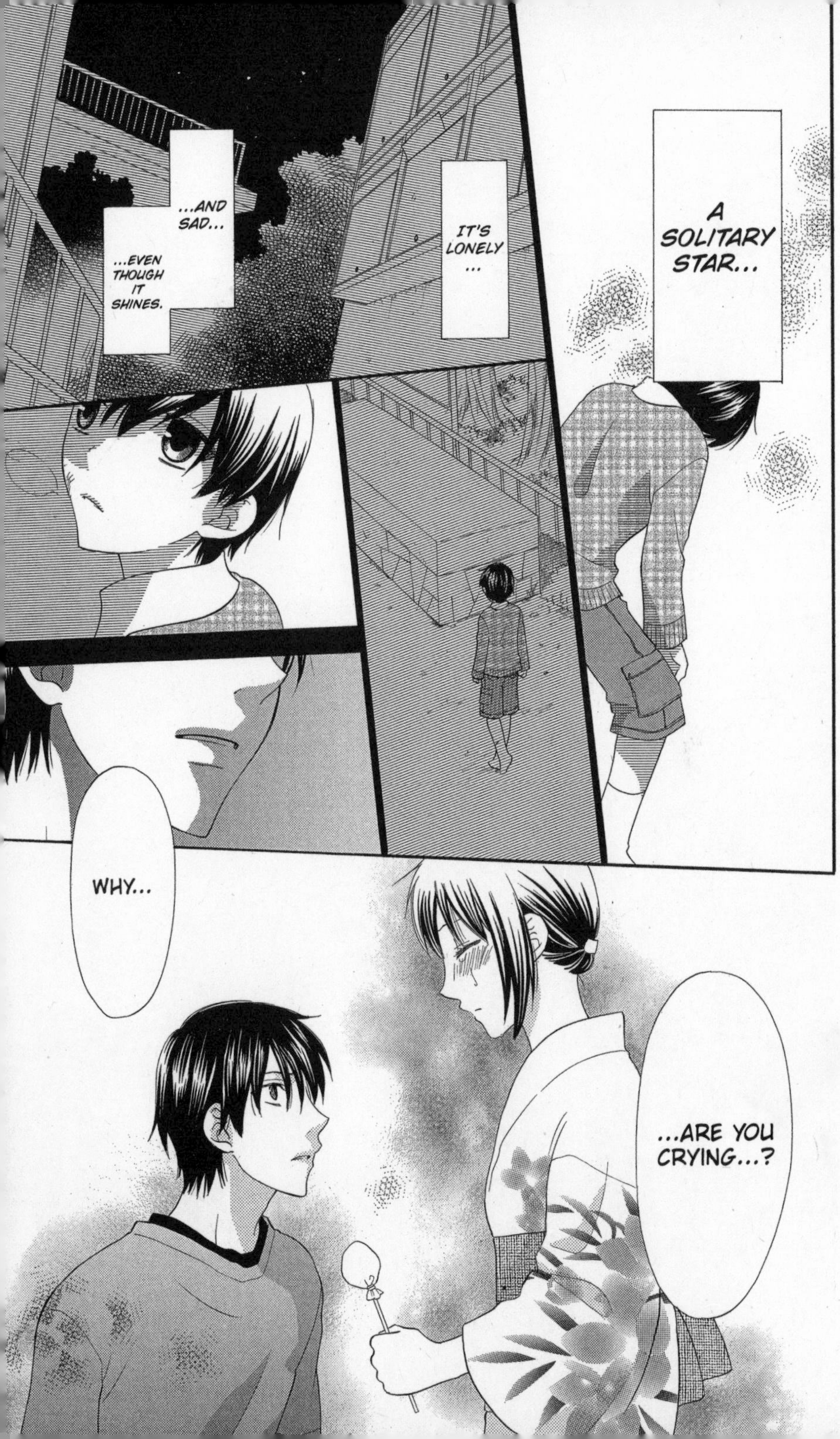
A SOLITARY STAR...
IT'S LONELY ...
...AND SAD...
...EVEN THOUGH IT SHINES.
WHY...
...ARE YOU CRYING...?

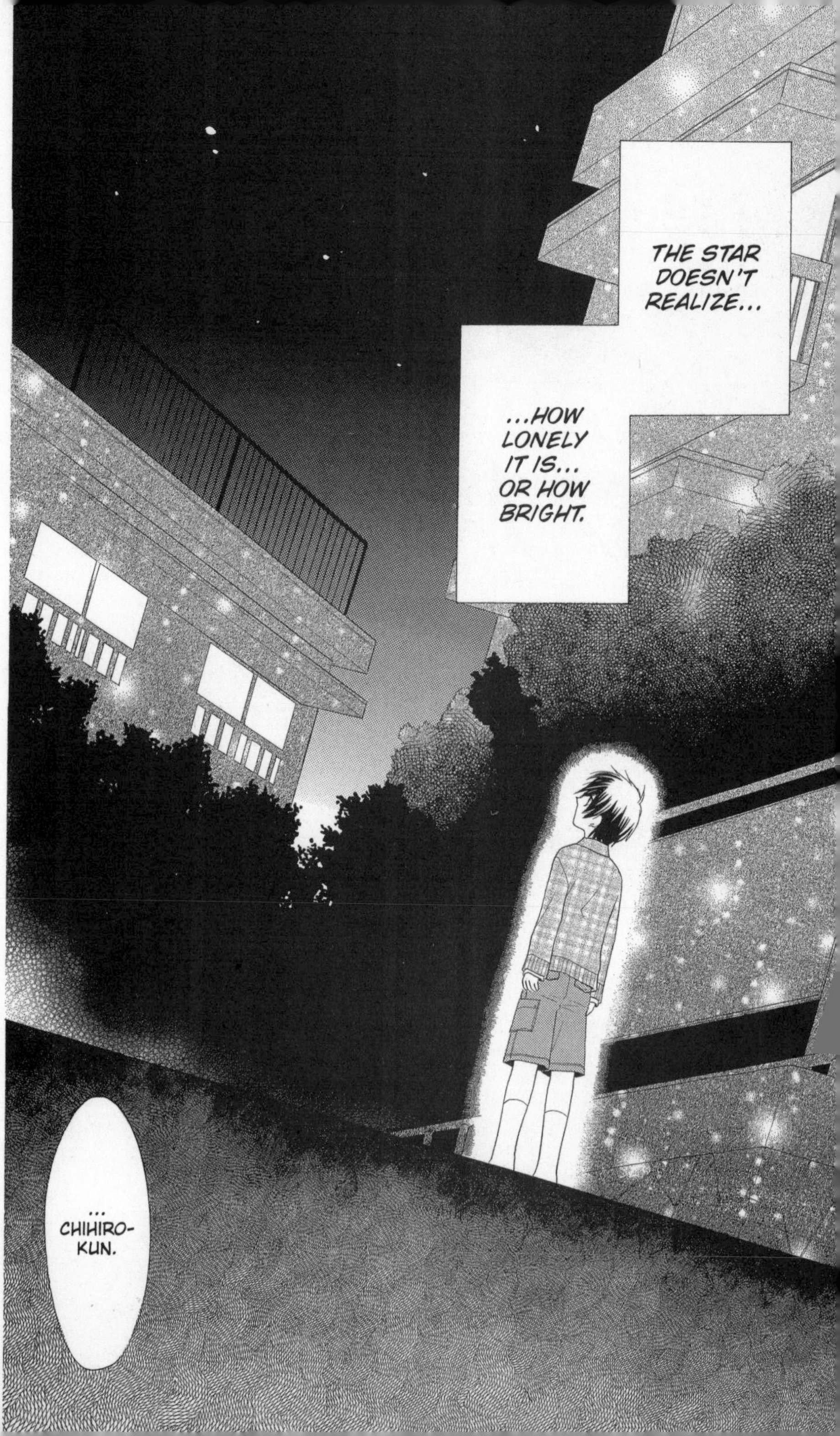
THE STAR DOESN'T REALIZE...
...HOW LONELY IT IS... OR HOW BRIGHT.
...CHIHIRO-KUN.

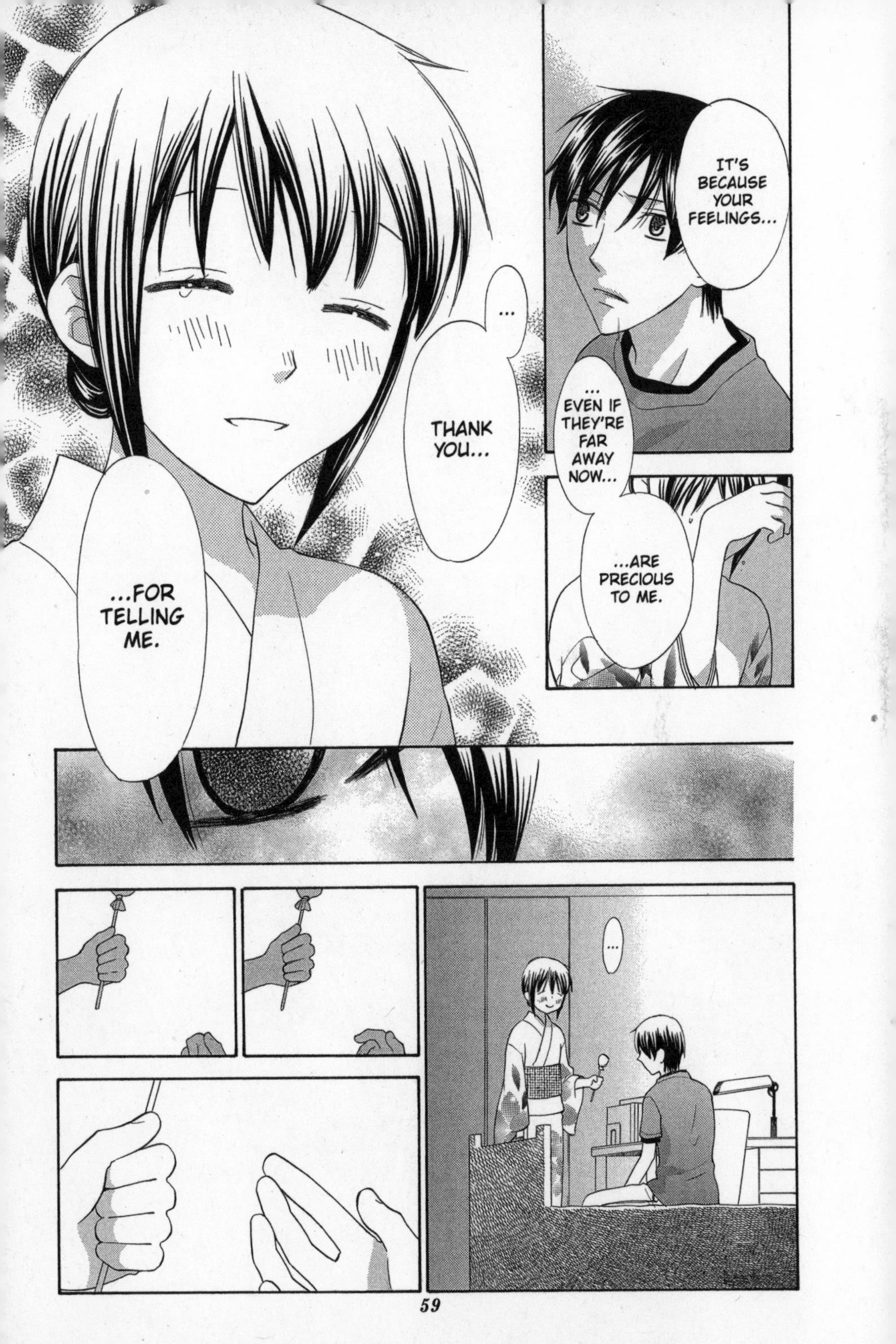
IT'S BECAUSE YOUR FEELINGS...
... EVEN IF THEY'RE FAR AWAY NOW...
...ARE PRECIOUS TO ME.
...
THANK YOU...
...FOR TELLING ME.
...

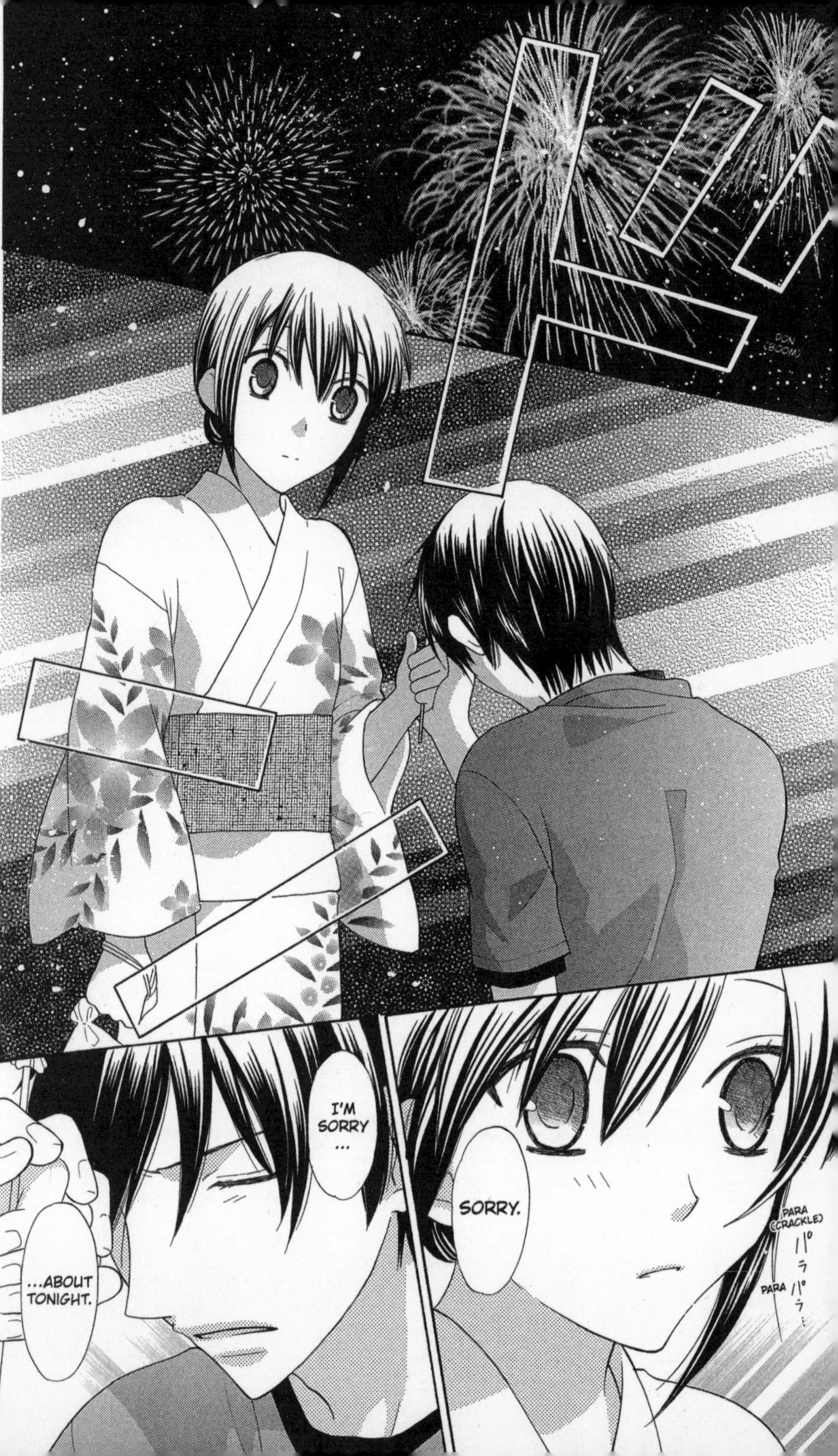
DON (BOOM)
SORRY.
PARA (CRACKLE) パ ラ
PARA パ ラ …
I'M SORRY …
…ABOUT TONIGHT.

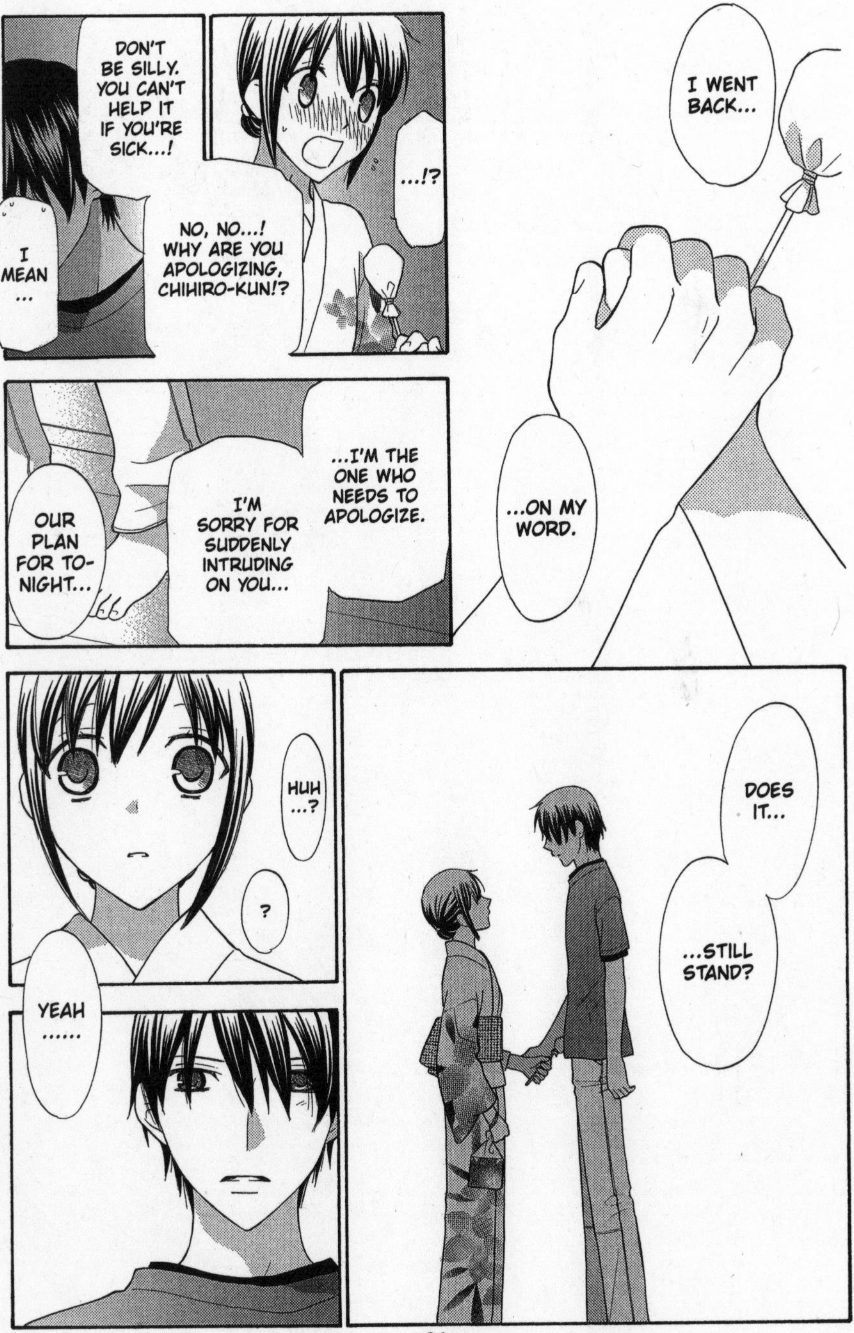
I WENT BACK...
...ON MY WORD.
...!?
NO, NO...! WHY ARE YOU APOLOGIZING, CHIHIRO-KUN!?
DON'T BE SILLY. YOU CAN'T HELP IT IF YOU'RE SICK...!
I MEAN ...
...I'M THE ONE WHO NEEDS TO APOLOGIZE.
I'M SORRY FOR SUDDENLY INTRUDING ON YOU...
OUR PLAN FOR TO-NIGHT...
DOES IT...
...STILL STAND?
HUH ...?
?
YEAH ......

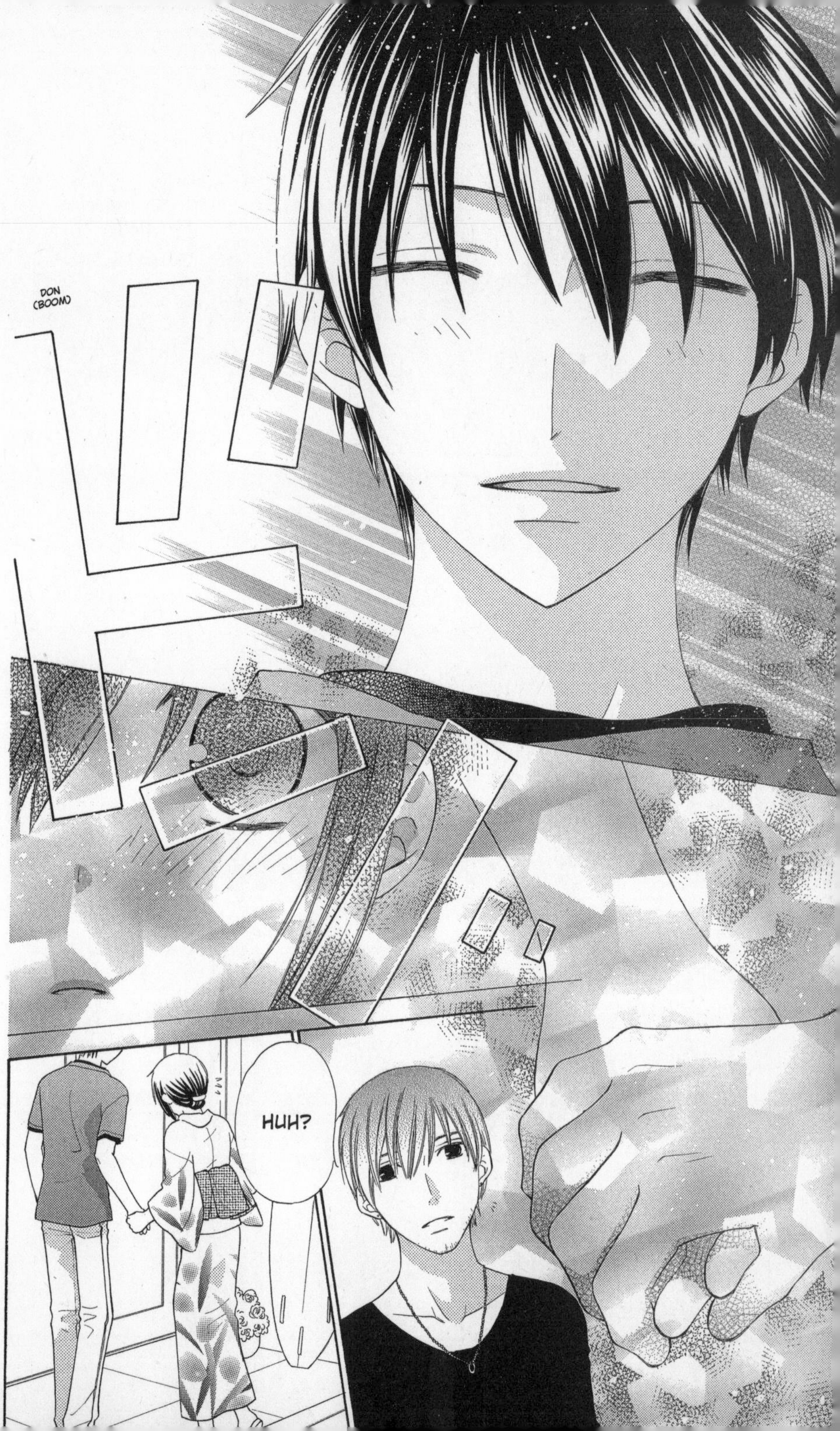
DON (BOOM)
HUH?

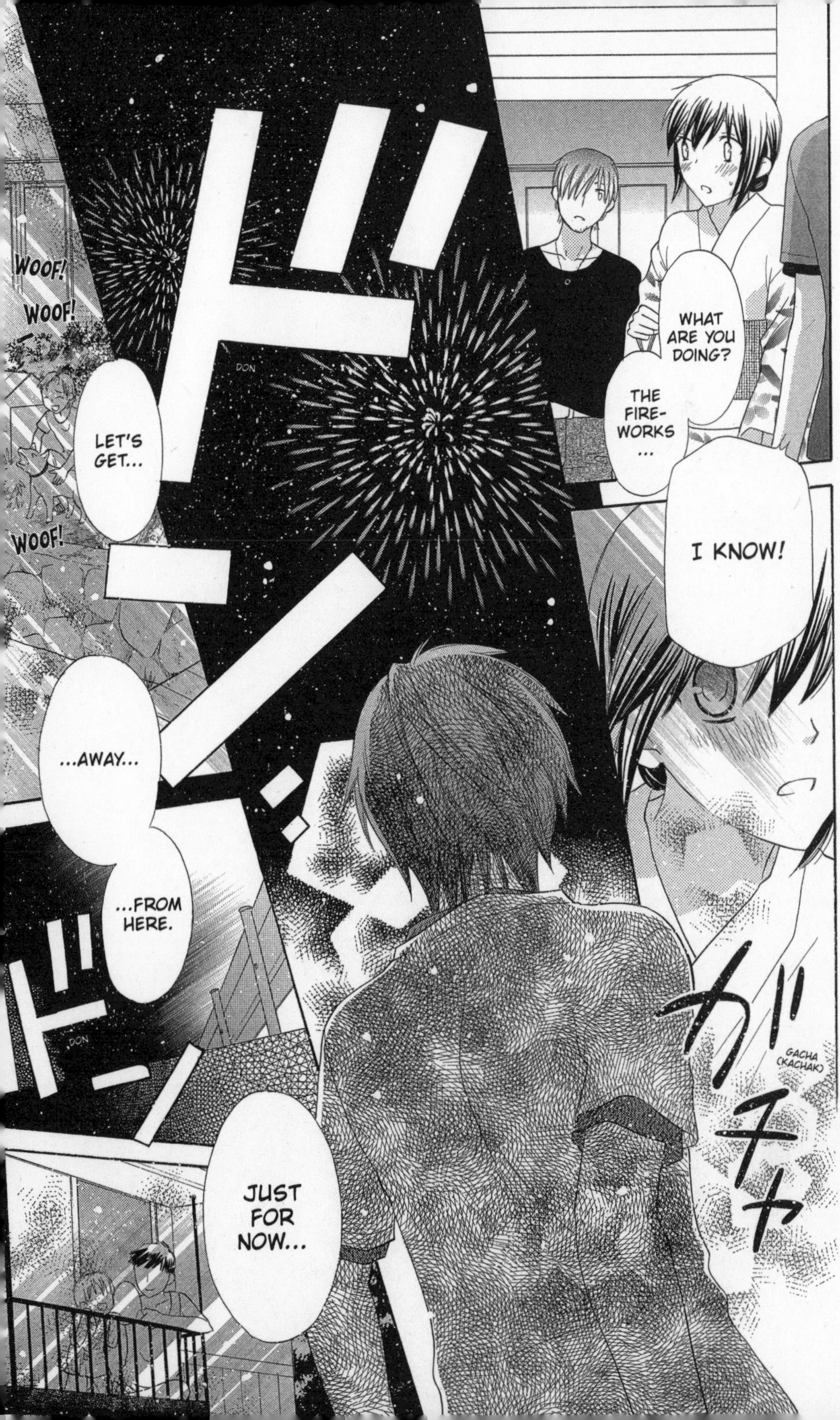
WHAT ARE YOU DOING?
THE FIRE-WORKS...
DON
WOOF!
WOOF!
LET'S GET...
WOOF!
I KNOW!
GACHA (KACHAK)
...AWAY...
...FROM HERE.
DON
JUST FOR NOW...

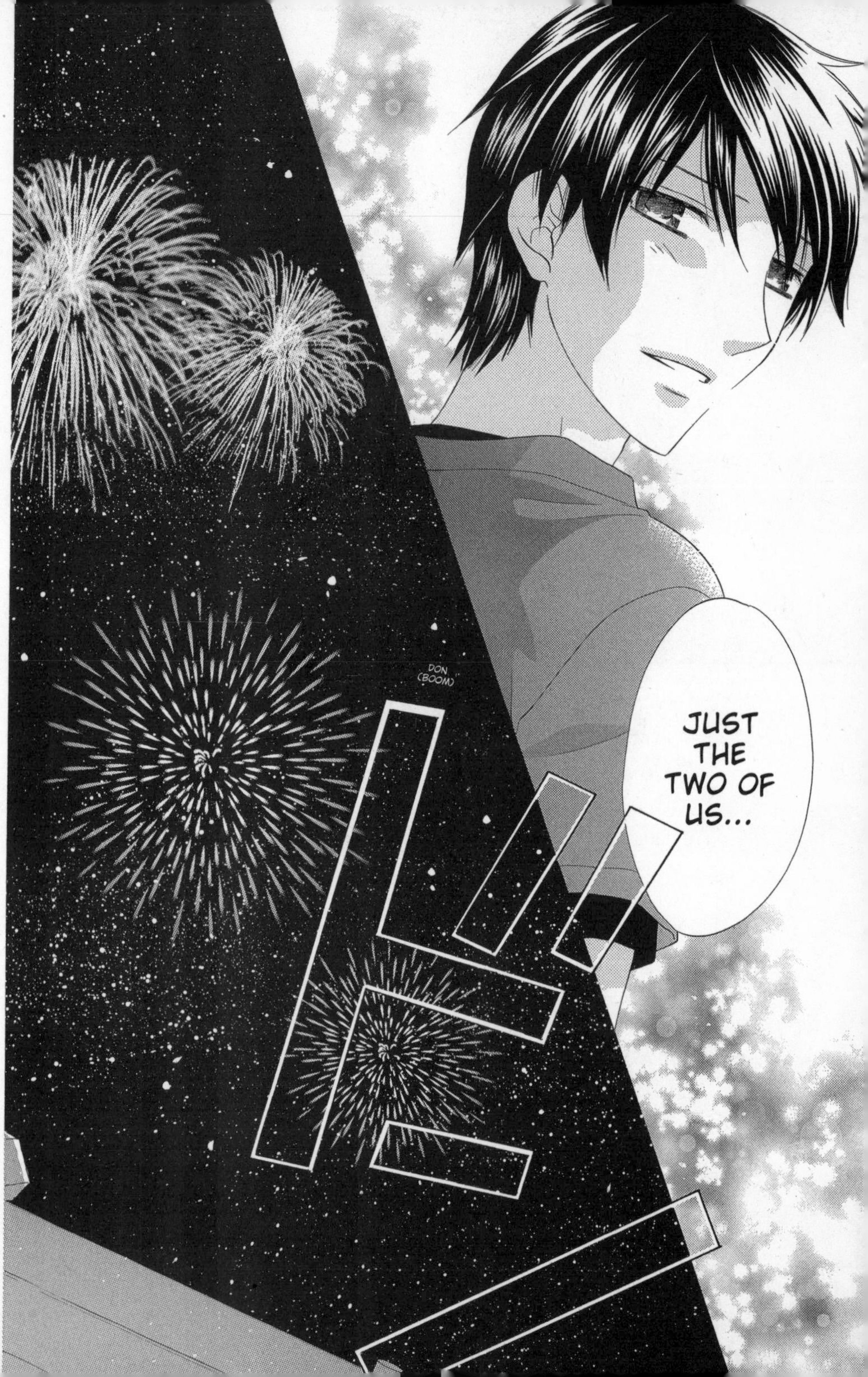
JUST THE TWO OF US...
DON (BOOM)

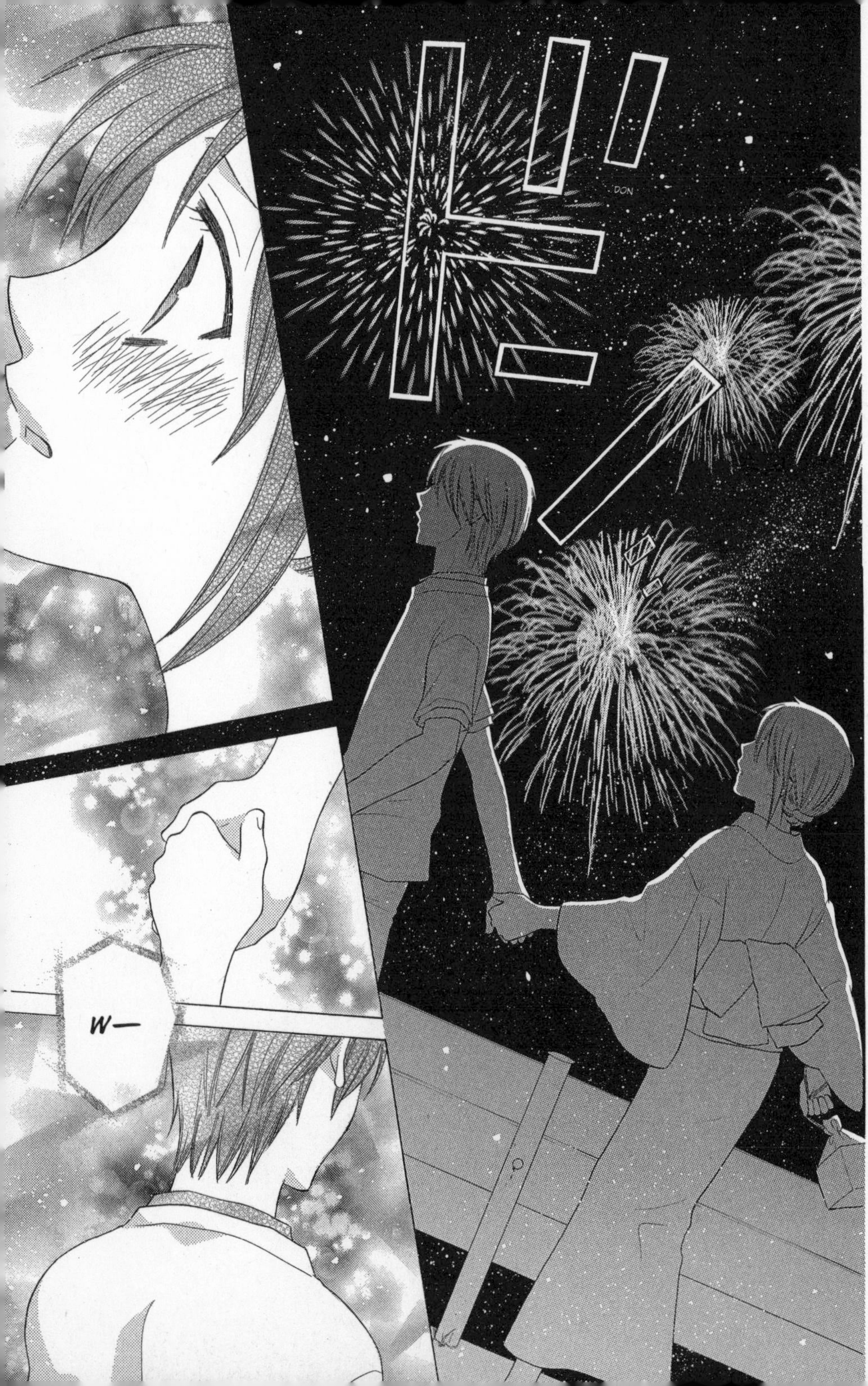
DON
W—

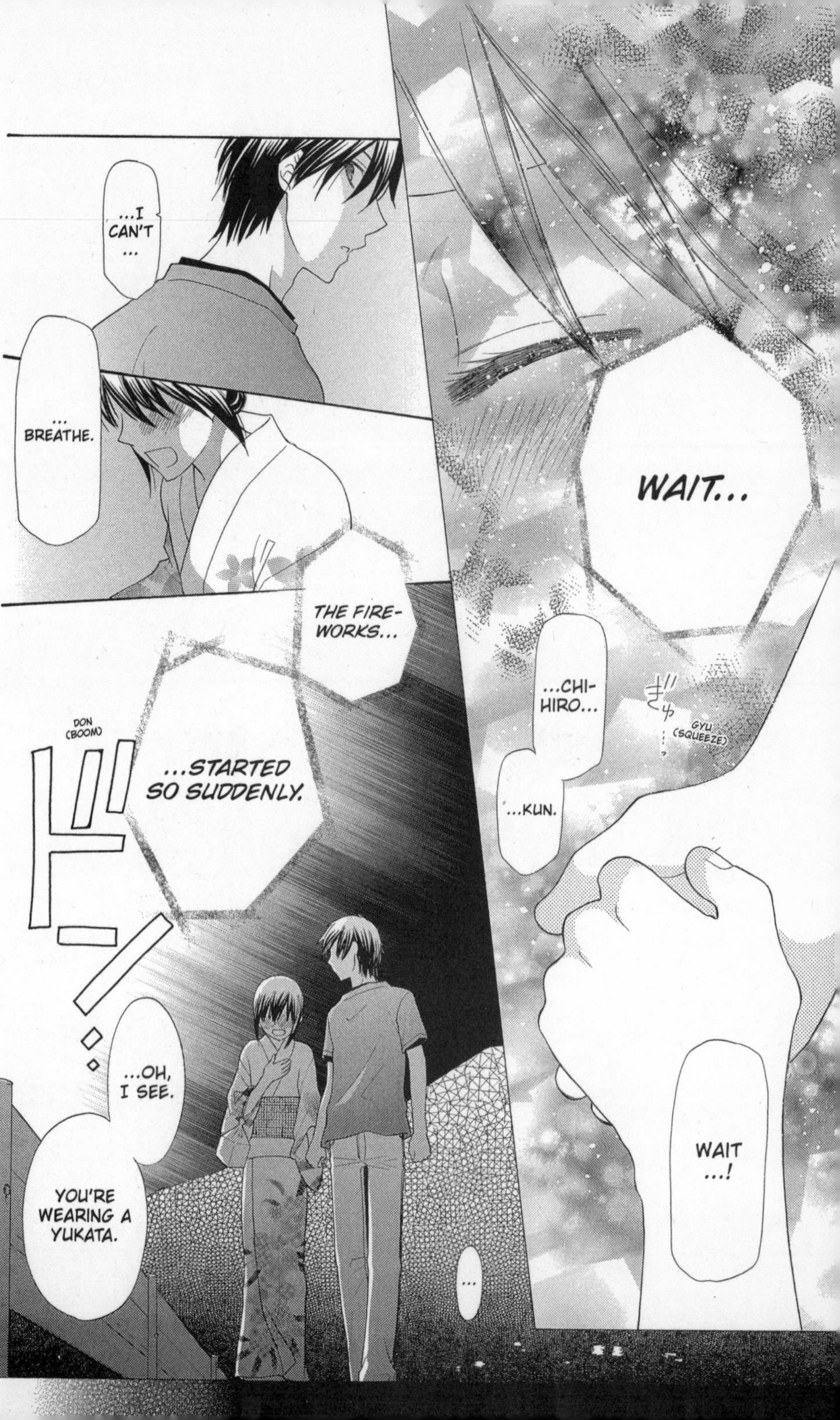
WAIT...
...CHI-HIRO...
ぎゅ
GYU (SQUEEZE)
...KUN.
WAIT ...!
...I CAN'T ...
... BREATHE.
THE FIRE-WORKS...
...STARTED SO SUDDENLY.
ドン
DON (BOOM)
...OH, I SEE.
YOU'RE WEARING A YUKATA.
...

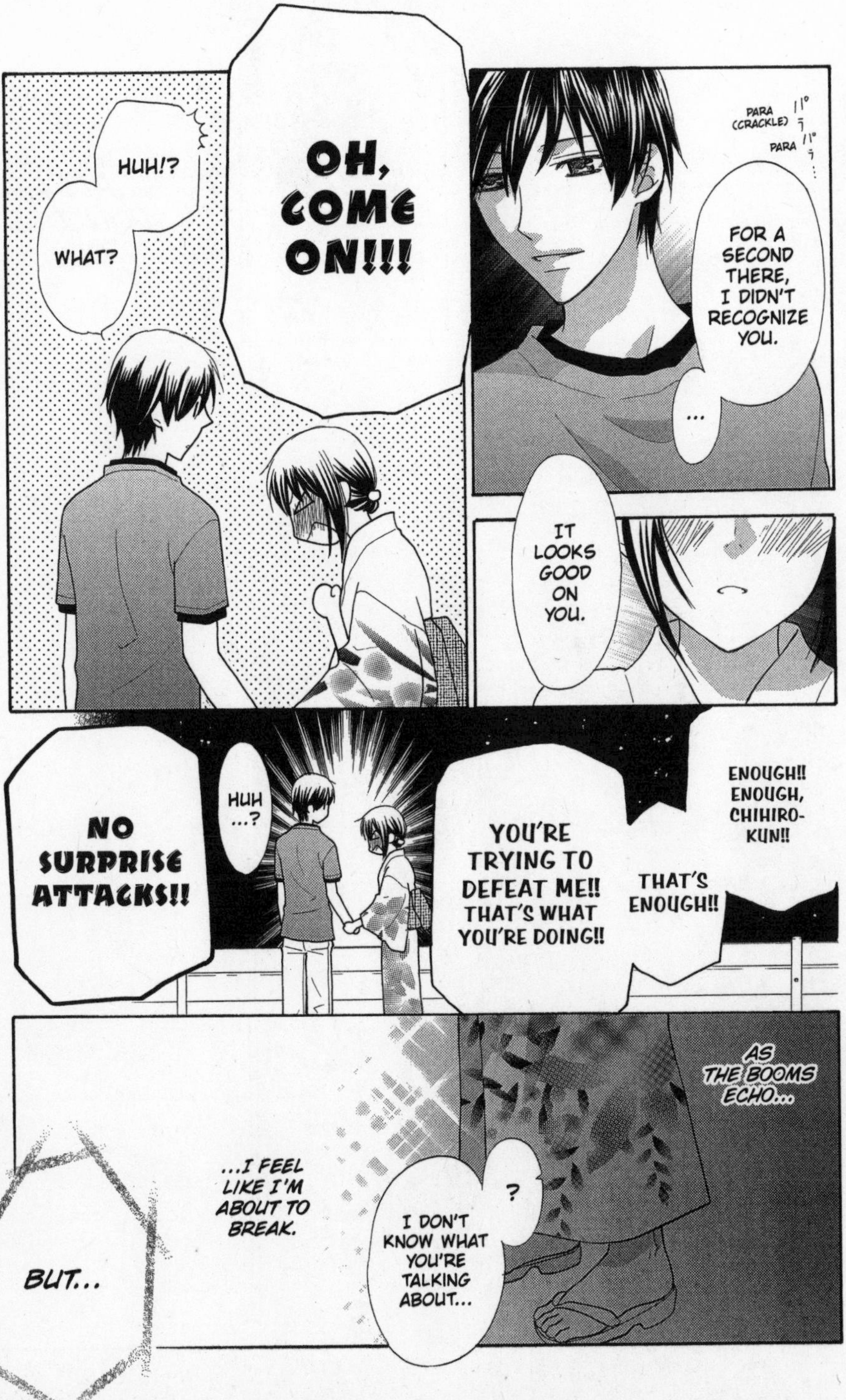
PARA (CRACKLE)
PARA
FOR A SECOND THERE, I DIDN'T RECOGNIZE YOU.
...
IT LOOKS GOOD ON YOU.
OH, COME ON!!!
HUH!?
WHAT?
ENOUGH!! ENOUGH, CHIHIRO-KUN!!
THAT'S ENOUGH!!
YOU'RE TRYING TO DEFEAT ME!! THAT'S WHAT YOU'RE DOING!!
HUH ...?
NO SURPRISE ATTACKS!!
AS THE BOOMS ECHO...
?
I DON'T KNOW WHAT YOU'RE TALKING ABOUT...
...I FEEL LIKE I'M ABOUT TO BREAK.
BUT...

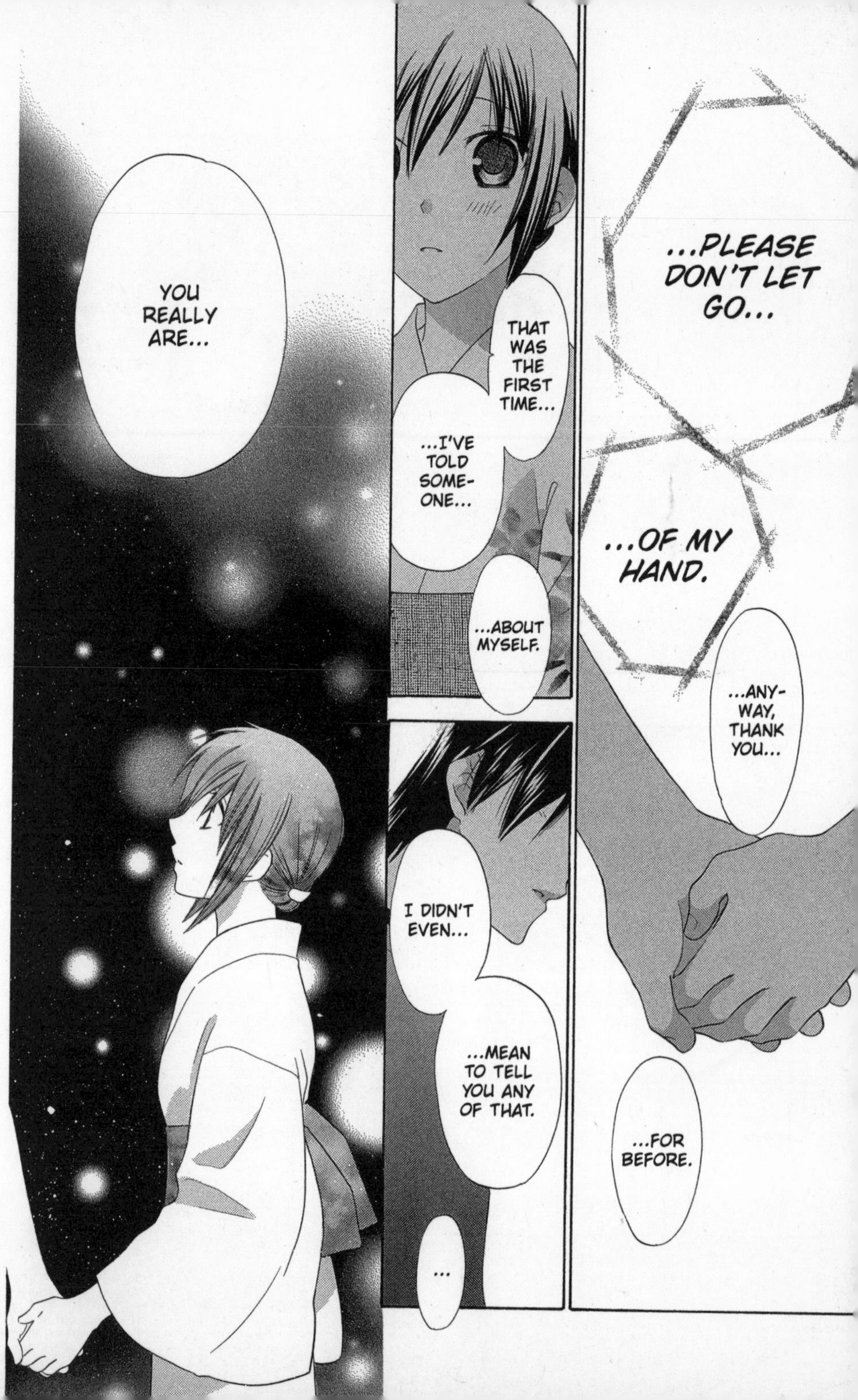
...PLEASE DON'T LET GO...
...OF MY HAND.
...ANY-WAY, THANK YOU...
...FOR BEFORE.
THAT WAS THE FIRST TIME...
...I'VE TOLD SOME-ONE...
...ABOUT MYSELF.
I DIDN'T EVEN...
...MEAN TO TELL YOU ANY OF THAT.
...
YOU REALLY ARE...

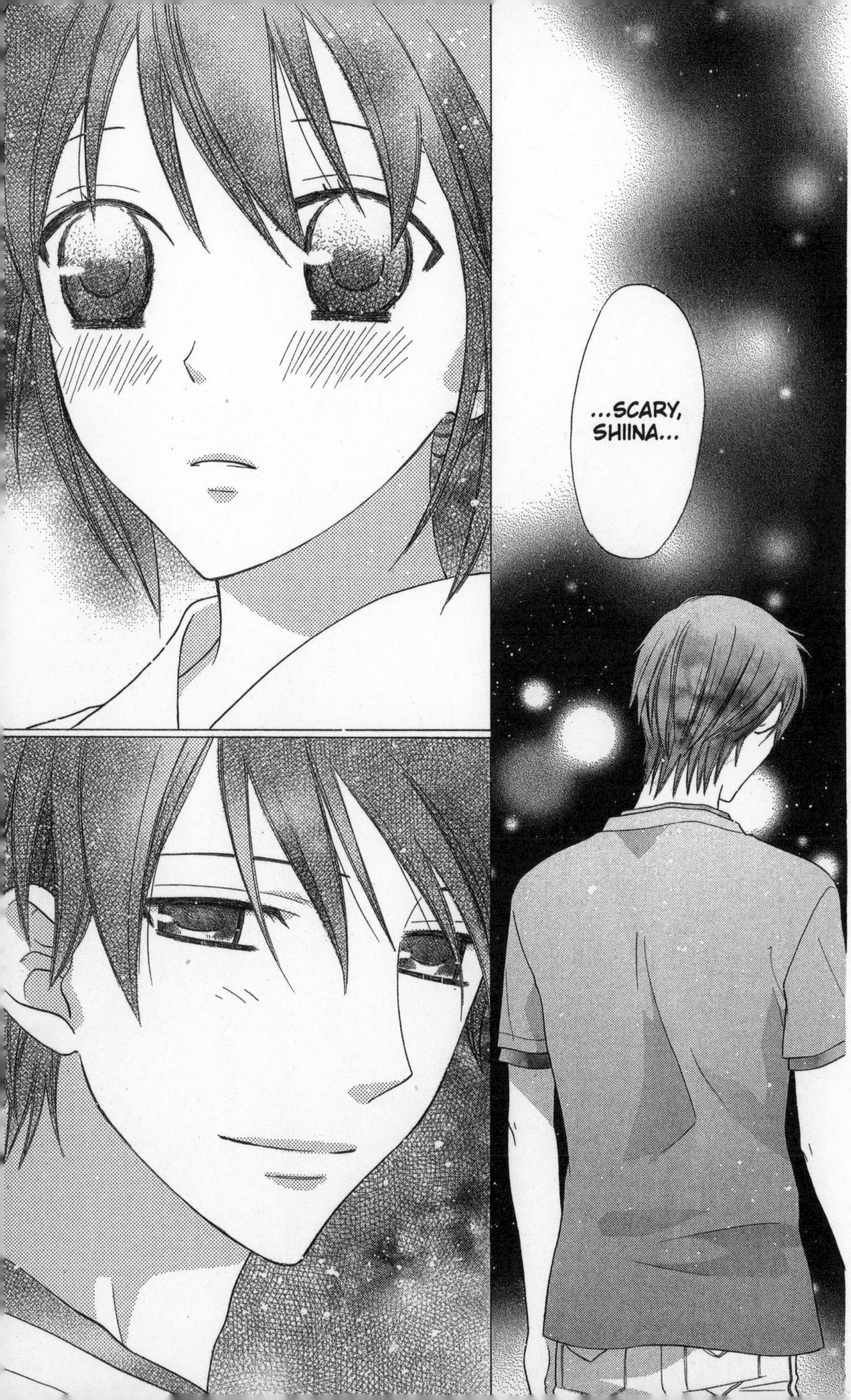
...SCARY, SHIINA...

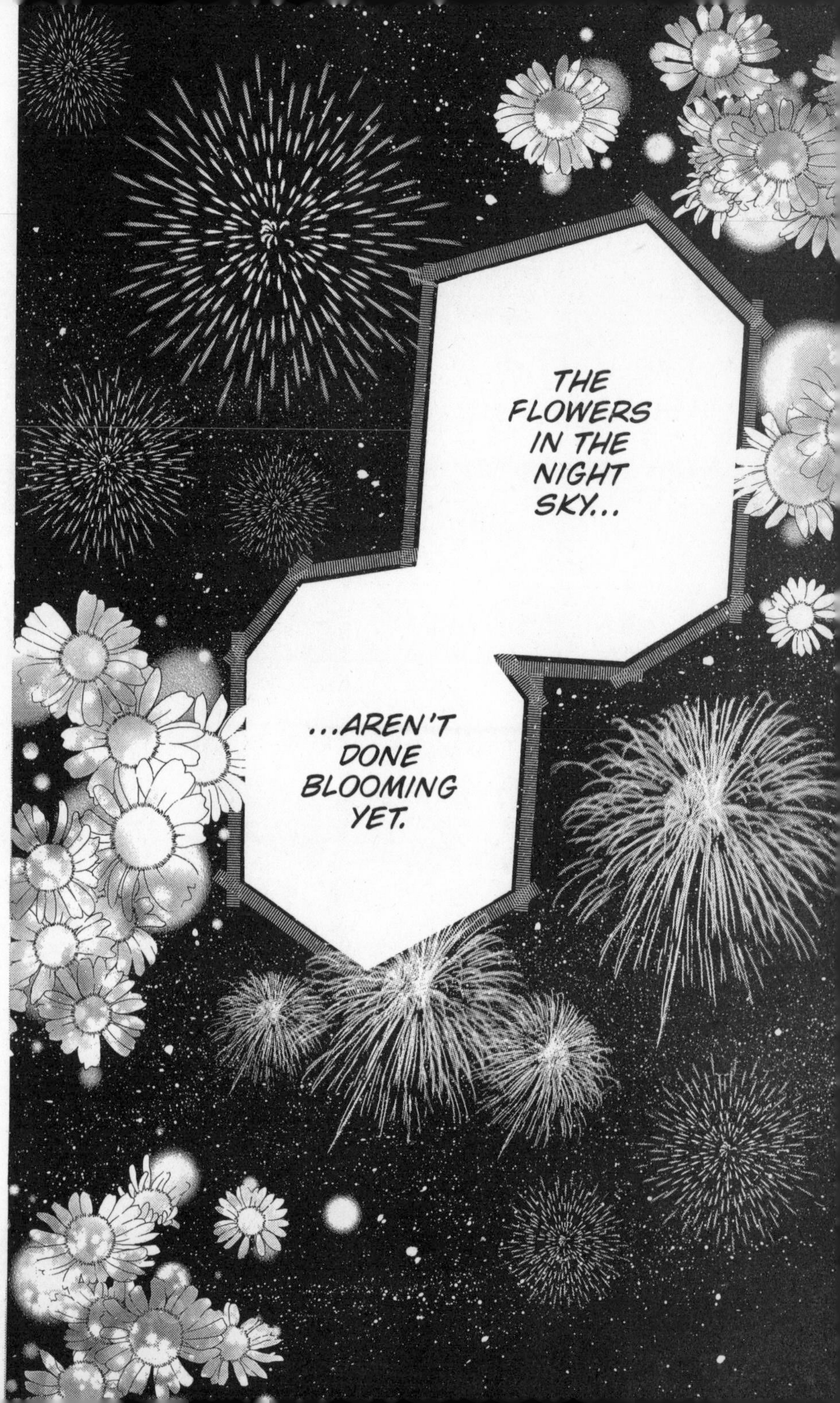
THE FLOWERS IN THE NIGHT SKY...
...AREN'T DONE BLOOMING YET.

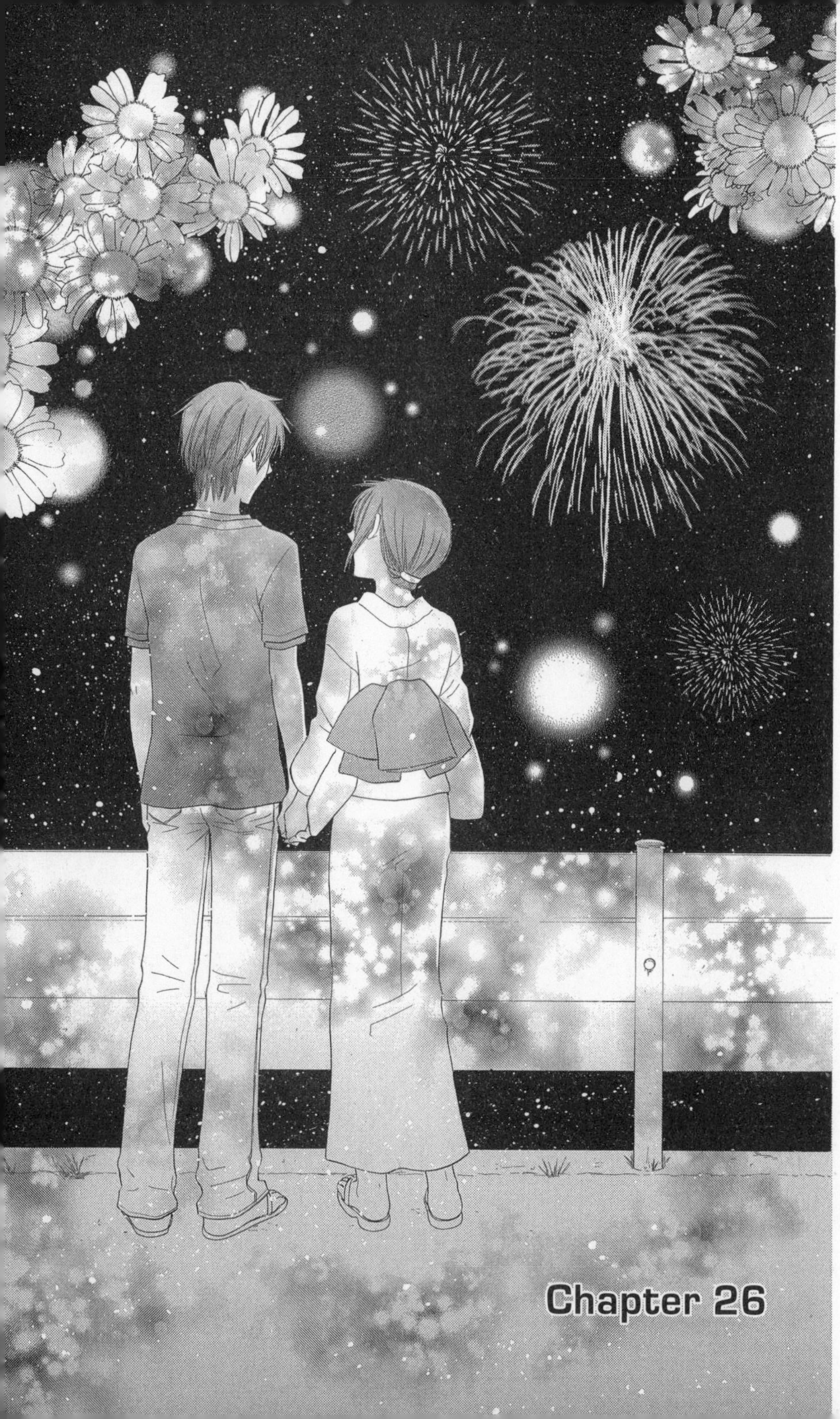
Chapter 26

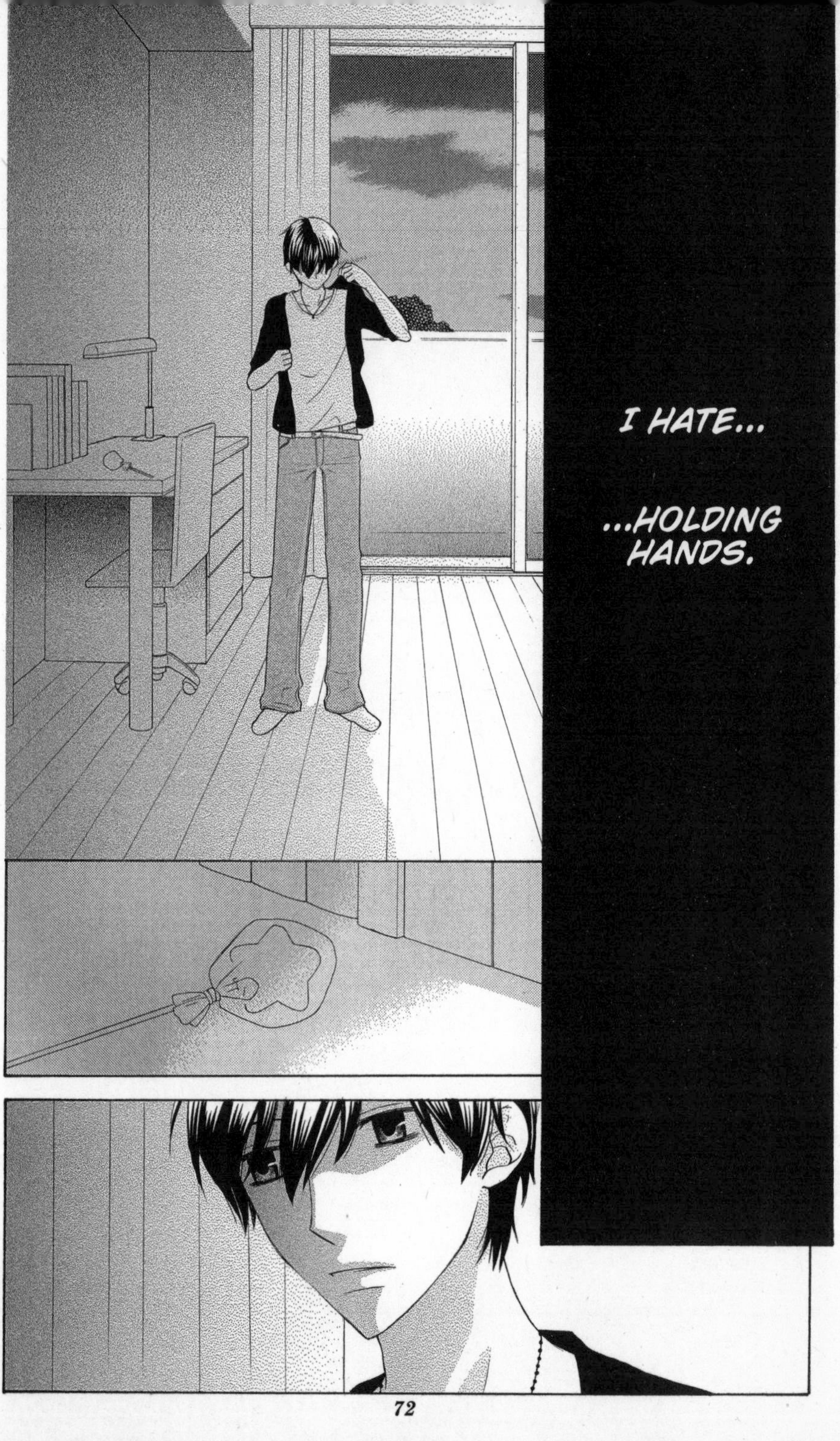
I HATE...
...HOLDING HANDS.

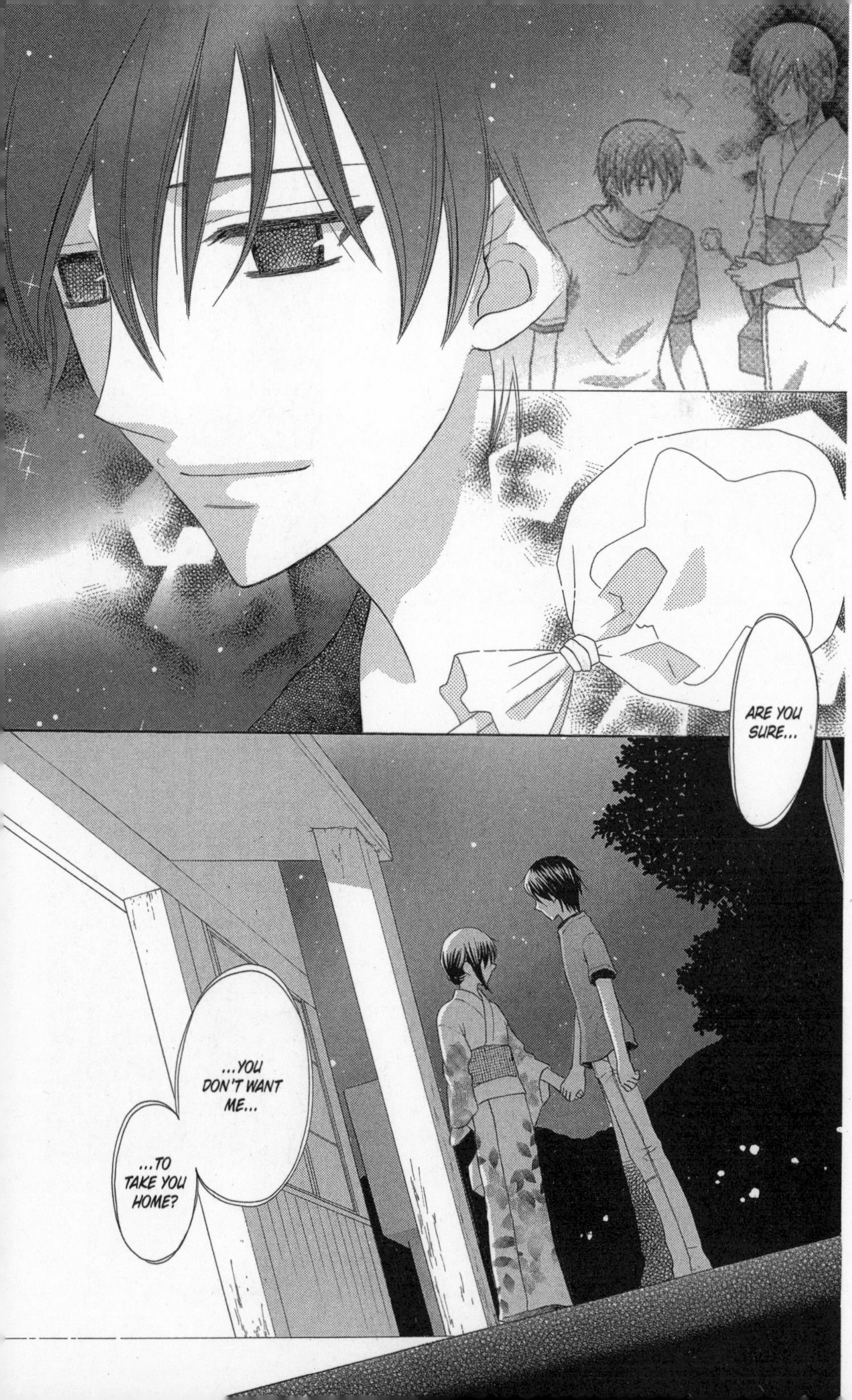
ARE YOU SURE...
...YOU DON'T WANT ME...
...TO TAKE YOU HOME?

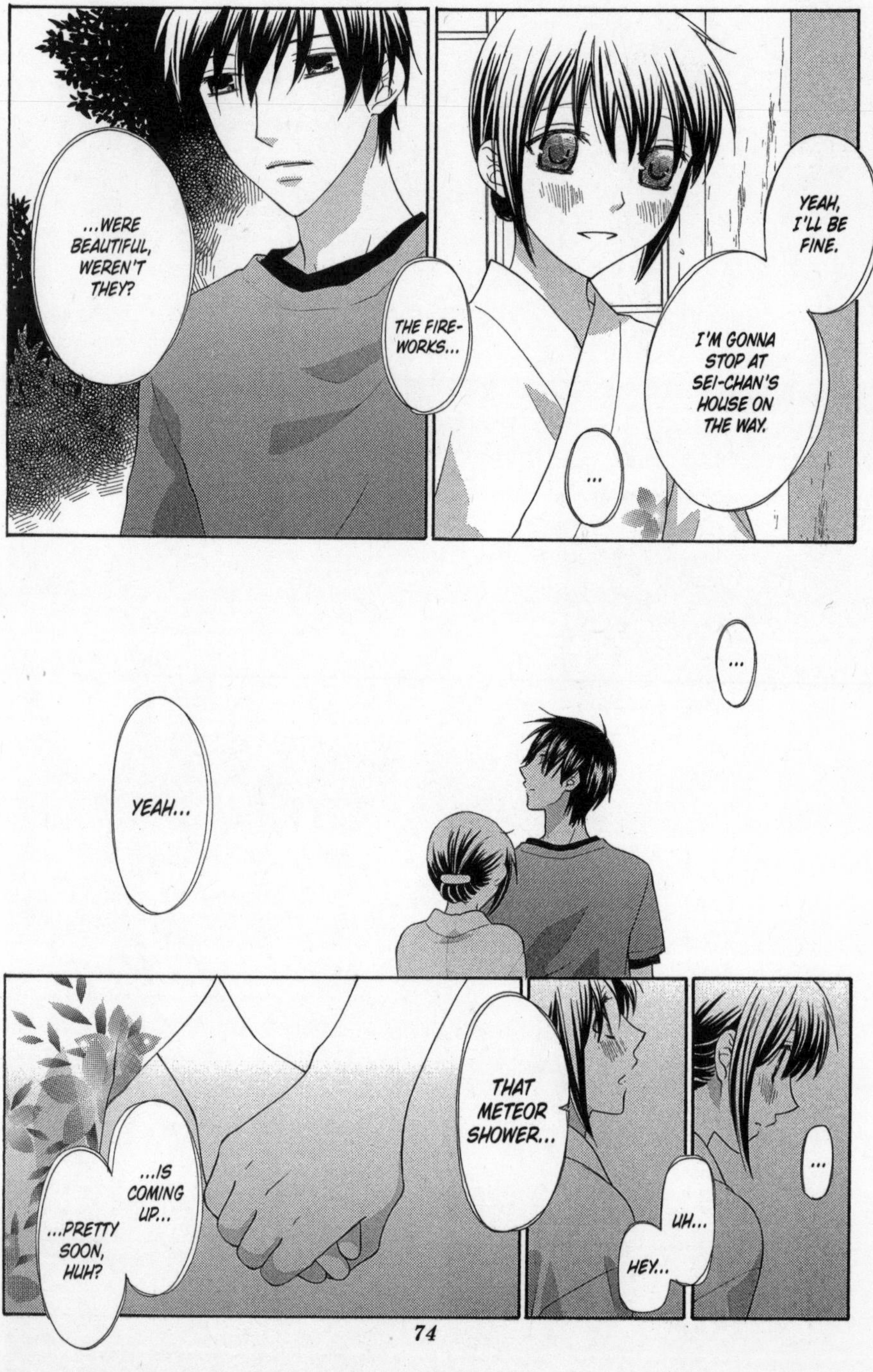
YEAH, I'LL BE FINE.
I'M GONNA STOP AT SEI-CHAN'S HOUSE ON THE WAY.
...
THE FIRE-WORKS...
...WERE BEAUTIFUL, WEREN'T THEY?
...
YEAH...
...
THAT METEOR SHOWER...
UH...
HEY...
...IS COMING UP...
...PRETTY SOON, HUH?

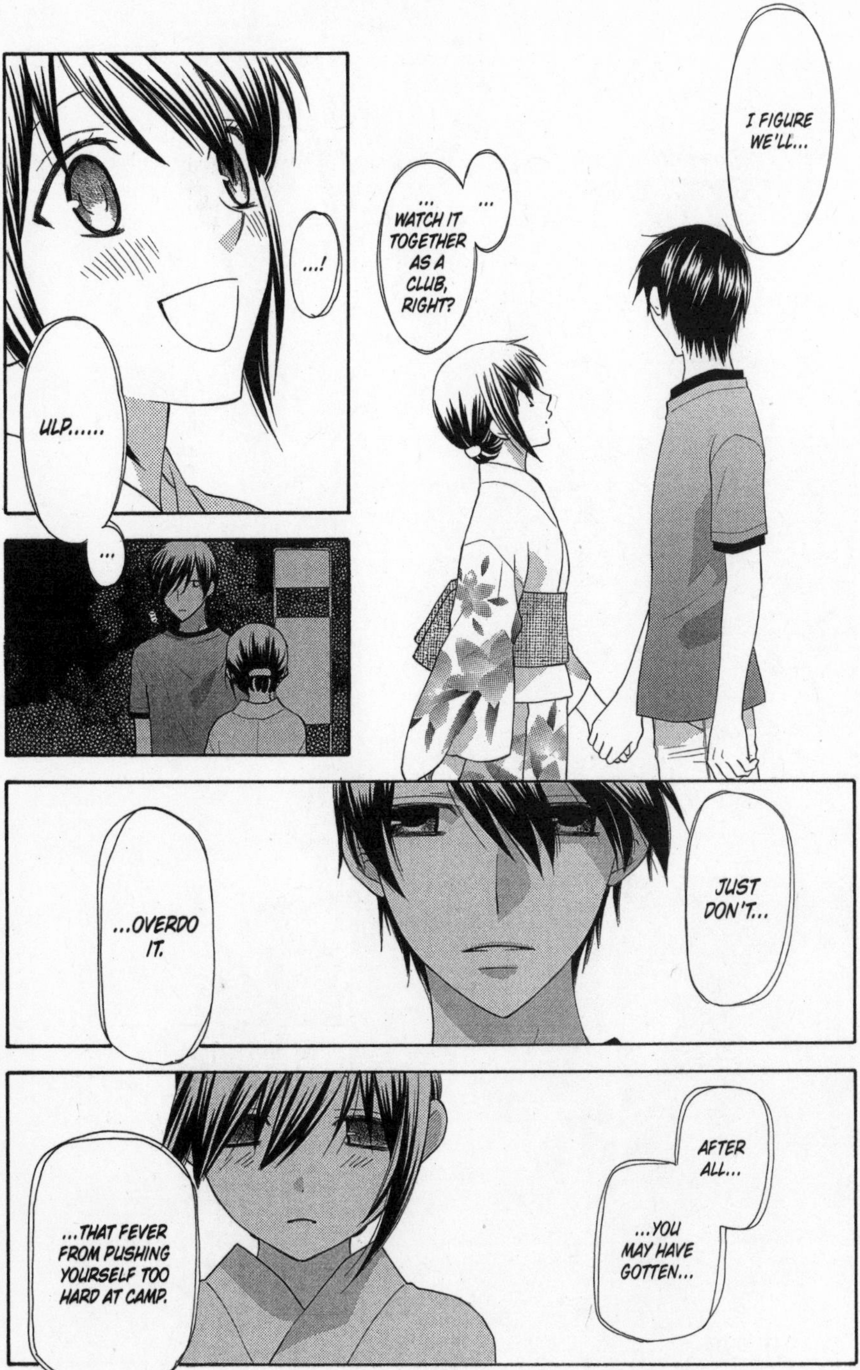
I FIGURE WE'LL...
... ... WATCH IT TOGETHER AS A CLUB, RIGHT?
...!
ULP......
...
JUST DON'T...
...OVERDO IT.
AFTER ALL...
...YOU MAY HAVE GOTTEN...
...THAT FEVER FROM PUSHING YOURSELF TOO HARD AT CAMP.

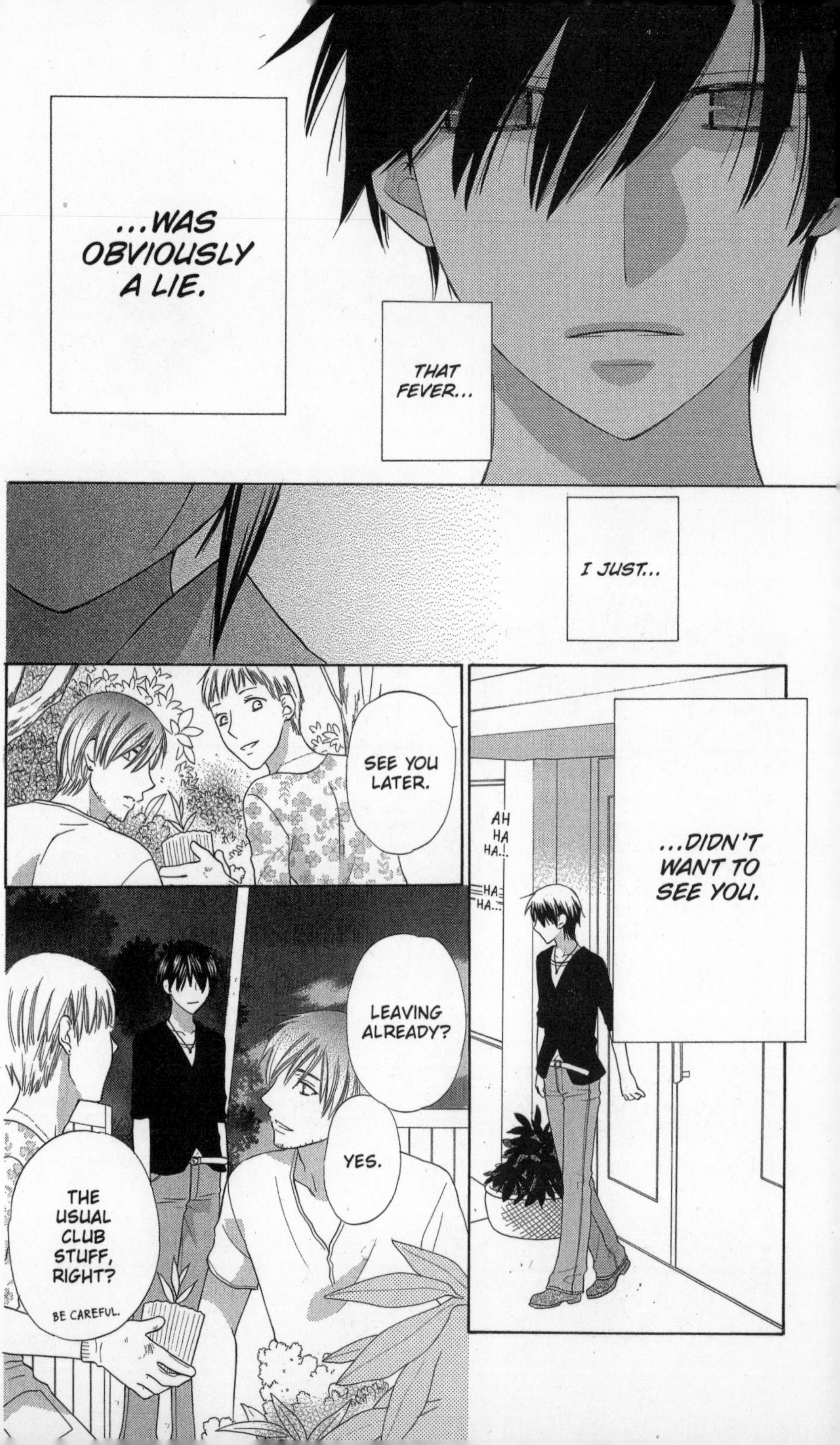
THAT FEVER...
...WAS OBVIOUSLY A LIE.
I JUST...
...DIDN'T WANT TO SEE YOU.
AH HA HA...
HA HA...
SEE YOU LATER.
LEAVING ALREADY?
YES.
THE USUAL CLUB STUFF, RIGHT?
BE CAREFUL.

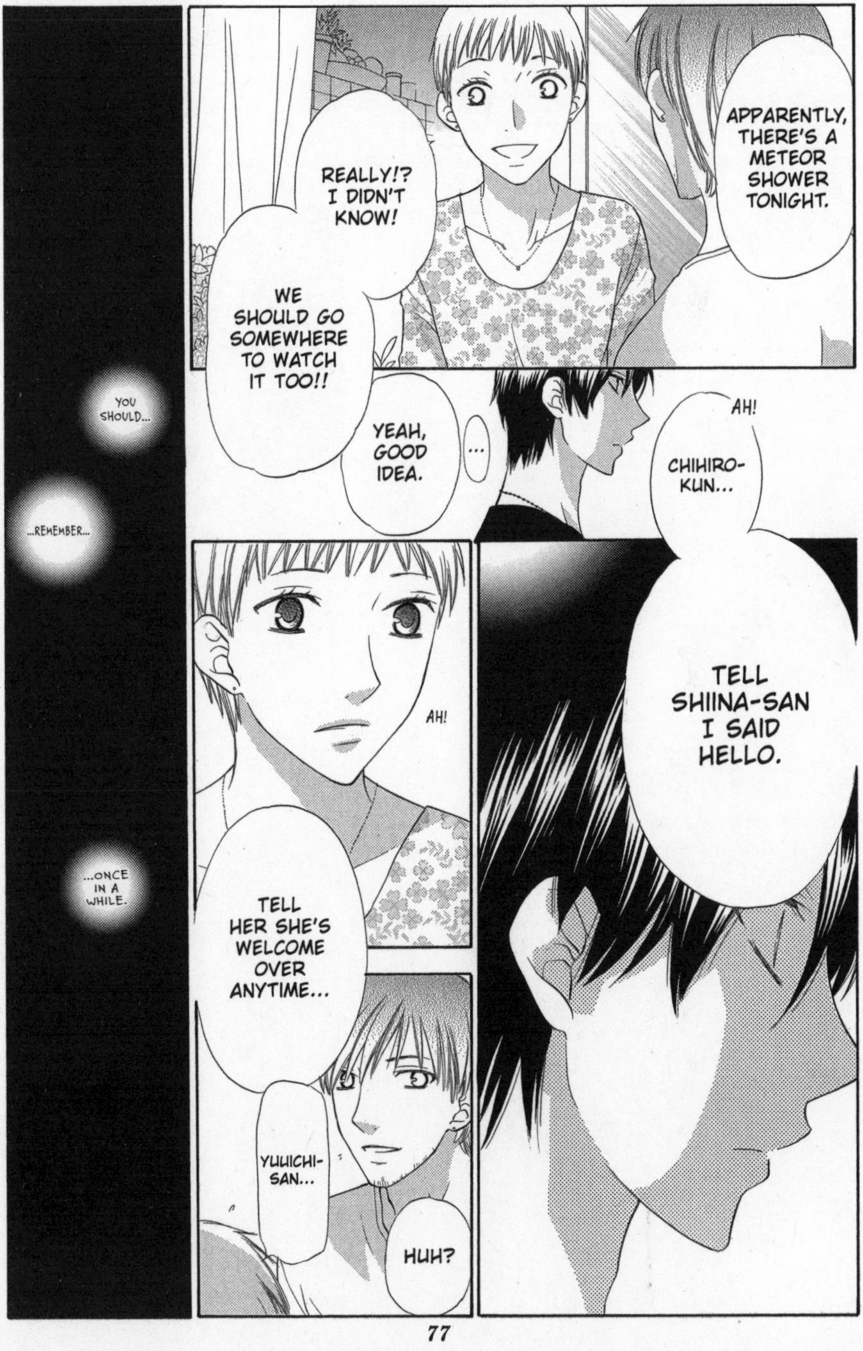

APPARENTLY, THERE'S A METEOR SHOWER TONIGHT.
REALLY!? I DIDN'T KNOW!
WE SHOULD GO SOMEWHERE TO WATCH IT TOO!!
AH!
CHIHIRO-KUN...
...
YEAH, GOOD IDEA.
TELL SHIINA-SAN I SAID HELLO.
AH!
TELL HER SHE'S WELCOME OVER ANYTIME...
YUUICHI-SAN...
HUH?
YOU SHOULD...
...REMEMBER...
...ONCE IN A WHILE.

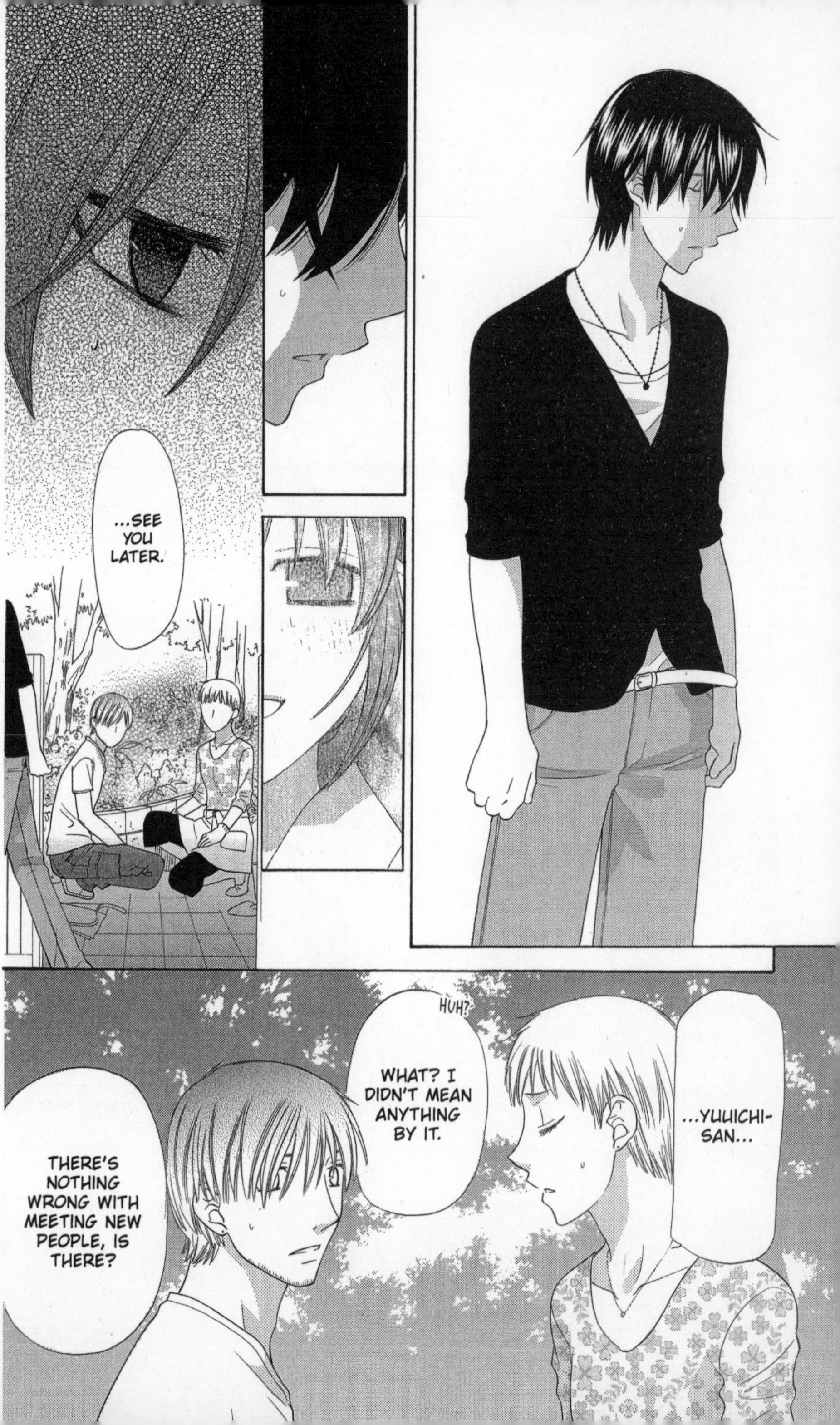
...SEE YOU LATER.
...YUUICHI-SAN...
HUH?
WHAT? I DIDN'T MEAN ANYTHING BY IT.
THERE'S NOTHING WRONG WITH MEETING NEW PEOPLE, IS THERE?

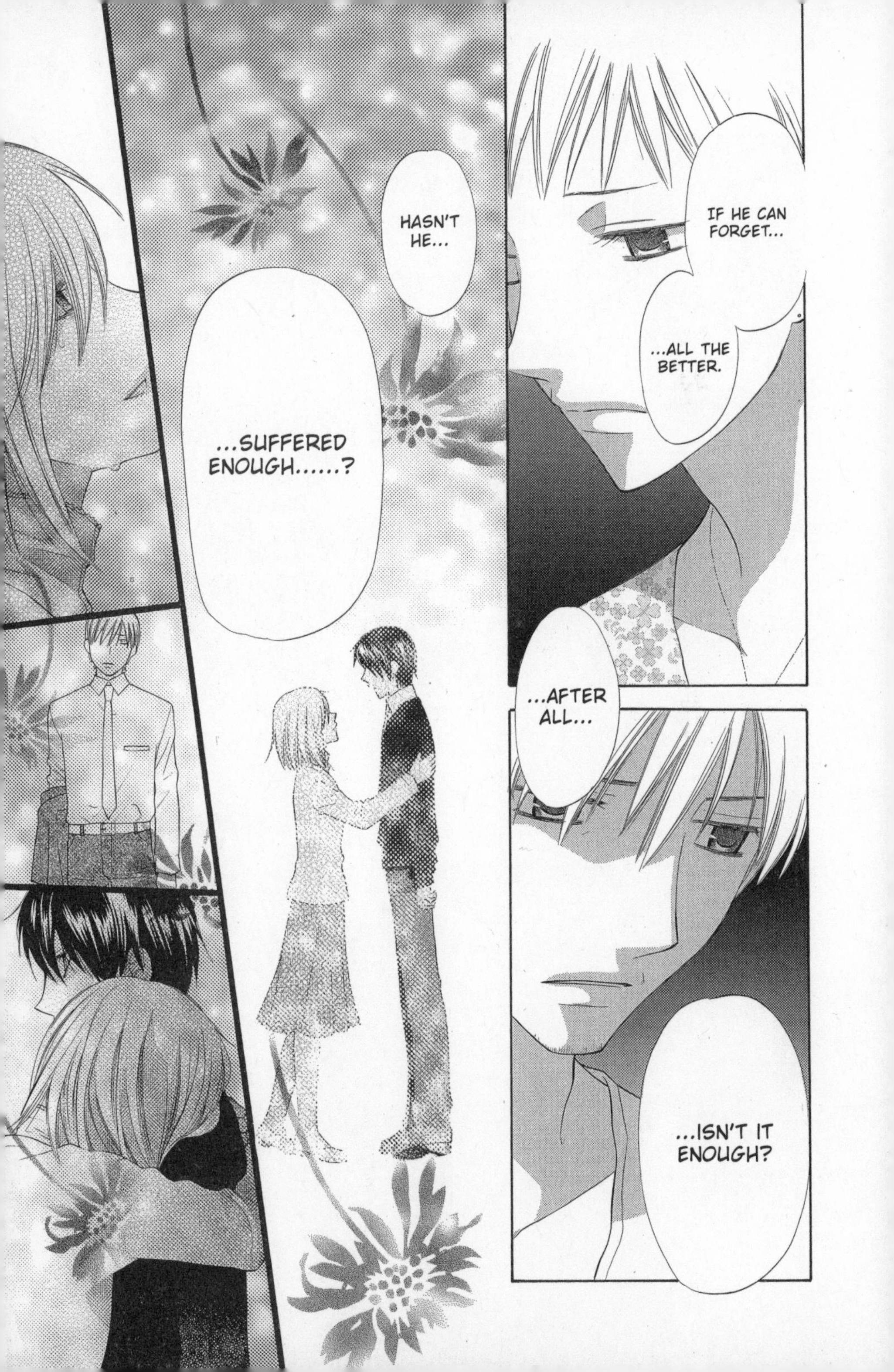
IF HE CAN FORGET...
...ALL THE BETTER.
...AFTER ALL...
...ISN'T IT ENOUGH?
HASN'T HE...
...SUFFERED ENOUGH......?

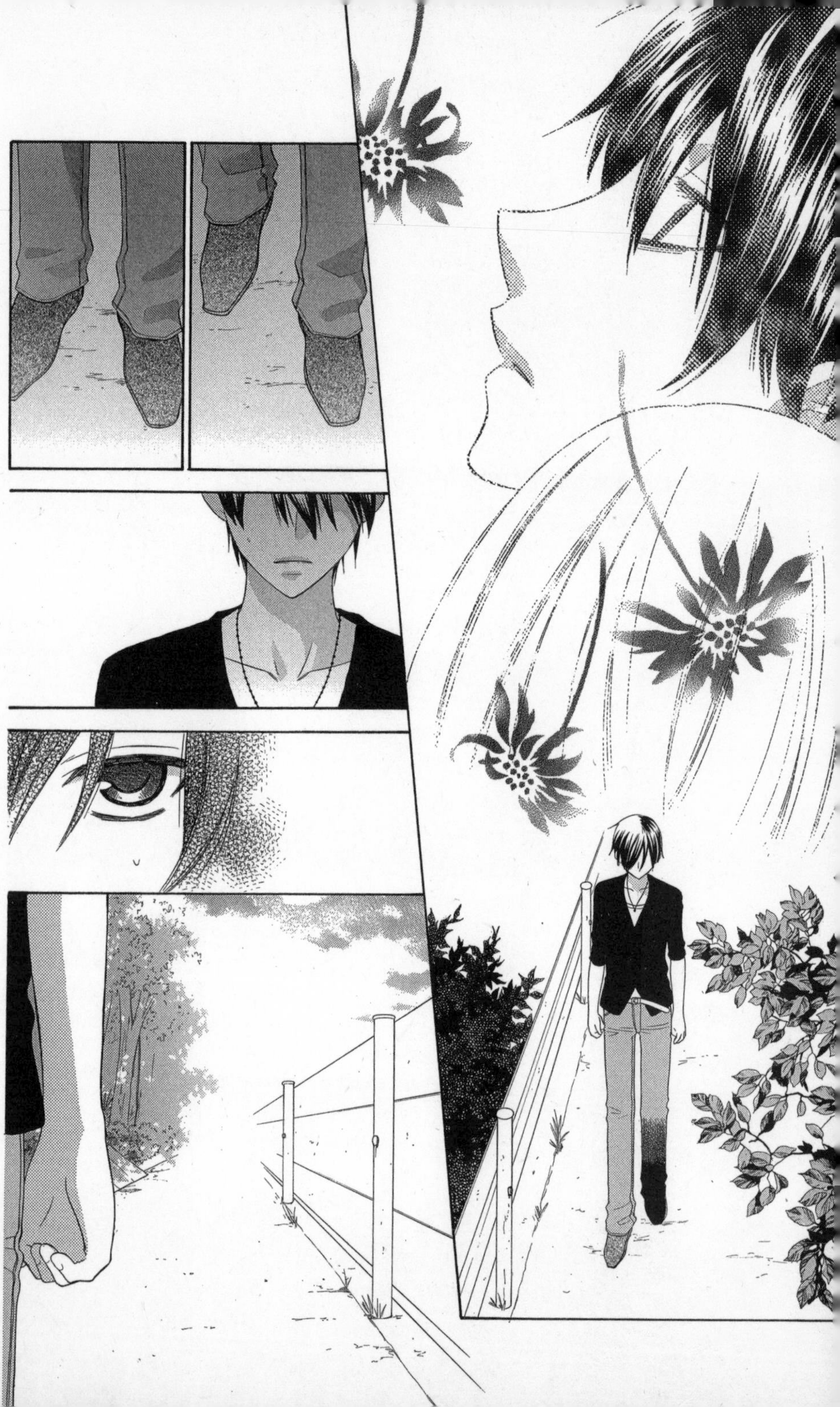

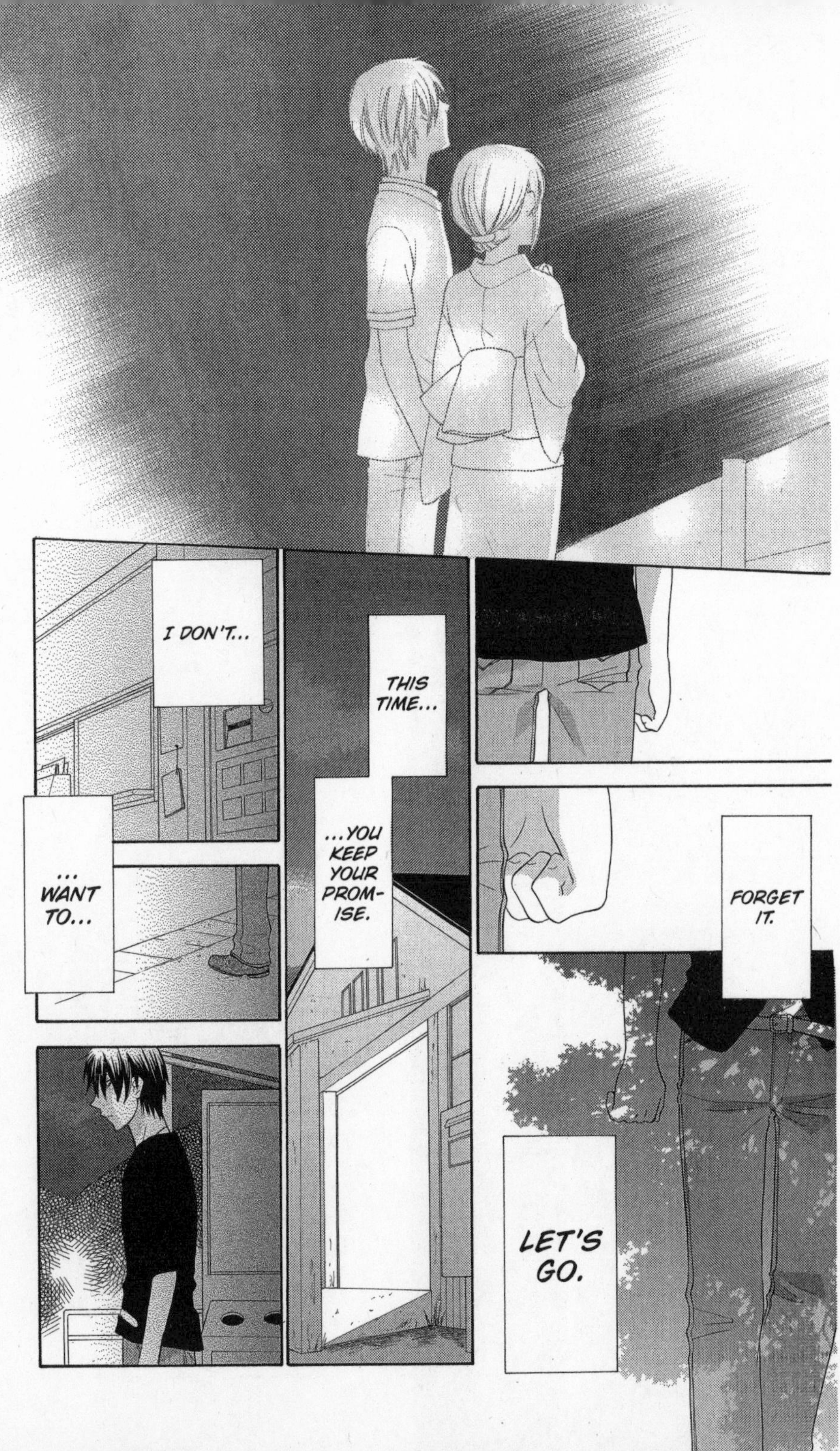
FORGET IT.
LET'S GO.
THIS TIME...
...YOU KEEP YOUR PROMISE.
I DON'T...
...WANT TO...

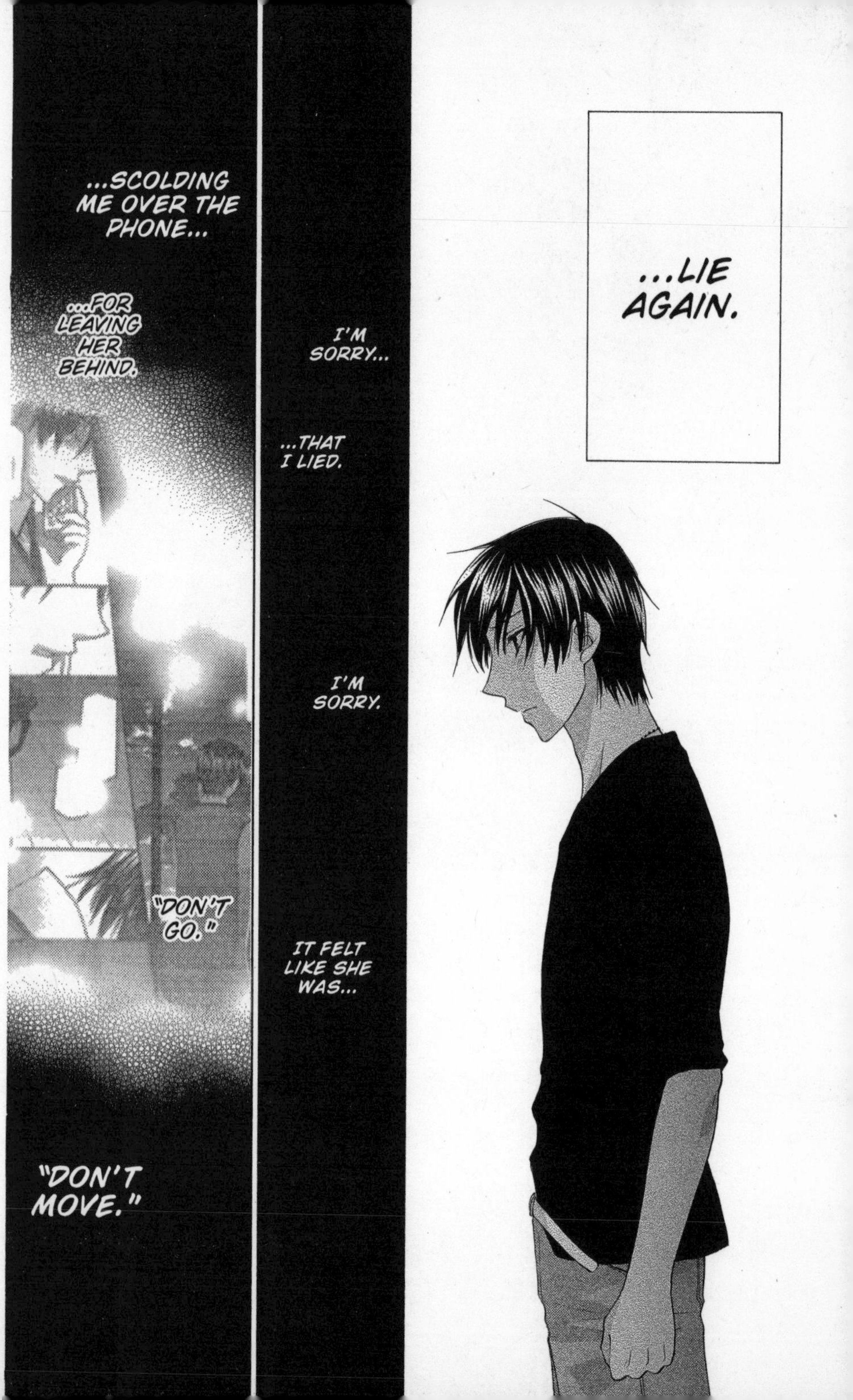
...LIE AGAIN.
I'M SORRY...
...THAT I LIED.
I'M SORRY.
IT FELT LIKE SHE WAS...
...SCOLDING ME OVER THE PHONE...
...FOR LEAVING HER BEHIND.
"DON'T GO."
"DON'T MOVE."

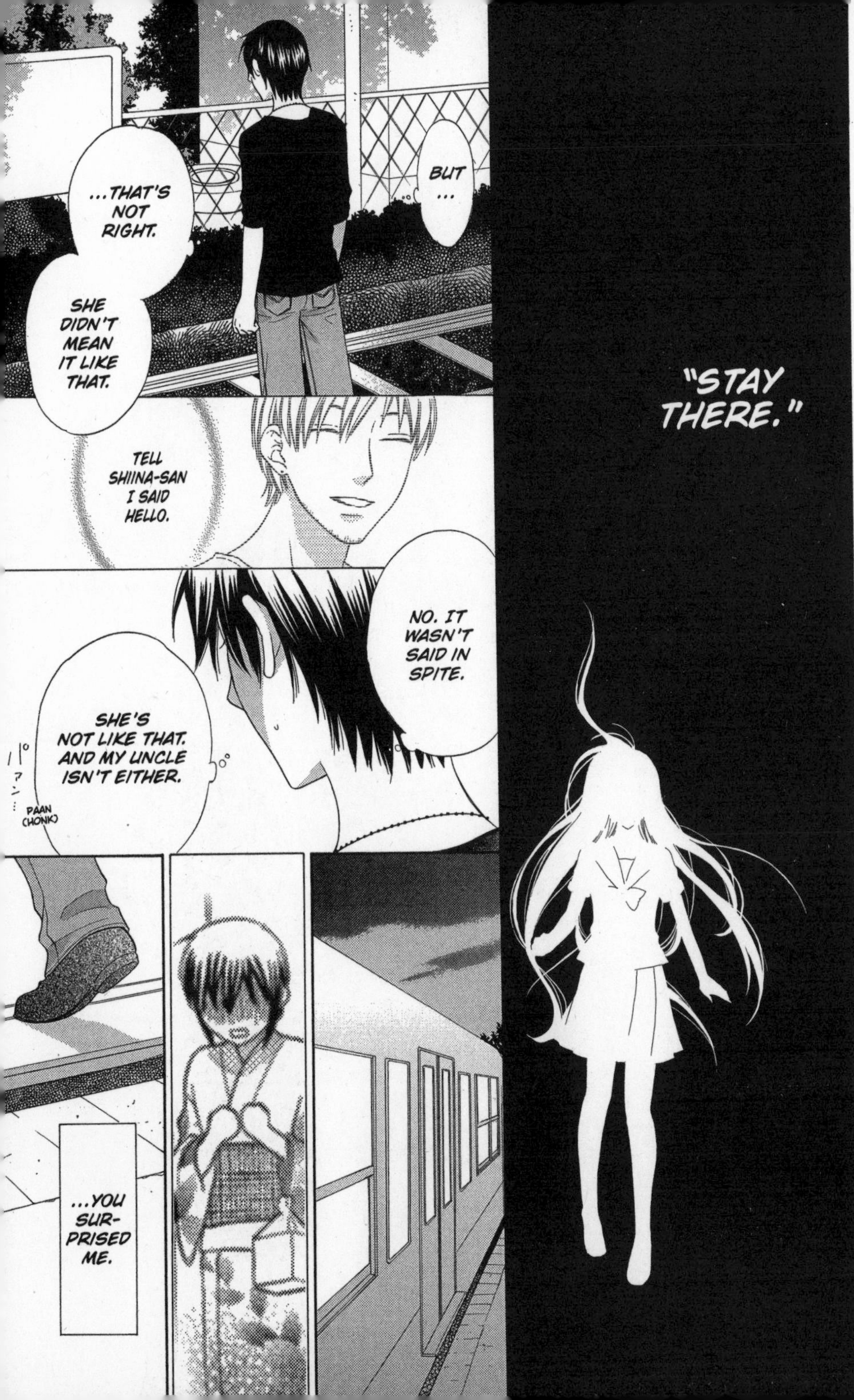
"STAY THERE."
BUT...
...THAT'S NOT RIGHT.
SHE DIDN'T MEAN IT LIKE THAT.
TELL SHIINA-SAN I SAID HELLO.
NO. IT WASN'T SAID IN SPITE.
SHE'S NOT LIKE THAT. AND MY UNCLE ISN'T EITHER.
パァン…
PAAN (HONK)
...YOU SUR-PRISED ME.

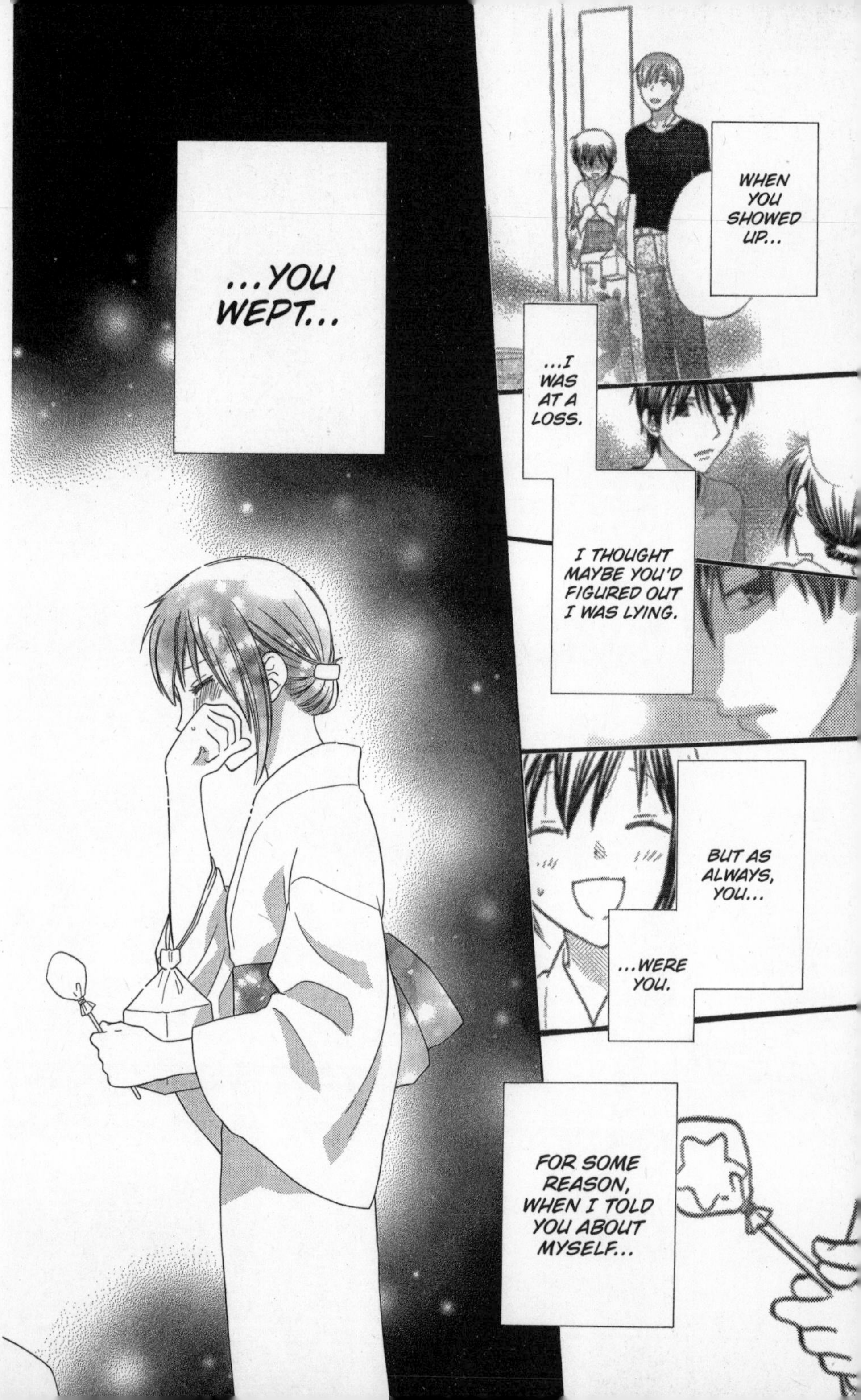
WHEN YOU SHOWED UP...
...I WAS AT A LOSS.
I THOUGHT MAYBE YOU'D FIGURED OUT I WAS LYING.
BUT AS ALWAYS, YOU...
...WERE YOU.
FOR SOME REASON, WHEN I TOLD YOU ABOUT MYSELF...
...YOU WEPT...

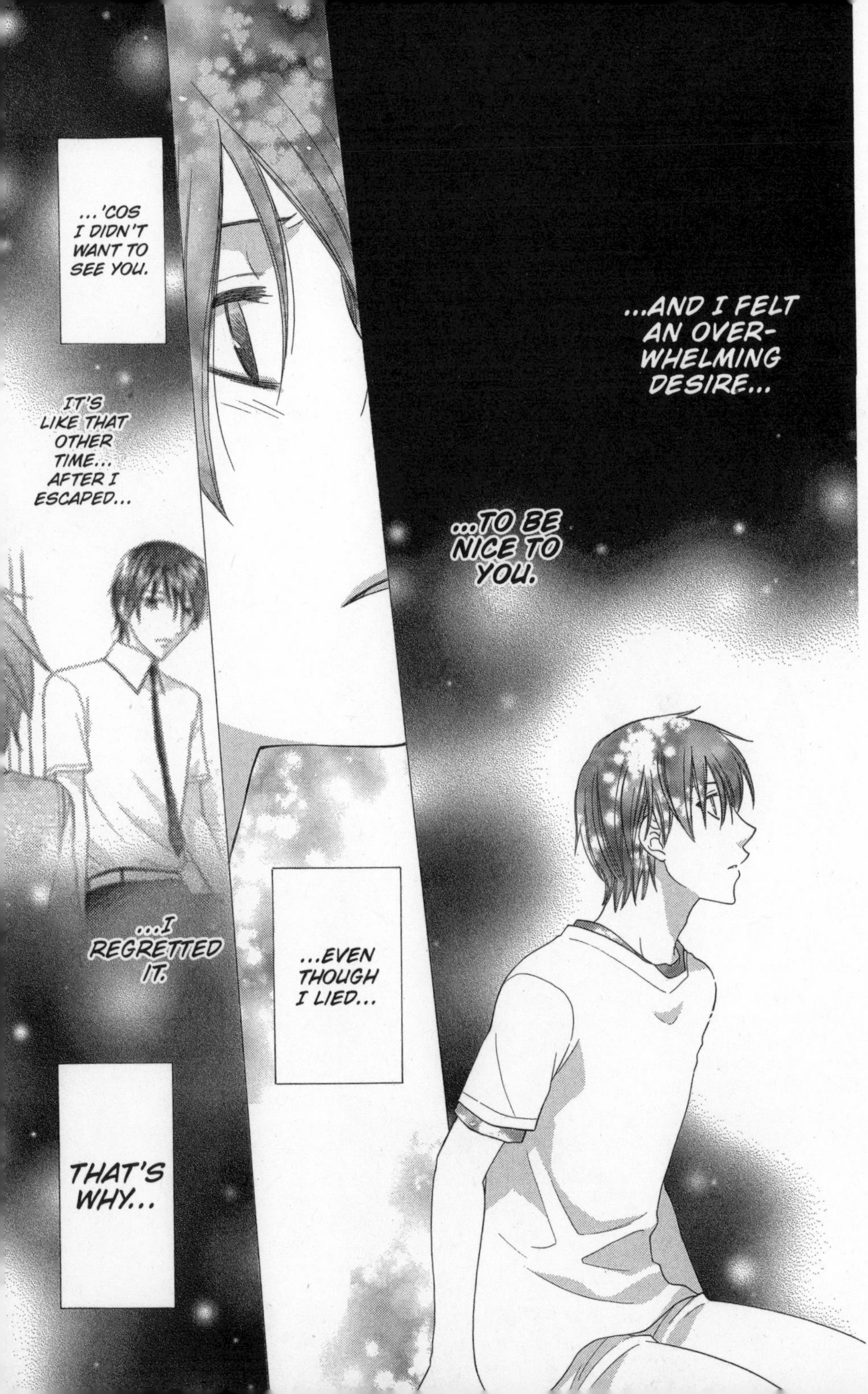
...AND I FELT AN OVER-WHELMING DESIRE...
...TO BE NICE TO YOU.
...EVEN THOUGH I LIED...
...'COS I DIDN'T WANT TO SEE YOU.
IT'S LIKE THAT OTHER TIME... AFTER I ESCAPED...
...I REGRETTED IT.
THAT'S WHY...

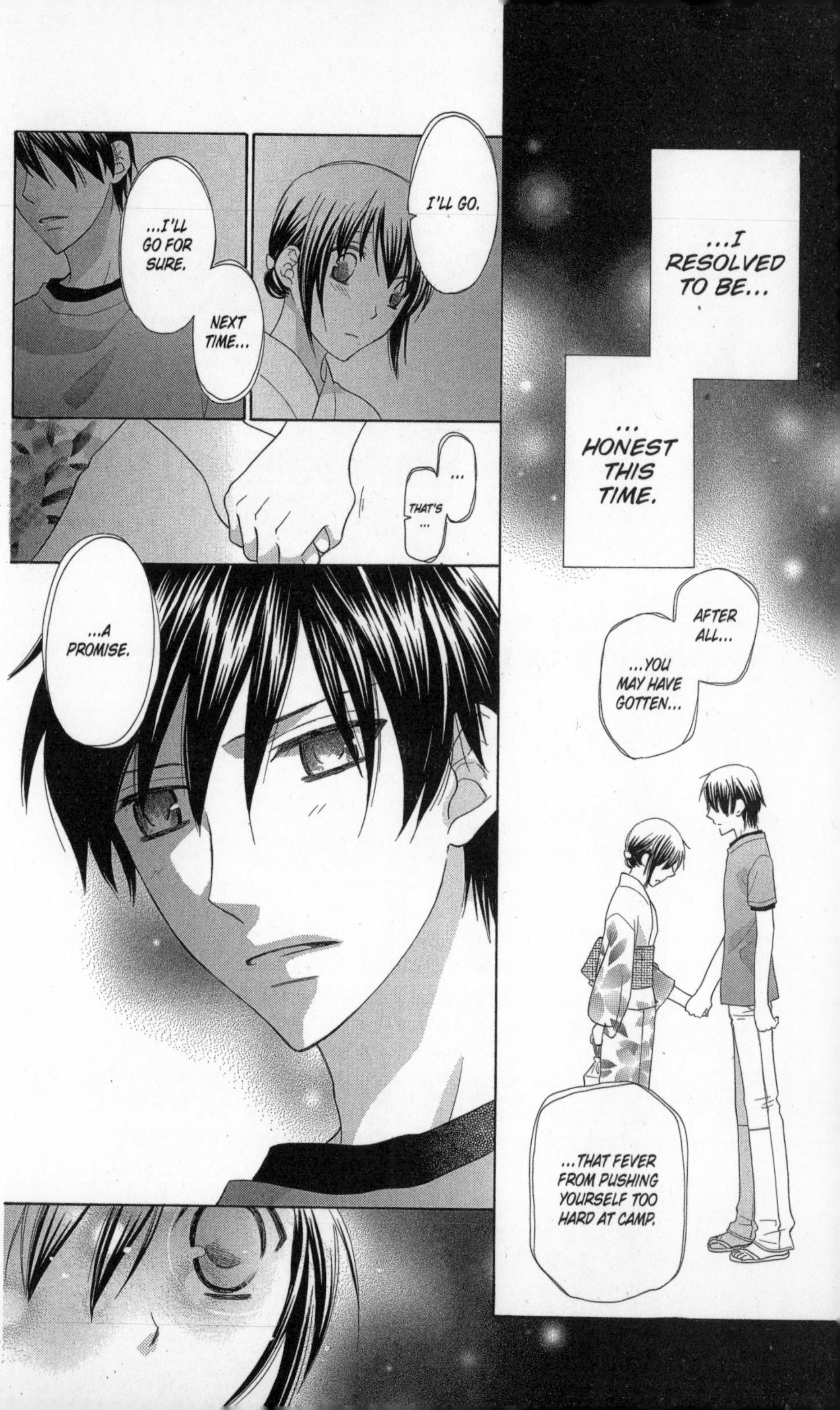
...I RESOLVED TO BE...
...HONEST THIS TIME.
AFTER ALL...
...YOU MAY HAVE GOTTEN...
...THAT FEVER FROM PUSHING YOURSELF TOO HARD AT CAMP.
I'LL GO.
NEXT TIME...
...I'LL GO FOR SURE.
...THAT'S...
...A PROMISE.

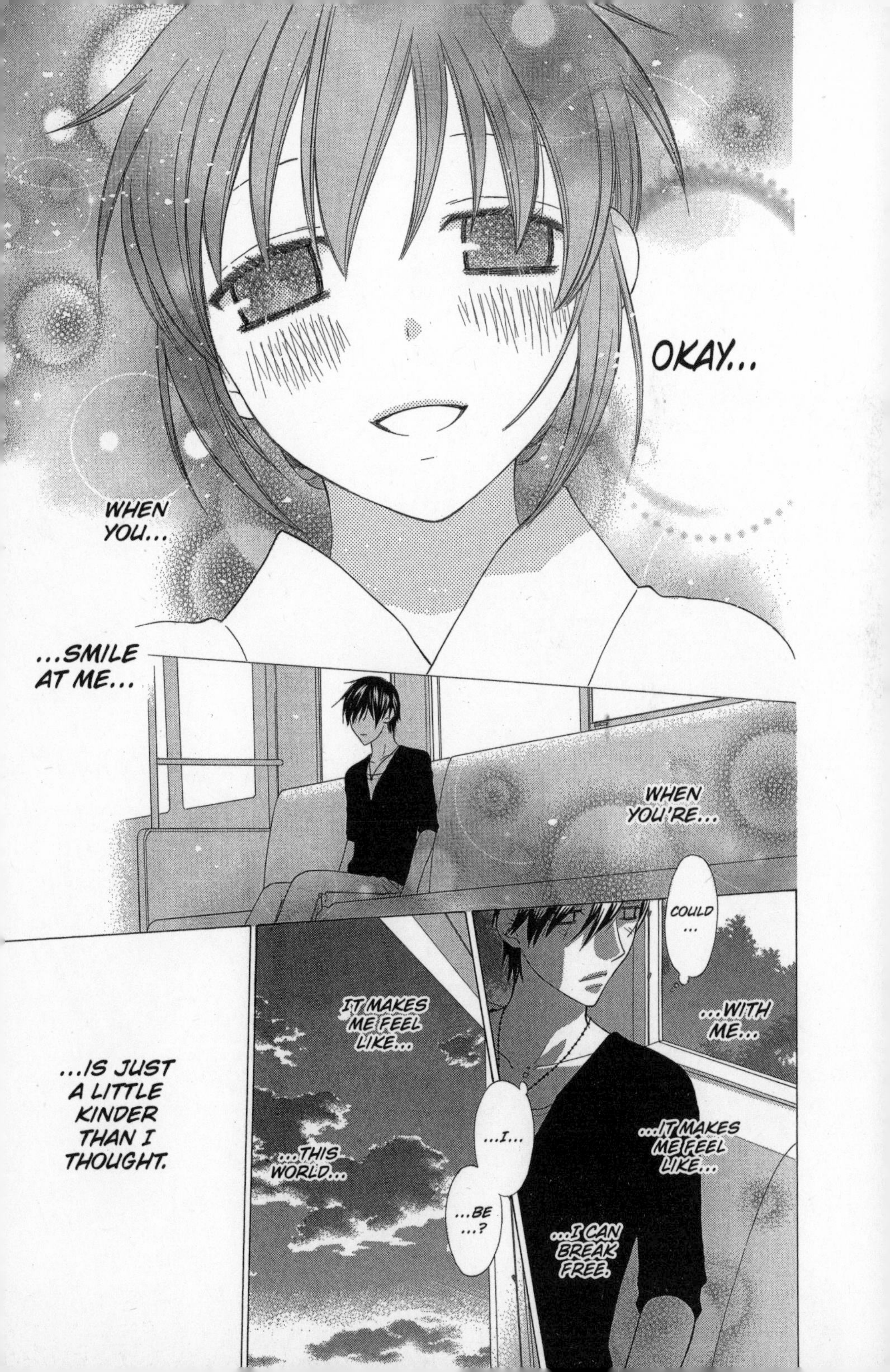
OKAY...
WHEN YOU...
...SMILE AT ME...
WHEN YOU'RE...
COULD ...
...WITH ME...
...IT MAKES ME FEEL LIKE...
IT MAKES ME FEEL LIKE...
...I...
...THIS WORLD...
...BE ...?
...I CAN BREAK FREE.
...IS JUST A LITTLE KINDER THAN I THOUGHT.

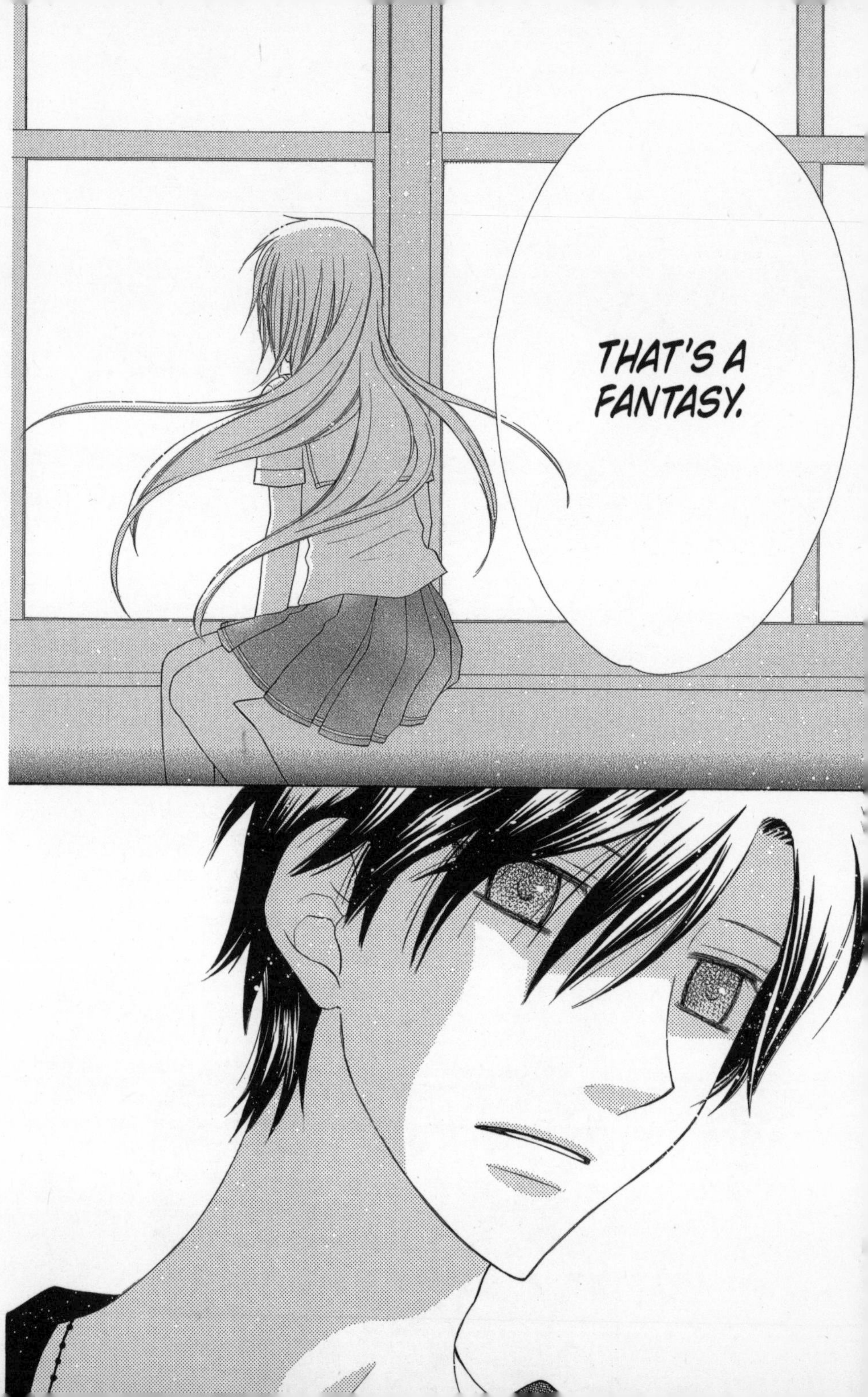
THAT'S A FANTASY.

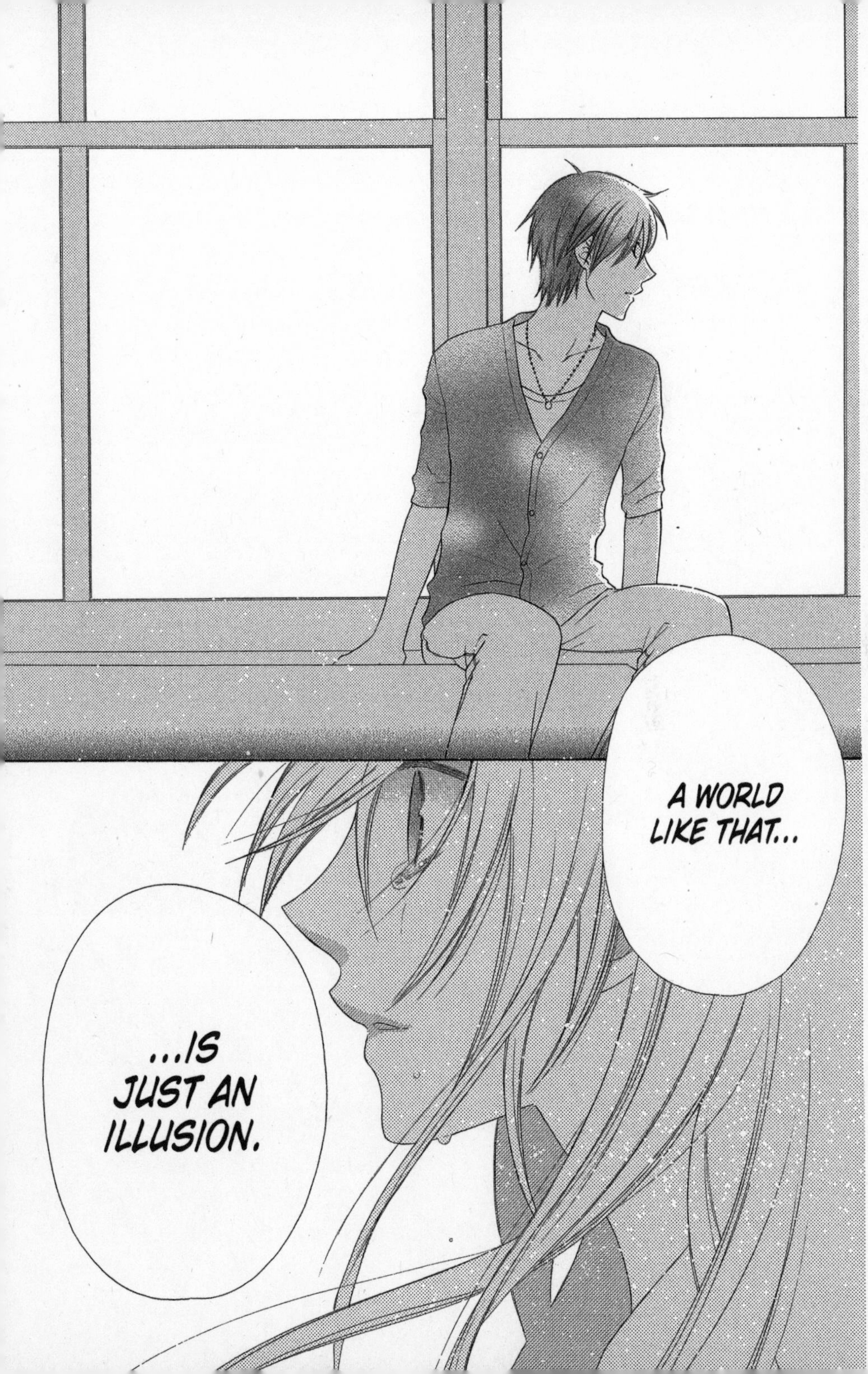
A WORLD LIKE THAT...
...IS JUST AN ILLUSION.

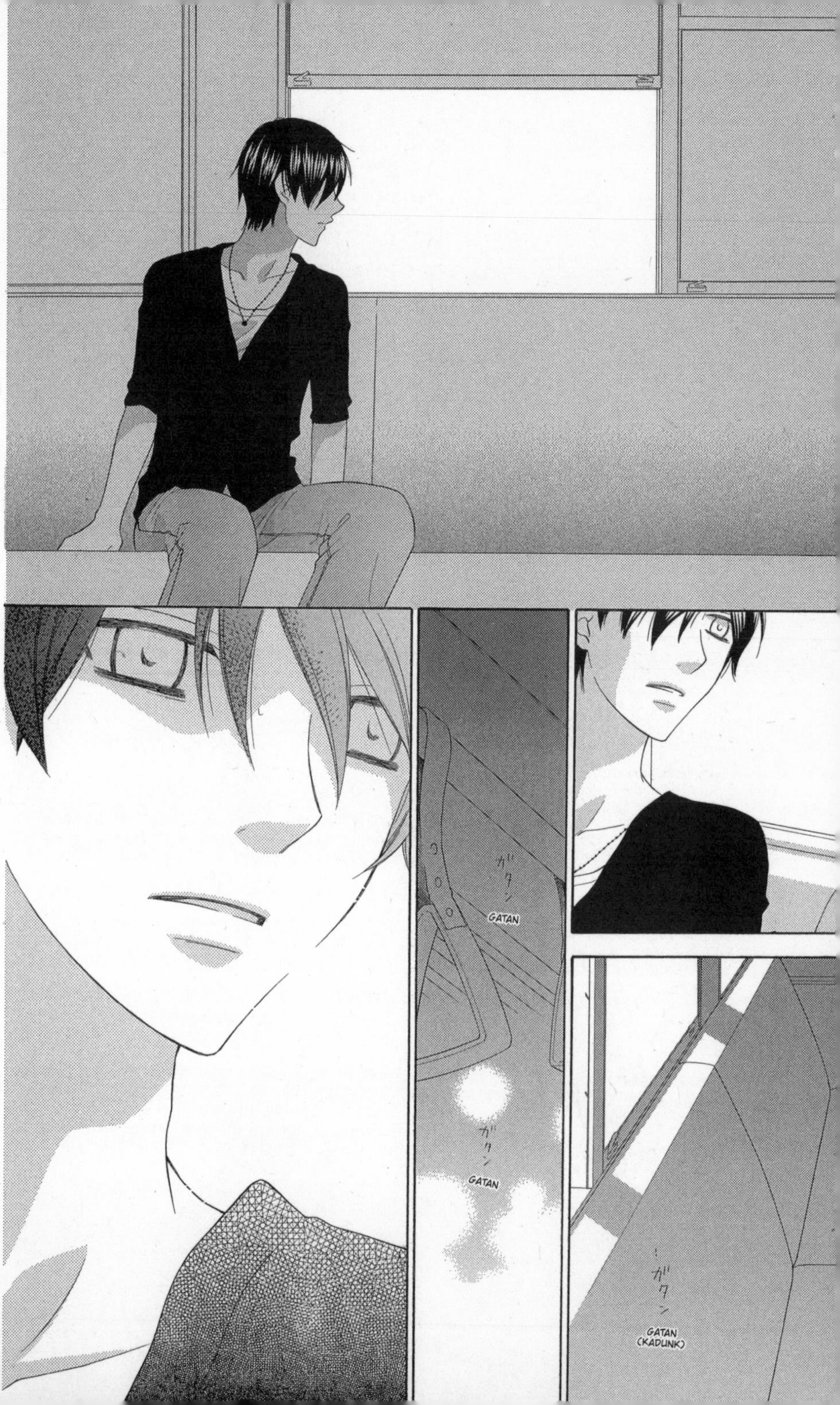
ガタン
GATAN (KADUNK)
ガタン
GATAN
ガタン
GATAN

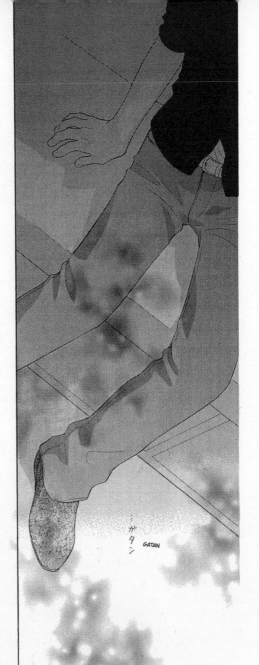

...OH, IT'S YOU.

I WAS HOPIN' YOU WOULDN'T MAKE IT TONIGHT.

WAIT...

ガタン GATAN

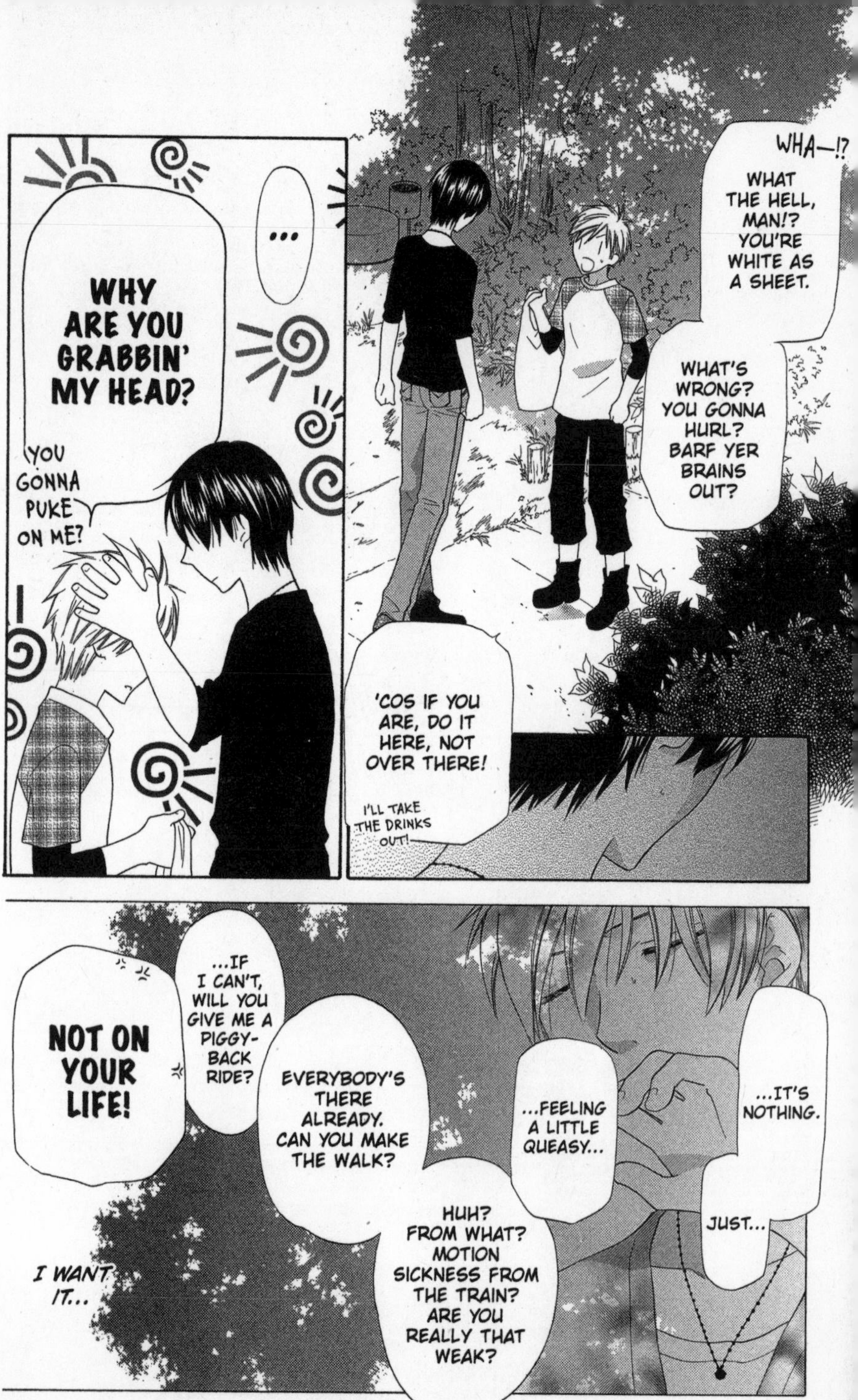
WHA—!?
WHAT THE HELL, MAN!? YOU'RE WHITE AS A SHEET.
WHAT'S WRONG? YOU GONNA HURL? BARF YER BRAINS OUT?
'COS IF YOU ARE, DO IT HERE, NOT OVER THERE!
I'LL TAKE THE DRINKS OUT!
...
WHY ARE YOU GRABBIN' MY HEAD?
YOU GONNA PUKE ON ME?
...IT'S NOTHING.
JUST...
...FEELING A LITTLE QUEASY...
HUH? FROM WHAT? MOTION SICKNESS FROM THE TRAIN? ARE YOU REALLY THAT WEAK?
EVERYBODY'S THERE ALREADY. CAN YOU MAKE THE WALK?
...IF I CAN'T, WILL YOU GIVE ME A PIGGY-BACK RIDE?
NOT ON YOUR LIFE!
I WANT IT...

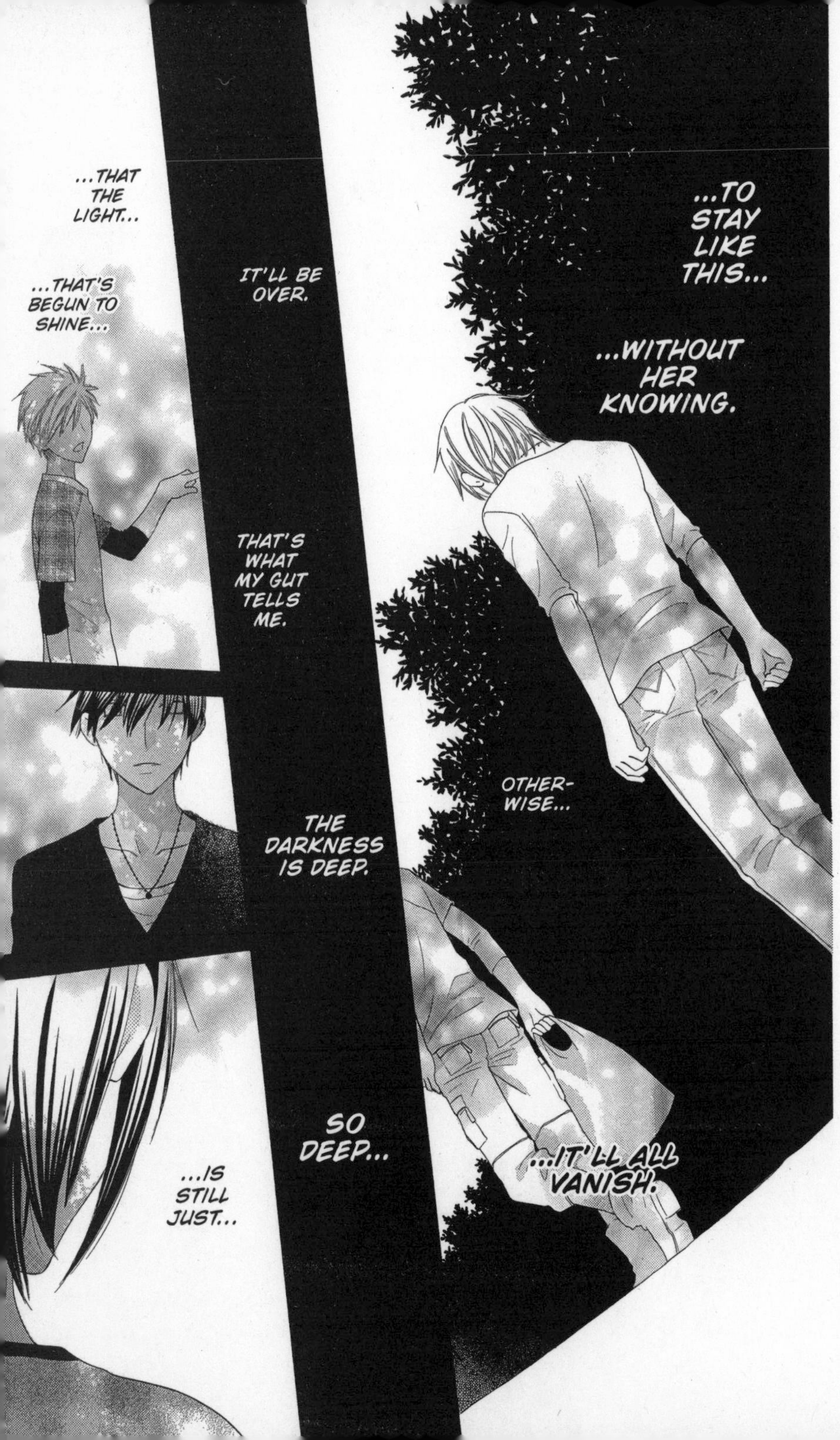
...TO STAY LIKE THIS...
...WITHOUT HER KNOWING.
OTHER-WISE...
...IT'LL ALL VANISH.
IT'LL BE OVER.
THAT'S WHAT MY GUT TELLS ME.
THE DARKNESS IS DEEP.
SO DEEP...
...THAT THE LIGHT...
...THAT'S BEGUN TO SHINE...
...IS STILL JUST...

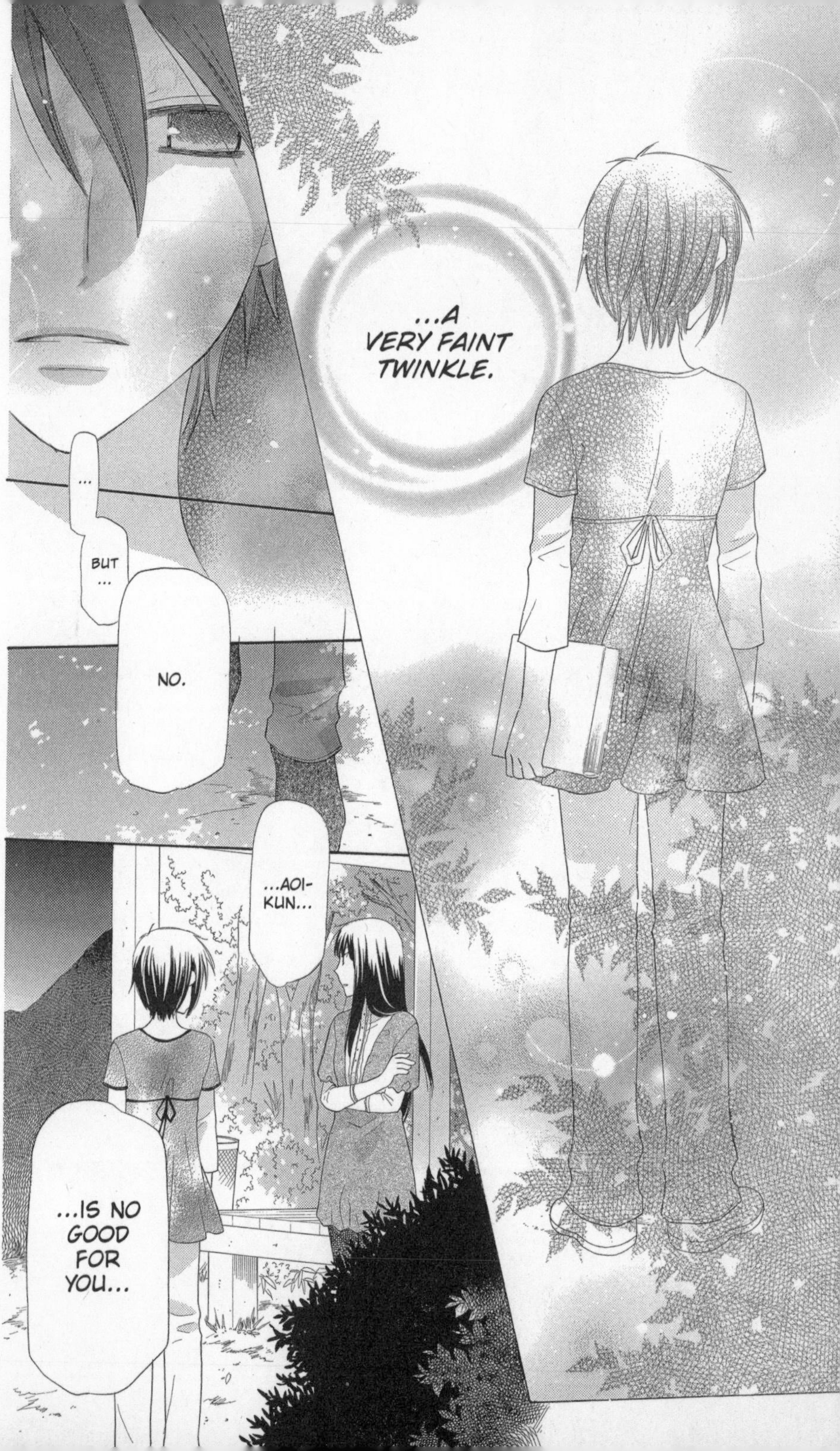
...A VERY FAINT TWINKLE.
...
BUT ...
NO.
...AOI-KUN...
...IS NO GOOD FOR YOU...

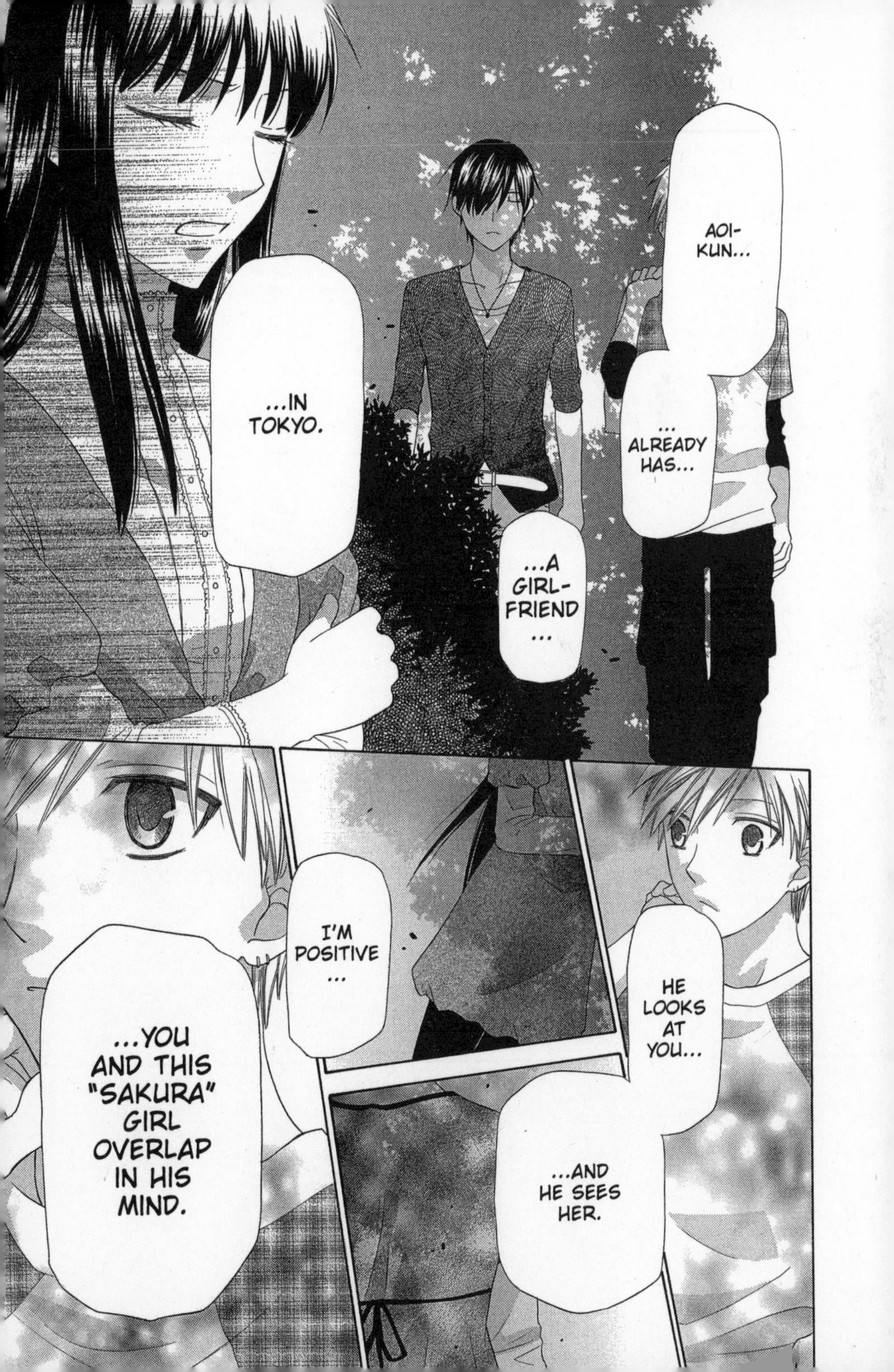
AOI-KUN...
...ALREADY HAS...
...A GIRLFRIEND...
...IN TOKYO.
HE LOOKS AT YOU...
...AND HE SEES HER.
I'M POSITIVE...
...YOU AND THIS "SAKURA" GIRL OVERLAP IN HIS MIND.

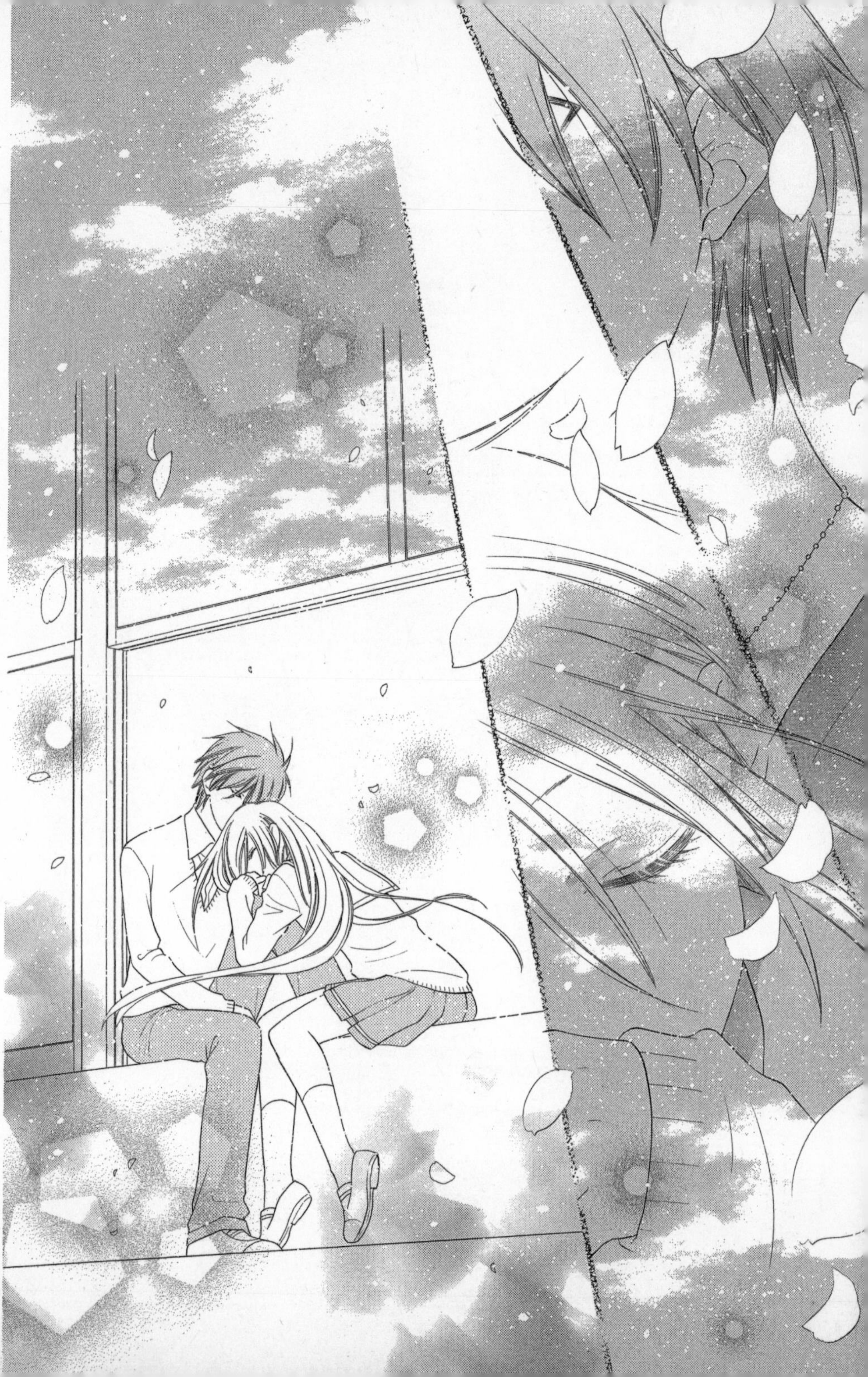

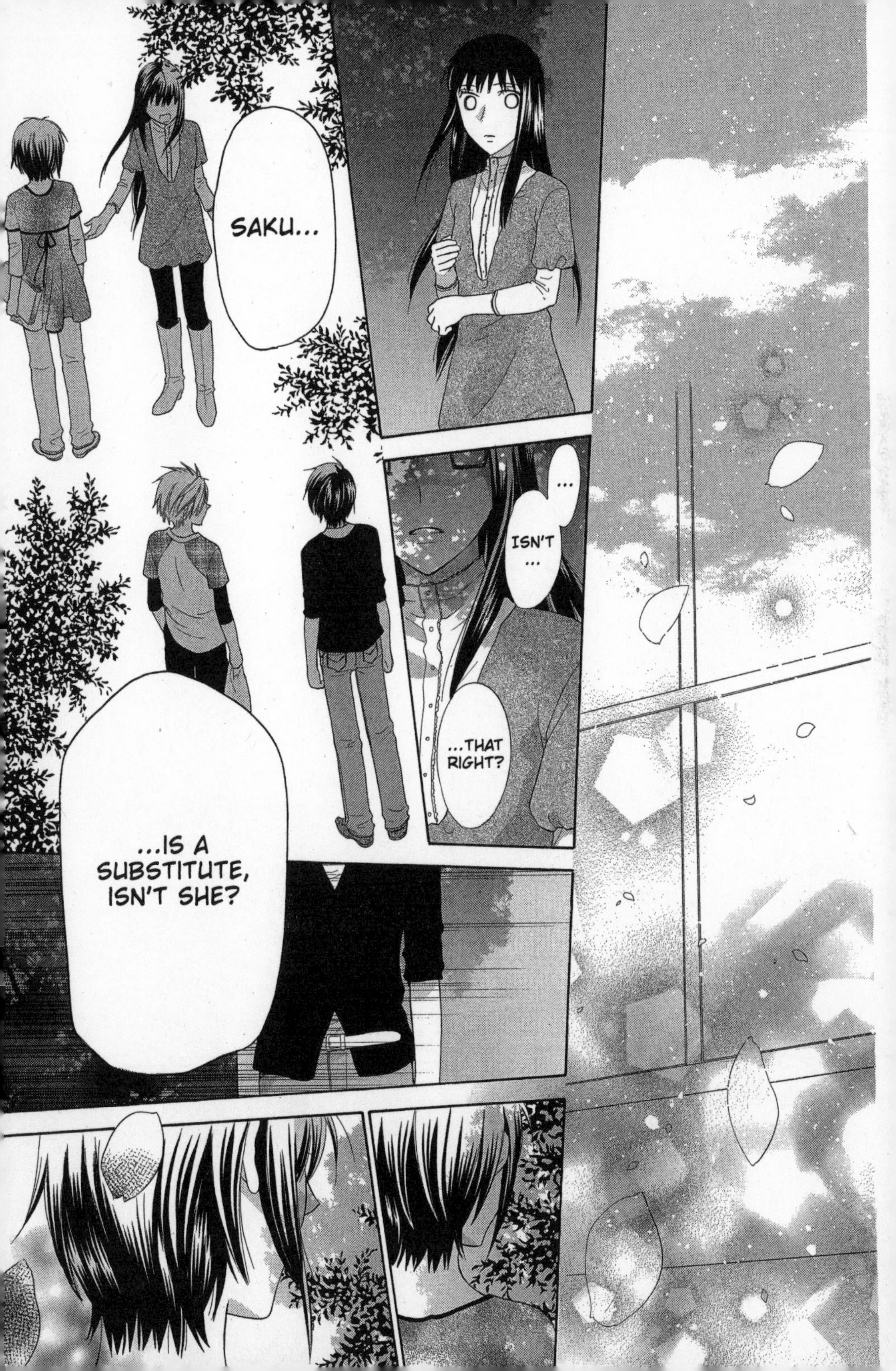
SAKU...
...
ISN'T ...
...THAT RIGHT?
...IS A SUBSTITUTE, ISN'T SHE?

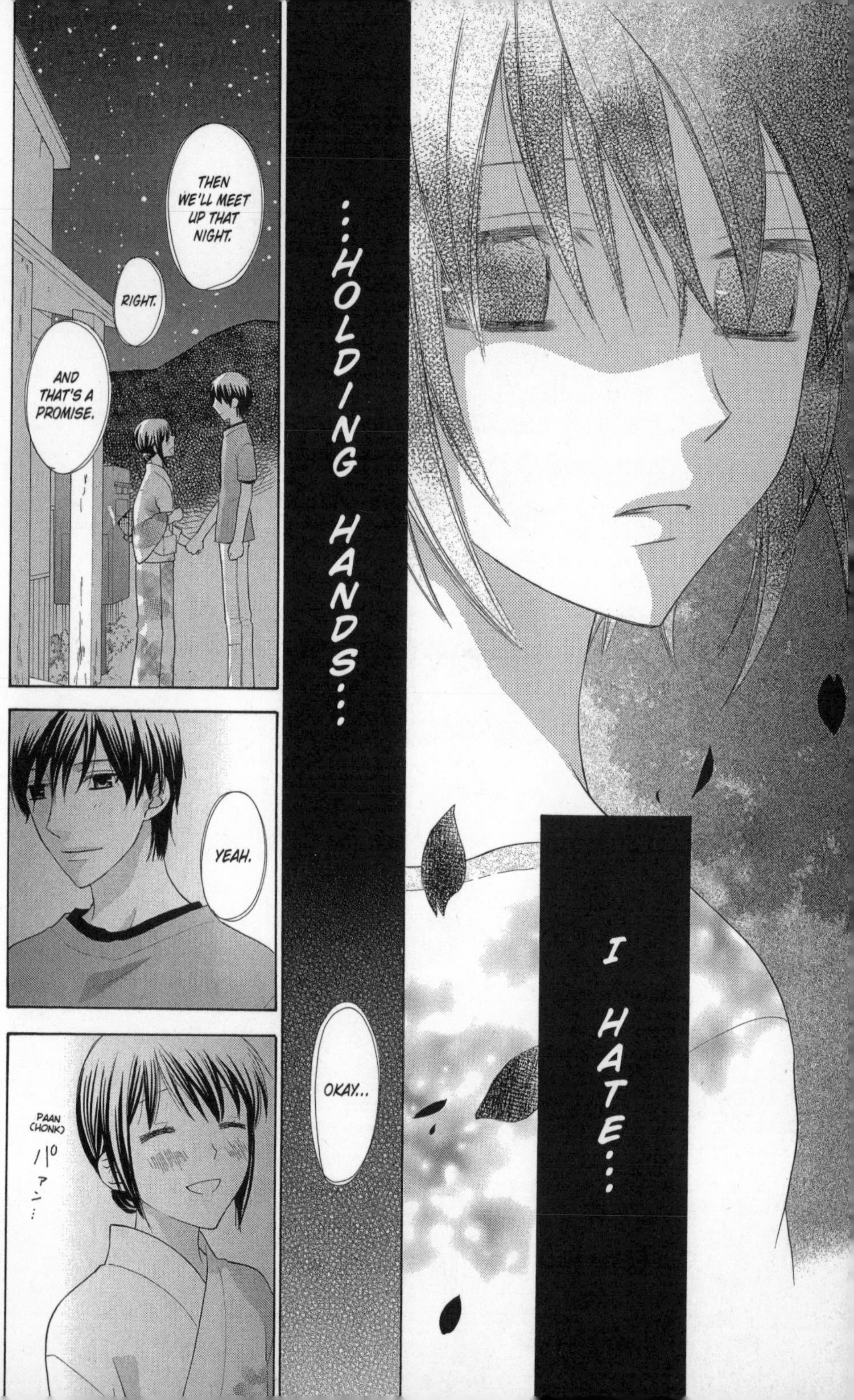
I HATE...
...HOLDING HANDS...
OKAY...
THEN WE'LL MEET UP THAT NIGHT.
RIGHT.
AND THAT'S A PROMISE.
YEAH.
PAAN (CHONK)
パァン…

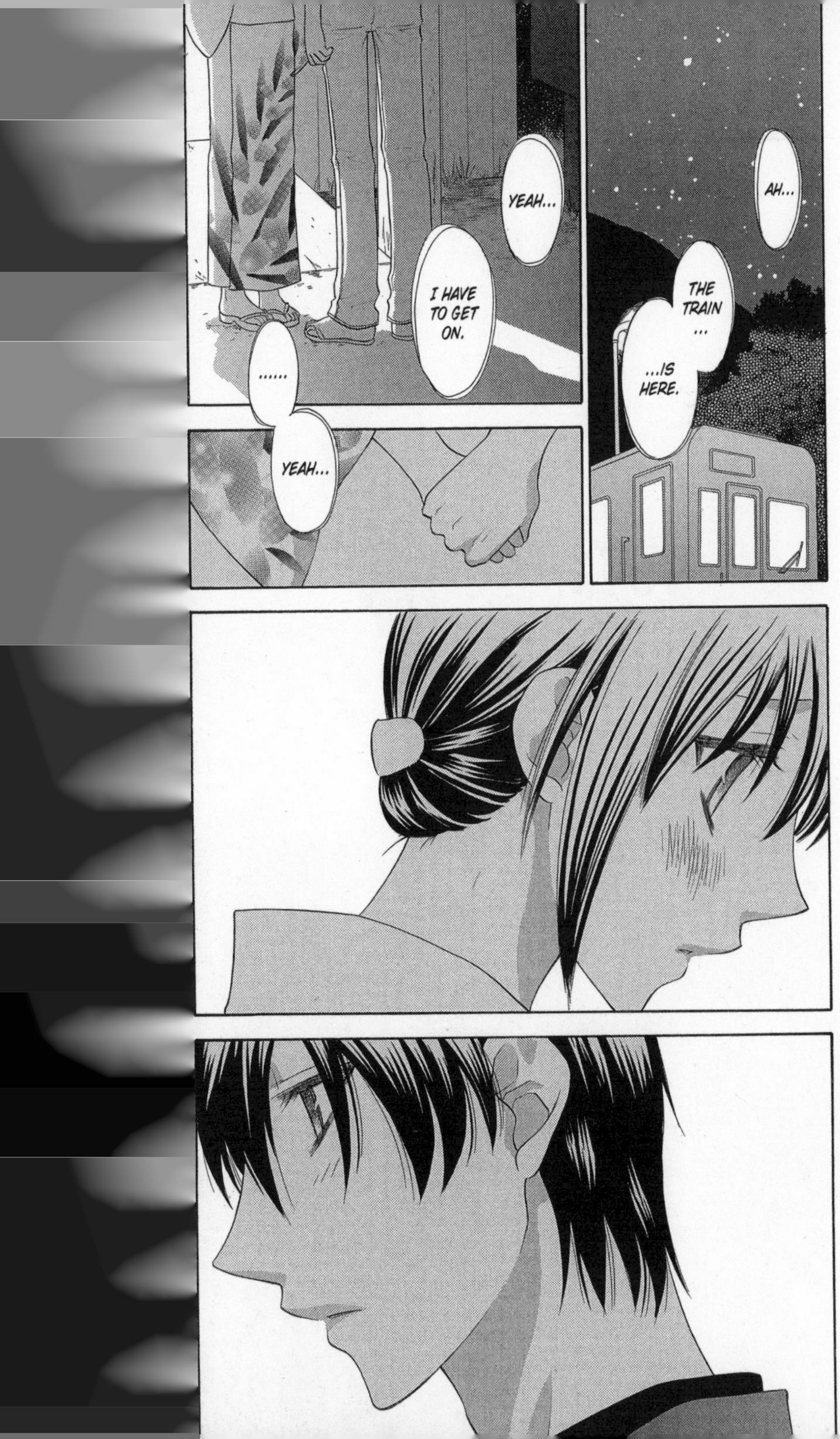
AH...
THE TRAIN ...
...IS HERE.
YEAH...
I HAVE TO GET ON.
......
YEAH...

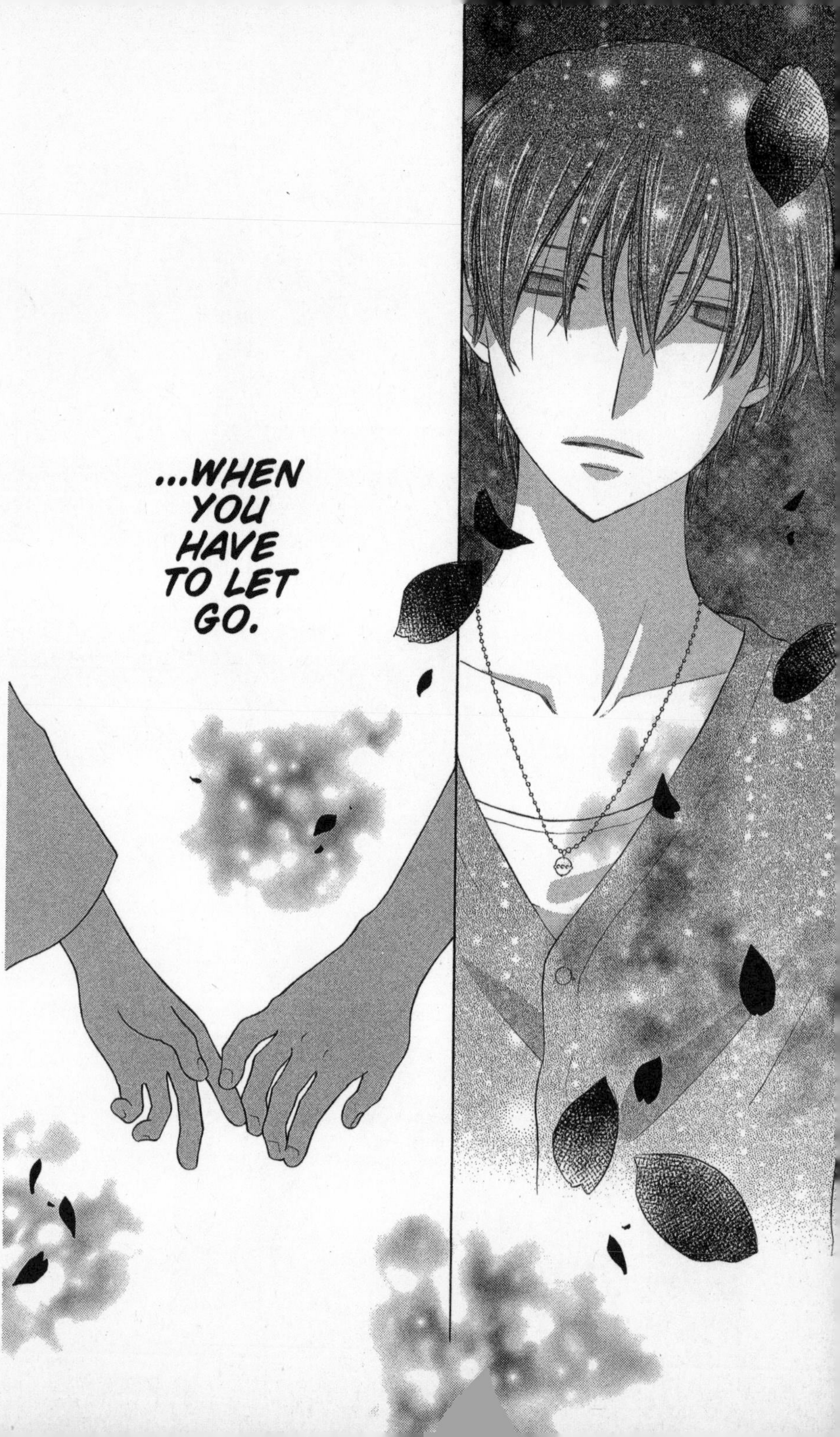
...WHEN YOU HAVE TO LET GO.

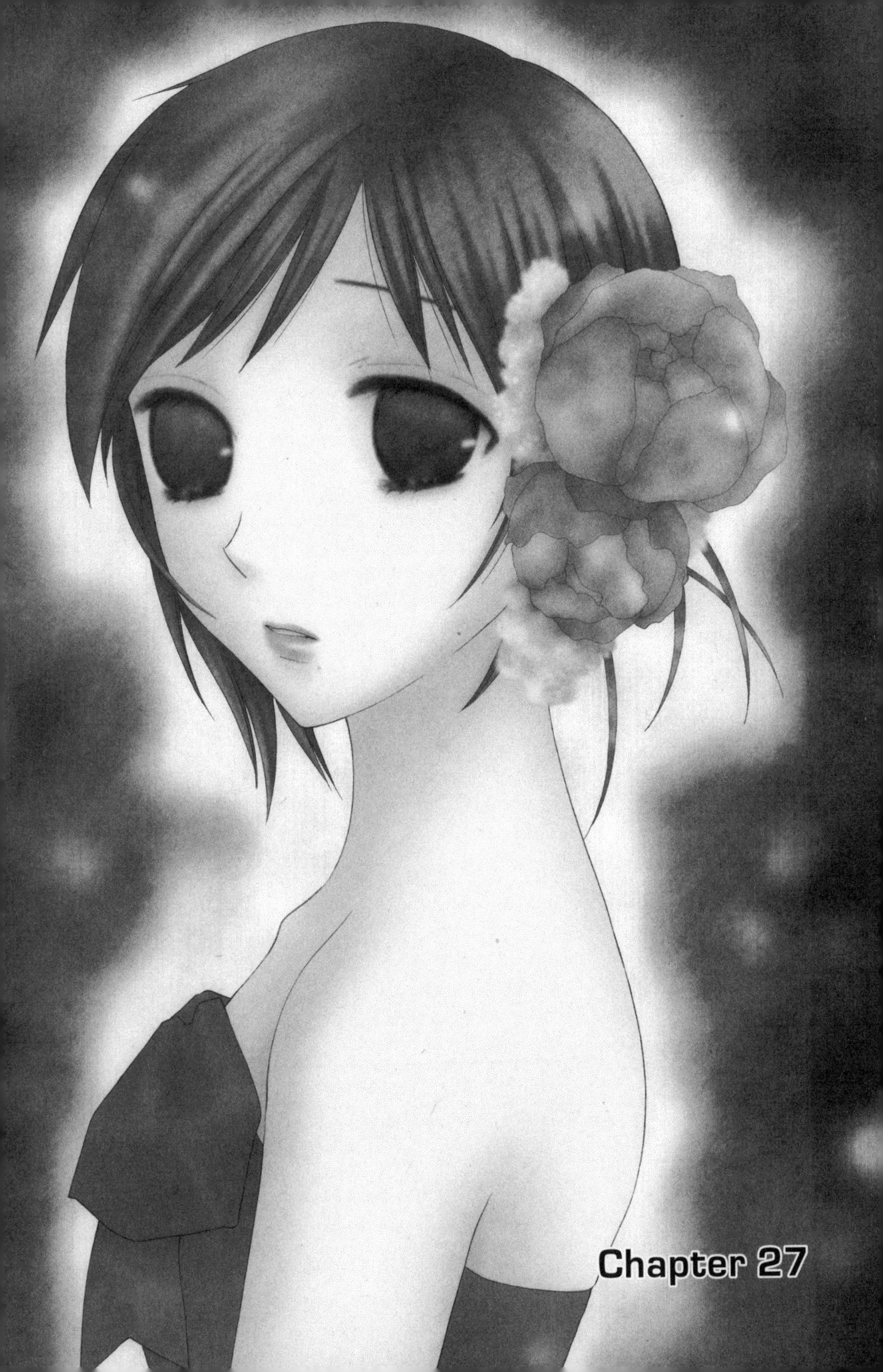
Chapter 27

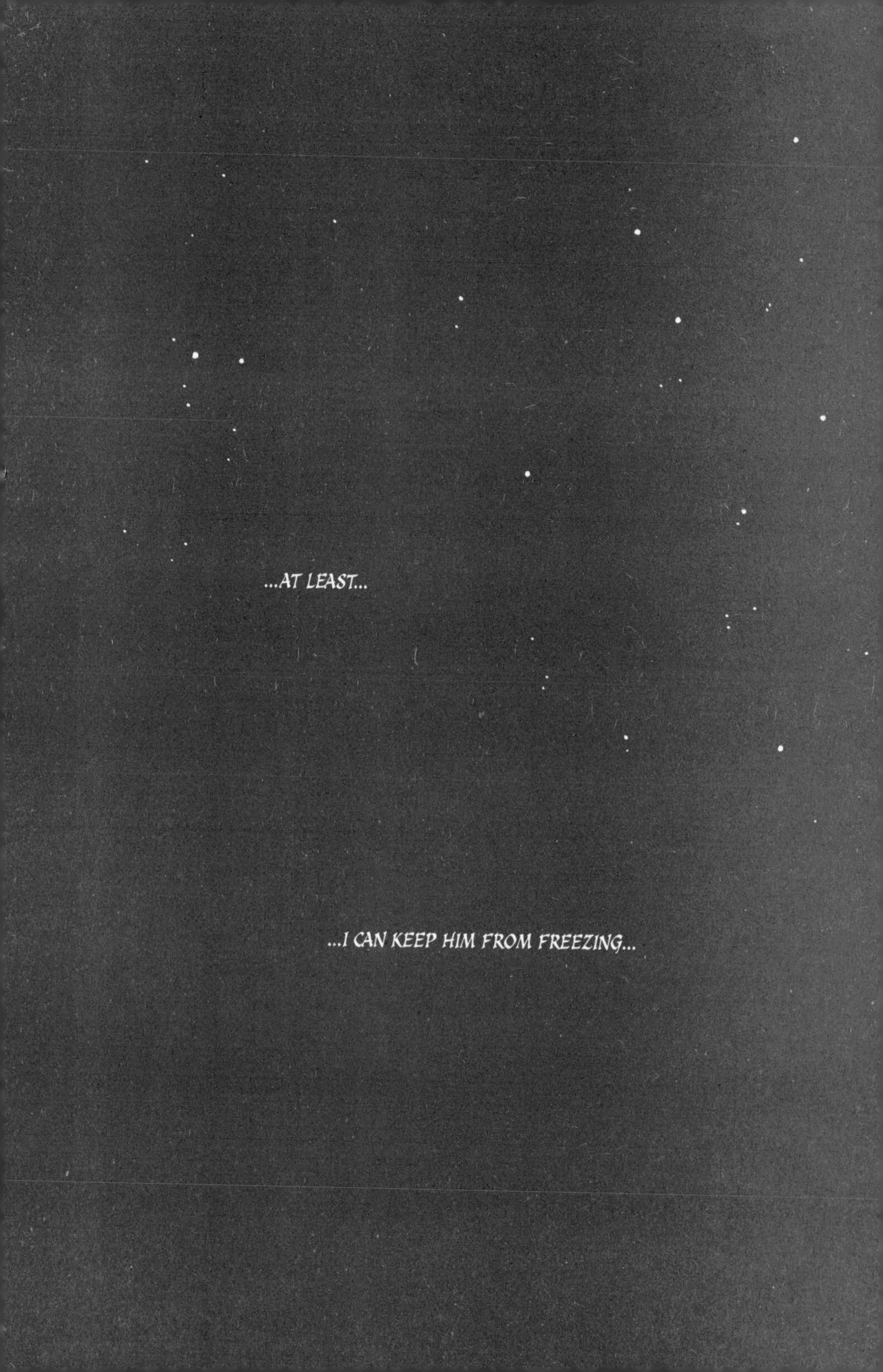
...AT LEAST...
...I CAN KEEP HIM FROM FREEZING...

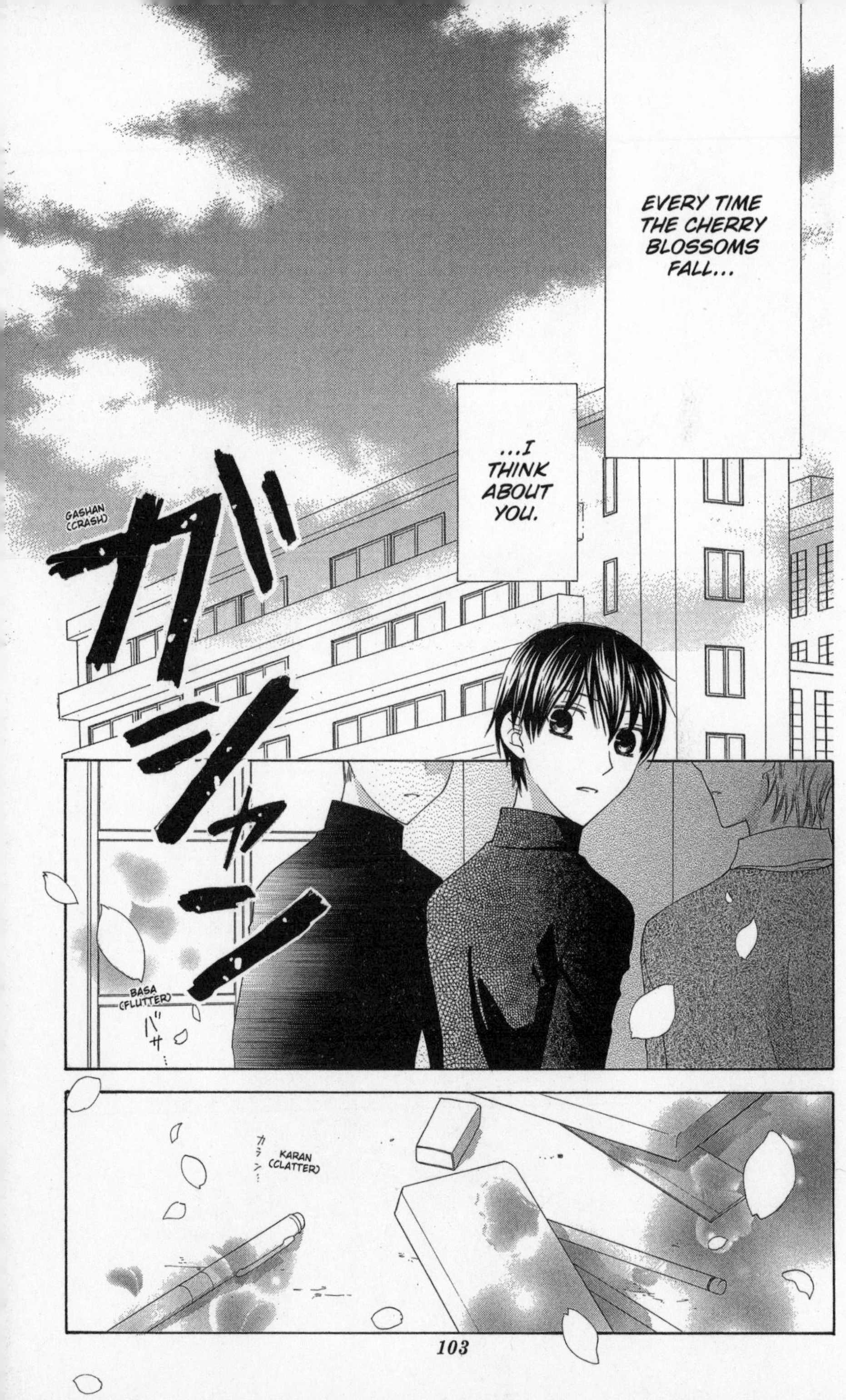
EVERY TIME THE CHERRY BLOSSOMS FALL...
...I THINK ABOUT YOU.
ガシャーン
GASHAN (CRASH)
バサ…
BASA (FLUTTER)
カラン…
KARAN (CLATTER)

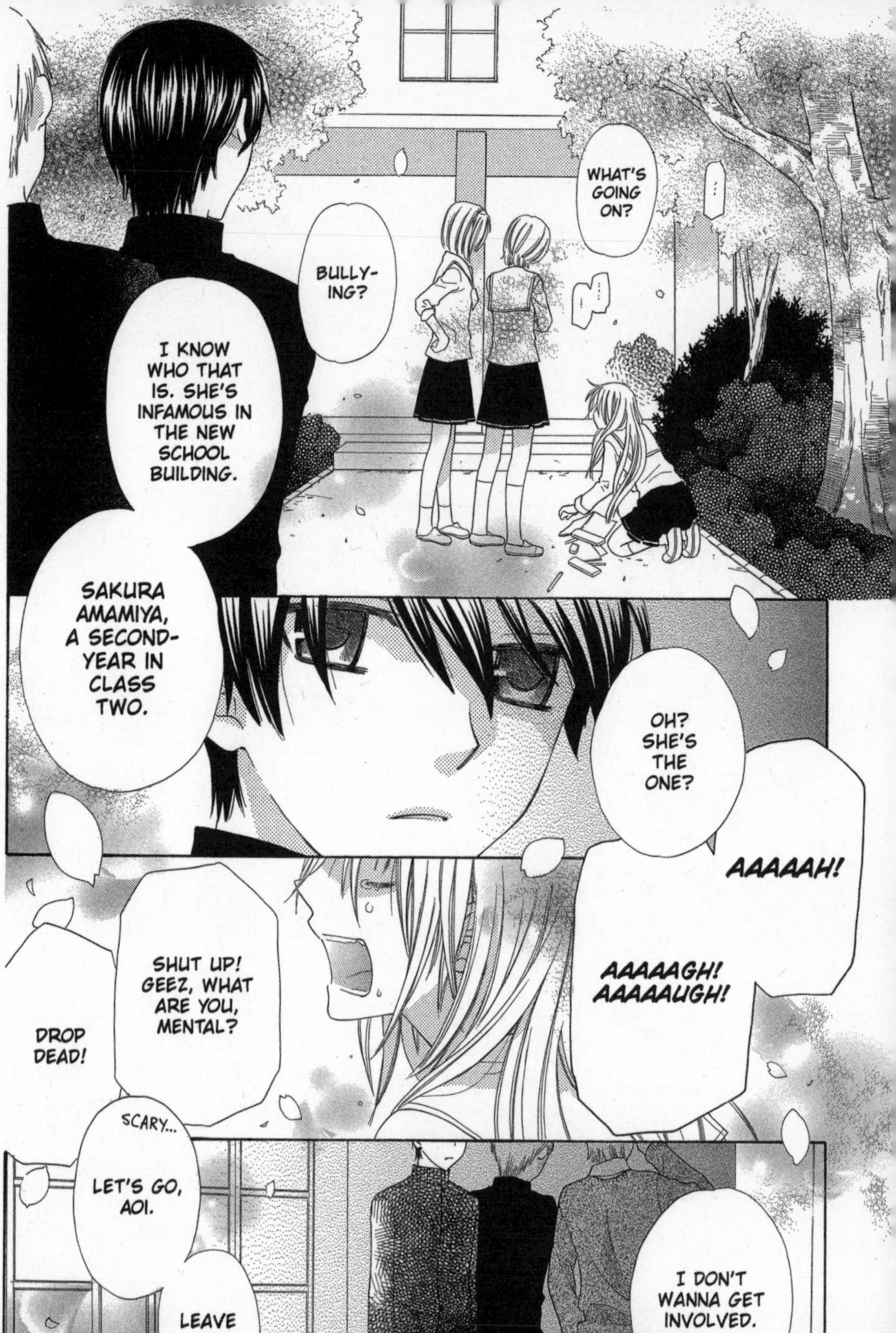
...
WHAT'S GOING ON?
BULLY-ING?
...
I KNOW WHO THAT IS. SHE'S INFAMOUS IN THE NEW SCHOOL BUILDING.
SAKURA AMAMIYA, A SECOND-YEAR IN CLASS TWO.
OH? SHE'S THE ONE?
AAAAAH!
AAAAAGH! AAAAAUGH!
SHUT UP! GEEZ, WHAT ARE YOU, MENTAL?
DROP DEAD!
I DON'T WANNA GET INVOLVED.
SCARY...
LET'S GO, AOI.
LEAVE IT.

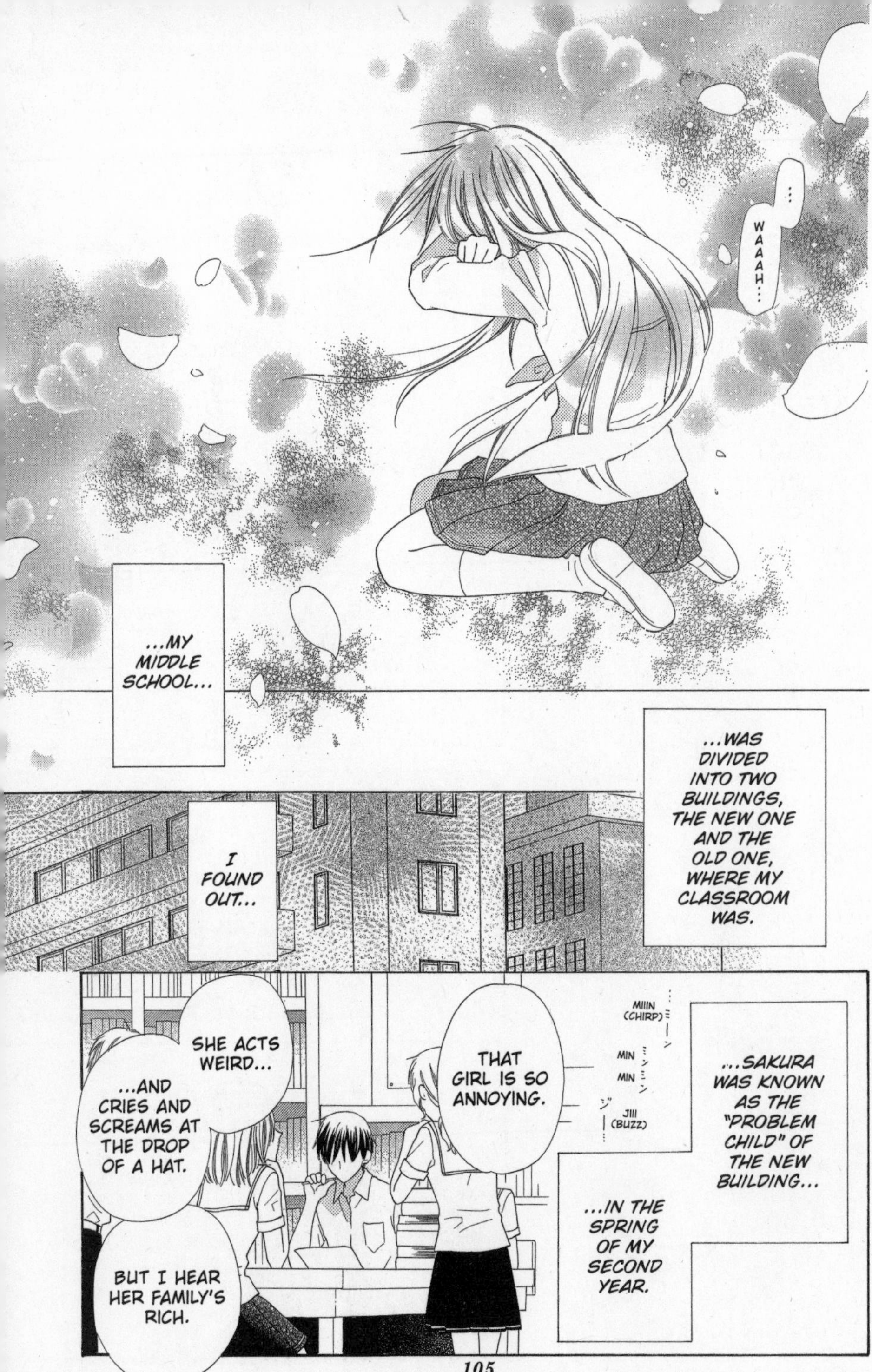

...WAAAH...
...MY MIDDLE SCHOOL...
...WAS DIVIDED INTO TWO BUILDINGS, THE NEW ONE AND THE OLD ONE, WHERE MY CLASSROOM WAS.
I FOUND OUT...
...SAKURA WAS KNOWN AS THE "PROBLEM CHILD" OF THE NEW BUILDING...
...IN THE SPRING OF MY SECOND YEAR.
MIIIN (CHIRP)
MIN MIN
JIII (BUZZ)
THAT GIRL IS SO ANNOYING.
SHE ACTS WEIRD...
...AND CRIES AND SCREAMS AT THE DROP OF A HAT.
BUT I HEAR HER FAMILY'S RICH.

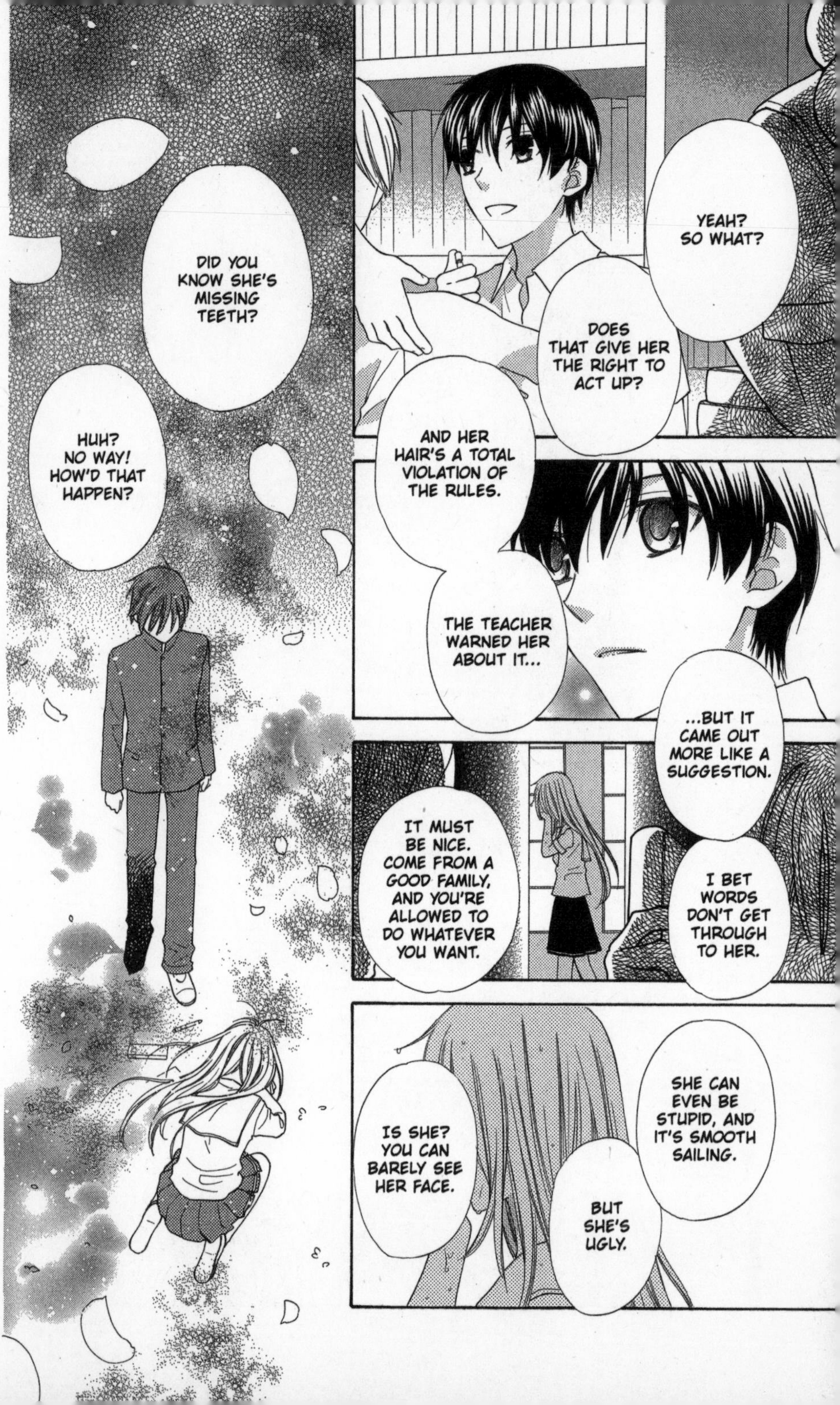
YEAH? SO WHAT?
DOES THAT GIVE HER THE RIGHT TO ACT UP?
AND HER HAIR'S A TOTAL VIOLATION OF THE RULES.
THE TEACHER WARNED HER ABOUT IT...
...BUT IT CAME OUT MORE LIKE A SUGGESTION.
I BET WORDS DON'T GET THROUGH TO HER.
IT MUST BE NICE. COME FROM A GOOD FAMILY, AND YOU'RE ALLOWED TO DO WHATEVER YOU WANT.
SHE CAN EVEN BE STUPID, AND IT'S SMOOTH SAILING.
BUT SHE'S UGLY.
IS SHE? YOU CAN BARELY SEE HER FACE.
DID YOU KNOW SHE'S MISSING TEETH?
HUH? NO WAY! HOW'D THAT HAPPEN?

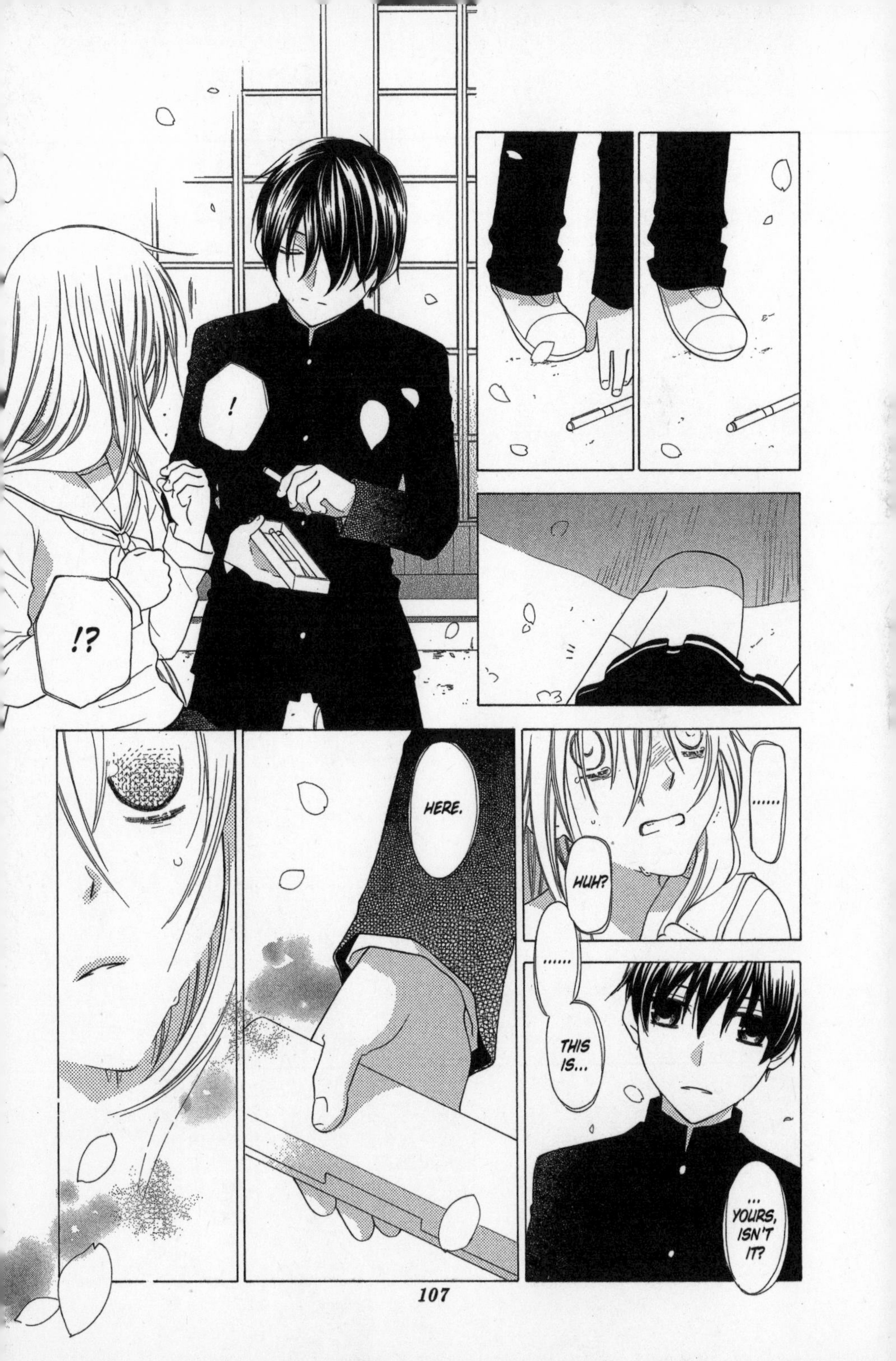
!
!?
......
HUH?
......
THIS IS...
... YOURS, ISN'T IT?
HERE.

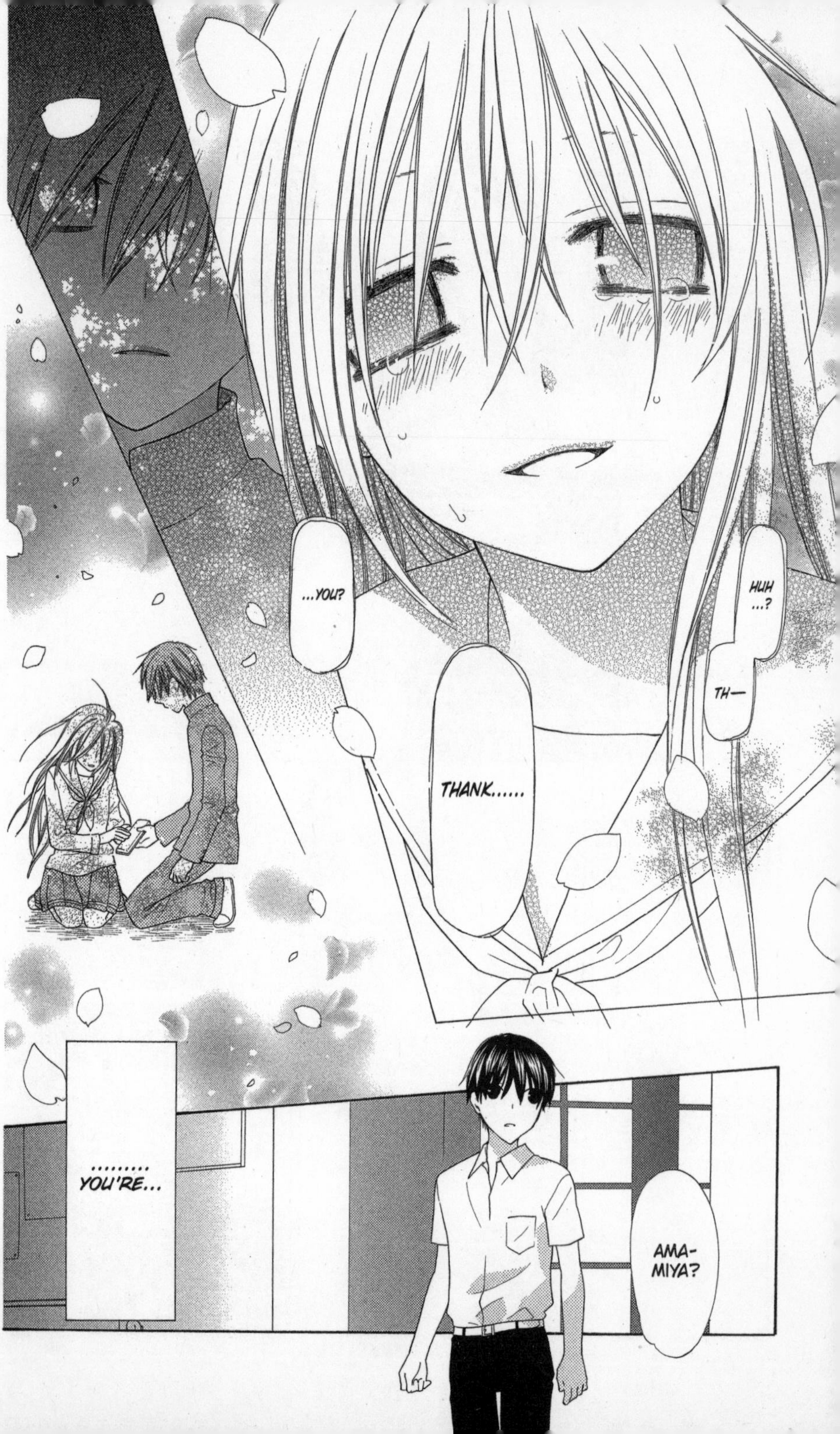
HUH ...?
TH—
THANK......
...YOU?
AMA-MIYA?
.... YOU'RE...

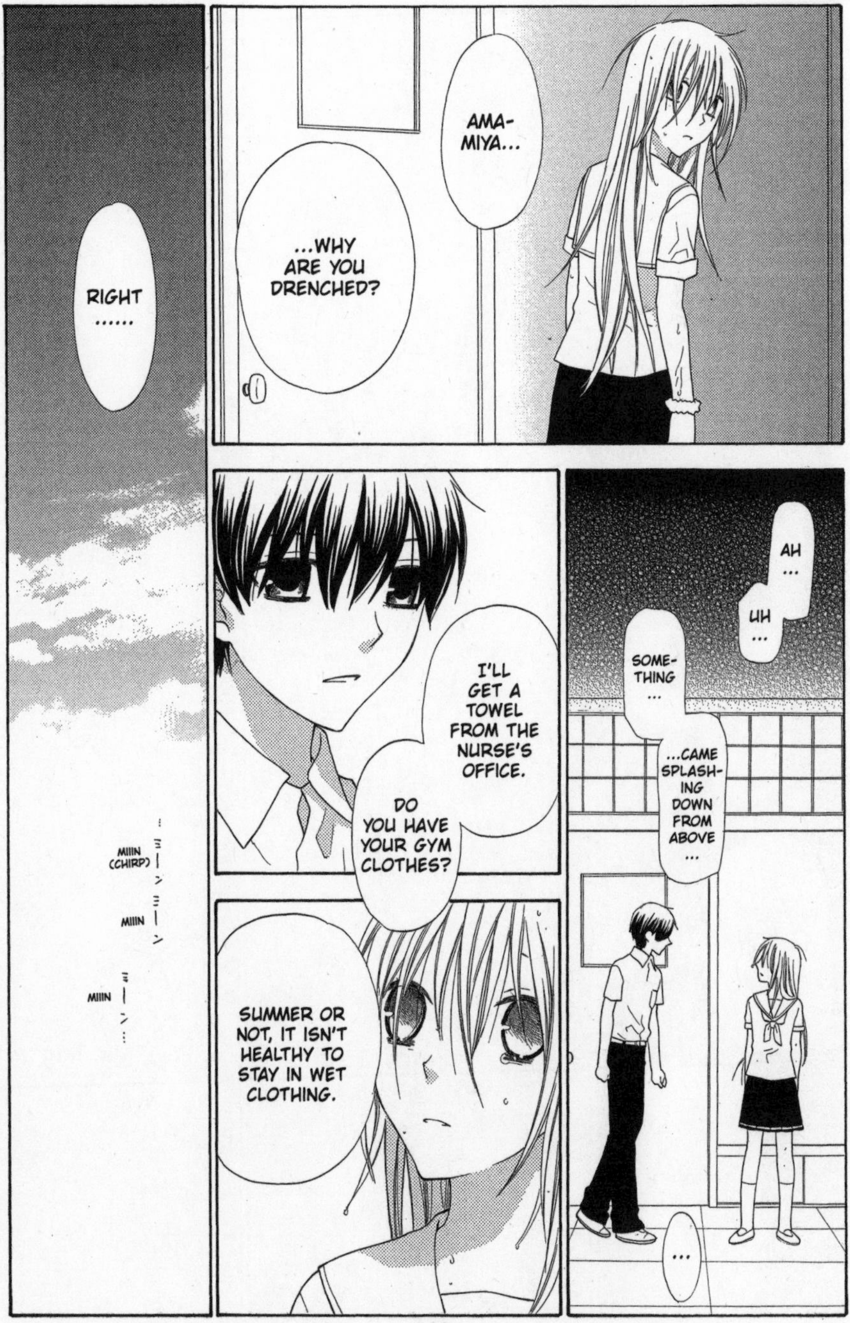
AMA-MIYA...
...WHY ARE YOU DRENCHED?
AH...
UH...
SOME-THING...
...CAME SPLASHING DOWN FROM ABOVE...
...
I'LL GET A TOWEL FROM THE NURSE'S OFFICE.
DO YOU HAVE YOUR GYM CLOTHES?
SUMMER OR NOT, IT ISN'T HEALTHY TO STAY IN WET CLOTHING.
RIGHT......
MIIIN (CHIRP)
MIIIN
MIIIN

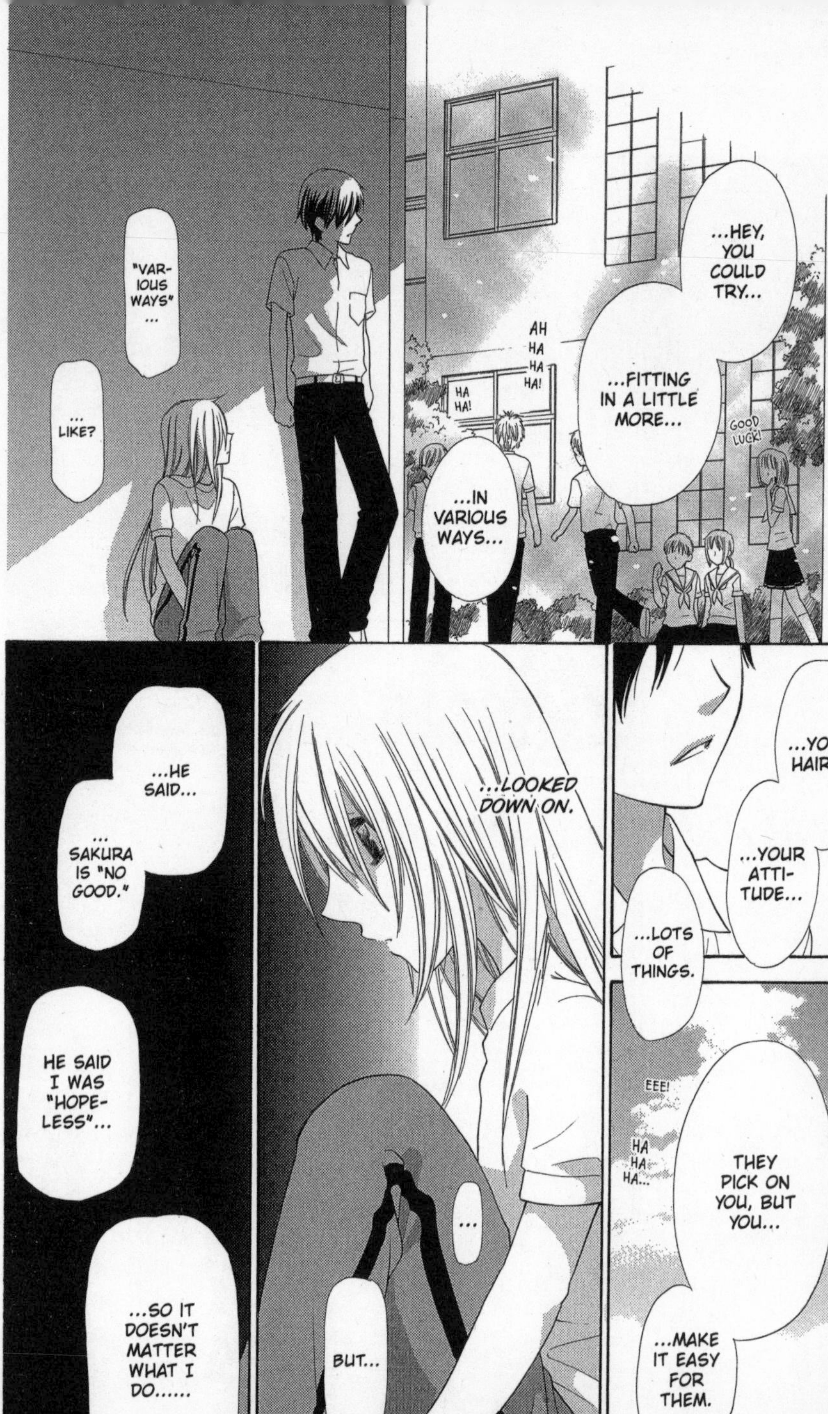
...HEY, YOU COULD TRY...
...FITTING IN A LITTLE MORE...
GOOD LUCK!
AH HA HA HA!
HA HA!
...IN VARIOUS WAYS...
"VARIOUS WAYS"...
...LIKE?
...YOUR HAIR...
...YOUR ATTITUDE...
...LOTS OF THINGS.
EEE!
THEY PICK ON YOU, BUT YOU...
HA HA HA...
...MAKE IT EASY FOR THEM.
...LOOKED DOWN ON.
...
BUT...
...HE SAID...
...SAKURA IS "NO GOOD."
HE SAID I WAS "HOPELESS"...
...SO IT DOESN'T MATTER WHAT I DO......

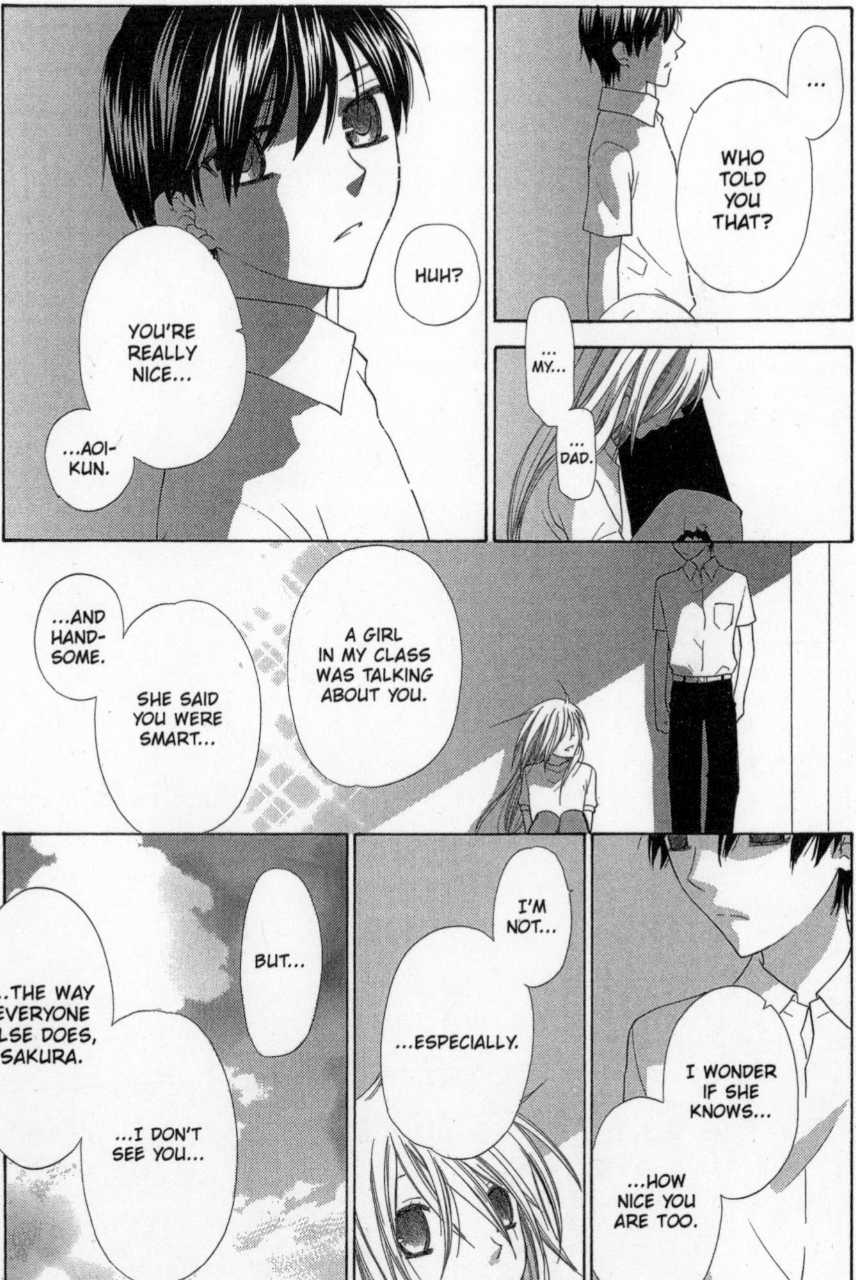
...
WHO TOLD YOU THAT?
...MY...
...DAD.
HUH?
YOU'RE REALLY NICE...
...AOI-KUN.
A GIRL IN MY CLASS WAS TALKING ABOUT YOU.
SHE SAID YOU WERE SMART...
...AND HANDSOME.
I WONDER IF SHE KNOWS...
...HOW NICE YOU ARE TOO.
I'M NOT...
...ESPECIALLY.
BUT...
...I DON'T SEE YOU...
...THE WAY EVERYONE ELSE DOES, SAKURA.

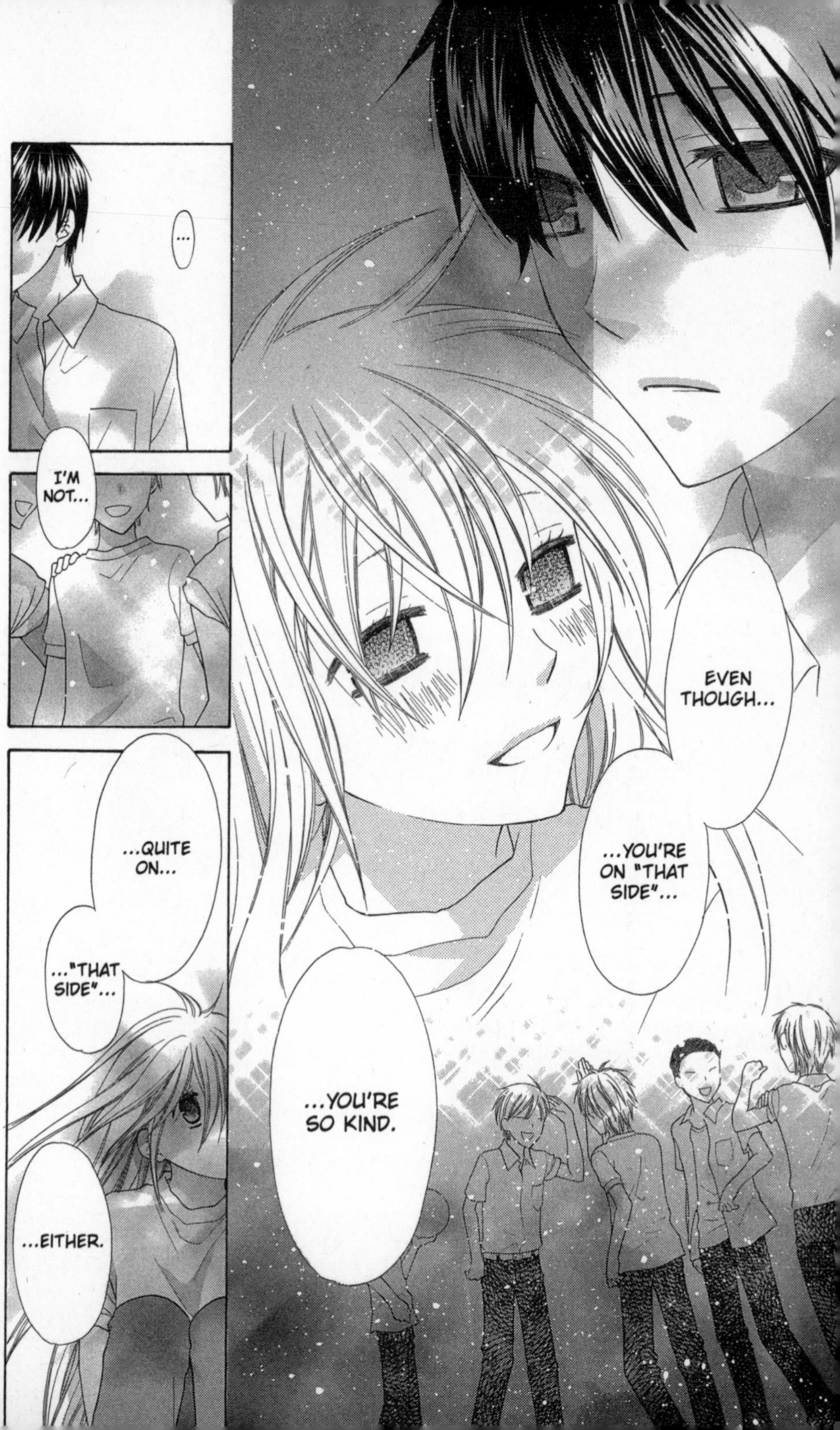
EVEN THOUGH...
...YOU'RE ON "THAT SIDE"...
...YOU'RE SO KIND.
...
I'M NOT...
...QUITE ON...
..."THAT SIDE"...
...EITHER.

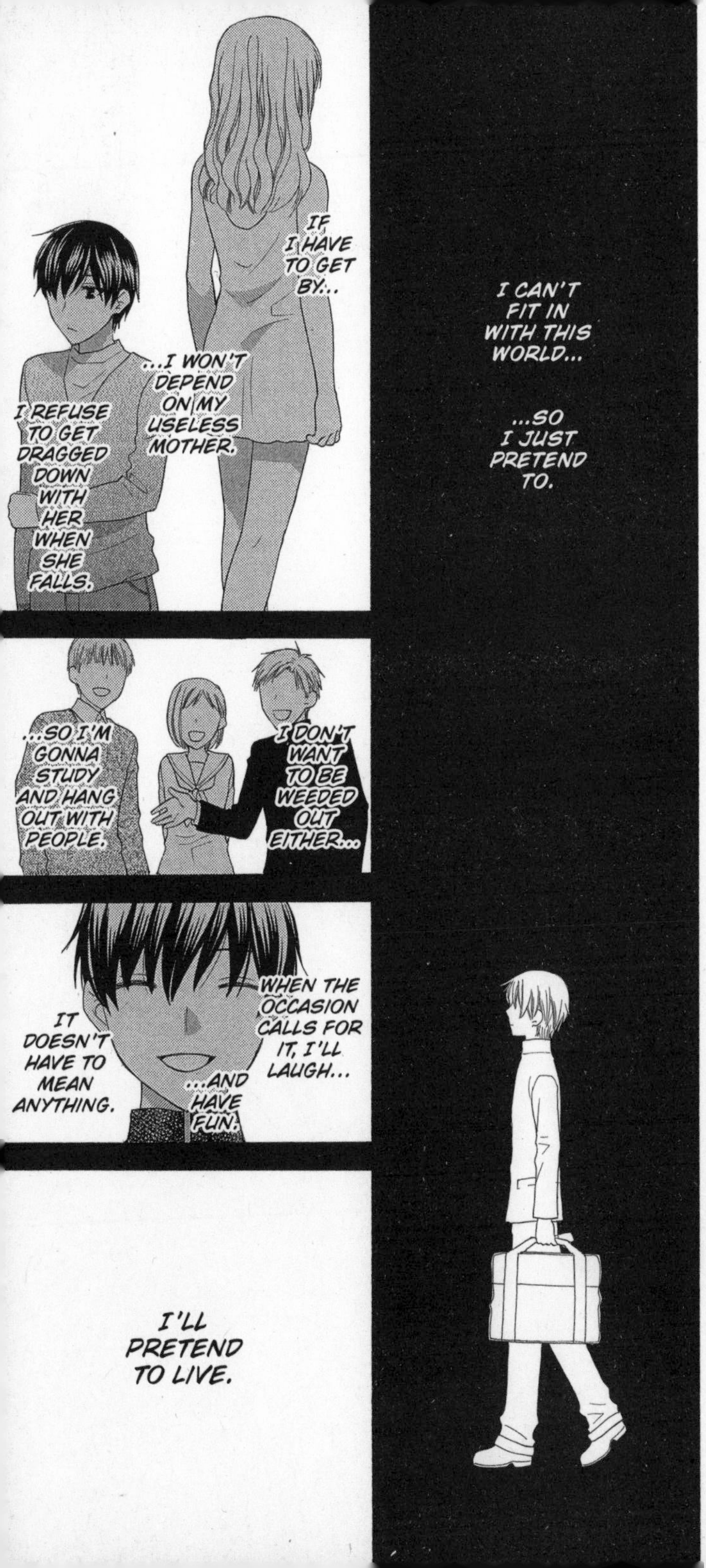
I CAN'T FIT IN WITH THIS WORLD...
...SO I JUST PRETEND TO.
IF I HAVE TO GET BY...
...I WON'T DEPEND ON MY USELESS MOTHER.
I REFUSE TO GET DRAGGED DOWN WITH HER WHEN SHE FALLS.
I DON'T WANT TO BE WEEDED OUT EITHER...
...SO I'M GONNA STUDY AND HANG OUT WITH PEOPLE.
WHEN THE OCCASION CALLS FOR IT, I'LL LAUGH...
...AND HAVE FUN.
IT DOESN'T HAVE TO MEAN ANYTHING.
I'LL PRETEND TO LIVE.

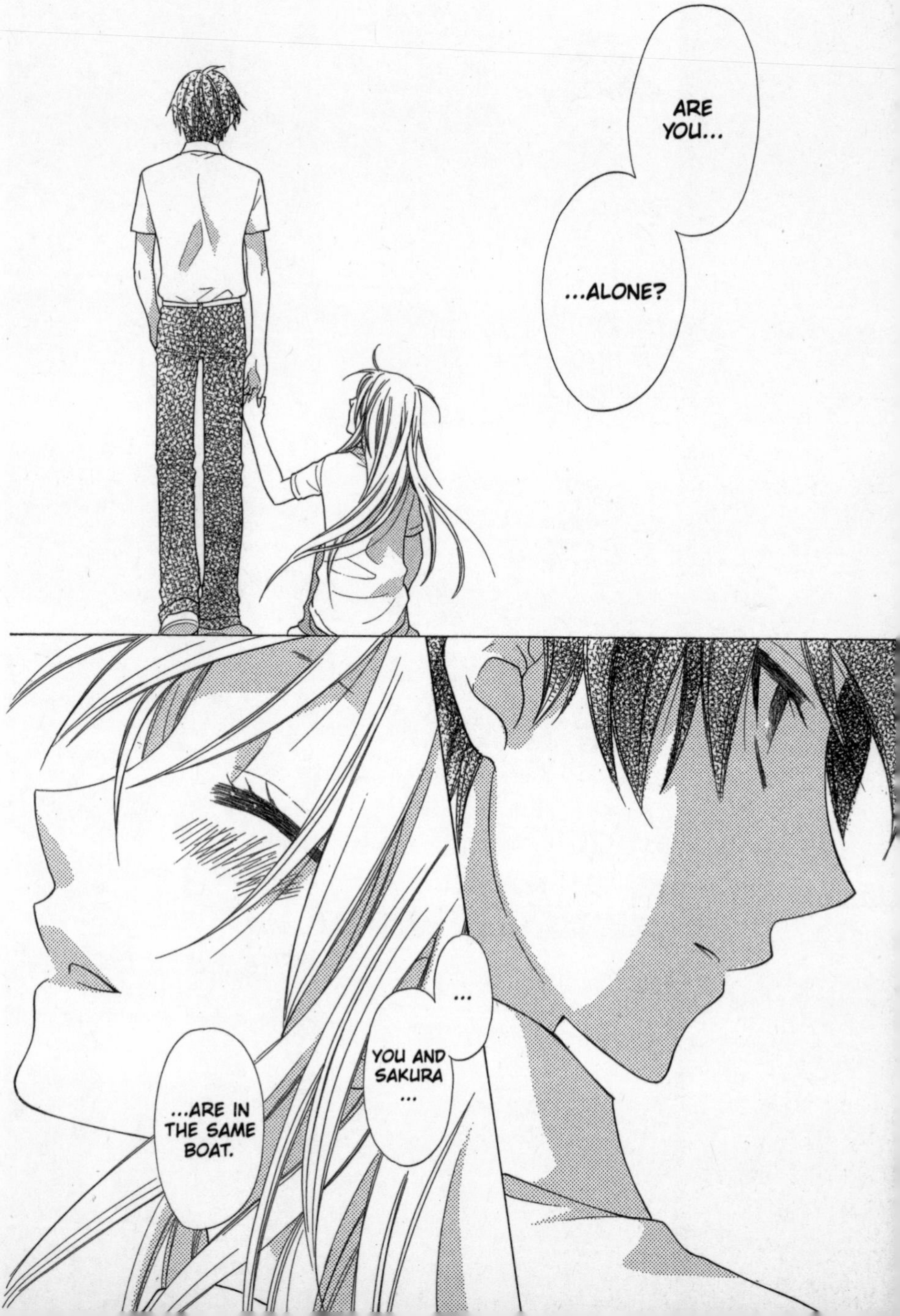
ARE YOU...
...ALONE?
...
YOU AND SAKURA ...
...ARE IN THE SAME BOAT.

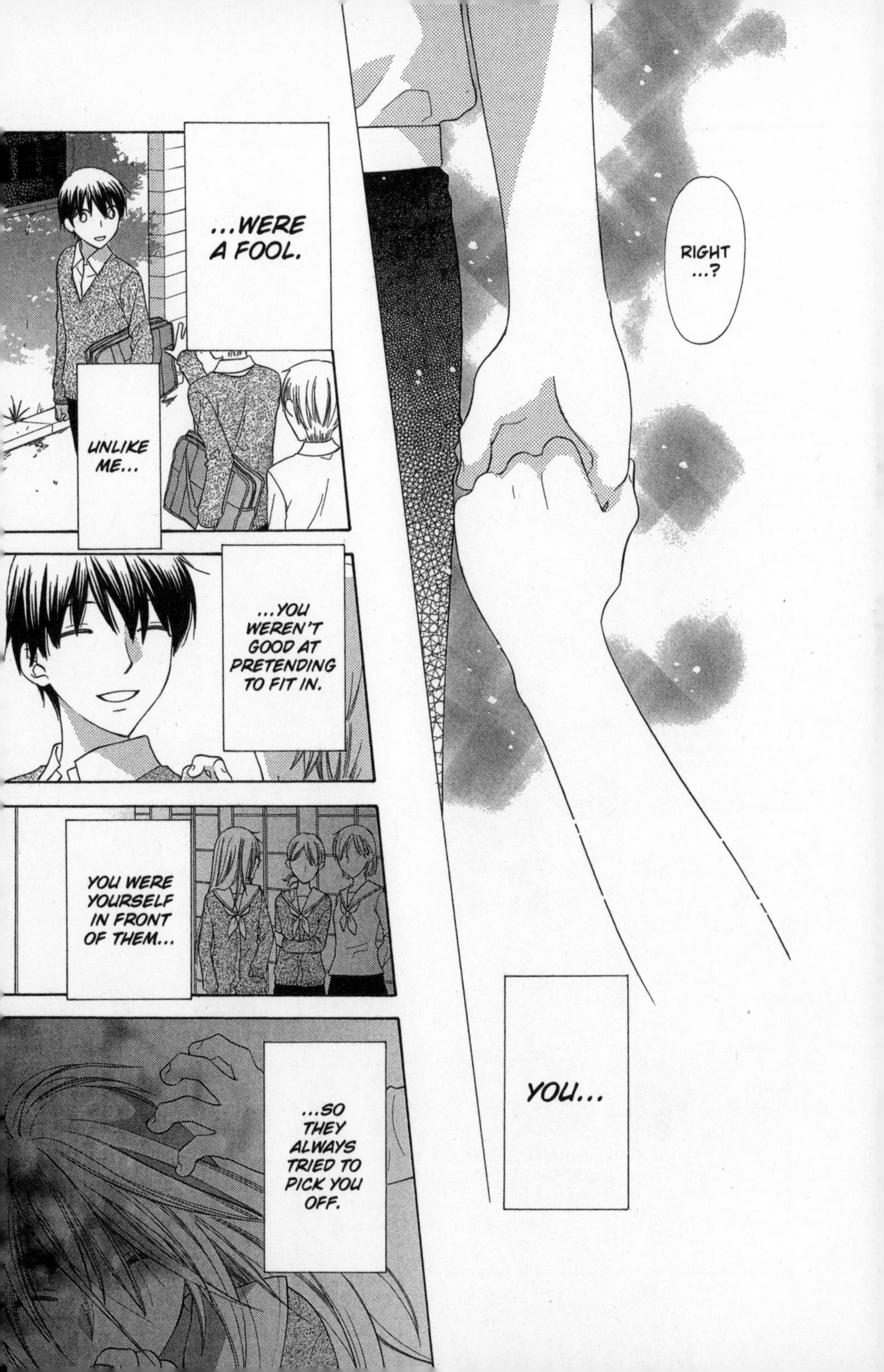
RIGHT ...?
YOU...
...WERE A FOOL.
UNLIKE ME...
...YOU WEREN'T GOOD AT PRETENDING TO FIT IN.
YOU WERE YOURSELF IN FRONT OF THEM...
...SO THEY ALWAYS TRIED TO PICK YOU OFF.

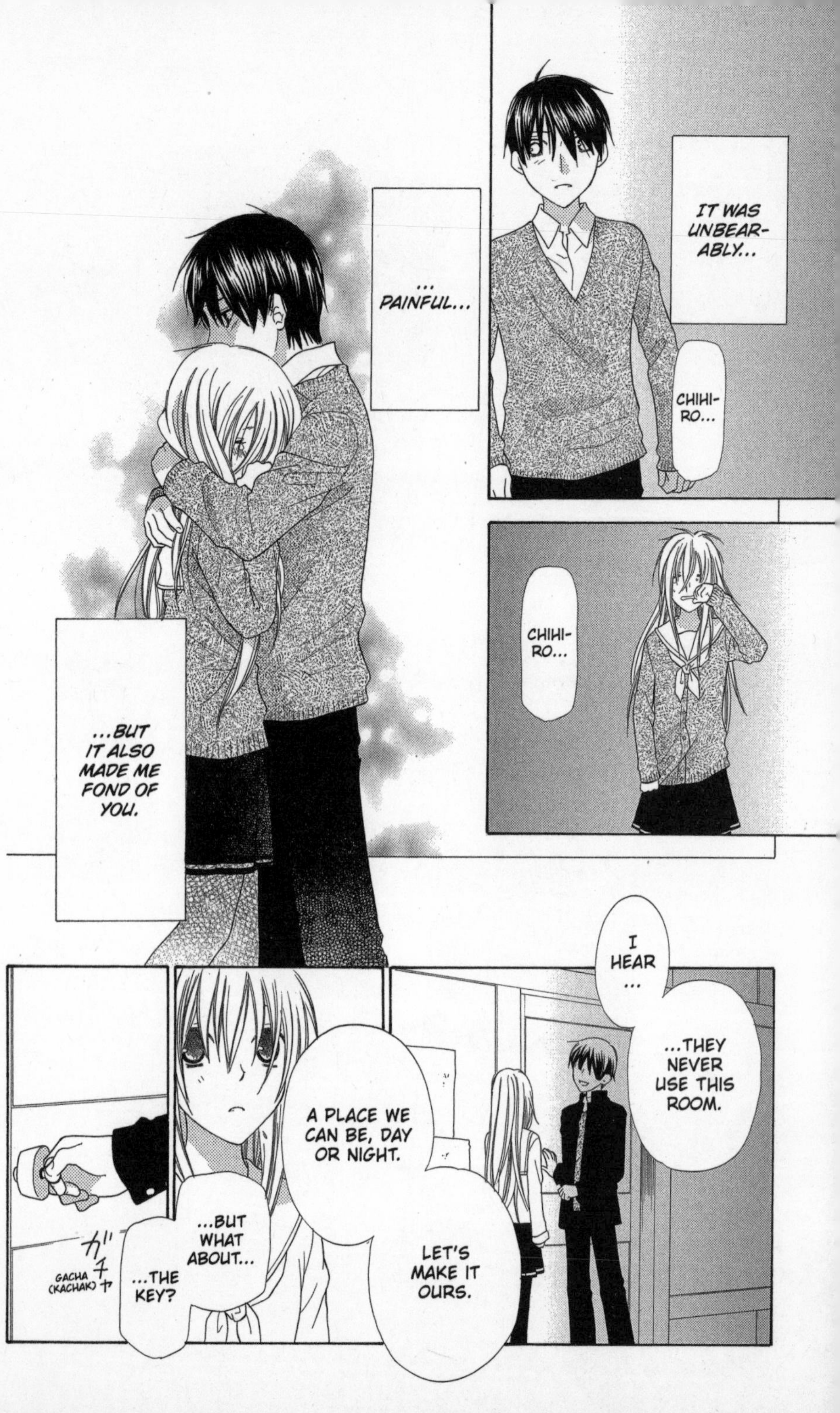
IT WAS UNBEARABLY...
CHIHIRO...
CHIHIRO...
...PAINFUL...
...BUT IT ALSO MADE ME FOND OF YOU.
I HEAR...
...THEY NEVER USE THIS ROOM.
A PLACE WE CAN BE, DAY OR NIGHT.
LET'S MAKE IT OURS.
...BUT WHAT ABOUT...
...THE KEY?
ガチャ
GACHA (KACHAK)

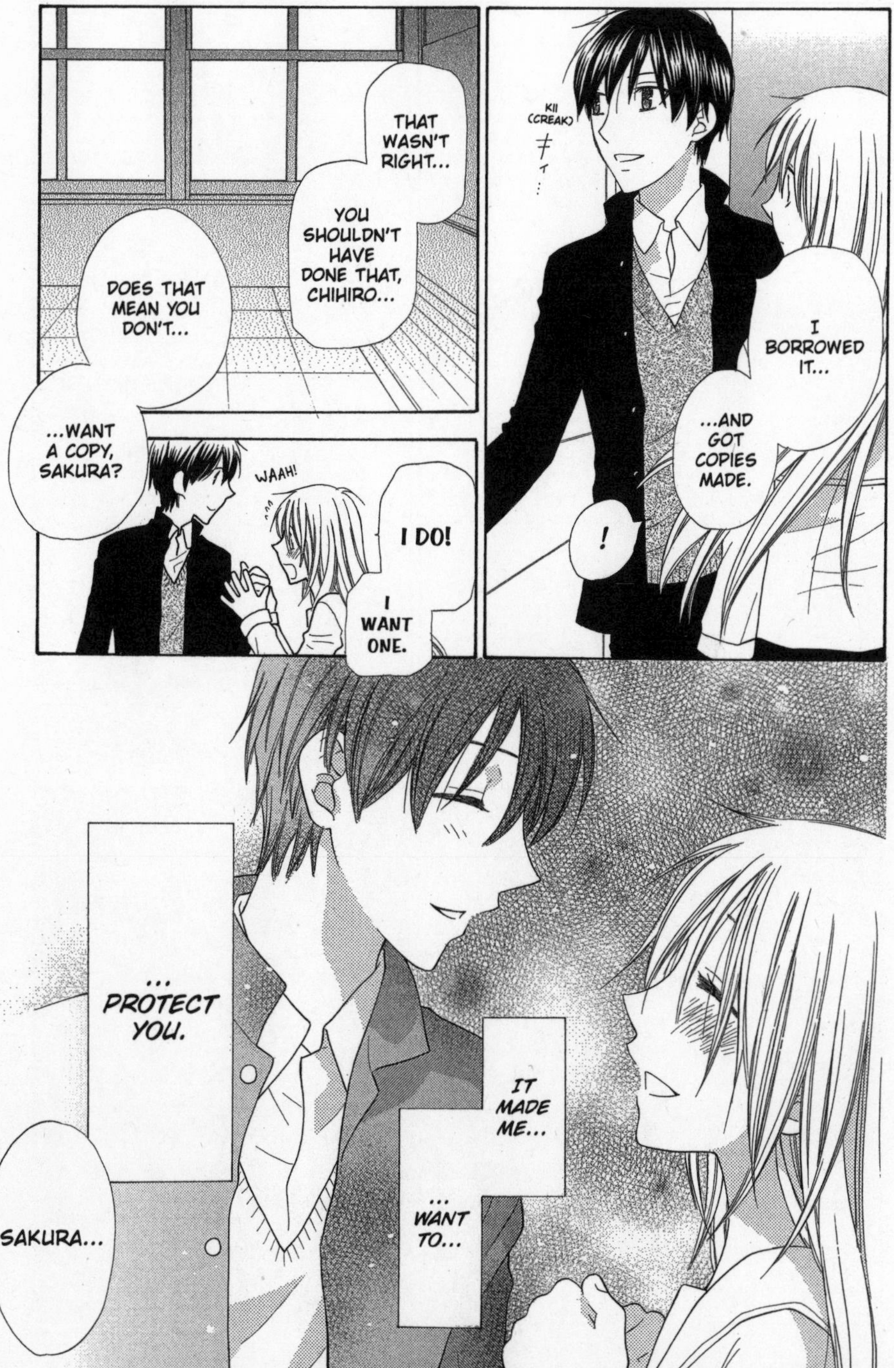

KII (CREAK)
キィ…
I BORROWED IT...
...AND GOT COPIES MADE.
!
THAT WASN'T RIGHT...
YOU SHOULDN'T HAVE DONE THAT, CHIHIRO...
DOES THAT MEAN YOU DON'T...
...WANT A COPY, SAKURA?
WAAH!
I DO!
I WANT ONE.
IT MADE ME...
...WANT TO...
...PROTECT YOU.
SAKURA...

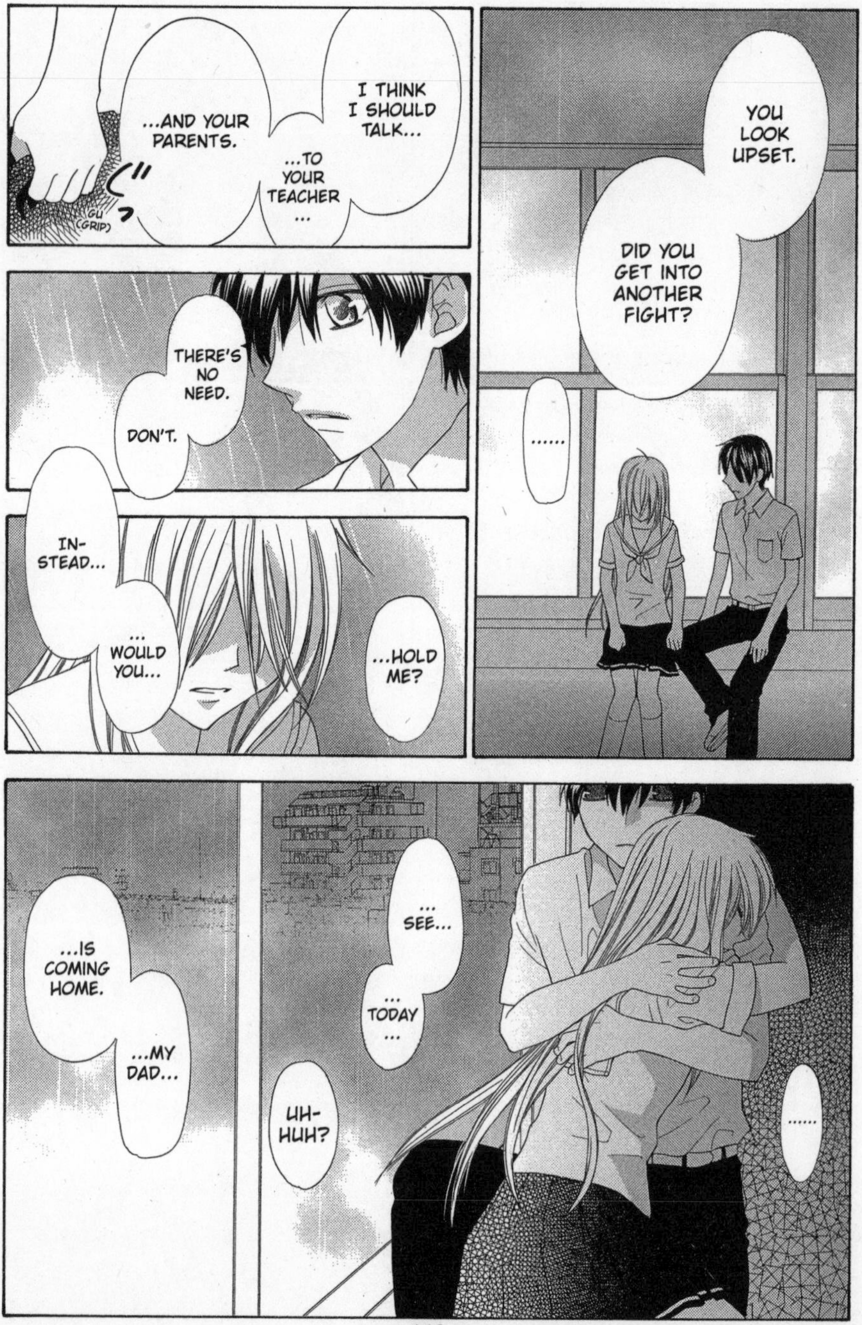
YOU LOOK UPSET.
DID YOU GET INTO ANOTHER FIGHT?
......
I THINK I SHOULD TALK...
...TO YOUR TEACHER...
...AND YOUR PARENTS.
GU (GRIP)
THERE'S NO NEED.
DON'T.
IN-STEAD...
...WOULD YOU...
...HOLD ME?
...SEE...
...TODAY...
...MY DAD...
...IS COMING HOME.
UH-HUH?
......

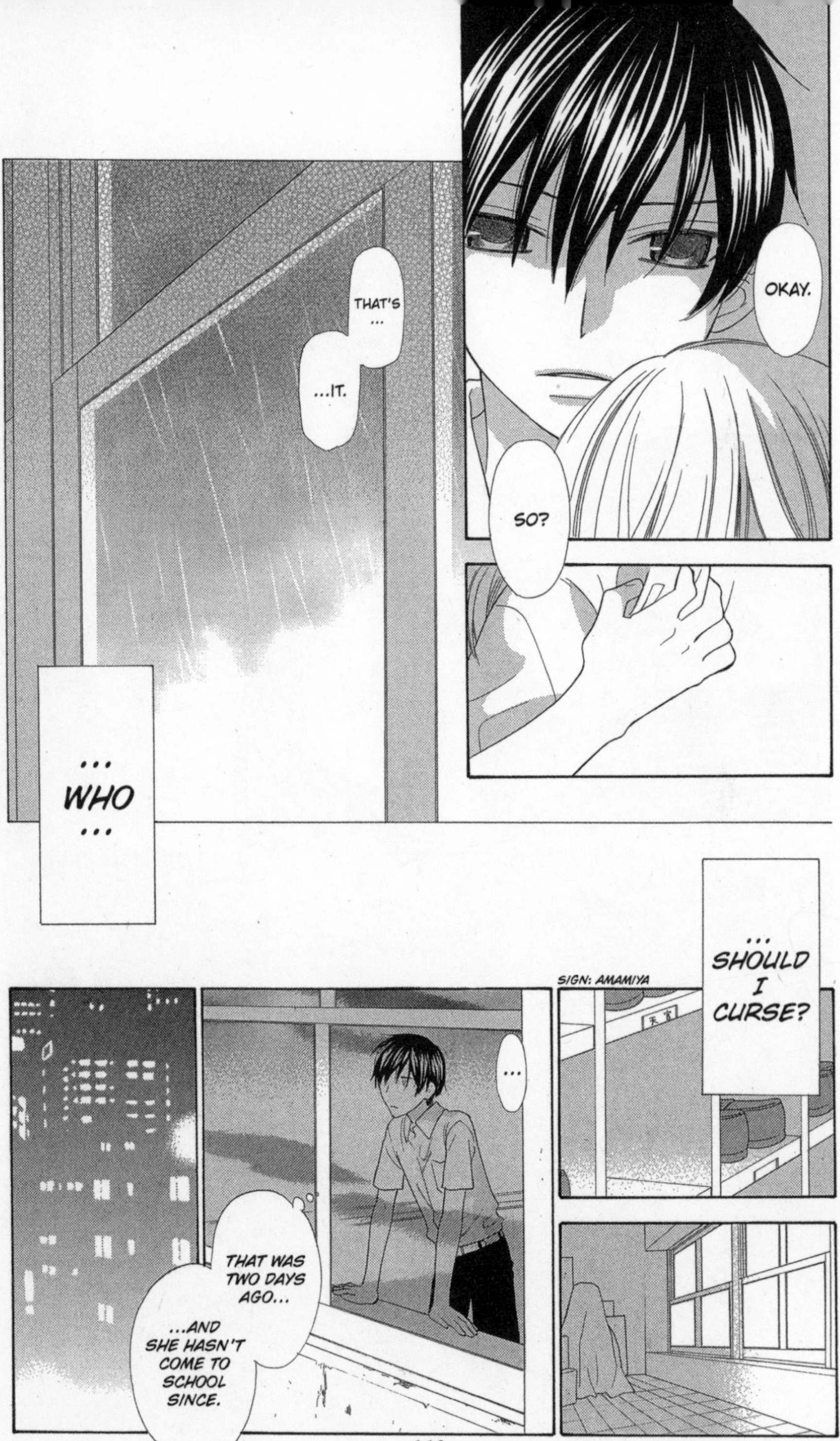
OKAY.
SO?
THAT'S...
...IT.
...WHO...
SIGN: AMAMIYA
...SHOULD I CURSE?
...
THAT WAS TWO DAYS AGO...
...AND SHE HASN'T COME TO SCHOOL SINCE.

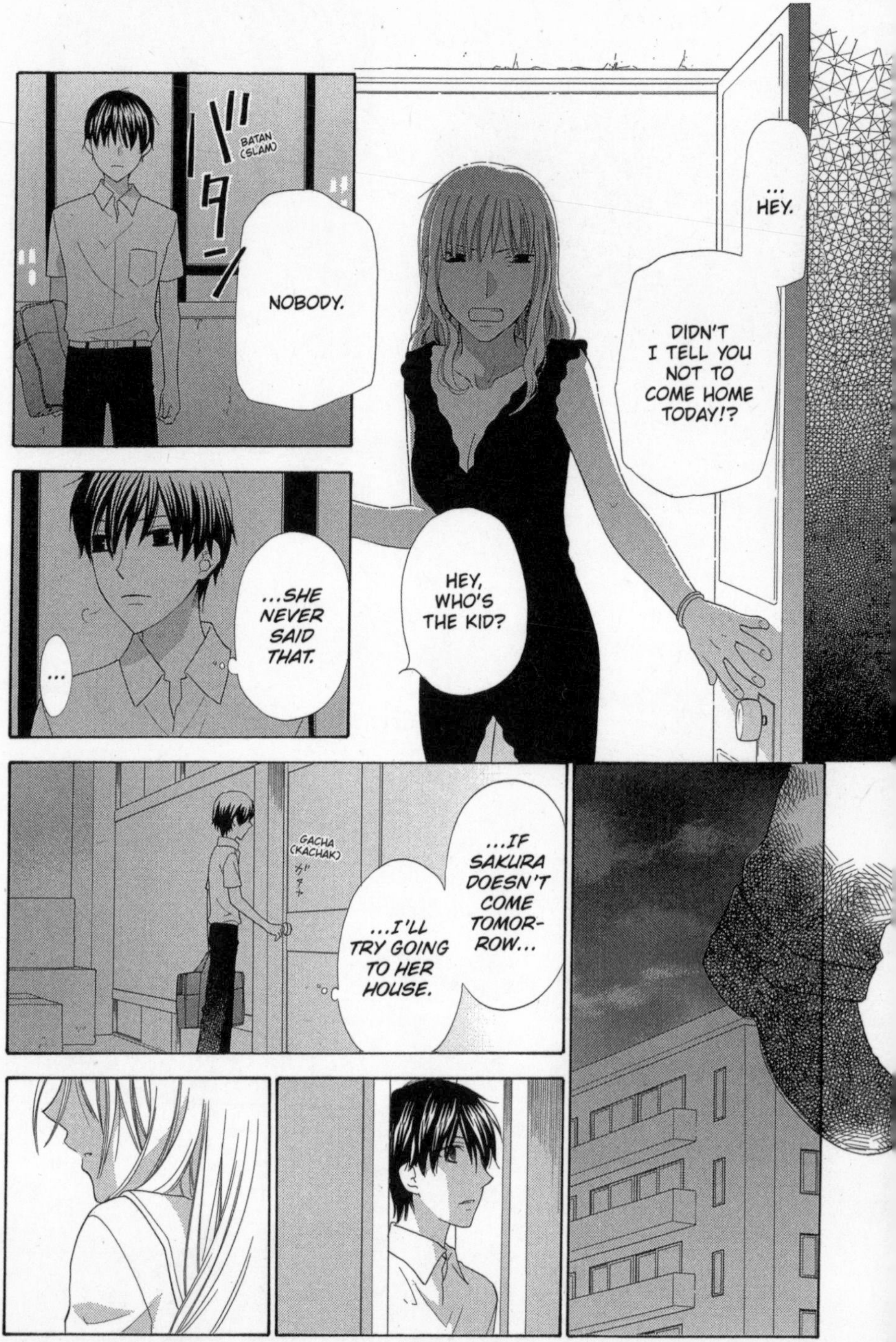
...HEY.
DIDN'T I TELL YOU NOT TO COME HOME TODAY!?
NOBODY.
HEY, WHO'S THE KID?
BATAN (SLAM)
バターン
...SHE NEVER SAID THAT.
...
...IF SAKURA DOESN'T COME TOMORROW...
...I'LL TRY GOING TO HER HOUSE.
GACHA (KACHAK)

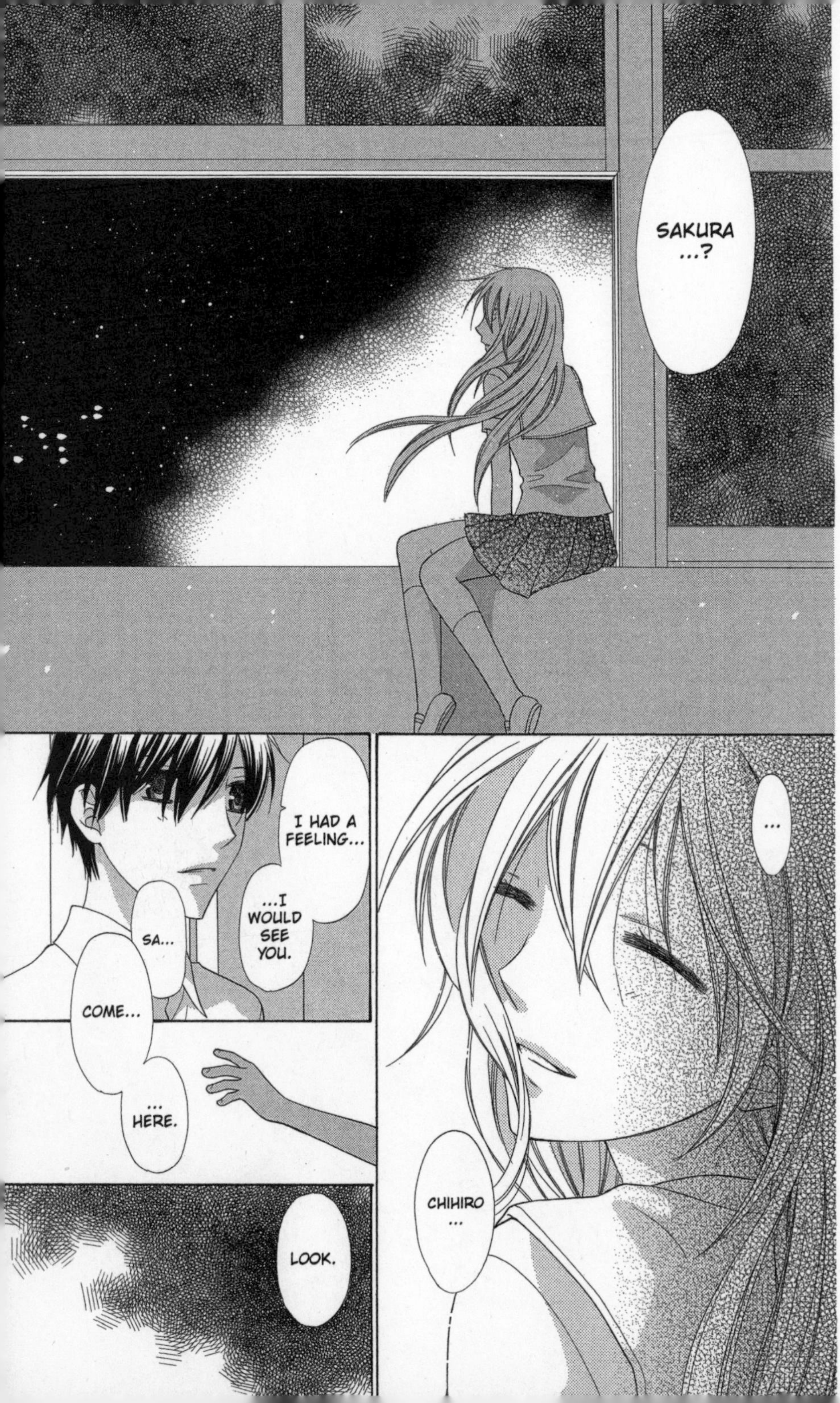
SAKURA ...?
...
CHIHIRO ...
I HAD A FEELING...
...I WOULD SEE YOU.
SA...
COME...
... HERE.
LOOK.

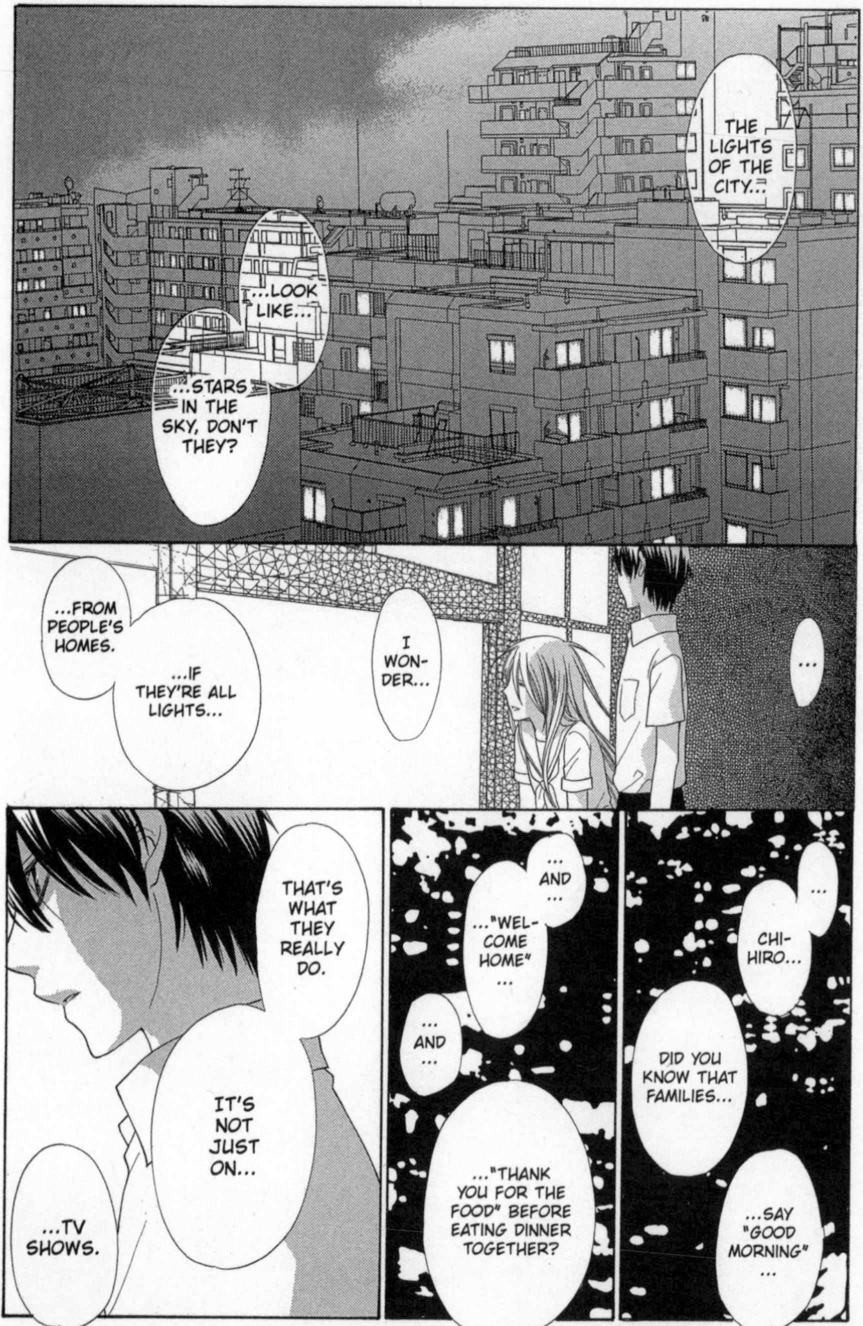
THE LIGHTS OF THE CITY...
...LOOK LIKE...
...STARS IN THE SKY, DON'T THEY?
...
I WONDER...
...IF THEY'RE ALL LIGHTS...
...FROM PEOPLE'S HOMES.
...
CHIHIRO...
DID YOU KNOW THAT FAMILIES...
...SAY "GOOD MORNING"...
...AND...
..."WELCOME HOME"...
...AND...
..."THANK YOU FOR THE FOOD" BEFORE EATING DINNER TOGETHER?
THAT'S WHAT THEY REALLY DO.
IT'S NOT JUST ON...
...TV SHOWS.

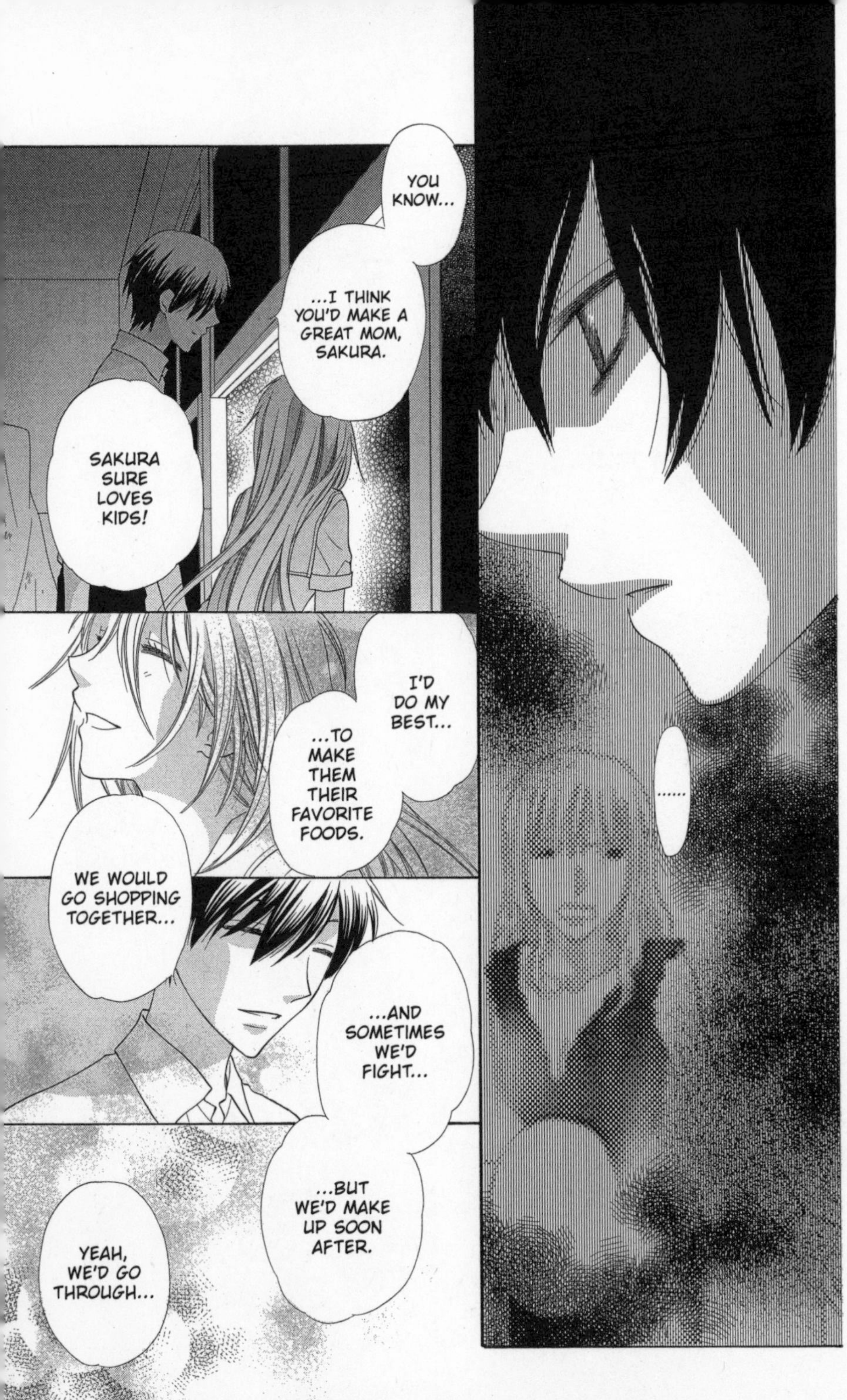
......
YOU KNOW...
...I THINK YOU'D MAKE A GREAT MOM, SAKURA.
SAKURA SURE LOVES KIDS!
I'D DO MY BEST...
...TO MAKE THEM THEIR FAVORITE FOODS.
WE WOULD GO SHOPPING TOGETHER...
...AND SOMETIMES WE'D FIGHT...
...BUT WE'D MAKE UP SOON AFTER.
YEAH, WE'D GO THROUGH...

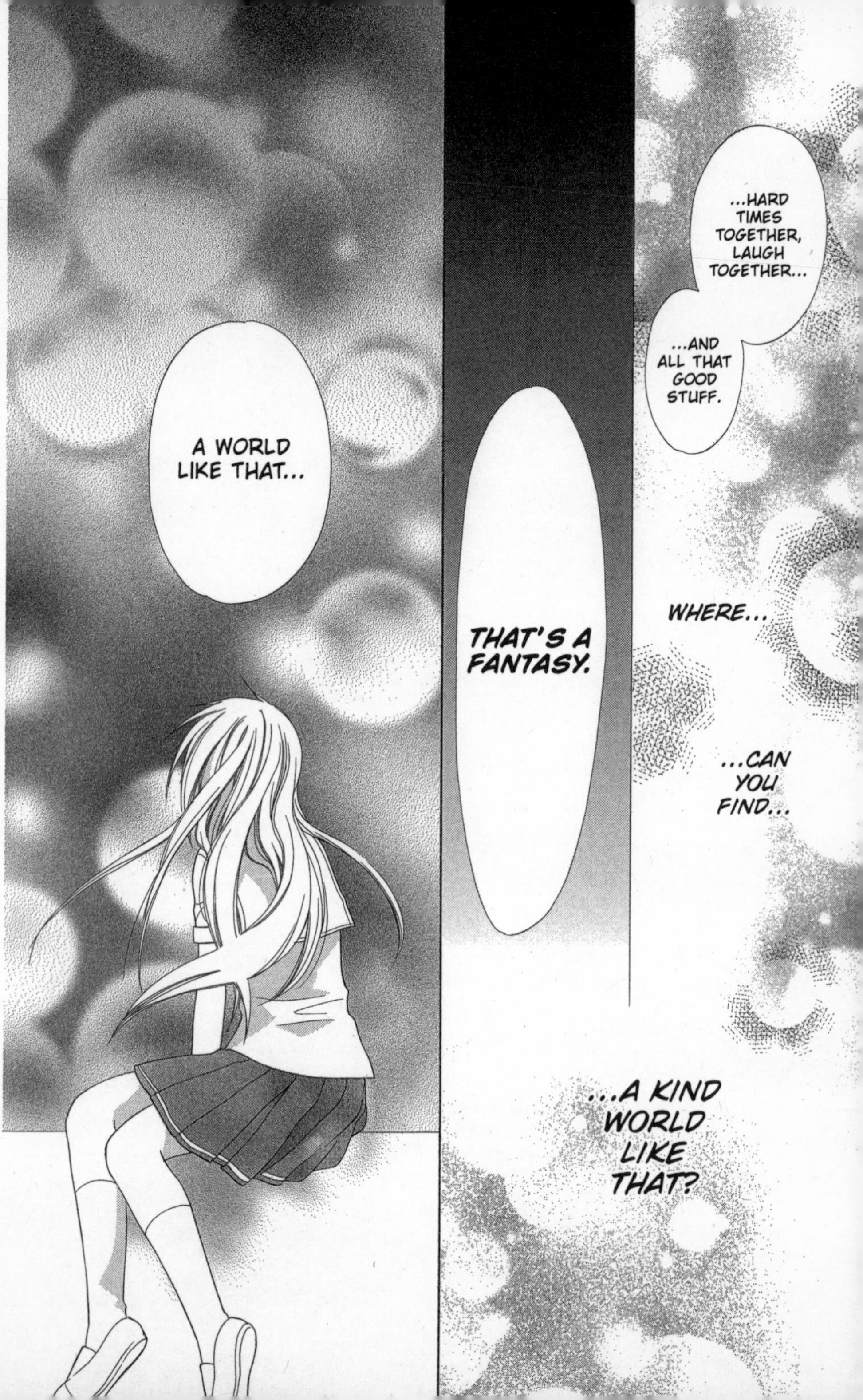
...HARD TIMES TOGETHER, LAUGH TOGETHER...
...AND ALL THAT GOOD STUFF.
WHERE...
...CAN YOU FIND...
...A KIND WORLD LIKE THAT?
THAT'S A FANTASY.
A WORLD LIKE THAT...

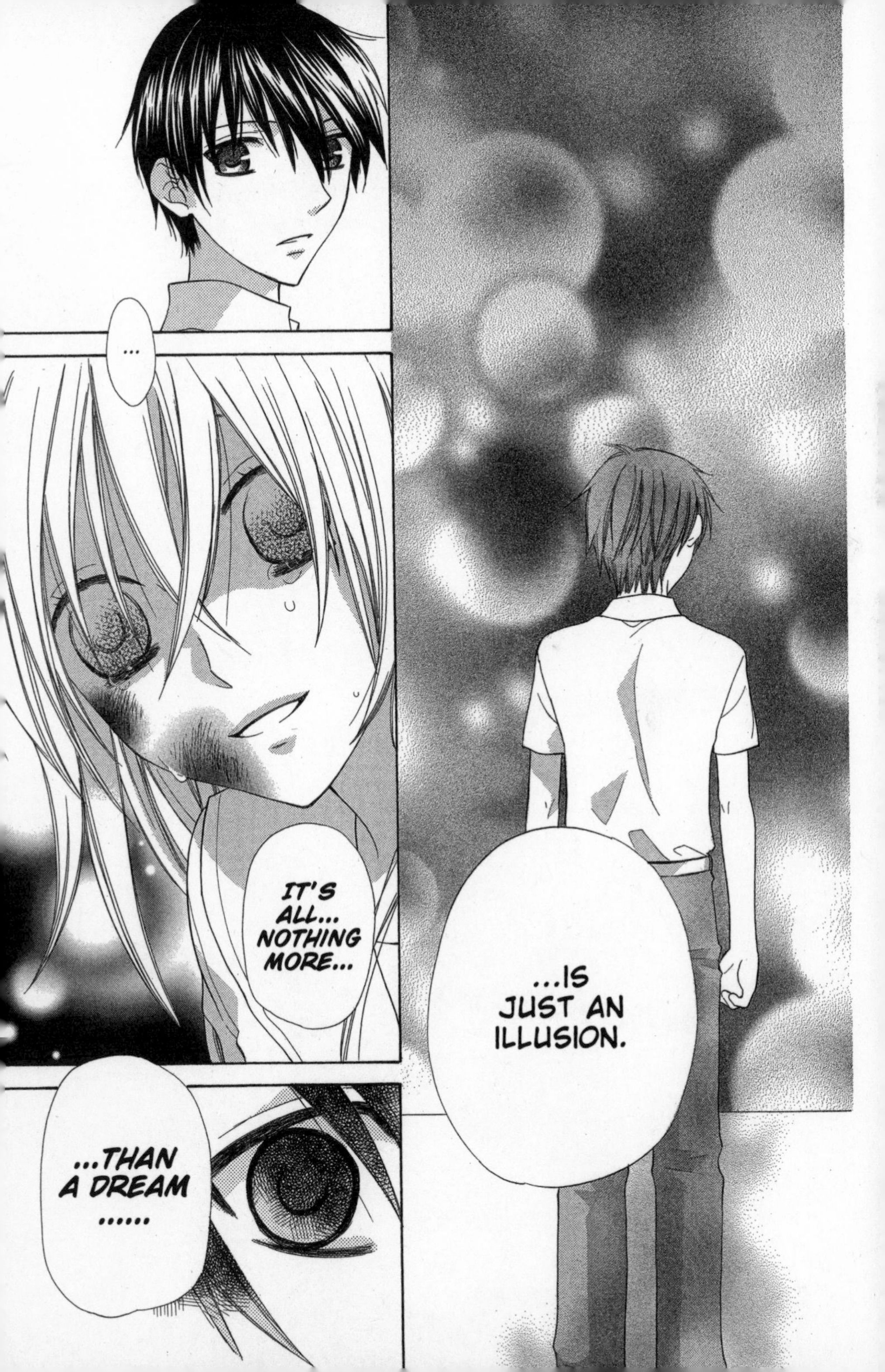
...IS JUST AN ILLUSION.
...
IT'S ALL... NOTHING MORE...
...THAN A DREAM ......

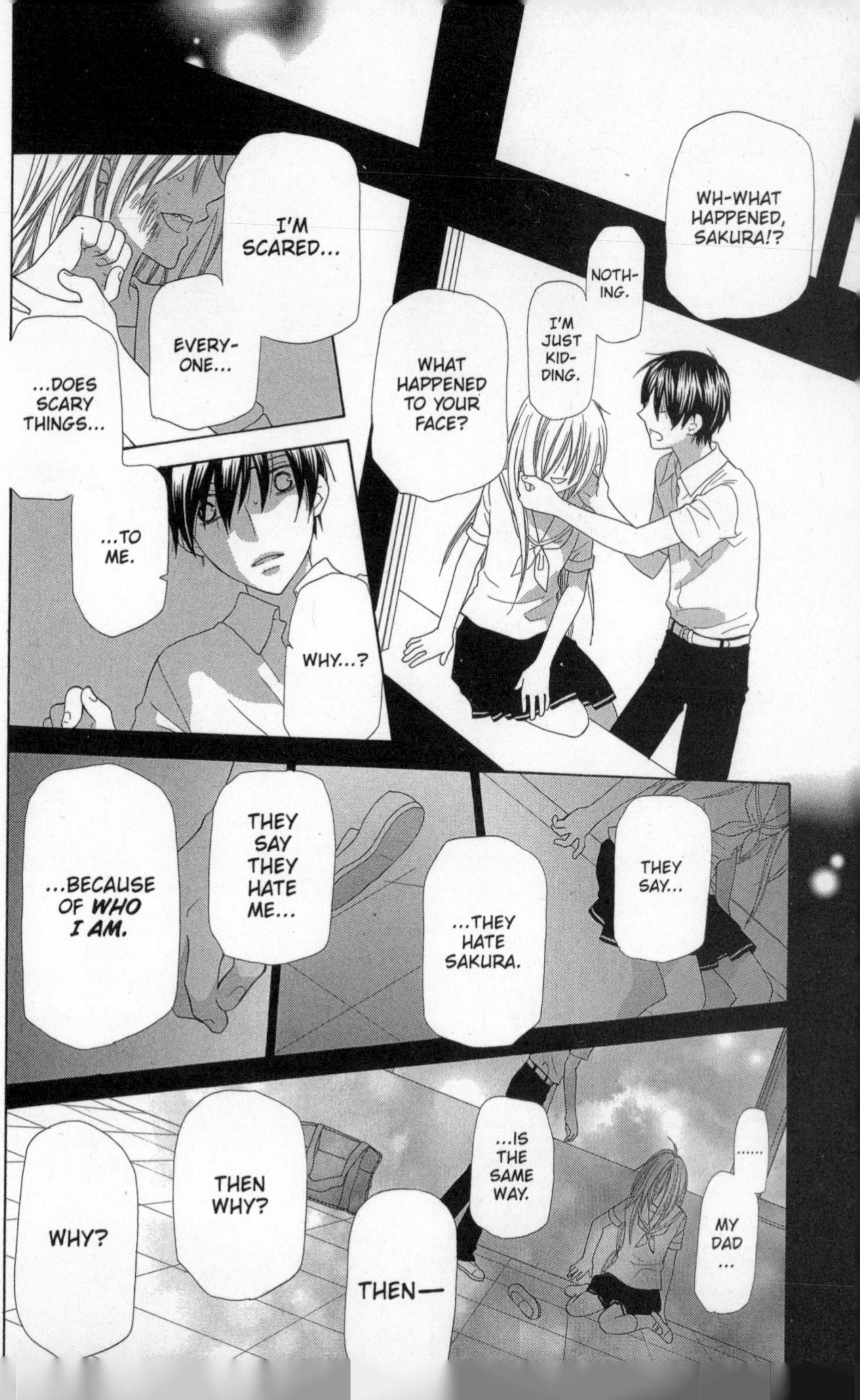
WH-WHAT HAPPENED, SAKURA!?
NOTH-ING.
I'M JUST KID-DING.
WHAT HAPPENED TO YOUR FACE?
I'M SCARED...
EVERY-ONE...
...DOES SCARY THINGS...
...TO ME.
WHY...?
THEY SAY...
...THEY HATE SAKURA.
THEY SAY THEY HATE ME...
...BECAUSE OF ***WHO I AM.***
......
MY DAD ...
...IS THE SAME WAY.
THEN—
THEN WHY?
WHY?

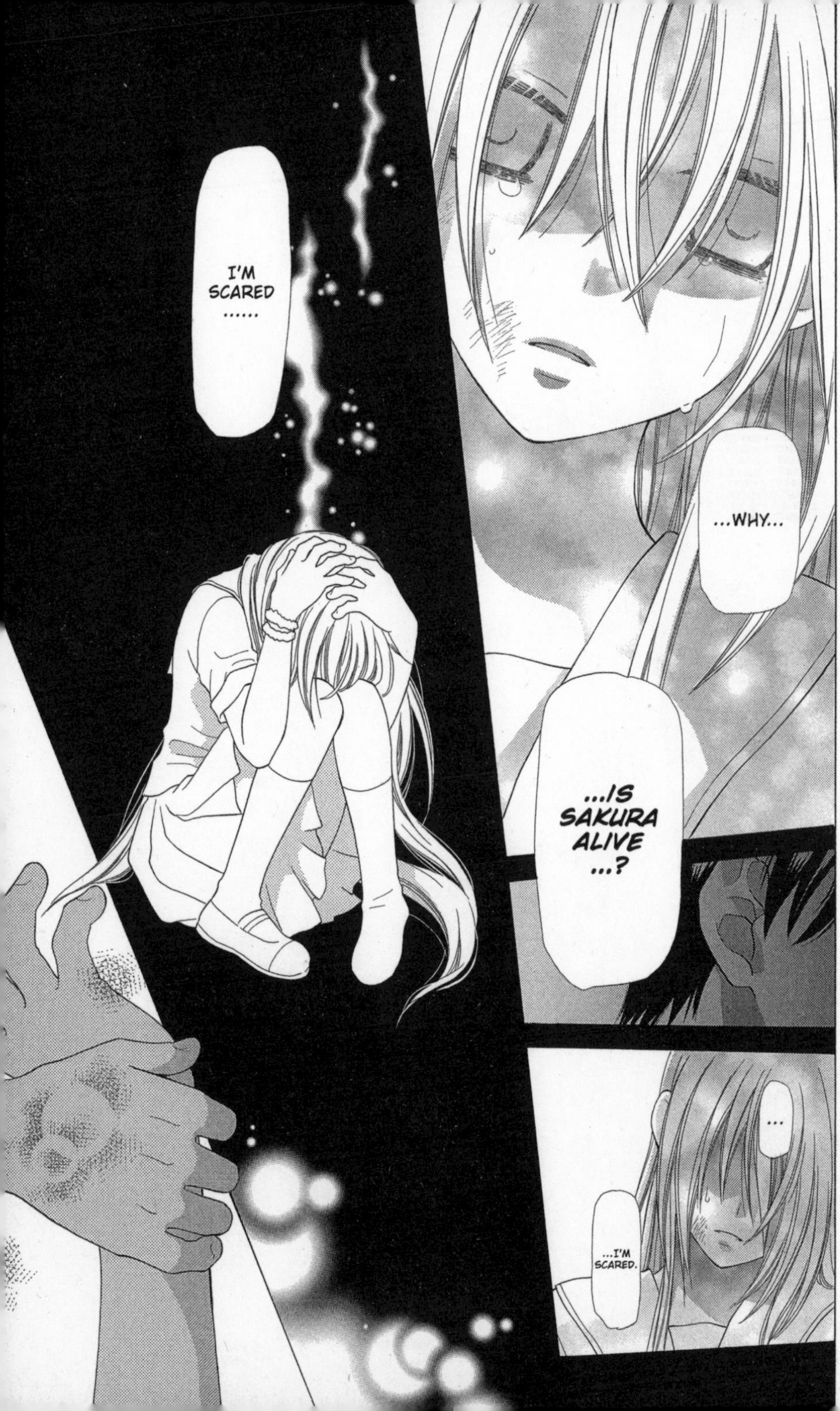
...WHY...
...IS SAKURA ALIVE ...?
...
...I'M SCARED.
I'M SCARED ......

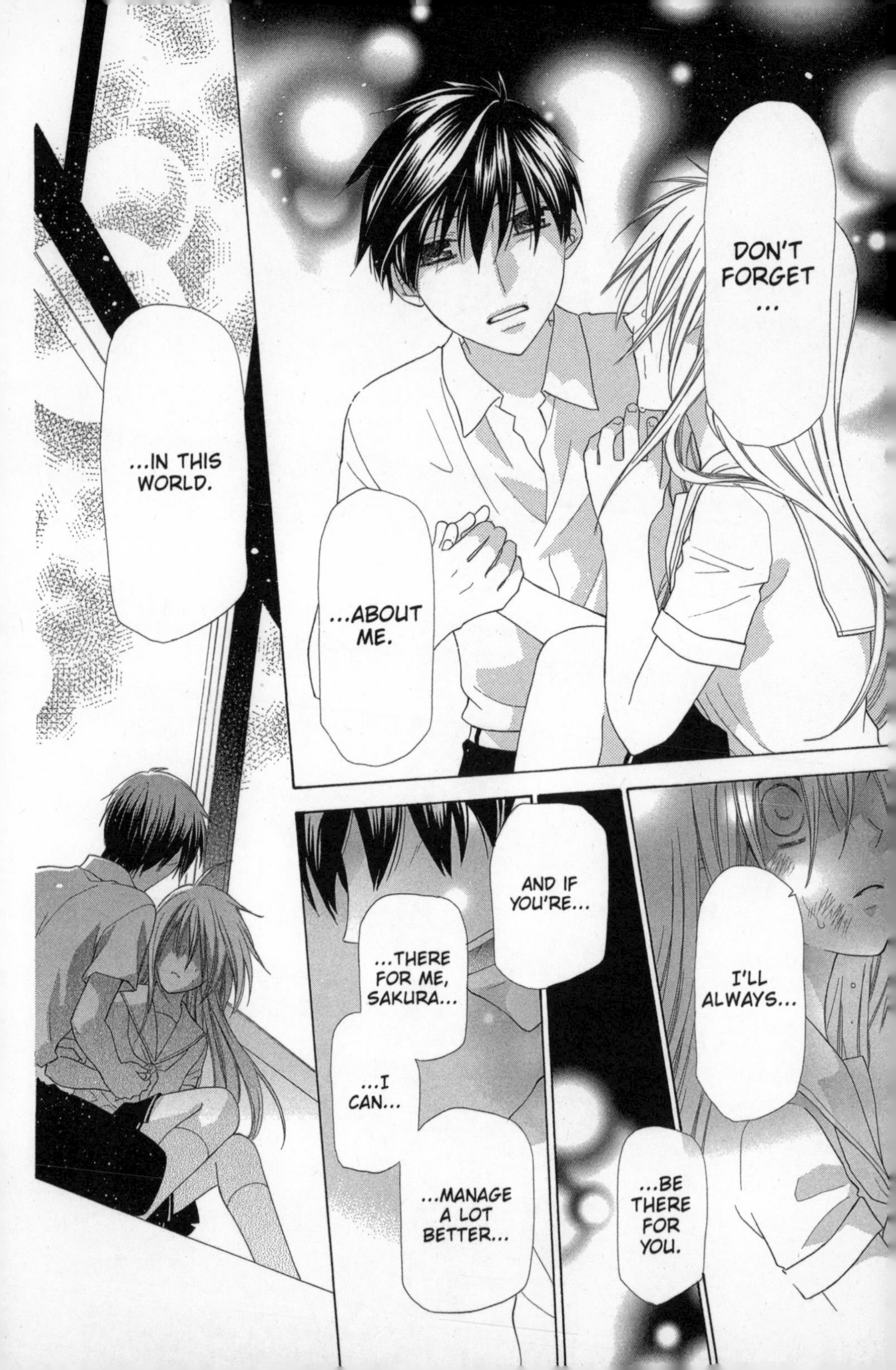
DON'T FORGET...
...ABOUT ME.
...IN THIS WORLD.
I'LL ALWAYS...
...BE THERE FOR YOU.
AND IF YOU'RE...
...THERE FOR ME, SAKURA...
...I CAN...
...MANAGE A LOT BETTER...

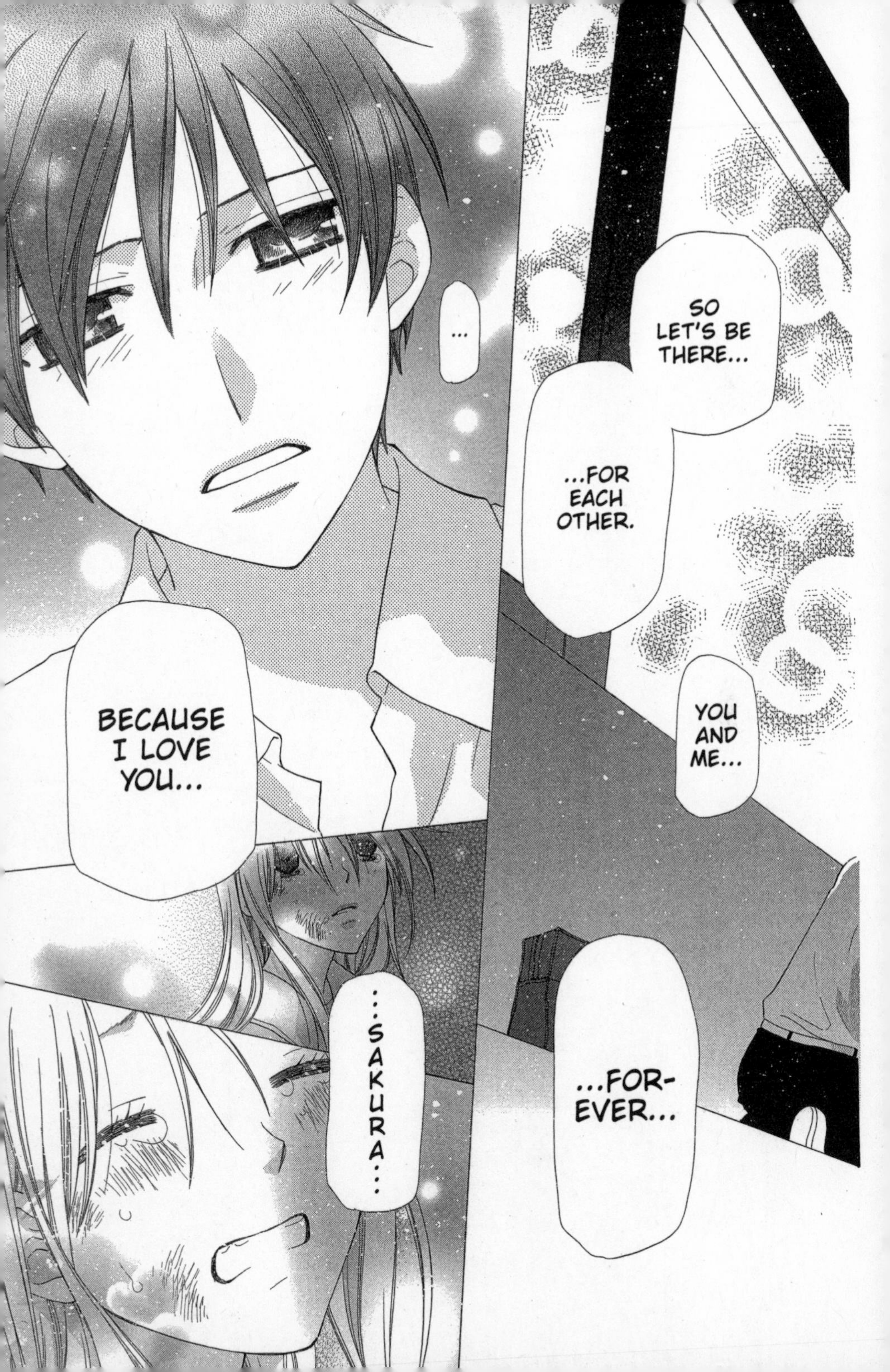
SO LET'S BE THERE...
...FOR EACH OTHER.
YOU AND ME...
...FOR-EVER...
...
BECAUSE I LOVE YOU...
...SAKURA...

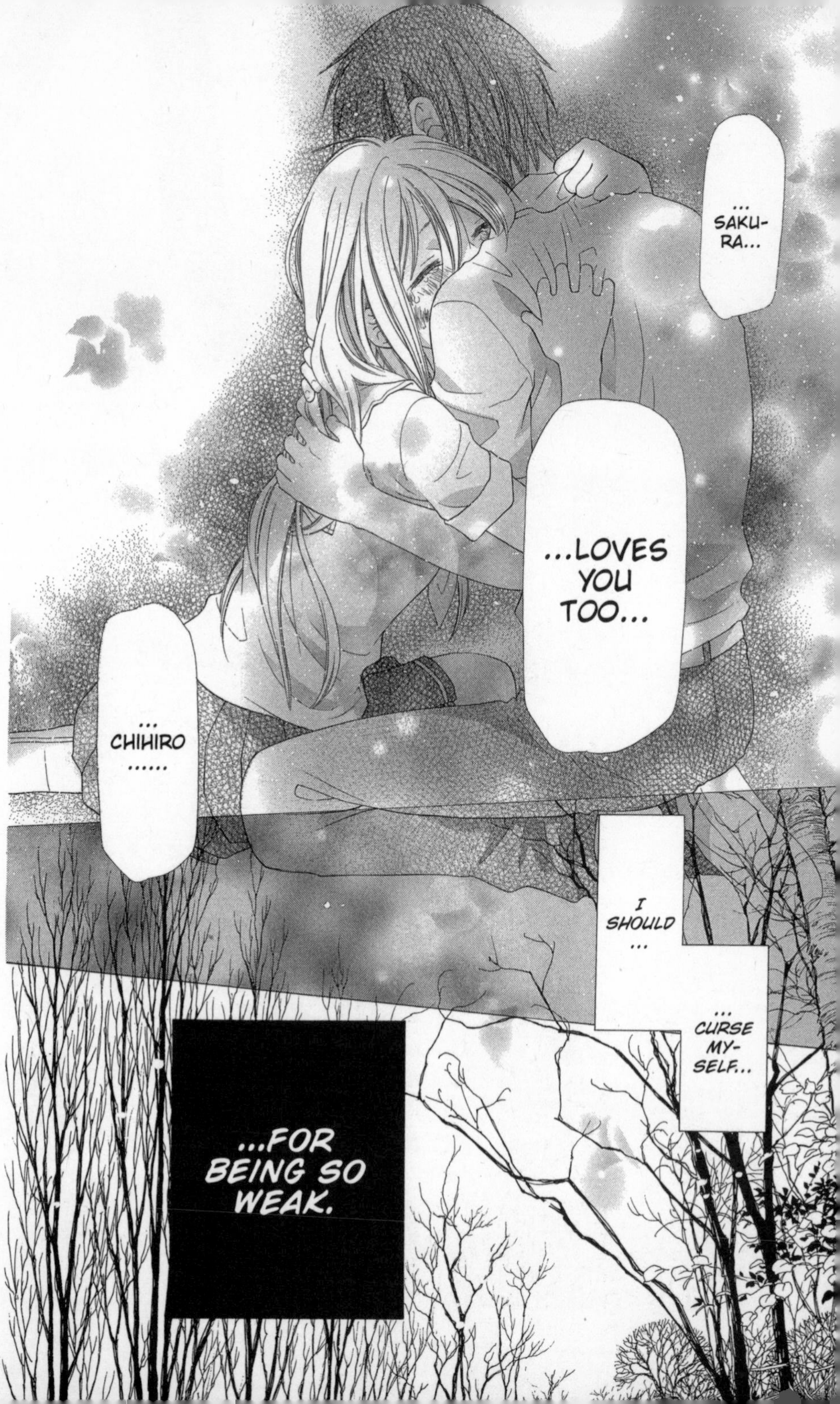
...SAKU-RA...
...LOVES YOU TOO...
...CHIHIRO......
I SHOULD...
...CURSE MY-SELF...
...FOR BEING SO WEAK.

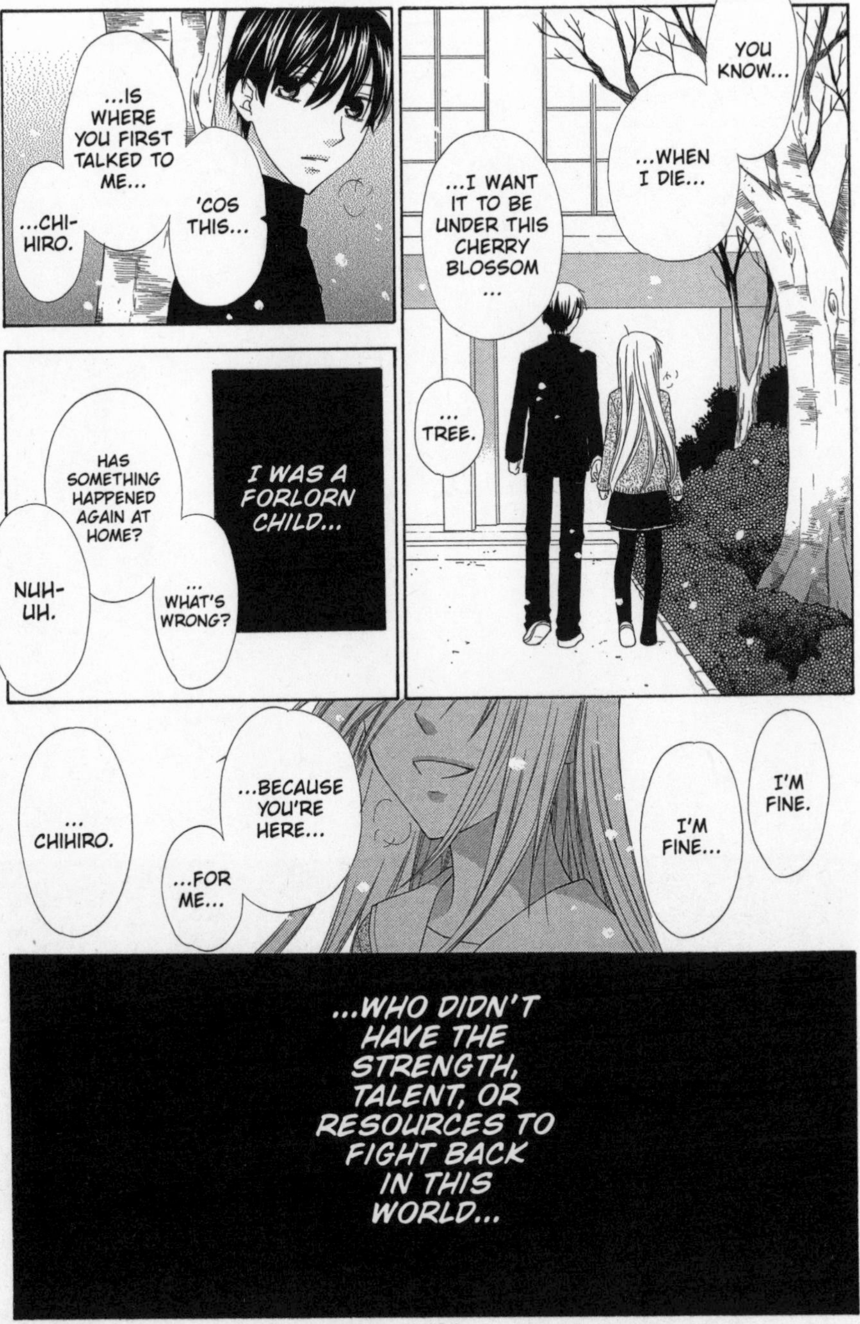
YOU KNOW...
...WHEN I DIE...
...I WANT IT TO BE UNDER THIS CHERRY BLOSSOM ...
... TREE.
'COS THIS...
...IS WHERE YOU FIRST TALKED TO ME...
...CHI-HIRO.
I WAS A FORLORN CHILD...
... WHAT'S WRONG?
HAS SOMETHING HAPPENED AGAIN AT HOME?
NUH-UH.
I'M FINE.
I'M FINE...
...BECAUSE YOU'RE HERE...
...FOR ME...
... CHIHIRO.
...WHO DIDN'T HAVE THE STRENGTH, TALENT, OR RESOURCES TO FIGHT BACK IN THIS WORLD...

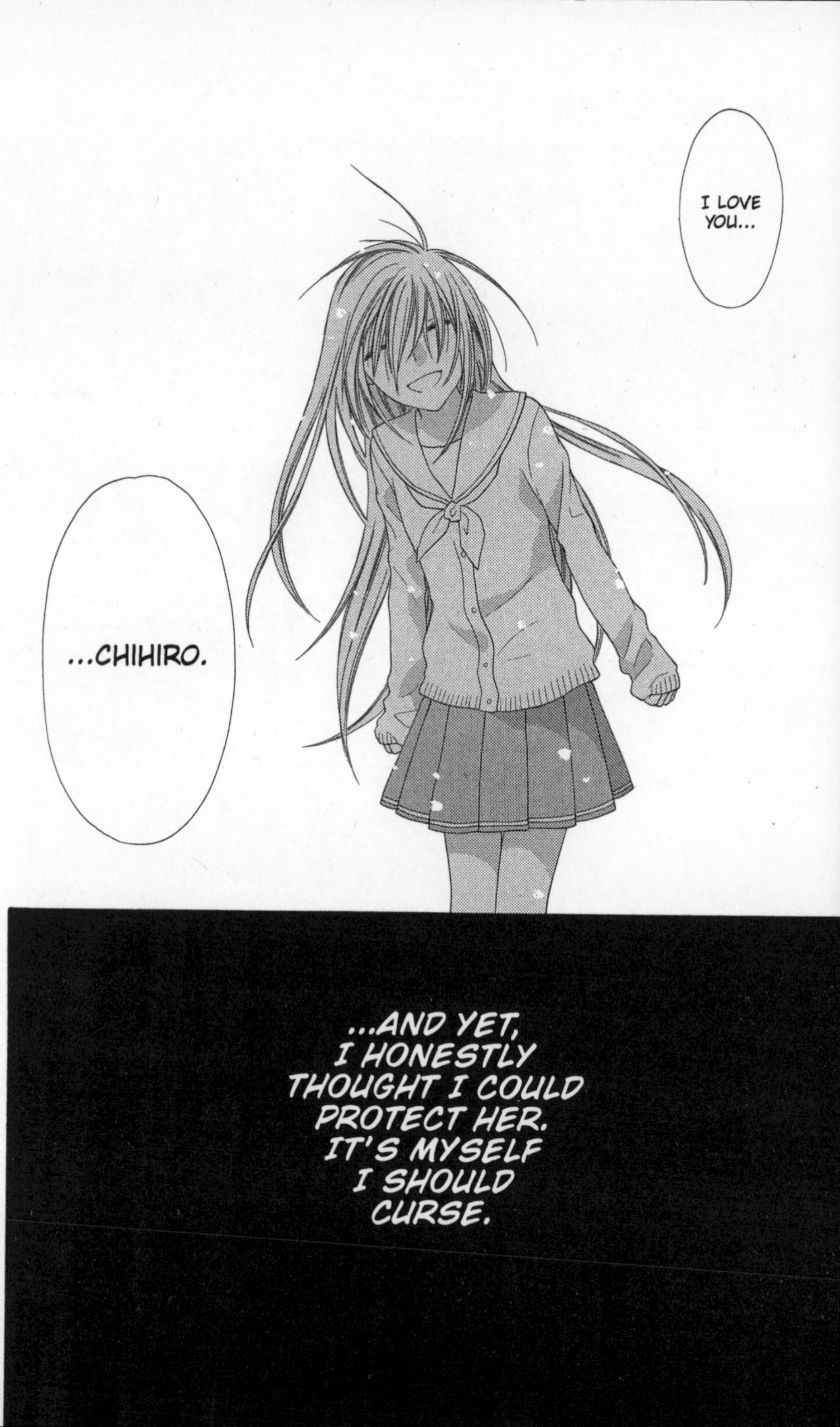

I LOVE YOU...
...CHIHIRO.
...AND YET, I HONESTLY THOUGHT I COULD PROTECT HER. IT'S MYSELF I SHOULD CURSE.

Chapter 28

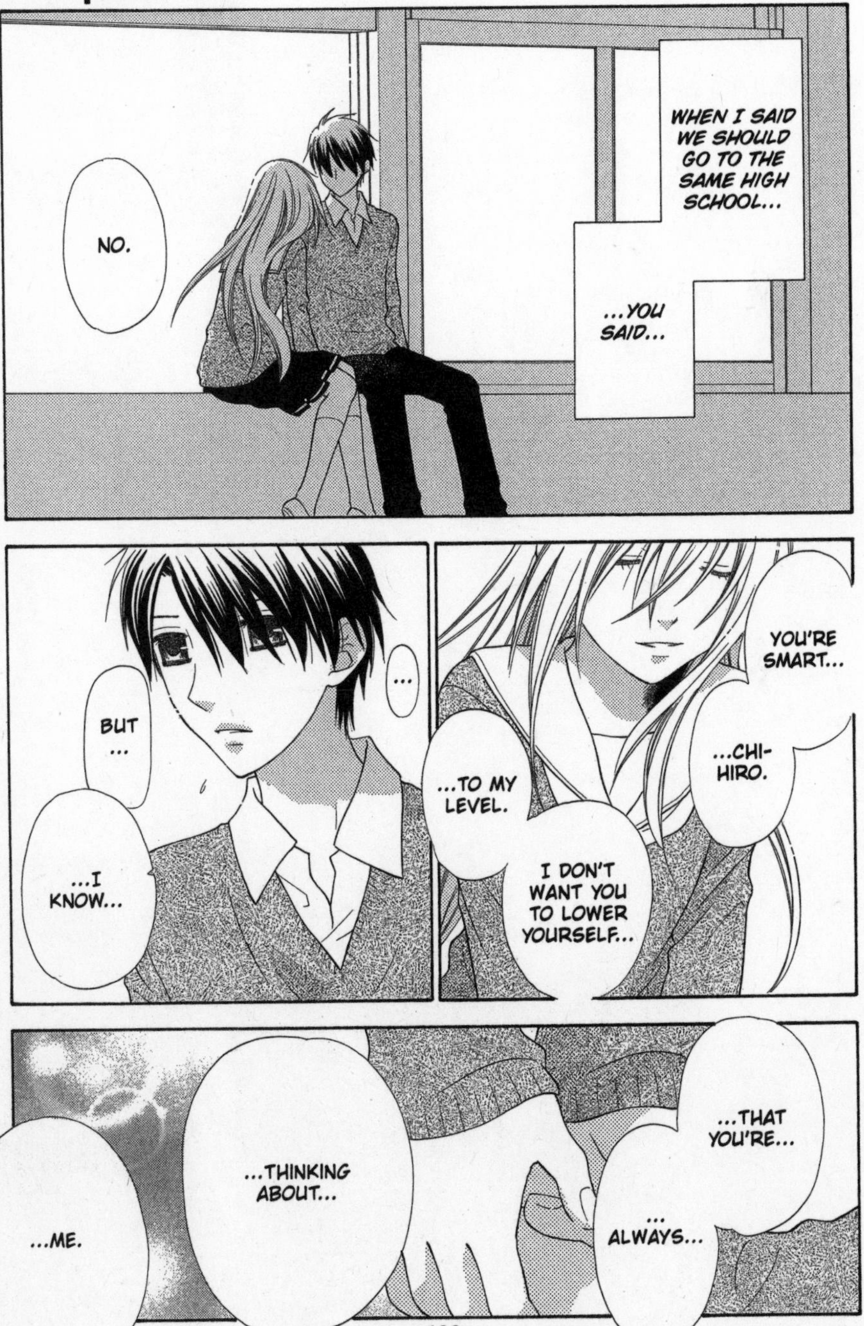
WHEN I SAID WE SHOULD GO TO THE SAME HIGH SCHOOL...
...YOU SAID...
NO.
YOU'RE SMART...
...CHI-HIRO.
I DON'T WANT YOU TO LOWER YOURSELF...
...TO MY LEVEL.
...
BUT ...
...I KNOW...
...THAT YOU'RE...
... ALWAYS...
...THINKING ABOUT...
...ME.

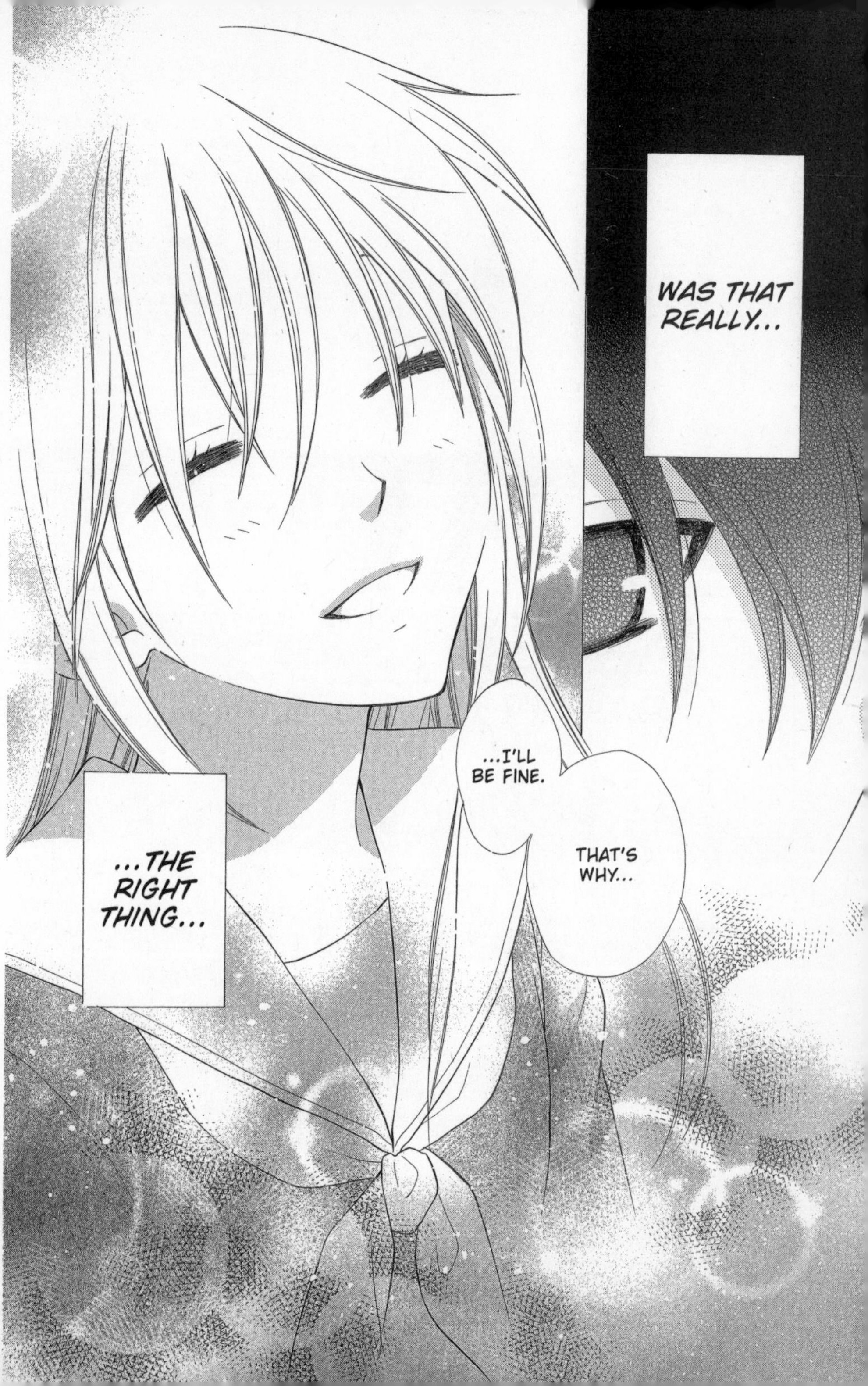
WAS THAT REALLY...
...I'LL BE FINE.
THAT'S WHY...
...THE RIGHT THING...

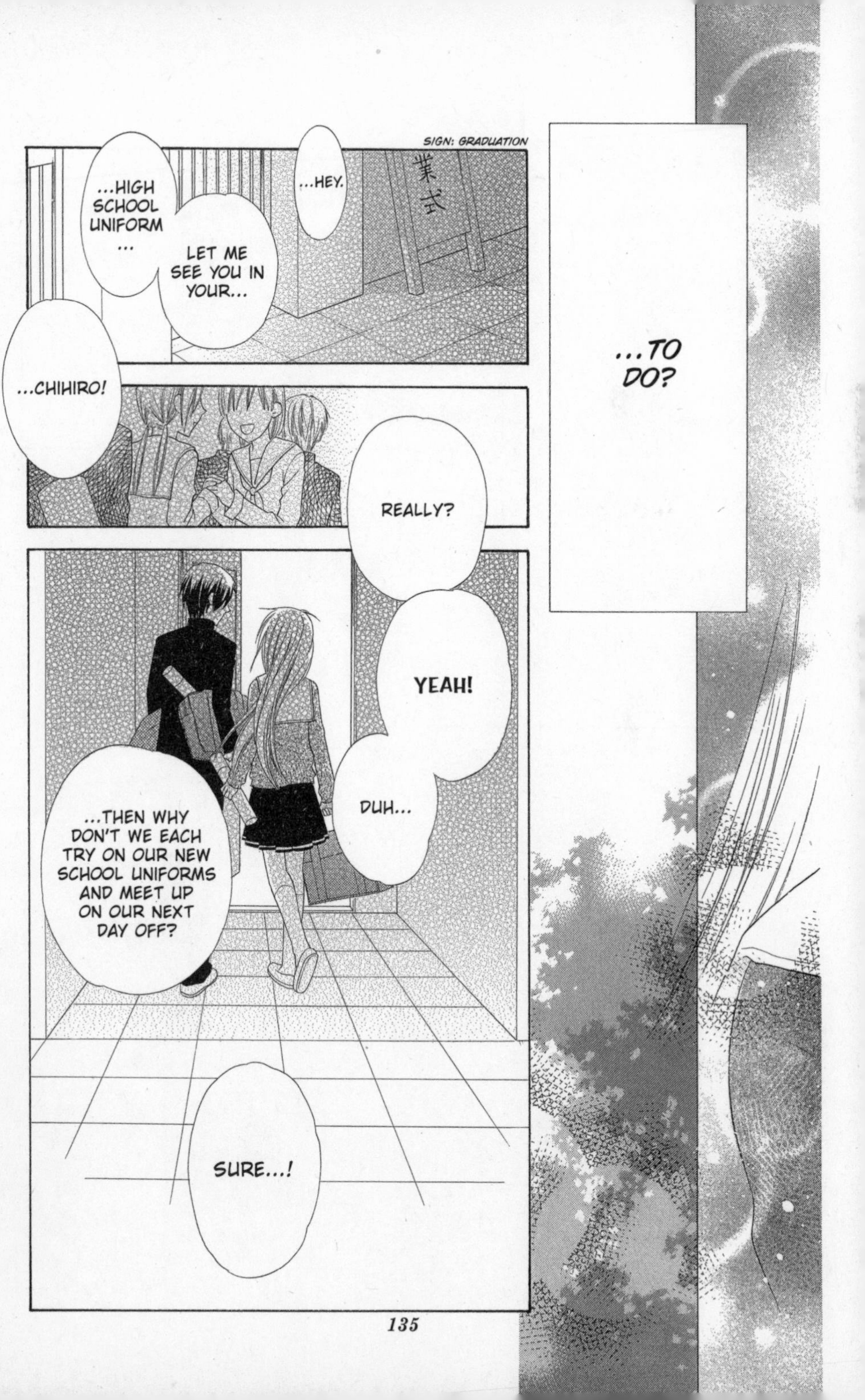
...TO DO?
SIGN: GRADUATION
...HEY.
LET ME SEE YOU IN YOUR...
...HIGH SCHOOL UNIFORM ...
...CHIHIRO!
REALLY?
YEAH!
DUH...
...THEN WHY DON'T WE EACH TRY ON OUR NEW SCHOOL UNIFORMS AND MEET UP ON OUR NEXT DAY OFF?
SURE...!

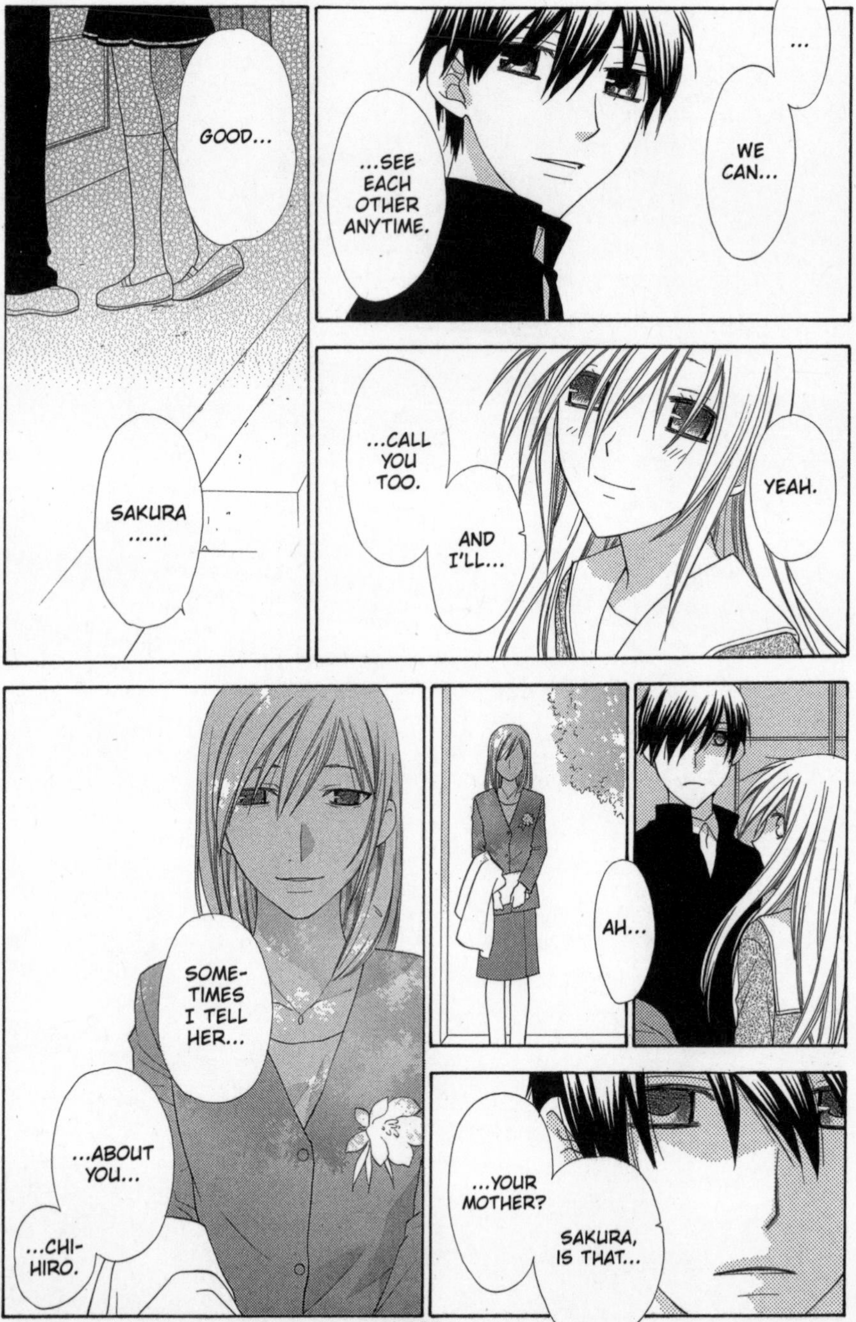
...
WE CAN...
...SEE EACH OTHER ANYTIME.
YEAH.
AND I'LL...
...CALL YOU TOO.
GOOD...
SAKURA ......
AH...
SAKURA, IS THAT...
...YOUR MOTHER?
SOME-TIMES I TELL HER...
...ABOUT YOU...
...CHI-HIRO.

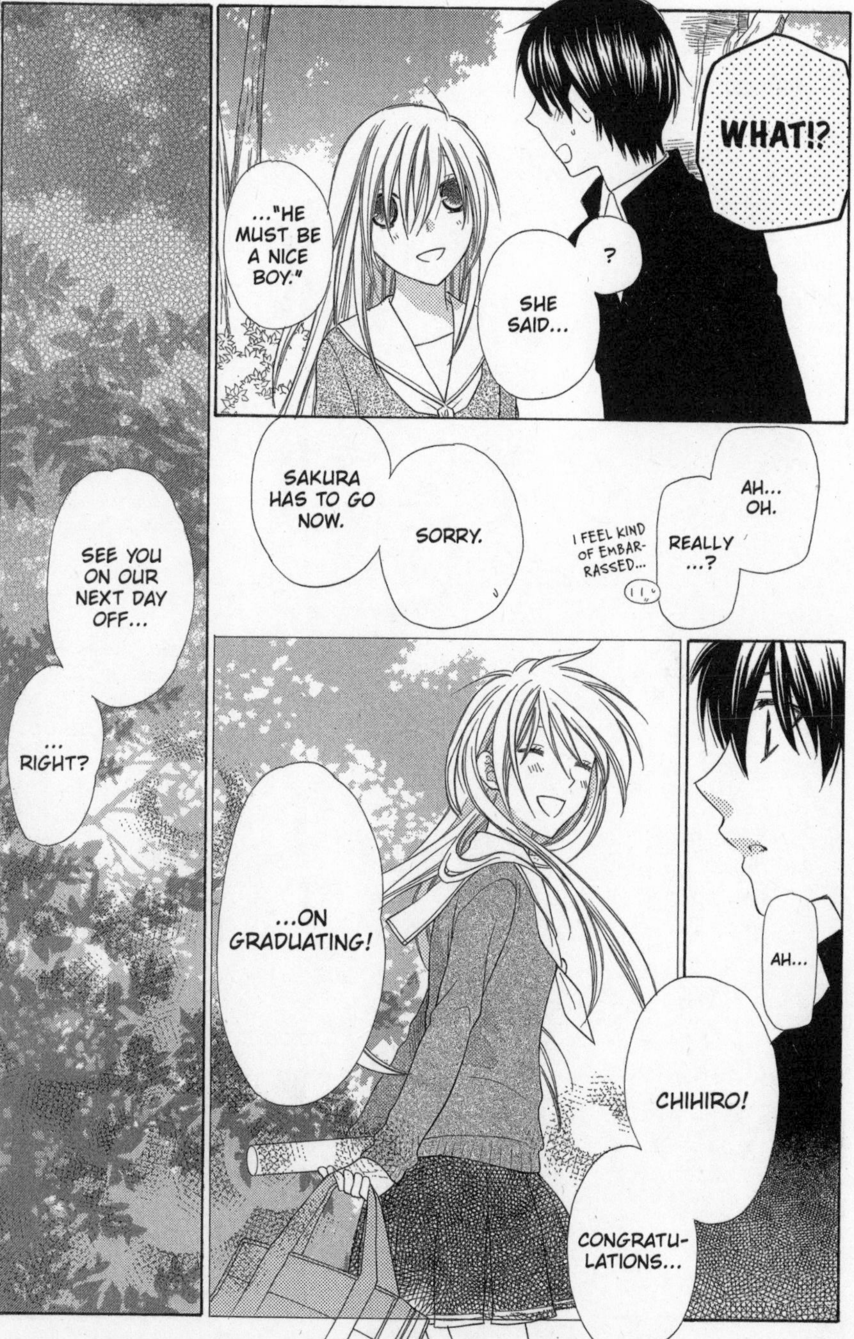
WHAT!?
?
SHE SAID...
..."HE MUST BE A NICE BOY."
AH... OH.
REALLY ...?
I FEEL KIND OF EMBARRASSED...
SORRY.
SAKURA HAS TO GO NOW.
AH...
CHIHIRO!
CONGRATULATIONS...
...ON GRADUATING!
SEE YOU ON OUR NEXT DAY OFF...
...RIGHT?

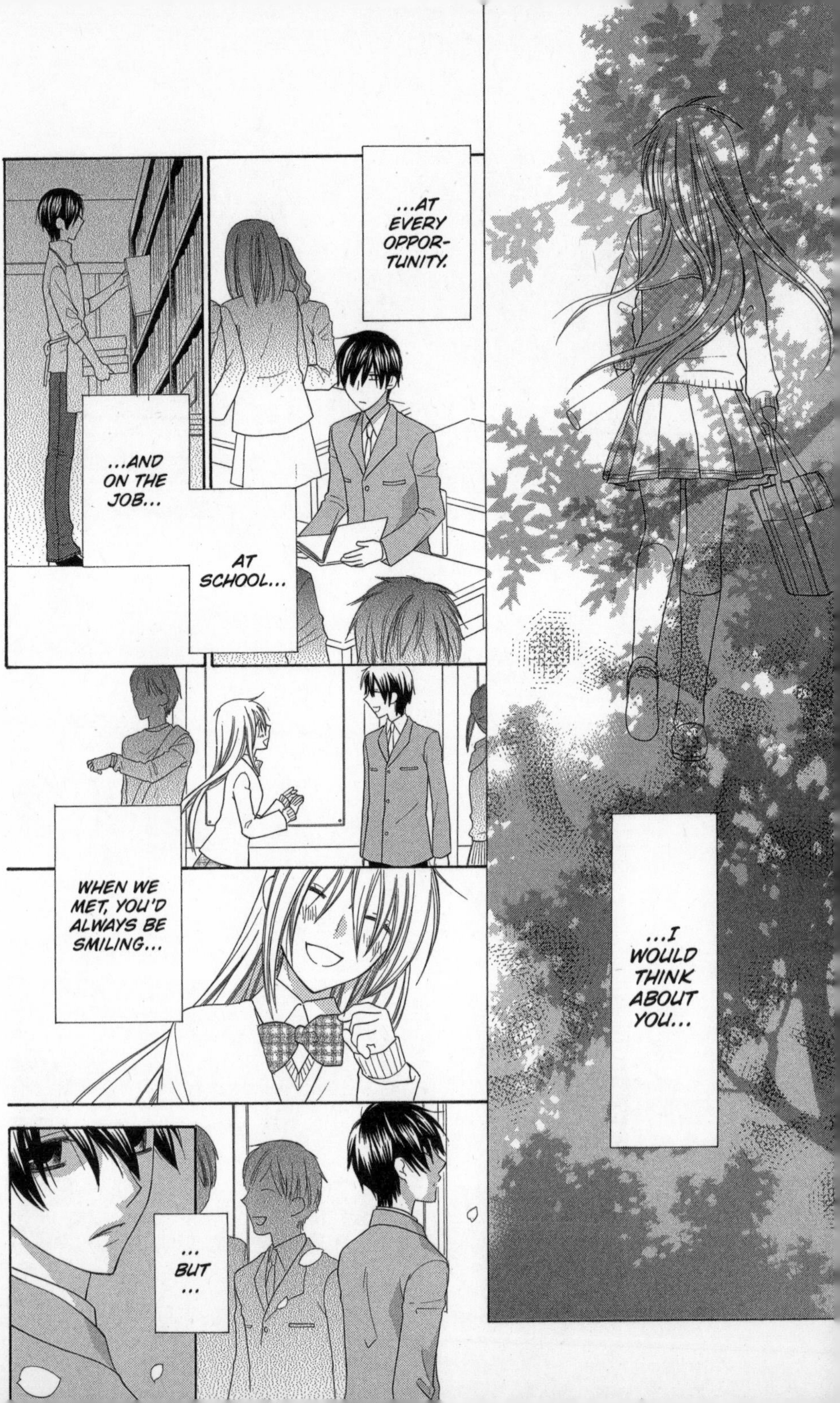
...I WOULD THINK ABOUT YOU...
...AT EVERY OPPORTUNITY.
AT SCHOOL...
...AND ON THE JOB...
WHEN WE MET, YOU'D ALWAYS BE SMILING...
...BUT...

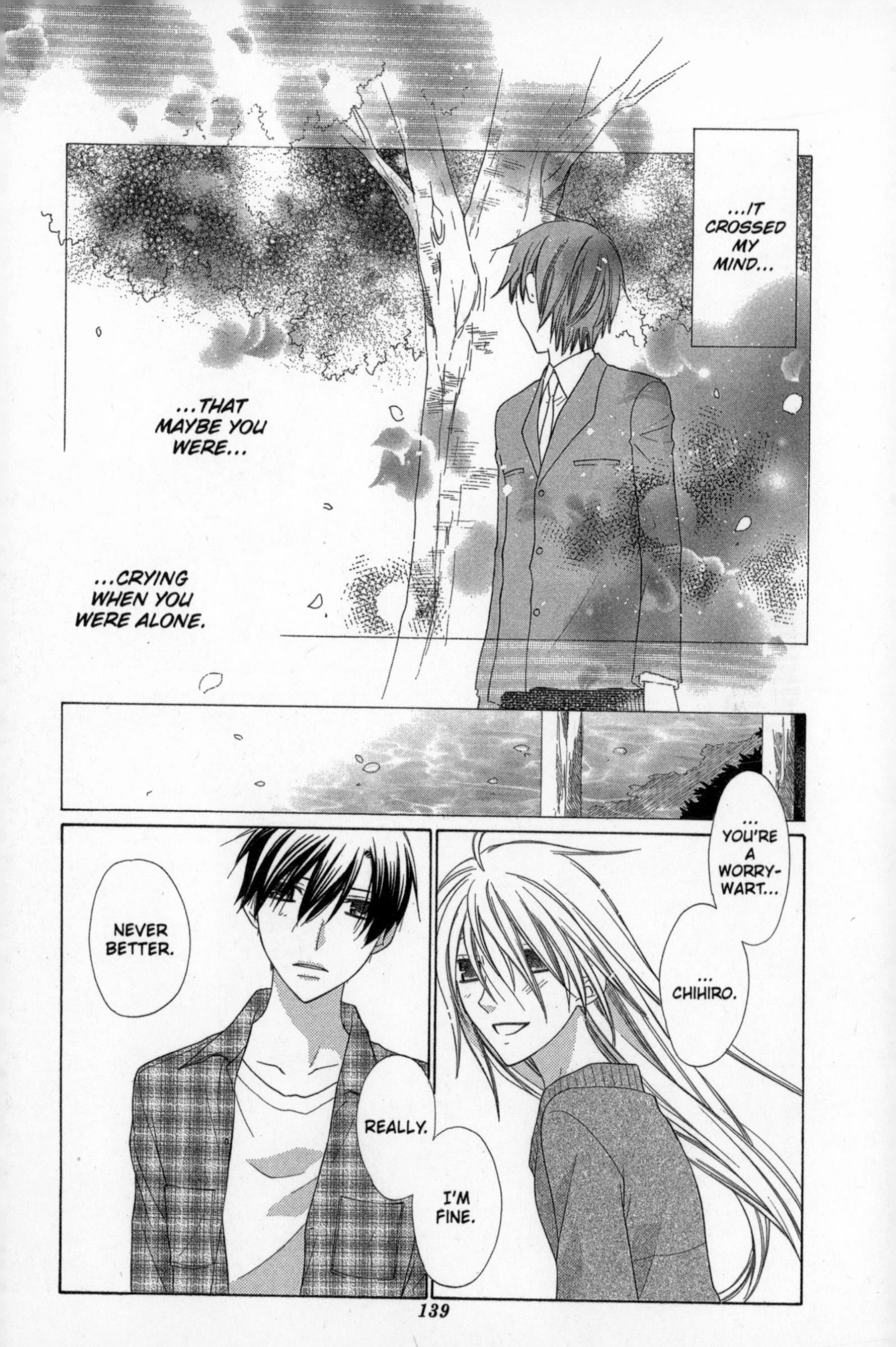
...IT CROSSED MY MIND...
...THAT MAYBE YOU WERE...
...CRYING WHEN YOU WERE ALONE.
...YOU'RE A WORRY-WART...
...CHIHIRO.
REALLY.
I'M FINE.
NEVER BETTER.

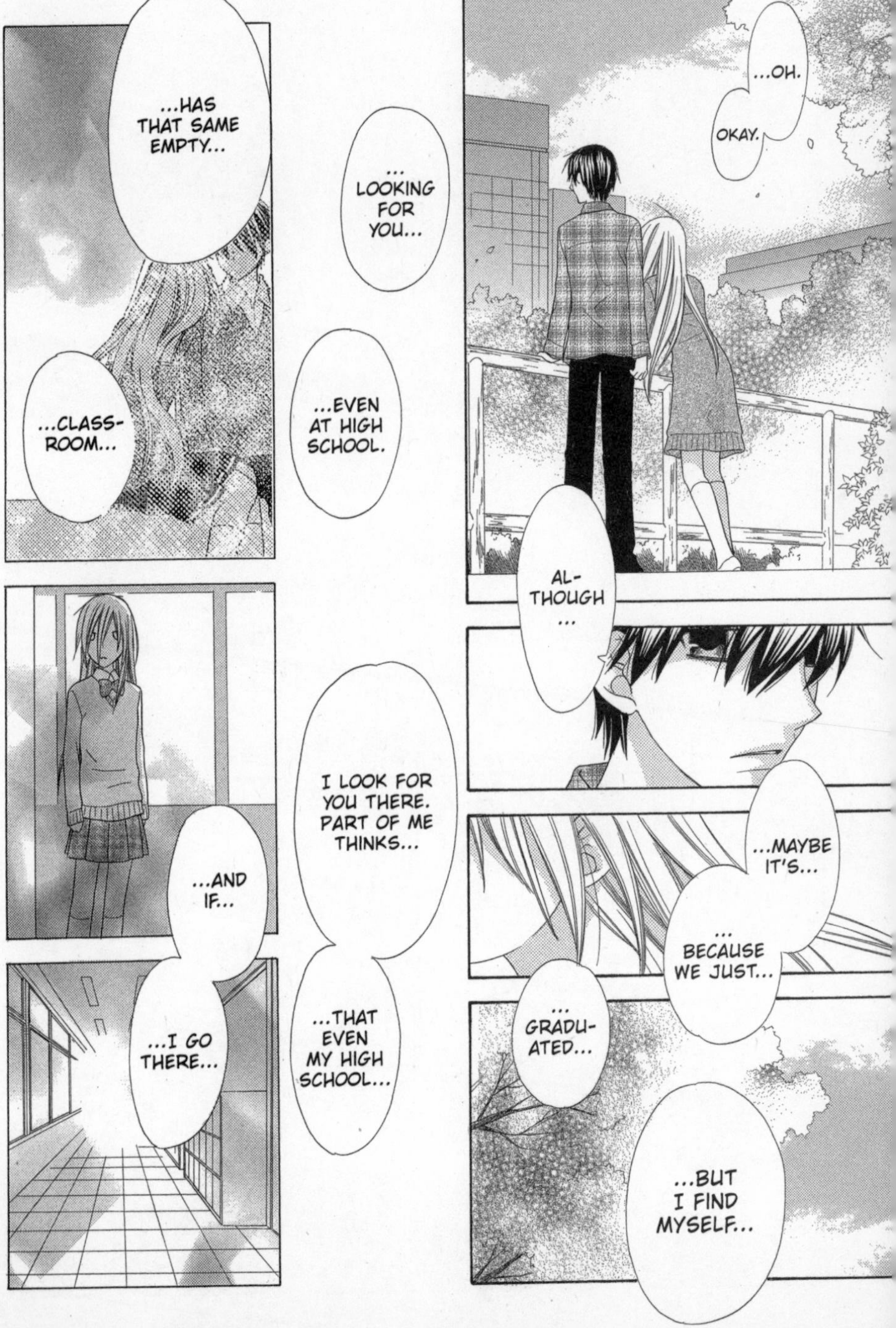
...OH.
OKAY.
AL-THOUGH...
...MAYBE IT'S...
...BECAUSE WE JUST...
...GRADUATED...
...BUT I FIND MYSELF...
...LOOKING FOR YOU...
...EVEN AT HIGH SCHOOL.
I LOOK FOR YOU THERE. PART OF ME THINKS...
...THAT EVEN MY HIGH SCHOOL...
...HAS THAT SAME EMPTY...
...CLASS-ROOM...
...AND IF...
...I GO THERE...

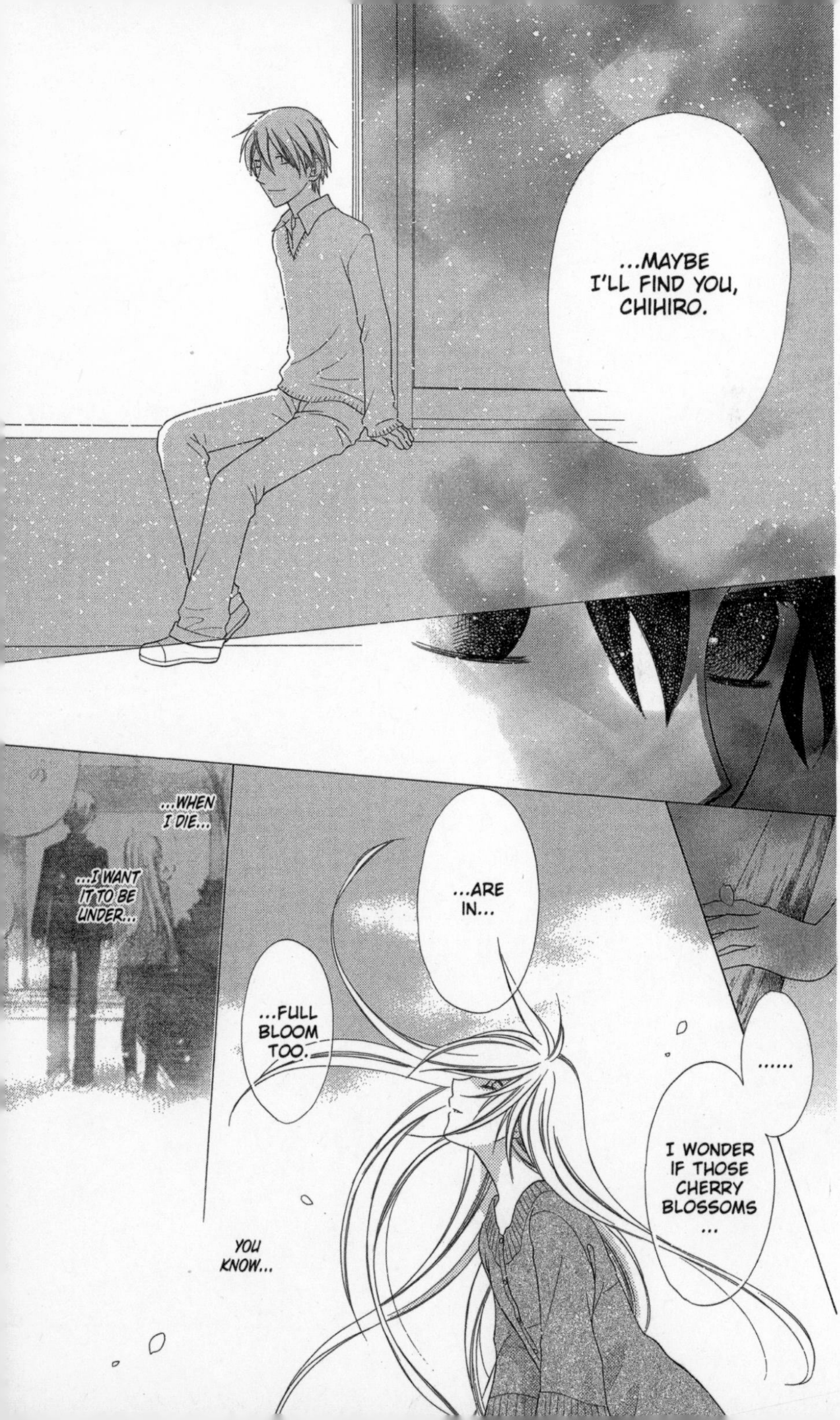
...MAYBE I'LL FIND YOU, CHIHIRO.
......
I WONDER IF THOSE CHERRY BLOSSOMS ...
...ARE IN...
...FULL BLOOM TOO.
YOU KNOW...
...WHEN I DIE...
...I WANT IT TO BE UNDER...

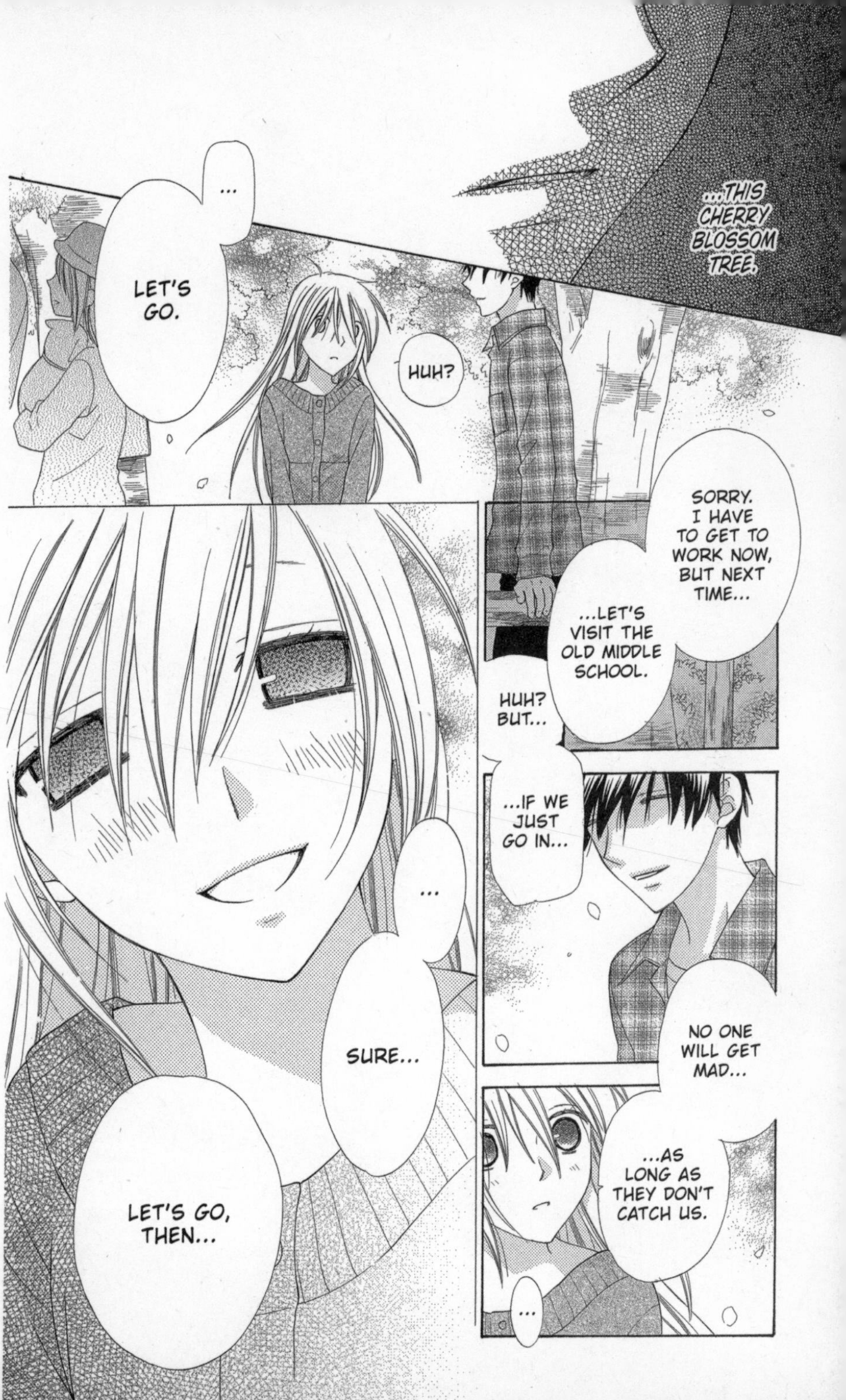
...THIS CHERRY BLOSSOM TREE.
...
LET'S GO.
HUH?
SORRY. I HAVE TO GET TO WORK NOW, BUT NEXT TIME...
...LET'S VISIT THE OLD MIDDLE SCHOOL.
HUH? BUT...
...IF WE JUST GO IN...
NO ONE WILL GET MAD...
...AS LONG AS THEY DON'T CATCH US.
...
...
SURE...
LET'S GO, THEN...

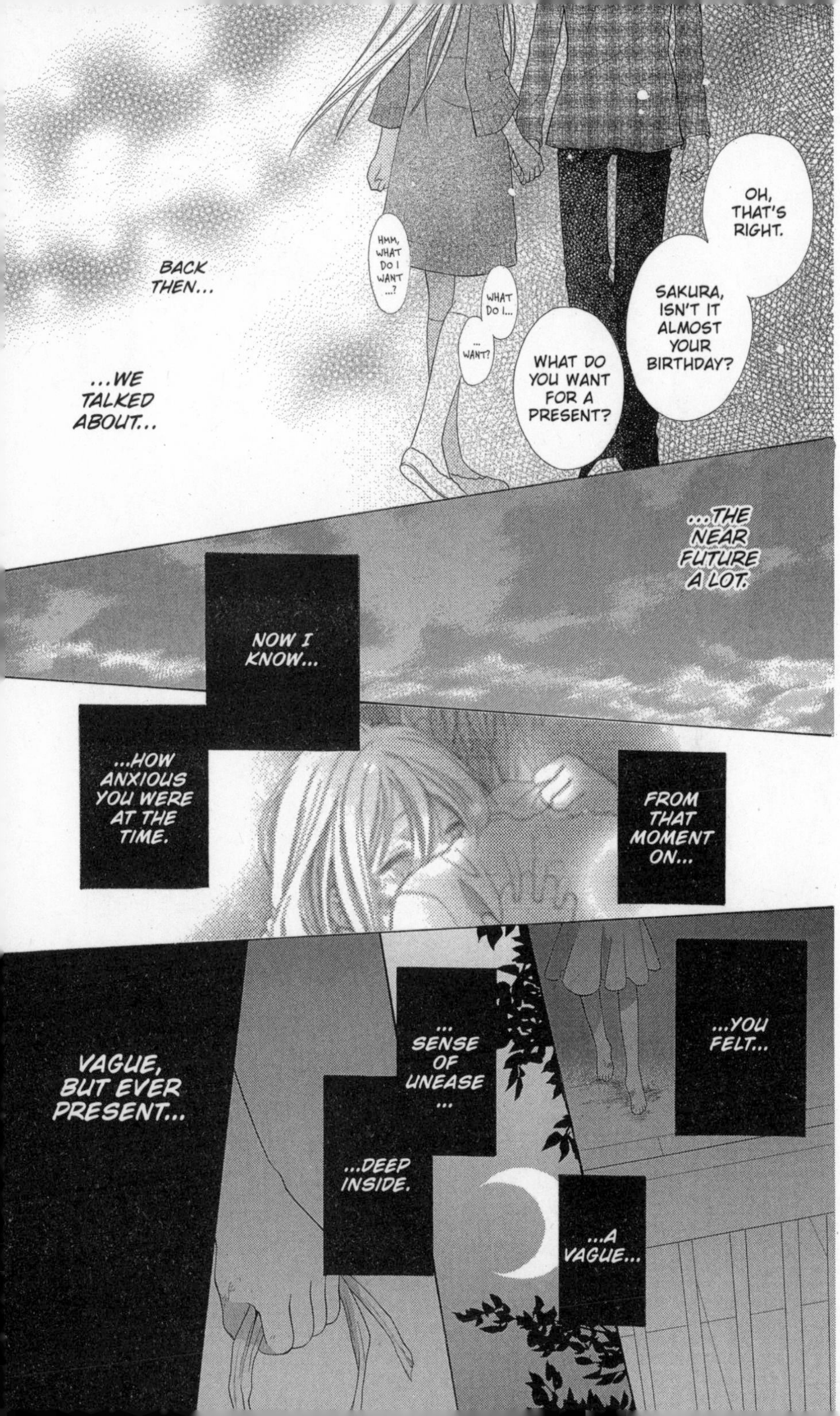
OH, THAT'S RIGHT.
SAKURA, ISN'T IT ALMOST YOUR BIRTHDAY?
WHAT DO YOU WANT FOR A PRESENT?
WHAT DO I...
...WANT?
HMM, WHAT DO I WANT ...?
BACK THEN...
...WE TALKED ABOUT...
...THE NEAR FUTURE A LOT.
NOW I KNOW...
...HOW ANXIOUS YOU WERE AT THE TIME.
FROM THAT MOMENT ON...
...YOU FELT...
...A VAGUE...
... SENSE OF UNEASE ...
...DEEP INSIDE.
VAGUE, BUT EVER PRESENT...

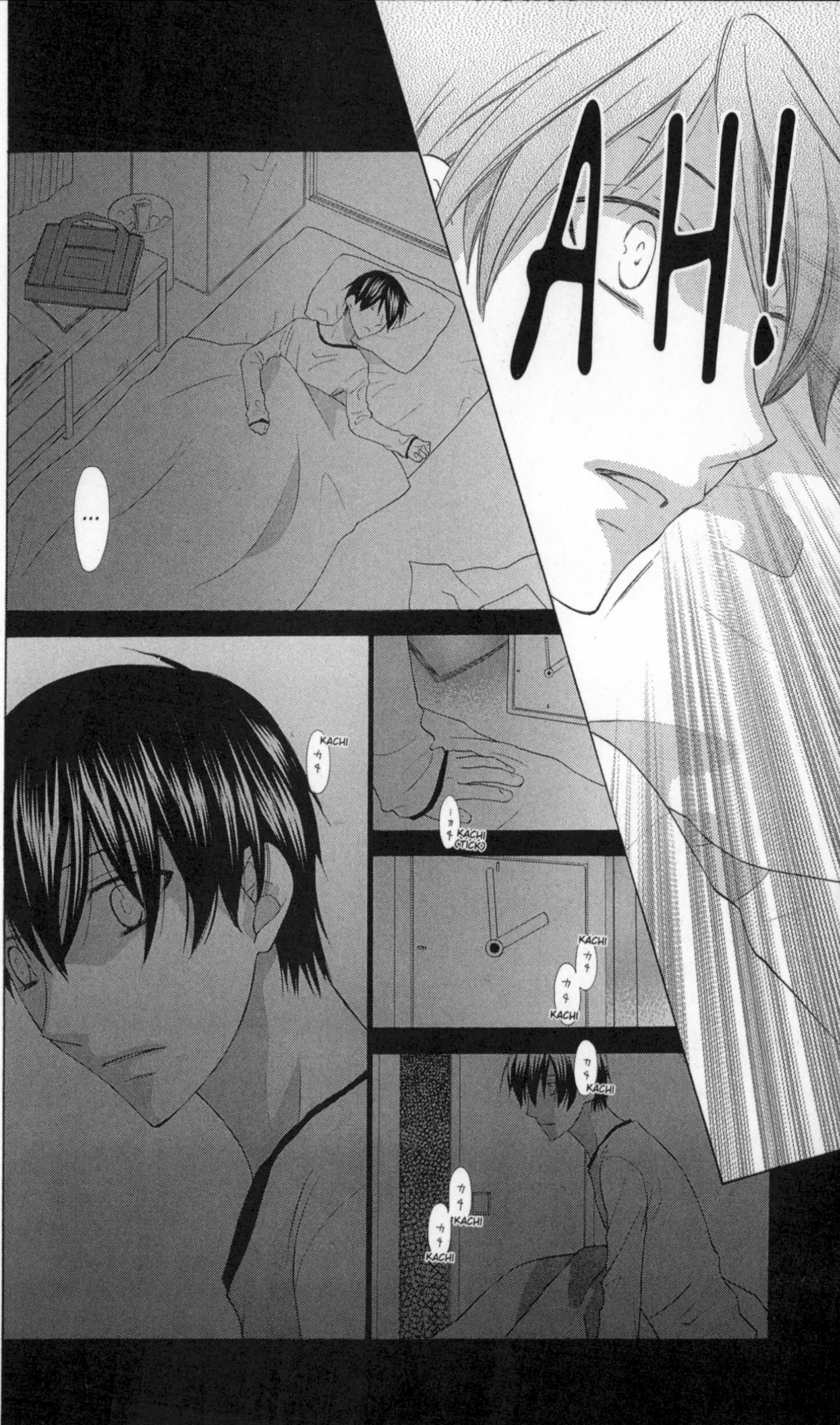
AH!
...
...カチ KACHI (TICK)
KACHI カチ
カチ KACHI
カチ KACHI
カチ KACHI
カチ KACHI
KACHI カチ

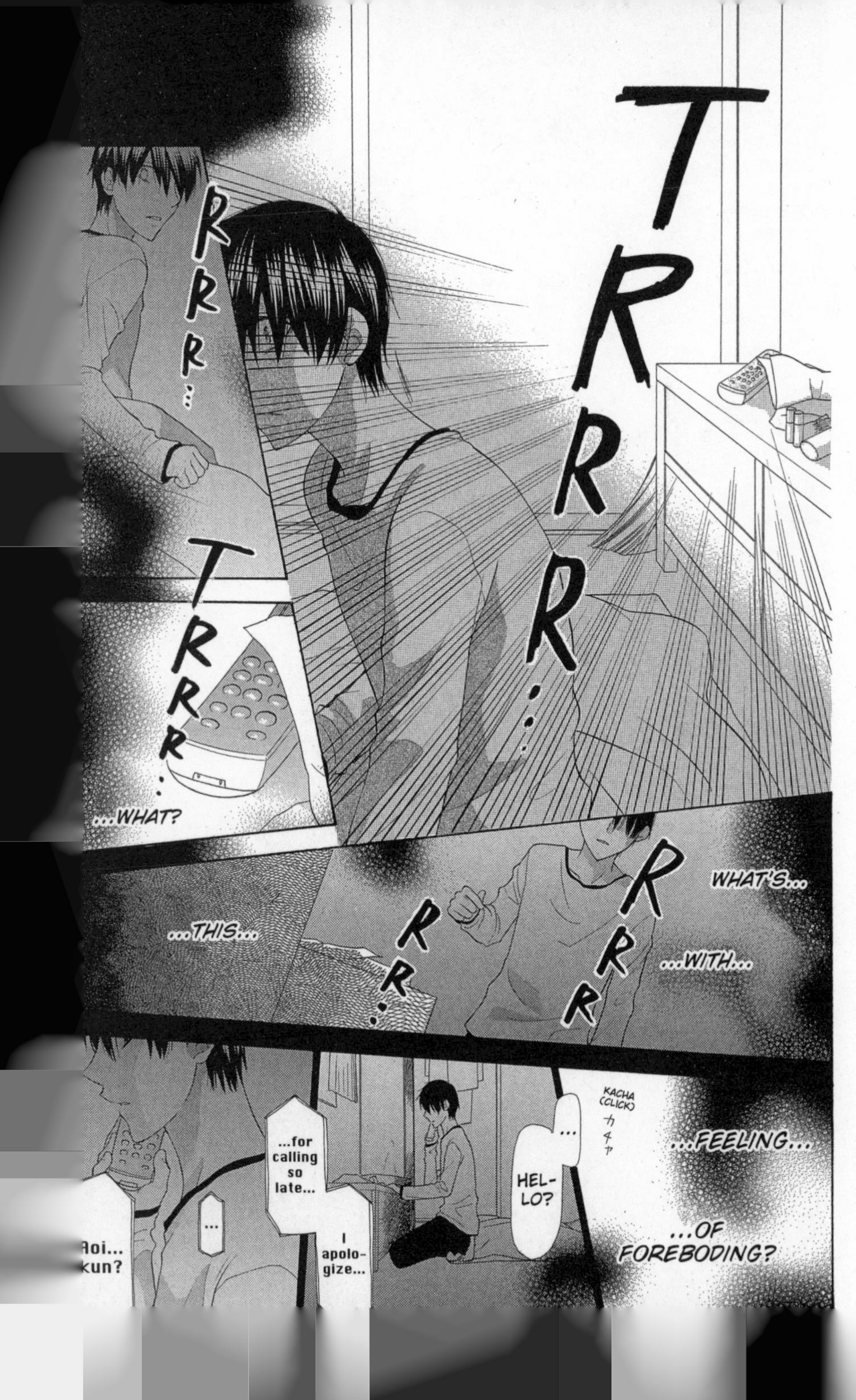
TRRRR...
RRRR...
TRRRR...
...WHAT?
WHAT'S...
RRRR
...WITH...
RRR...
...THIS...
...FEELING...
...OF FOREBODING?
KACHA (CLICK)
カチャ
...
HEL-LO?
...for calling so late...
I apolo-gize...
...
Aoi... kun?

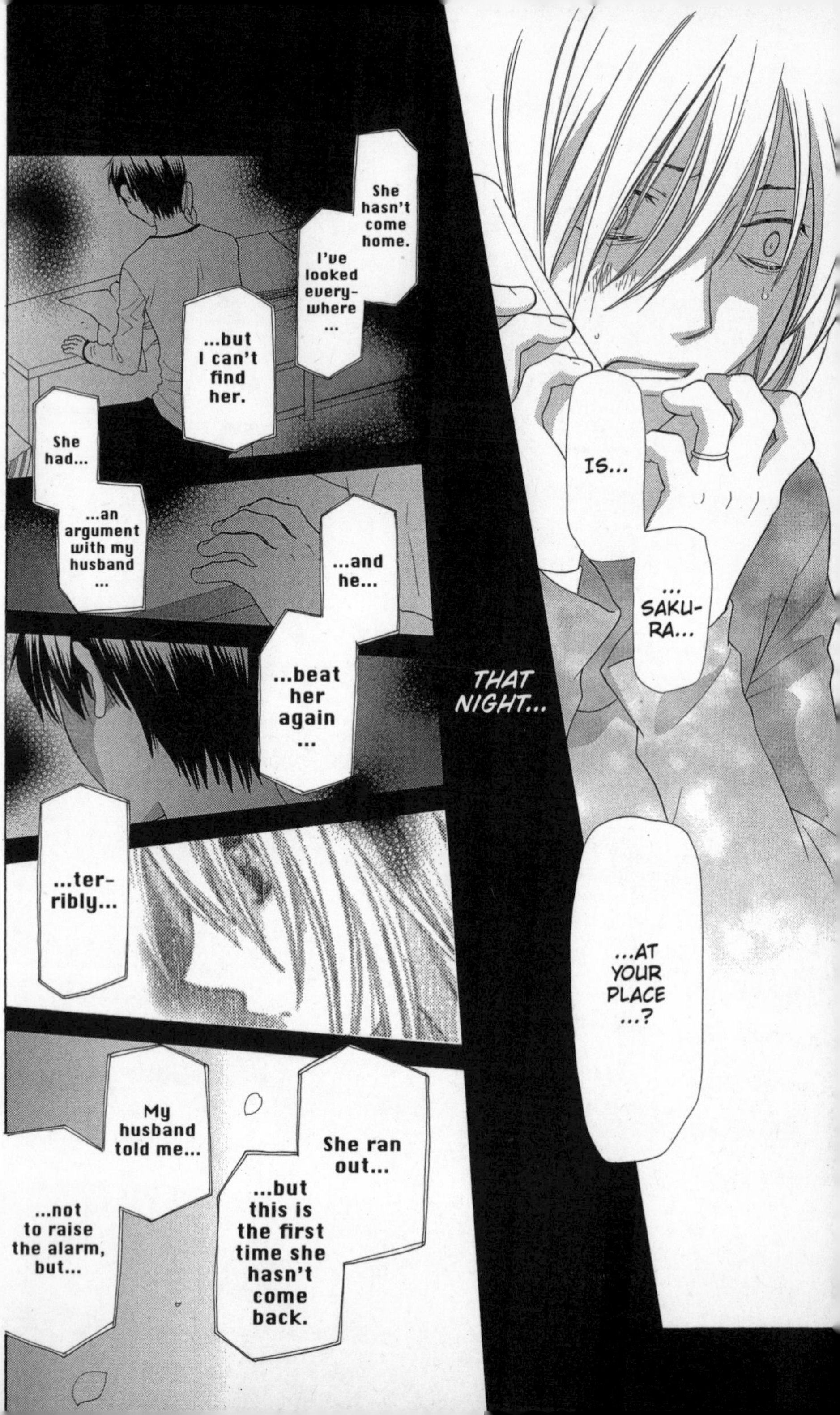
THAT NIGHT...
IS...
...SAKU-RA...
...AT YOUR PLACE...?
She hasn't come home.
I've looked every-where...
...but I can't find her.
She had...
...an argument with my husband...
...and he...
...beat her again...
...ter-ribly...
She ran out...
...but this is the first time she hasn't come back.
My husband told me...
...not to raise the alarm, but...

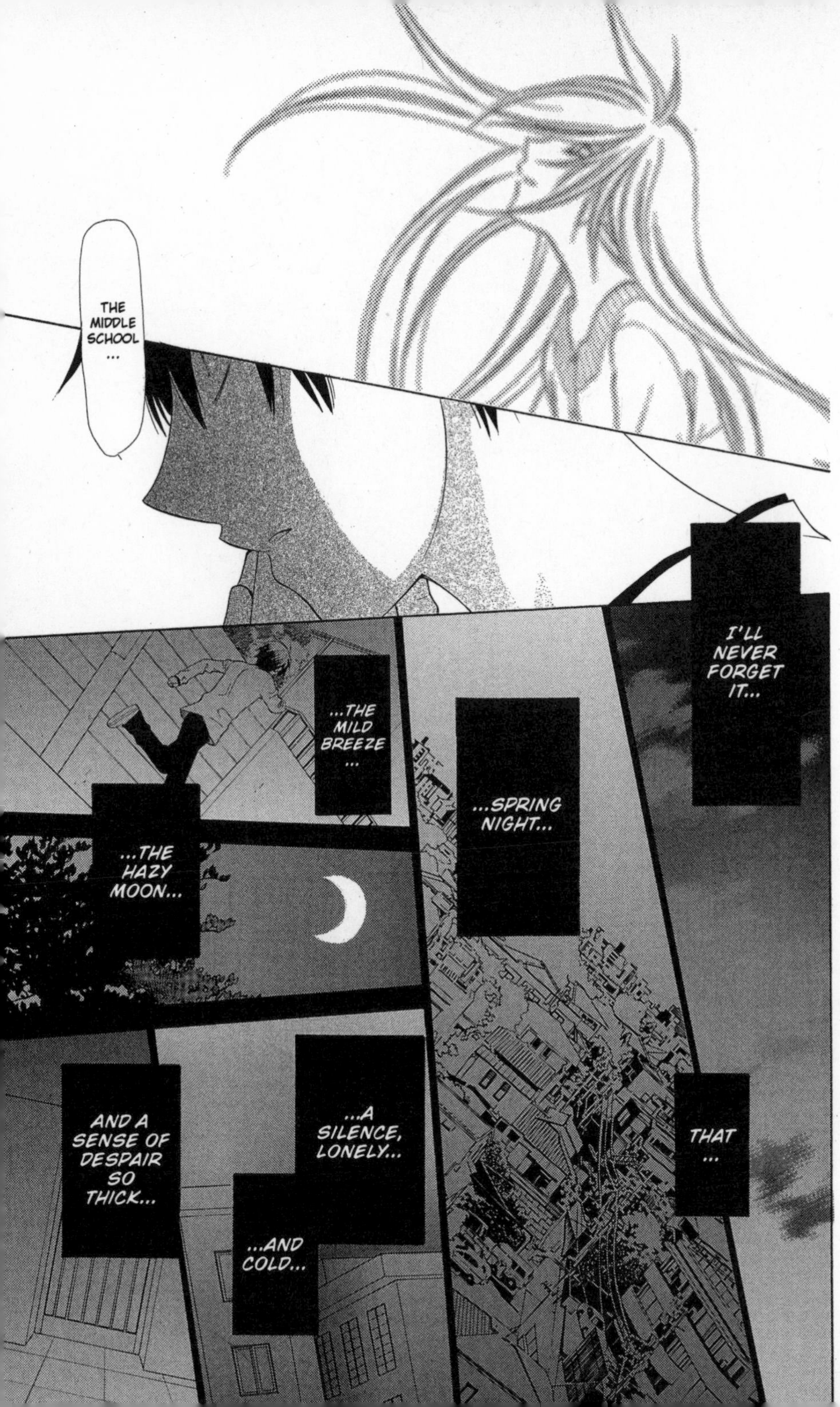
THE MIDDLE SCHOOL ...
I'LL NEVER FORGET IT...
THAT ...
...SPRING NIGHT...
...THE MILD BREEZE ...
...THE HAZY MOON...
...A SILENCE, LONELY...
...AND COLD...
AND A SENSE OF DESPAIR SO THICK...

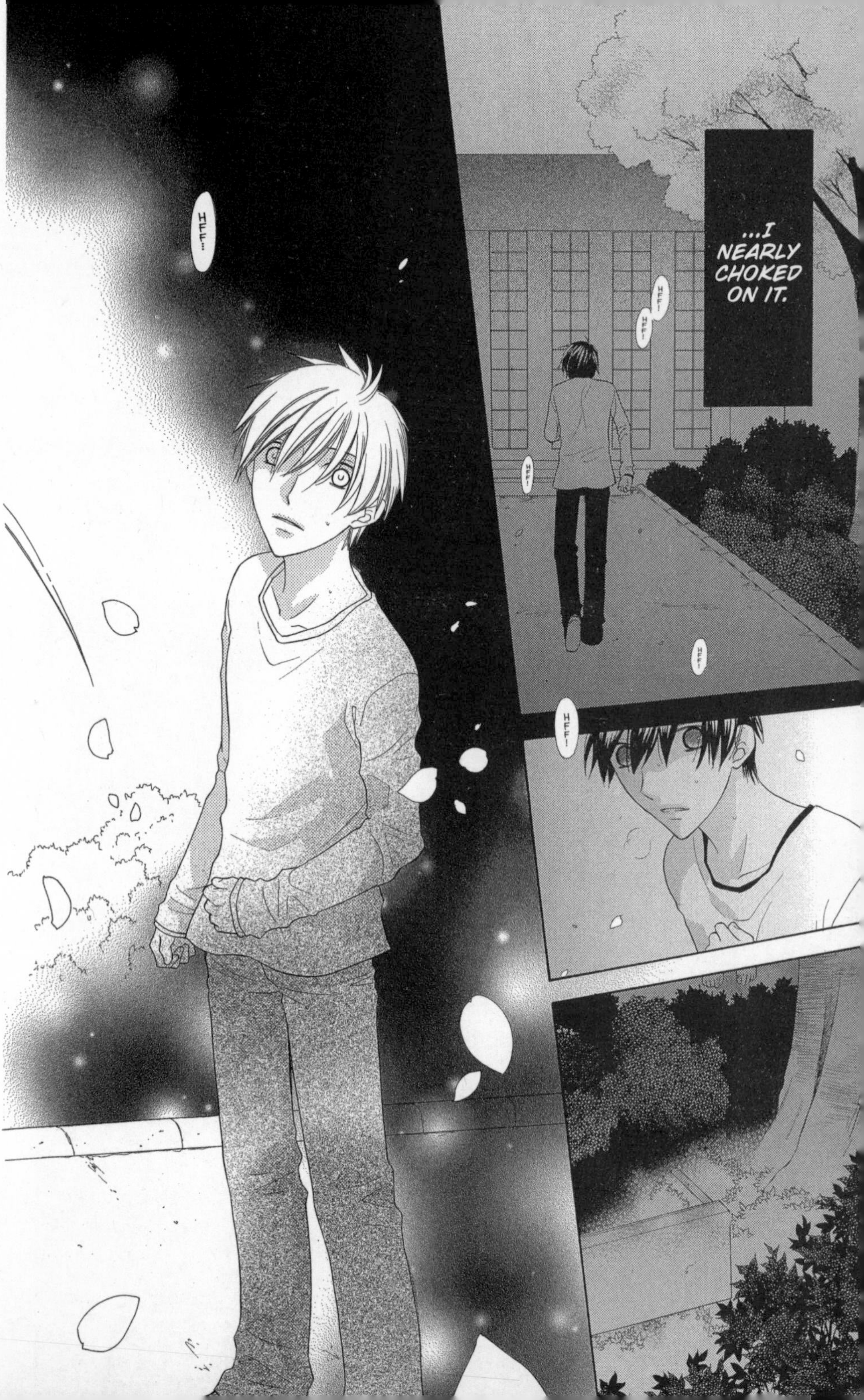
...I NEARLY CHOKED ON IT.
HFF!
HFF!
HFF!
HFF!
HFF!
HFF!

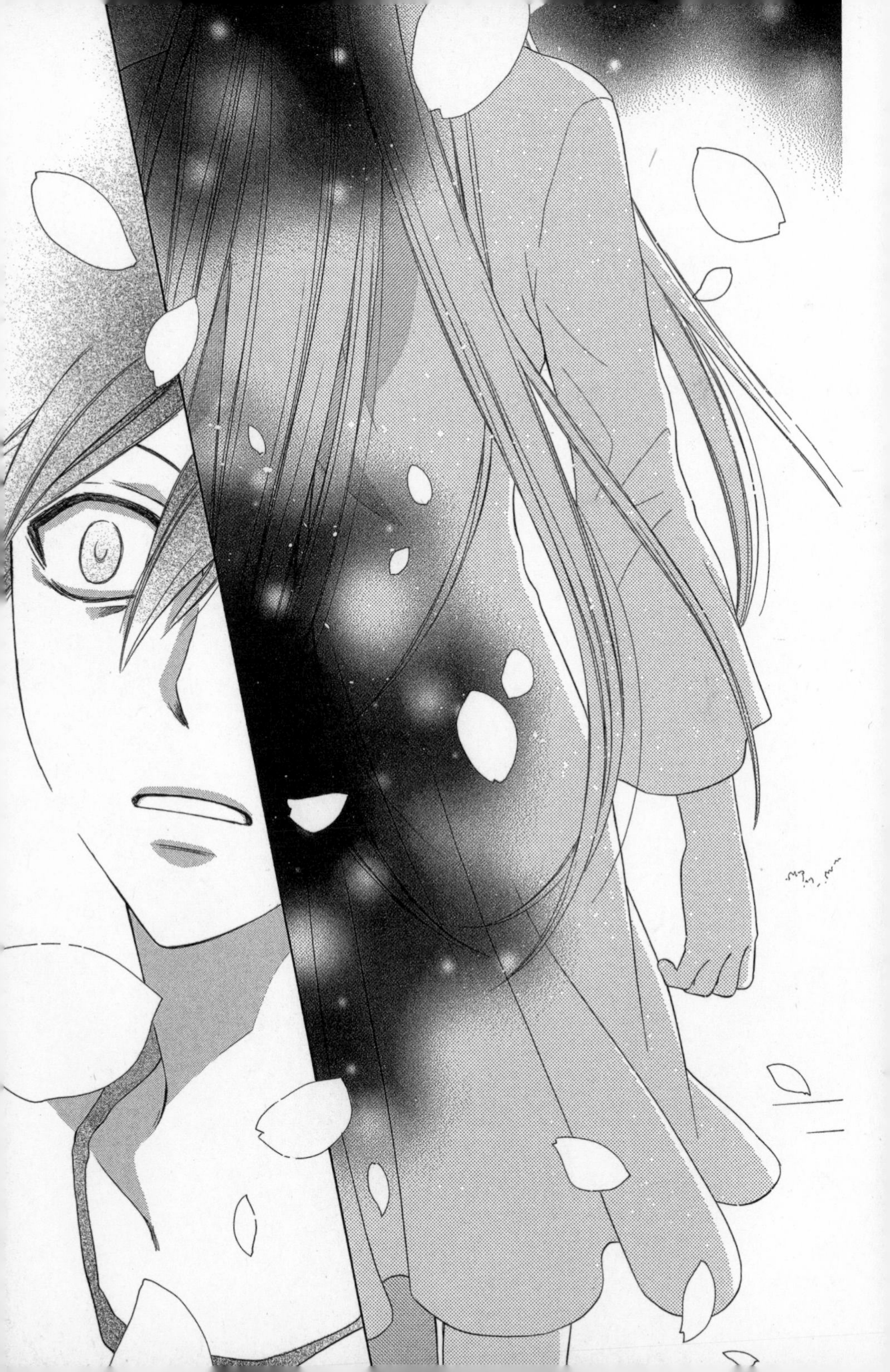

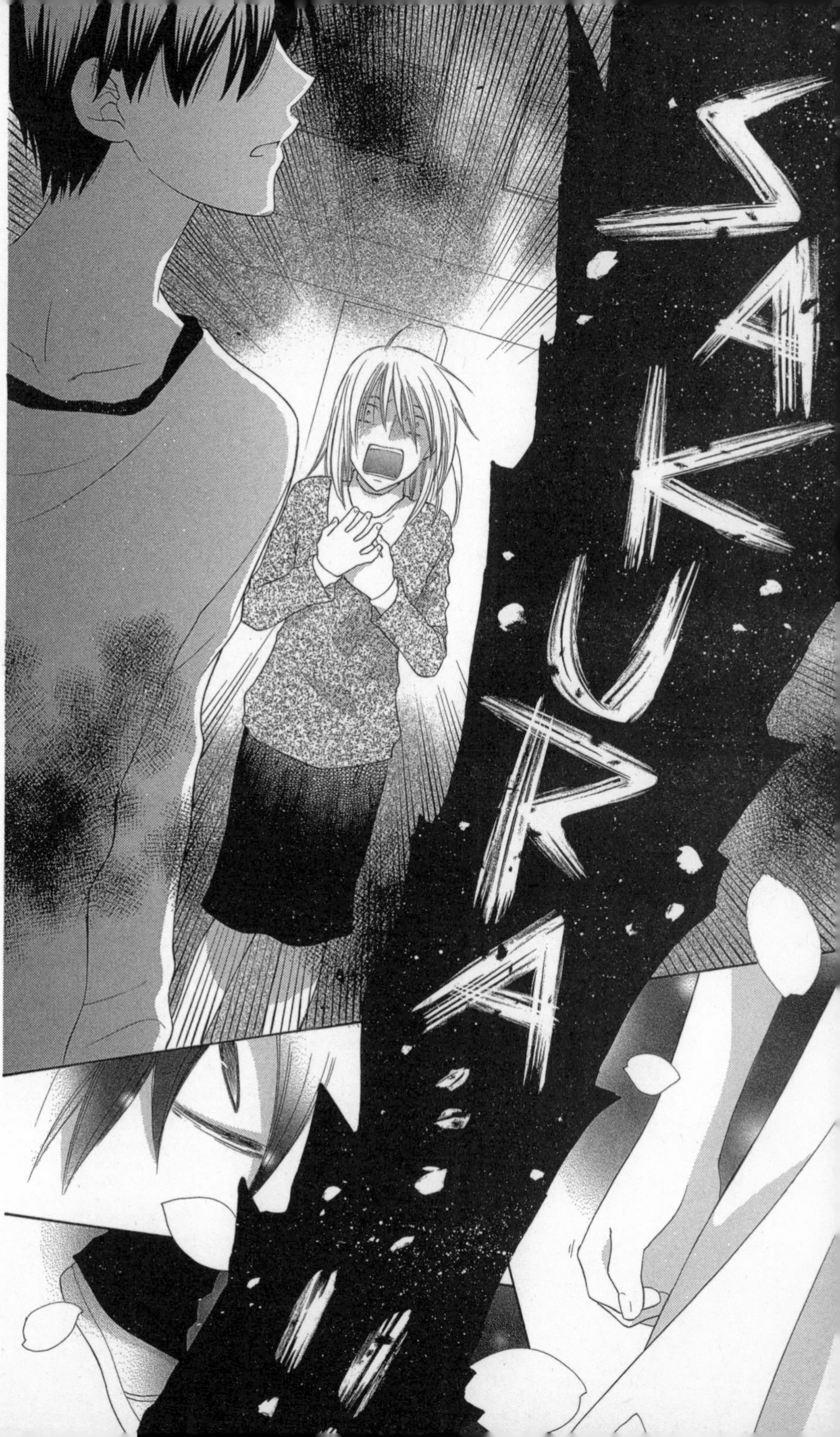
SAKURA

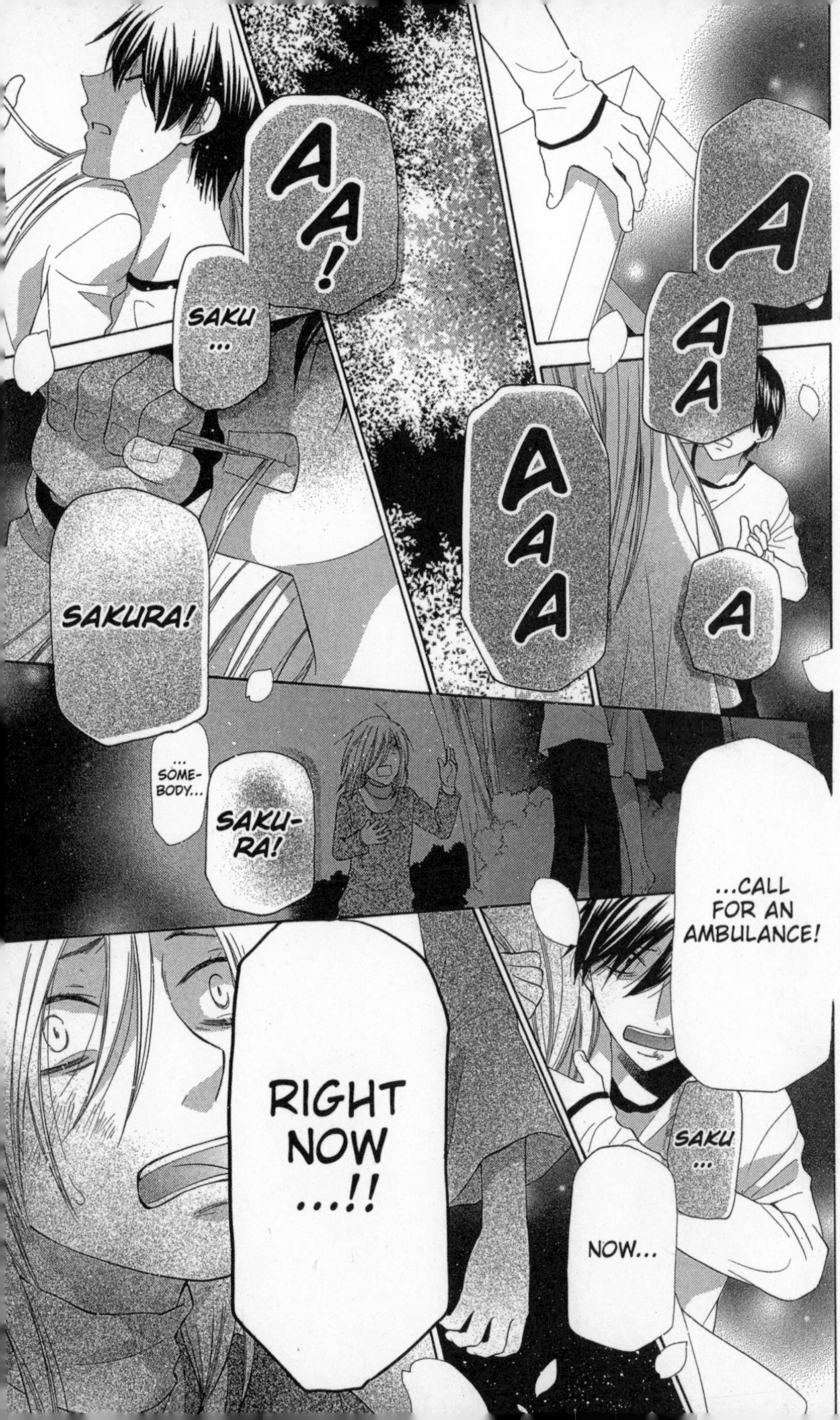
A
AA
AAA
A
AA!
SAKU ...
SAKURA!
SAKU-RA!
... SOME-BODY...
...CALL FOR AN AMBULANCE!
SAKU ...
NOW...
RIGHT NOW ...!!

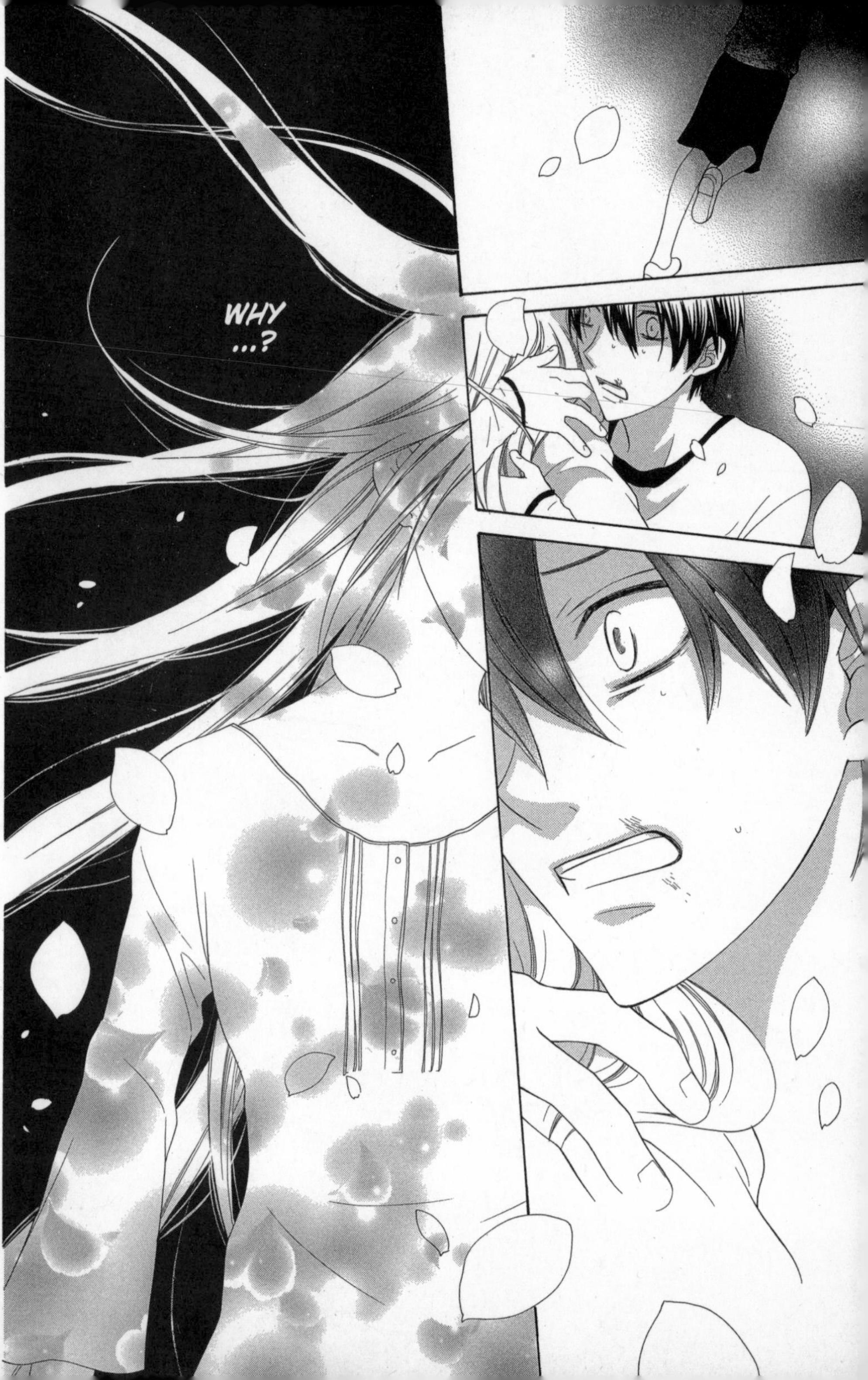
WHY ...?

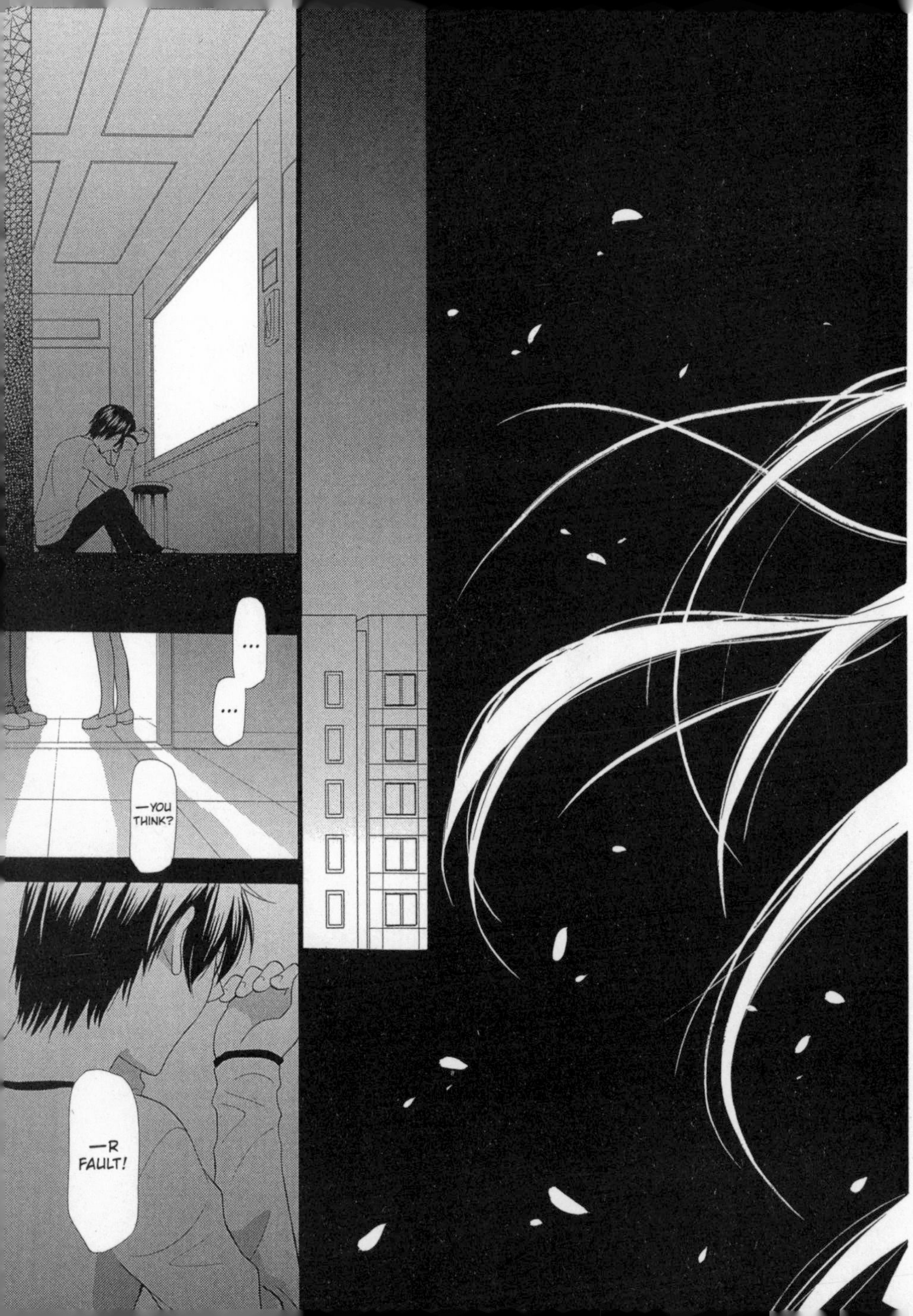
...
...
—YOU THINK?
—R FAULT!

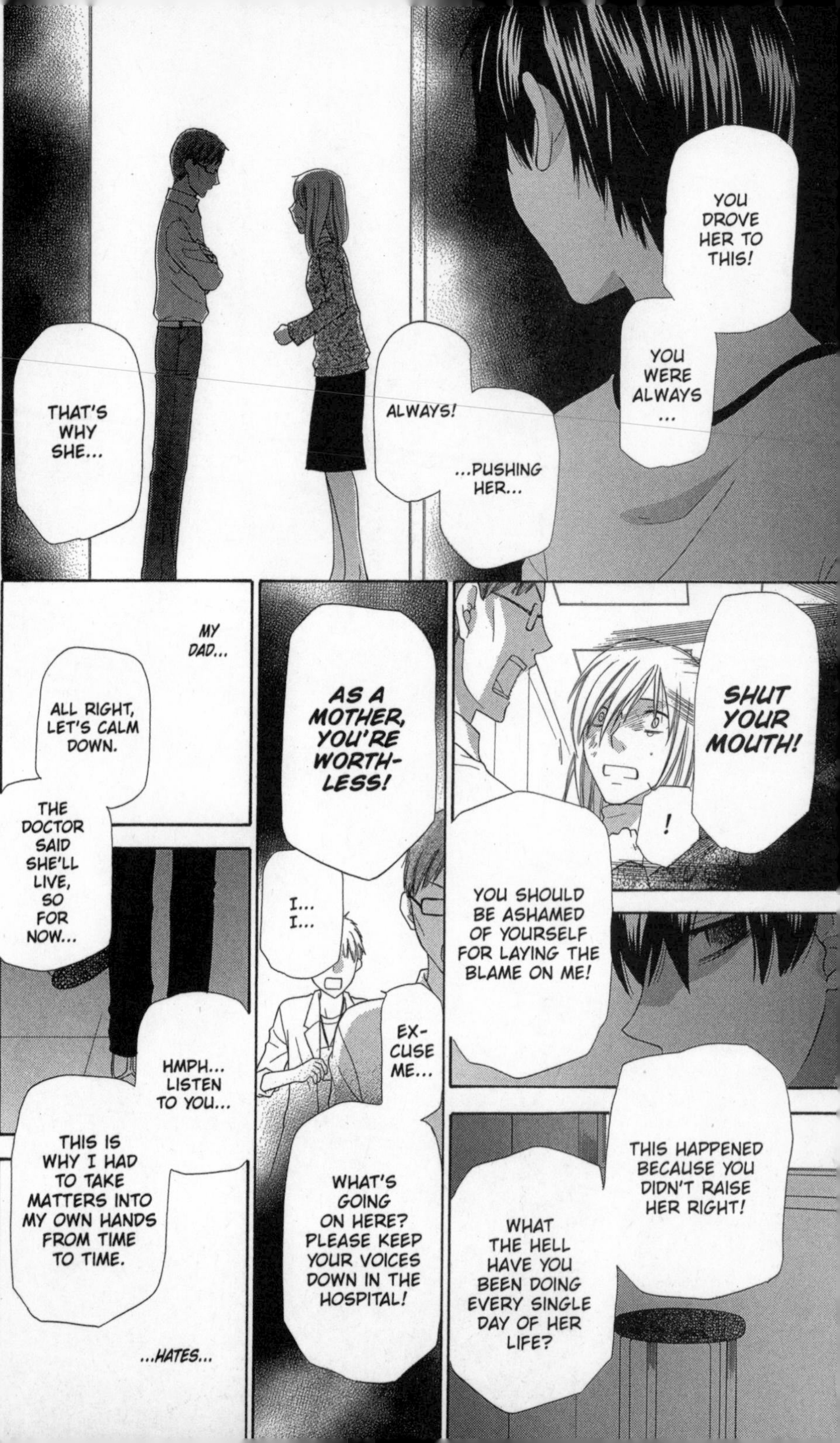
YOU DROVE HER TO THIS!
YOU WERE ALWAYS ...
...PUSHING HER...
ALWAYS!
THAT'S WHY SHE...
SHUT YOUR MOUTH!
!
AS A MOTHER, YOU'RE WORTHLESS!
YOU SHOULD BE ASHAMED OF YOURSELF FOR LAYING THE BLAME ON ME!
MY DAD...
ALL RIGHT, LET'S CALM DOWN.
THE DOCTOR SAID SHE'LL LIVE, SO FOR NOW...
I... I...
EX-CUSE ME...
THIS HAPPENED BECAUSE YOU DIDN'T RAISE HER RIGHT!
WHAT THE HELL HAVE YOU BEEN DOING EVERY SINGLE DAY OF HER LIFE?
WHAT'S GOING ON HERE? PLEASE KEEP YOUR VOICES DOWN IN THE HOSPITAL!
HMPH... LISTEN TO YOU...
THIS IS WHY I HAD TO TAKE MATTERS INTO MY OWN HANDS FROM TIME TO TIME.
...HATES...

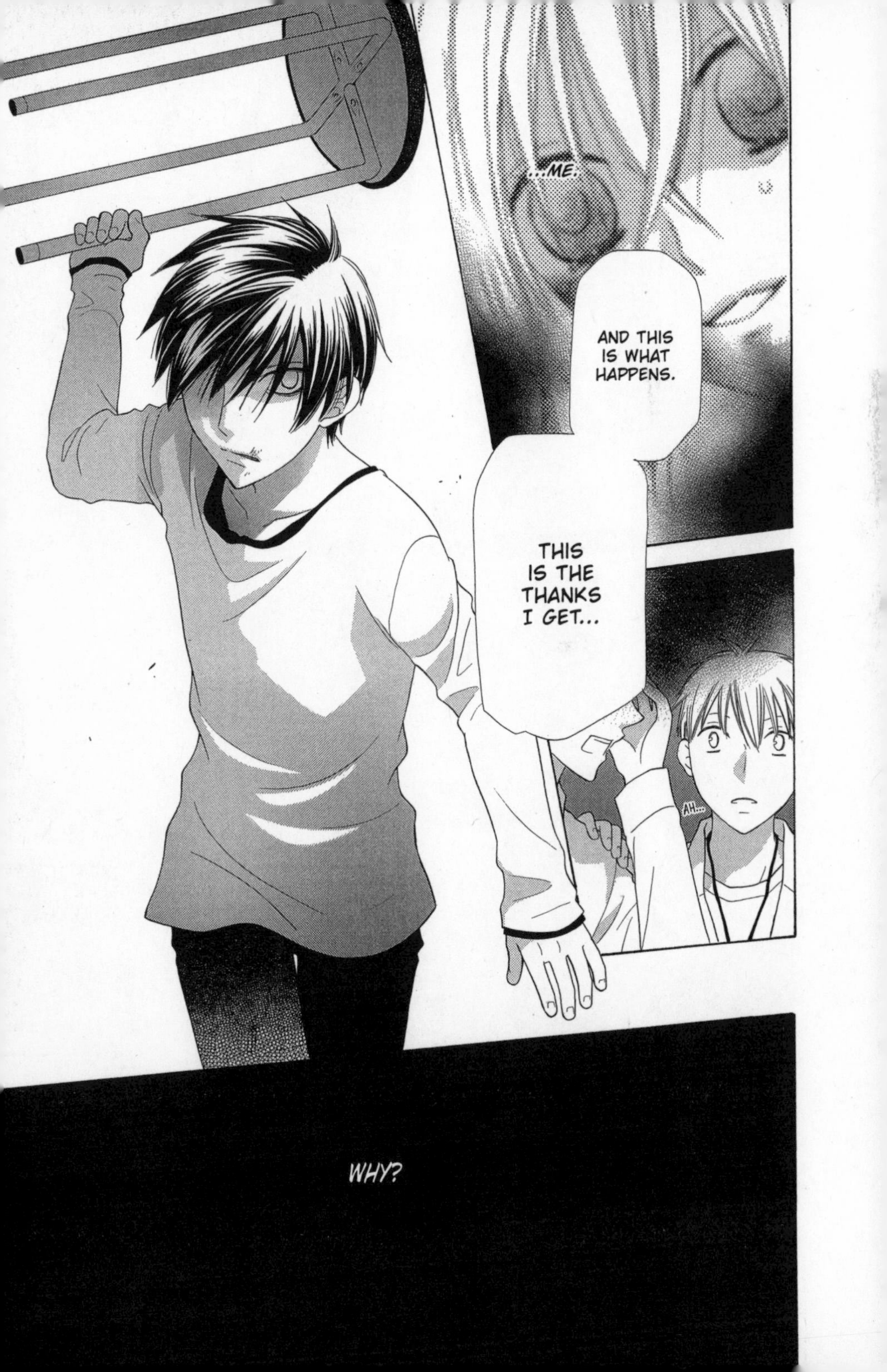
...ME.
AND THIS IS WHAT HAPPENS.
THIS IS THE THANKS I GET...
AH...
WHY?

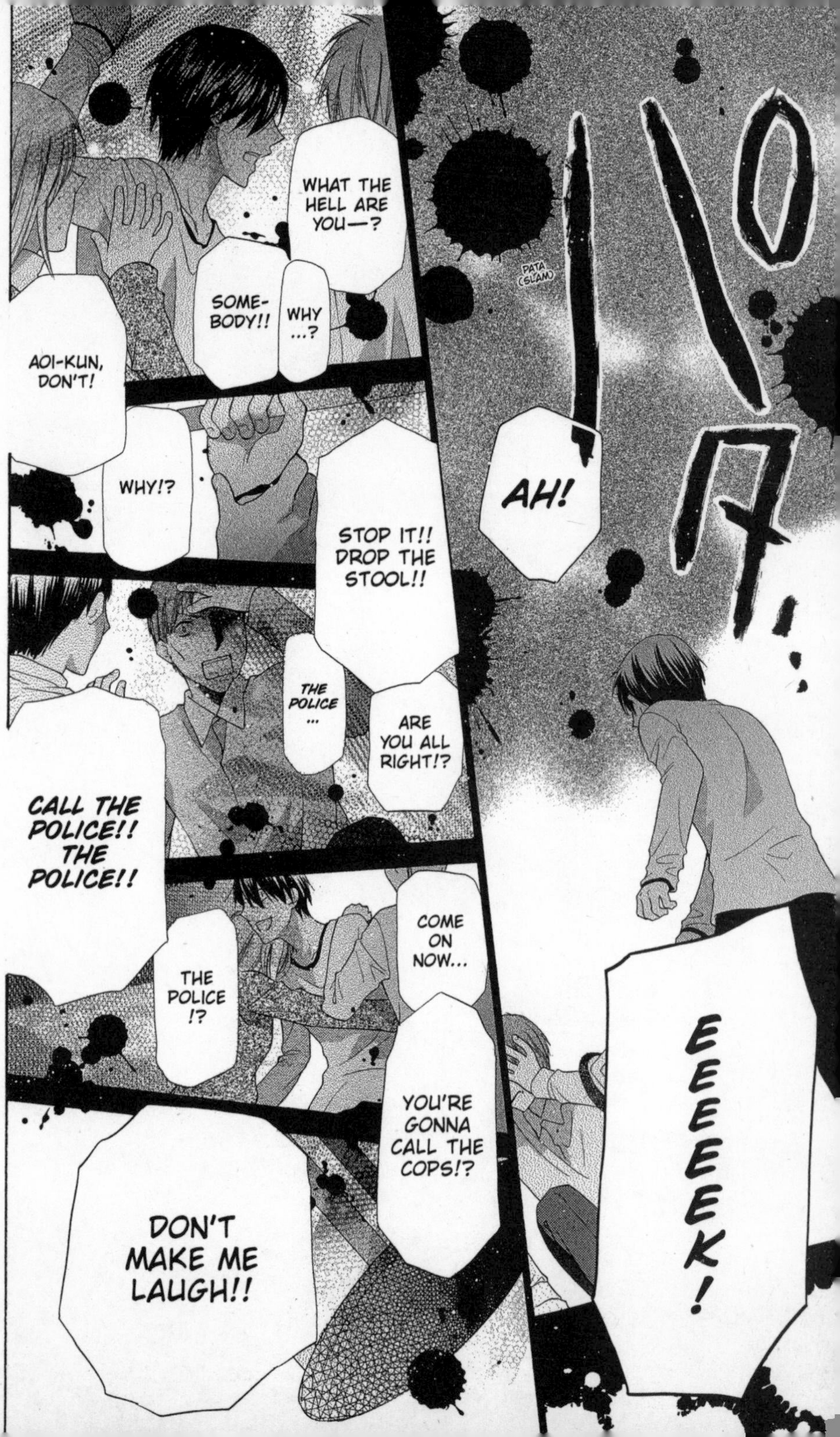
PATA (SLAM)
AH!
EEEEEK!
WHAT THE HELL ARE YOU—?
WHY ...?
SOME-BODY!!
AOI-KUN, DON'T!
STOP IT!! DROP THE STOOL!!
WHY!?
ARE YOU ALL RIGHT!?
THE POLICE ...
CALL THE POLICE!! THE POLICE!!
COME ON NOW...
THE POLICE !?
YOU'RE GONNA CALL THE COPS!?
DON'T MAKE ME LAUGH!!

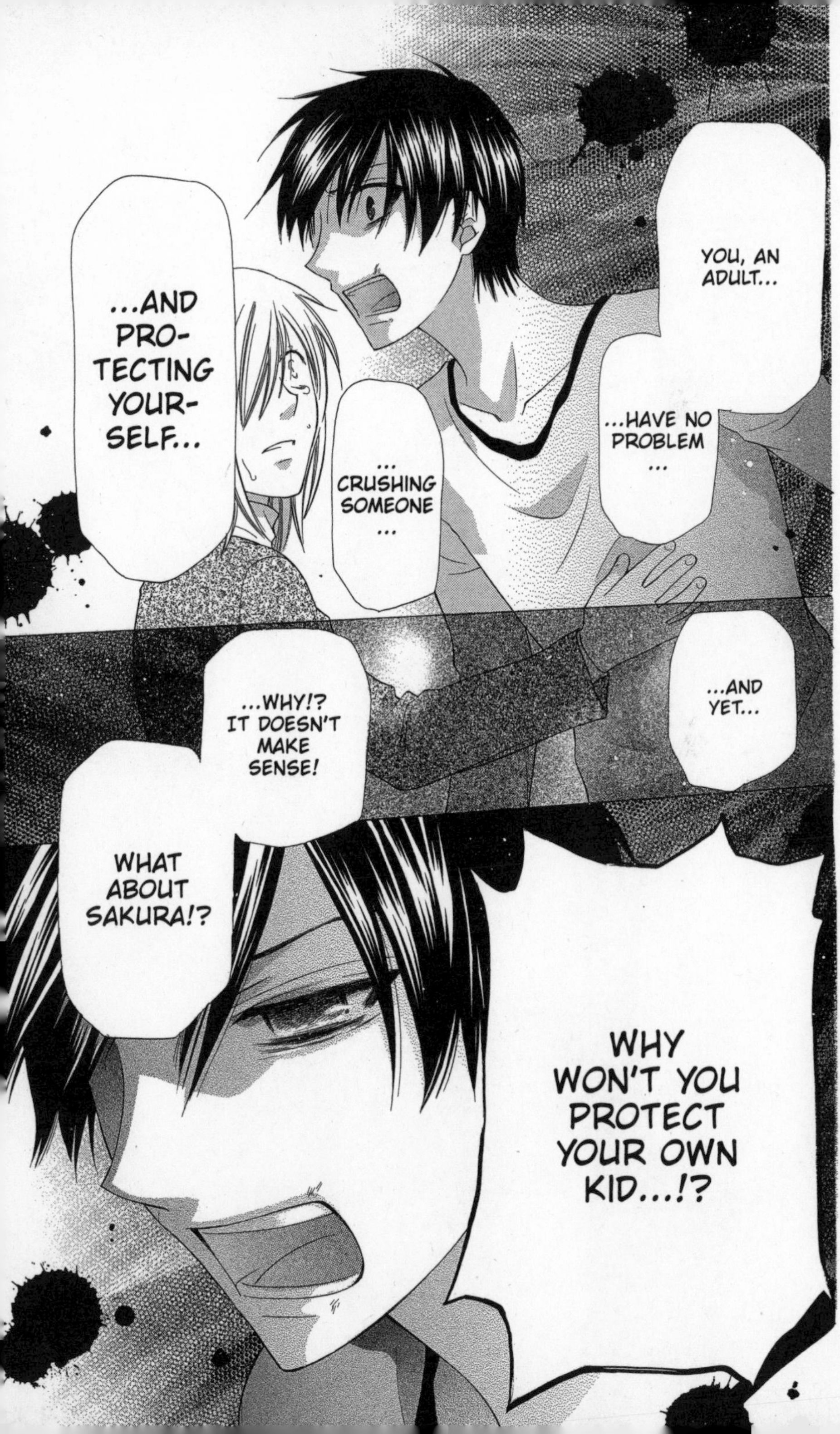
YOU, AN ADULT...
...HAVE NO PROBLEM ...
... CRUSHING SOMEONE ...
...AND PROTECTING YOURSELF...
...AND YET...
...WHY!? IT DOESN'T MAKE SENSE!
WHY WON'T YOU PROTECT YOUR OWN KID...!?
WHAT ABOUT SAKURA!?

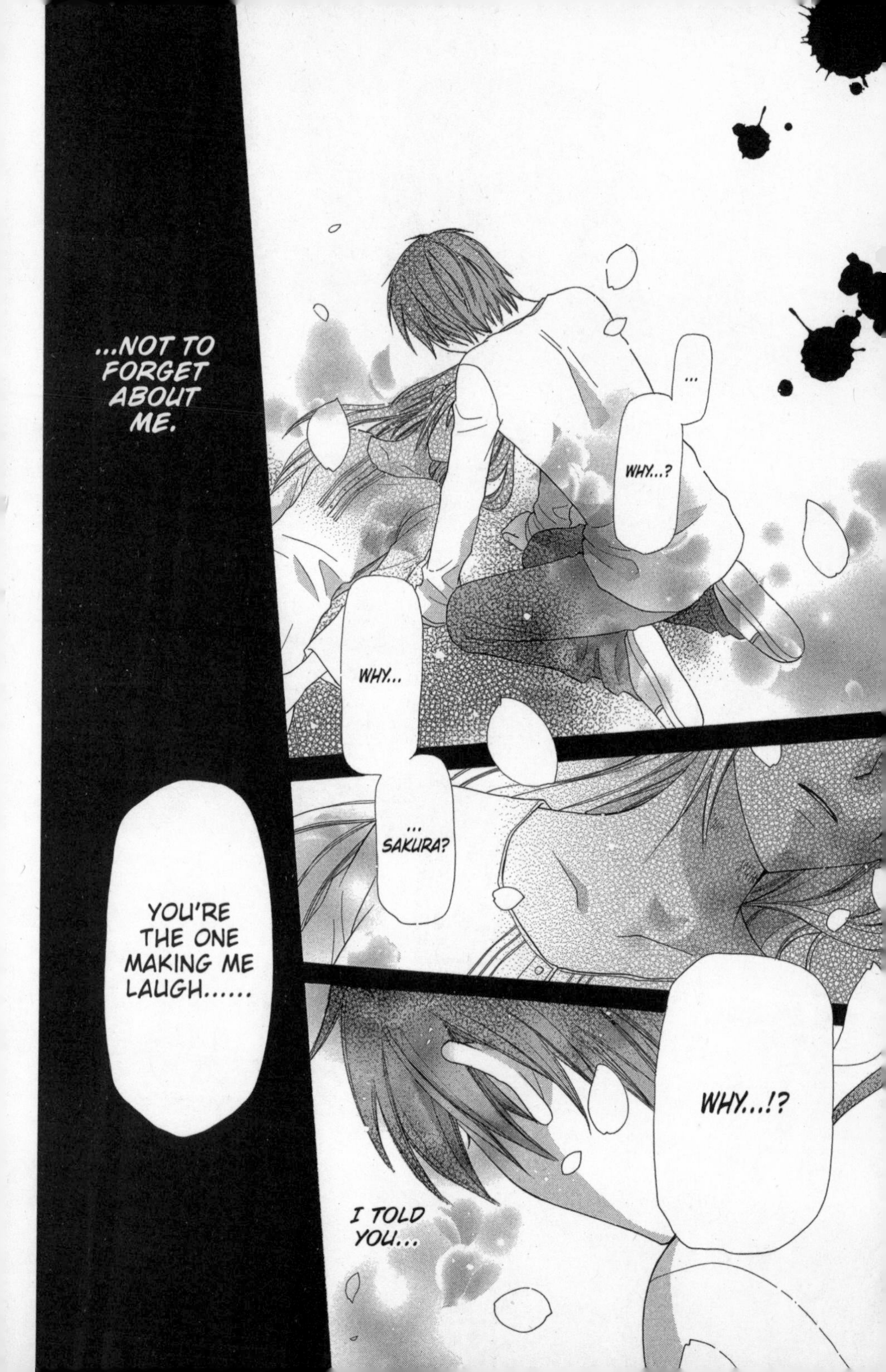
...
WHY...?
WHY...
...SAKURA?
WHY...!?
I TOLD YOU...
...NOT TO FORGET ABOUT ME.
YOU'RE THE ONE MAKING ME LAUGH......

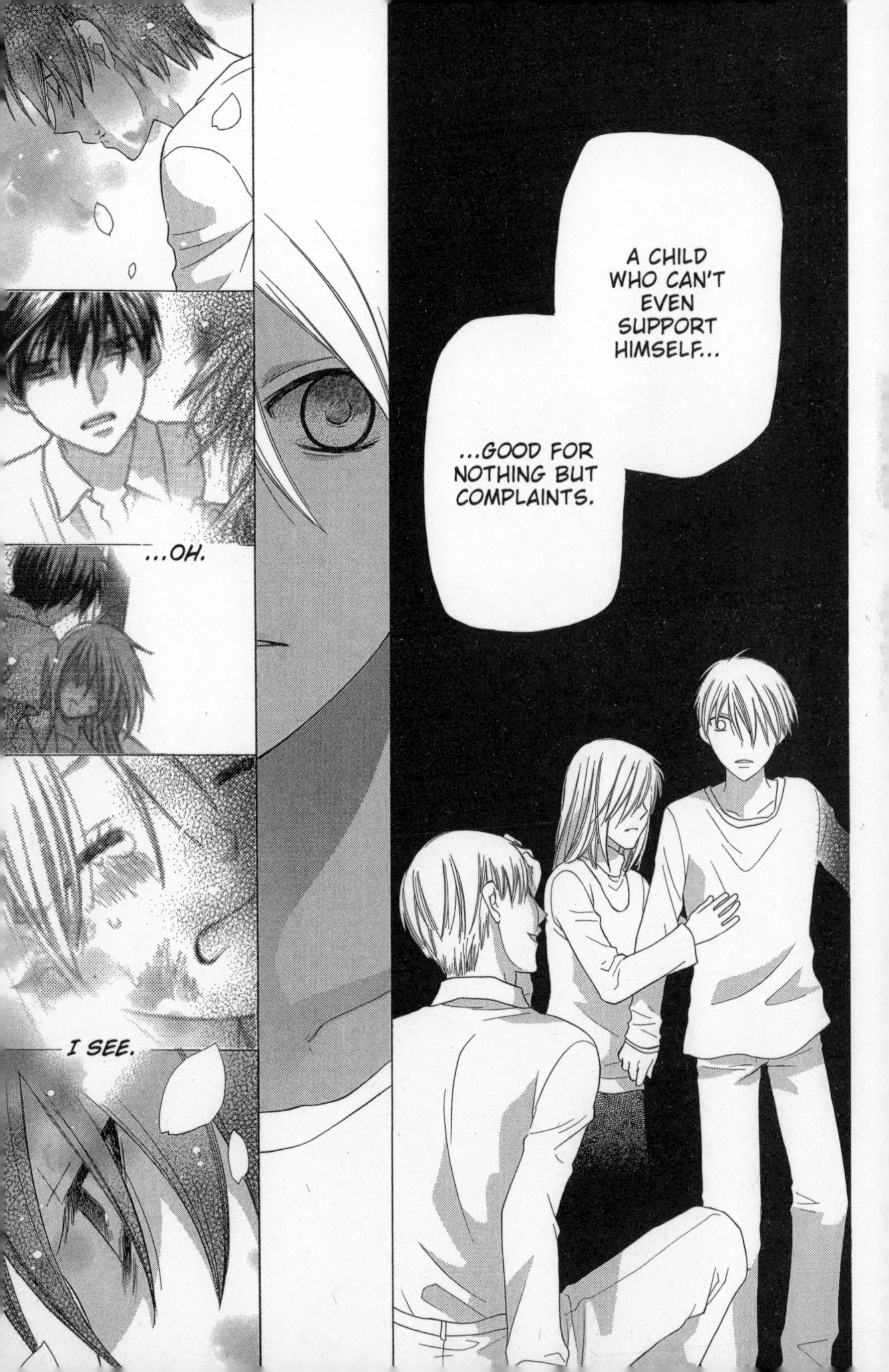
A CHILD WHO CAN'T EVEN SUPPORT HIMSELF...
...GOOD FOR NOTHING BUT COMPLAINTS.
...OH.
I SEE.

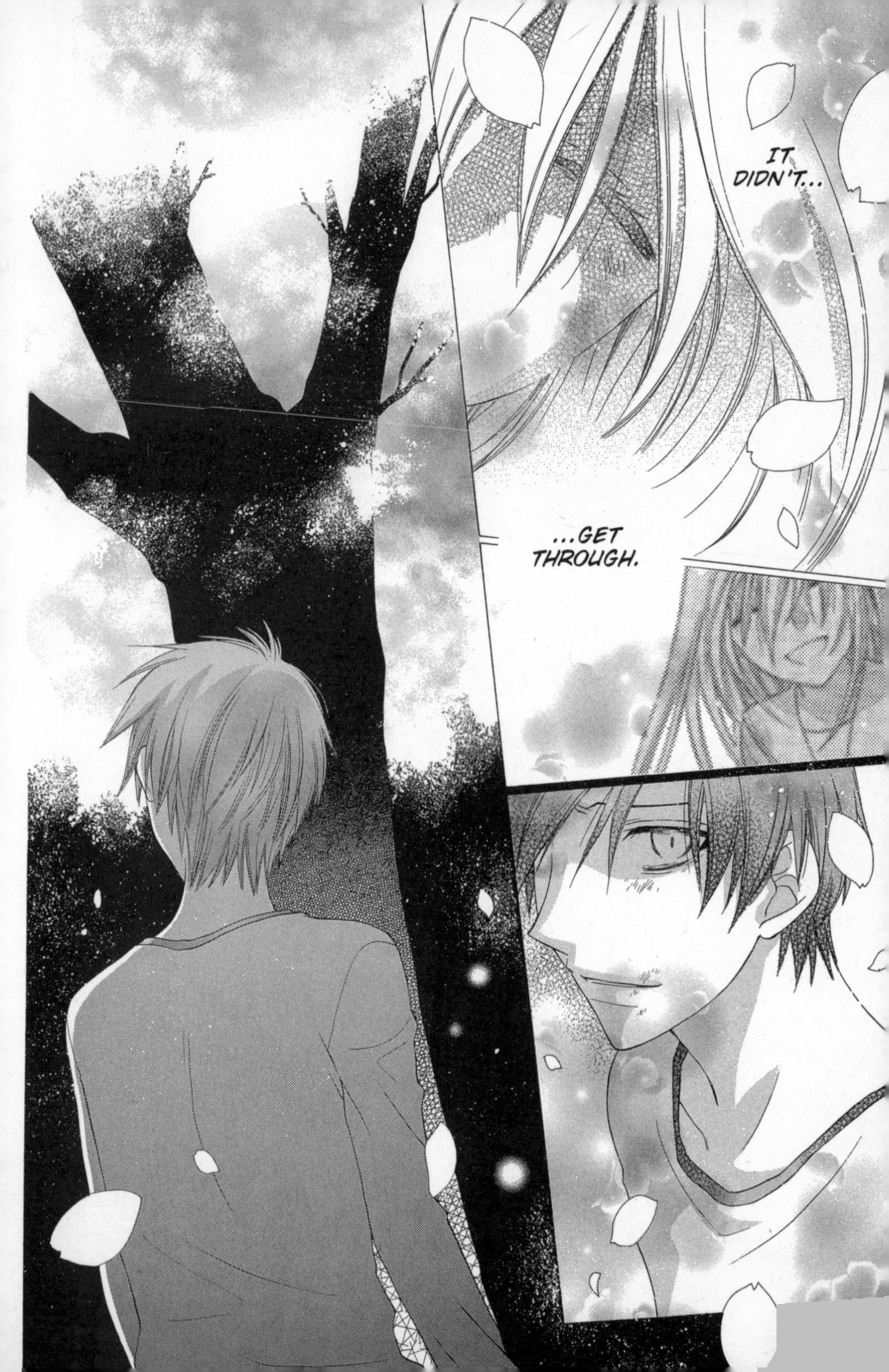
IT DIDN'T...
...GET THROUGH.

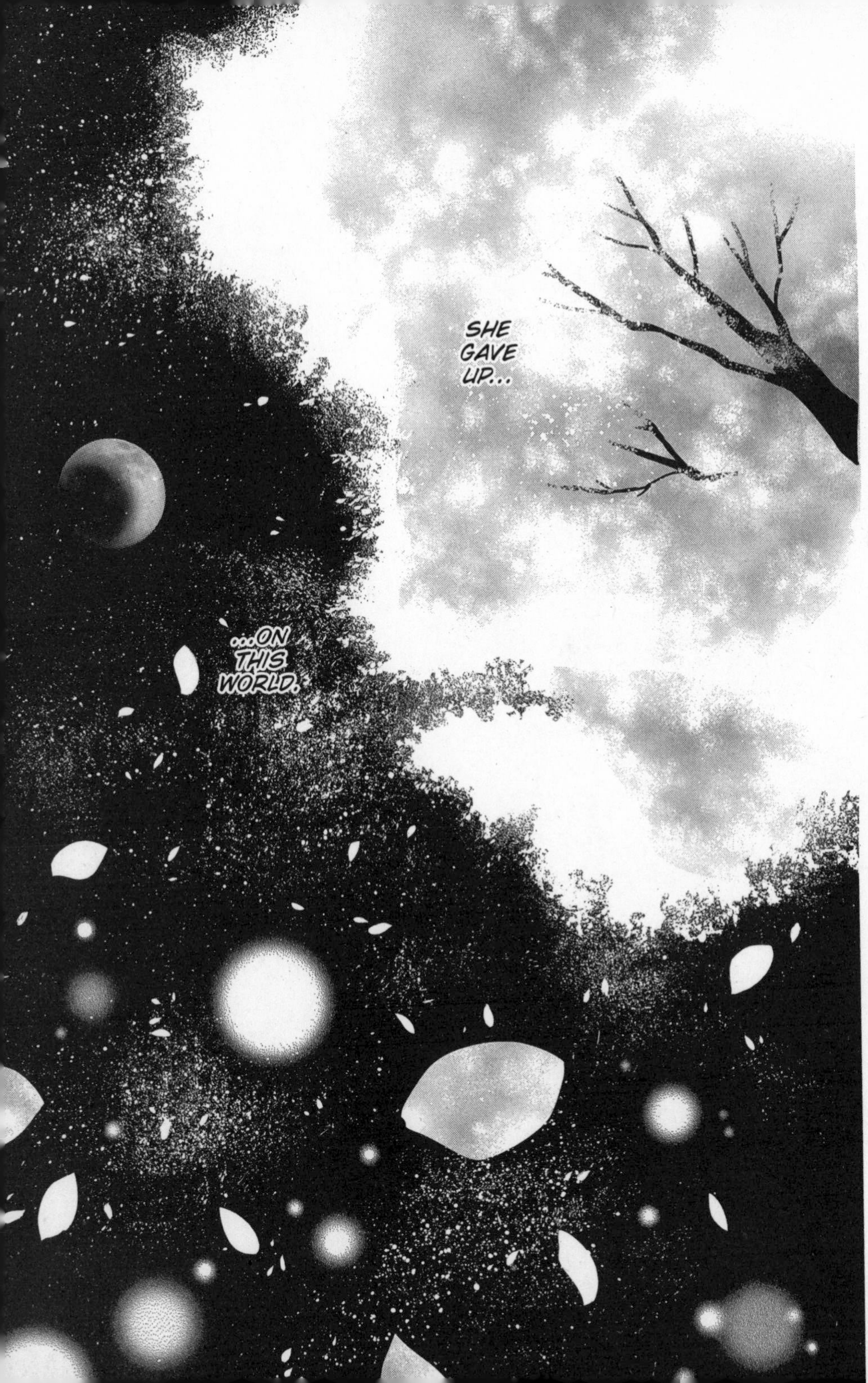
SHE GAVE UP...
...ON THIS WORLD.

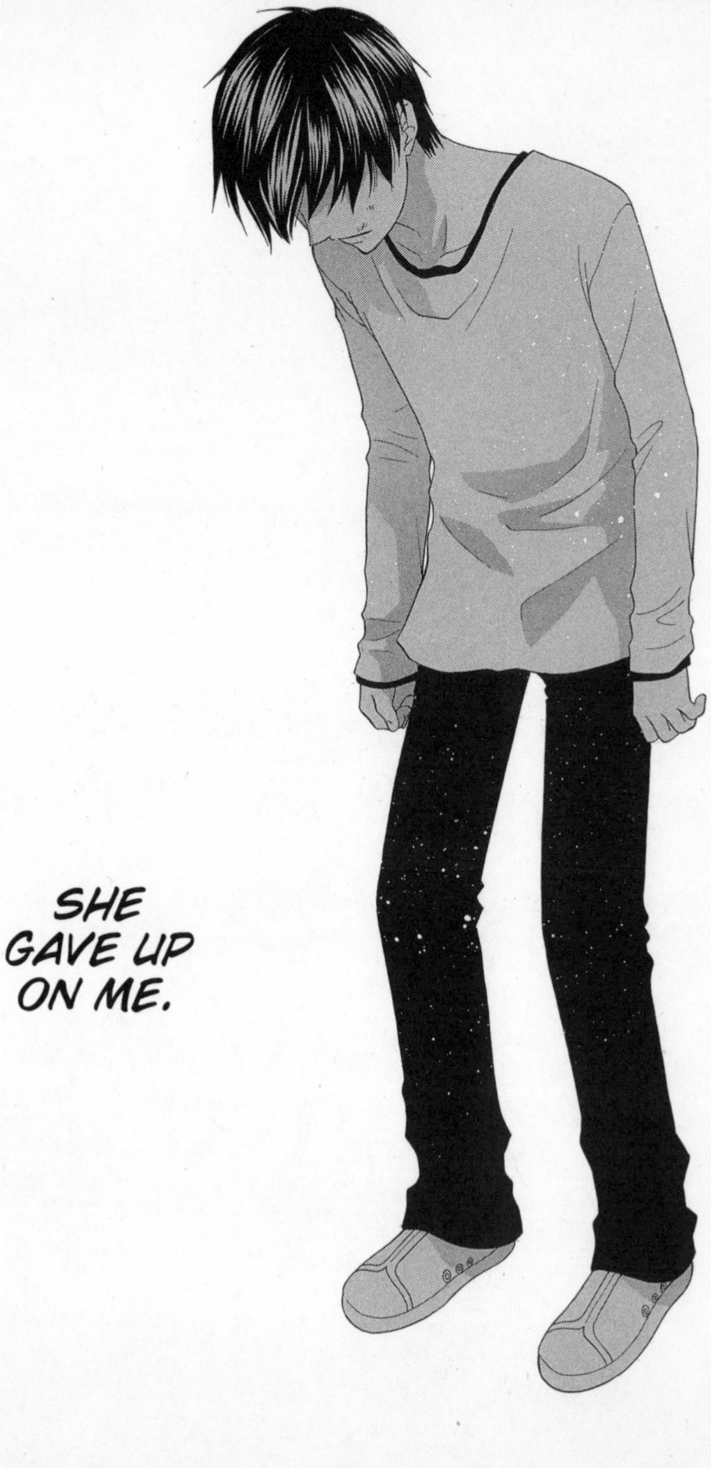
SHE GAVE UP ON ME.

Chapter 29

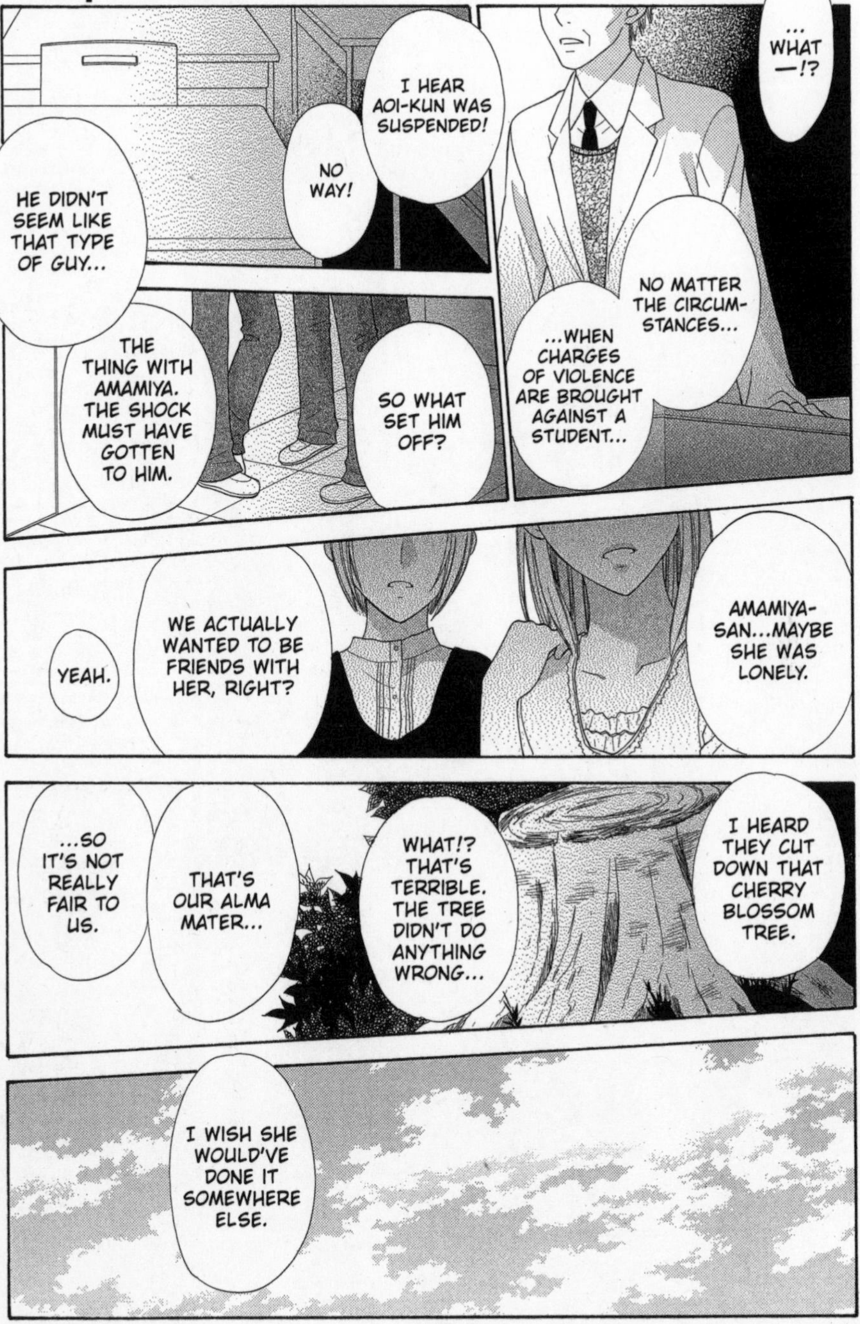
...WHAT—!?
NO MATTER THE CIRCUMSTANCES...
...WHEN CHARGES OF VIOLENCE ARE BROUGHT AGAINST A STUDENT...
I HEAR AOI-KUN WAS SUSPENDED!
NO WAY!
HE DIDN'T SEEM LIKE THAT TYPE OF GUY...
SO WHAT SET HIM OFF?
THE THING WITH AMAMIYA. THE SHOCK MUST HAVE GOTTEN TO HIM.
AMAMIYA-SAN...MAYBE SHE WAS LONELY.
WE ACTUALLY WANTED TO BE FRIENDS WITH HER, RIGHT?
YEAH.
I HEARD THEY CUT DOWN THAT CHERRY BLOSSOM TREE.
WHAT!? THAT'S TERRIBLE. THE TREE DIDN'T DO ANYTHING WRONG...
THAT'S OUR ALMA MATER...
...SO IT'S NOT REALLY FAIR TO US.
I WISH SHE WOULD'VE DONE IT SOMEWHERE ELSE.

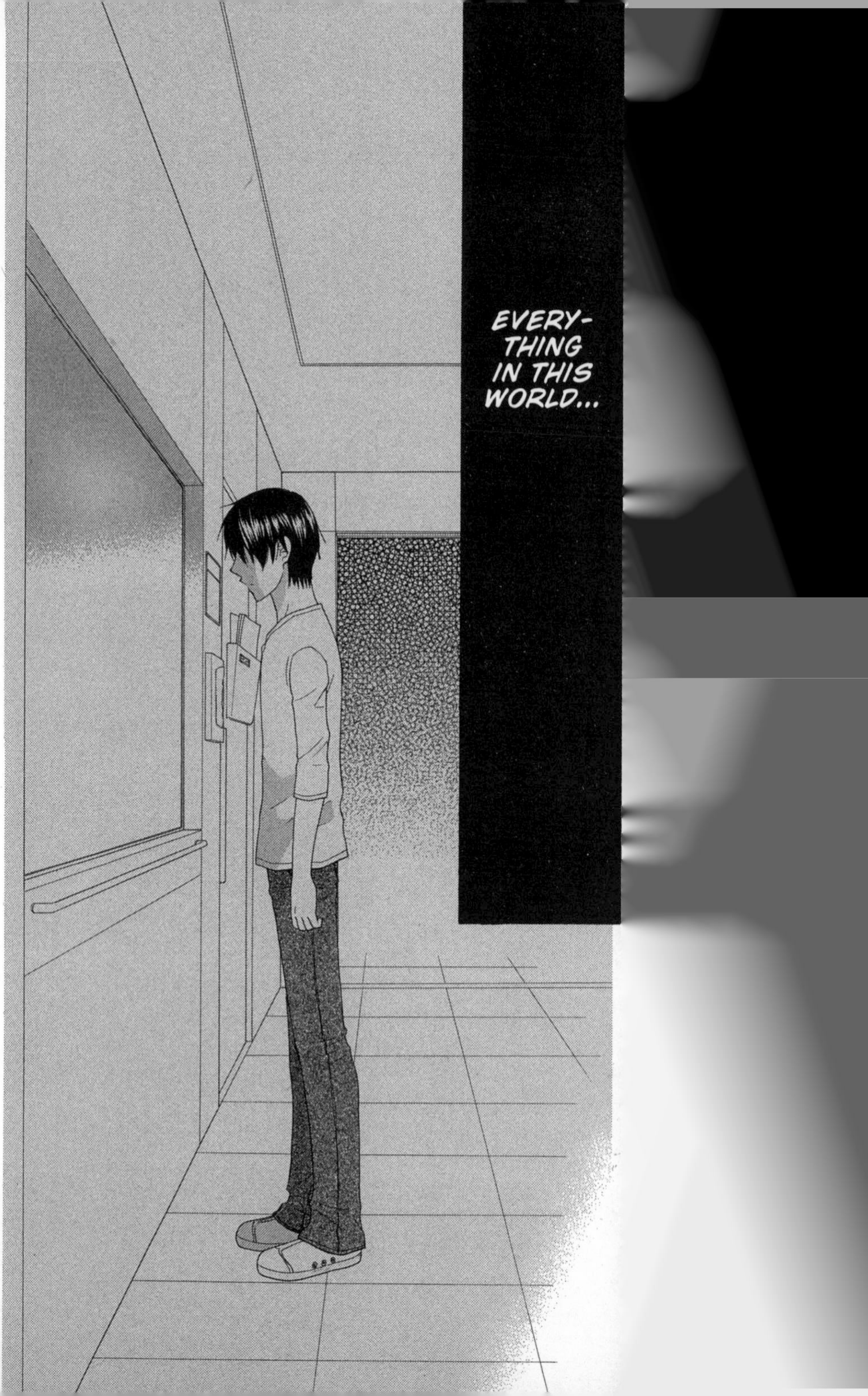
EVERY-THING IN THIS WORLD...

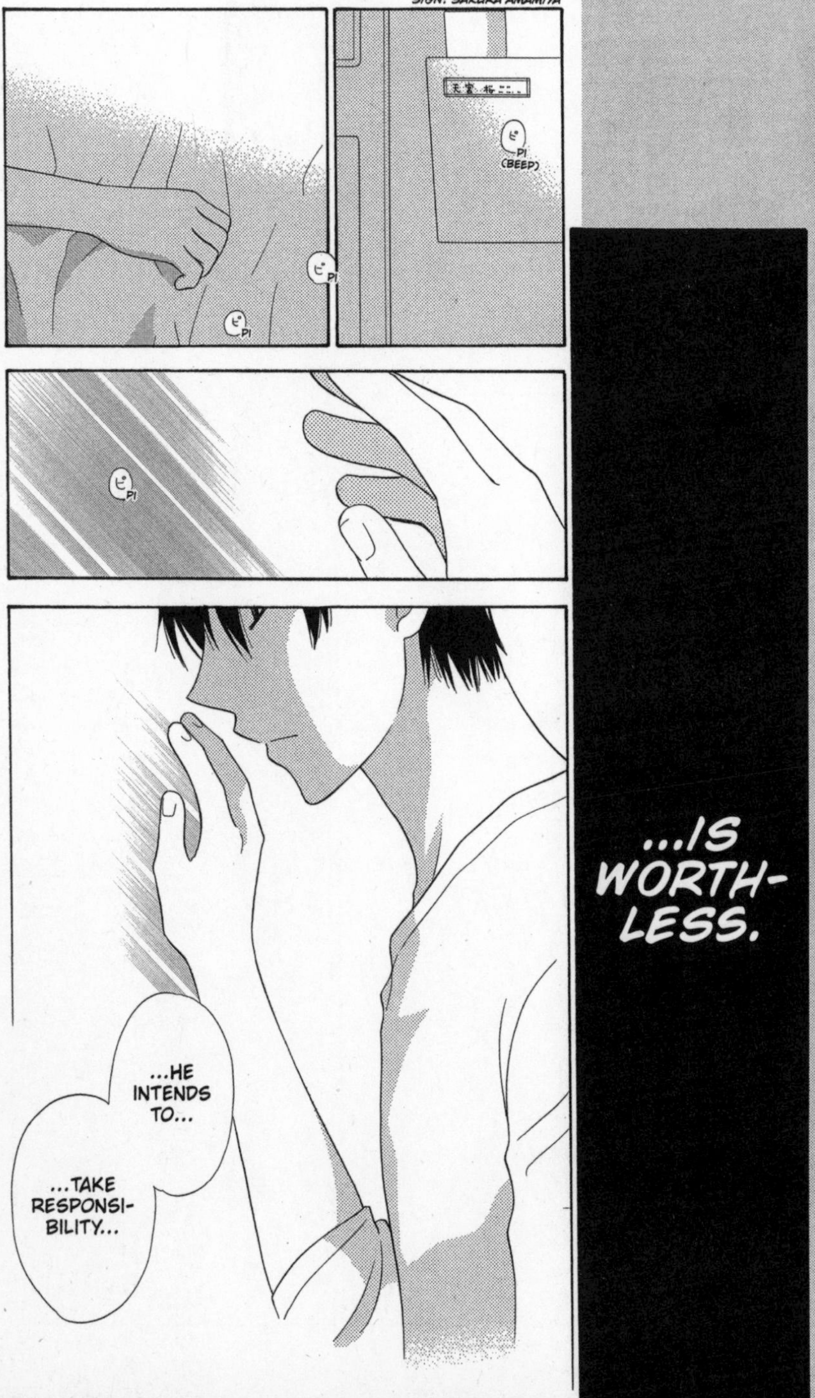
SIGN: SAKURA AMAMIYA
ピ PI (BEEP)
ピ PI
ピ PI
ピ PI
...HE INTENDS TO...
...TAKE RESPONSI-BILITY...
...IS WORTH-LESS.

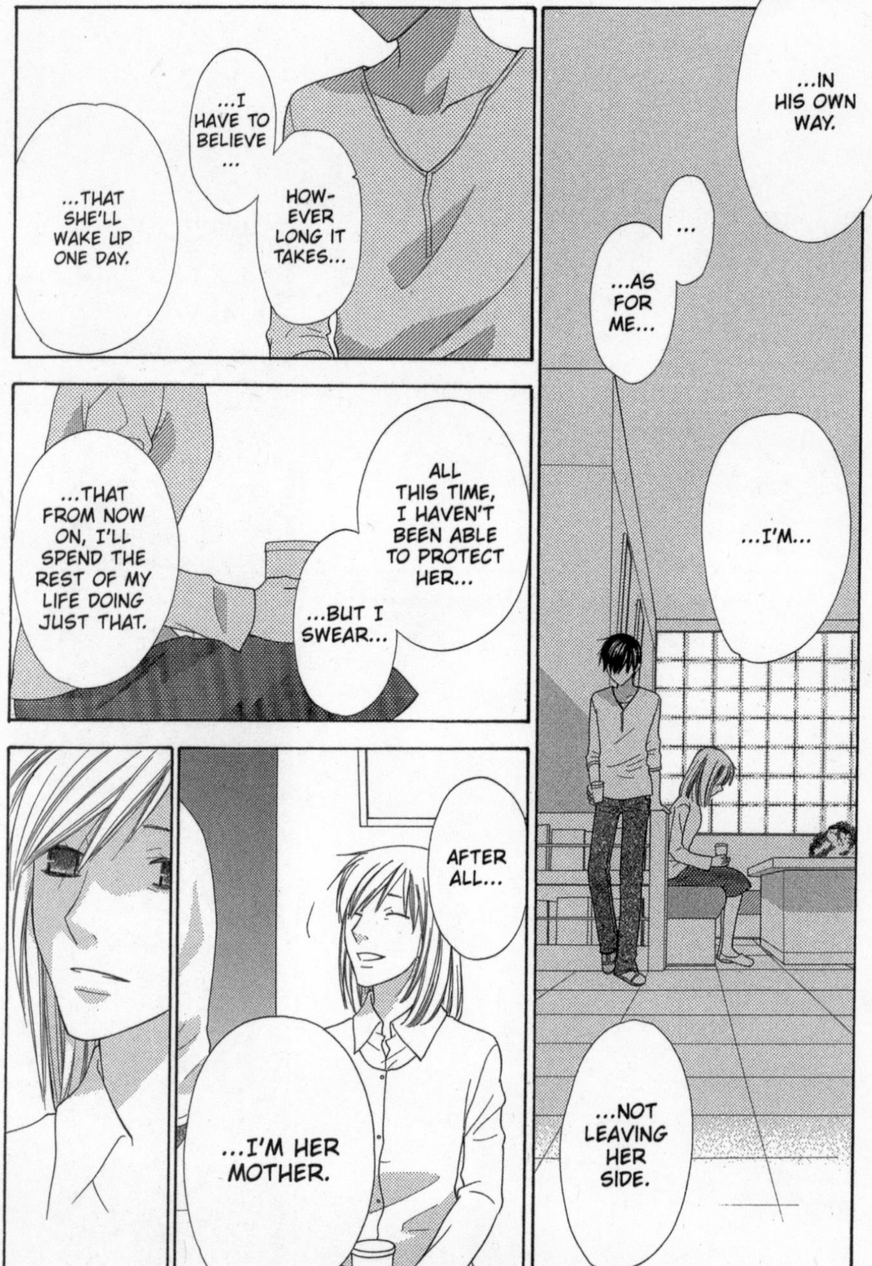

...IN HIS OWN WAY.
...
...AS FOR ME...
...I'M...
...NOT LEAVING HER SIDE.
...I HAVE TO BELIEVE ...
HOW-EVER LONG IT TAKES...
...THAT SHE'LL WAKE UP ONE DAY.
ALL THIS TIME, I HAVEN'T BEEN ABLE TO PROTECT HER...
...BUT I SWEAR...
...THAT FROM NOW ON, I'LL SPEND THE REST OF MY LIFE DOING JUST THAT.
AFTER ALL...
...I'M HER MOTHER.

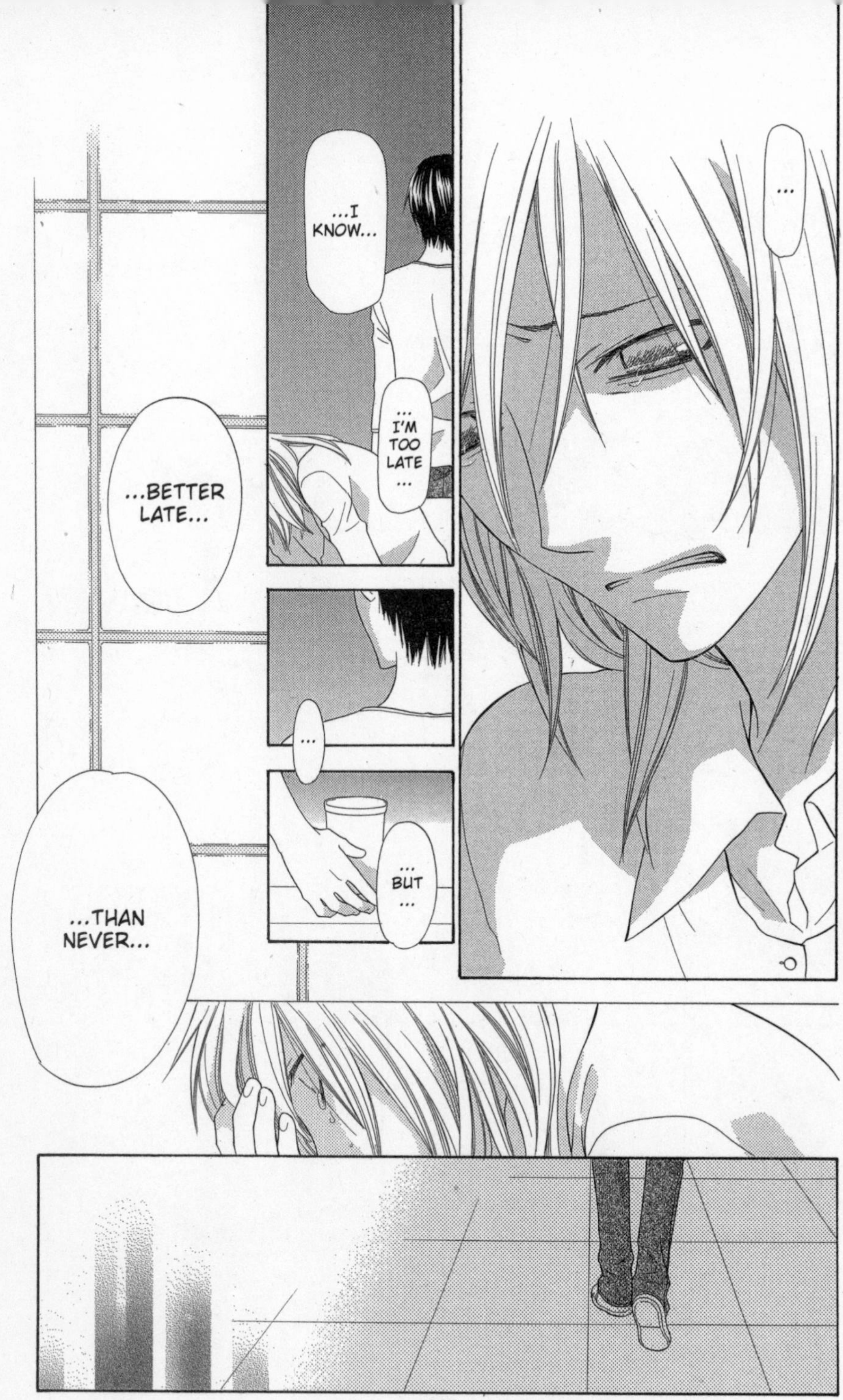
...
...I KNOW...
...I'M TOO LATE...
...
...BUT...
...BETTER LATE...
...THAN NEVER...

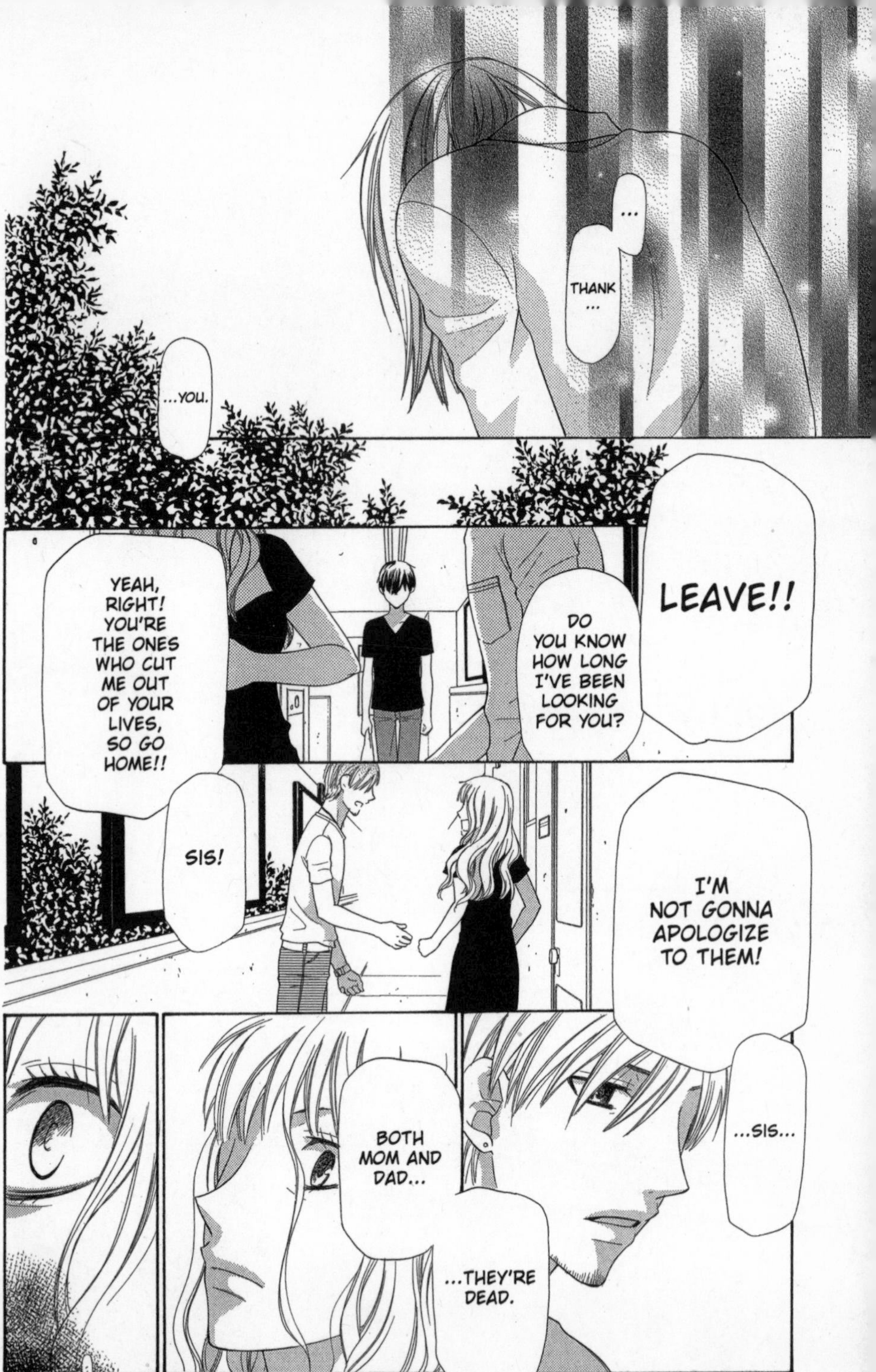
...
THANK ...
...YOU.
LEAVE!!
DO YOU KNOW HOW LONG I'VE BEEN LOOKING FOR YOU?
YEAH, RIGHT! YOU'RE THE ONES WHO CUT ME OUT OF YOUR LIVES, SO GO HOME!!
I'M NOT GONNA APOLOGIZE TO THEM!
SIS!
...SIS...
BOTH MOM AND DAD...
...THEY'RE DEAD.
...

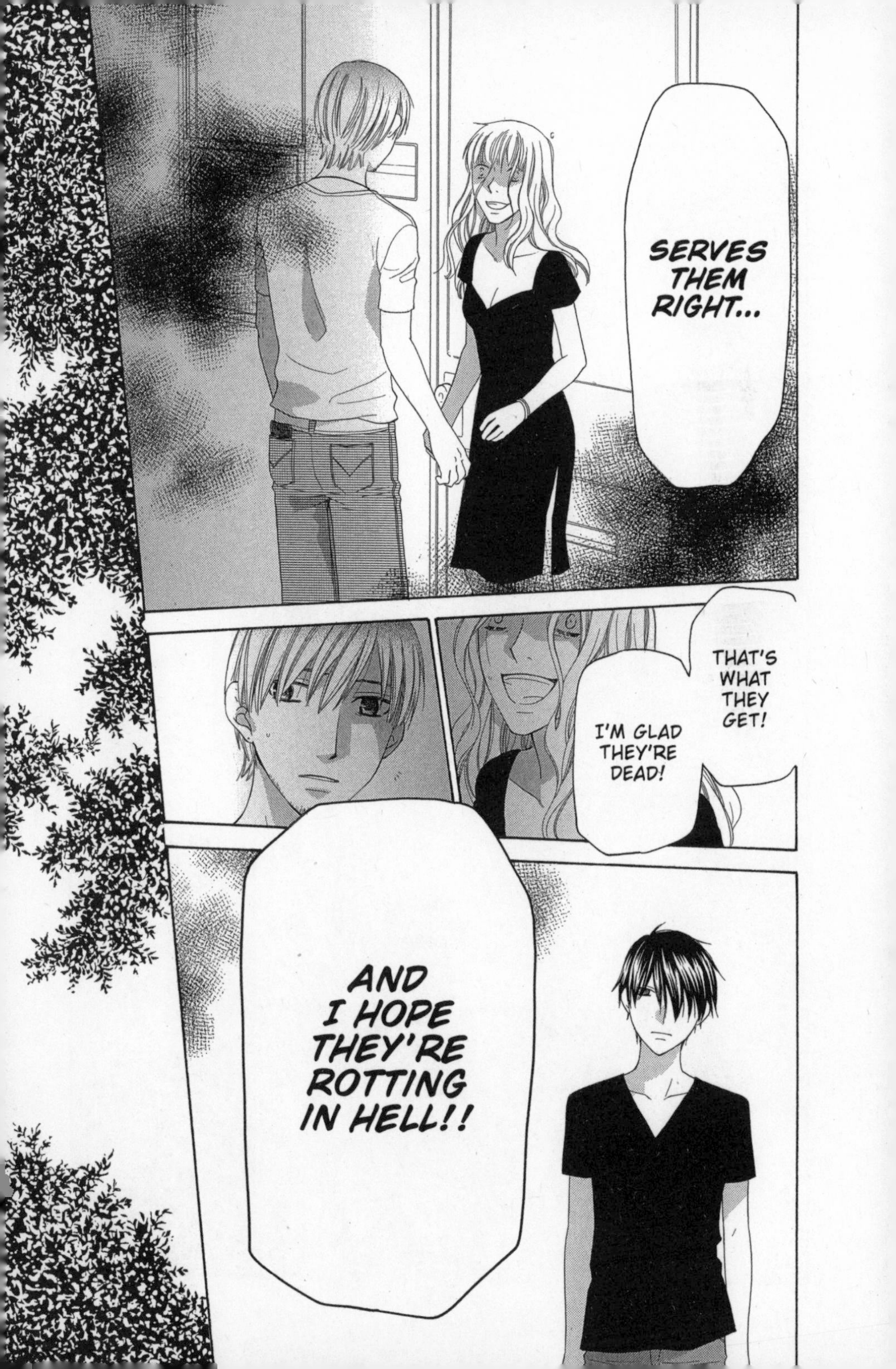
SERVES THEM RIGHT...
THAT'S WHAT THEY GET!
I'M GLAD THEY'RE DEAD!
AND I HOPE THEY'RE ROTTING IN HELL!!

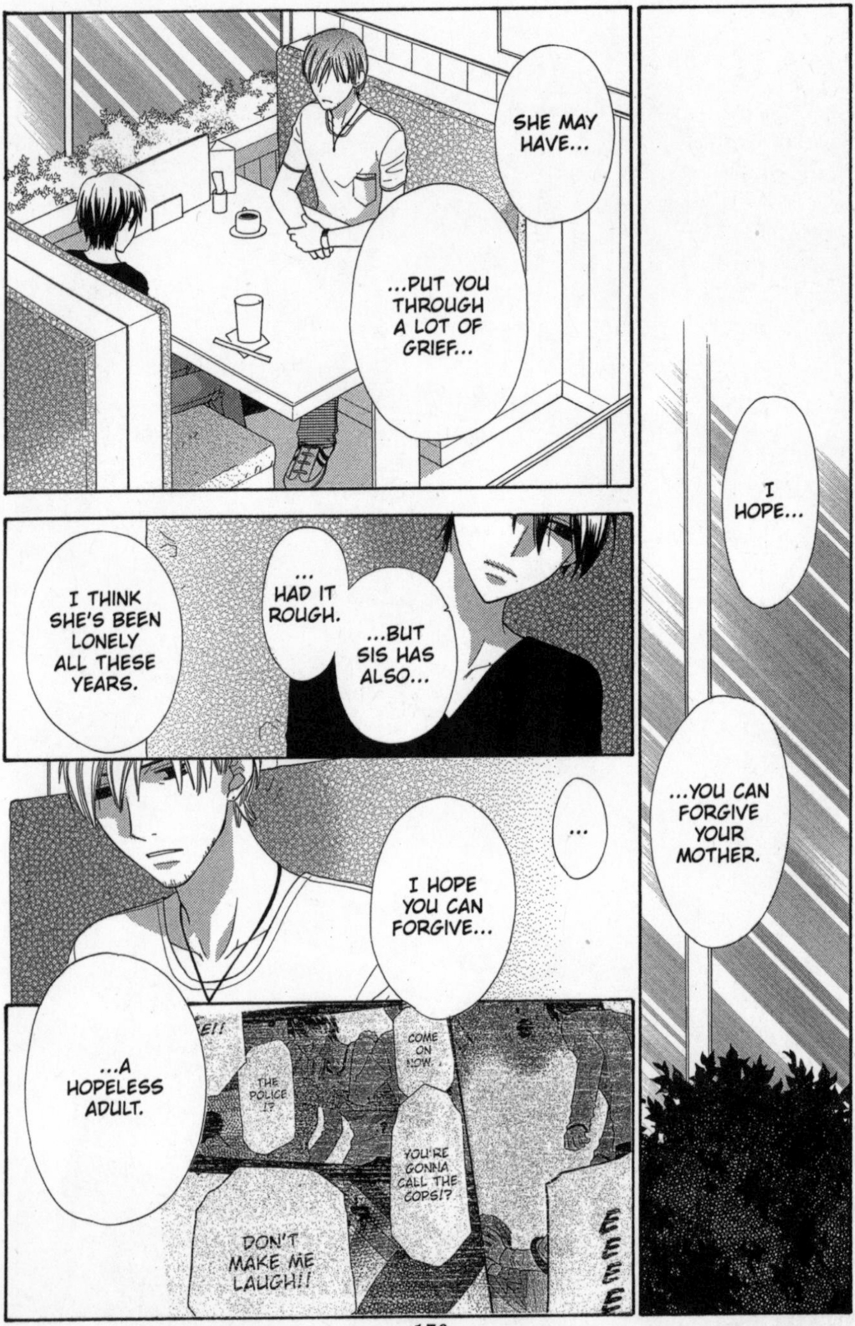
I HOPE...
...YOU CAN FORGIVE YOUR MOTHER.
SHE MAY HAVE...
...PUT YOU THROUGH A LOT OF GRIEF...
...BUT SIS HAS ALSO...
... HAD IT ROUGH.
I THINK SHE'S BEEN LONELY ALL THESE YEARS.
...
I HOPE YOU CAN FORGIVE...
...A HOPELESS ADULT.
COME ON NOW.
THE POLICE !?
YOU'RE GONNA CALL THE COPS!?
DON'T MAKE ME LAUGH!!
EEEE

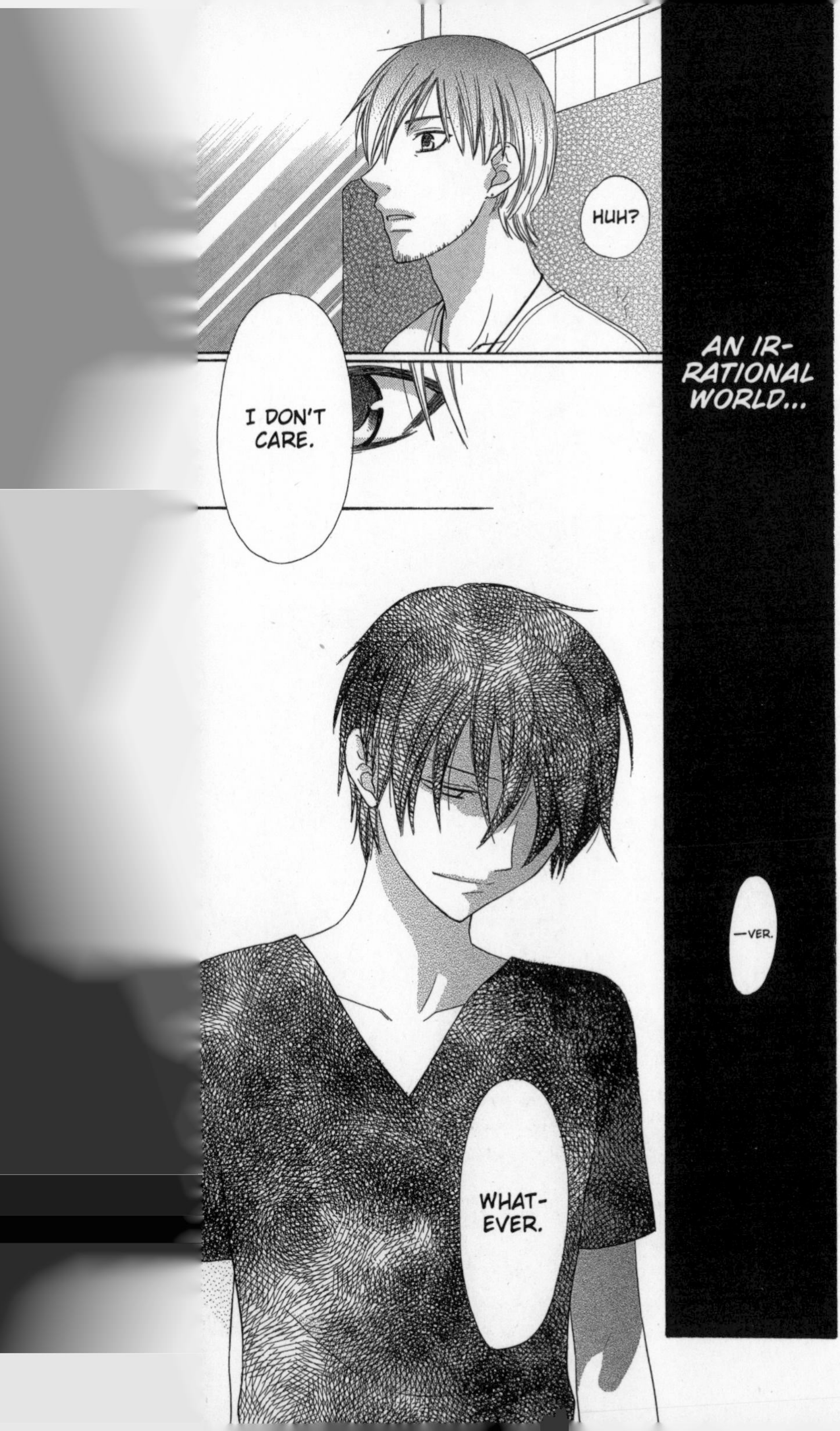
AN IR-RATIONAL WORLD...
—VER.
HUH?
I DON'T CARE.
WHAT-EVER.

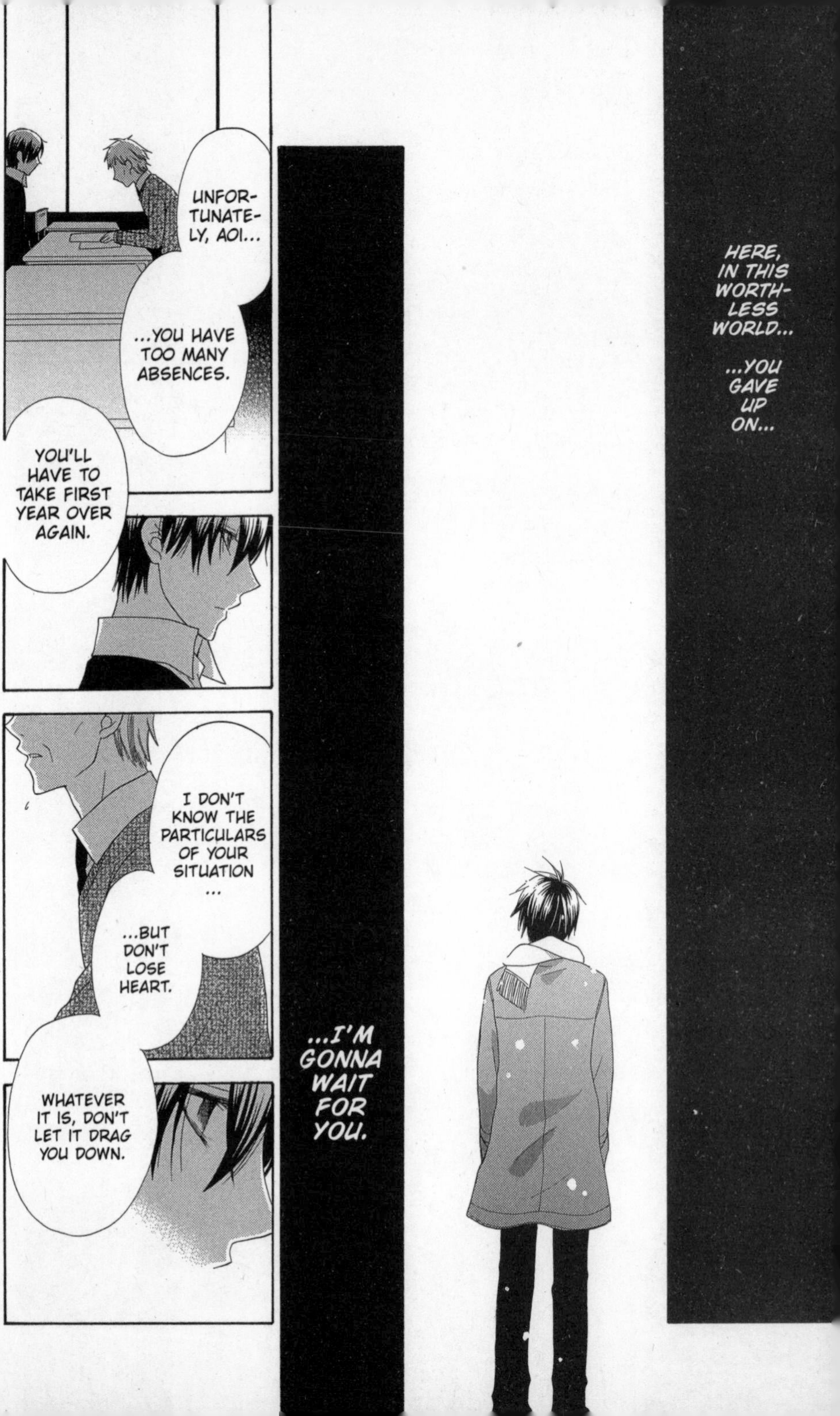
HERE, IN THIS WORTHLESS WORLD...
...YOU GAVE UP ON...
...I'M GONNA WAIT FOR YOU.
UNFORTUNATELY, AOI...
...YOU HAVE TOO MANY ABSENCES.
YOU'LL HAVE TO TAKE FIRST YEAR OVER AGAIN.
I DON'T KNOW THE PARTICULARS OF YOUR SITUATION...
...BUT DON'T LOSE HEART.
WHATEVER IT IS, DON'T LET IT DRAG YOU DOWN.

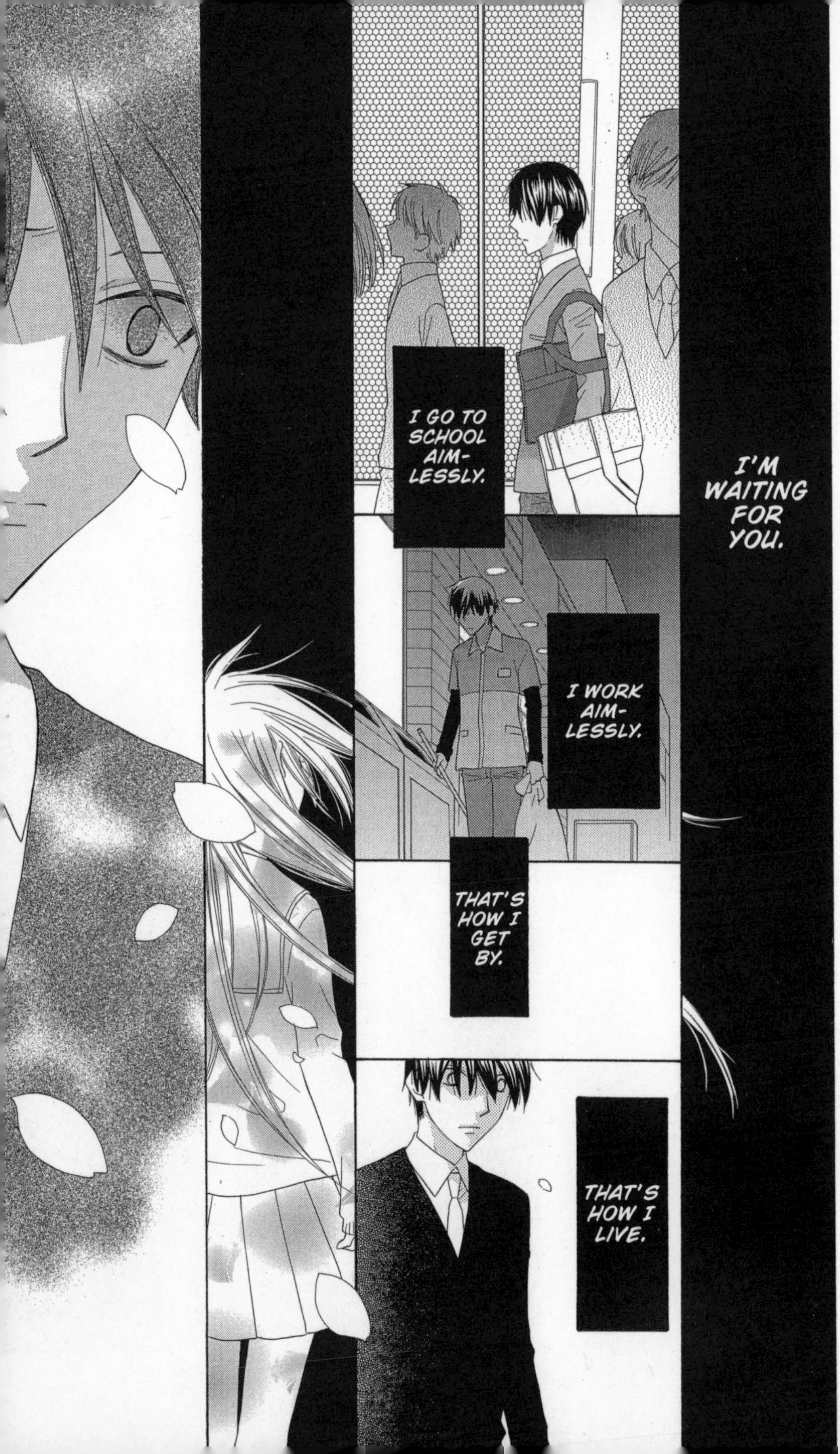
I'M WAITING FOR YOU.
I GO TO SCHOOL AIM-LESSLY.
I WORK AIM-LESSLY.
THAT'S HOW I GET BY.
THAT'S HOW I LIVE.

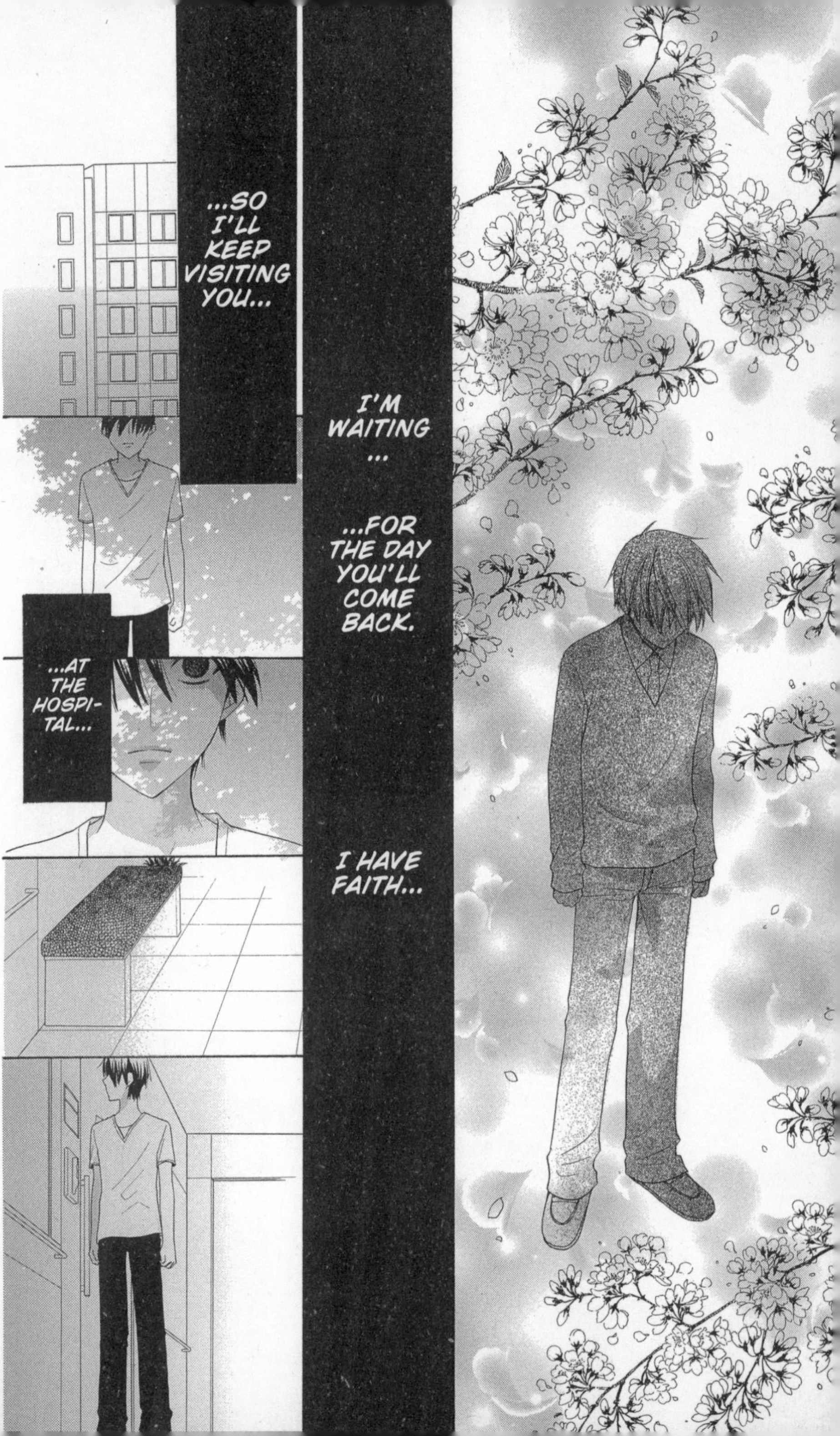
I'M WAITING ...
...FOR THE DAY YOU'LL COME BACK.
I HAVE FAITH...
...SO I'LL KEEP VISITING YOU...
...AT THE HOSPITAL...

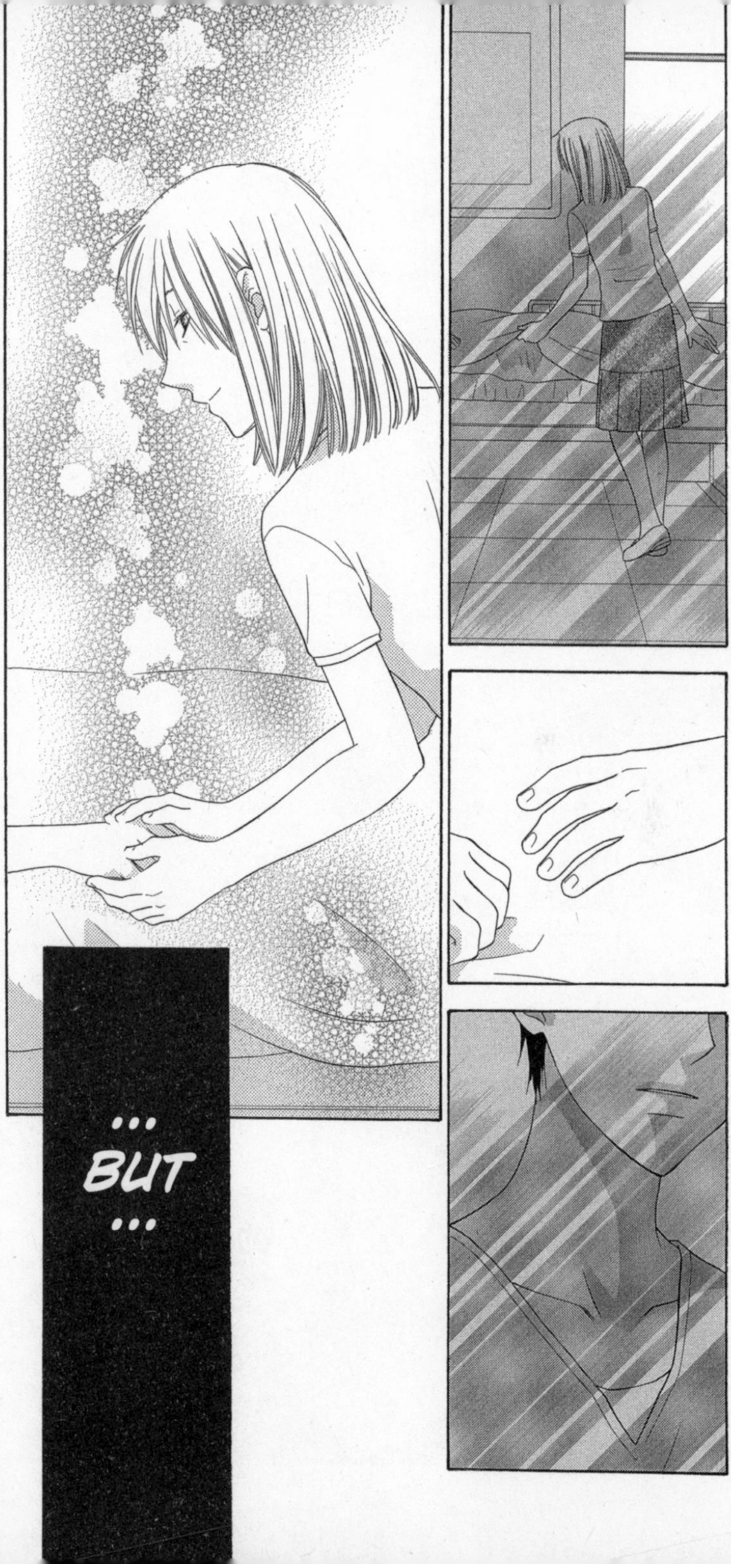
... BUT ...

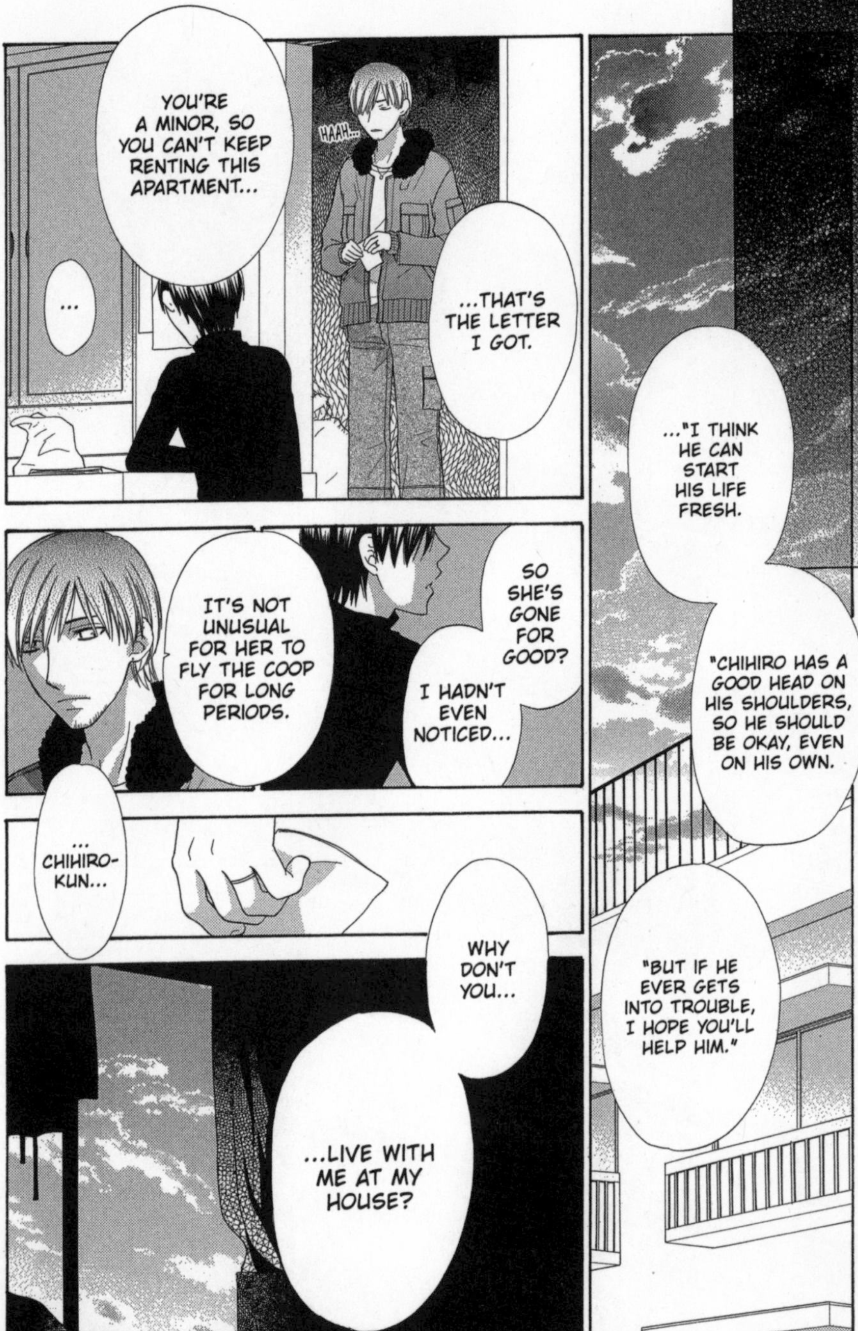
..."I THINK HE CAN START HIS LIFE FRESH.
"CHIHIRO HAS A GOOD HEAD ON HIS SHOULDERS, SO HE SHOULD BE OKAY, EVEN ON HIS OWN.
"BUT IF HE EVER GETS INTO TROUBLE, I HOPE YOU'LL HELP HIM."
YOU'RE A MINOR, SO YOU CAN'T KEEP RENTING THIS APARTMENT...
HAAH...
...THAT'S THE LETTER I GOT.
...
SO SHE'S GONE FOR GOOD?
I HADN'T EVEN NOTICED...
IT'S NOT UNUSUAL FOR HER TO FLY THE COOP FOR LONG PERIODS.
WHY DON'T YOU...
... CHIHIRO-KUN...
...LIVE WITH ME AT MY HOUSE?

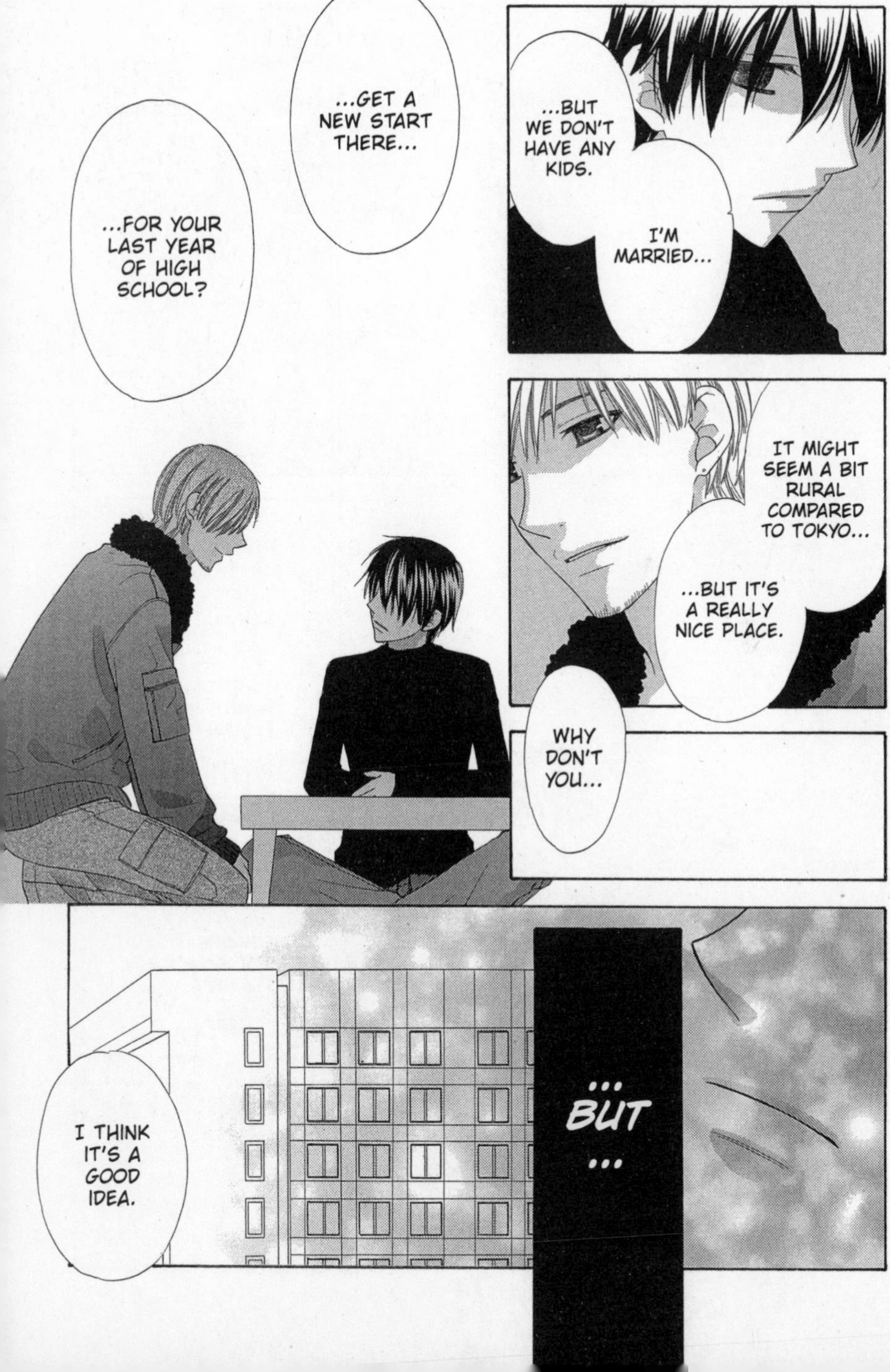

I'M MARRIED...
...BUT WE DON'T HAVE ANY KIDS.
IT MIGHT SEEM A BIT RURAL COMPARED TO TOKYO...
...BUT IT'S A REALLY NICE PLACE.
WHY DON'T YOU...
...GET A NEW START THERE...
...FOR YOUR LAST YEAR OF HIGH SCHOOL?
... BUT ...
I THINK IT'S A GOOD IDEA.

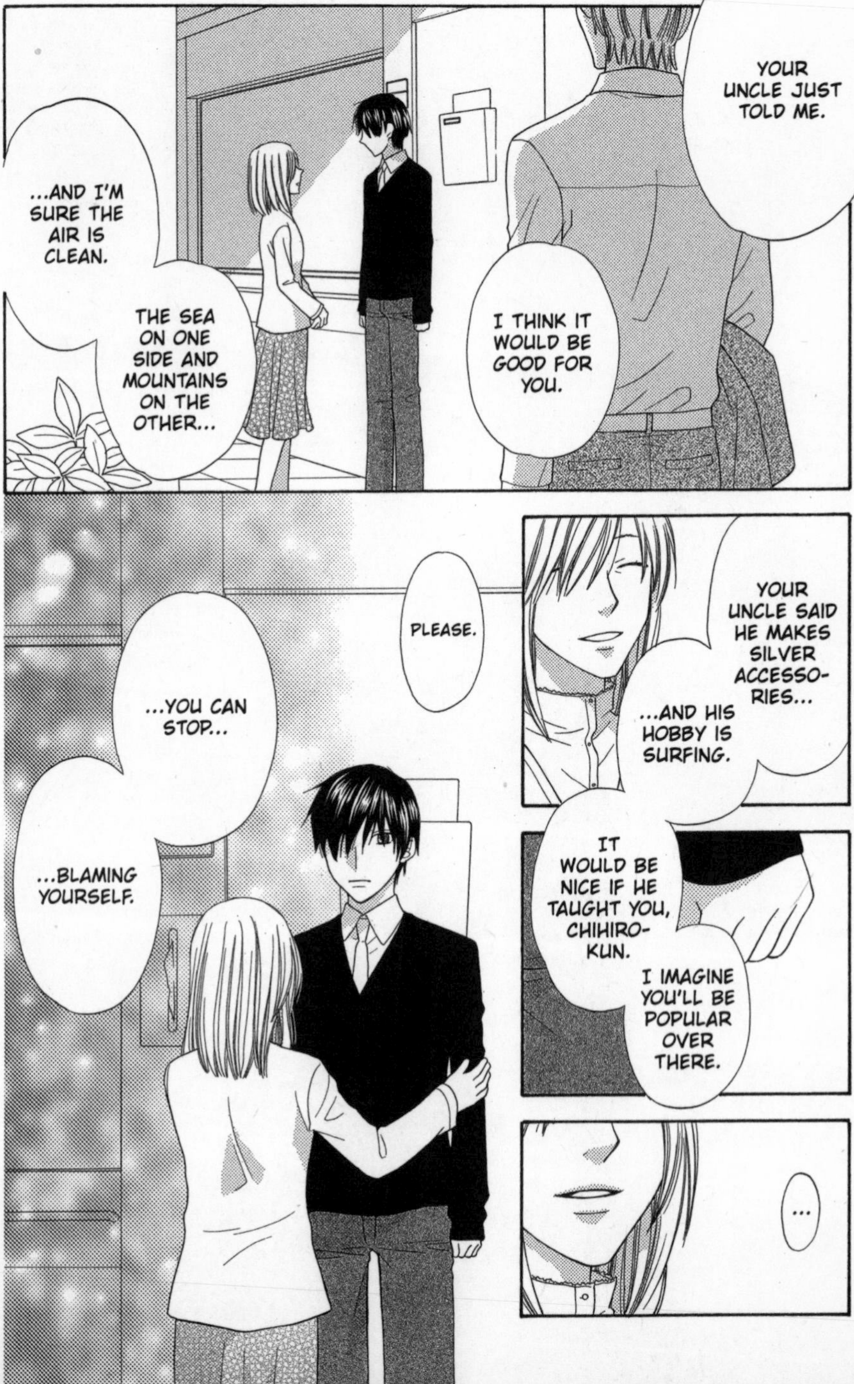
YOUR UNCLE JUST TOLD ME.
I THINK IT WOULD BE GOOD FOR YOU.
THE SEA ON ONE SIDE AND MOUNTAINS ON THE OTHER...
...AND I'M SURE THE AIR IS CLEAN.
YOUR UNCLE SAID HE MAKES SILVER ACCESSO-RIES...
...AND HIS HOBBY IS SURFING.
IT WOULD BE NICE IF HE TAUGHT YOU, CHIHIRO-KUN.
I IMAGINE YOU'LL BE POPULAR OVER THERE.
...
PLEASE.
...YOU CAN STOP...
...BLAMING YOURSELF.

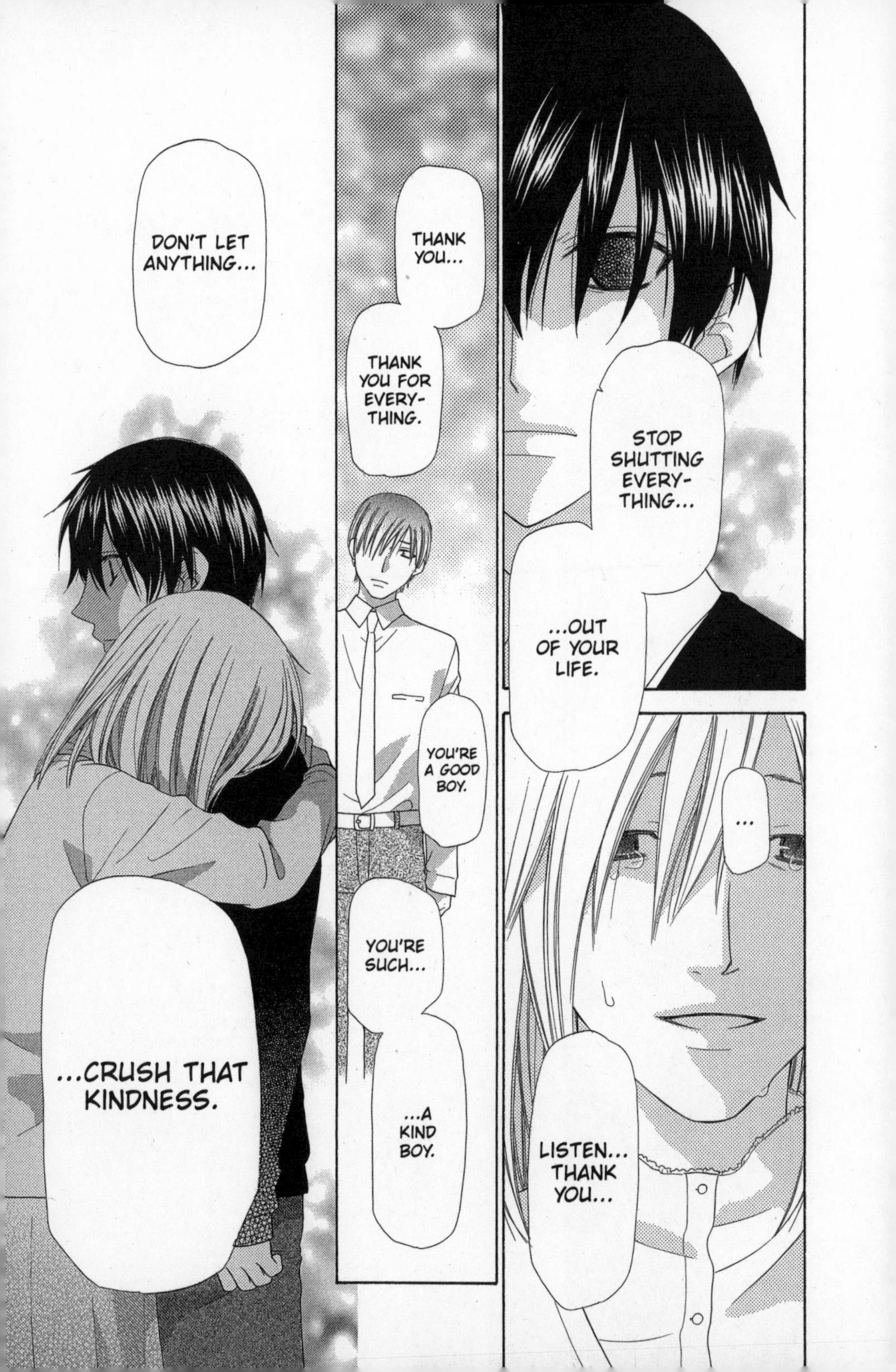
STOP SHUTTING EVERY-THING...
...OUT OF YOUR LIFE.
...
LISTEN... THANK YOU...
THANK YOU...
THANK YOU FOR EVERY-THING.
YOU'RE A GOOD BOY.
YOU'RE SUCH...
...A KIND BOY.
DON'T LET ANYTHING...
...CRUSH THAT KINDNESS.

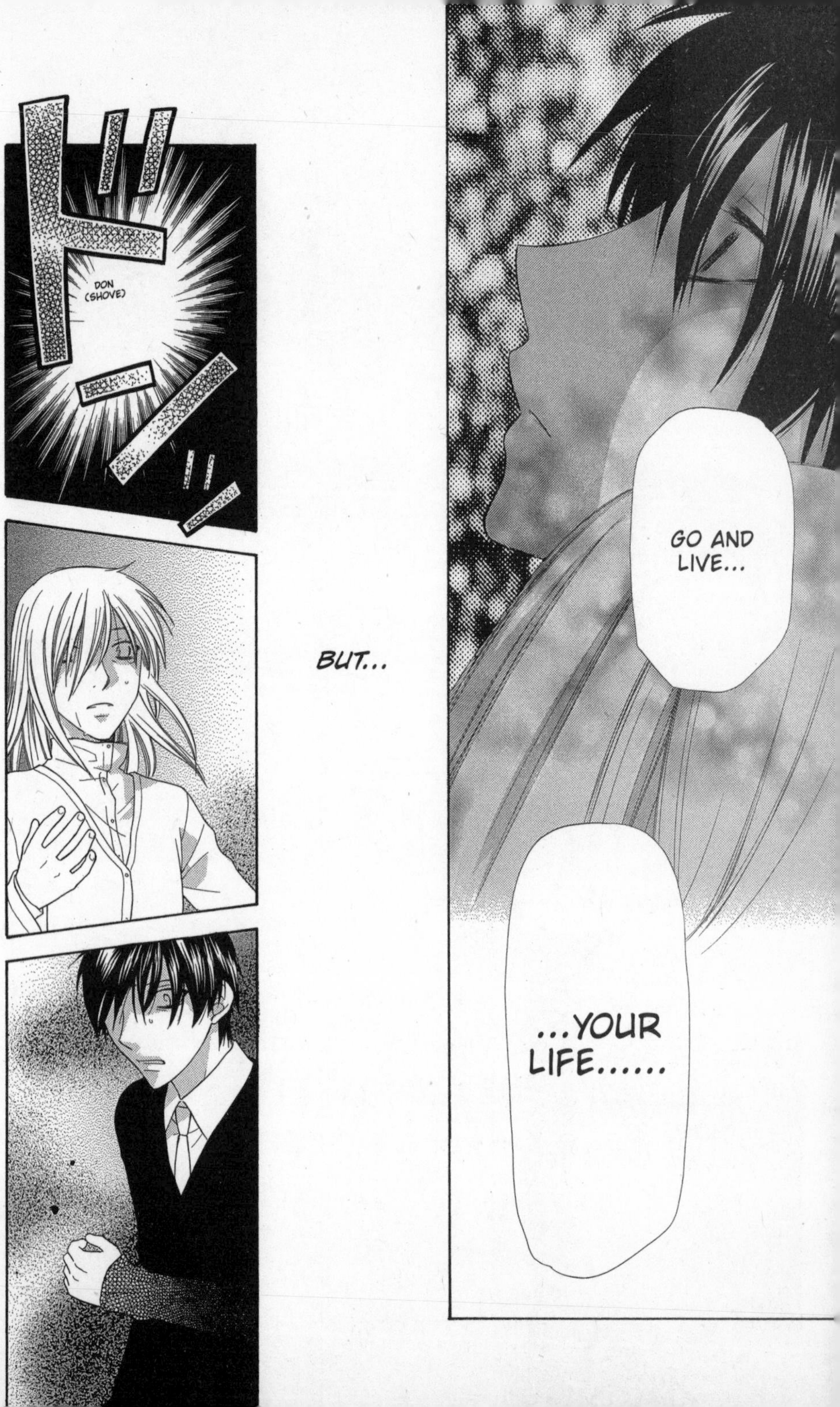
GO AND LIVE...
...YOUR LIFE......
BUT...
DON (SHOVE)

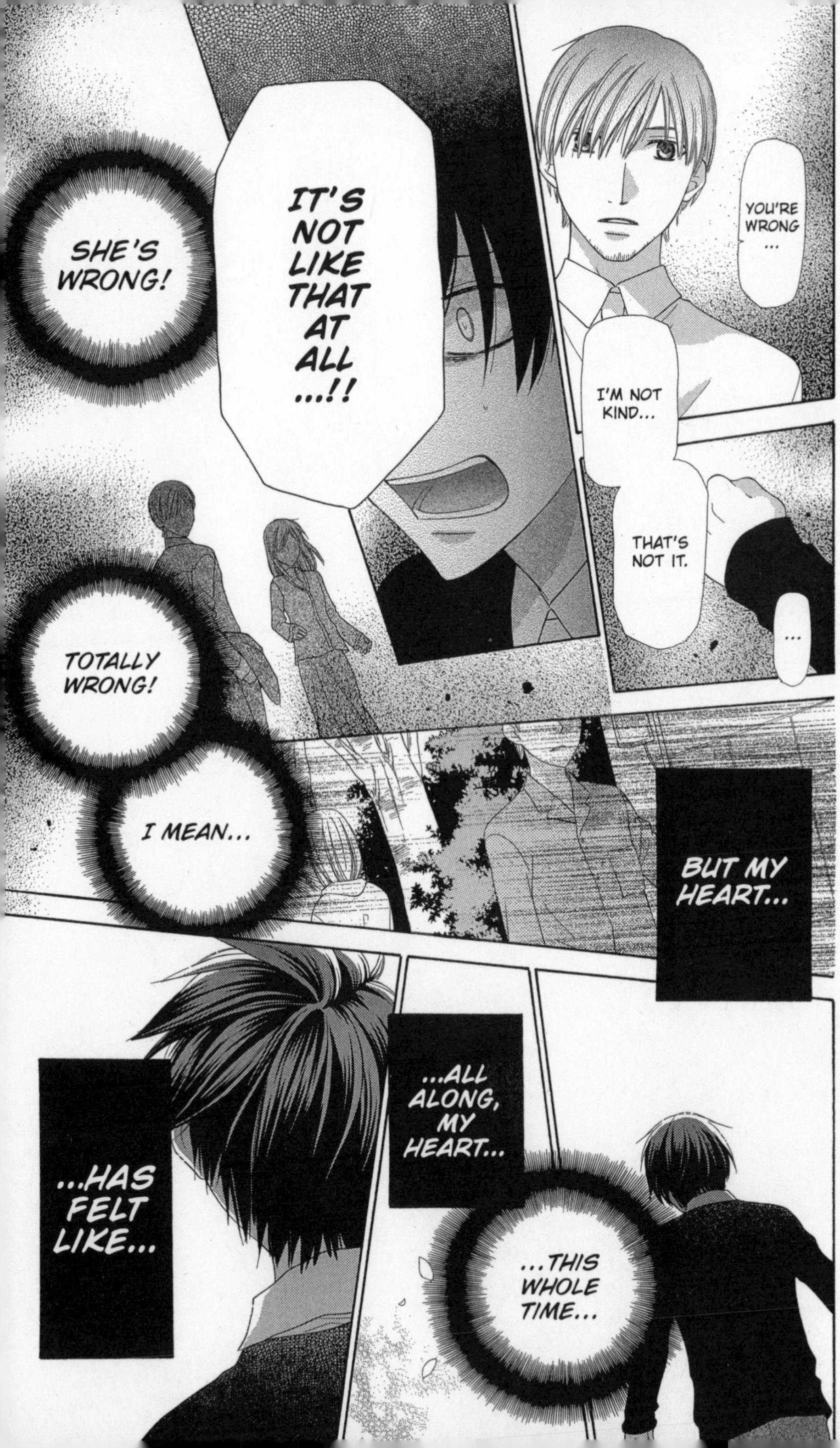
YOU'RE WRONG...
I'M NOT KIND...
THAT'S NOT IT.
...
IT'S NOT LIKE THAT AT ALL...!!
SHE'S WRONG!
TOTALLY WRONG!
I MEAN...
BUT MY HEART...
...ALL ALONG, MY HEART...
...THIS WHOLE TIME...
...HAS FELT LIKE...

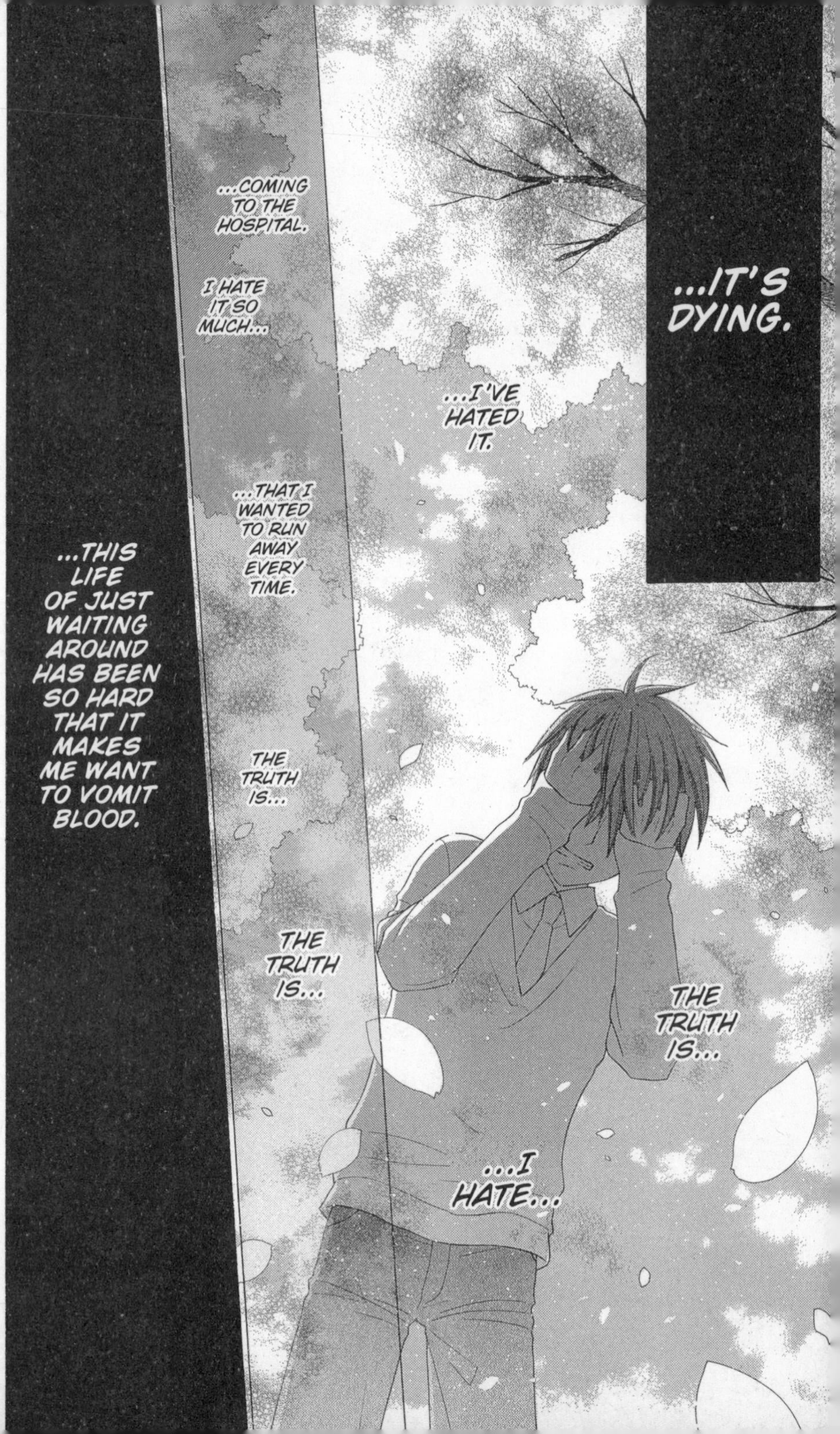
...IT'S DYING.
THE TRUTH IS...
THE TRUTH IS...
THE TRUTH IS...
...I HATE...
...COMING TO THE HOSPITAL.
I HATE IT SO MUCH...
...THAT I WANTED TO RUN AWAY EVERY TIME.
...I'VE HATED IT.
...THIS LIFE OF JUST WAITING AROUND HAS BEEN SO HARD THAT IT MAKES ME WANT TO VOMIT BLOOD.

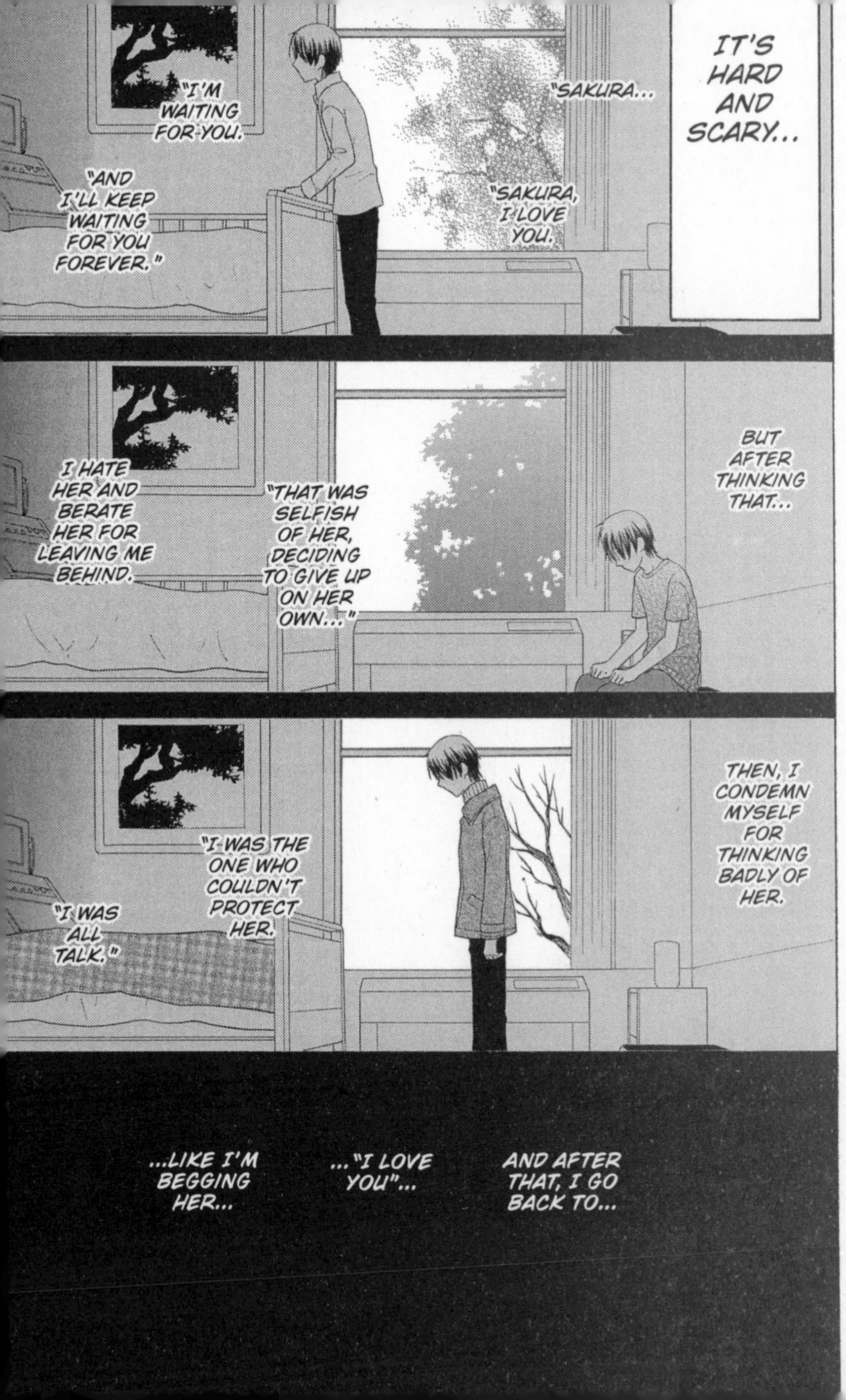
IT'S HARD AND SCARY...
"SAKURA...
"SAKURA, I LOVE YOU.
"I'M WAITING FOR YOU.
"AND I'LL KEEP WAITING FOR YOU FOREVER."
BUT AFTER THINKING THAT...
"THAT WAS SELFISH OF HER, DECIDING TO GIVE UP ON HER OWN..."
I HATE HER AND BERATE HER FOR LEAVING ME BEHIND.
THEN, I CONDEMN MYSELF FOR THINKING BADLY OF HER.
"I WAS THE ONE WHO COULDN'T PROTECT HER.
"I WAS ALL TALK."
AND AFTER THAT, I GO BACK TO...
..."I LOVE YOU"...
...LIKE I'M BEGGING HER...

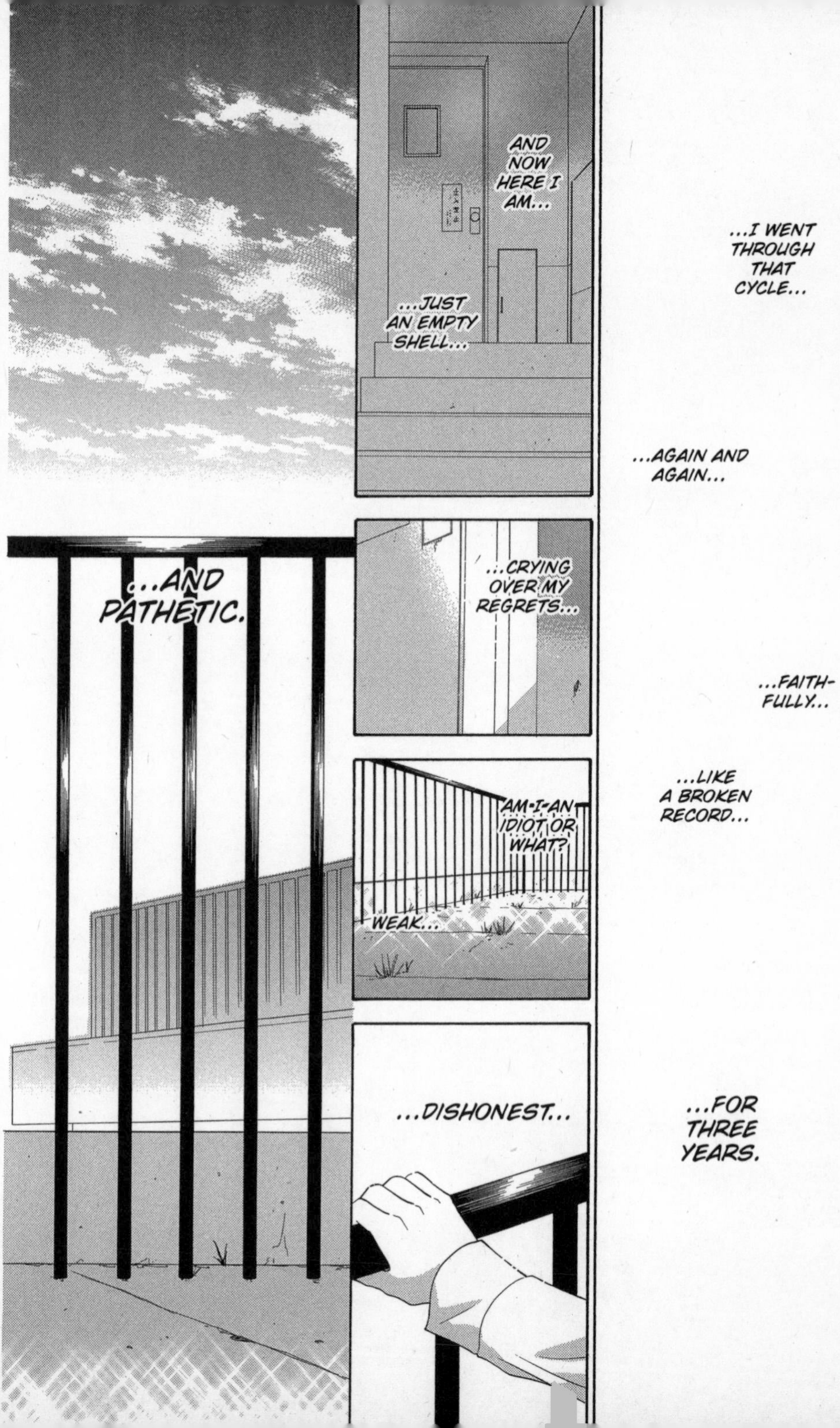
...I WENT THROUGH THAT CYCLE...
...AGAIN AND AGAIN...
...FAITH-FULLY...
...LIKE A BROKEN RECORD...
...FOR THREE YEARS.
AND NOW HERE I AM...
...JUST AN EMPTY SHELL...
...CRYING OVER MY REGRETS...
AM-I-AN IDIOT OR WHAT?
WEAK...
...DISHONEST...
...AND PATHETIC.

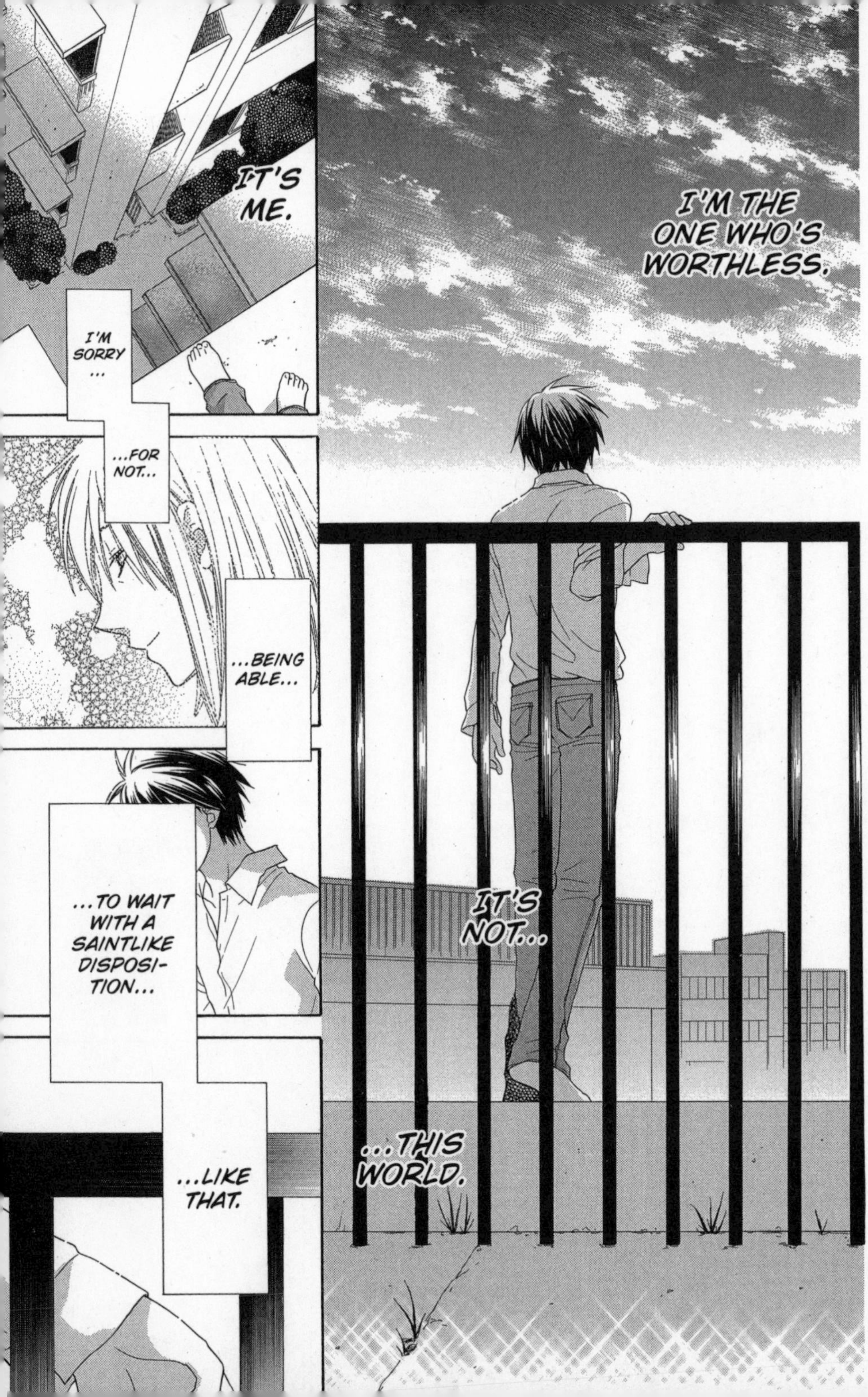
I'M THE ONE WHO'S WORTHLESS.
IT'S NOT...
...THIS WORLD.
IT'S ME.
I'M SORRY...
...FOR NOT...
...BEING ABLE...
...TO WAIT WITH A SAINTLIKE DISPOSITION...
...LIKE THAT.

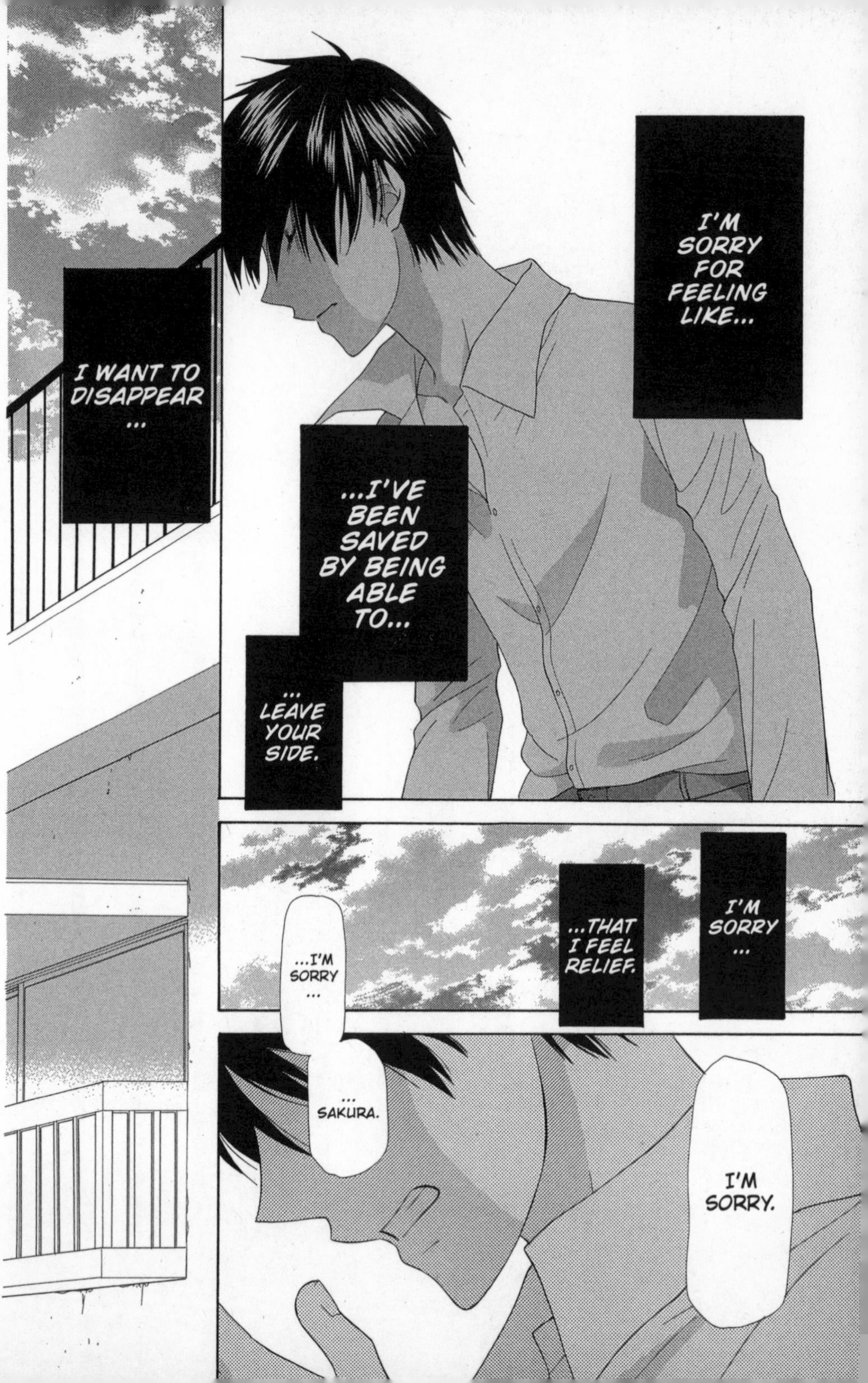

I'M SORRY FOR FEELING LIKE...
I WANT TO DISAPPEAR ...
...I'VE BEEN SAVED BY BEING ABLE TO...
... LEAVE YOUR SIDE.
I'M SORRY ...
...THAT I FEEL RELIEF.
...I'M SORRY ...
I'M SORRY.
... SAKURA.

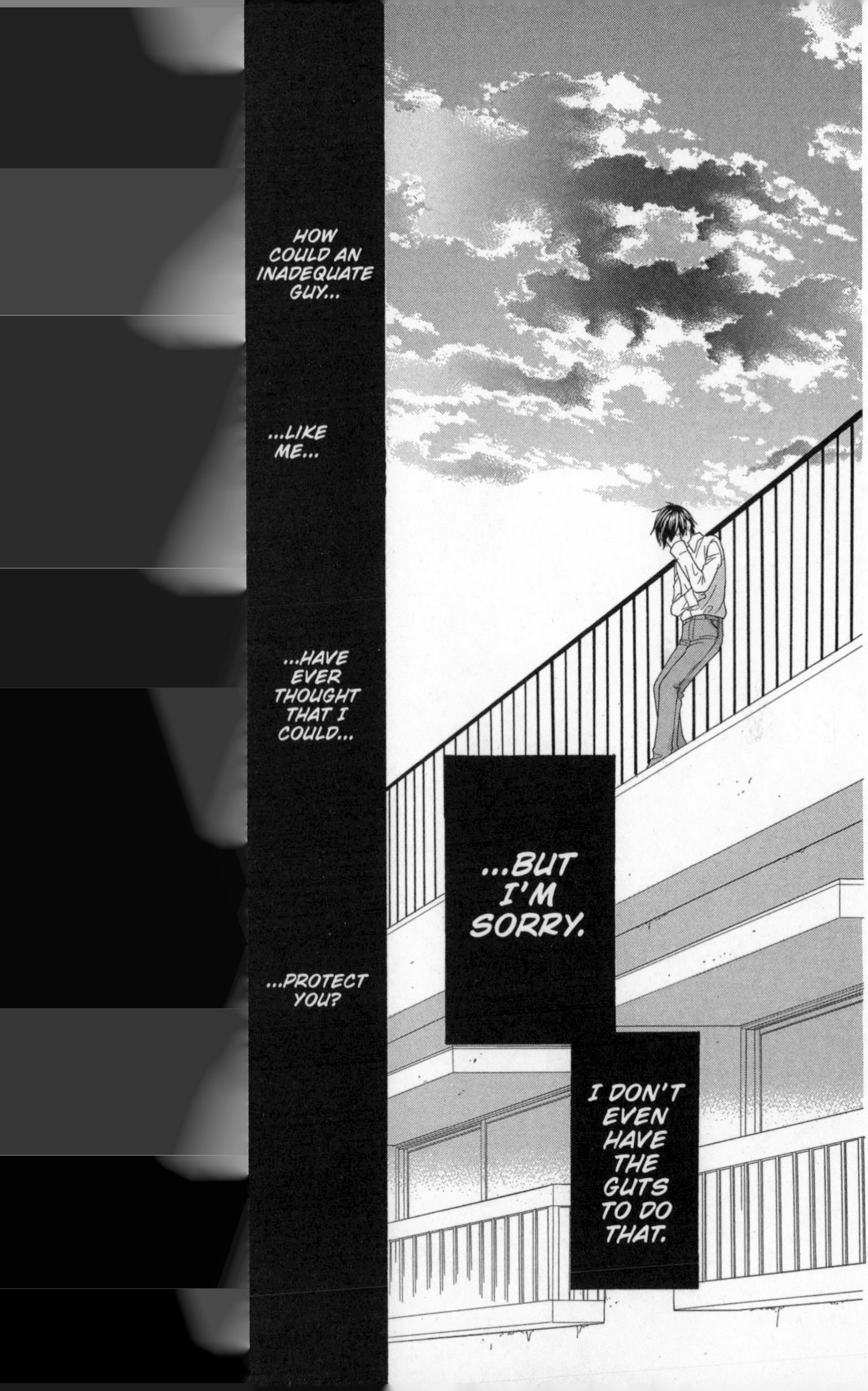
HOW COULD AN INADEQUATE GUY...
...LIKE ME...
...HAVE EVER THOUGHT THAT I COULD...
...PROTECT YOU?
...BUT I'M SORRY.
I DON'T EVEN HAVE THE GUTS TO DO THAT.

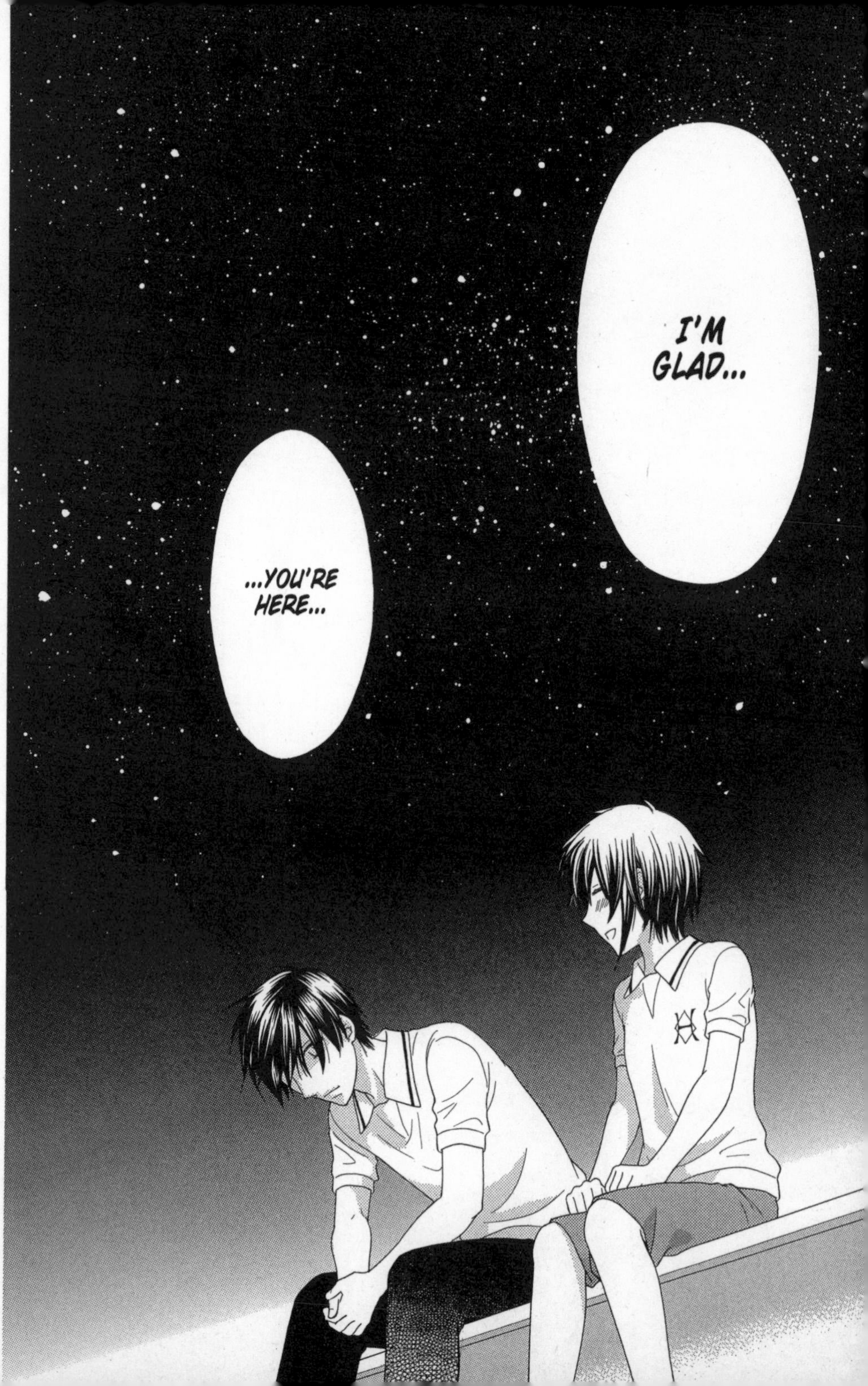
I'M GLAD...
...YOU'RE HERE...

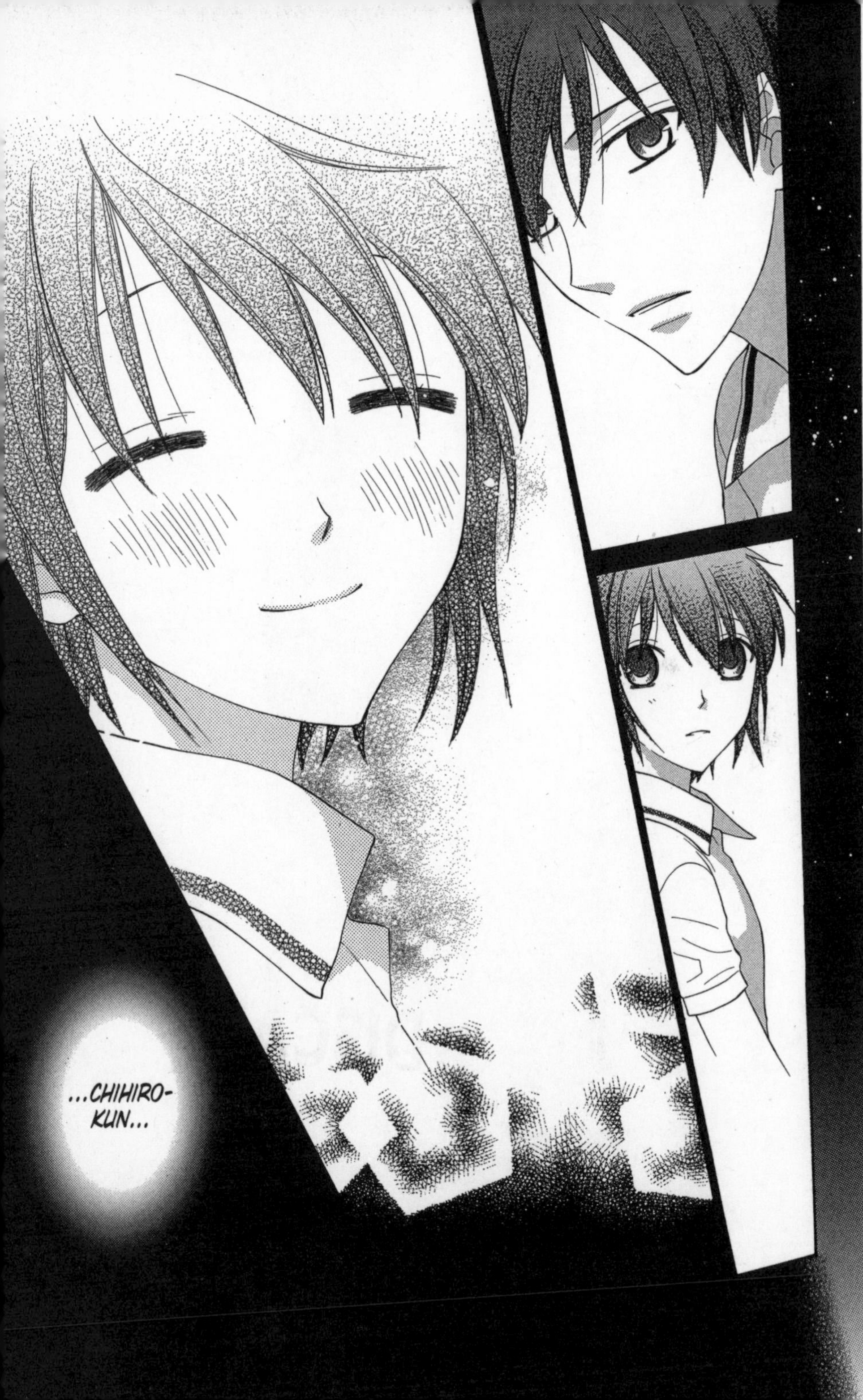
...CHIHIRO-KUN...

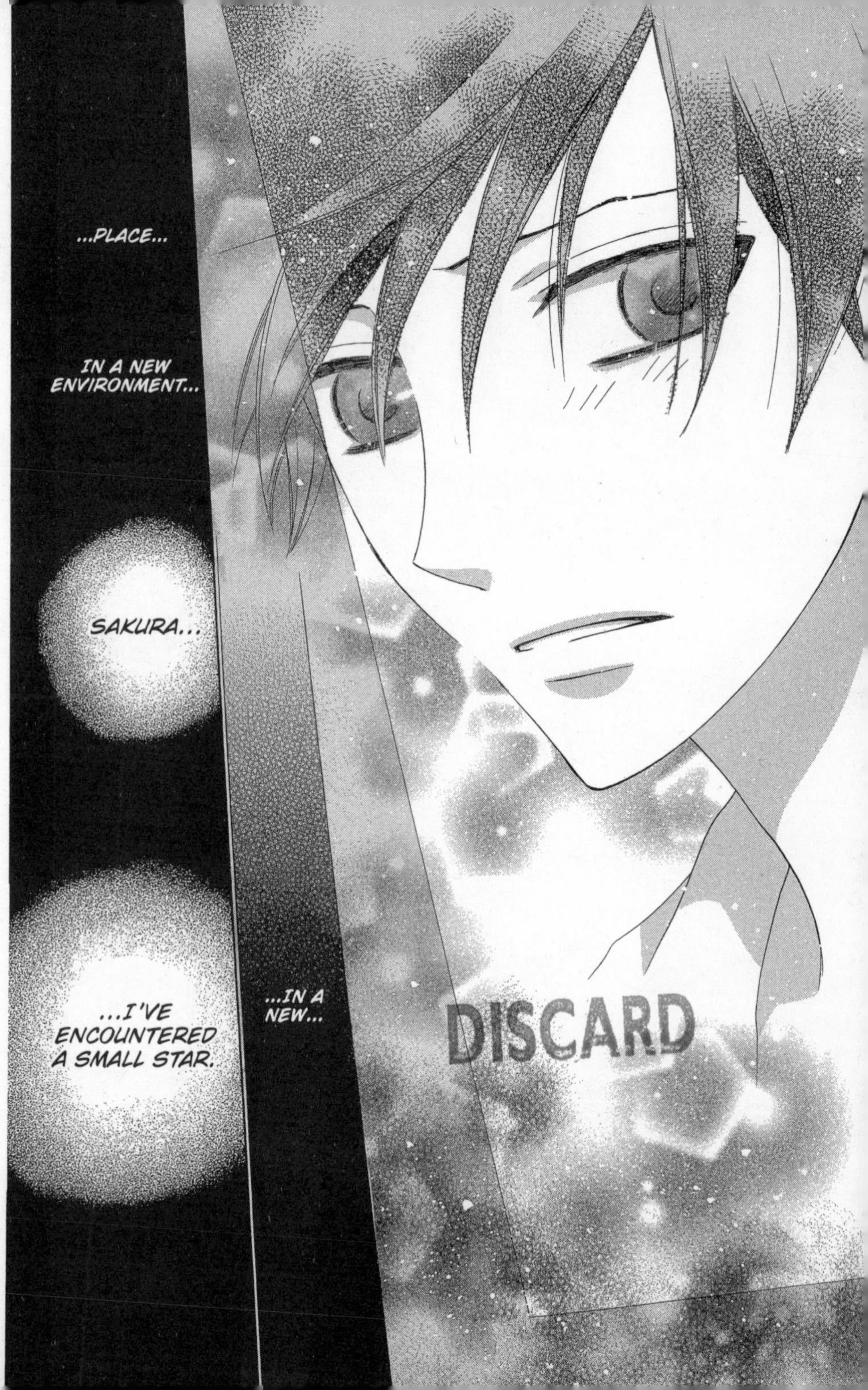
...IN A NEW...
...PLACE...
IN A NEW ENVIRONMENT...
SAKURA...
...I'VE ENCOUNTERED A SMALL STAR.

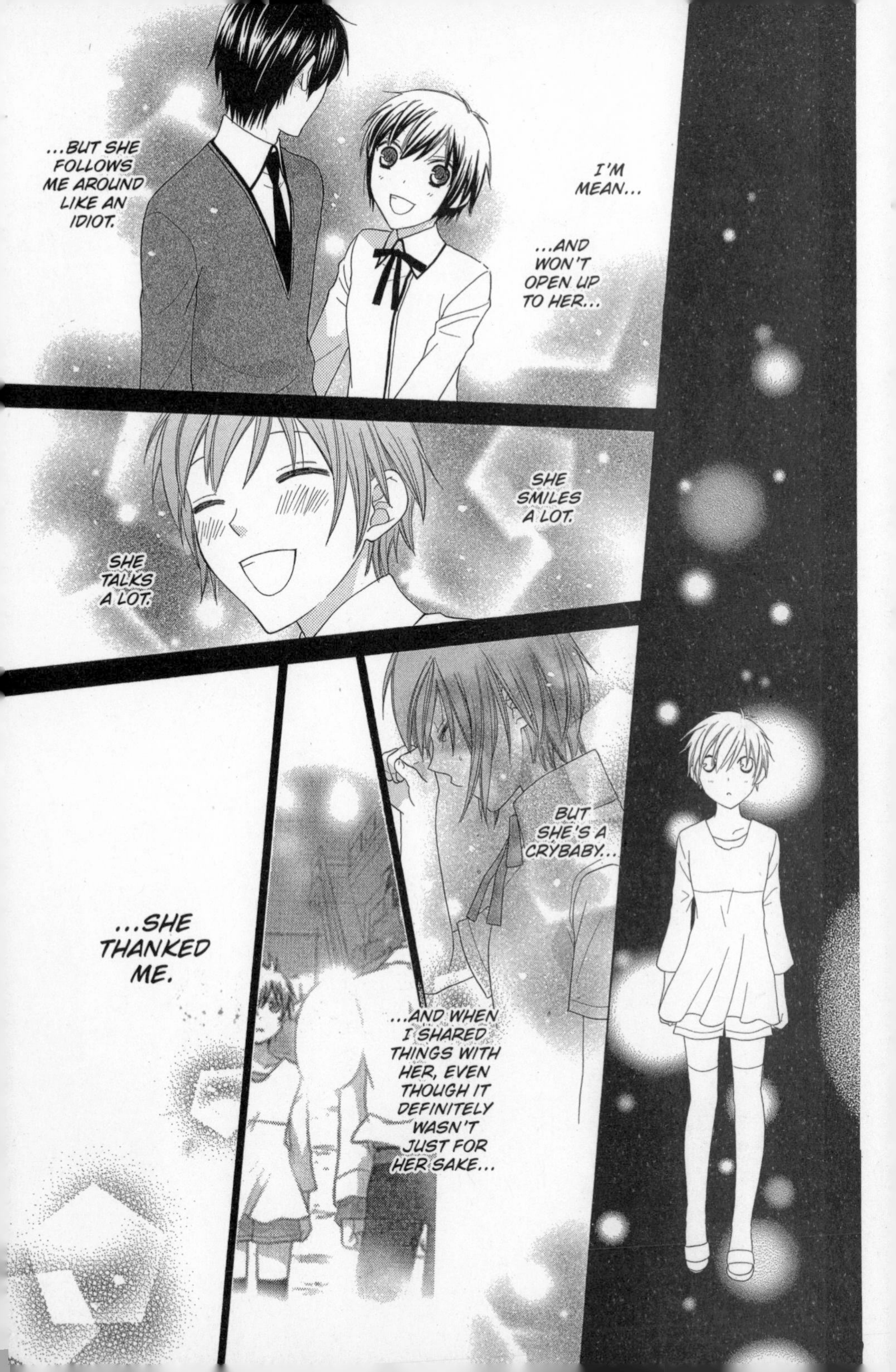
I'M MEAN...
...AND WON'T OPEN UP TO HER...
...BUT SHE FOLLOWS ME AROUND LIKE AN IDIOT.
SHE SMILES A LOT.
SHE TALKS A LOT.
BUT SHE'S A CRYBABY...
...AND WHEN I SHARED THINGS WITH HER, EVEN THOUGH IT DEFINITELY WASN'T JUST FOR HER SAKE...
...SHE THANKED ME.

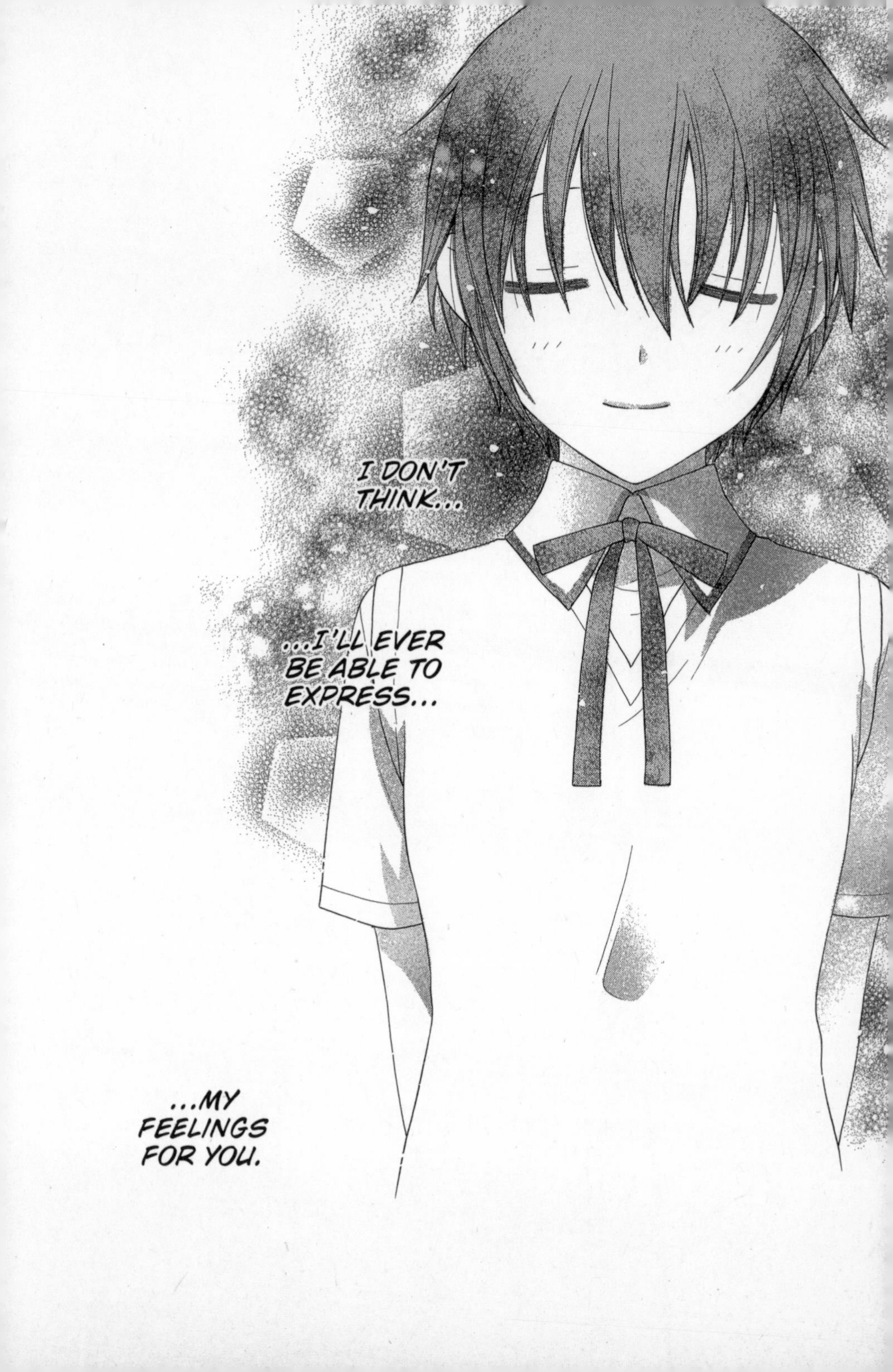
I DON'T THINK...
...I'LL EVER BE ABLE TO EXPRESS...
...MY FEELINGS FOR YOU.

Feelings of Gratitude ♪

Harada-sama   Araki-sama

Mother   My editor

Everyone who supports me
and reads this series

高屋 奈月。
Natsuki Takaya

TwinkleStars

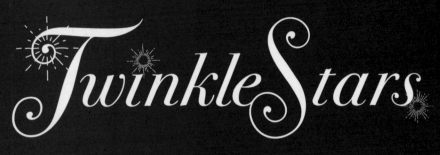

Twinkle Stars

Natsuki Takaya

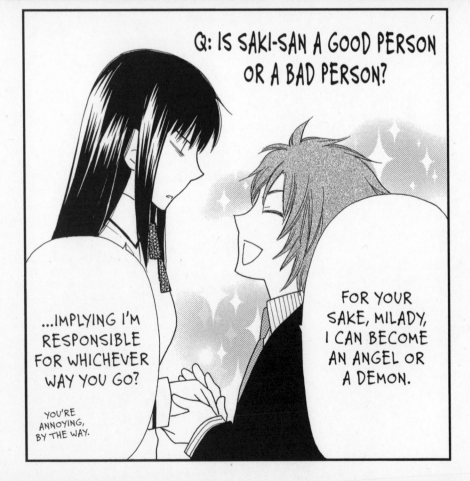

Q: IS SAKI-SAN A GOOD PERSON OR A BAD PERSON?
FOR YOUR SAKE, MILADY, I CAN BECOME AN ANGEL OR A DEMON.
...IMPLYING I'M RESPONSIBLE FOR WHICHEVER WAY YOU GO?
YOU'RE ANNOYING, BY THE WAY.

Twinkle Stars

Chapter 30

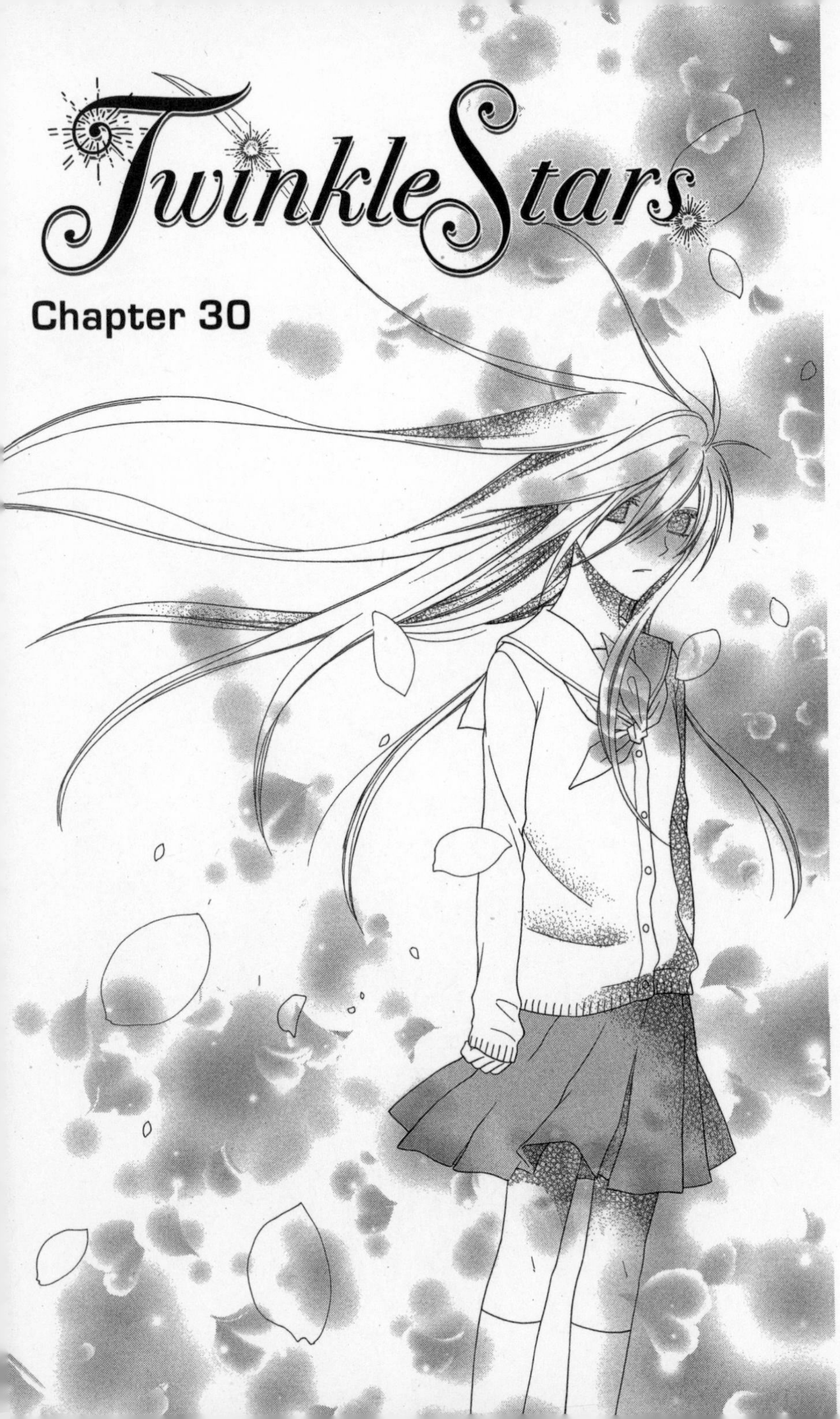

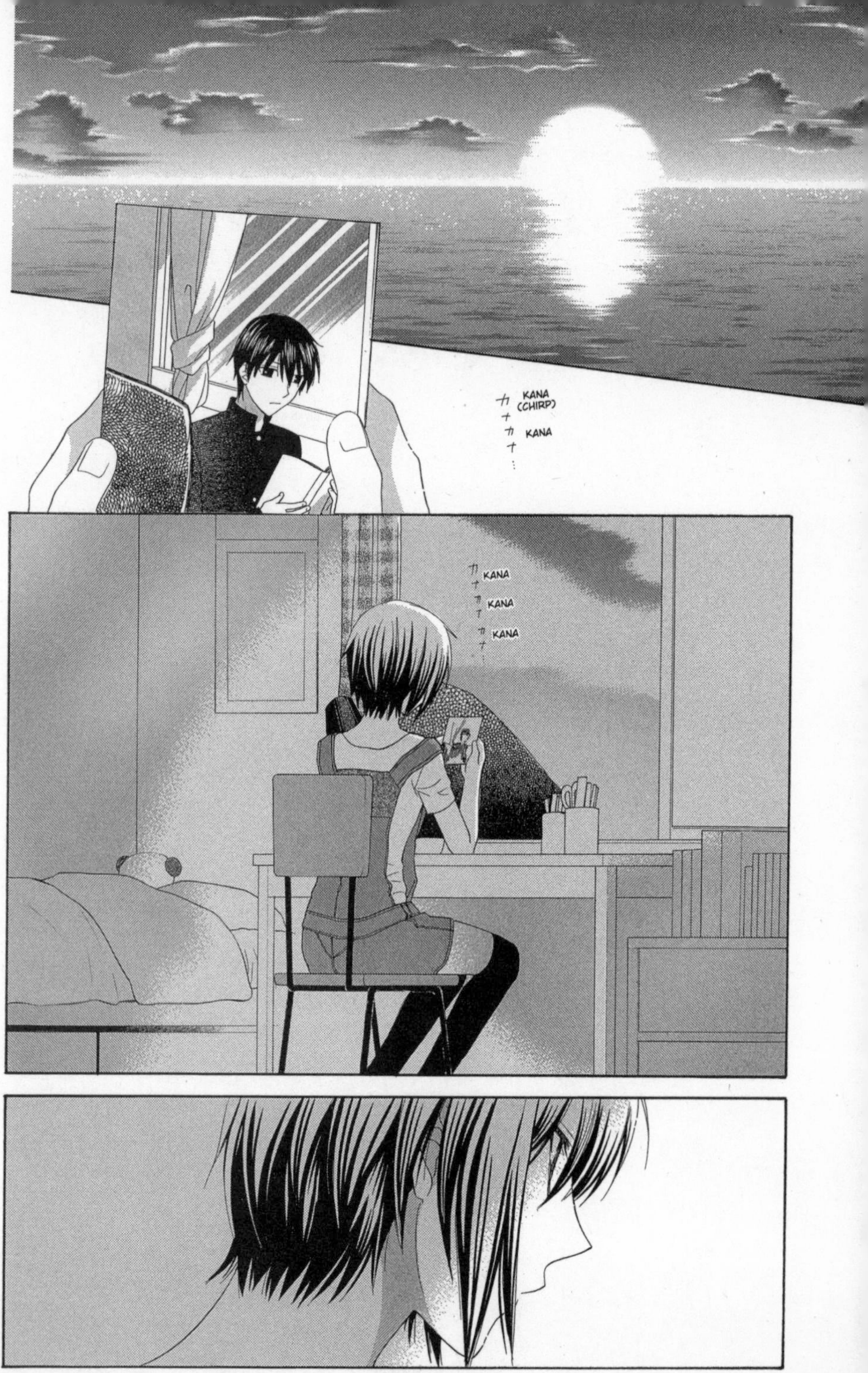
カナカナ…
KANA (CHIRP)
KANA
カナカナカナ…
KANA
KANA
KANA

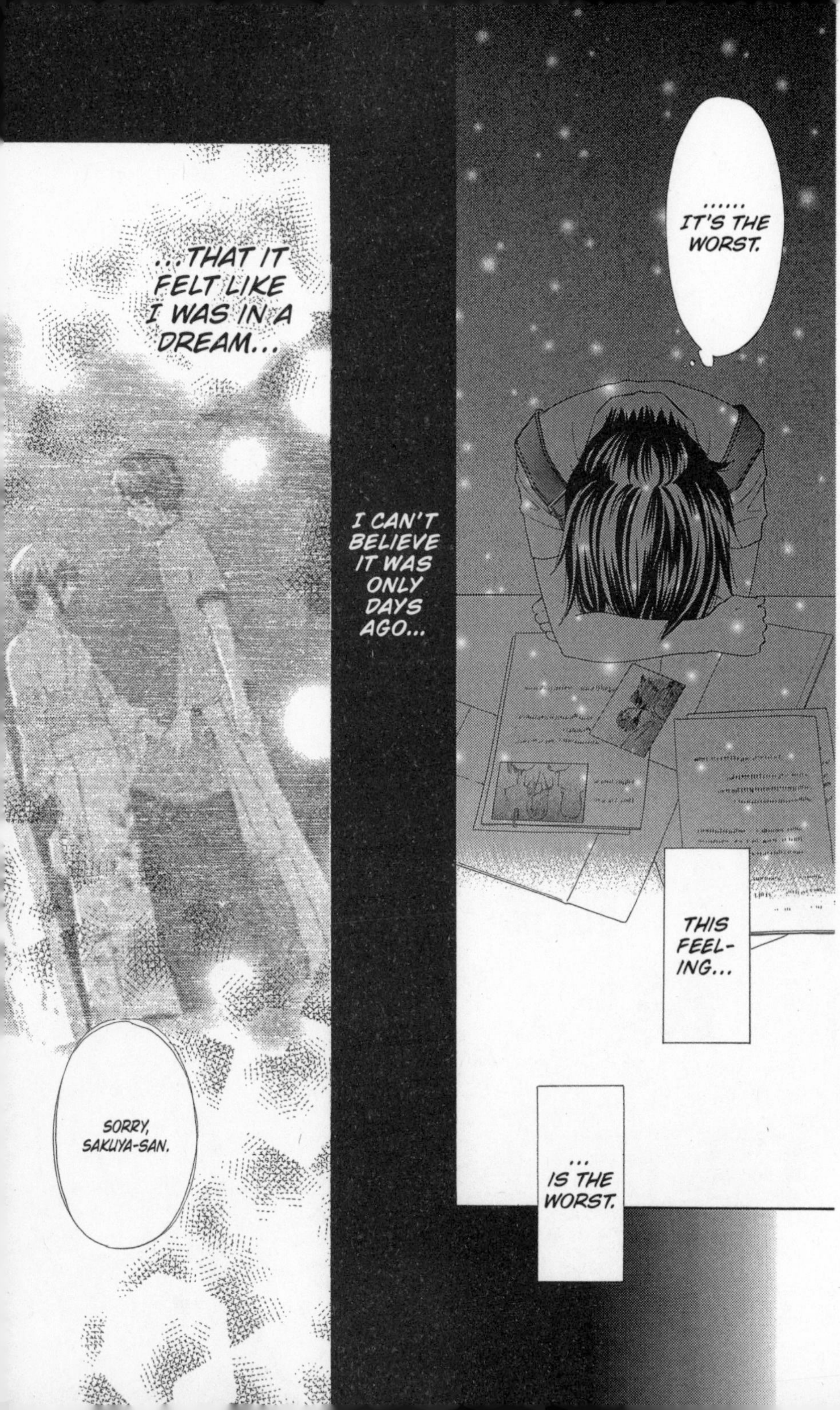

...... IT'S THE WORST.
THIS FEEL-ING...
... IS THE WORST.
I CAN'T BELIEVE IT WAS ONLY DAYS AGO...
...THAT IT FELT LIKE I WAS IN A DREAM...
SORRY, SAKUYA-SAN.

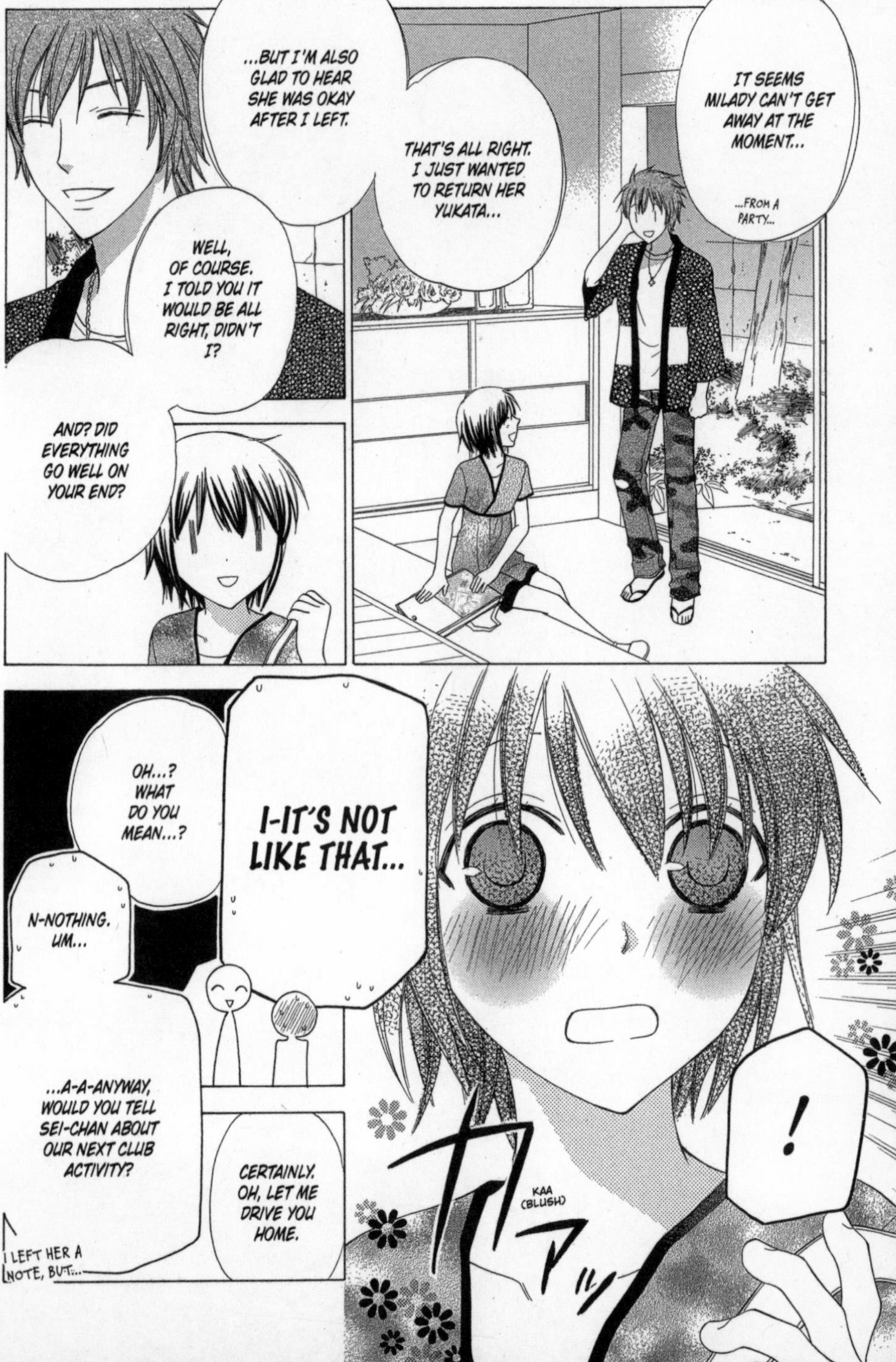
IT SEEMS MILADY CAN'T GET AWAY AT THE MOMENT...
...FROM A PARTY...
THAT'S ALL RIGHT. I JUST WANTED TO RETURN HER YUKATA...
...BUT I'M ALSO GLAD TO HEAR SHE WAS OKAY AFTER I LEFT.
WELL, OF COURSE. I TOLD YOU IT WOULD BE ALL RIGHT, DIDN'T I?
AND? DID EVERYTHING GO WELL ON YOUR END?
!
KAA (BLUSH)
I-IT'S NOT LIKE THAT...
OH...? WHAT DO YOU MEAN...?
N-NOTHING. UM...
...A-A-ANYWAY, WOULD YOU TELL SEI-CHAN ABOUT OUR NEXT CLUB ACTIVITY?
CERTAINLY. OH, LET ME DRIVE YOU HOME.
I LEFT HER A NOTE, BUT...

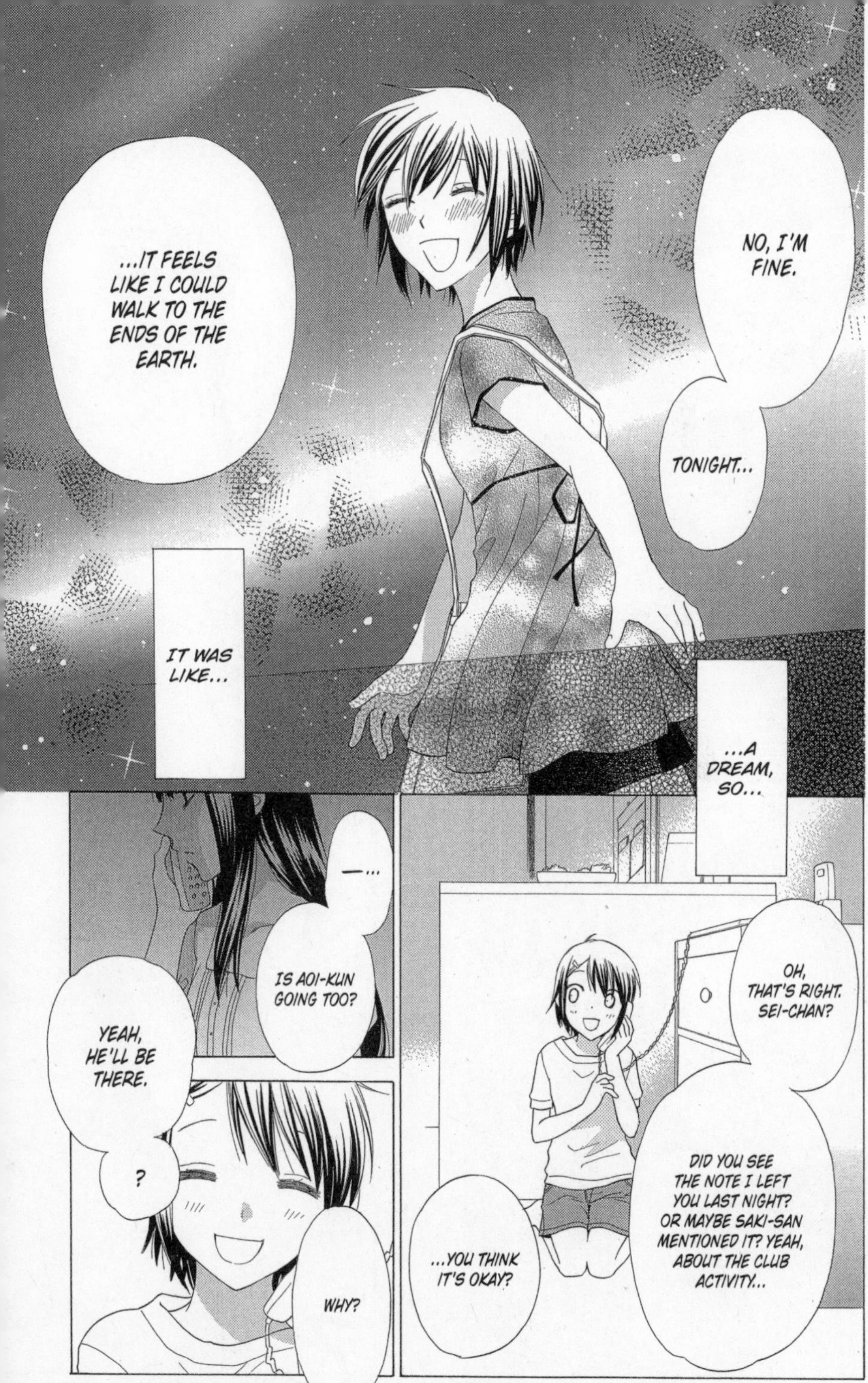

NO, I'M FINE.
TONIGHT...
...IT FEELS LIKE I COULD WALK TO THE ENDS OF THE EARTH.
IT WAS LIKE...
...A DREAM, SO...
OH, THAT'S RIGHT. SEI-CHAN?
DID YOU SEE THE NOTE I LEFT YOU LAST NIGHT? OR MAYBE SAKI-SAN MENTIONED IT? YEAH, ABOUT THE CLUB ACTIVITY...
...YOU THINK IT'S OKAY?
—...
IS AOI-KUN GOING TOO?
YEAH, HE'LL BE THERE.
?
WHY?

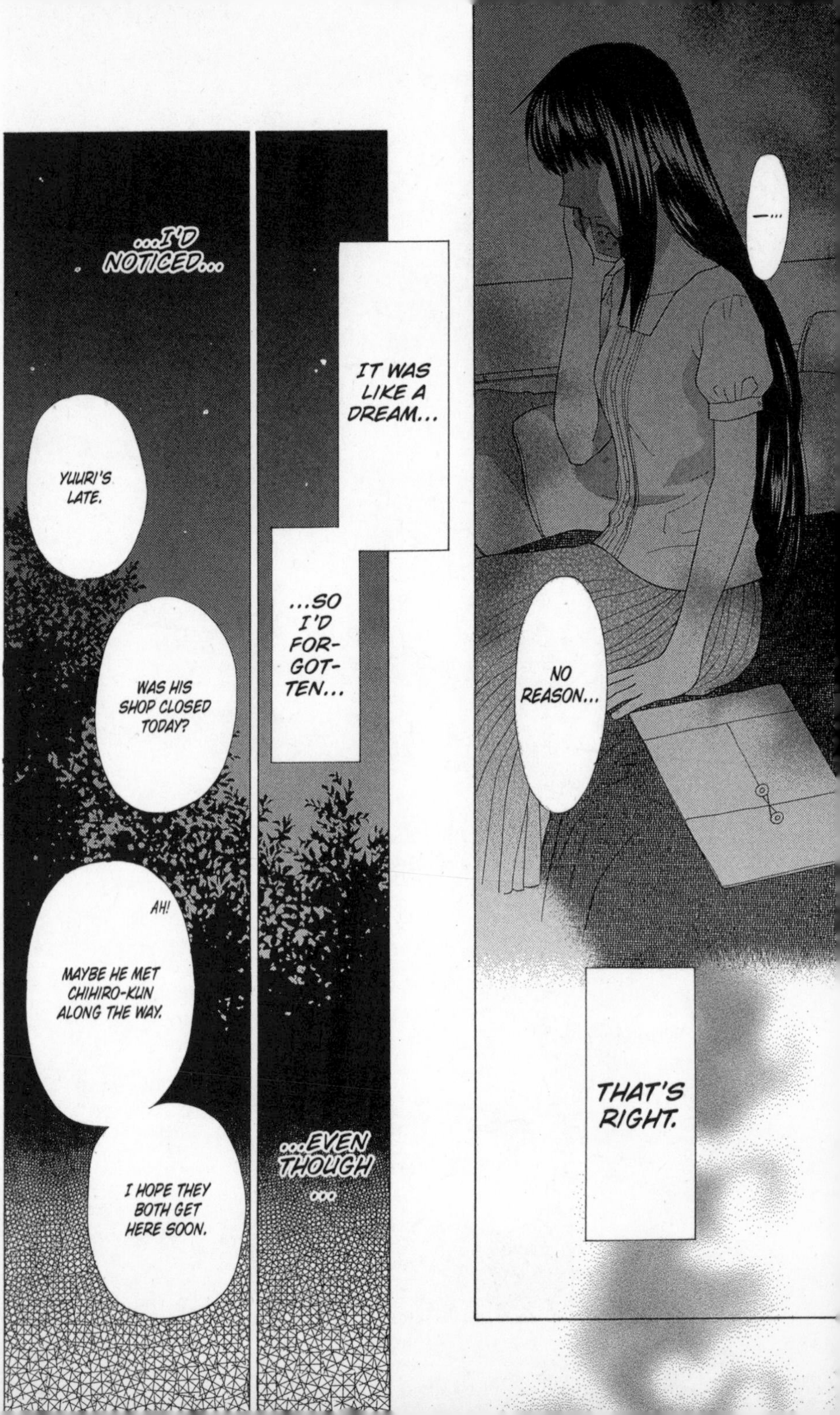
—...
NO REASON...
THAT'S RIGHT.
IT WAS LIKE A DREAM...
...SO I'D FORGOTTEN...
...EVEN THOUGH...
...I'D NOTICED...
YUURI'S LATE.
WAS HIS SHOP CLOSED TODAY?
AH!
MAYBE HE MET CHIHIRO-KUN ALONG THE WAY.
I HOPE THEY BOTH GET HERE SOON.

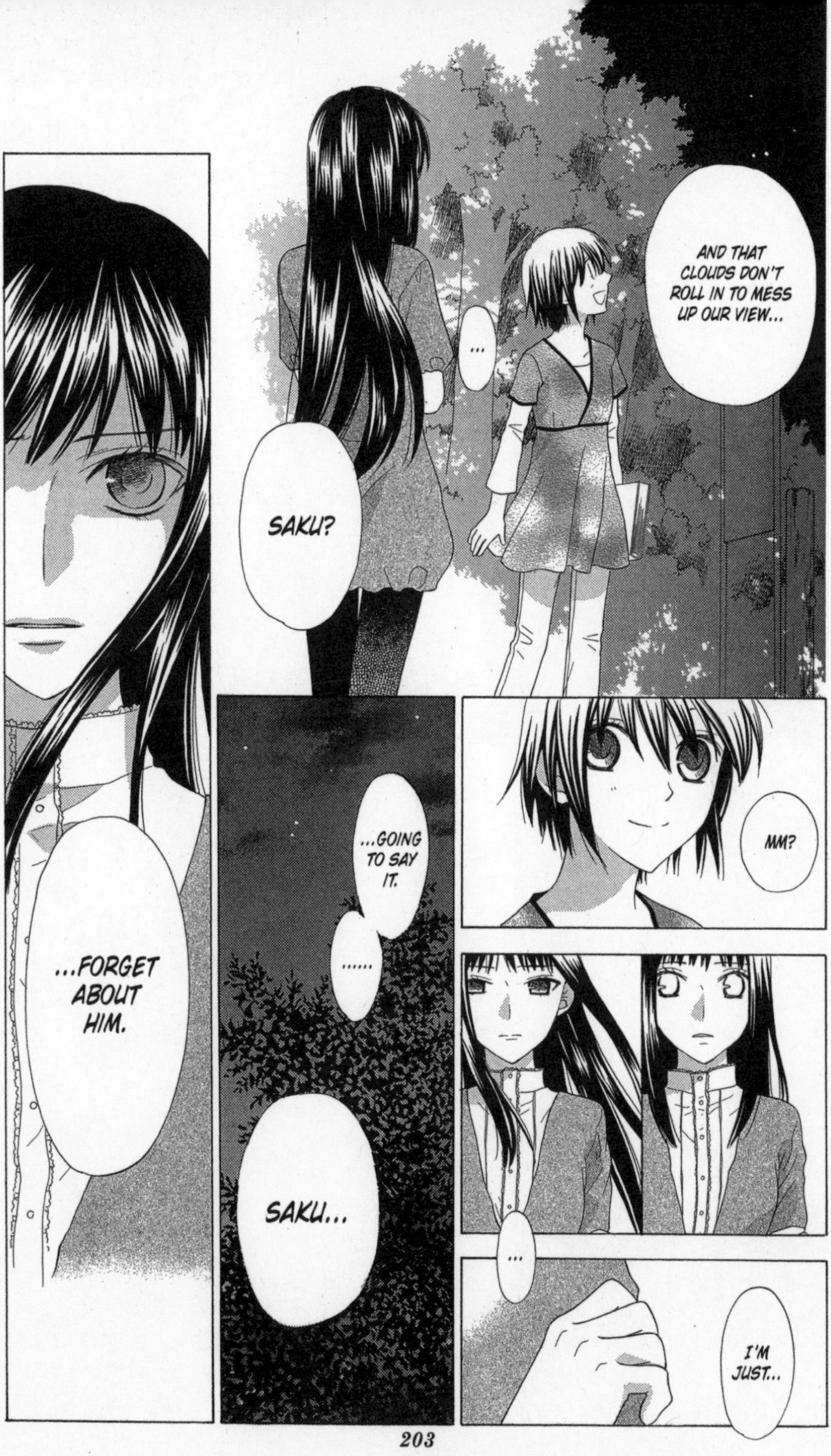
AND THAT CLOUDS DON'T ROLL IN TO MESS UP OUR VIEW...
...
SAKU?
MM?
...
I'M JUST...
...GOING TO SAY IT.
......
SAKU...
...FORGET ABOUT HIM.

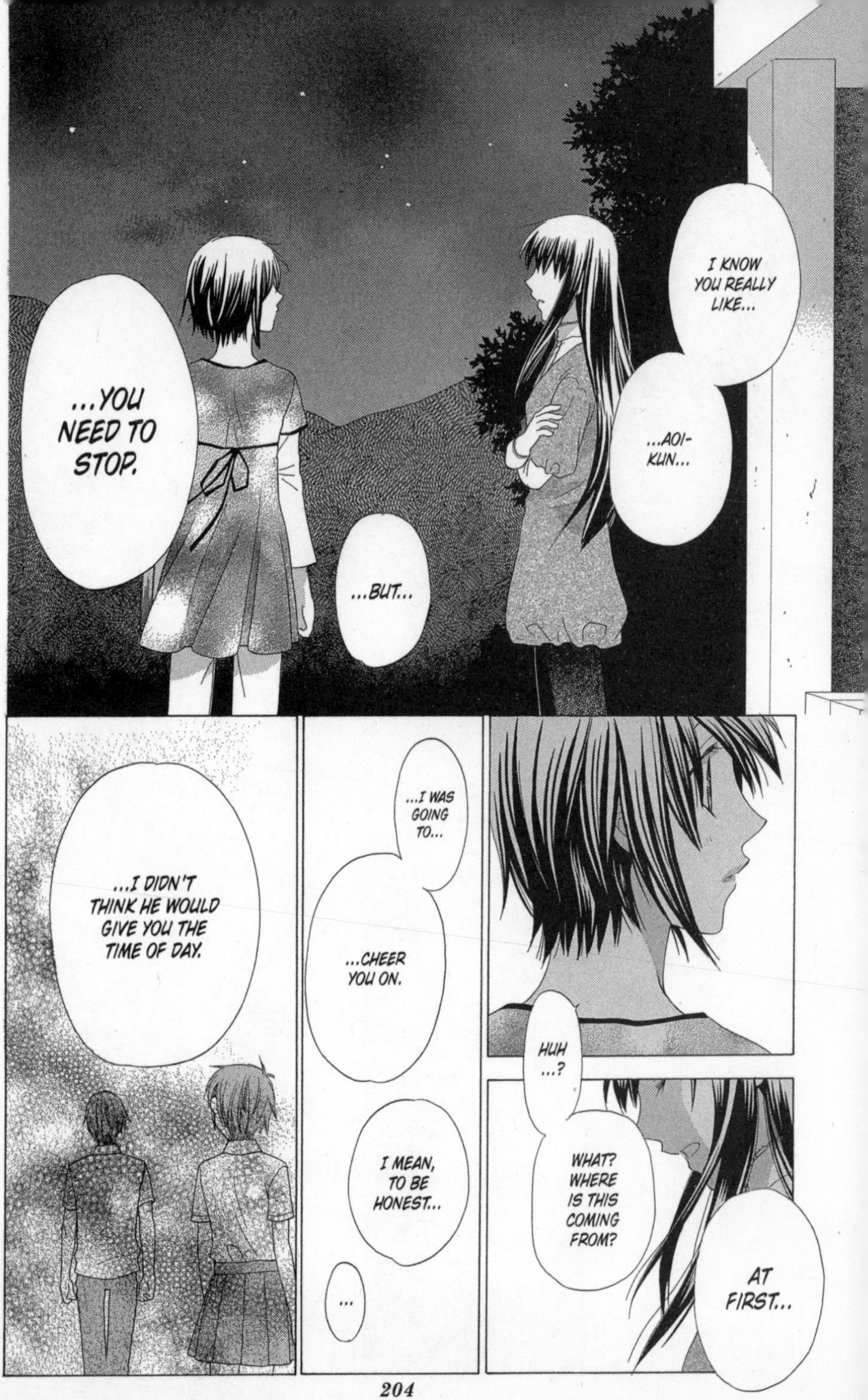
I KNOW YOU REALLY LIKE...
...AOI-KUN...
...BUT...
...YOU NEED TO STOP.
HUH ...?
WHAT? WHERE IS THIS COMING FROM?
AT FIRST...
...I WAS GOING TO...
...CHEER YOU ON.
I MEAN, TO BE HONEST...
...
...I DIDN'T THINK HE WOULD GIVE YOU THE TIME OF DAY.

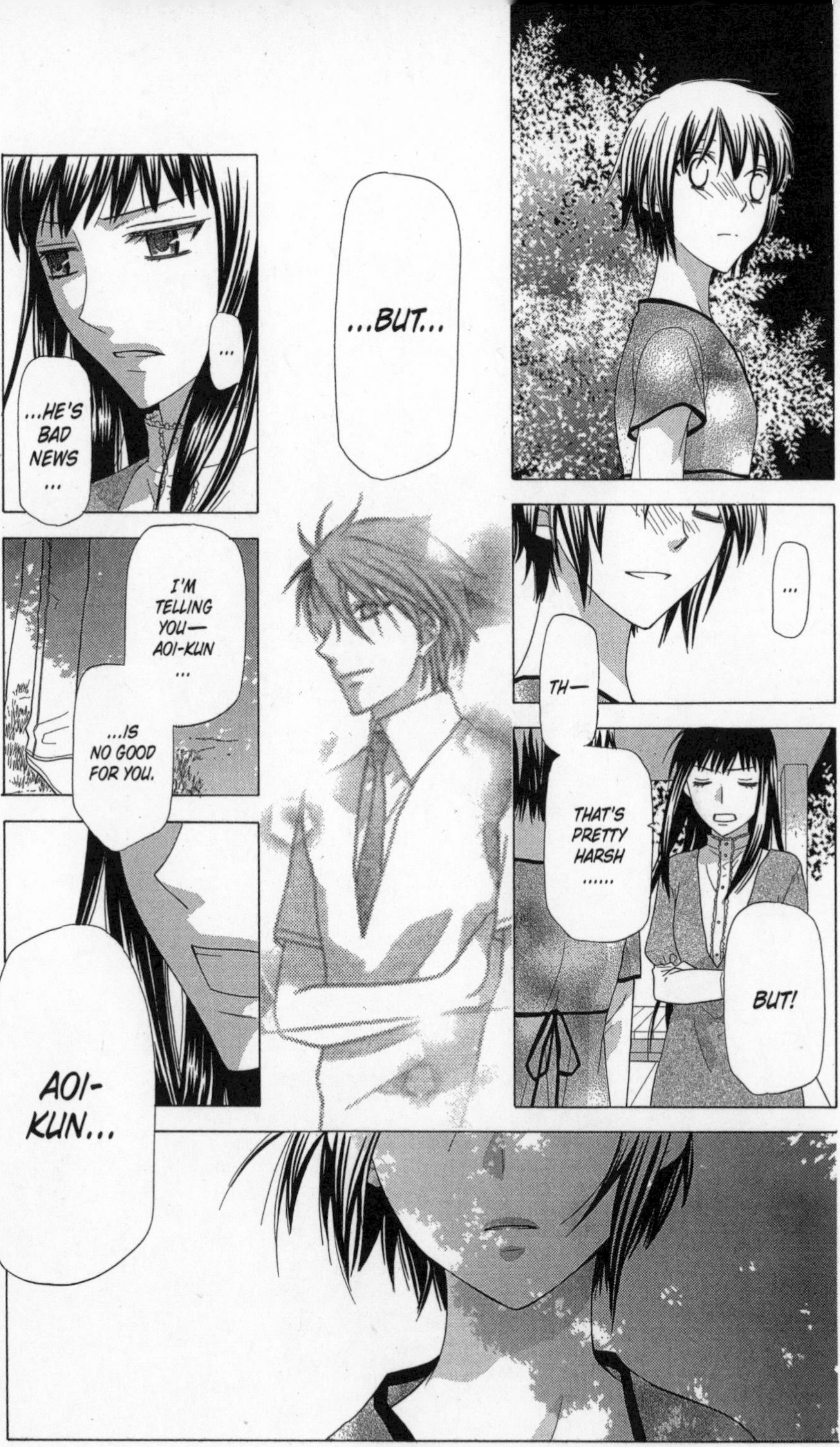
...BUT...
...
...HE'S BAD NEWS ...
...
TH—
THAT'S PRETTY HARSH ......
BUT!
I'M TELLING YOU— AOI-KUN ...
...IS NO GOOD FOR YOU.
AOI-KUN...

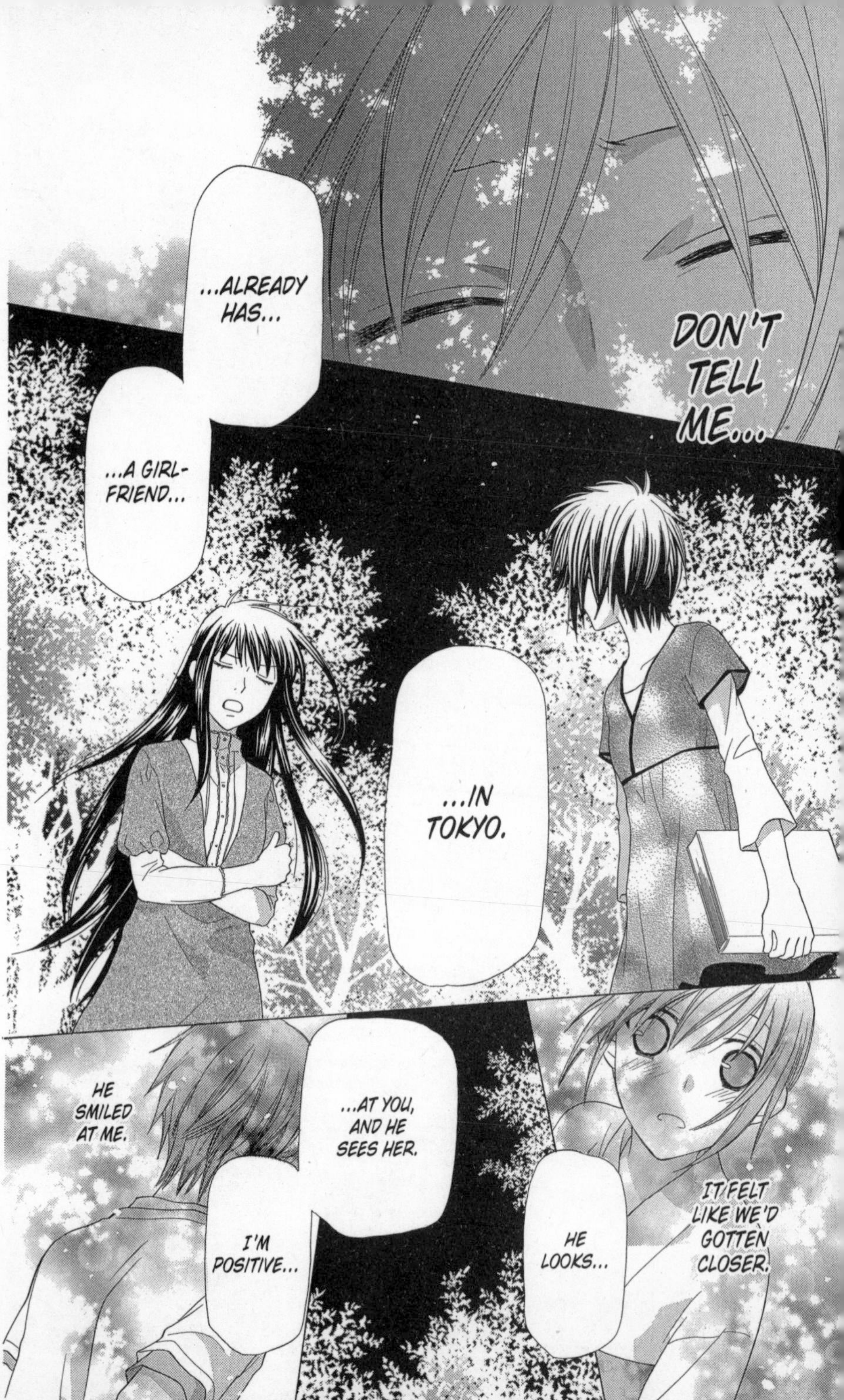
DON'T TELL ME...
...ALREADY HAS...
...A GIRL-FRIEND...
...IN TOKYO.
IT FELT LIKE WE'D GOTTEN CLOSER.
HE LOOKS...
...AT YOU, AND HE SEES HER.
HE SMILED AT ME.
I'M POSITIVE...

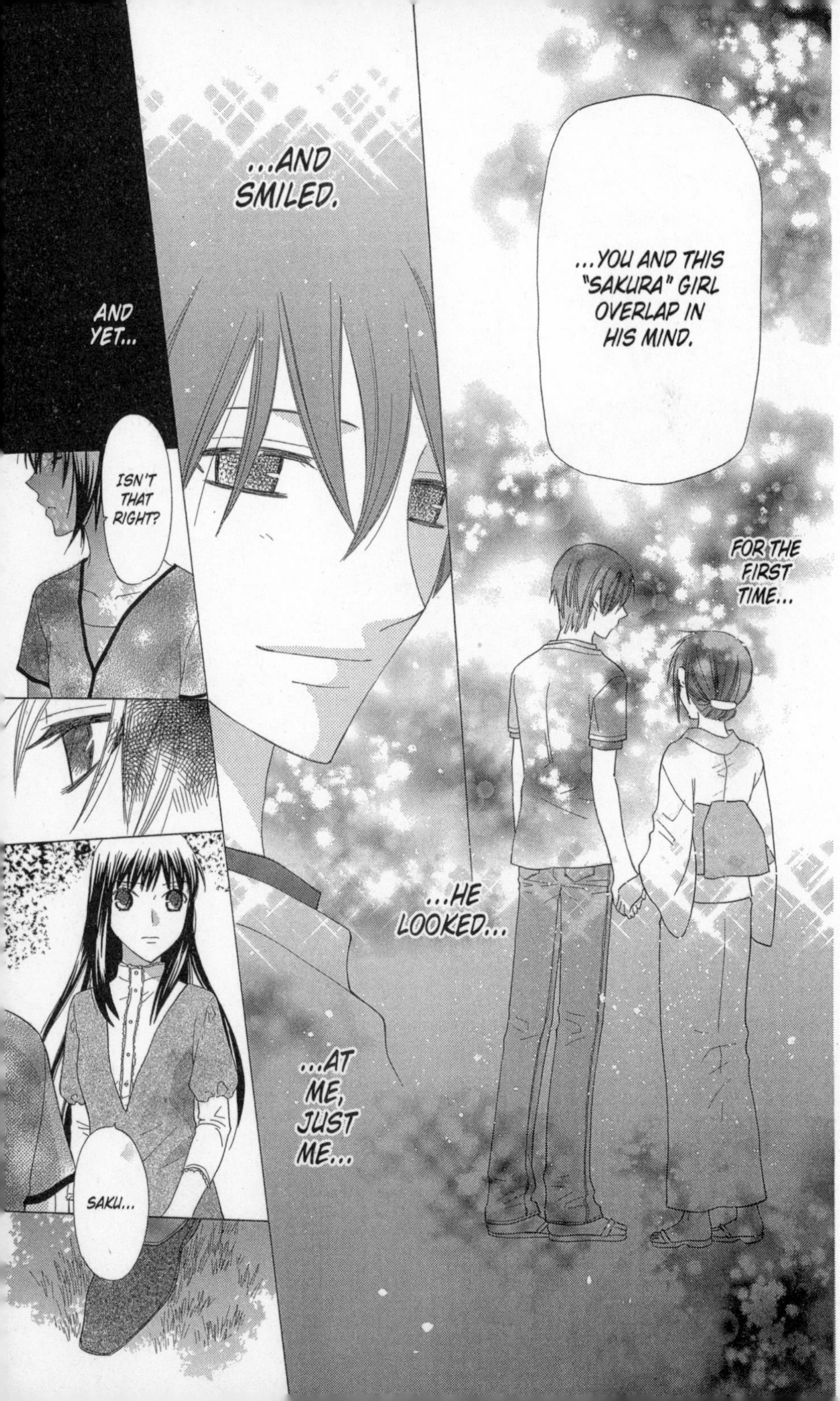
...YOU AND THIS "SAKURA" GIRL OVERLAP IN HIS MIND.
FOR THE FIRST TIME...
...HE LOOKED...
...AT ME, JUST ME...
...AND SMILED.
AND YET...
ISN'T THAT RIGHT?
SAKU...

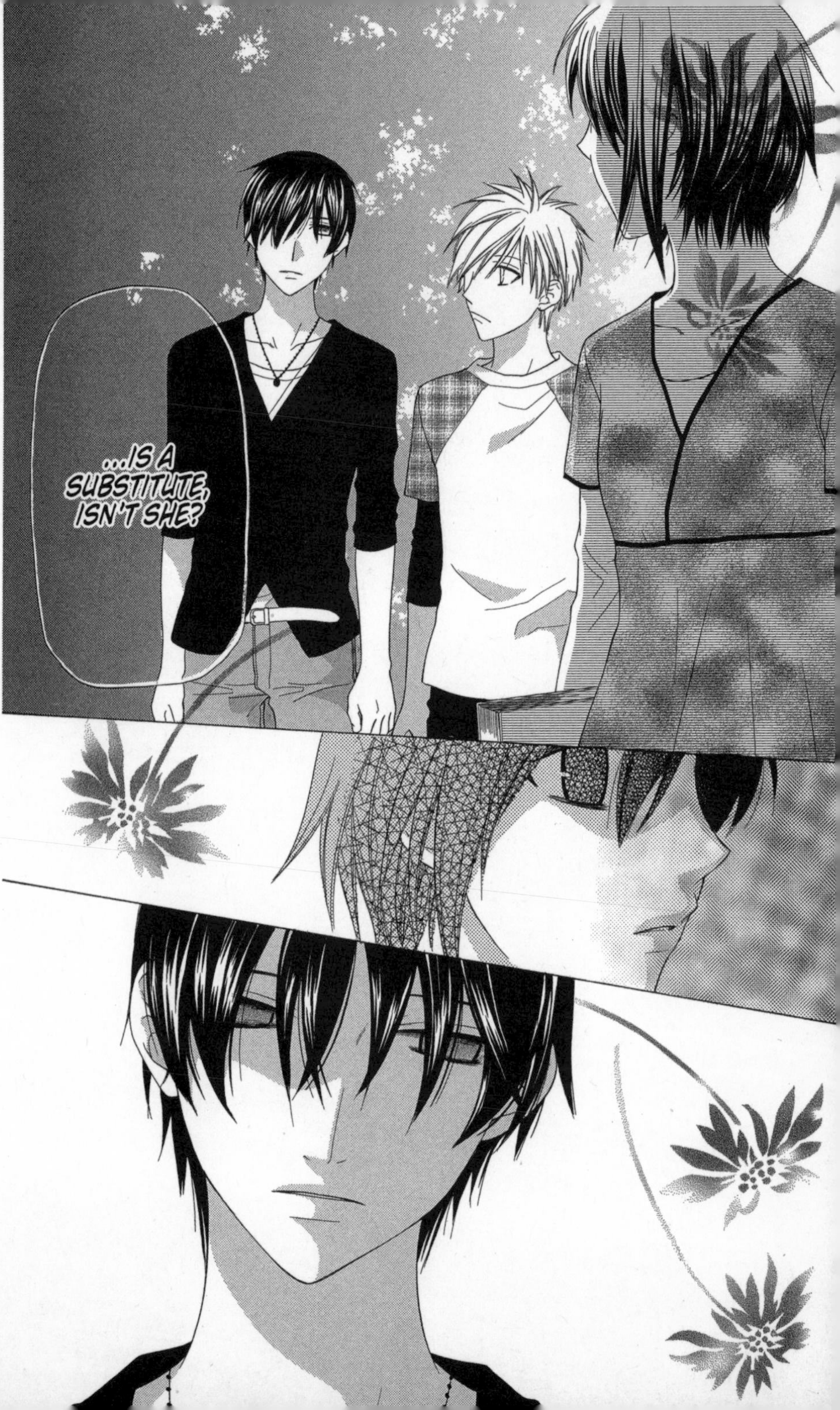
...IS A SUBSTITUTE, ISN'T SHE?

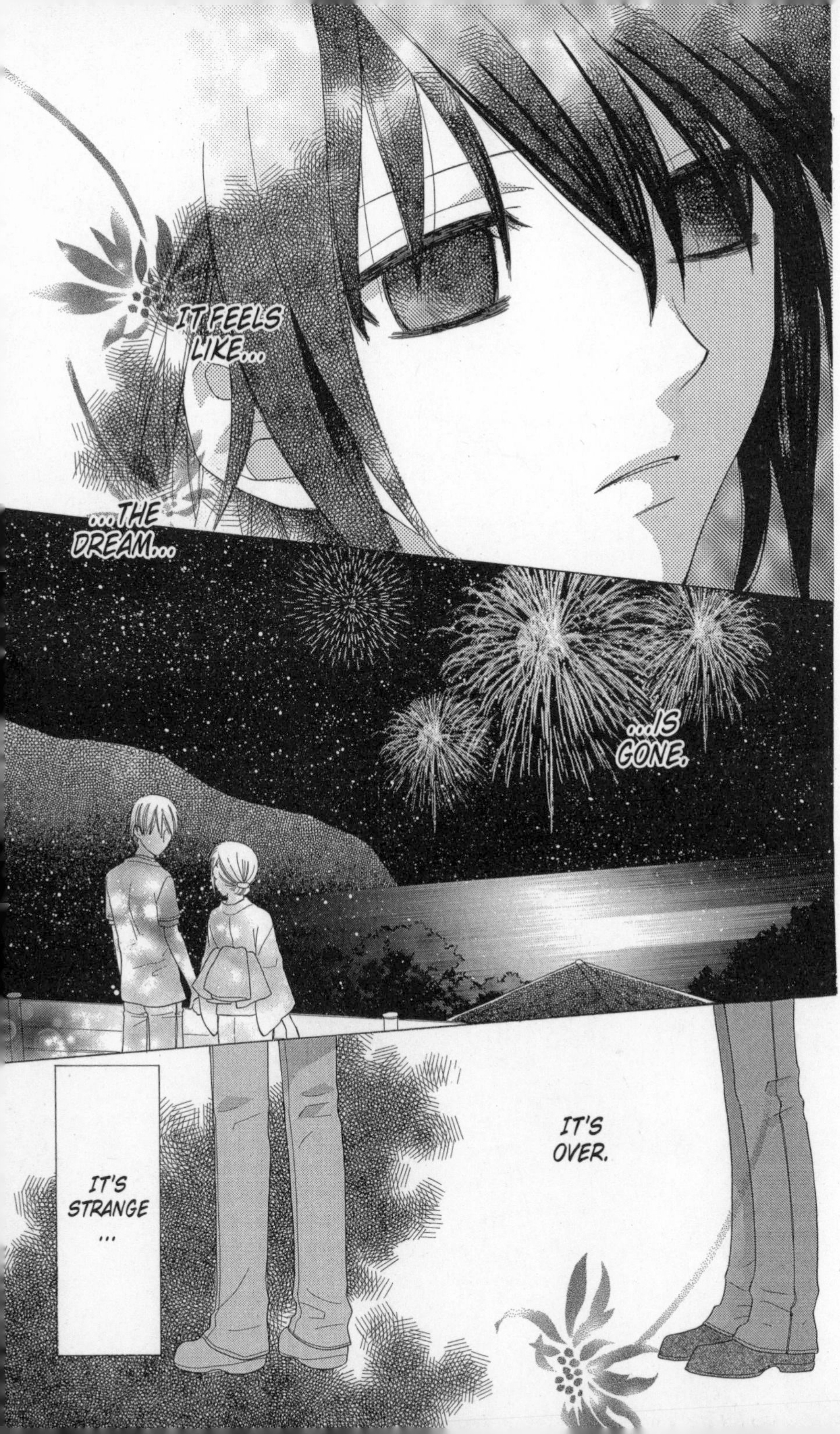
IT FEELS LIKE...
...THE DREAM...
...IS GONE.
IT'S OVER.
IT'S STRANGE ...

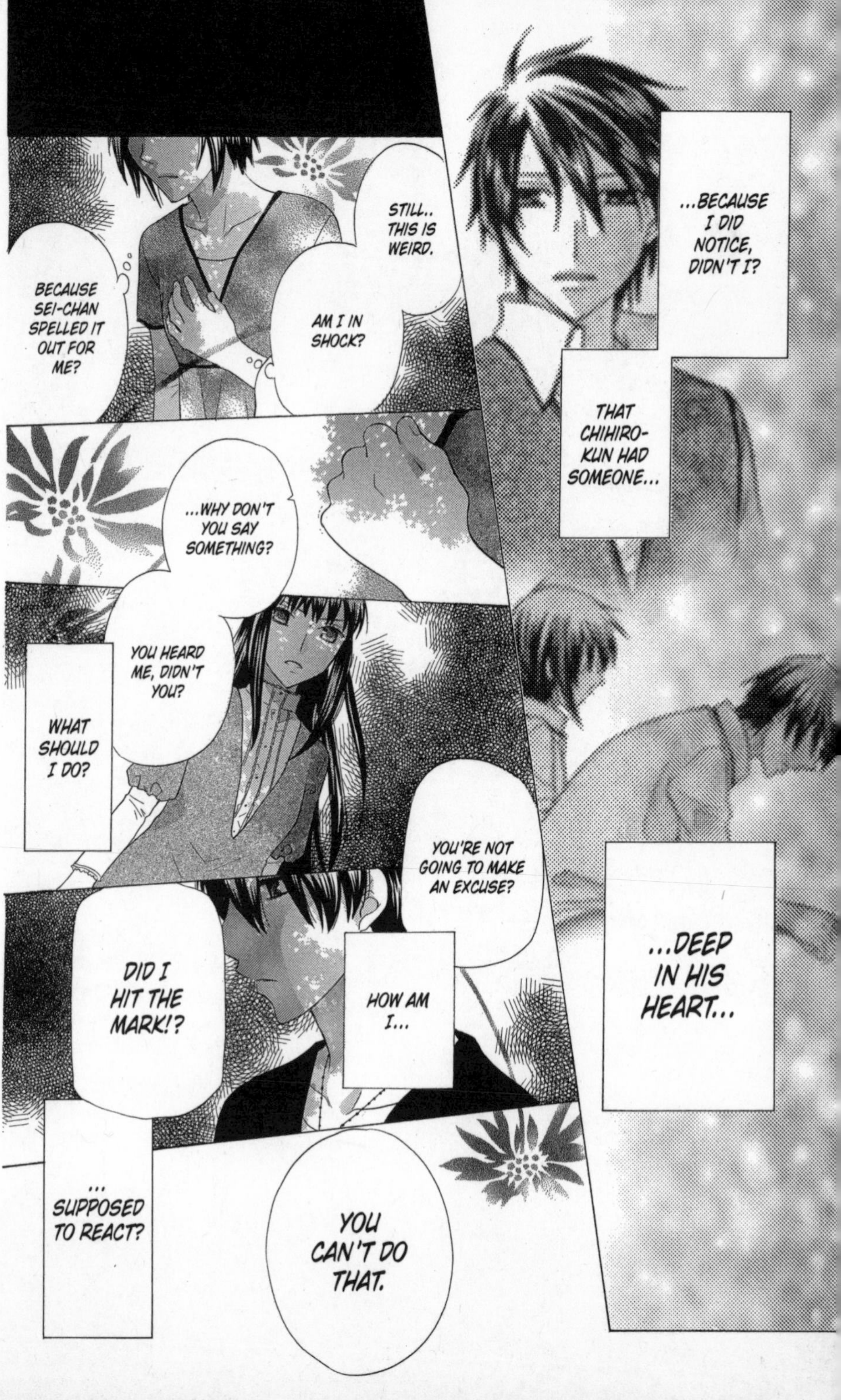
...BECAUSE I DID NOTICE, DIDN'T I?
THAT CHIHIRO-KUN HAD SOMEONE...
...DEEP IN HIS HEART...
STILL.. THIS IS WEIRD.
AM I IN SHOCK?
BECAUSE SEI-CHAN SPELLED IT OUT FOR ME?
...WHY DON'T YOU SAY SOMETHING?
YOU HEARD ME, DIDN'T YOU?
WHAT SHOULD I DO?
YOU'RE NOT GOING TO MAKE AN EXCUSE?
HOW AM I...
DID I HIT THE MARK!?
...SUPPOSED TO REACT?
YOU CAN'T DO THAT.

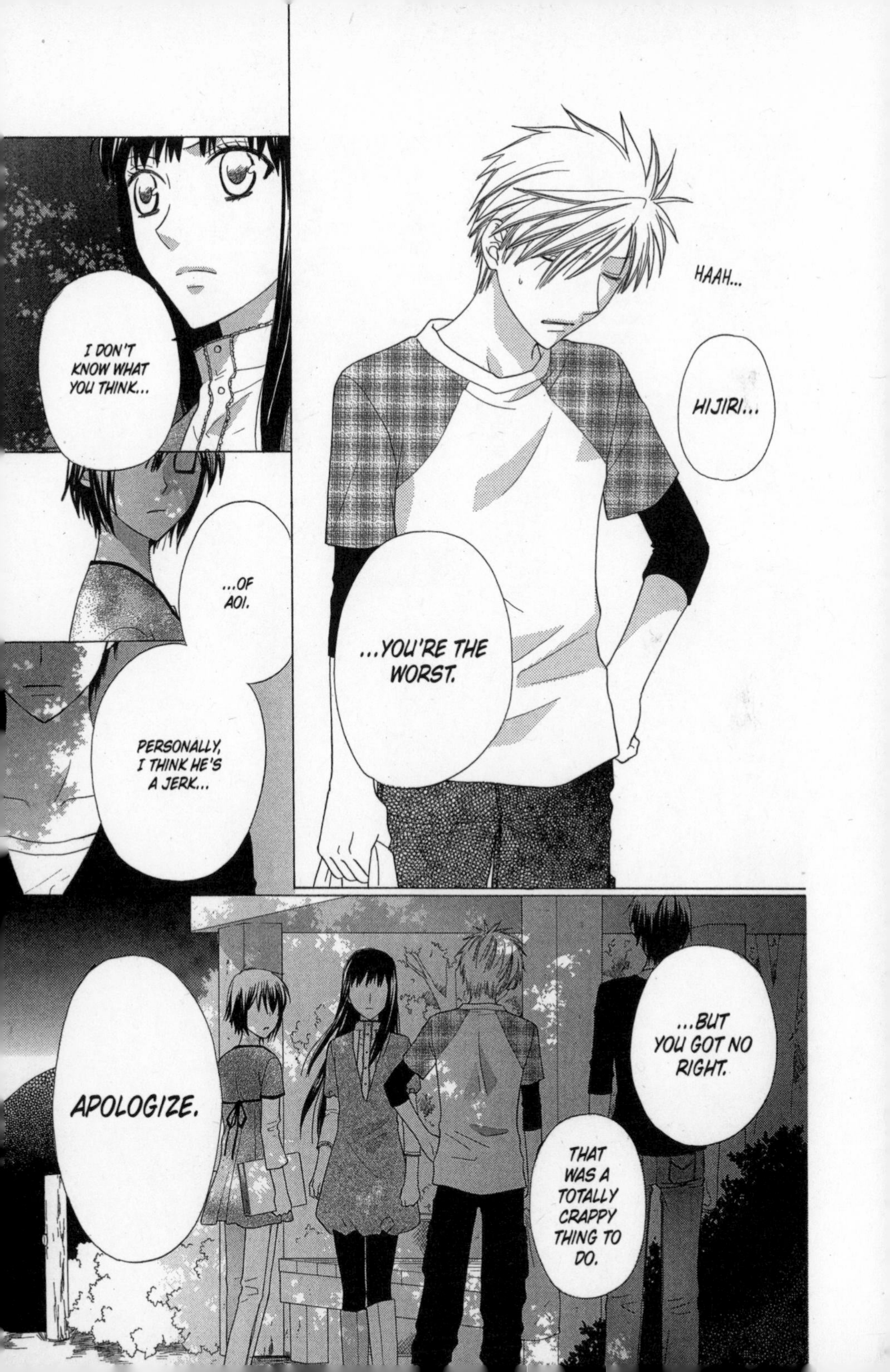
HAAH...
HIJIRI...
...YOU'RE THE WORST.
I DON'T KNOW WHAT YOU THINK...
...OF AOI.
PERSONALLY, I THINK HE'S A JERK...
...BUT YOU GOT NO RIGHT.
THAT WAS A TOTALLY CRAPPY THING TO DO.
APOLOGIZE.

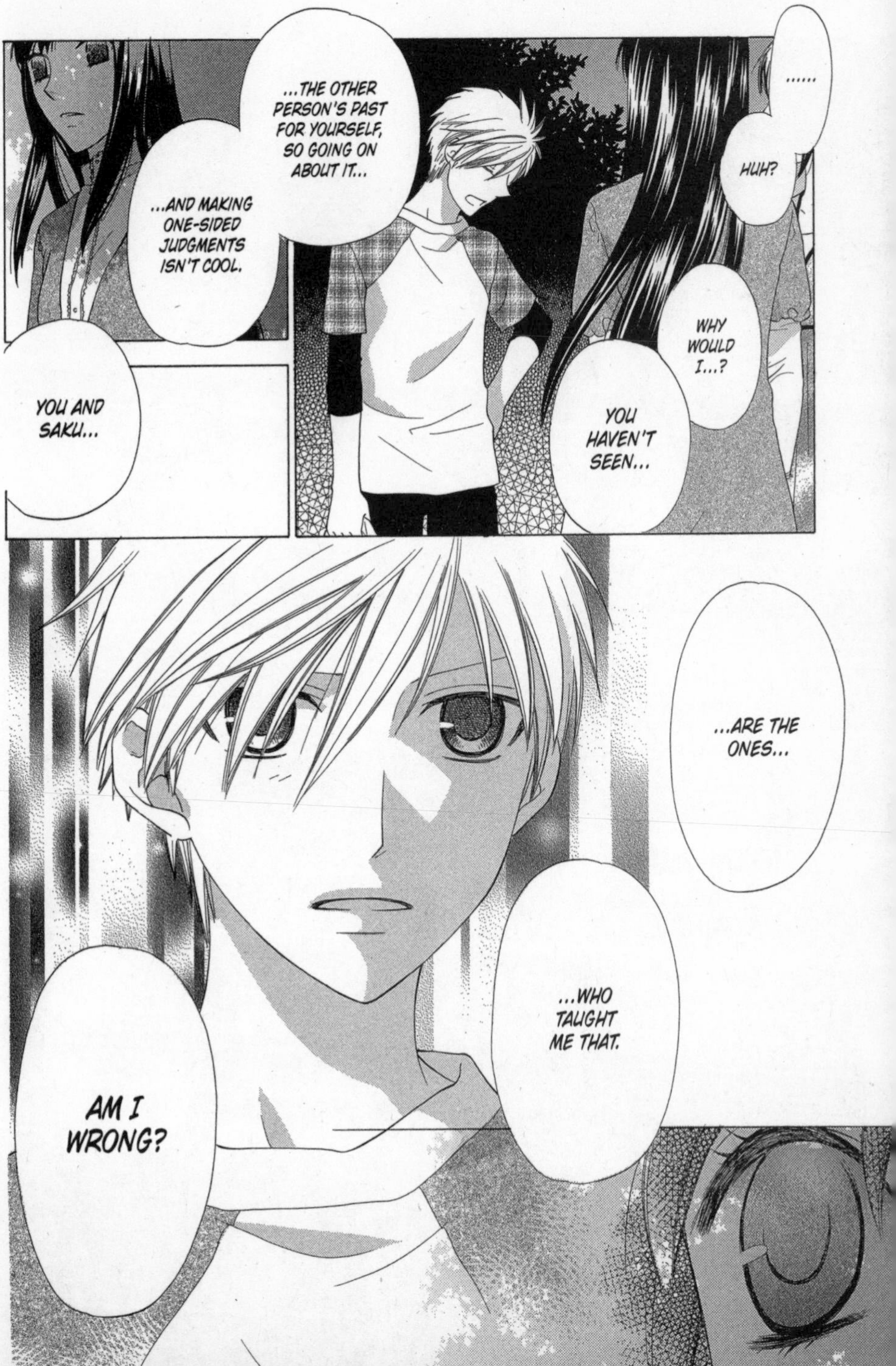
......
HUH?
WHY WOULD I...?
YOU HAVEN'T SEEN...
...THE OTHER PERSON'S PAST FOR YOURSELF, SO GOING ON ABOUT IT...
...AND MAKING ONE-SIDED JUDGMENTS ISN'T COOL.
YOU AND SAKU...
...ARE THE ONES...
...WHO TAUGHT ME THAT.
AM I WRONG?

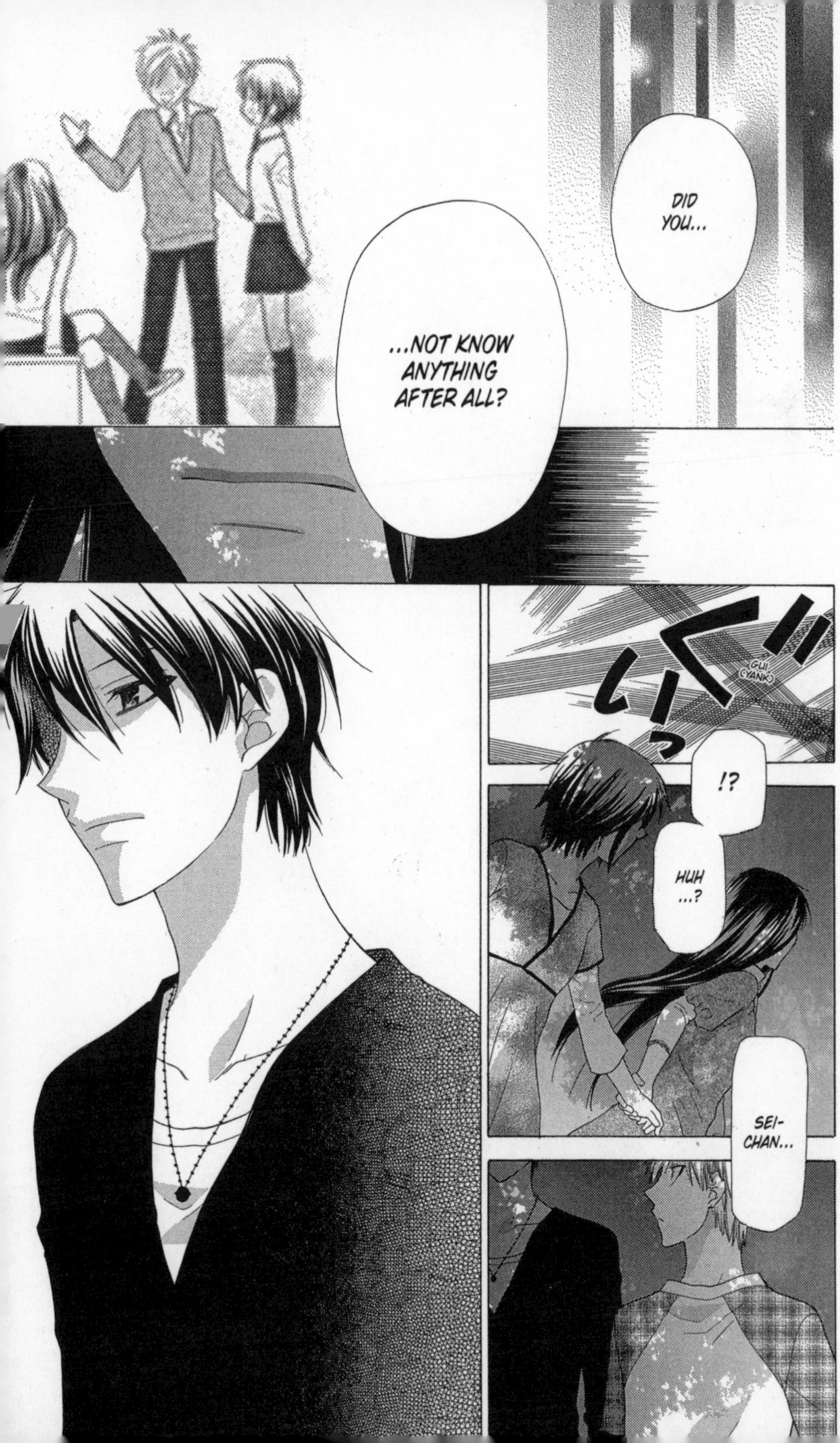
DID YOU...
...NOT KNOW ANYTHING AFTER ALL?
GUI (YANK)
!?
HUH ...?
SEI-CHAN...

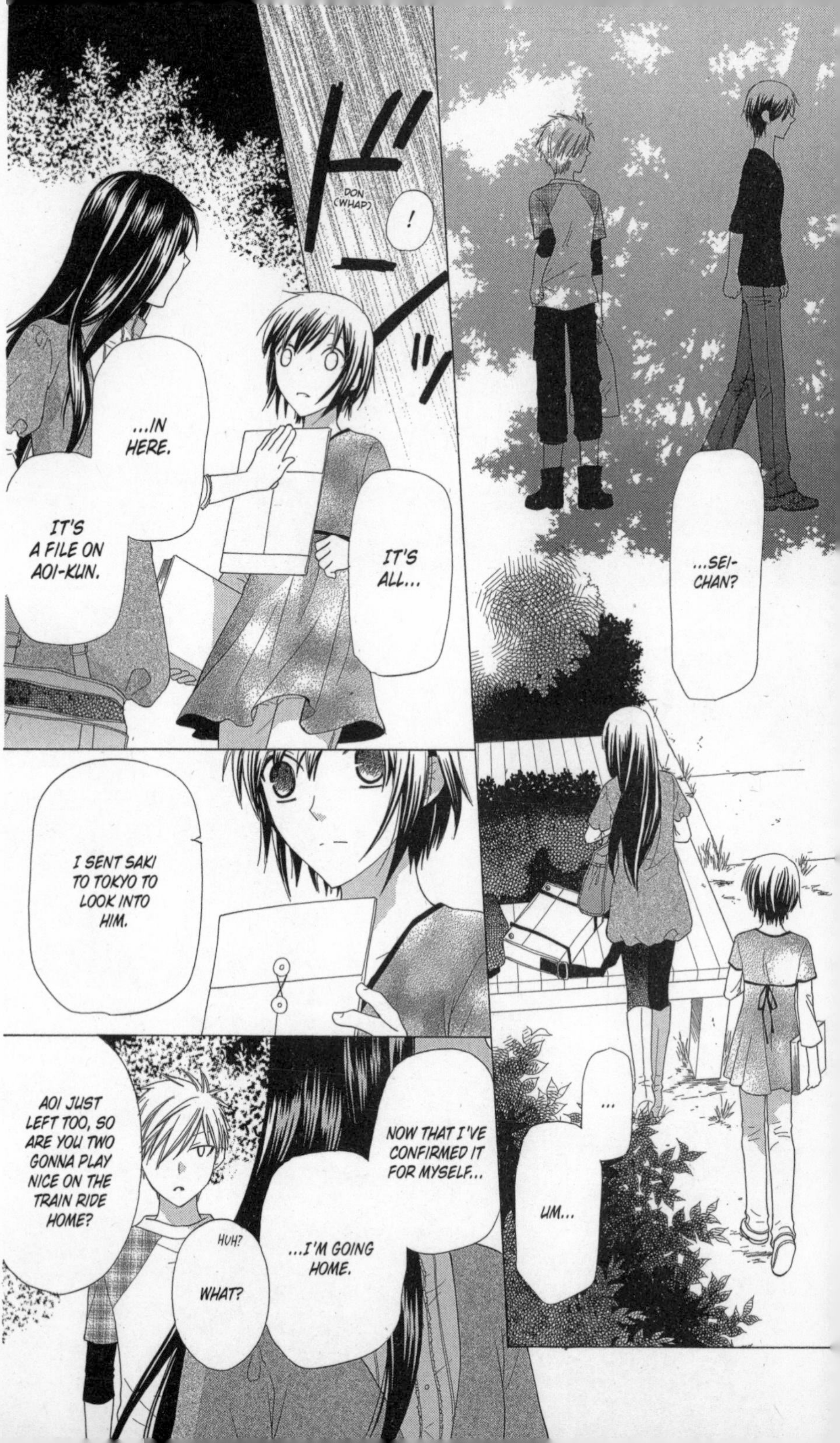
...SEI-CHAN?
DON (WHAP)
!
IT'S ALL...
...IN HERE.
IT'S A FILE ON AOI-KUN.
...
UM...
I SENT SAKI TO TOKYO TO LOOK INTO HIM.
NOW THAT I'VE CONFIRMED IT FOR MYSELF...
...I'M GOING HOME.
HUH?
WHAT?
AOI JUST LEFT TOO, SO ARE YOU TWO GONNA PLAY NICE ON THE TRAIN RIDE HOME?

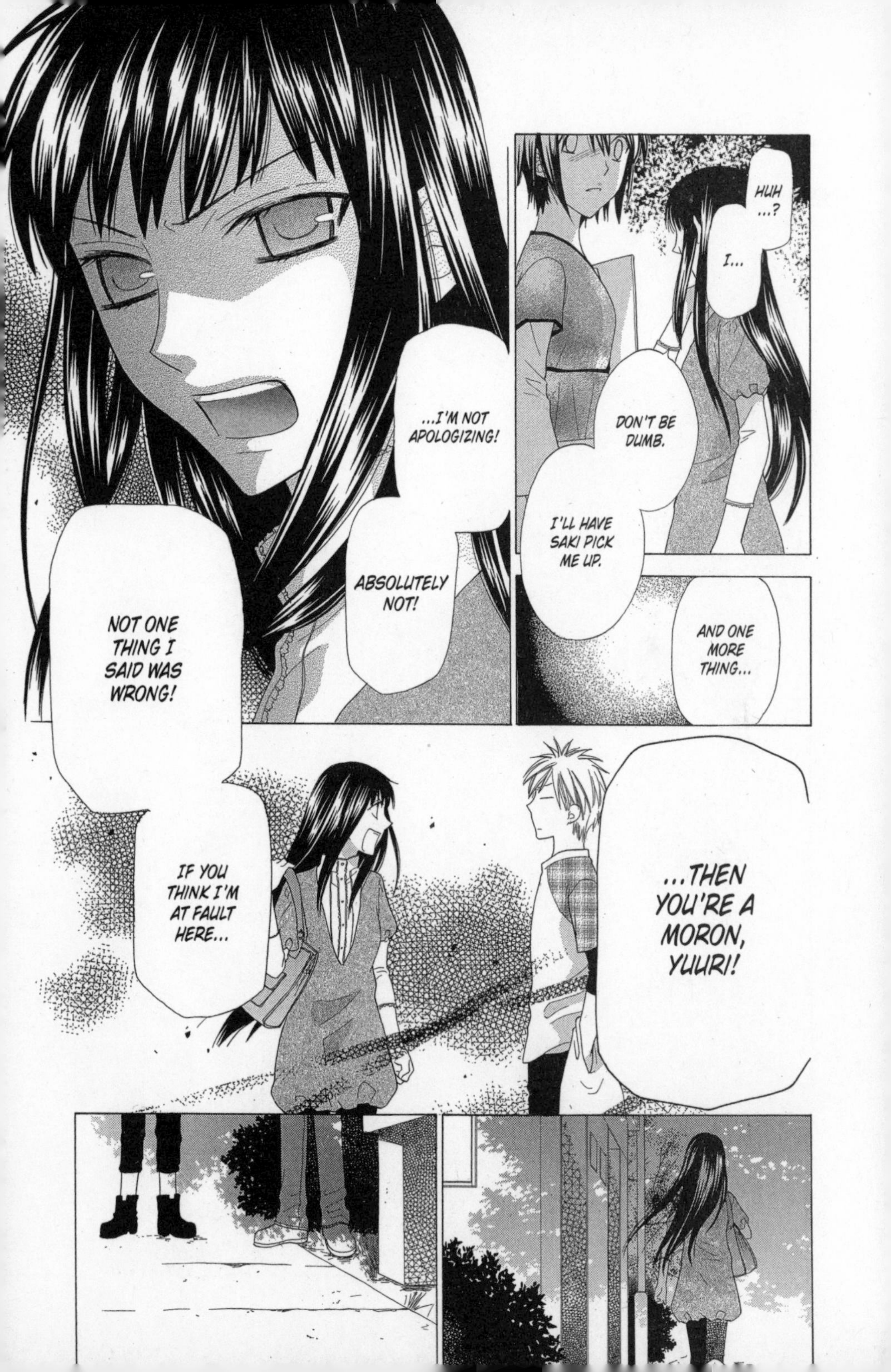
HUH ...?
I...
DON'T BE DUMB.
I'LL HAVE SAKI PICK ME UP.
AND ONE MORE THING...
...I'M NOT APOLOGIZING!
ABSOLUTELY NOT!
NOT ONE THING I SAID WAS WRONG!
IF YOU THINK I'M AT FAULT HERE...
...THEN YOU'RE A MORON, YUURI!

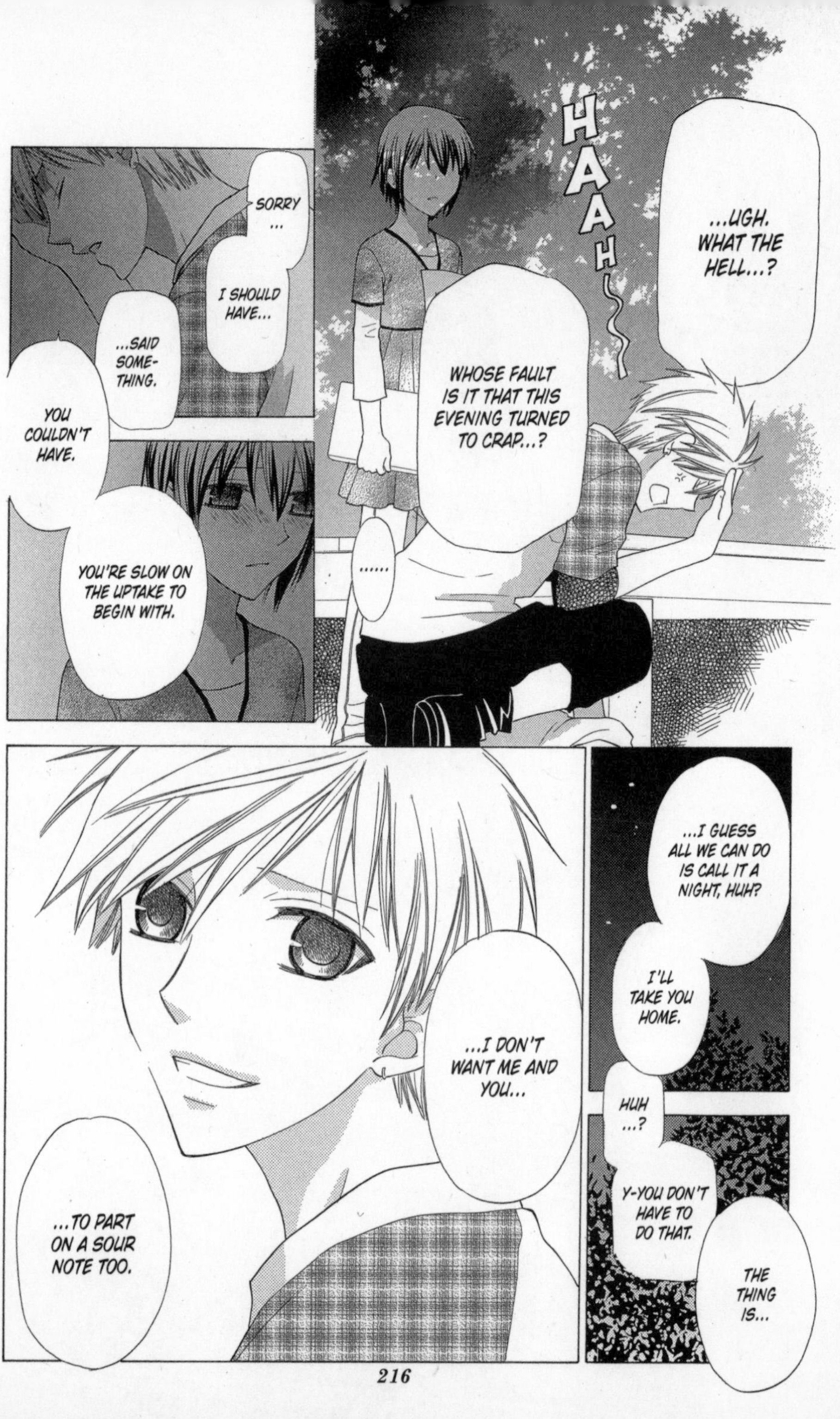

...UGH. WHAT THE HELL...?
HAAAH~
WHOSE FAULT IS IT THAT THIS EVENING TURNED TO CRAP...?
......
SORRY ...
I SHOULD HAVE...
...SAID SOMETHING.
YOU COULDN'T HAVE.
YOU'RE SLOW ON THE UPTAKE TO BEGIN WITH.
...I GUESS ALL WE CAN DO IS CALL IT A NIGHT, HUH?
I'LL TAKE YOU HOME.
HUH ...?
Y-YOU DON'T HAVE TO DO THAT.
THE THING IS...
...I DON'T WANT ME AND YOU...
...TO PART ON A SOUR NOTE TOO.

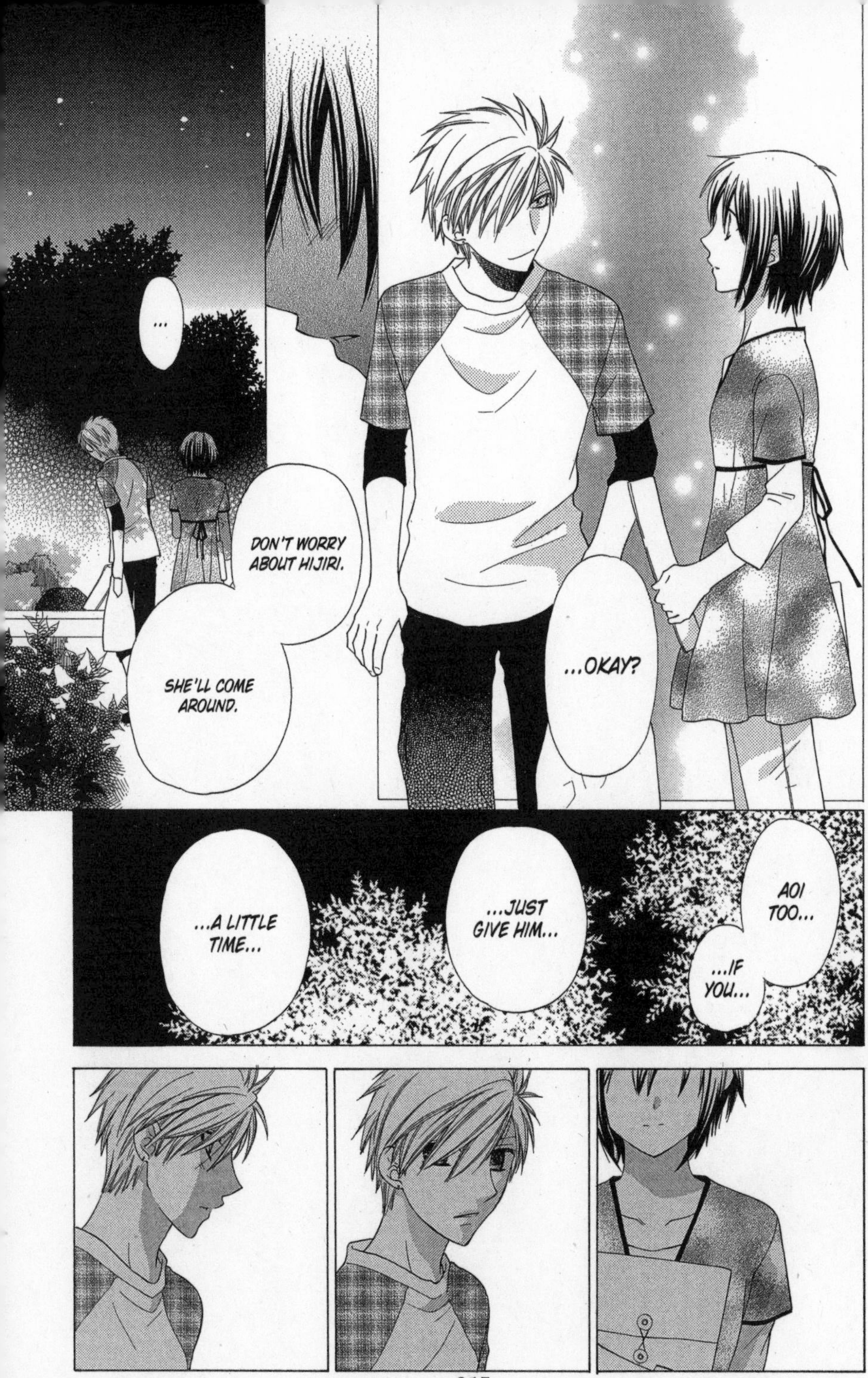
DON'T WORRY ABOUT HIJIRI.
SHE'LL COME AROUND.
...OKAY?
...
AOI TOO...
...IF YOU...
...JUST GIVE HIM...
...A LITTLE TIME...

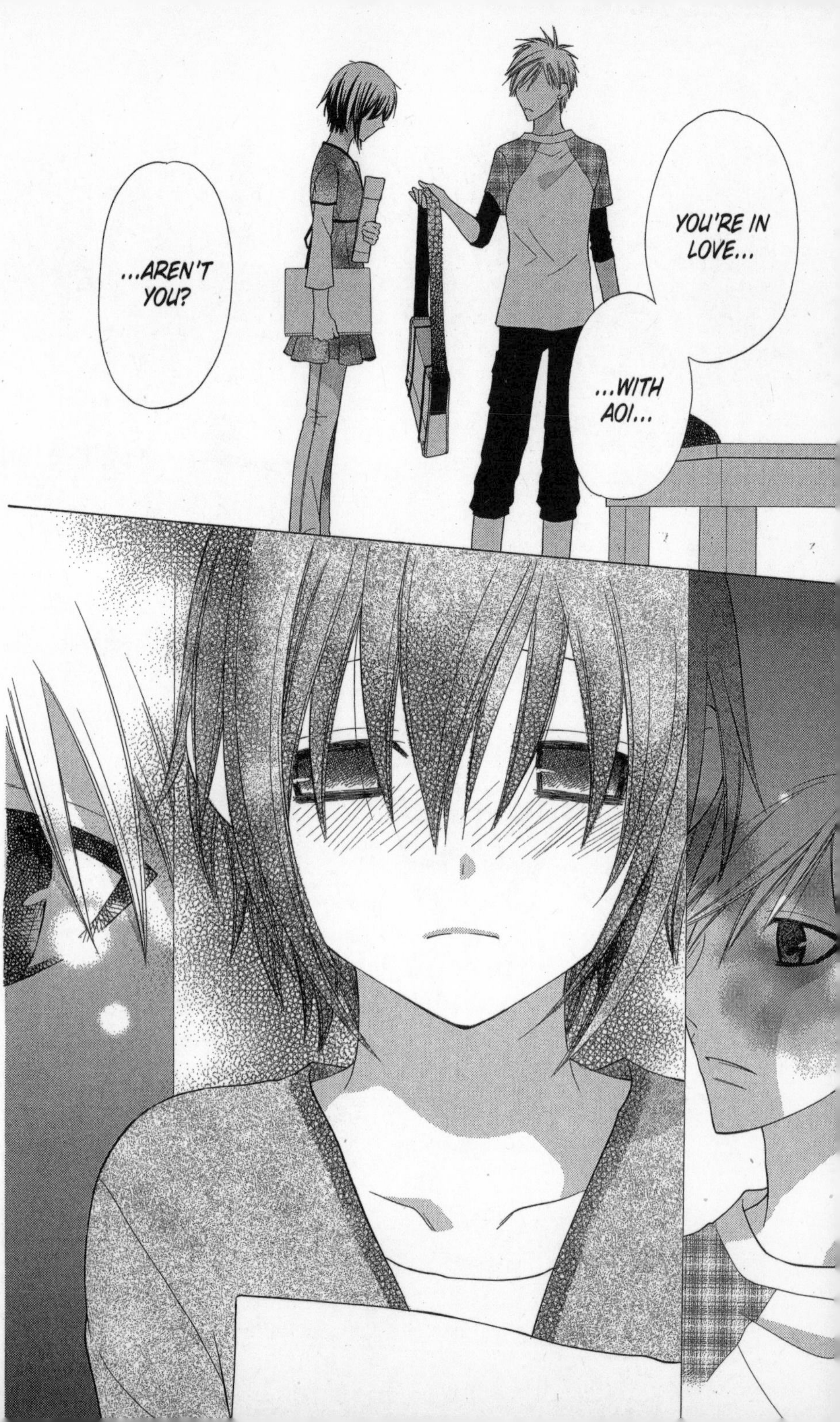
YOU'RE IN LOVE...
...WITH AOI...
...AREN'T YOU?

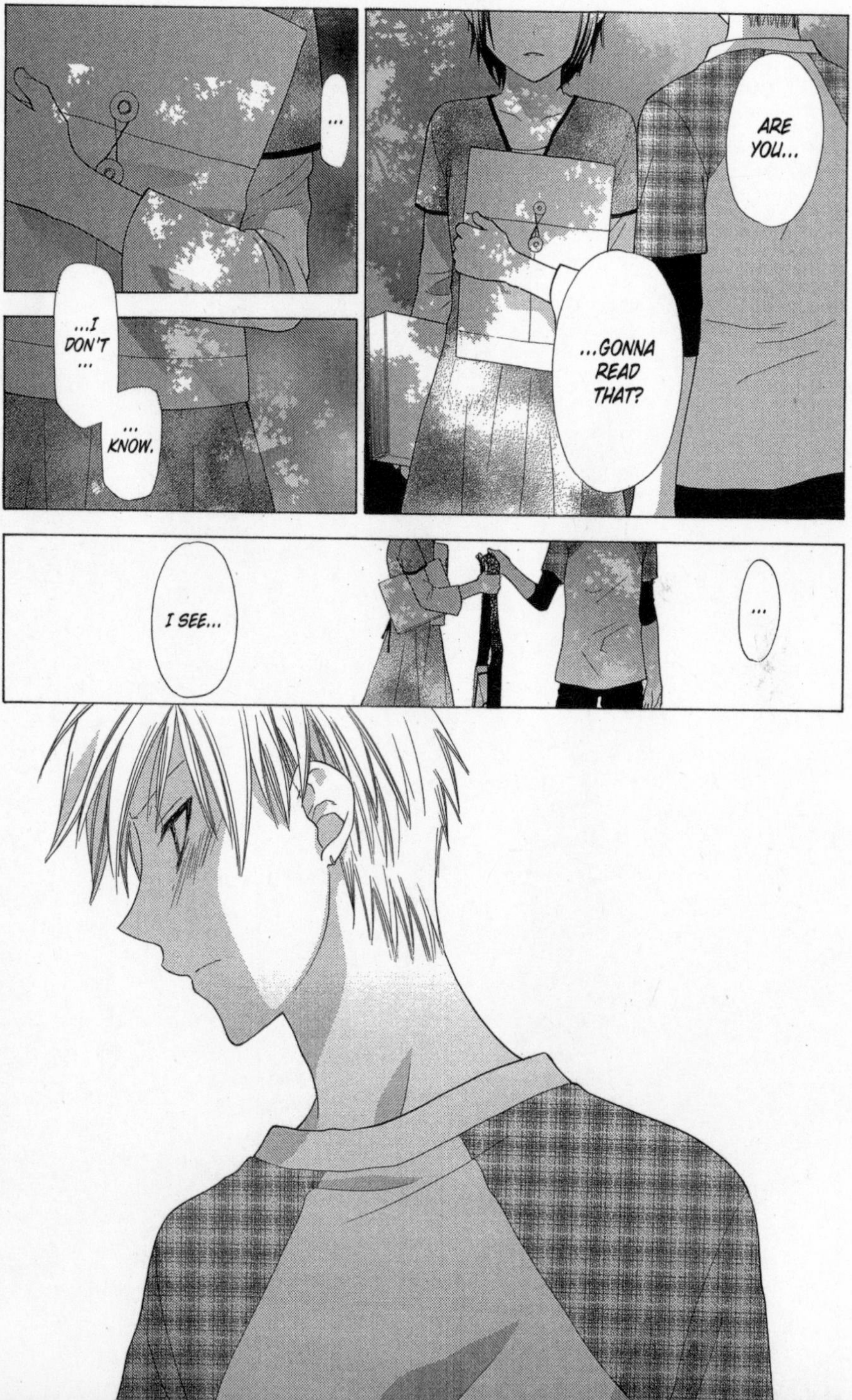
ARE YOU...
...GONNA READ THAT?
...
...I DON'T ...
... KNOW.
...
I SEE...

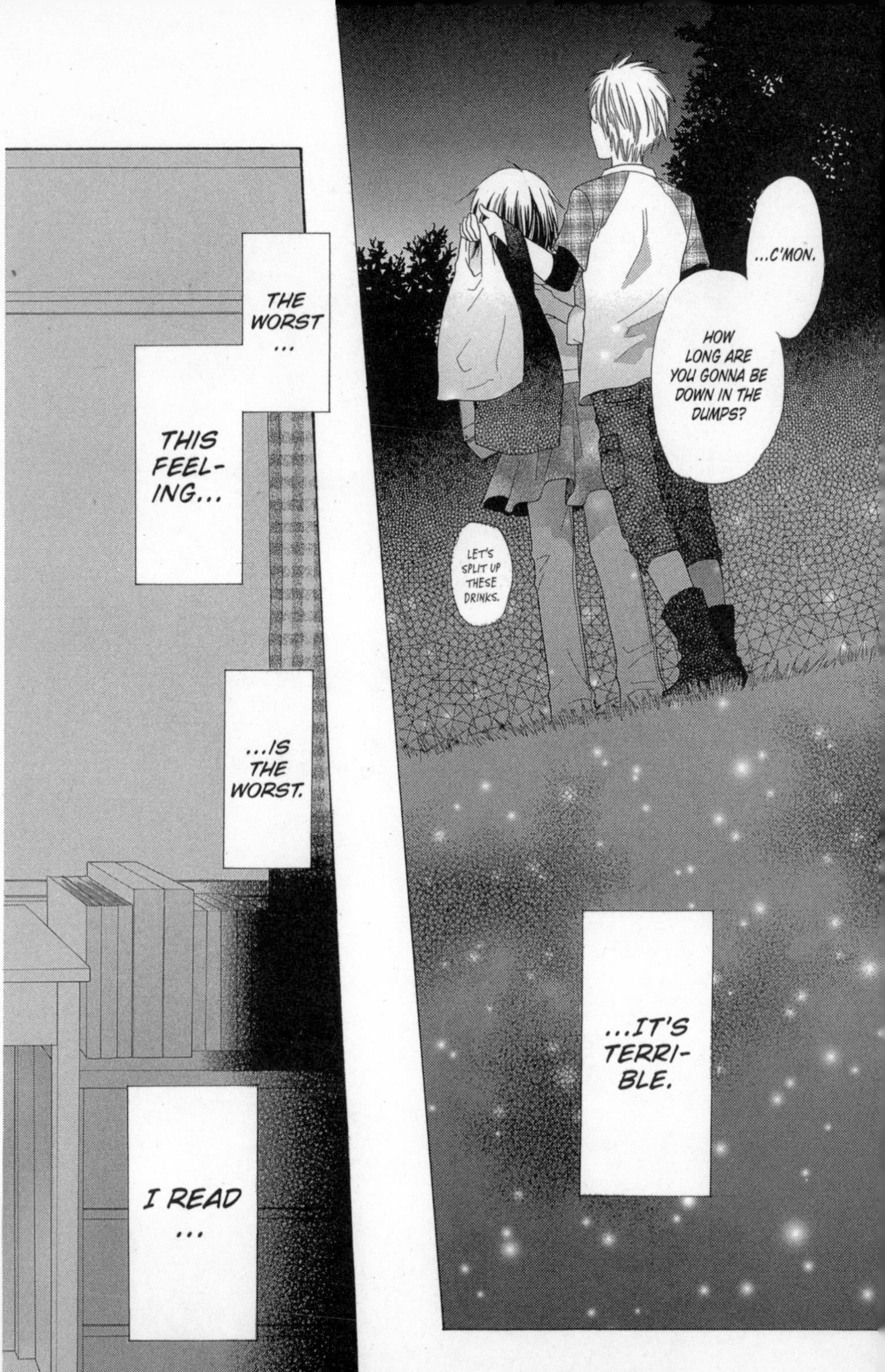
...C'MON.
HOW LONG ARE YOU GONNA BE DOWN IN THE DUMPS?
LET'S SPLIT UP THESE DRINKS.
...IT'S TERRIBLE.
THE WORST...
THIS FEELING...
...IS THE WORST.
I READ...

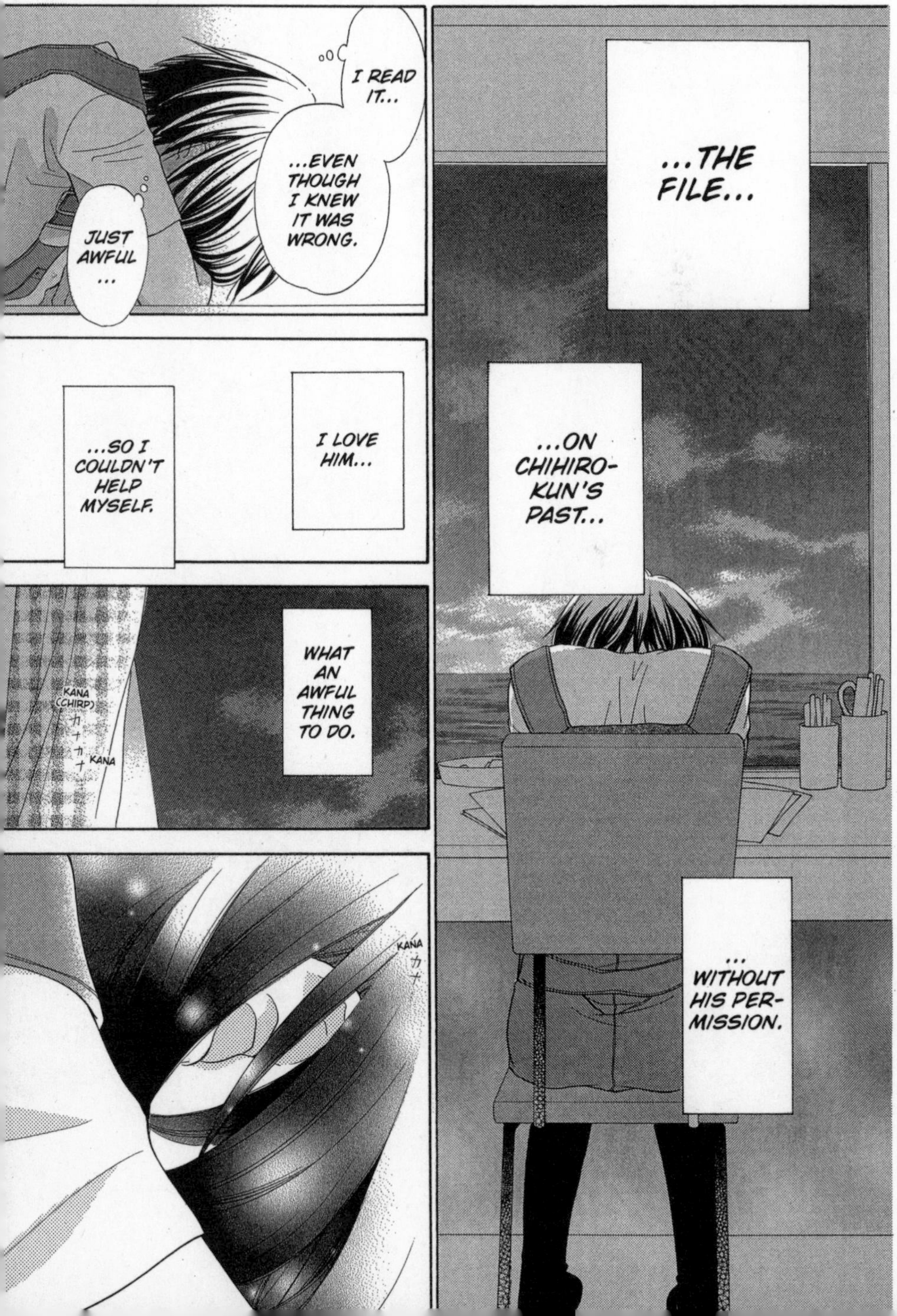
...THE FILE...
...ON CHIHIRO-KUN'S PAST...
...WITHOUT HIS PERMISSION.
I READ IT...
...EVEN THOUGH I KNEW IT WAS WRONG.
JUST AWFUL ...
I LOVE HIM...
...SO I COULDN'T HELP MYSELF.
WHAT AN AWFUL THING TO DO.
KANA (CHIRP)
カナカナ
KANA
KANA
カナ

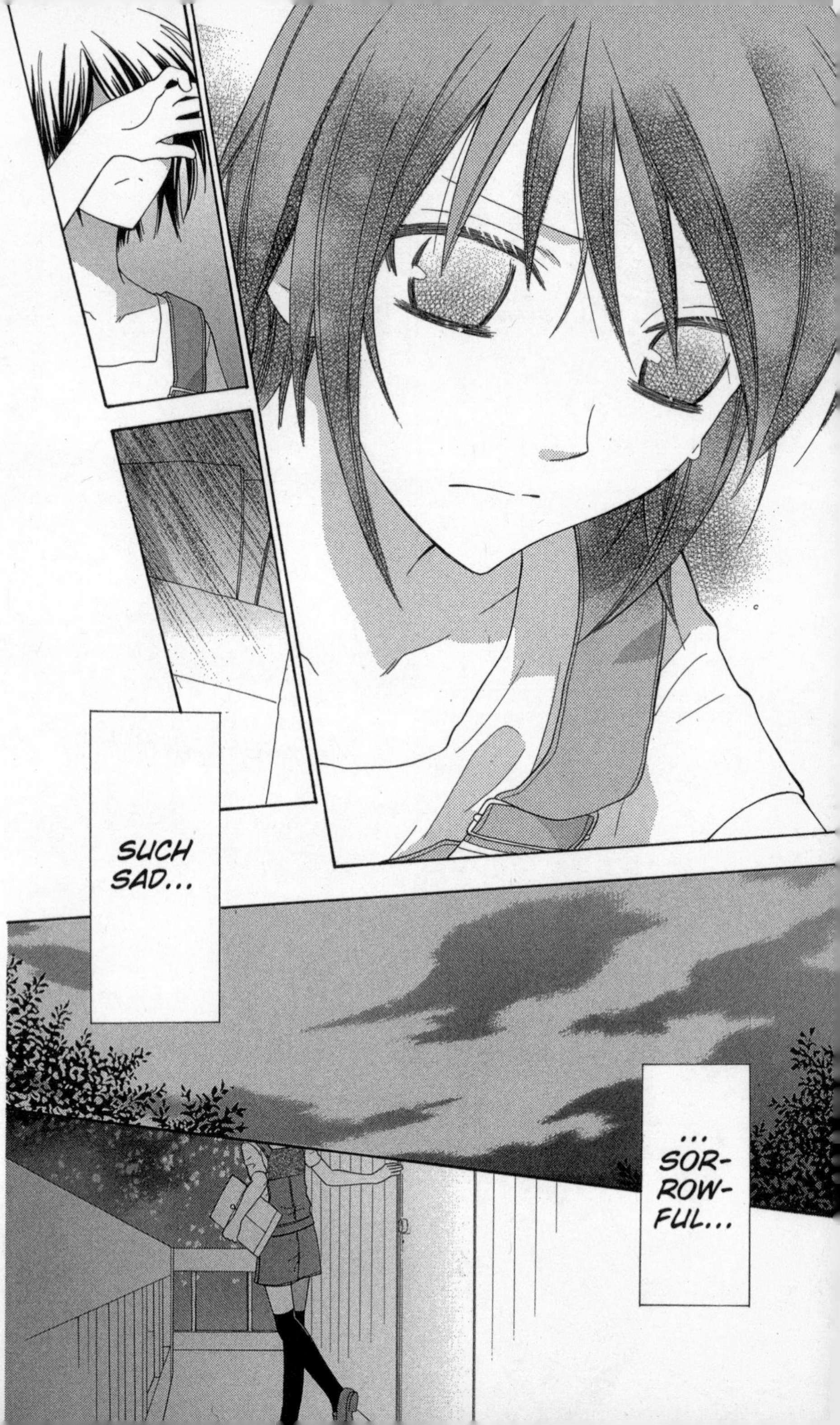
SUCH SAD...
...SOR-ROW-FUL...

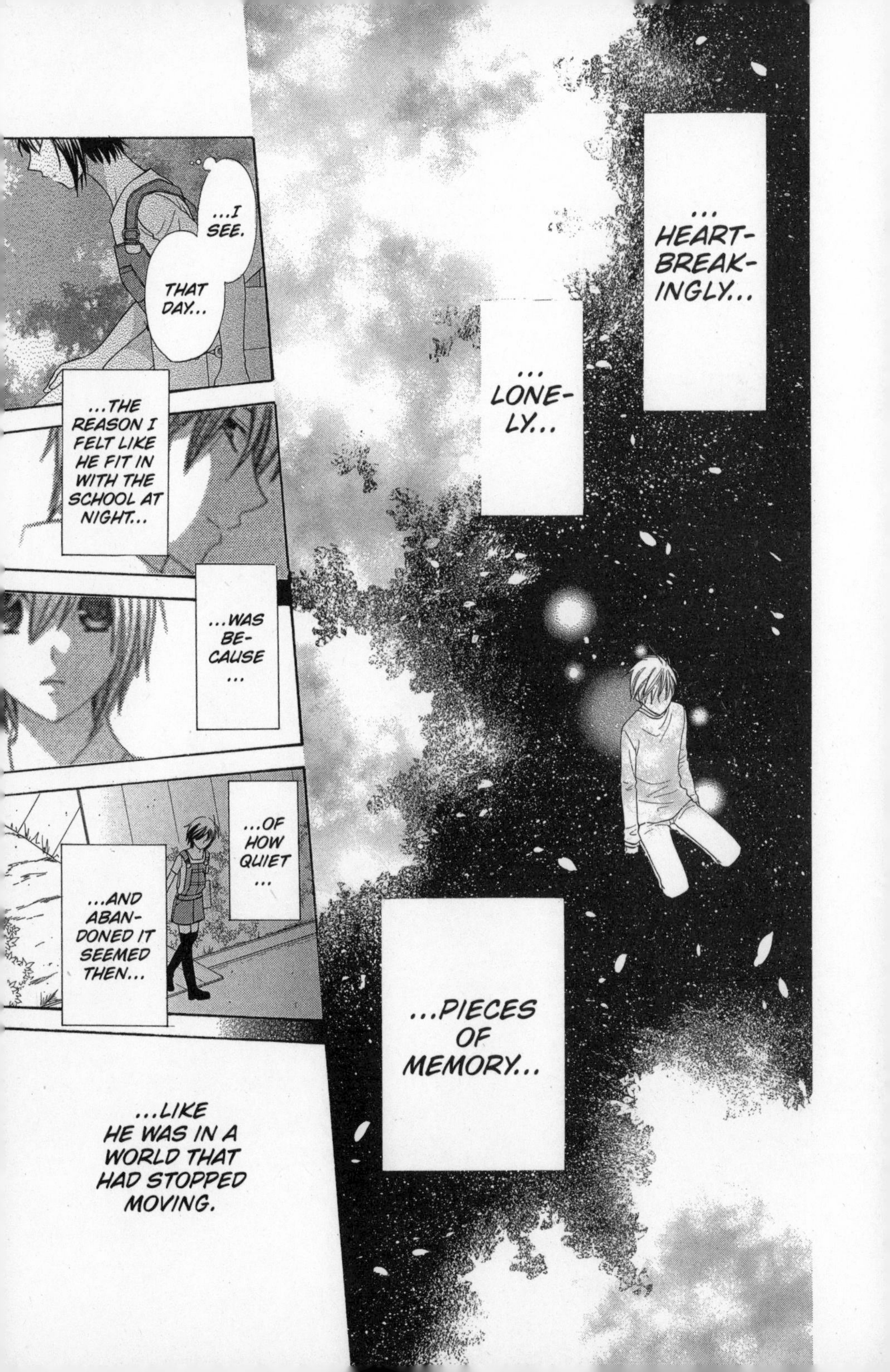
...HEART-BREAK-INGLY...
...LONE-LY...
...PIECES OF MEMORY...
...I SEE.
THAT DAY...
...THE REASON I FELT LIKE HE FIT IN WITH THE SCHOOL AT NIGHT...
...WAS BE-CAUSE...
...OF HOW QUIET...
...AND ABAN-DONED IT SEEMED THEN...
...LIKE HE WAS IN A WORLD THAT HAD STOPPED MOVING.

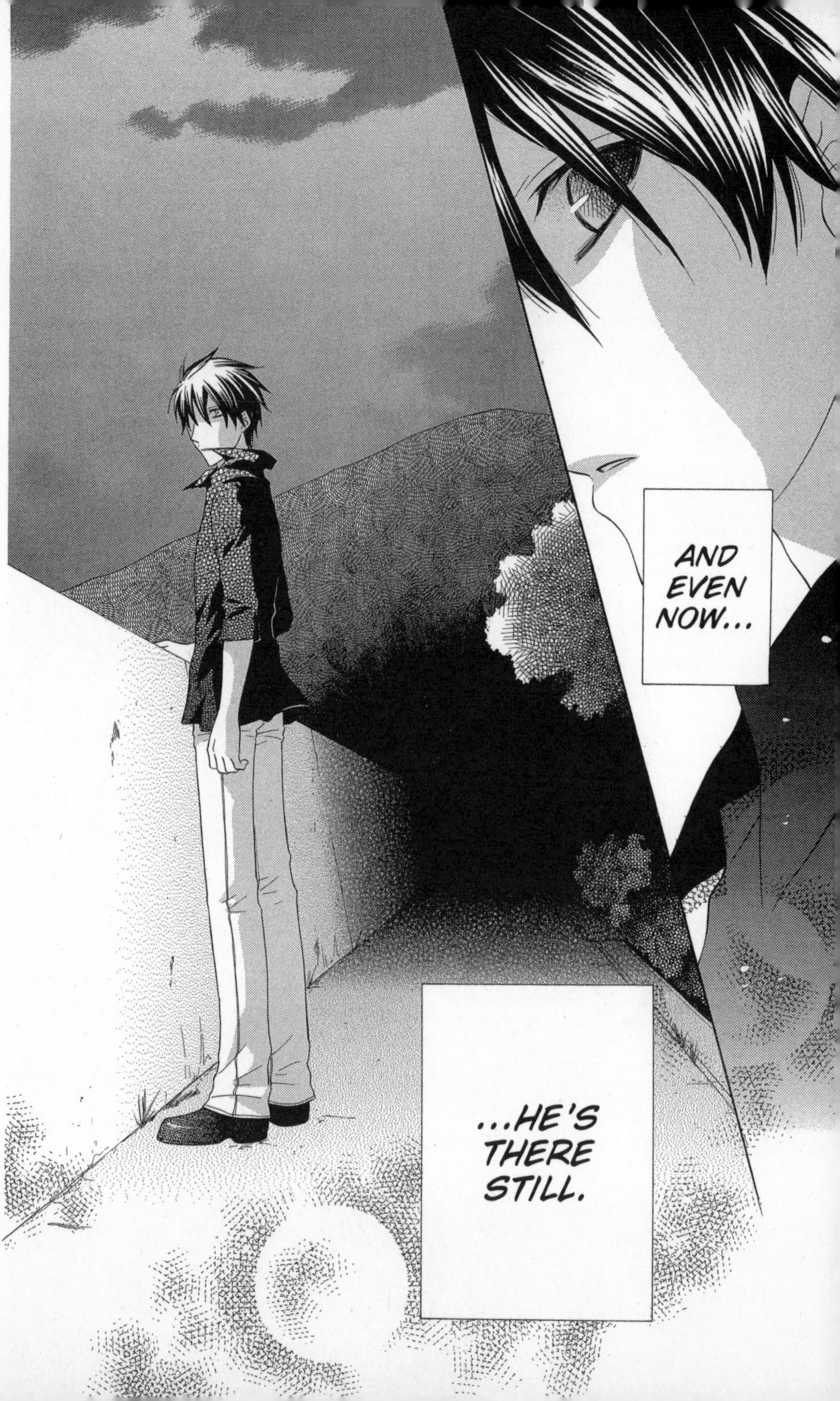
AND EVEN NOW...
...HE'S THERE STILL.

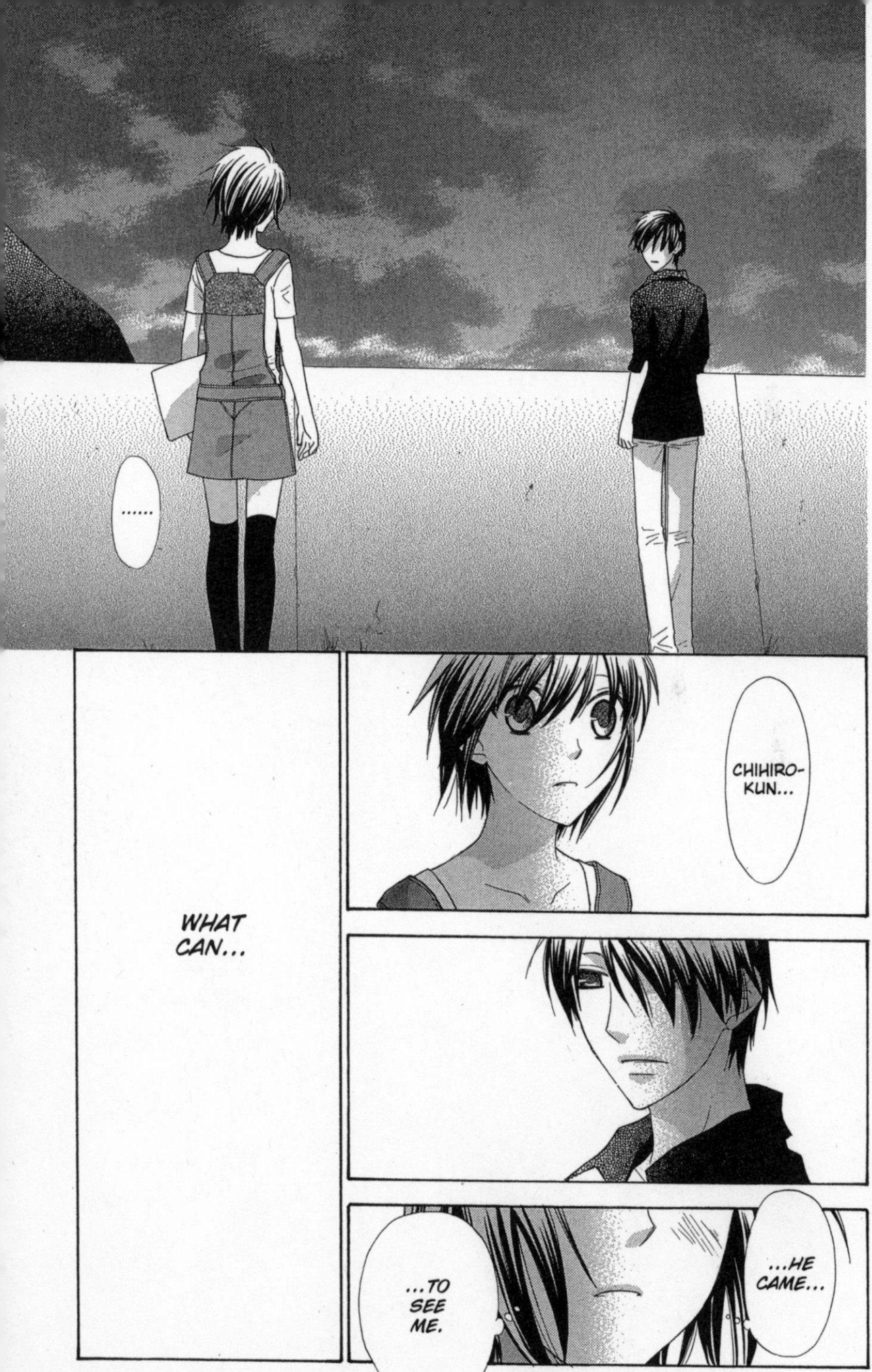
......
CHIHIRO-KUN...
...HE CAME...
...TO SEE ME.
WHAT CAN...

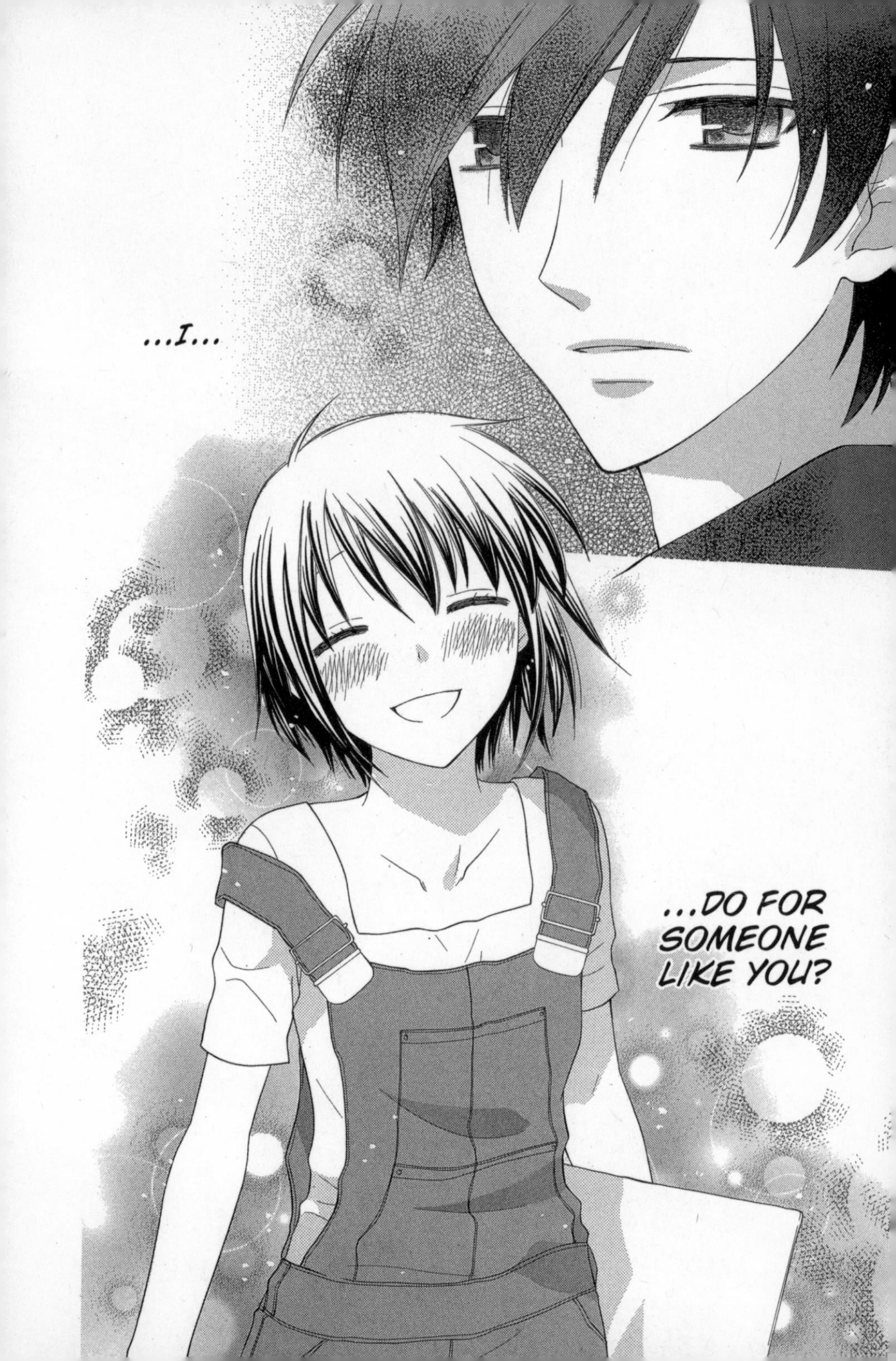
...I...
...DO FOR SOMEONE LIKE YOU?

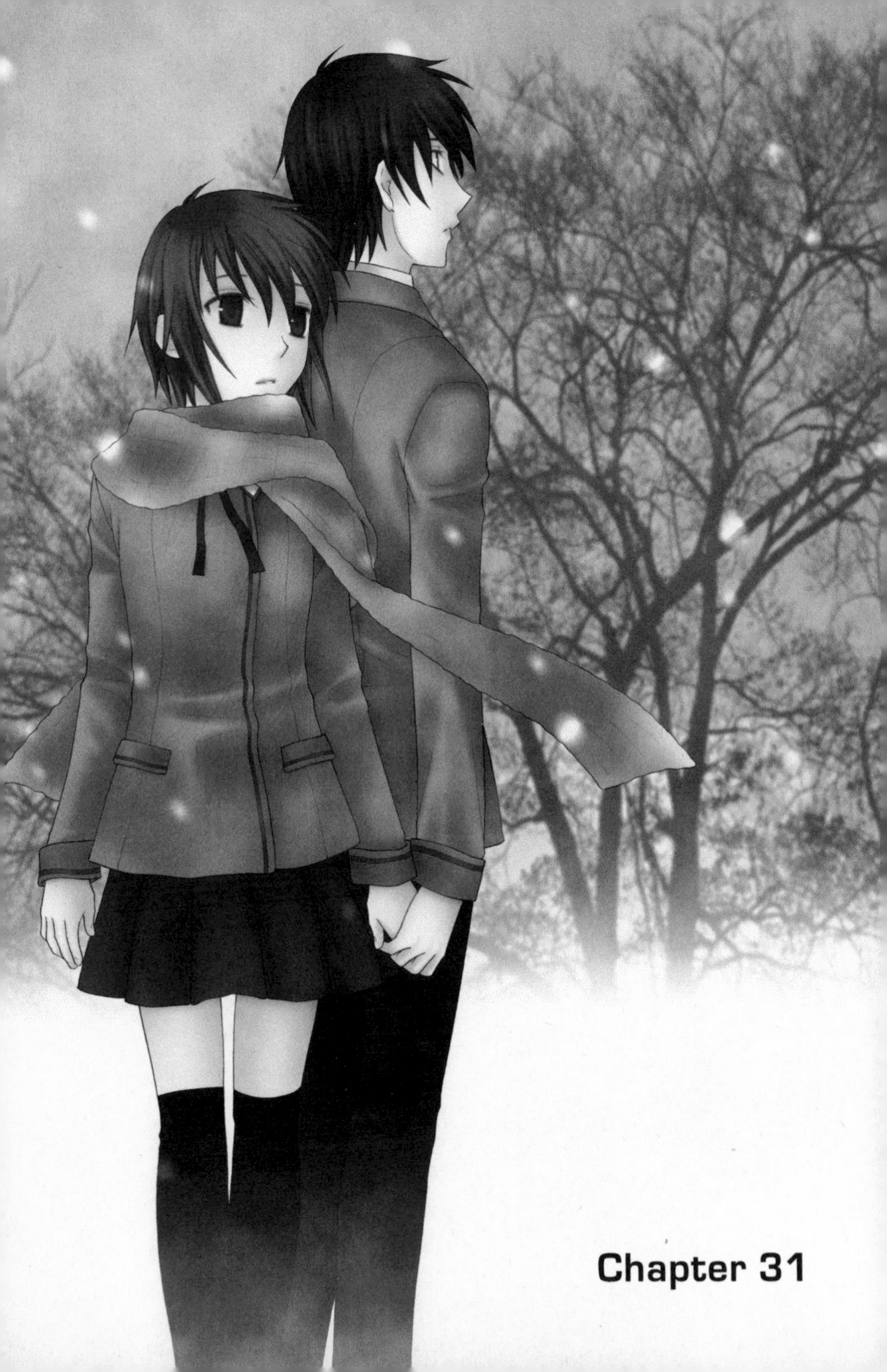

Chapter 31

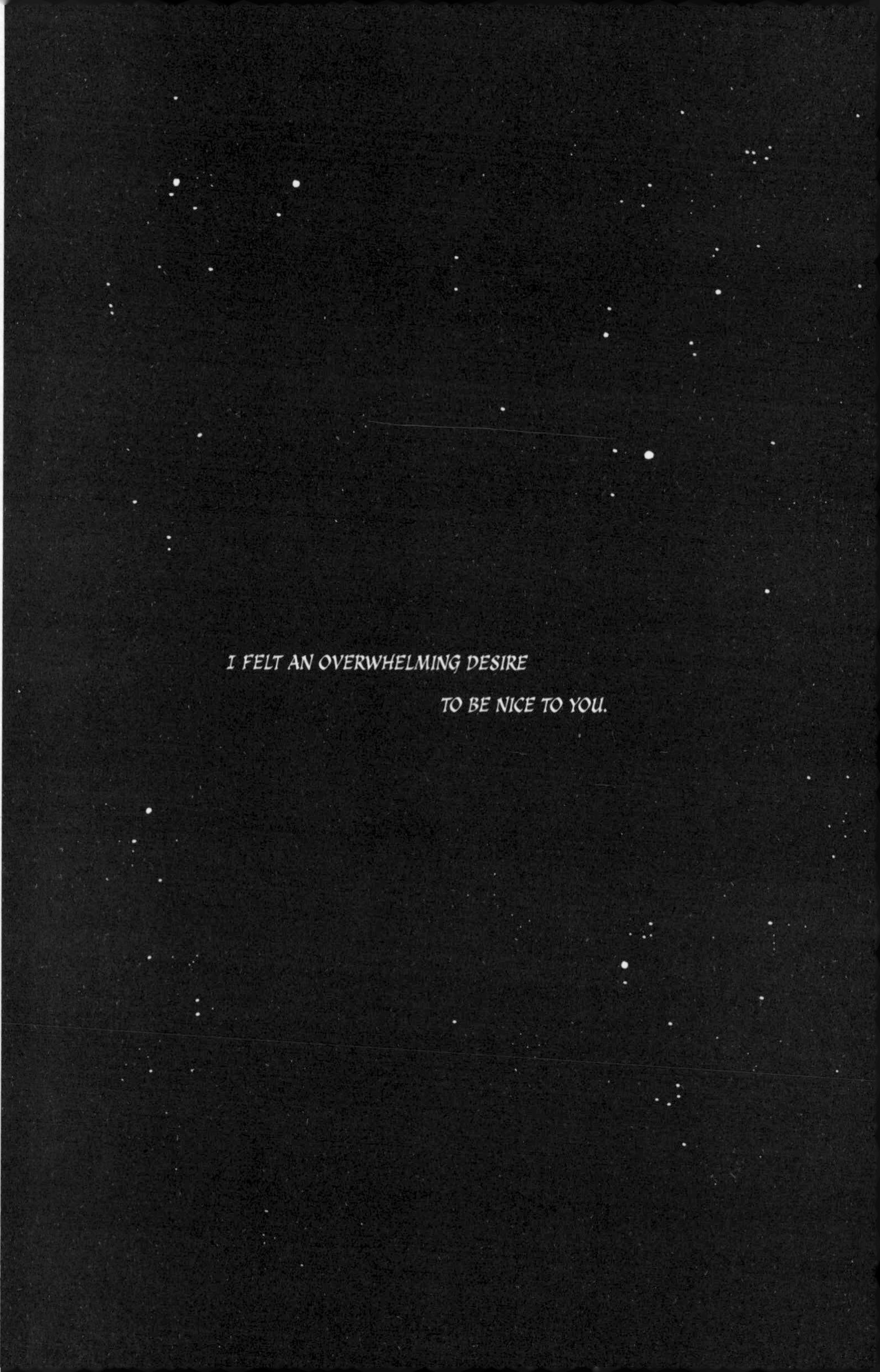
I FELT AN OVERWHELMING DESIRE
TO BE NICE TO YOU.

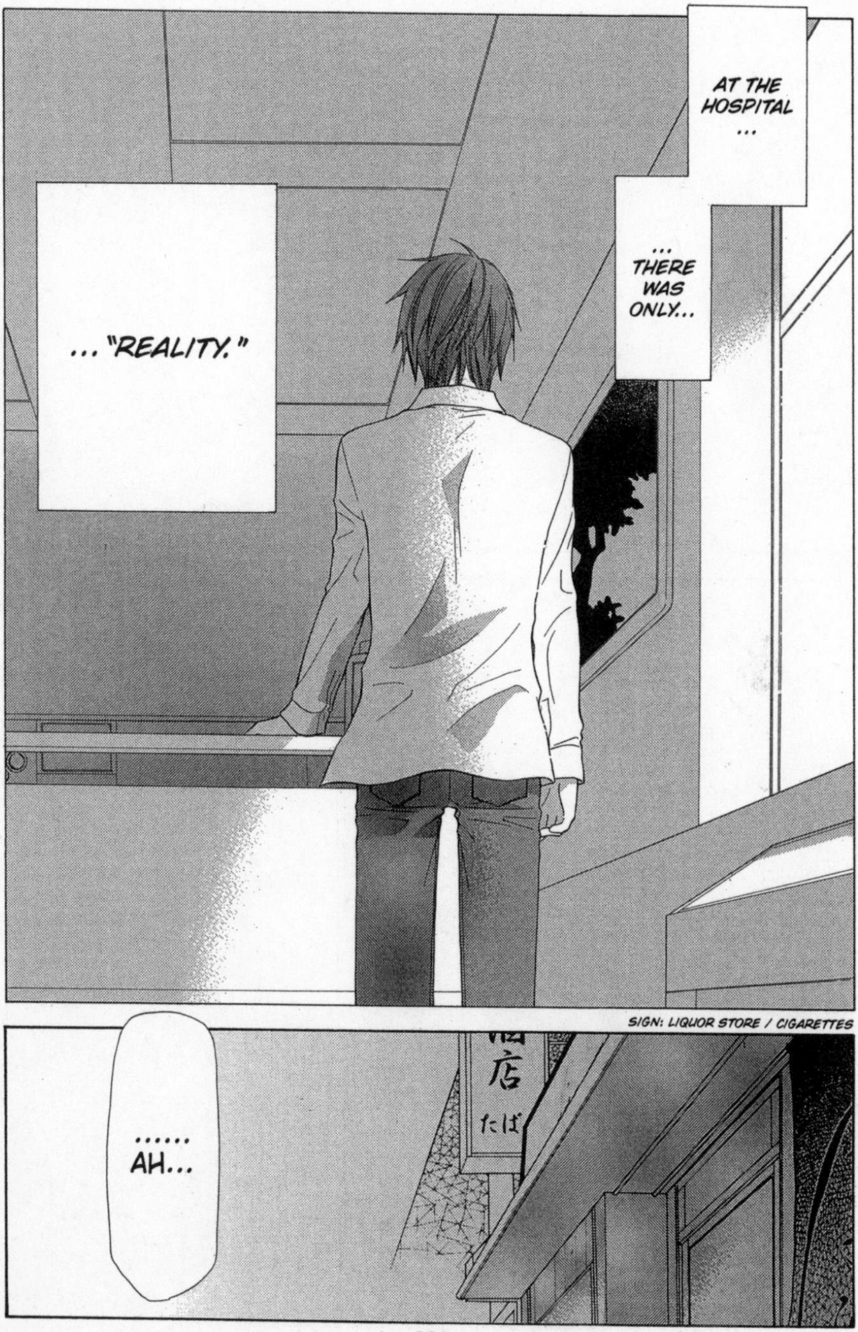
AT THE HOSPITAL ...
... THERE WAS ONLY...
... "REALITY."
SIGN: LIQUOR STORE / CIGARETTES
店
たば
...... AH...

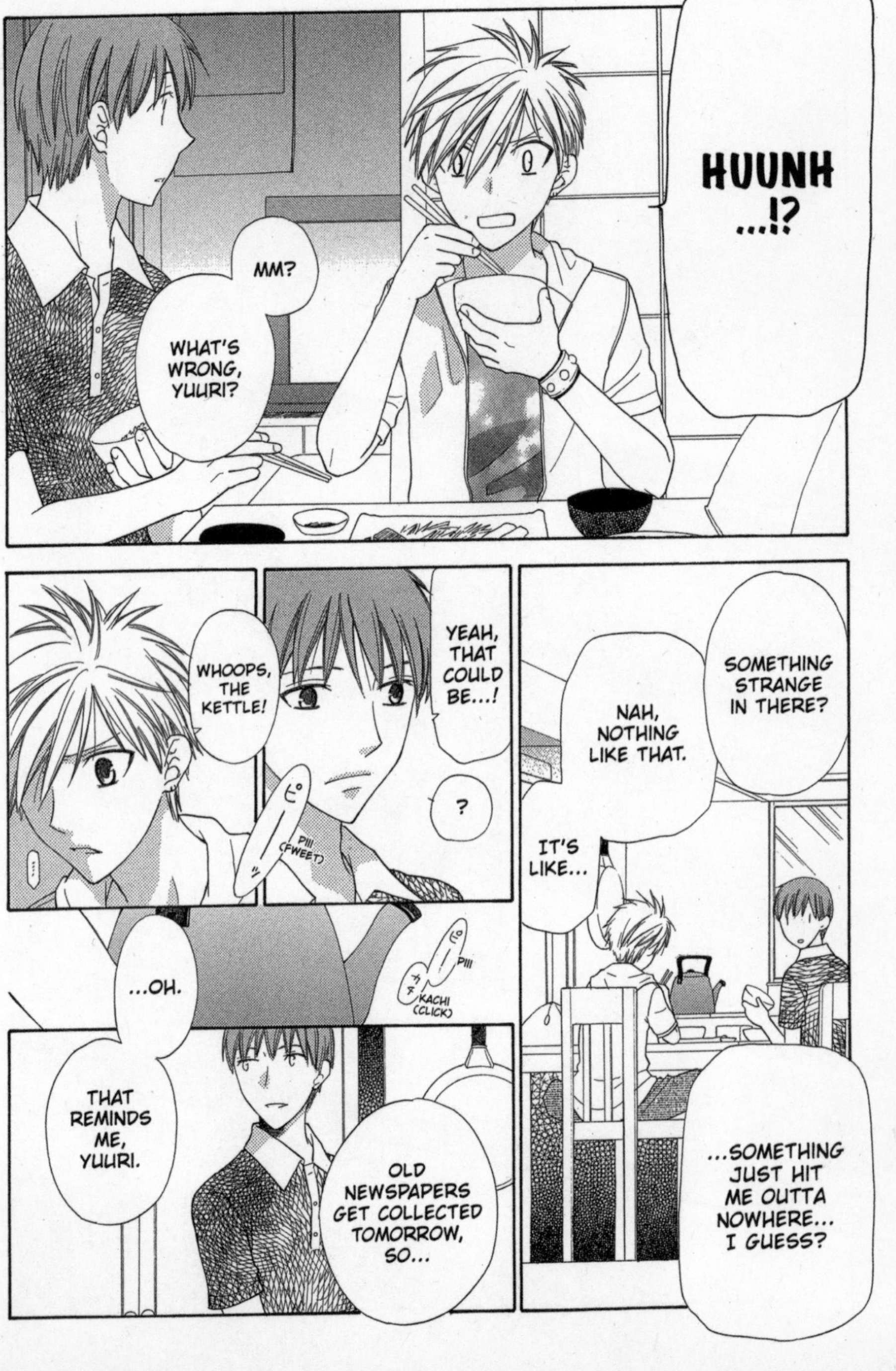
HUUNH ...!?
MM?
WHAT'S WRONG, YUURI?
SOMETHING STRANGE IN THERE?
NAH, NOTHING LIKE THAT.
IT'S LIKE...
...SOMETHING JUST HIT ME OUTTA NOWHERE... I GUESS?
YEAH, THAT COULD BE...!
?
PIII (FWEET)
WHOOPS, THE KETTLE!
PIII
KACHI (CLICK)
...OH.
THAT REMINDS ME, YUURI.
OLD NEWSPAPERS GET COLLECTED TOMORROW, SO...

Twinkle Stars

Nice to meet you and hello. I'm Takaya. We made it to Volume 6 of Twinkle Stars. Thank you!✿✿ By Volume 5, I had all the main characters (except for Sakura) on the cover, so from this volume on, I'm going to feature secondary characters on the cover.

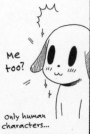

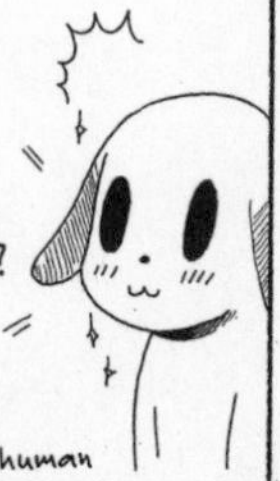
Me too?
Only human characters...

And so, Volume 6 begins...

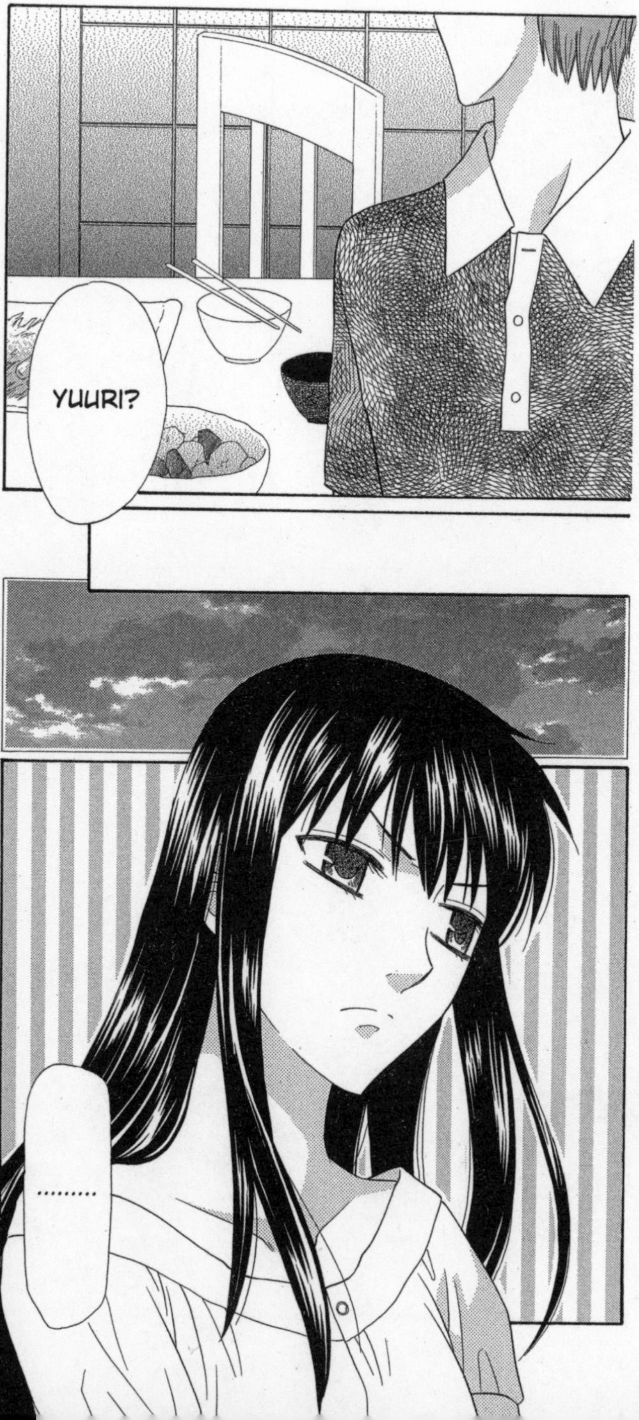
YUURI?
....

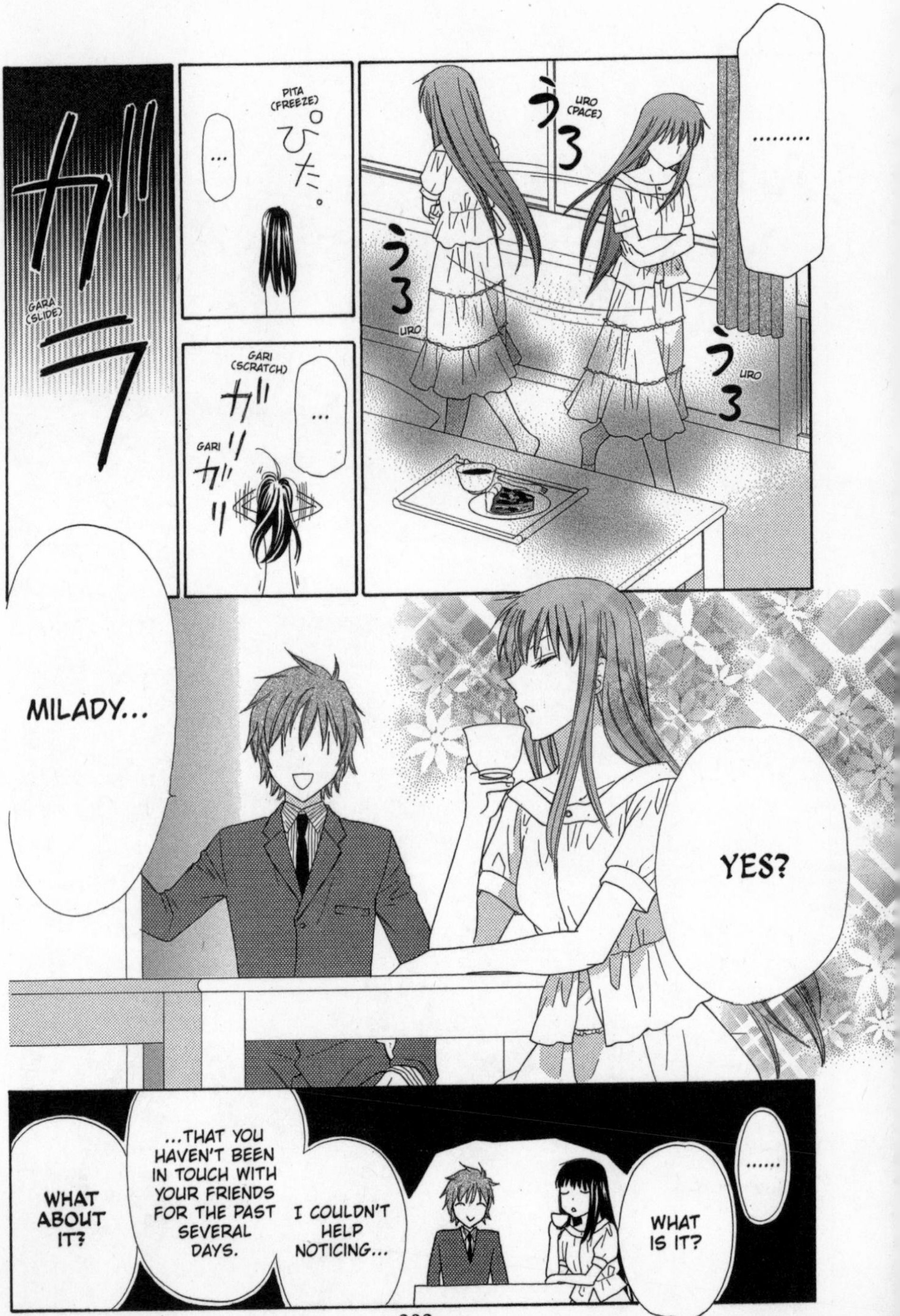
....
うろ
URO (PACE)
うろ
URO
うろ
URO
...
ぴた。
PITA (FREEZE)
...
ガリ
GARI (SCRATCH)
ガリ
GARI
ガラ
GARA (SLIDE)
MILADY...
YES?
......
WHAT IS IT?
I COULDN'T HELP NOTICING...
...THAT YOU HAVEN'T BEEN IN TOUCH WITH YOUR FRIENDS FOR THE PAST SEVERAL DAYS.
WHAT ABOUT IT?

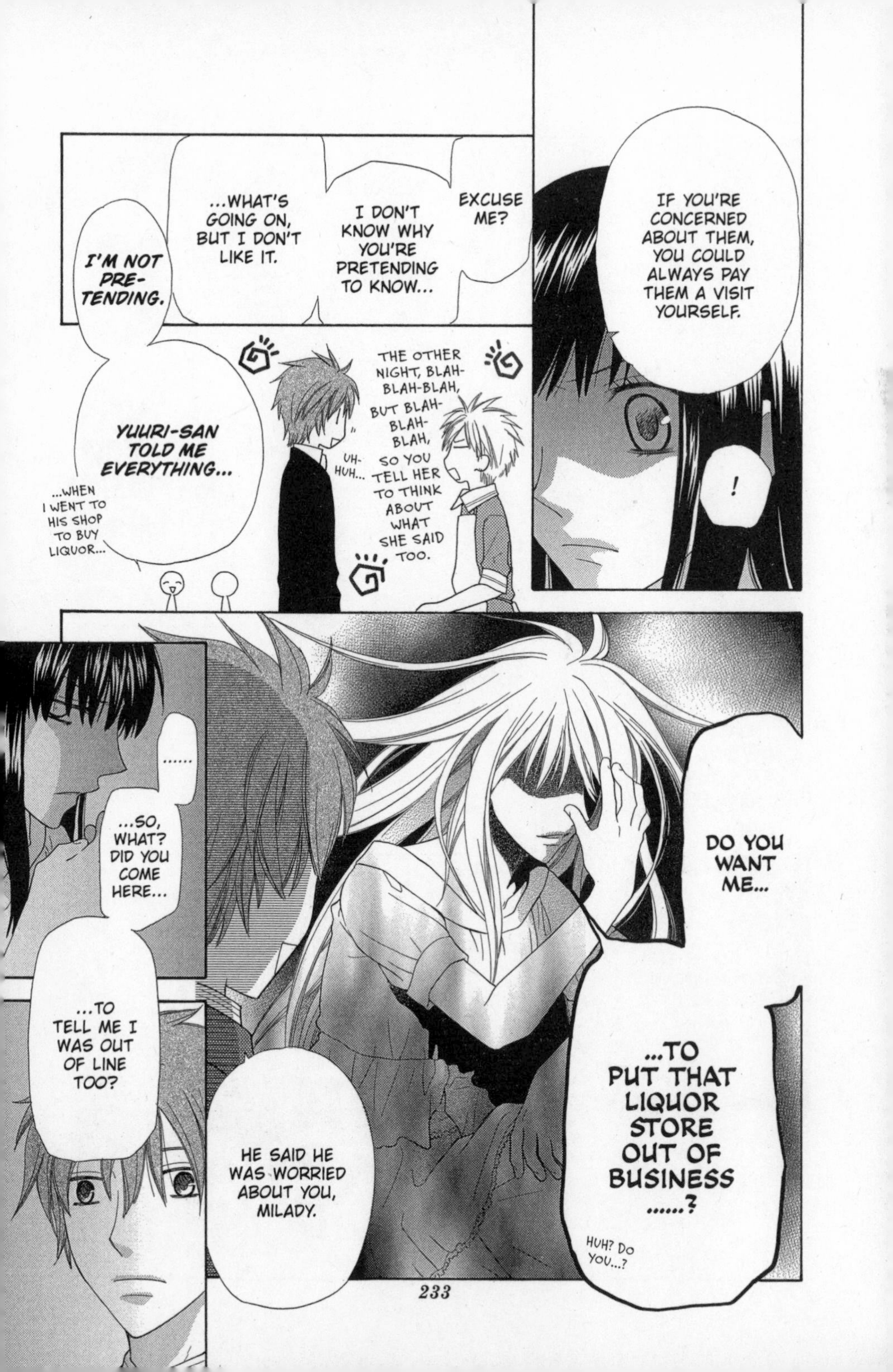
IF YOU'RE CONCERNED ABOUT THEM, YOU COULD ALWAYS PAY THEM A VISIT YOURSELF.
!
EXCUSE ME?
I DON'T KNOW WHY YOU'RE PRETENDING TO KNOW...
...WHAT'S GOING ON, BUT I DON'T LIKE IT.
I'M NOT PRETENDING.
YUURI-SAN TOLD ME EVERYTHING...
...WHEN I WENT TO HIS SHOP TO BUY LIQUOR...
THE OTHER NIGHT, BLAH-BLAH-BLAH, BUT BLAH-BLAH-BLAH, SO YOU TELL HER TO THINK ABOUT WHAT SHE SAID TOO.
UH-HUH...
DO YOU WANT ME...
...TO PUT THAT LIQUOR STORE OUT OF BUSINESS......?
HUH? DO YOU...?
HE SAID HE WAS WORRIED ABOUT YOU, MILADY.
......
...SO, WHAT? DID YOU COME HERE...
...TO TELL ME I WAS OUT OF LINE TOO?

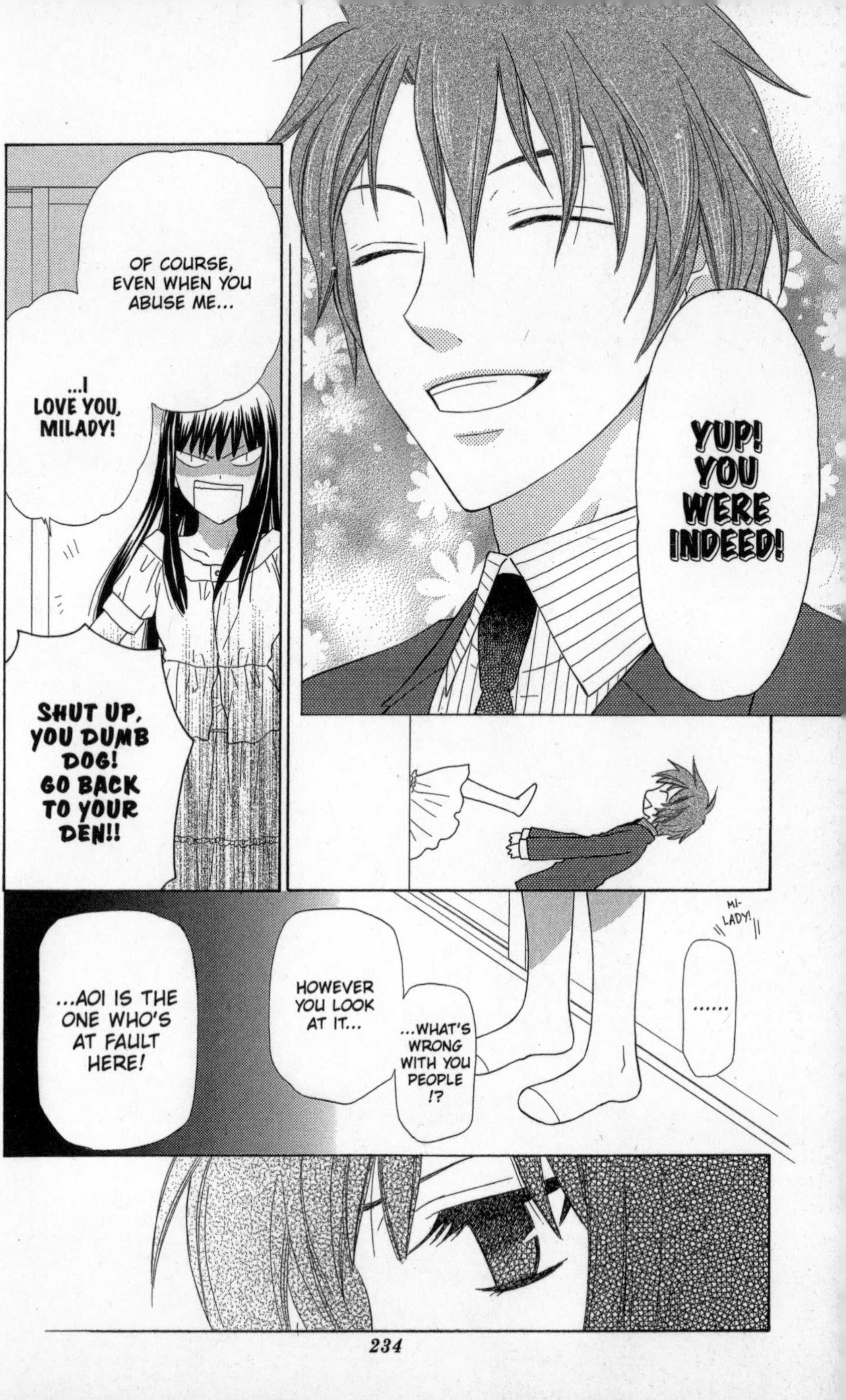
YUP! YOU WERE INDEED!
OF COURSE, EVEN WHEN YOU ABUSE ME...
...I LOVE YOU, MILADY!
SHUT UP, YOU DUMB DOG! GO BACK TO YOUR DEN!!
MI-LADY!
......
HOWEVER YOU LOOK AT IT...
...WHAT'S WRONG WITH YOU PEOPLE !?
...AOI IS THE ONE WHO'S AT FAULT HERE!

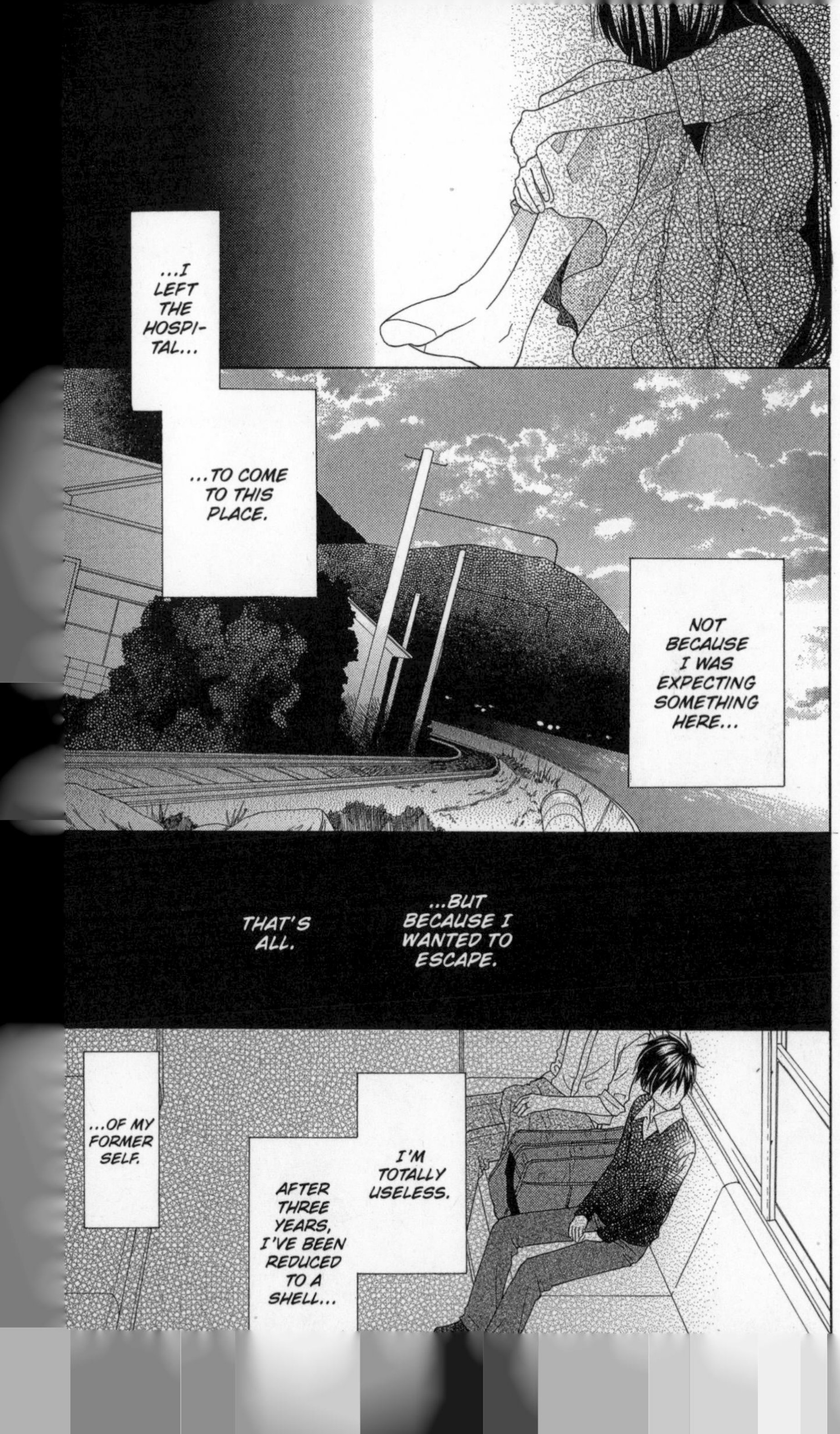
...I LEFT THE HOSPITAL...
...TO COME TO THIS PLACE.
NOT BECAUSE I WAS EXPECTING SOMETHING HERE...
...BUT BECAUSE I WANTED TO ESCAPE.
THAT'S ALL.
I'M TOTALLY USELESS.
AFTER THREE YEARS, I'VE BEEN REDUCED TO A SHELL...
...OF MY FORMER SELF.

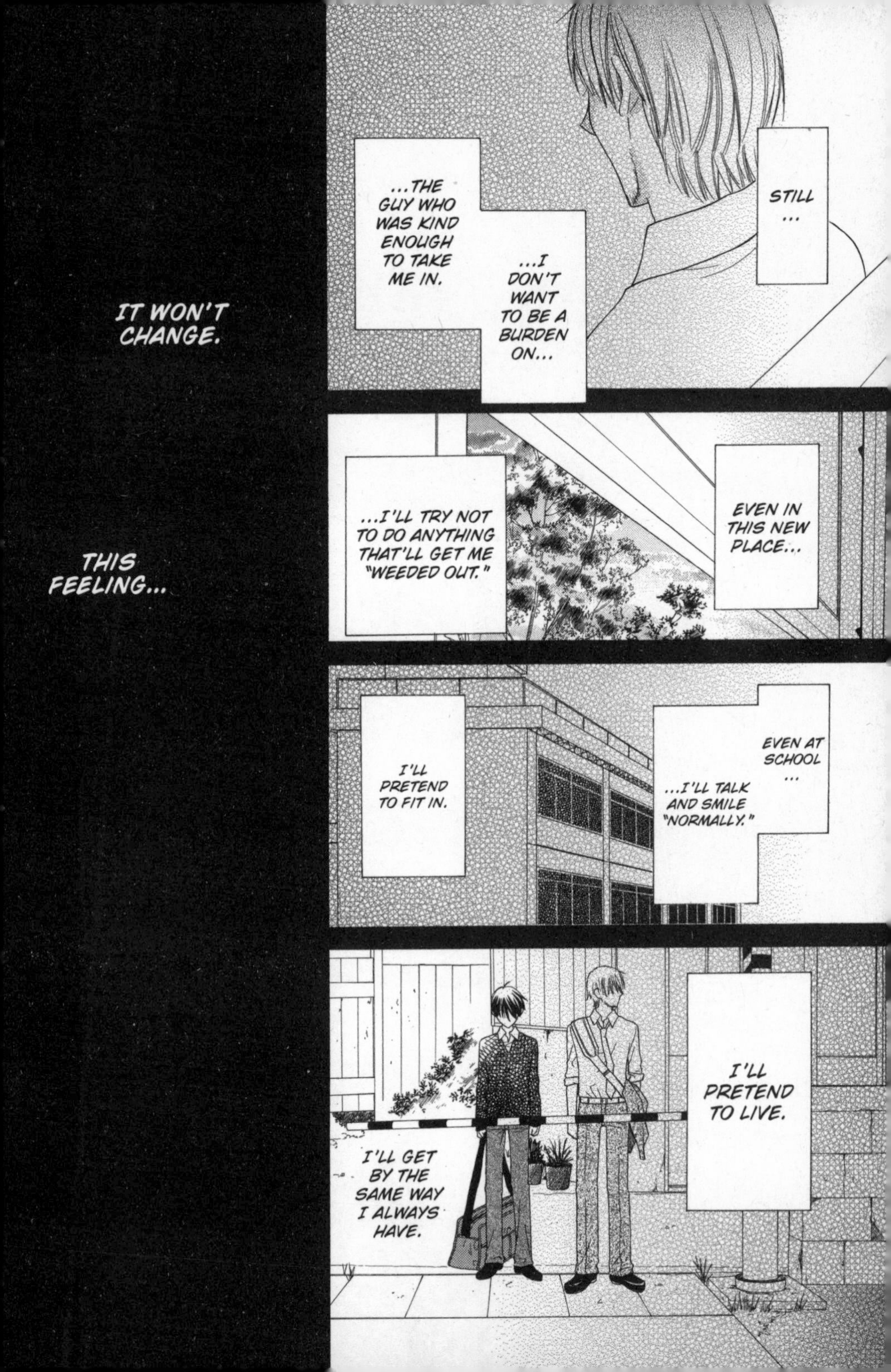
STILL...
...I DON'T WANT TO BE A BURDEN ON...
...THE GUY WHO WAS KIND ENOUGH TO TAKE ME IN.
EVEN IN THIS NEW PLACE...
...I'LL TRY NOT TO DO ANYTHING THAT'LL GET ME "WEEDED OUT."
EVEN AT SCHOOL...
...I'LL TALK AND SMILE "NORMALLY."
I'LL PRETEND TO FIT IN.
I'LL PRETEND TO LIVE.
I'LL GET BY THE SAME WAY I ALWAYS HAVE.
IT WON'T CHANGE.
THIS FEELING...

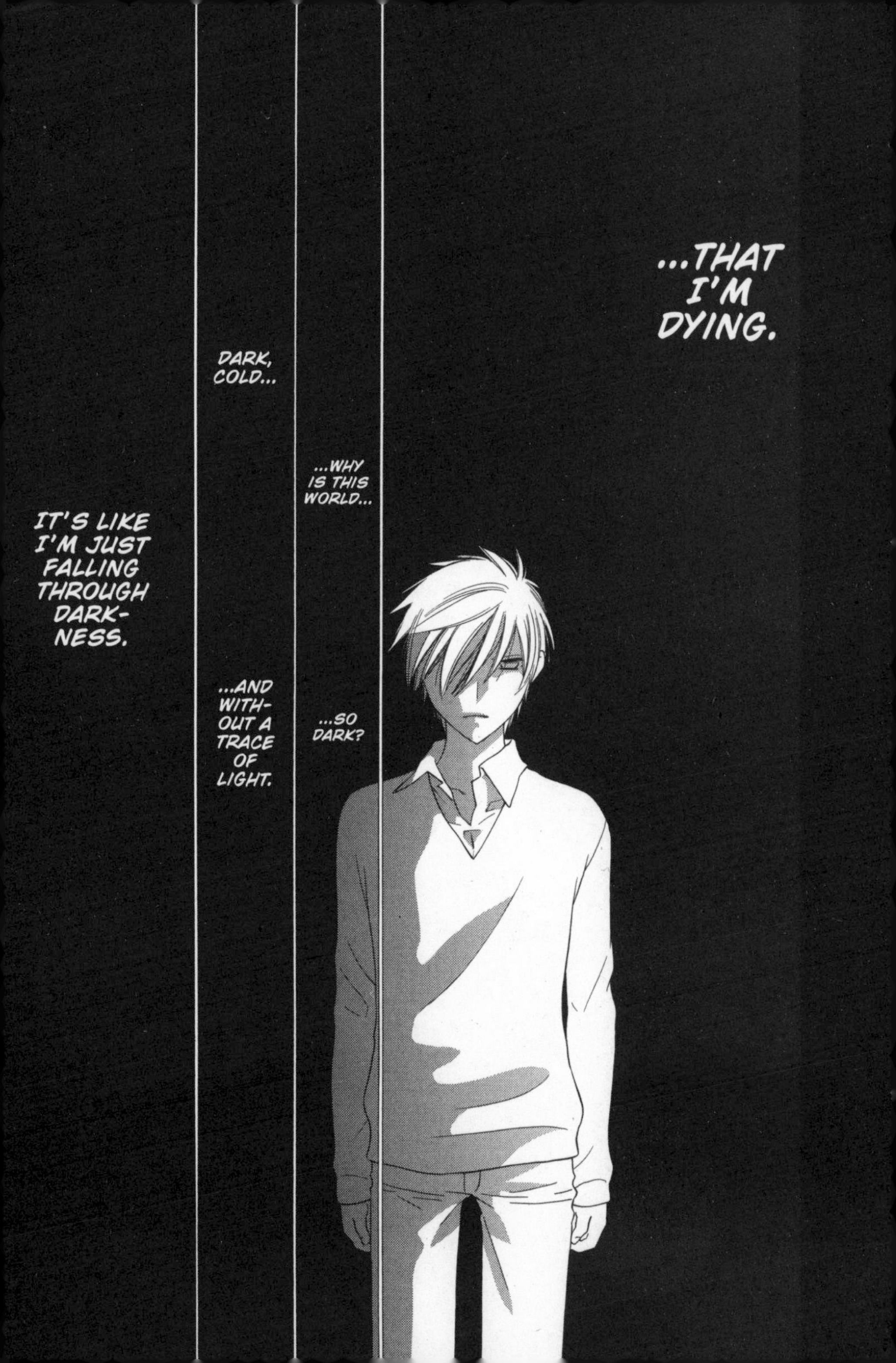
...THAT I'M DYING.
...WHY IS THIS WORLD...
...SO DARK?
DARK, COLD...
...AND WITH-OUT A TRACE OF LIGHT.
IT'S LIKE I'M JUST FALLING THROUGH DARK-NESS.

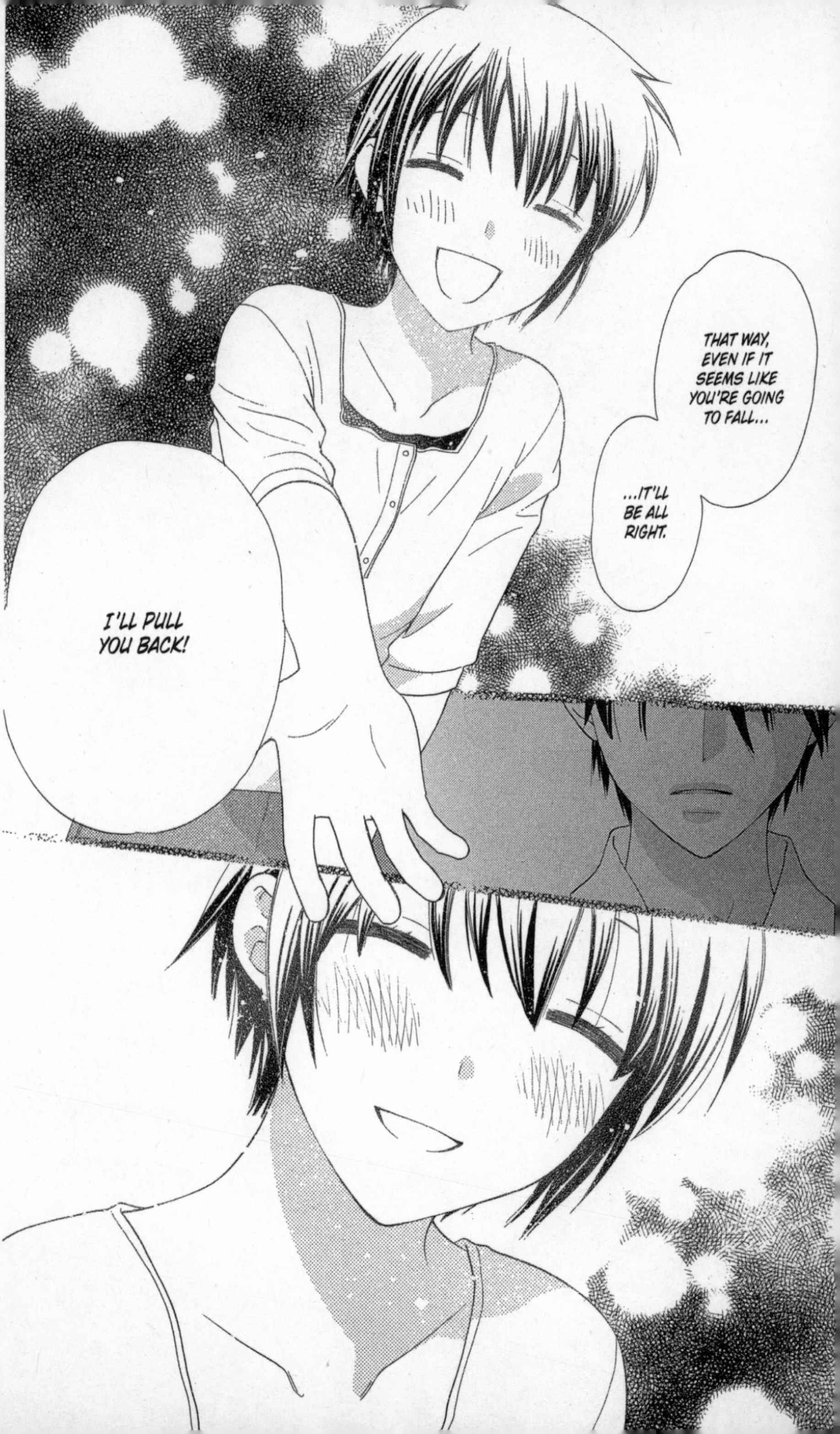
THAT WAY, EVEN IF IT SEEMS LIKE YOU'RE GOING TO FALL...
...IT'LL BE ALL RIGHT.
I'LL PULL YOU BACK!

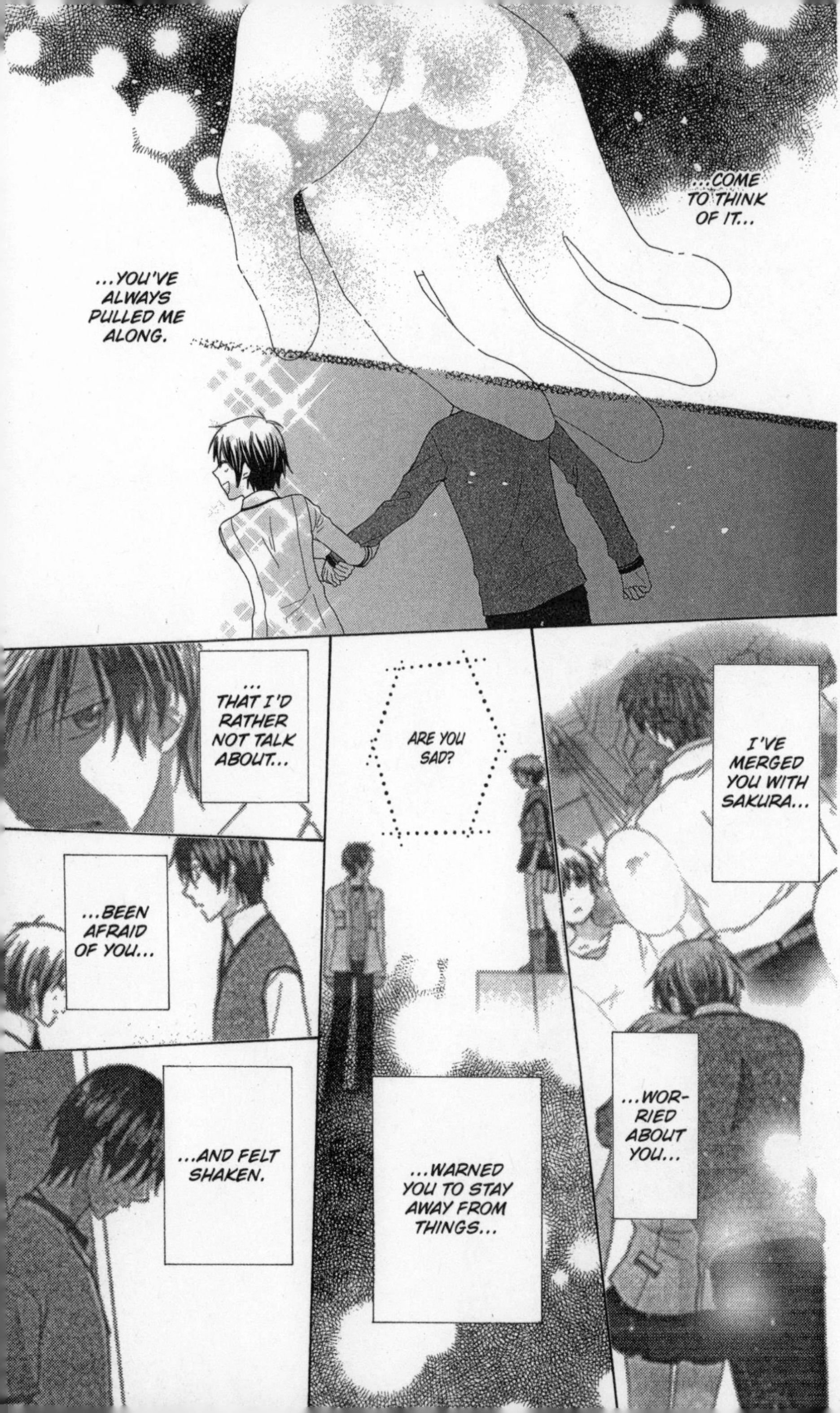
...COME TO THINK OF IT...
...YOU'VE ALWAYS PULLED ME ALONG.
I'VE MERGED YOU WITH SAKURA...
...WOR-RIED ABOUT YOU...
ARE YOU SAD?
...WARNED YOU TO STAY AWAY FROM THINGS...
...THAT I'D RATHER NOT TALK ABOUT...
...BEEN AFRAID OF YOU...
...AND FELT SHAKEN.

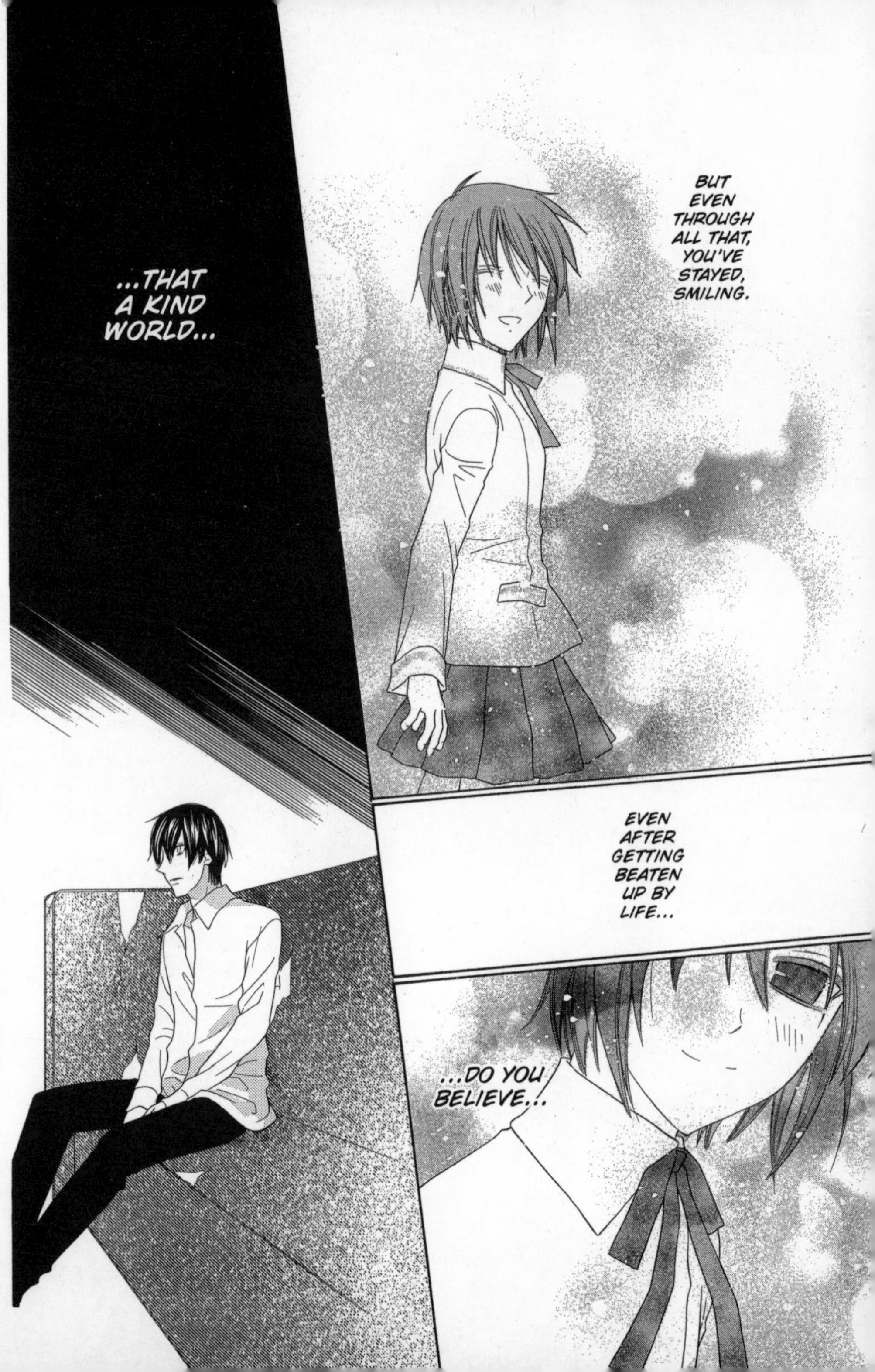
BUT EVEN THROUGH ALL THAT, YOU'VE STAYED, SMILING.
EVEN AFTER GETTING BEATEN UP BY LIFE...
...DO YOU BELIEVE...
...THAT A KIND WORLD...

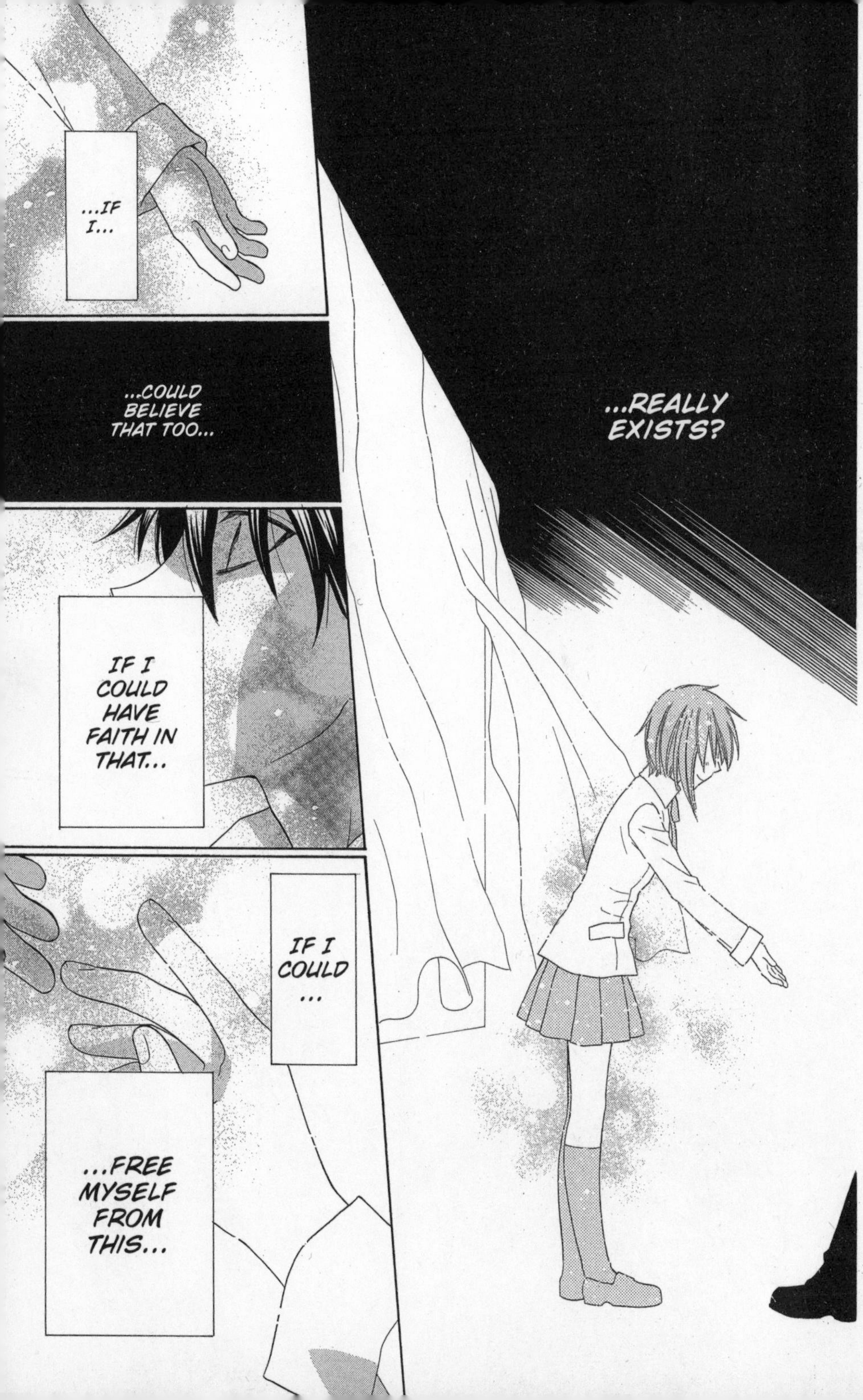
...REALLY EXISTS?
...IF I...
...COULD BELIEVE THAT TOO...
IF I COULD HAVE FAITH IN THAT...
IF I COULD ...
...FREE MYSELF FROM THIS...

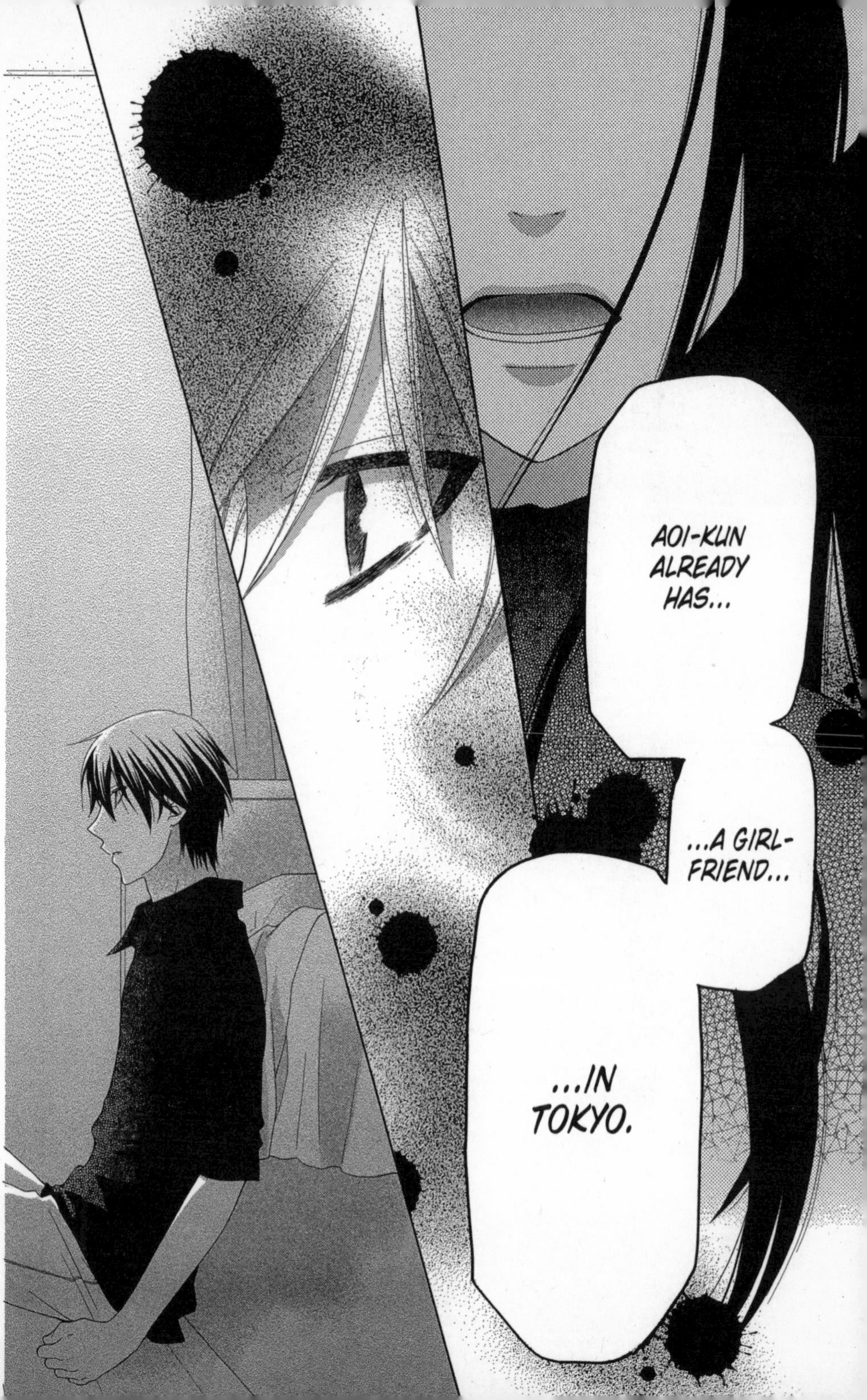
AOI-KUN ALREADY HAS...
...A GIRL-FRIEND...
...IN TOKYO.

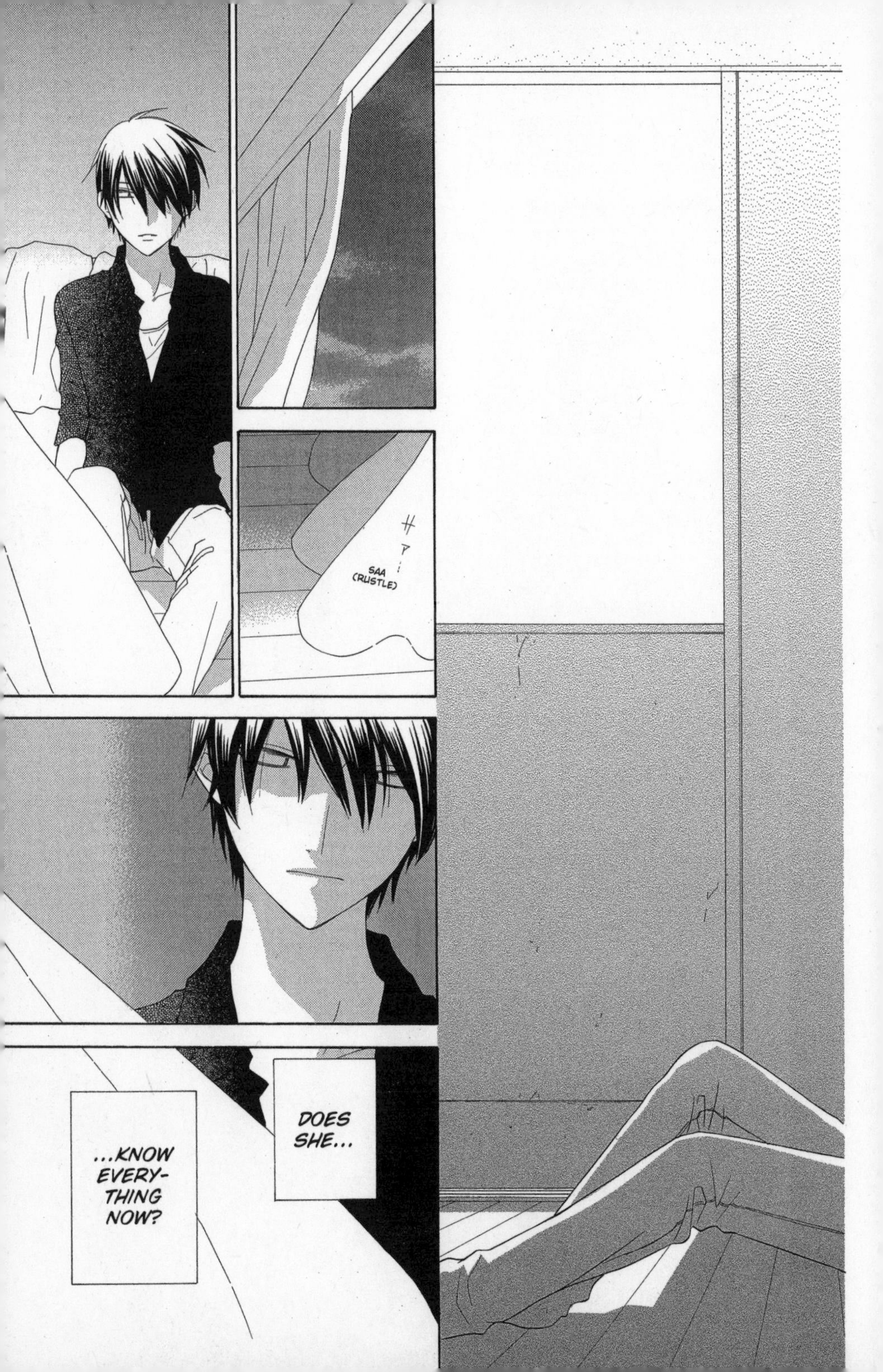
SAA (RUSTLE)
DOES SHE...
...KNOW EVERY-THING NOW?

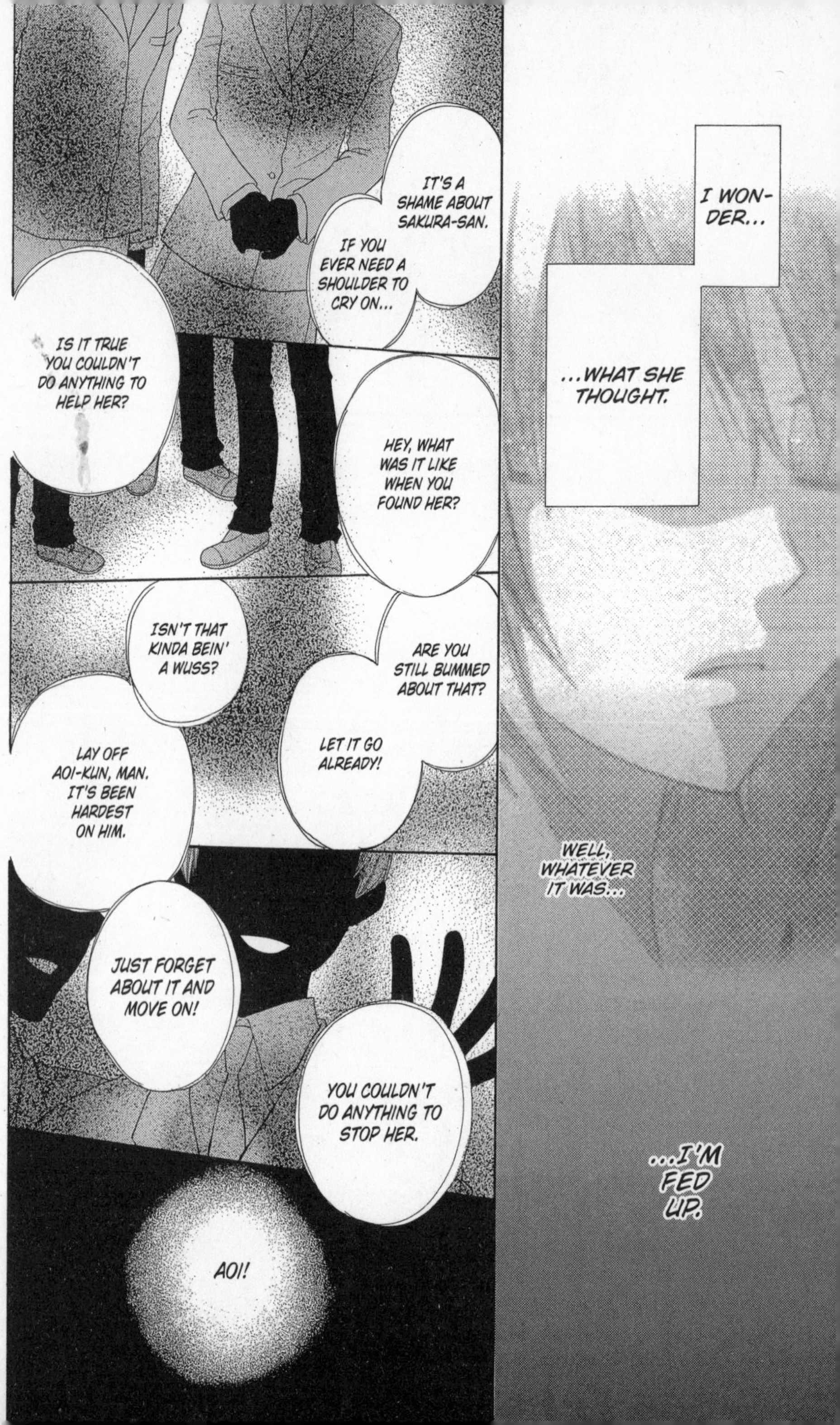
I WONDER...
...WHAT SHE THOUGHT.
WELL, WHATEVER IT WAS...
...I'M FED UP.
IT'S A SHAME ABOUT SAKURA-SAN.
IF YOU EVER NEED A SHOULDER TO CRY ON...
IS IT TRUE YOU COULDN'T DO ANYTHING TO HELP HER?
HEY, WHAT WAS IT LIKE WHEN YOU FOUND HER?
ARE YOU STILL BUMMED ABOUT THAT?
LET IT GO ALREADY!
ISN'T THAT KINDA BEIN' A WUSS?
LAY OFF AOI-KUN, MAN. IT'S BEEN HARDEST ON HIM.
JUST FORGET ABOUT IT AND MOVE ON!
YOU COULDN'T DO ANYTHING TO STOP HER.
AOI!

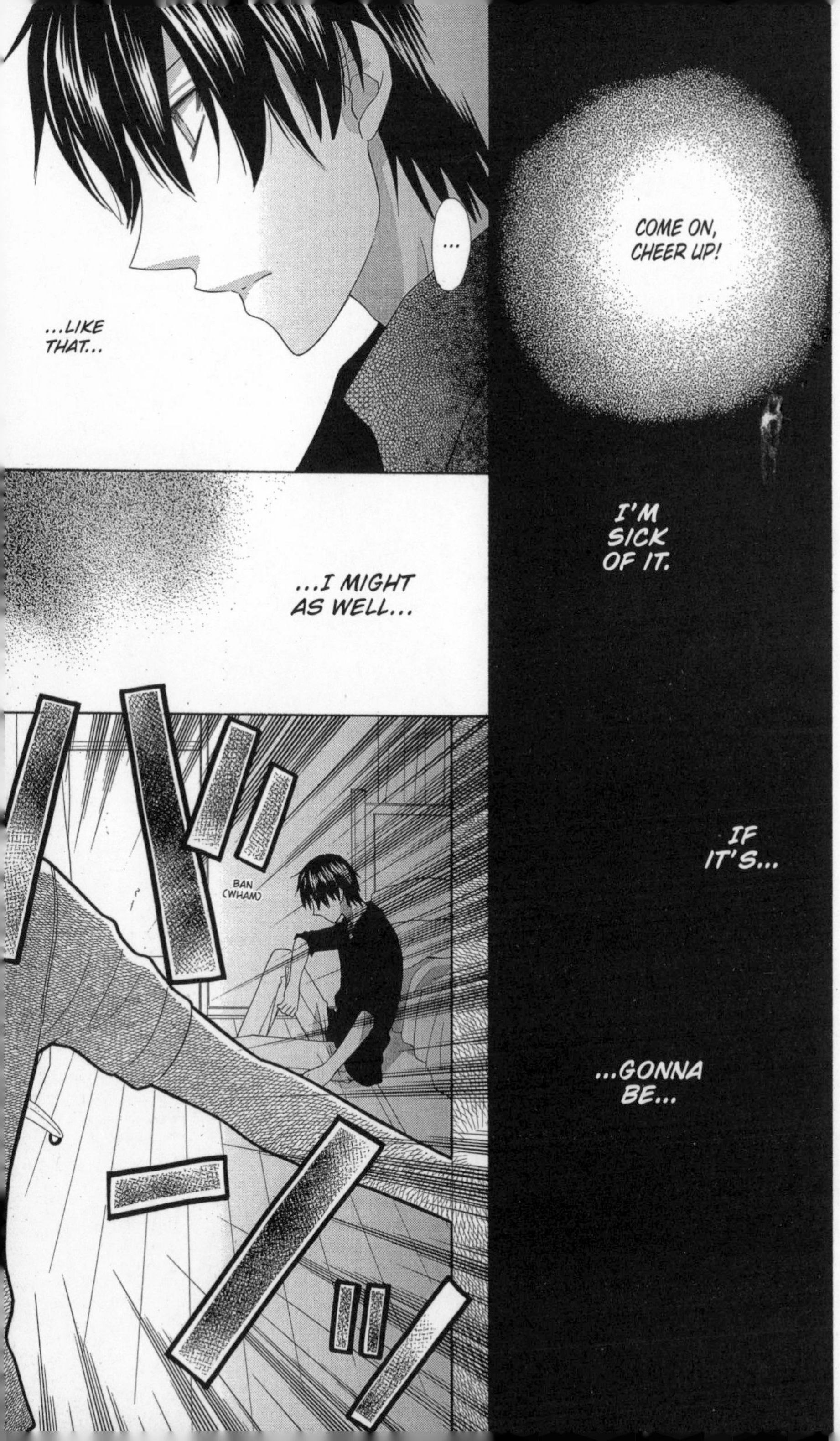
COME ON, CHEER UP!
I'M SICK OF IT.
IF IT'S...
...GONNA BE...
...
...LIKE THAT...
...I MIGHT AS WELL...
BAN (WHAM)

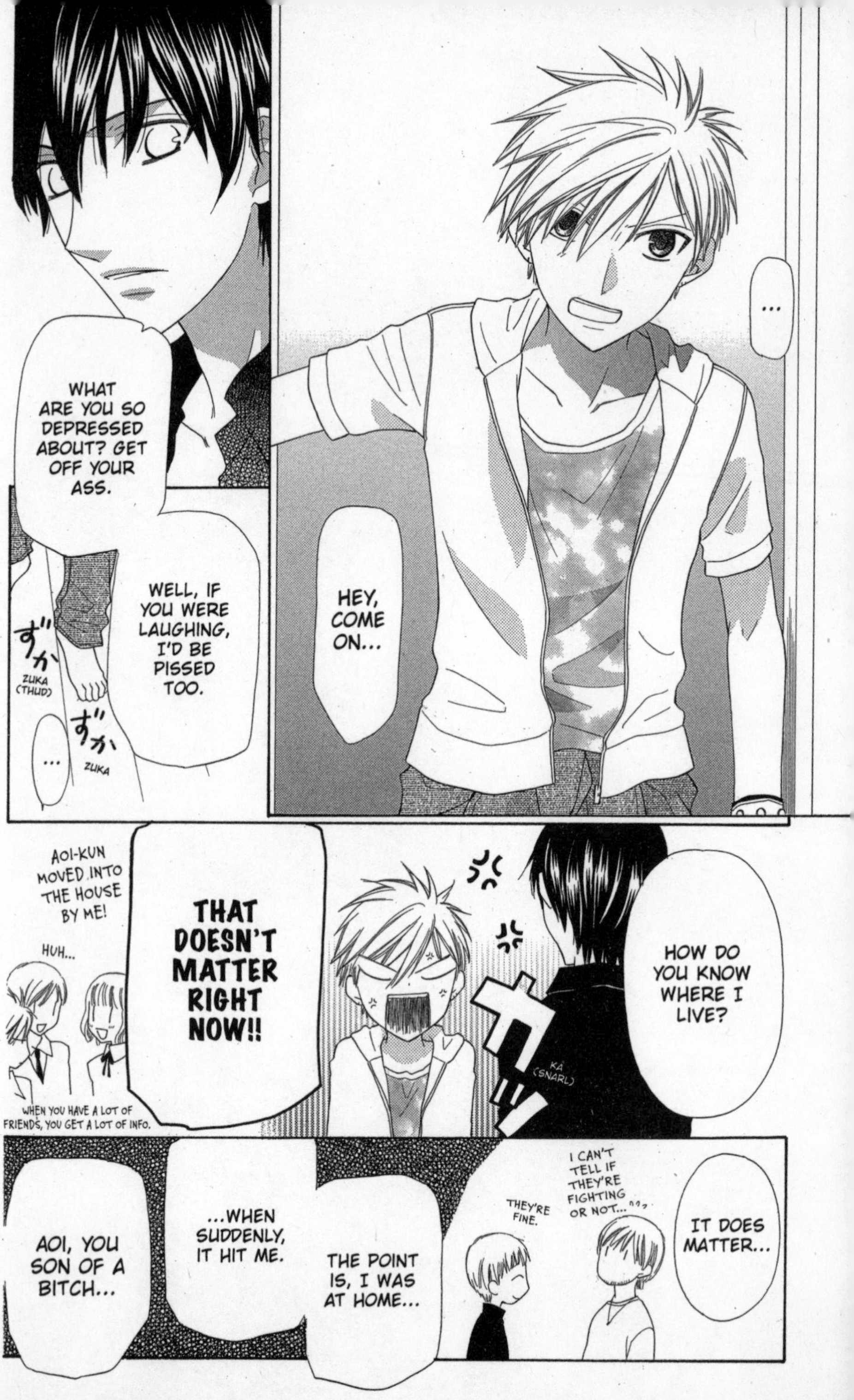
...
HEY, COME ON...
WHAT ARE YOU SO DEPRESSED ABOUT? GET OFF YOUR ASS.
WELL, IF YOU WERE LAUGHING, I'D BE PISSED TOO.
ずか
ZUKA (THUD)
ずか
ZUKA
...
HOW DO YOU KNOW WHERE I LIVE?
KA (SNARL)
THAT DOESN'T MATTER RIGHT NOW!!
AOI-KUN MOVED INTO THE HOUSE BY ME!
HUH...
WHEN YOU HAVE A LOT OF FRIENDS, YOU GET A LOT OF INFO.
IT DOES MATTER...
I CAN'T TELL IF THEY'RE FIGHTING OR NOT...???
THEY'RE FINE.
THE POINT IS, I WAS AT HOME...
...WHEN SUDDENLY, IT HIT ME.
AOI, YOU SON OF A BITCH...

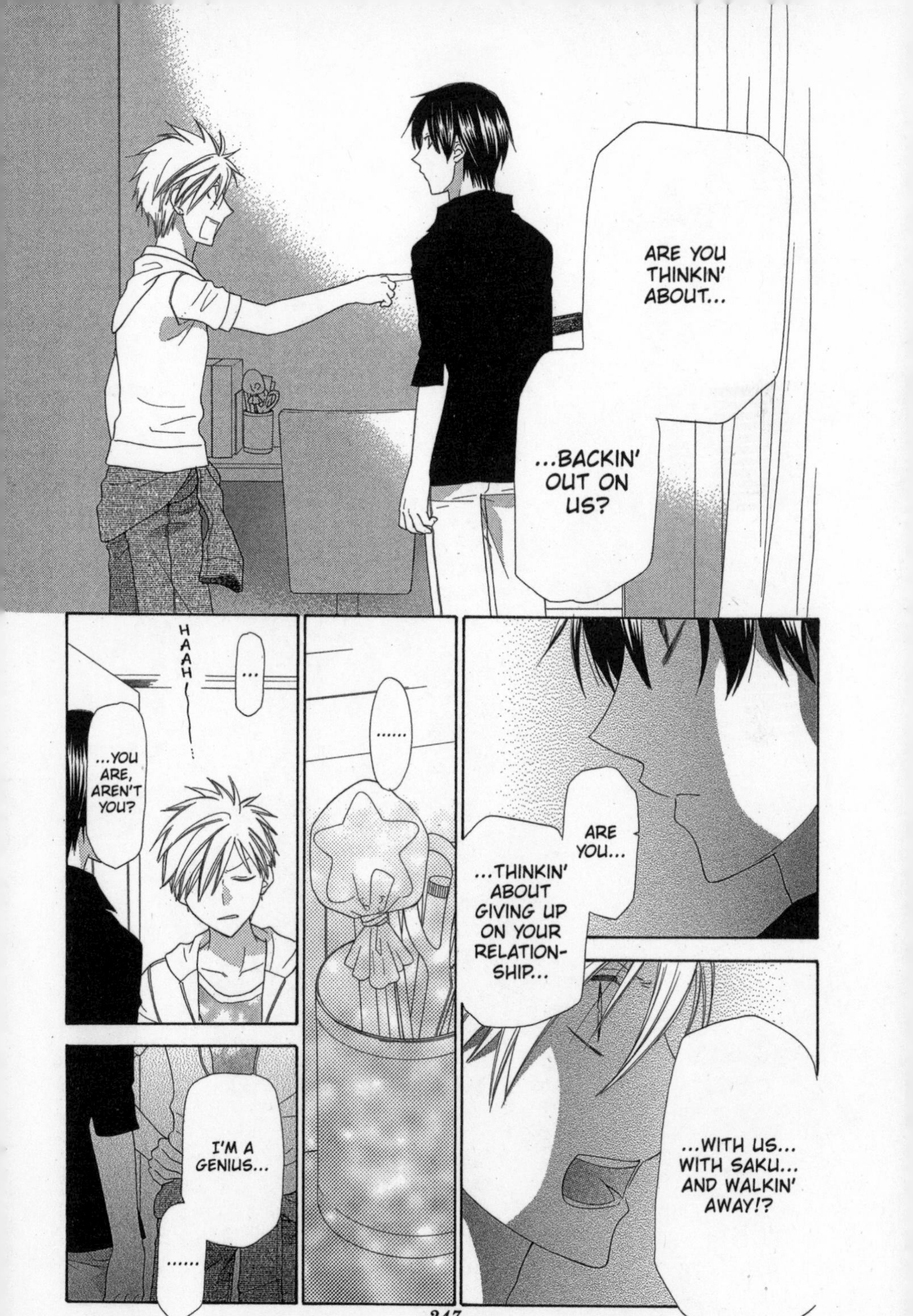
ARE YOU THINKIN' ABOUT...
...BACKIN' OUT ON US?
ARE YOU...
...THINKIN' ABOUT GIVING UP ON YOUR RELATION-SHIP...
...WITH US... WITH SAKU... AND WALKIN' AWAY!?
......
...
HAAH
...YOU ARE, AREN'T YOU?
I'M A GENIUS...
......

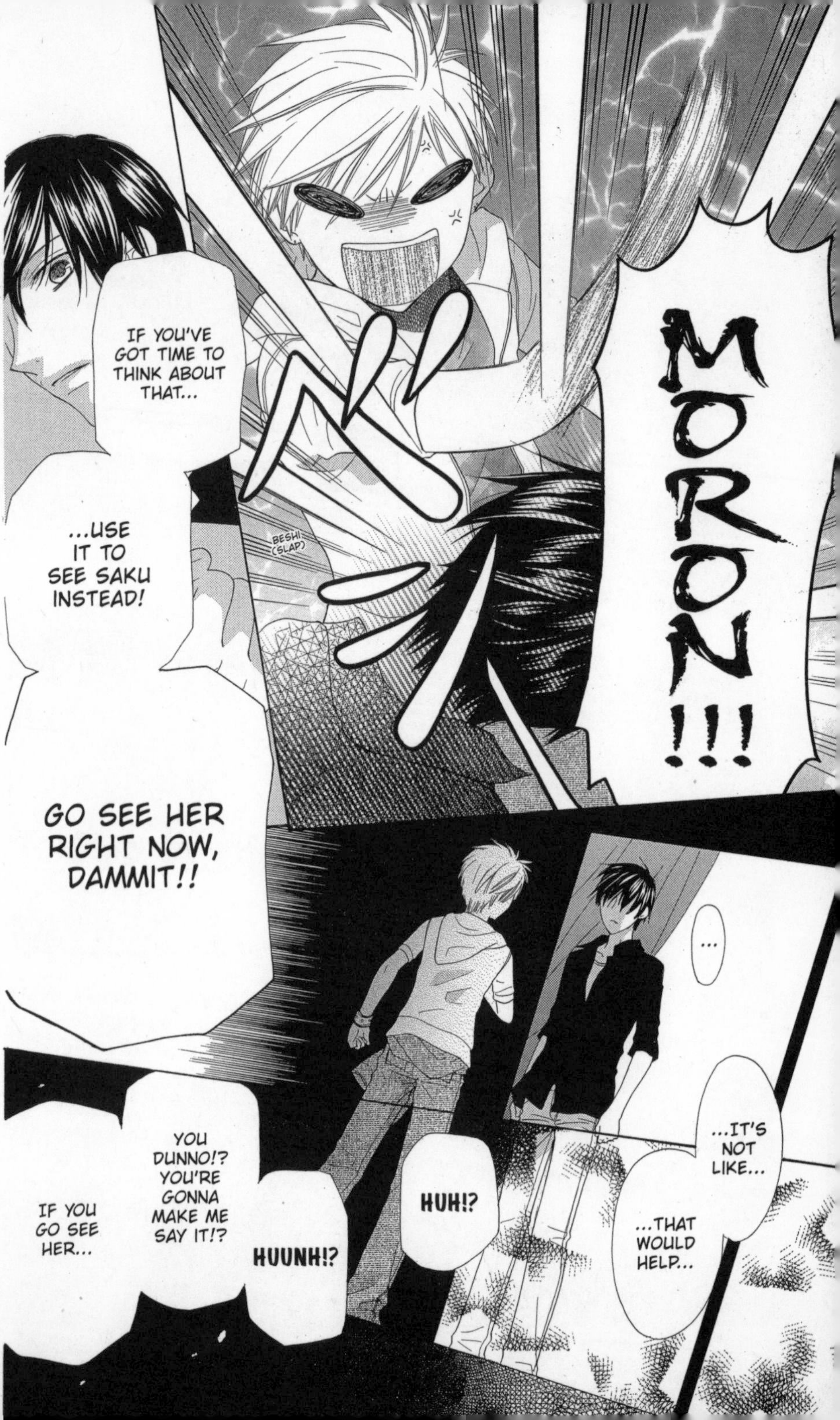
MORON!!!
BESHI (SLAP)
IF YOU'VE GOT TIME TO THINK ABOUT THAT...
...USE IT TO SEE SAKU INSTEAD!
GO SEE HER RIGHT NOW, DAMMIT!!
...
...IT'S NOT LIKE...
...THAT WOULD HELP...
HUH!?
HUUNH!?
YOU DUNNO!? YOU'RE GONNA MAKE ME SAY IT!?
IF YOU GO SEE HER...

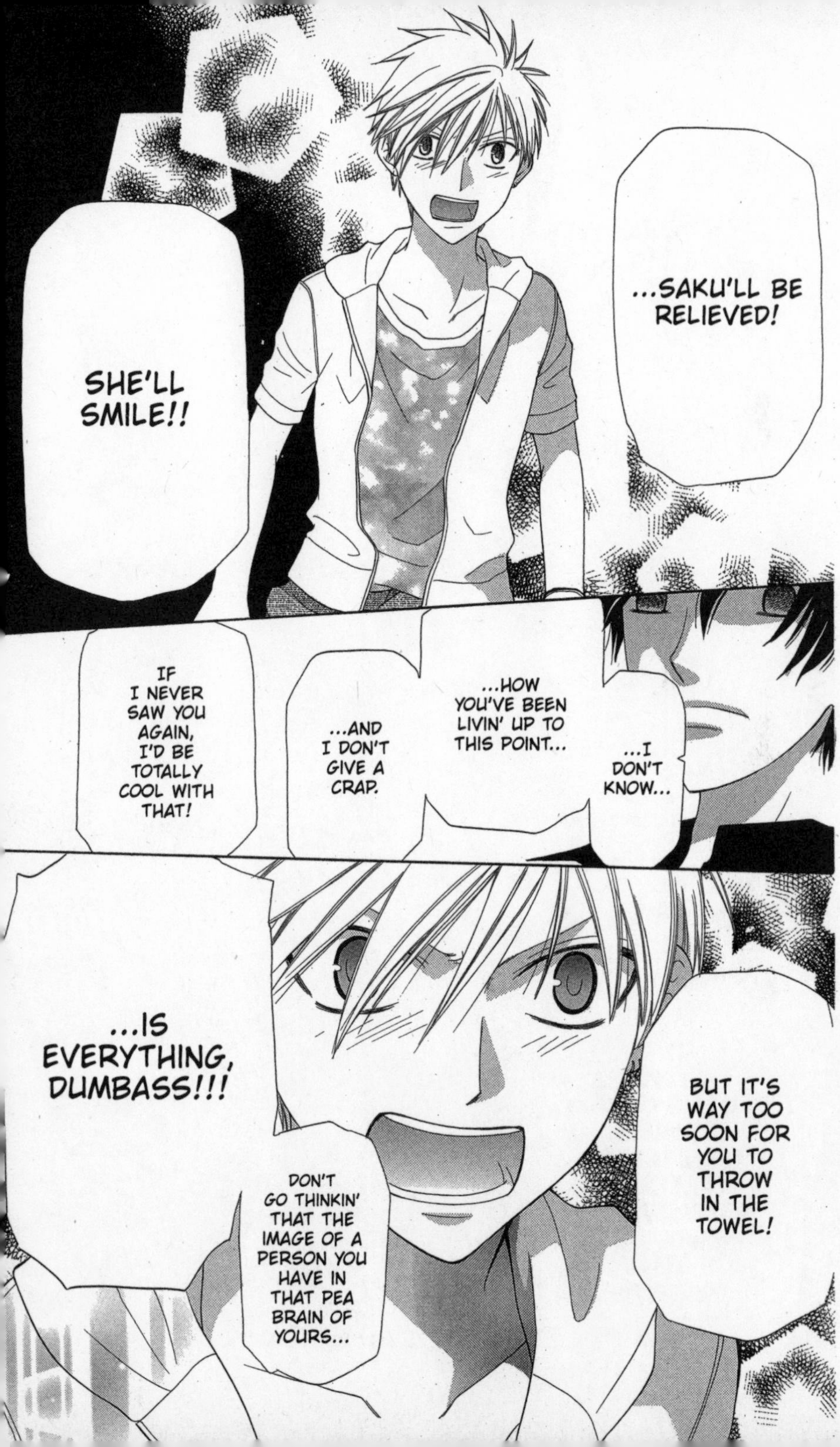
...SAKU'LL BE RELIEVED!
SHE'LL SMILE!!
...I DON'T KNOW...
...HOW YOU'VE BEEN LIVIN' UP TO THIS POINT...
...AND I DON'T GIVE A CRAP.
IF I NEVER SAW YOU AGAIN, I'D BE TOTALLY COOL WITH THAT!
BUT IT'S WAY TOO SOON FOR YOU TO THROW IN THE TOWEL!
DON'T GO THINKIN' THAT THE IMAGE OF A PERSON YOU HAVE IN THAT PEA BRAIN OF YOURS...
...IS EVERYTHING, DUMBASS!!!

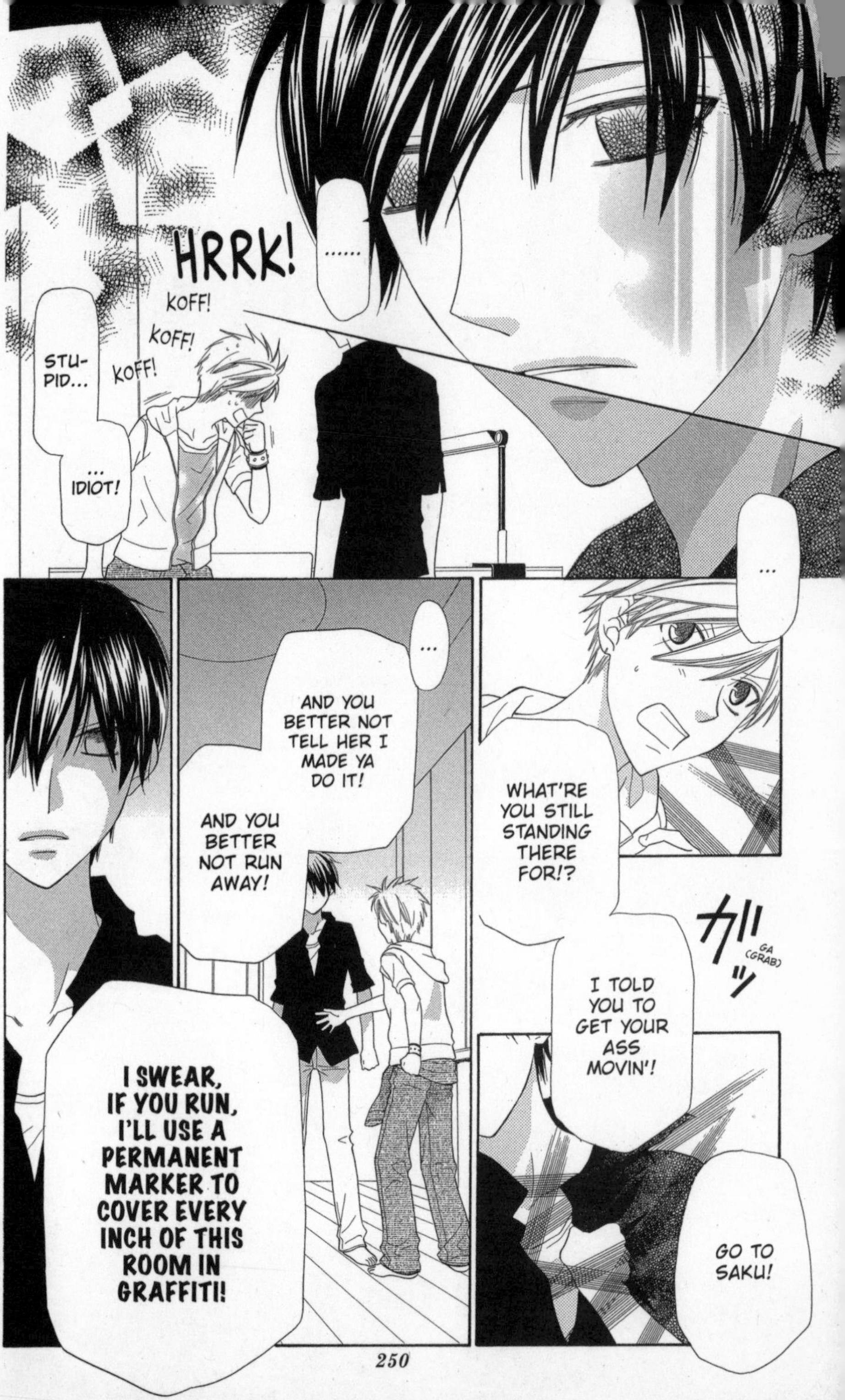
......
HRRK!
KOFF!
KOFF!
KOFF!
STU-PID...
...IDIOT!
...
WHAT'RE YOU STILL STANDING THERE FOR!?
ガッ
GA (GRAB)
I TOLD YOU TO GET YOUR ASS MOVIN'!
GO TO SAKU!
...
AND YOU BETTER NOT TELL HER I MADE YA DO IT!
AND YOU BETTER NOT RUN AWAY!
I SWEAR, IF YOU RUN, I'LL USE A PERMANENT MARKER TO COVER EVERY INCH OF THIS ROOM IN GRAFFITI!

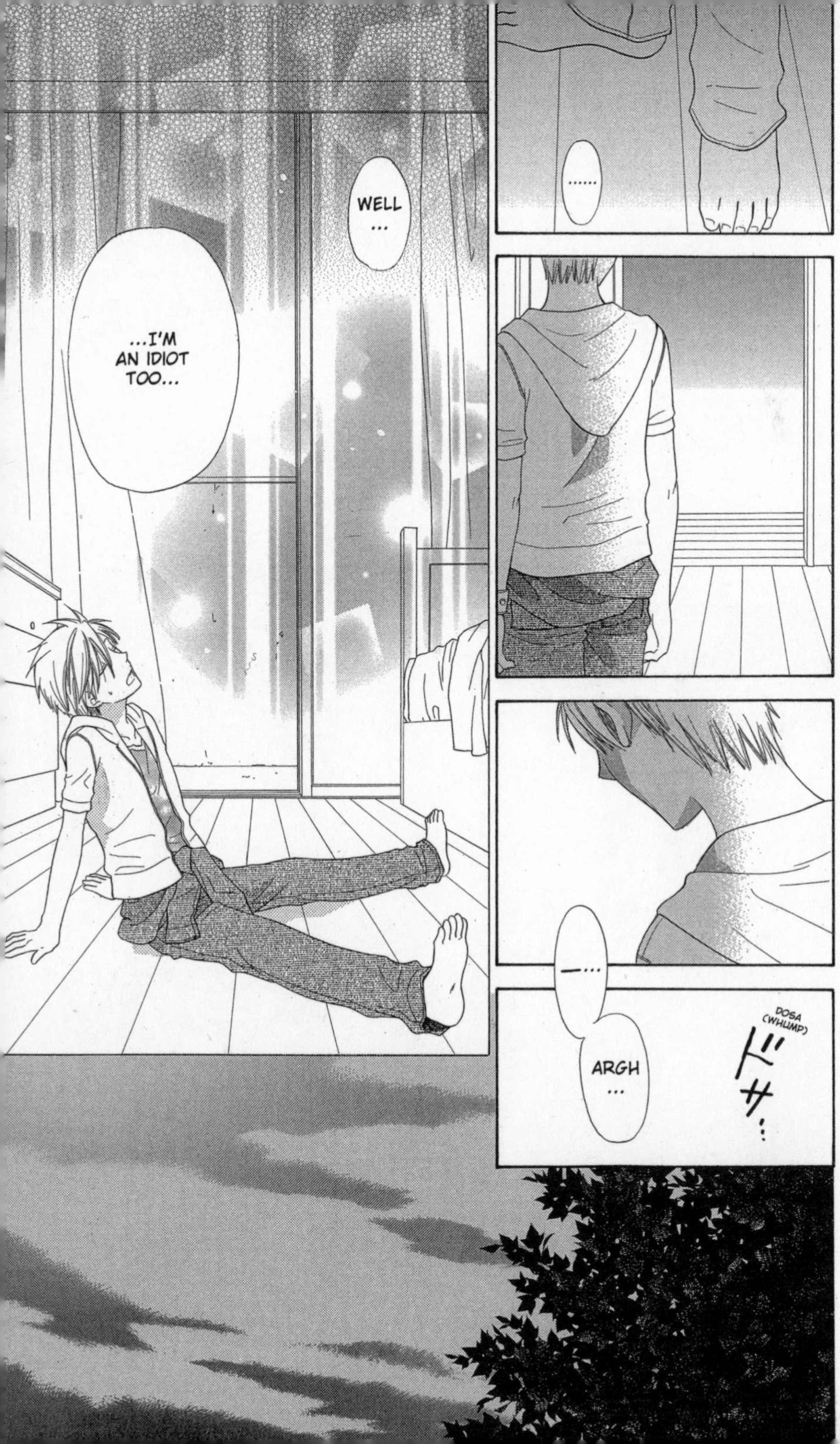
......
—...
ARGH ...
DOSA (WHUMP)
ドサ..
WELL ...
...I'M AN IDIOT TOO...

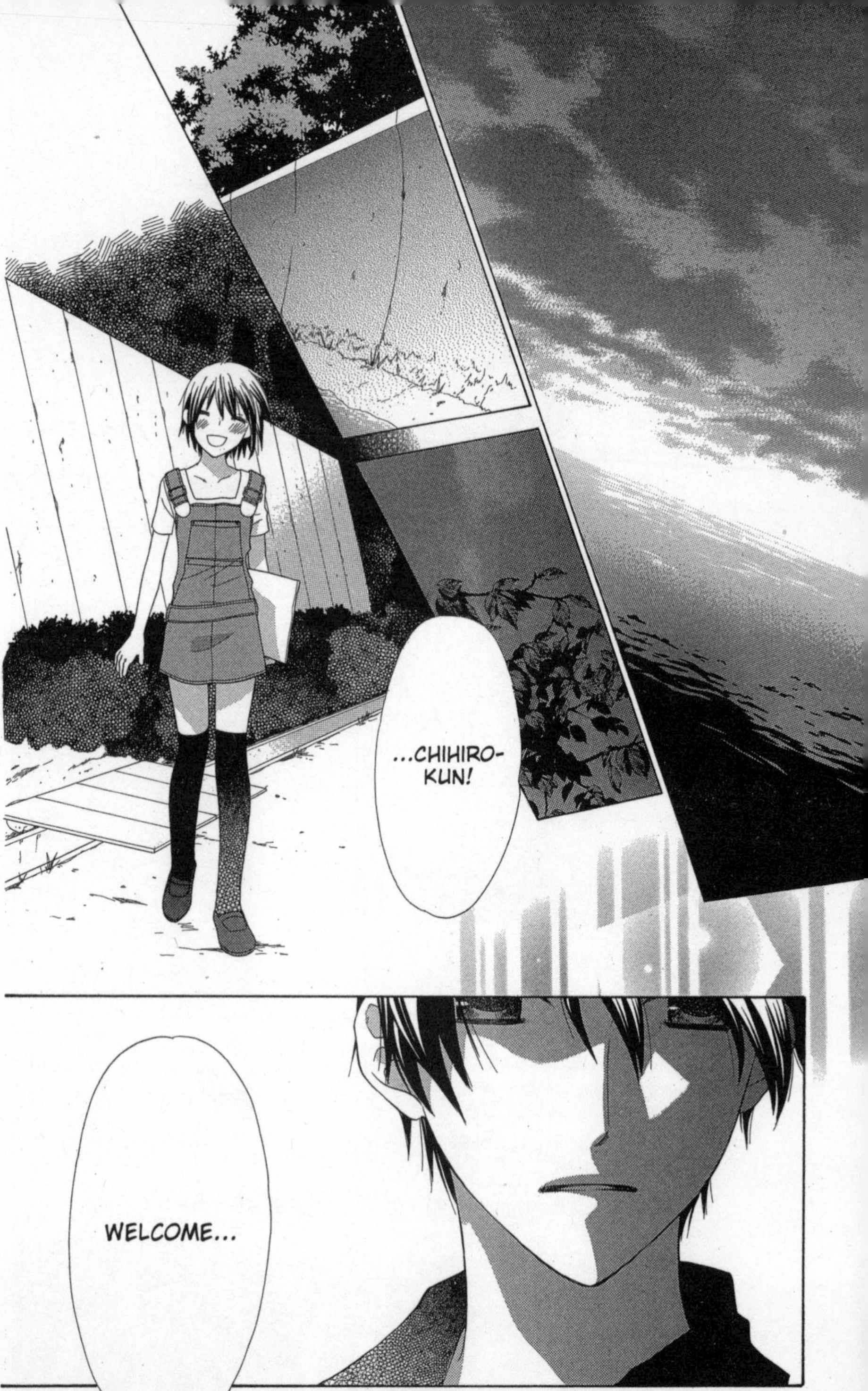
...CHIHIRO-KUN!
WELCOME...

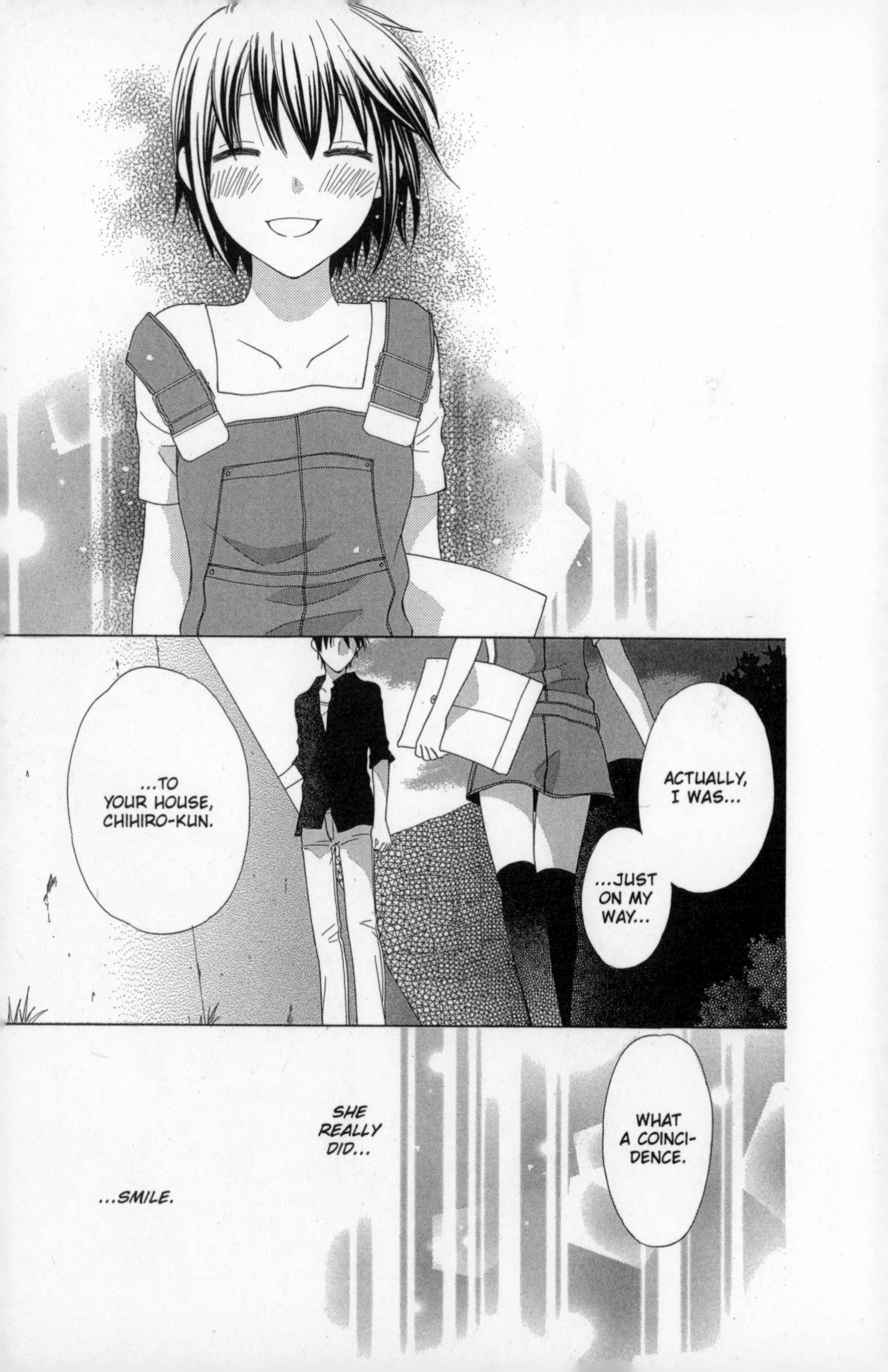
ACTUALLY, I WAS...
...JUST ON MY WAY...
...TO YOUR HOUSE, CHIHIRO-KUN.
WHAT A COINCI-DENCE.
SHE REALLY DID...
...SMILE.

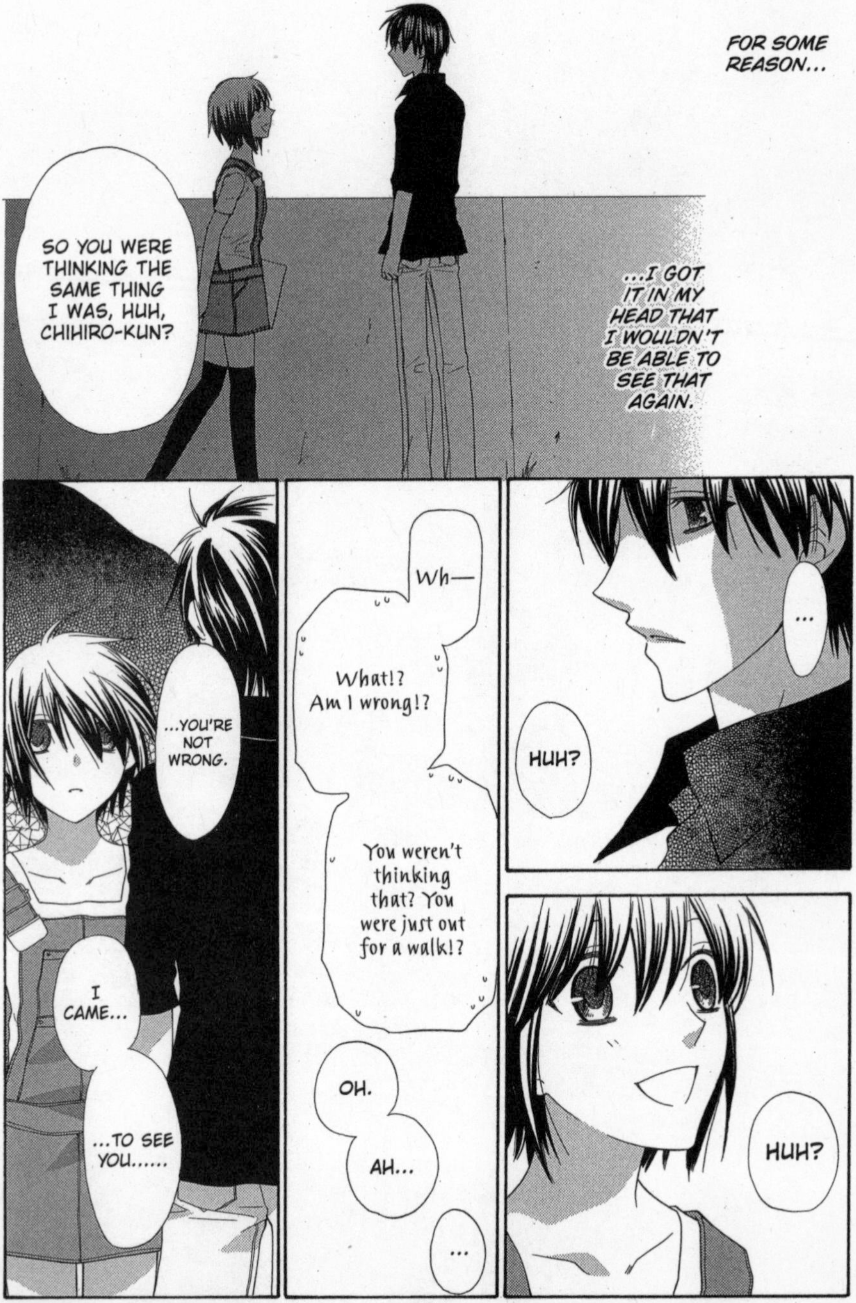

FOR SOME REASON...
...I GOT IT IN MY HEAD THAT I WOULDN'T BE ABLE TO SEE THAT AGAIN.
SO YOU WERE THINKING THE SAME THING I WAS, HUH, CHIHIRO-KUN?
...
HUH?
HUH?
Wh—
What!? Am I wrong!?
You weren't thinking that? You were just out for a walk!?
OH.
AH...
...
...YOU'RE NOT WRONG.
I CAME...
...TO SEE YOU......

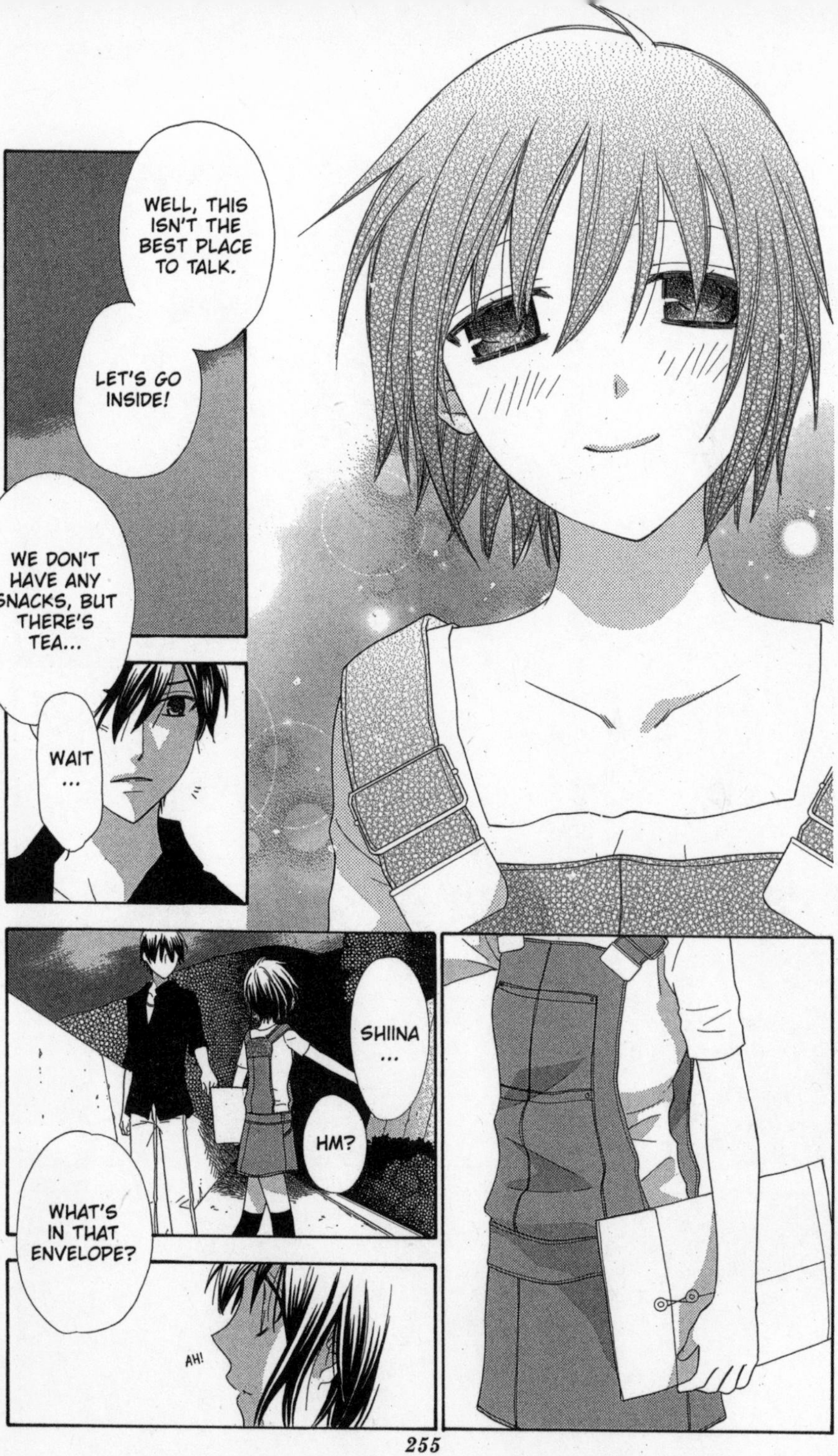
WELL, THIS ISN'T THE BEST PLACE TO TALK.
LET'S GO INSIDE!
WE DON'T HAVE ANY SNACKS, BUT THERE'S TEA...
WAIT ...
SHIINA ...
HM?
WHAT'S IN THAT ENVELOPE?
AH!

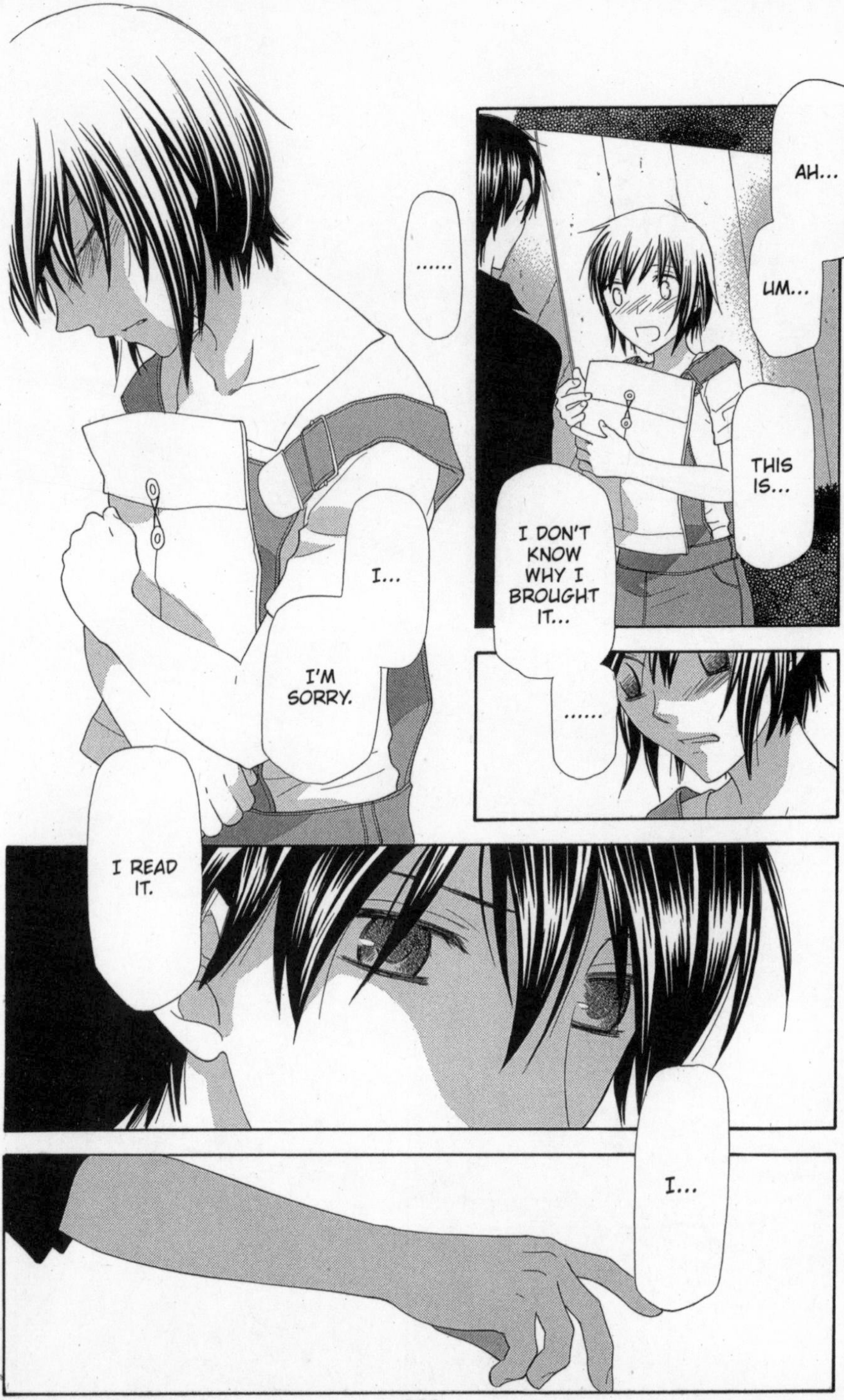
AH...
UM...
THIS IS...
I DON'T KNOW WHY I BROUGHT IT...
......
......
I...
I'M SORRY.
I READ IT.
I...

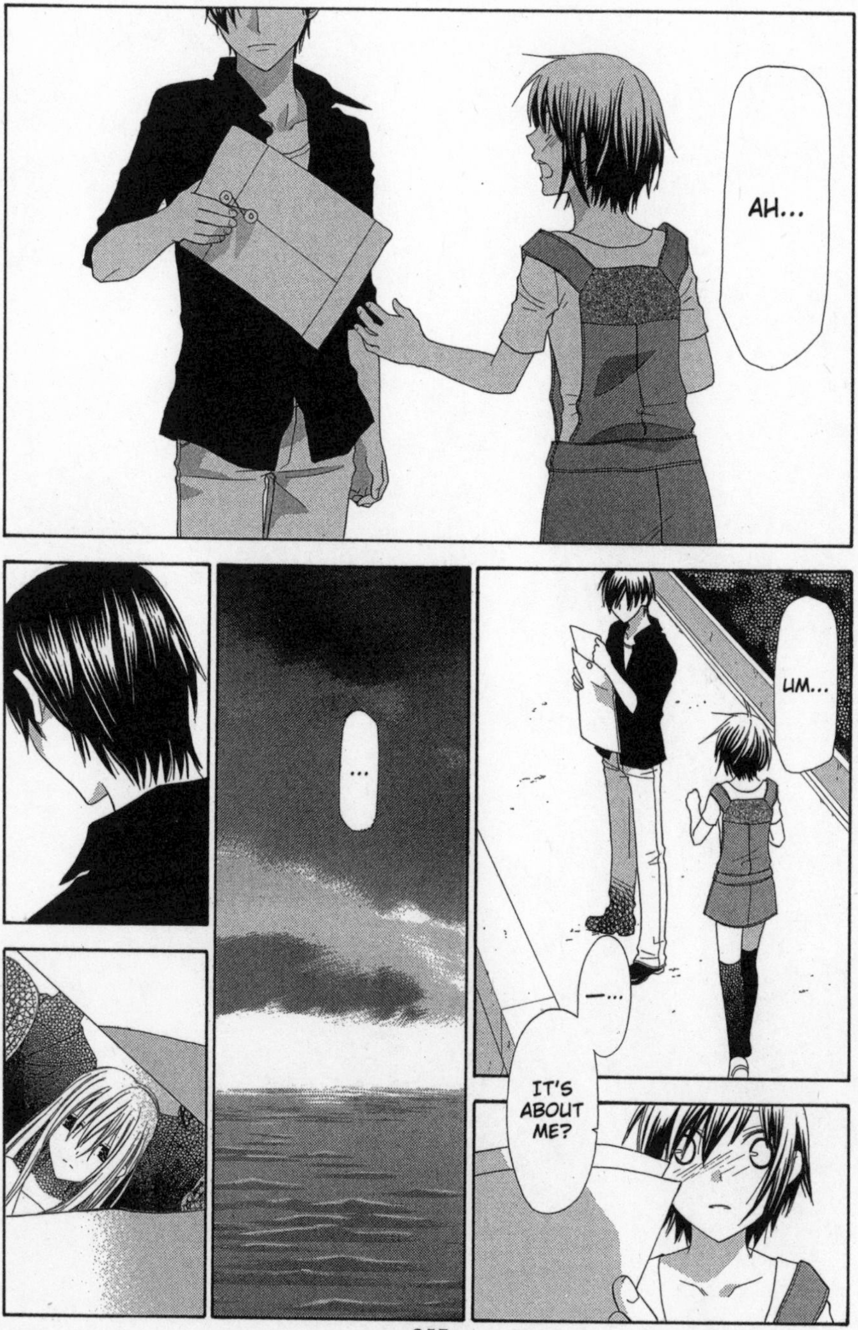
AH...
UM...
—...
IT'S ABOUT ME?
...

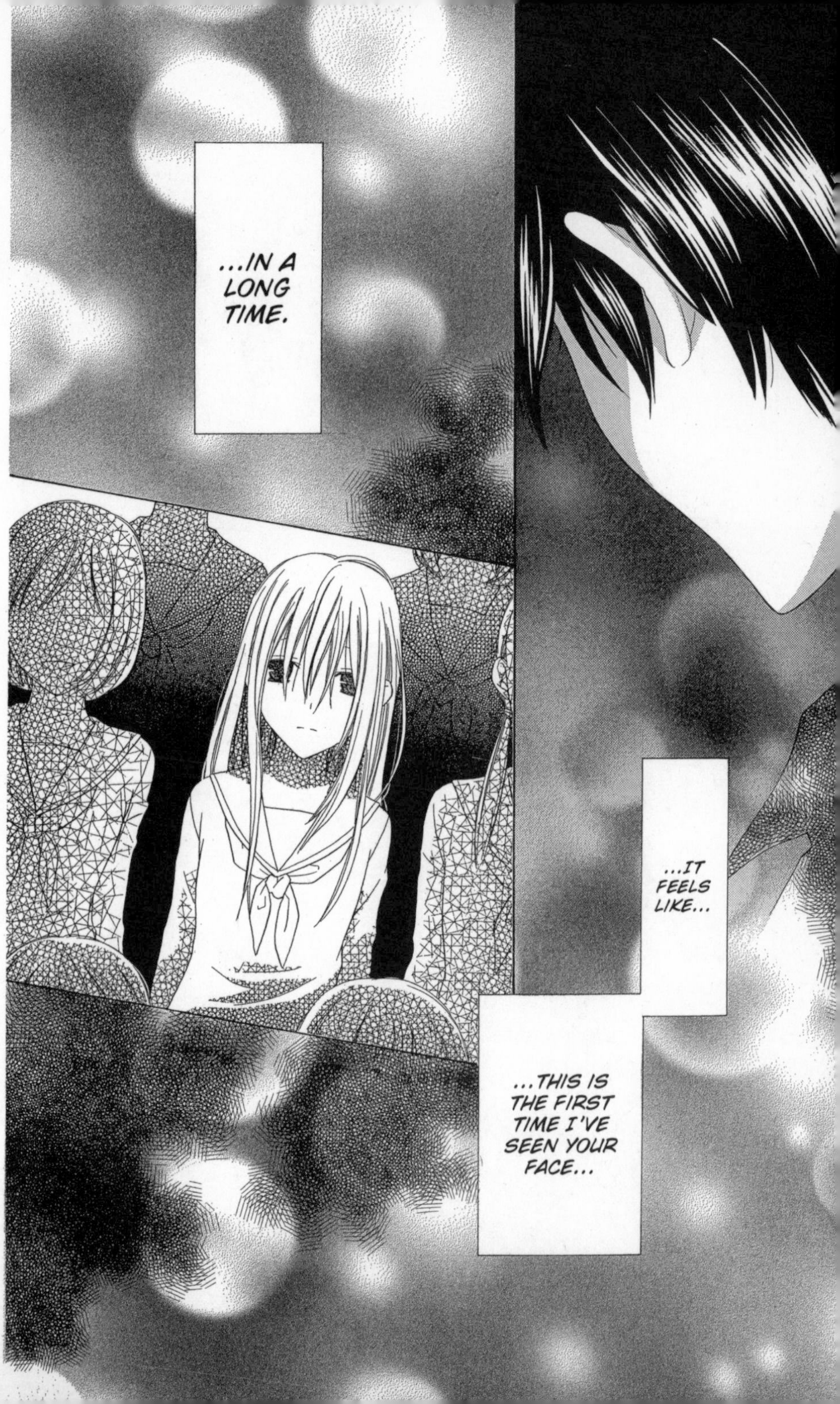
...IT FEELS LIKE...
...THIS IS THE FIRST TIME I'VE SEEN YOUR FACE...
...IN A LONG TIME.

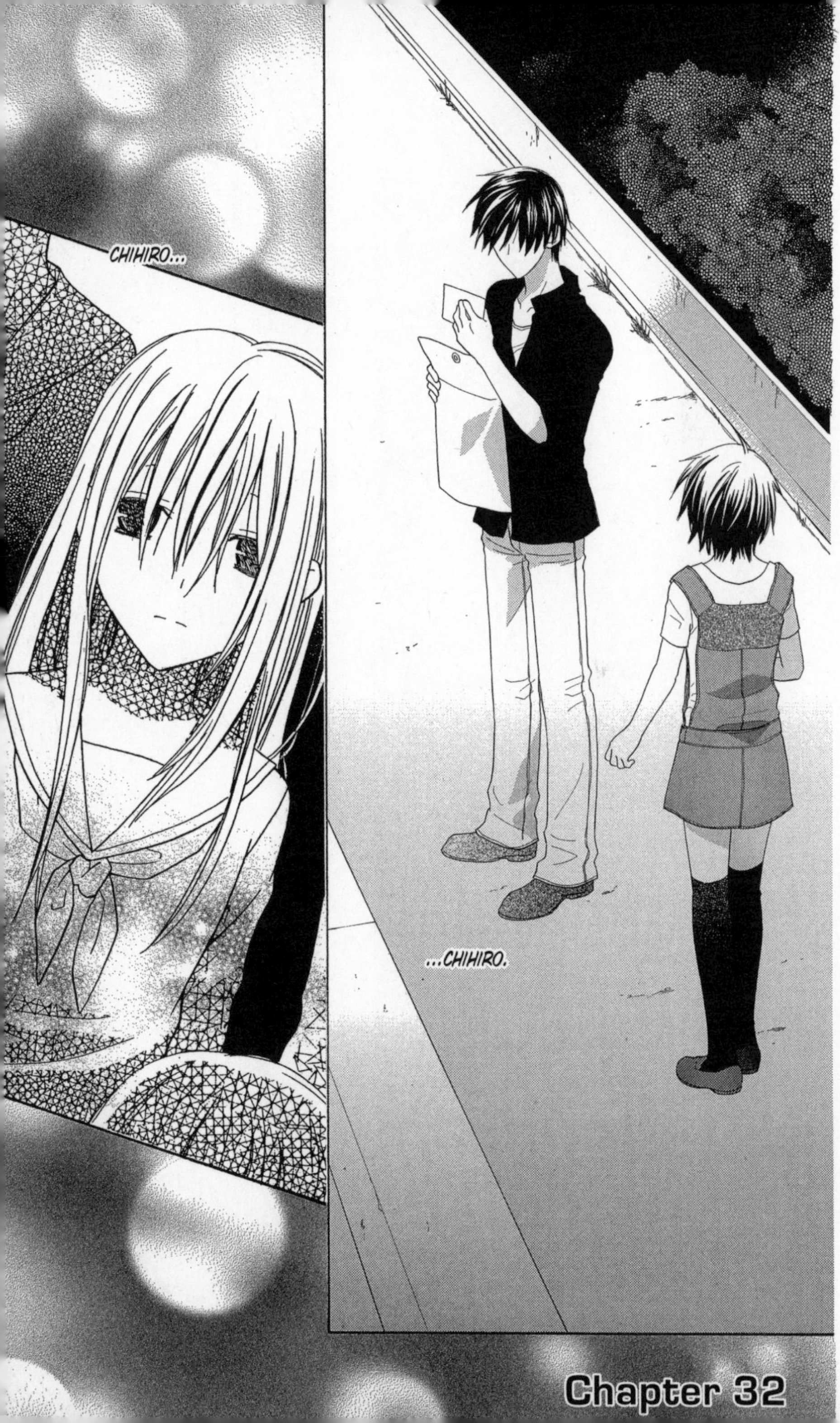
...CHIHIRO.
CHIHIRO...

Chapter 32

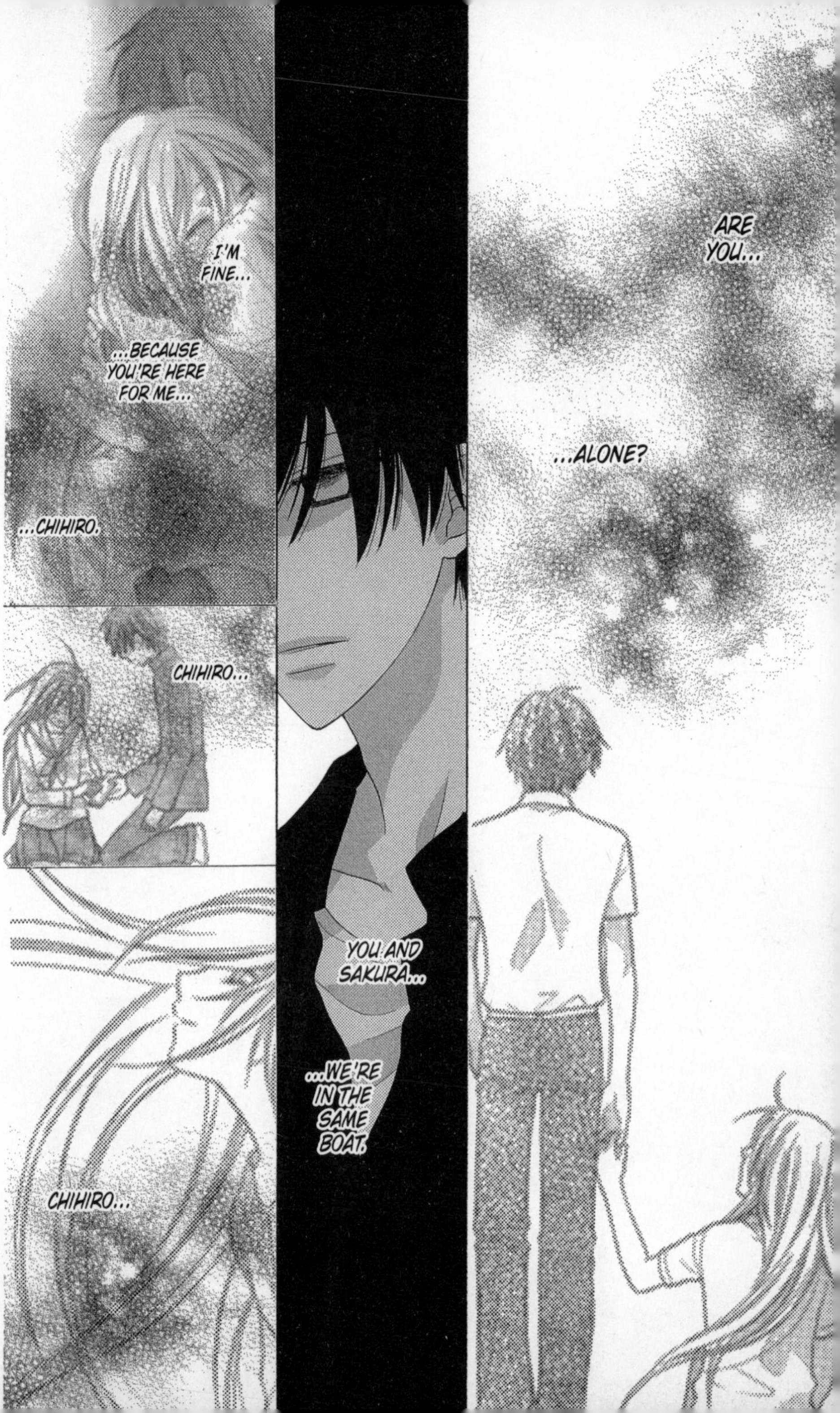
ARE YOU...
...ALONE?
YOU AND SAKURA...
...WE'RE IN THE SAME BOAT.
I'M FINE...
...BECAUSE YOU'RE HERE FOR ME...
...CHIHIRO.
CHIHIRO...
CHIHIRO...

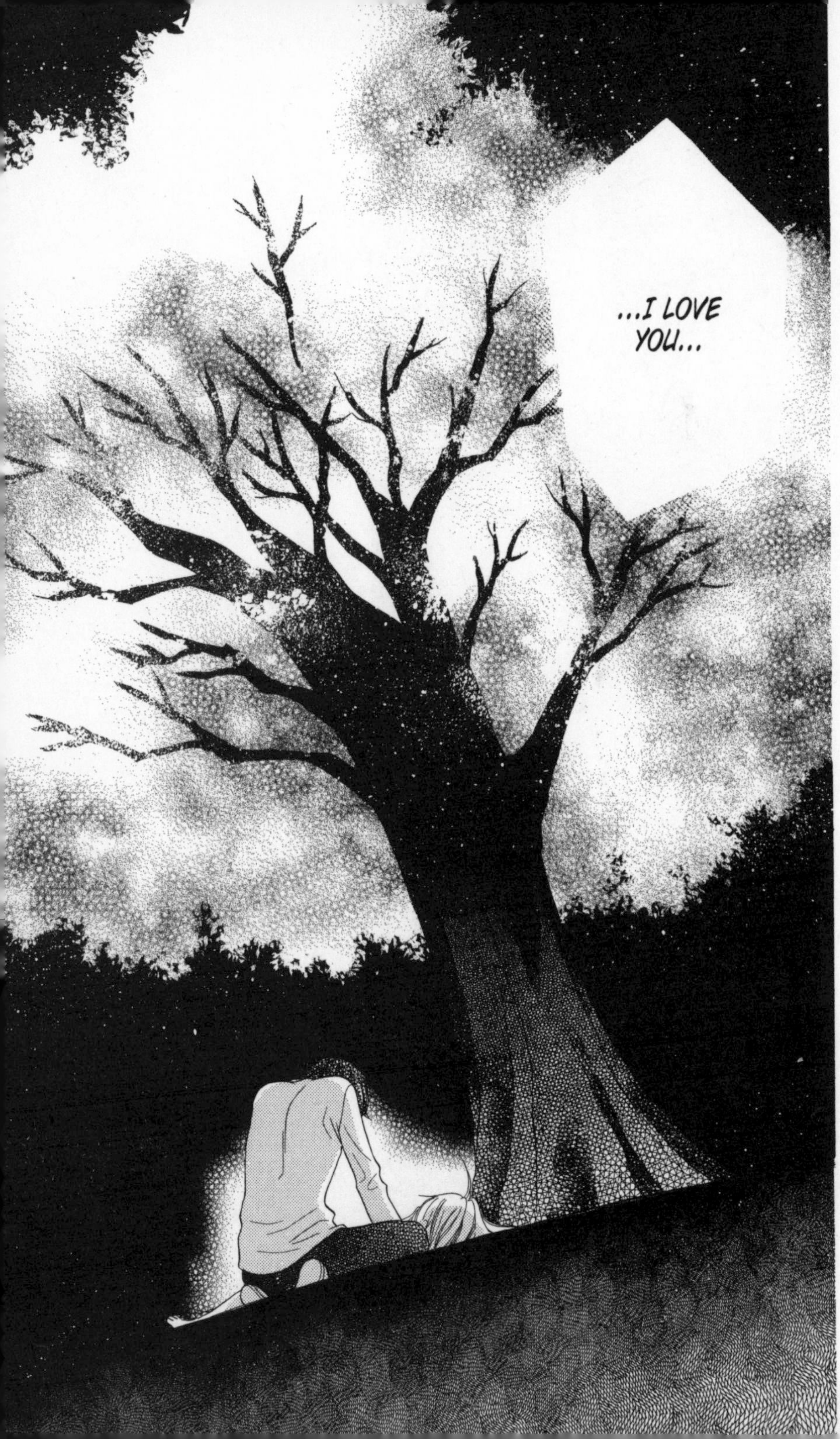
...I LOVE
YOU...

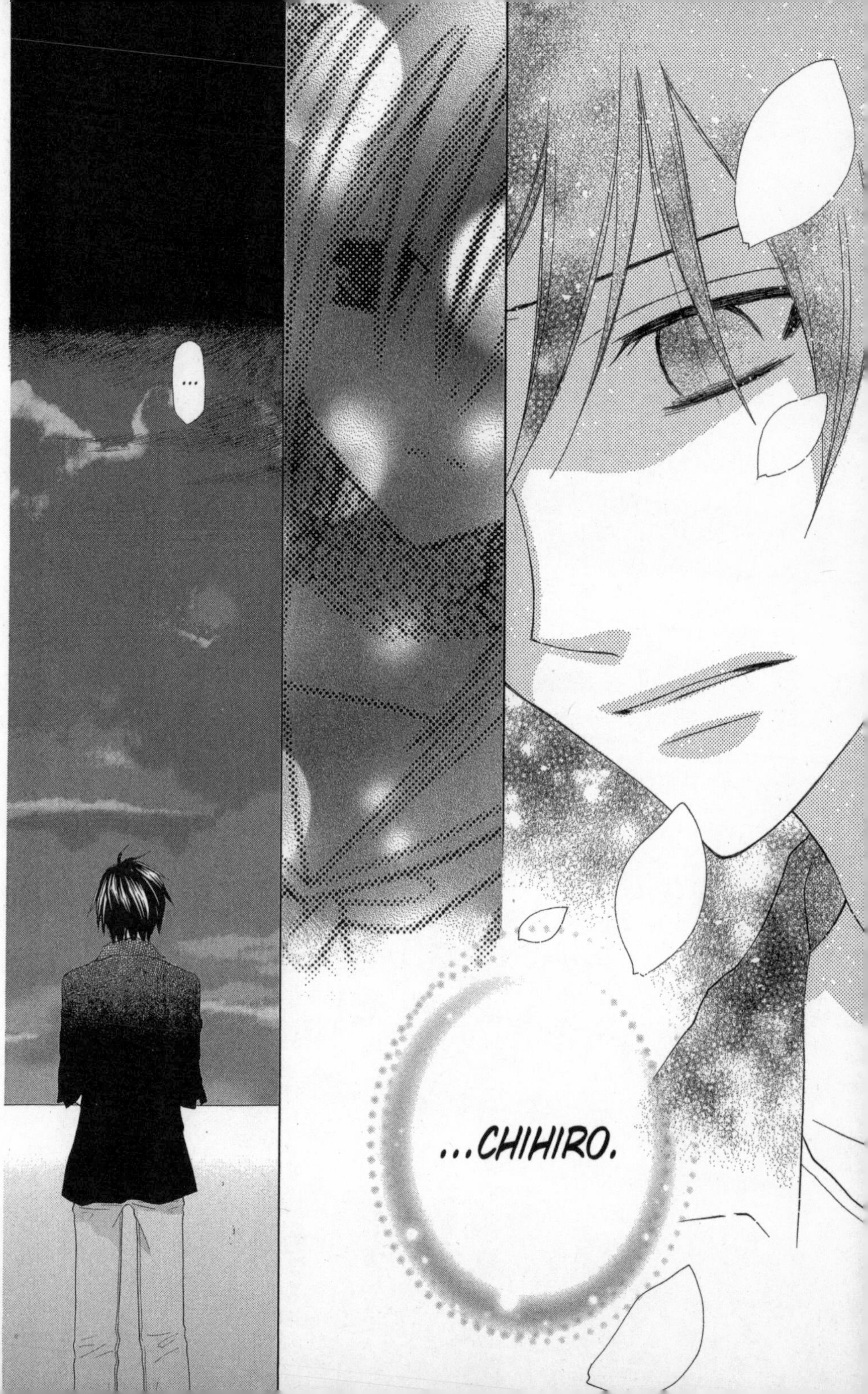
...CHIHIRO.
...

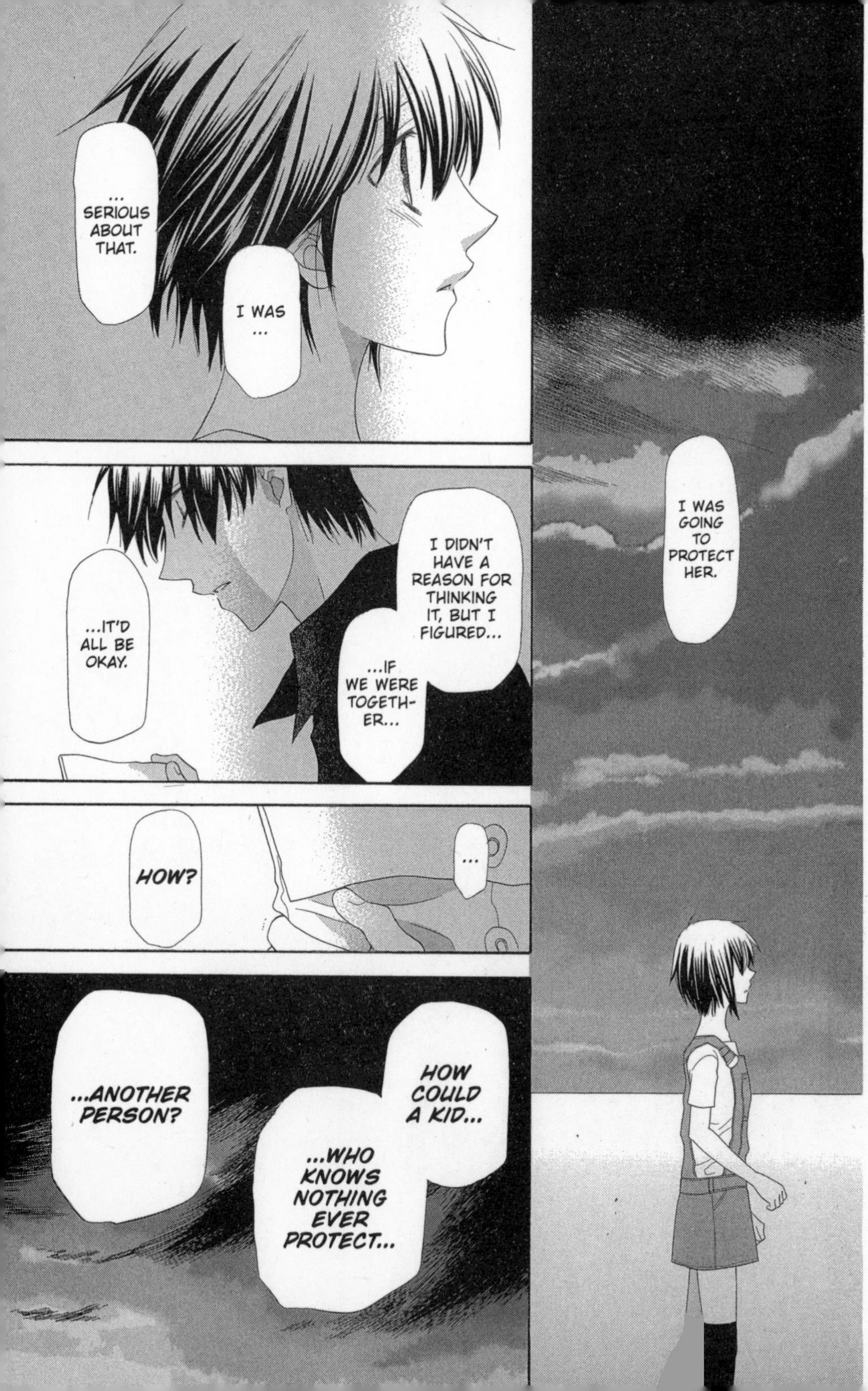
I WAS ...
... SERIOUS ABOUT THAT.
I WAS GOING TO PROTECT HER.
I DIDN'T HAVE A REASON FOR THINKING IT, BUT I FIGURED...
...IF WE WERE TOGETH-ER...
...IT'D ALL BE OKAY.
...
HOW?
HOW COULD A KID...
...WHO KNOWS NOTHING EVER PROTECT...
...ANOTHER PERSON?

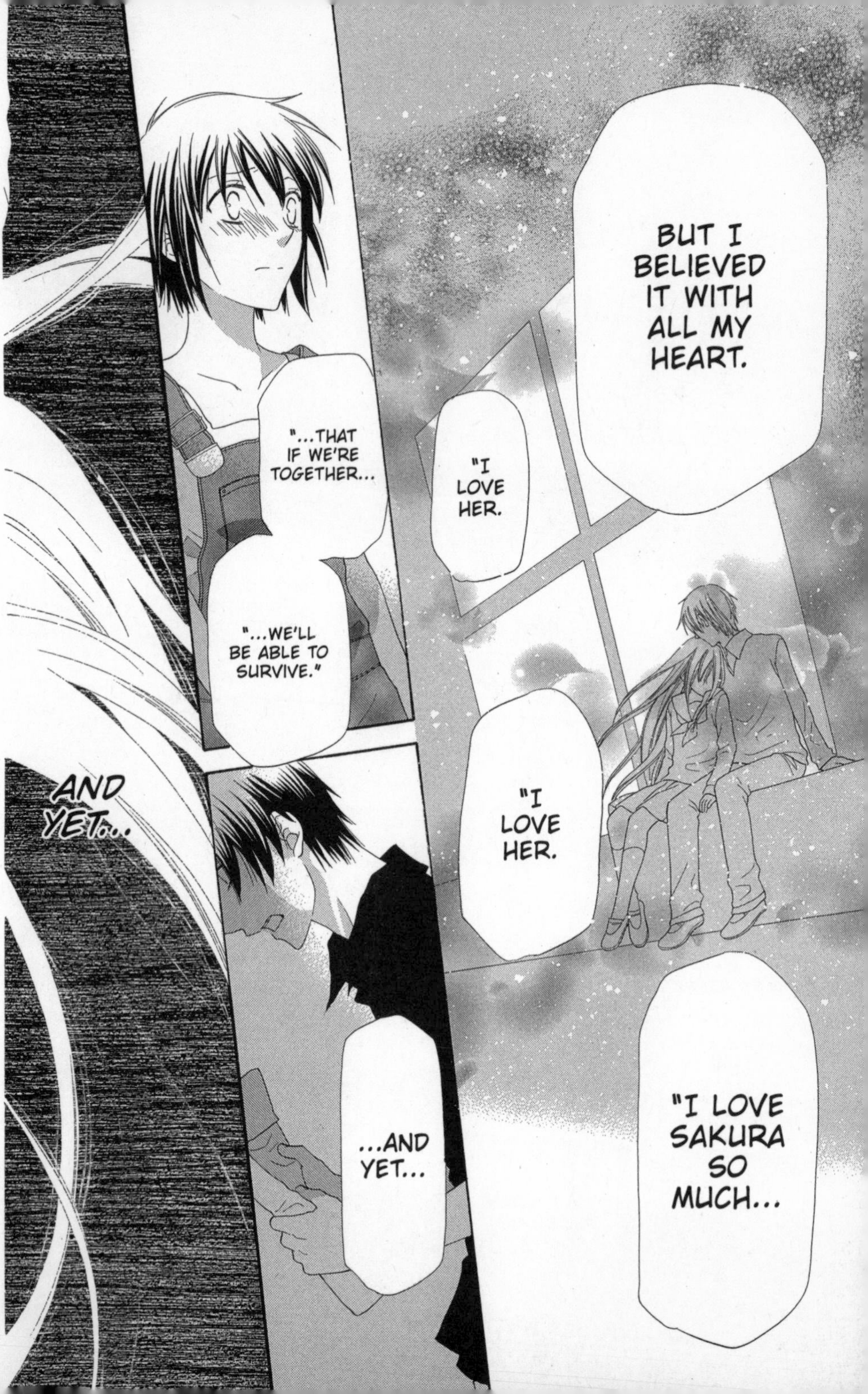

BUT I BELIEVED IT WITH ALL MY HEART.
"I LOVE HER.
"I LOVE HER.
"I LOVE SAKURA SO MUCH...
"...THAT IF WE'RE TOGETHER...
"...WE'LL BE ABLE TO SURVIVE."
...AND YET...
AND YET...

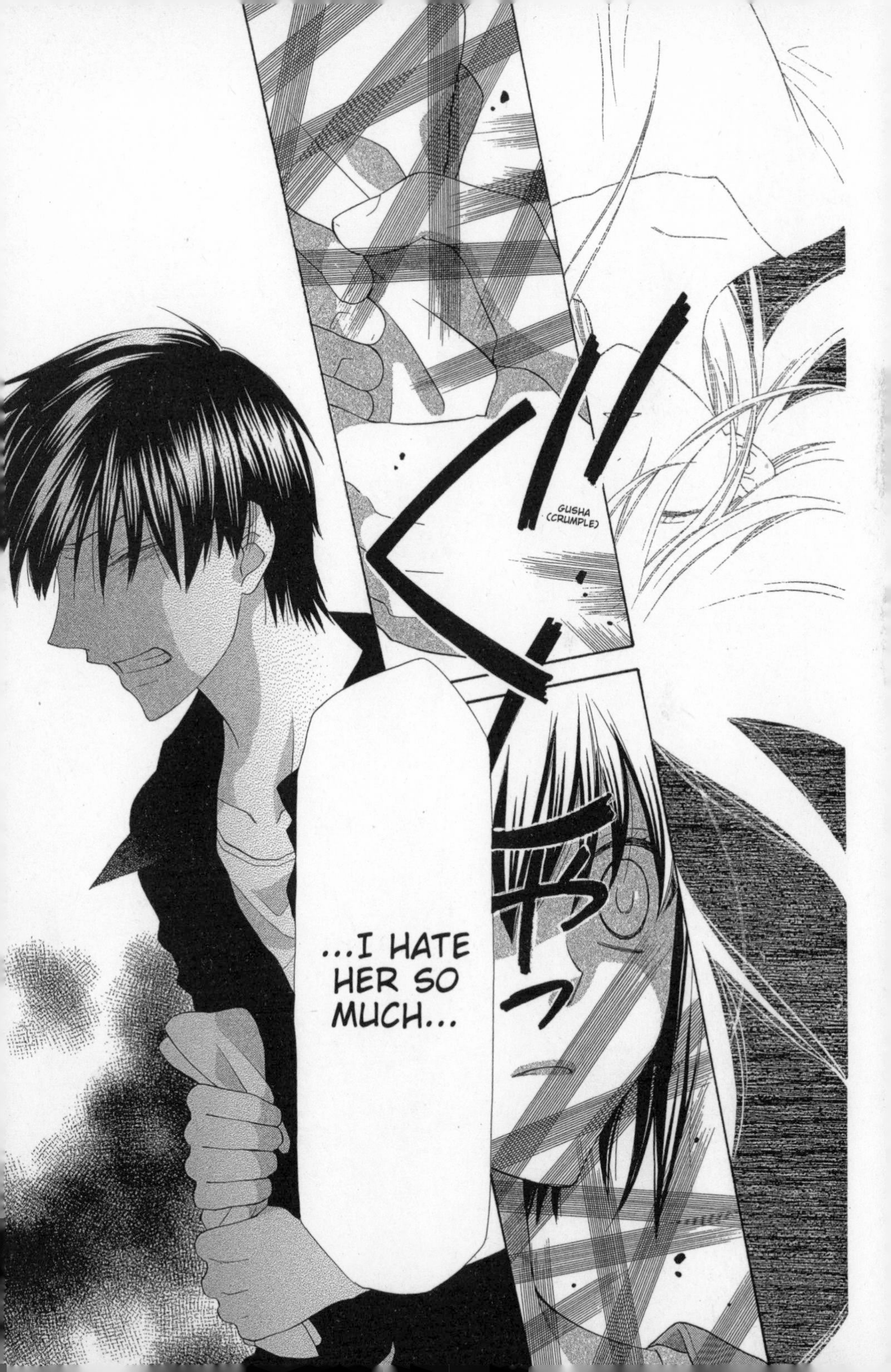
GUSHA (CRUMPLE)
...I HATE HER SO MUCH...

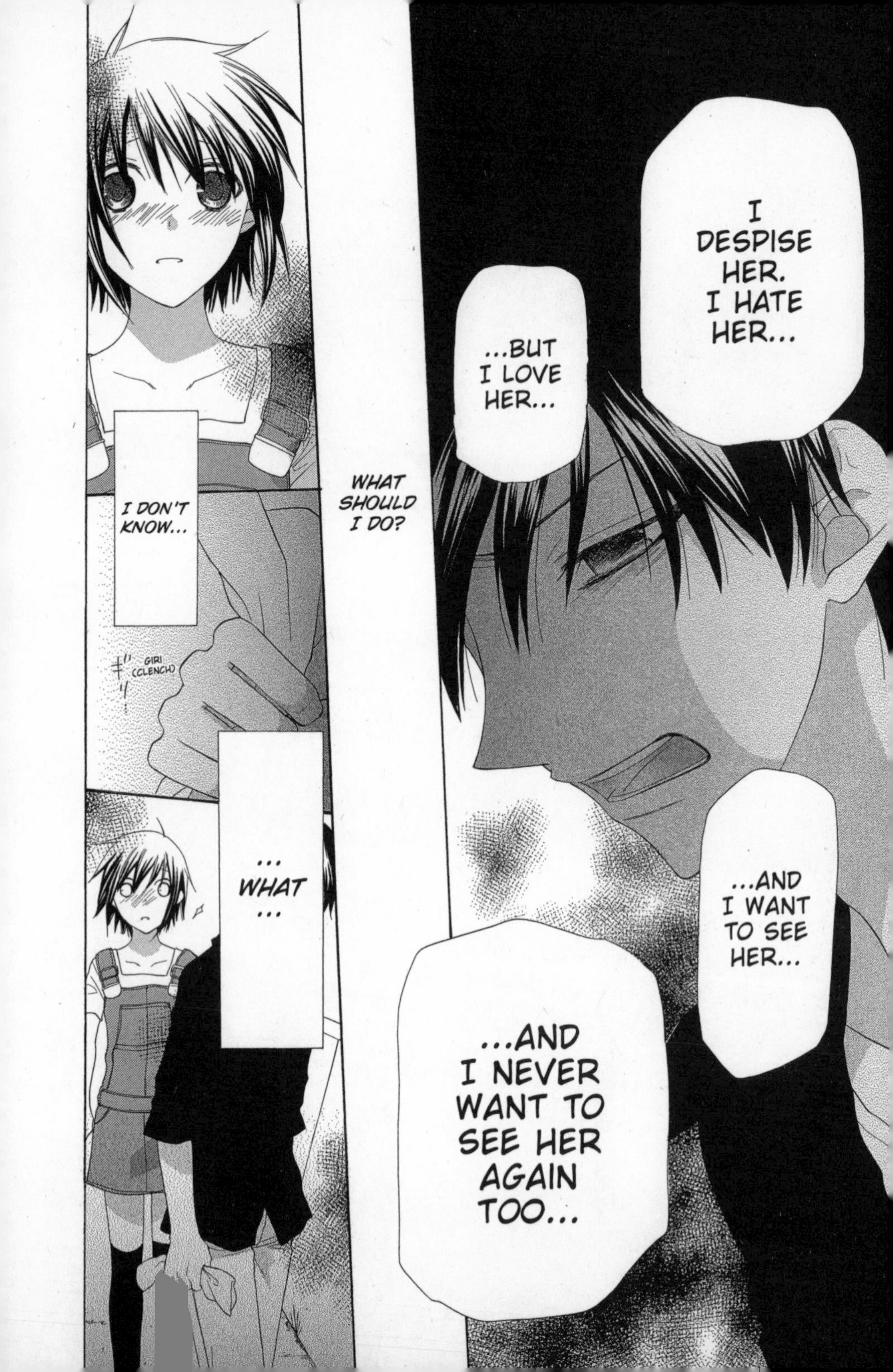
I DESPISE HER. I HATE HER...
...BUT I LOVE HER...
...AND I WANT TO SEE HER...
...AND I NEVER WANT TO SEE HER AGAIN TOO...
WHAT SHOULD I DO?
I DON'T KNOW...
GIRI (CLENCH)
... WHAT ...

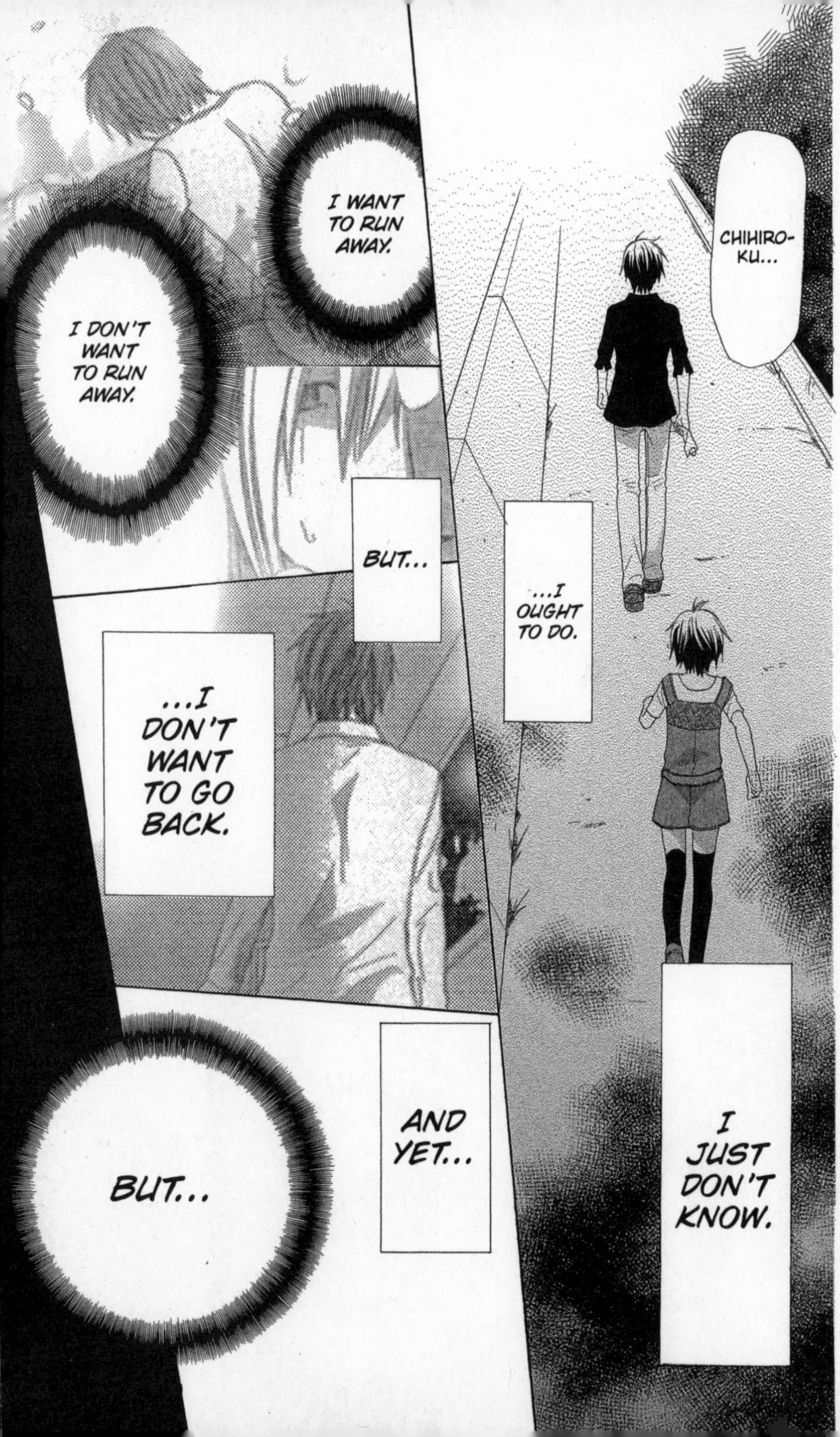

CHIHIRO-KU...
...I OUGHT TO DO.
I JUST DON'T KNOW.
I WANT TO RUN AWAY.
I DON'T WANT TO RUN AWAY.
BUT...
...I DON'T WANT TO GO BACK.
AND YET...
BUT...

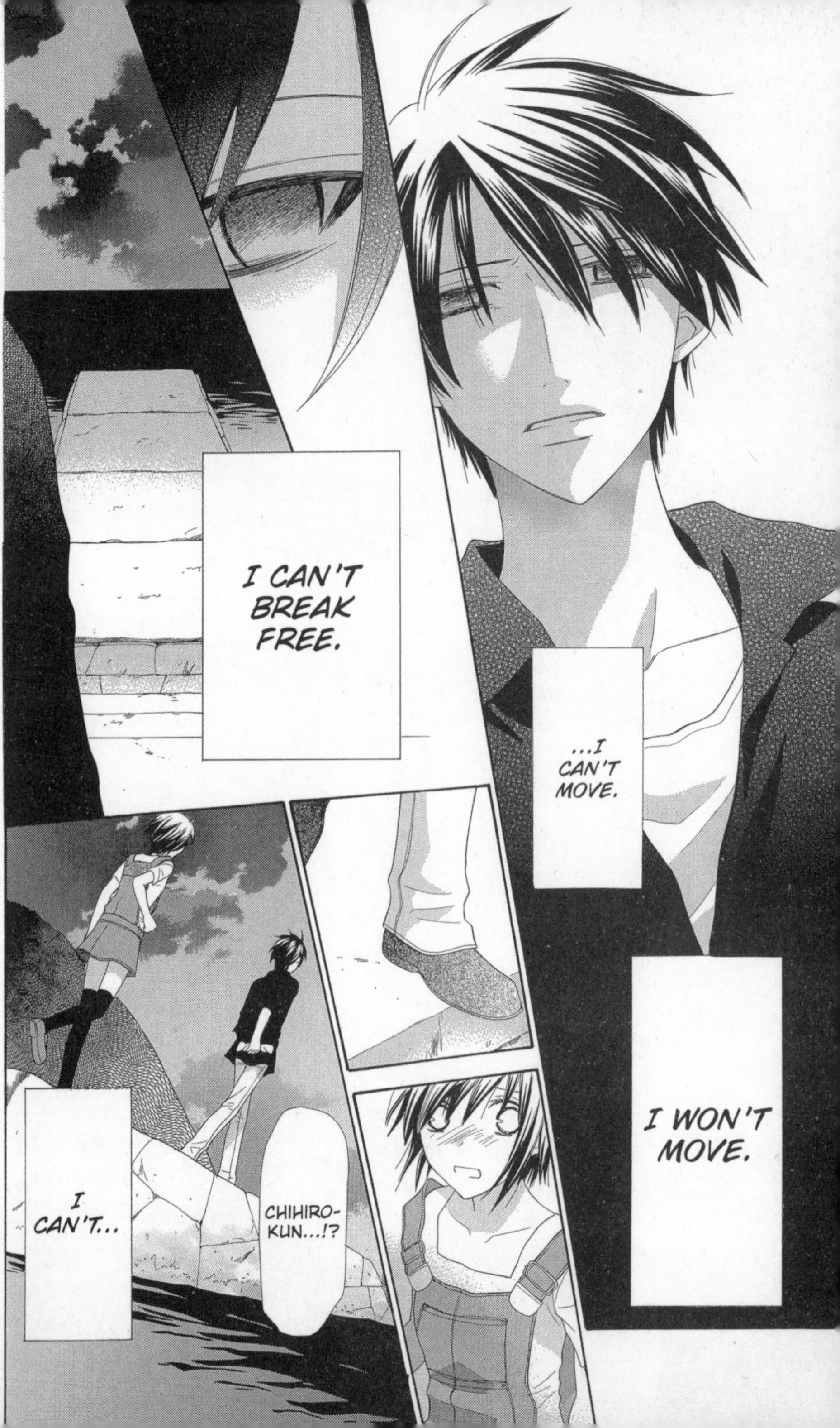
I CAN'T BREAK FREE.
...I CAN'T MOVE.
I WON'T MOVE.
CHIHIRO-KUN...!?
I CAN'T...

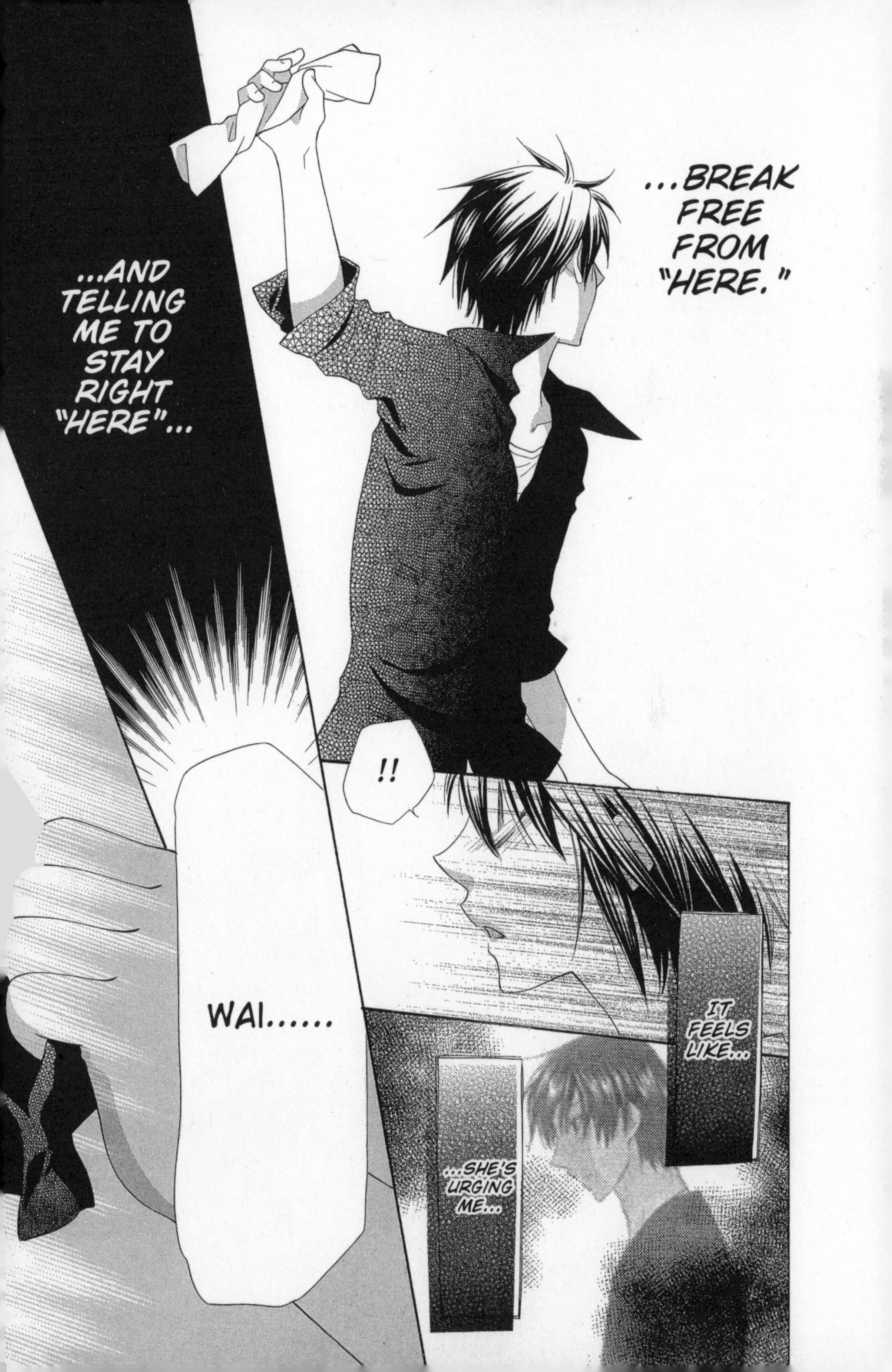
...BREAK FREE FROM "HERE."
...AND TELLING ME TO STAY RIGHT "HERE"...
!!
WAI......
IT FEELS LIKE...
...SHE'S URGING ME...

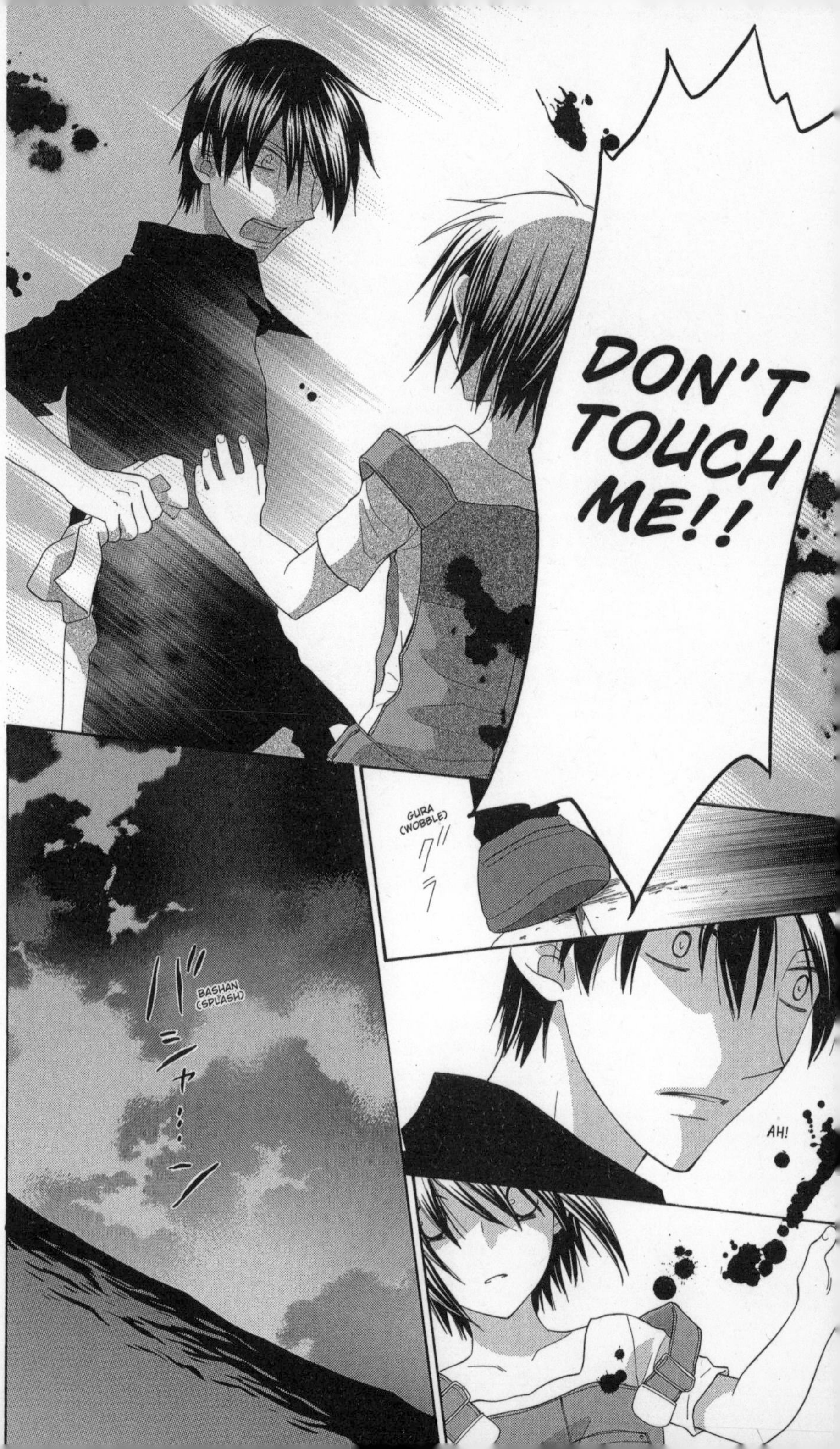
DON'T TOUCH ME!!
GURA (WOBBLE)
グラ
AH!
BASHAN (SPLASH)
バシャ…ン

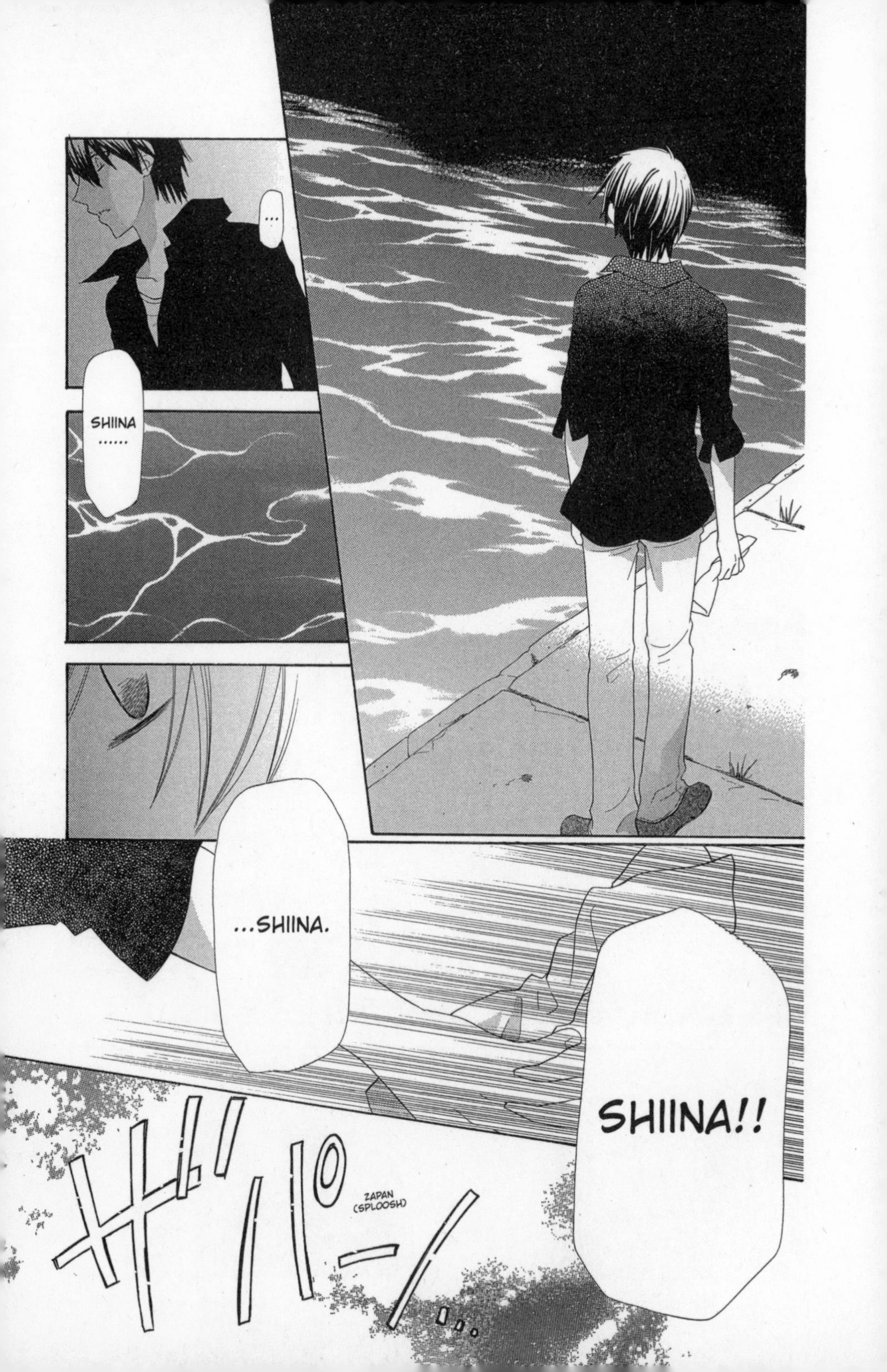
...
SHIINA ......
...SHIINA.
SHIINA!!
ZAPAN (SPLOOSH)

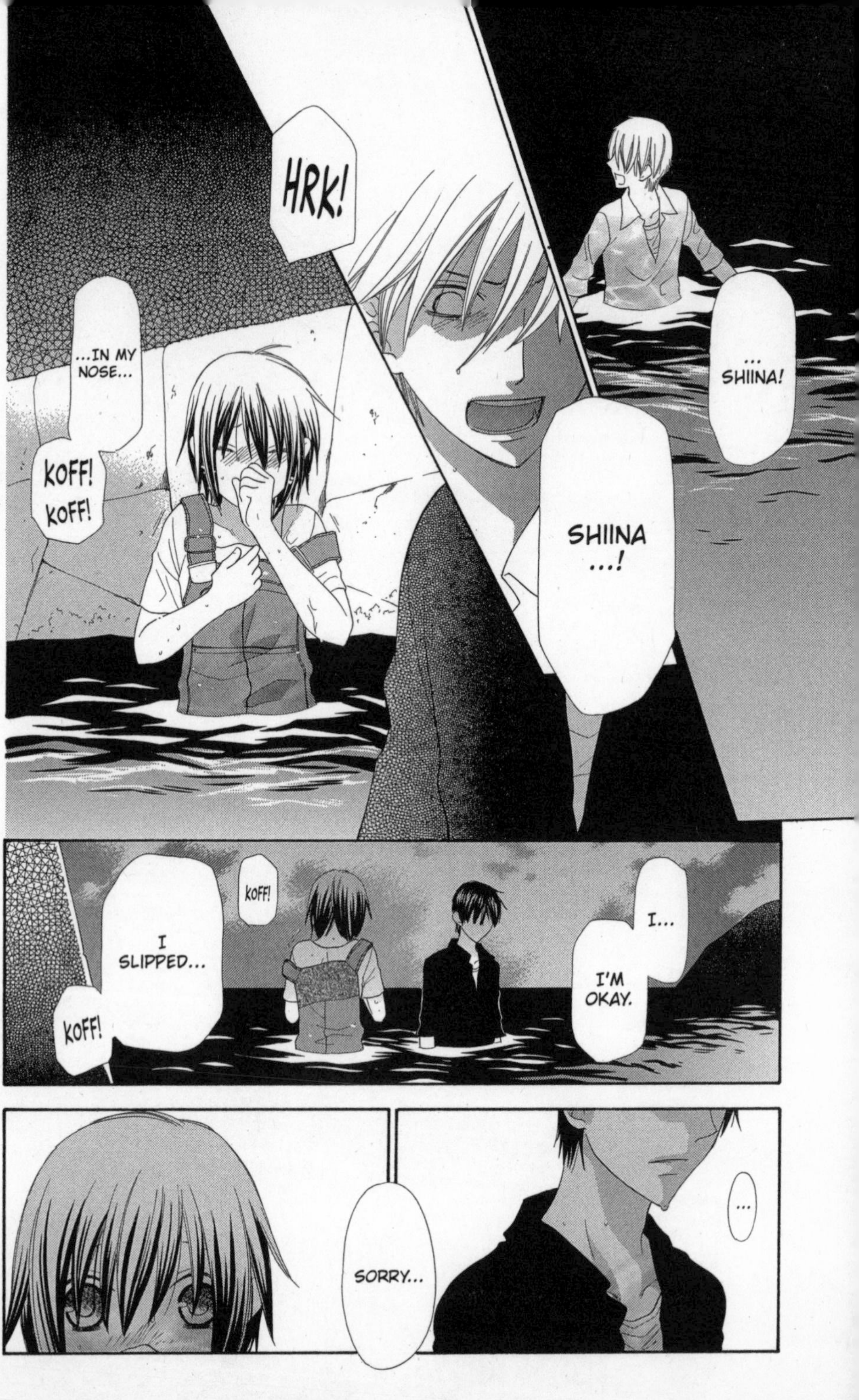
... SHIINA!
HRK!
SHIINA ...!
...IN MY NOSE...
KOFF! KOFF!
I... I'M OKAY.
KOFF!
I SLIPPED...
KOFF!
...
SORRY...

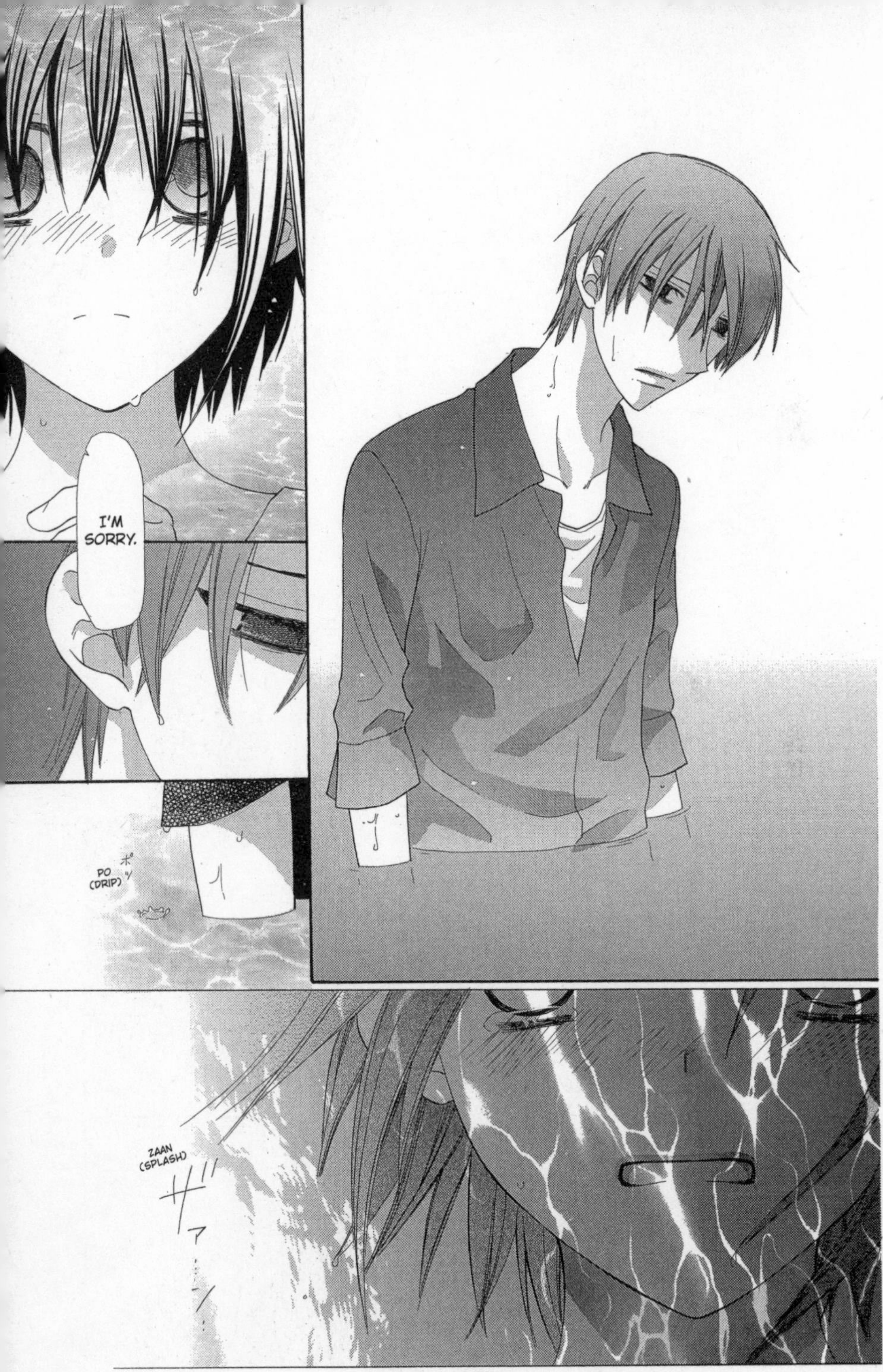
I'M SORRY.
ポッ
PO (DRIP)
ザァ…ン
ZAAN (SPLASH)

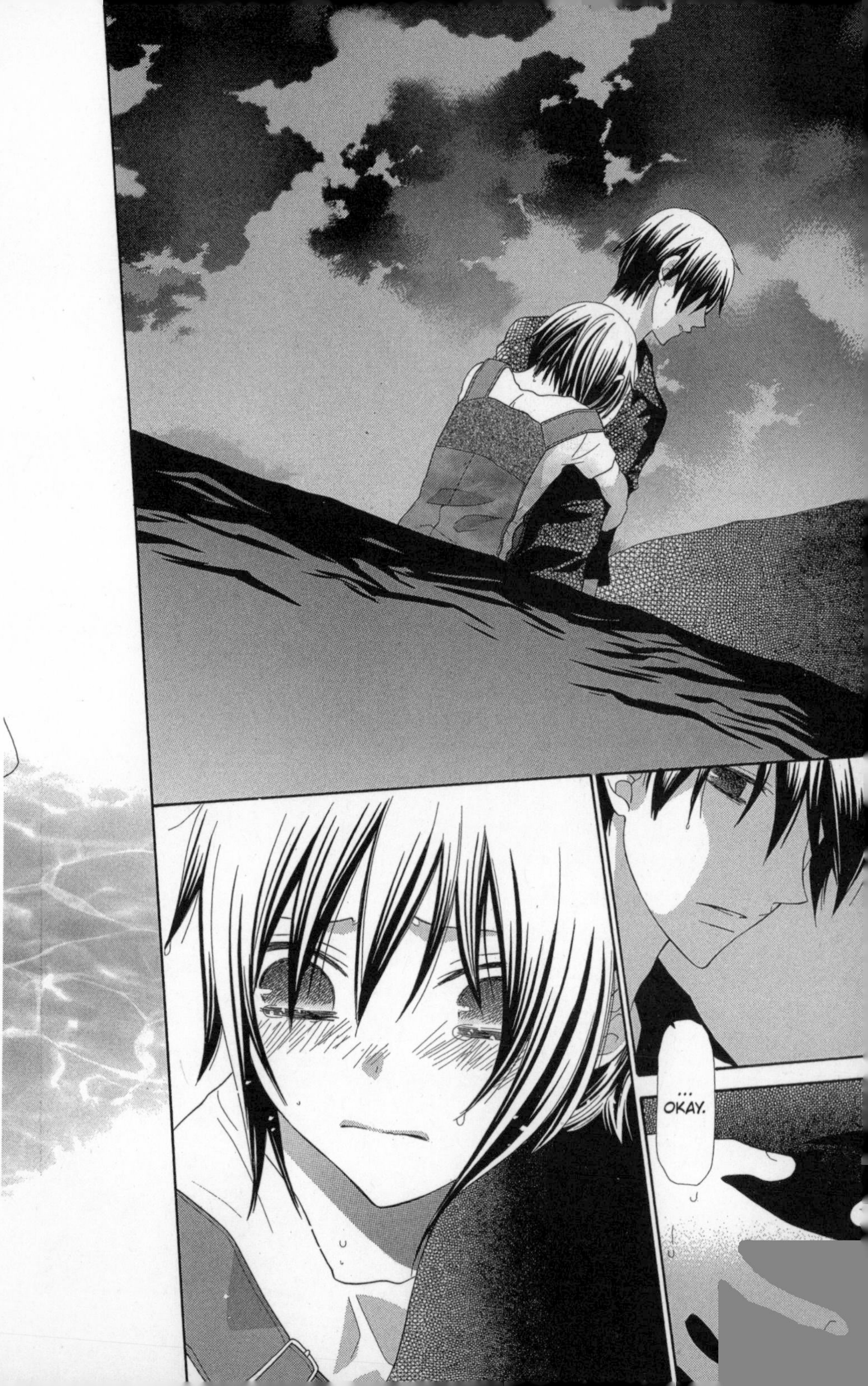

...OKAY.

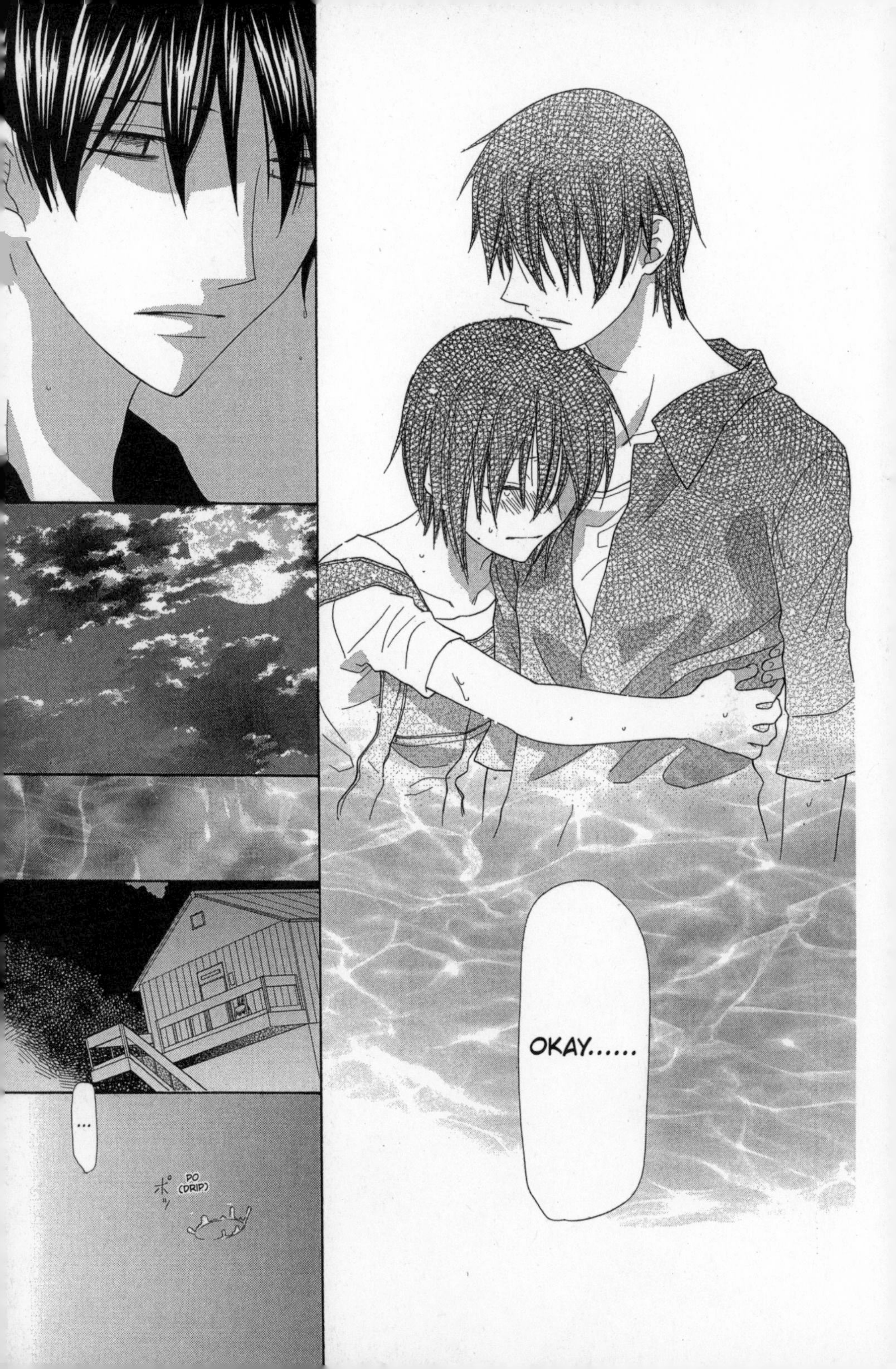
OKAY......
...
ポッ
PO (DRIP)

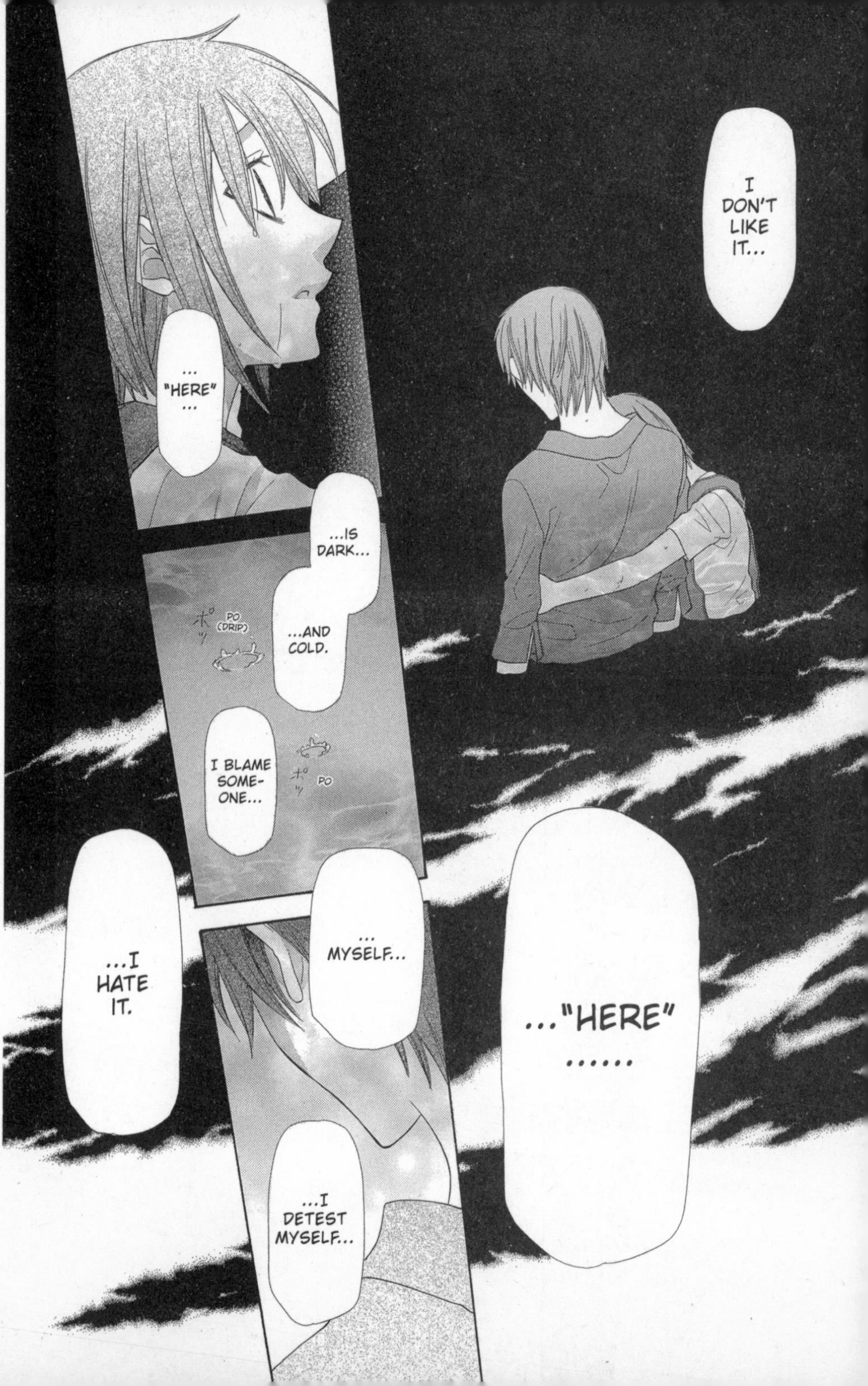
I DON'T LIKE IT...
... "HERE" ...
...IS DARK...
PO (DRIP)
...AND COLD.
I BLAME SOME-ONE...
PO
..."HERE" ......
... MYSELF...
...I DETEST MYSELF...
...I HATE IT.

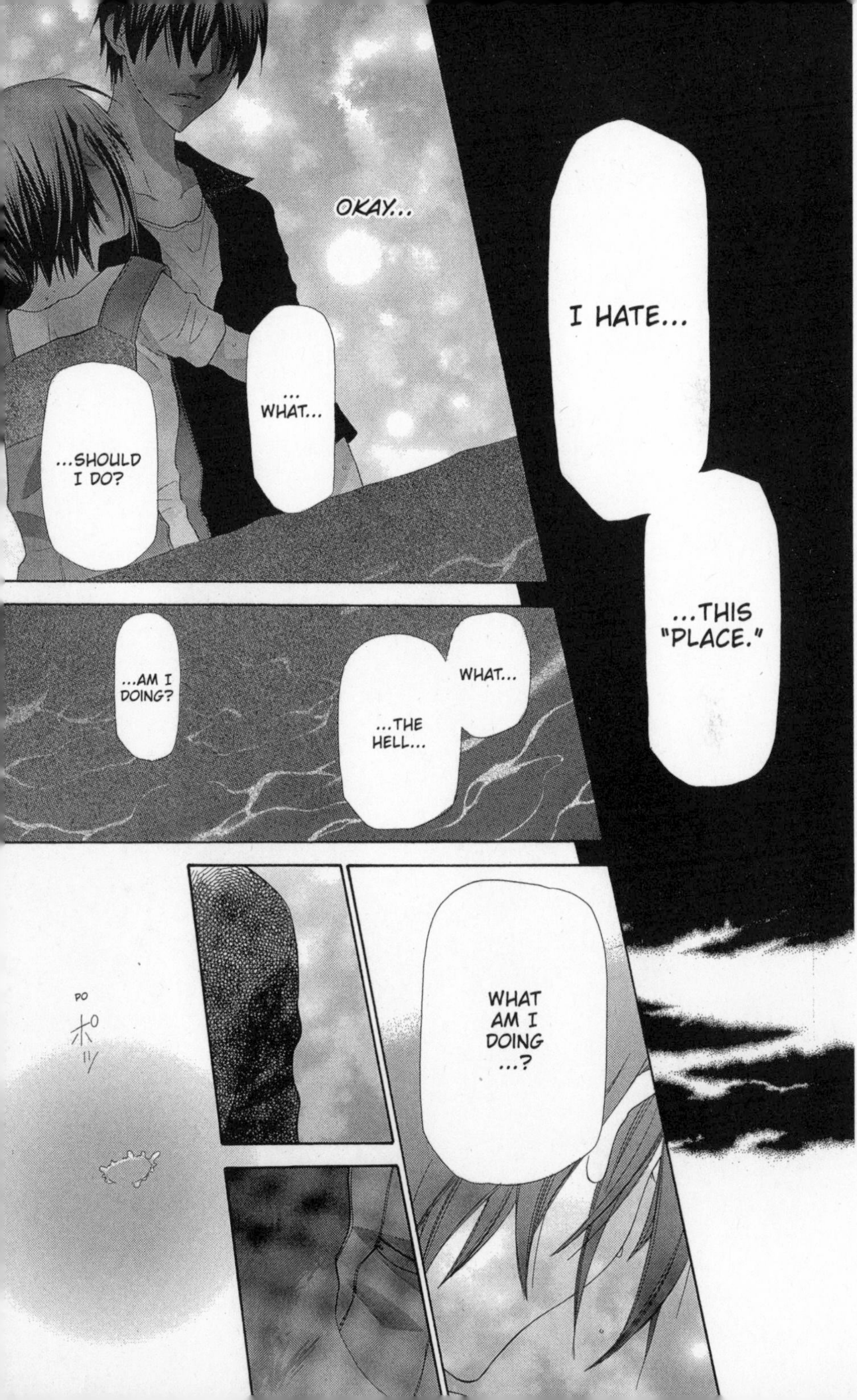
I HATE...
...THIS "PLACE."
OKAY...
...WHAT...
...SHOULD I DO?
WHAT...
...THE HELL...
...AM I DOING?
WHAT AM I DOING ...?
PO
ポツ

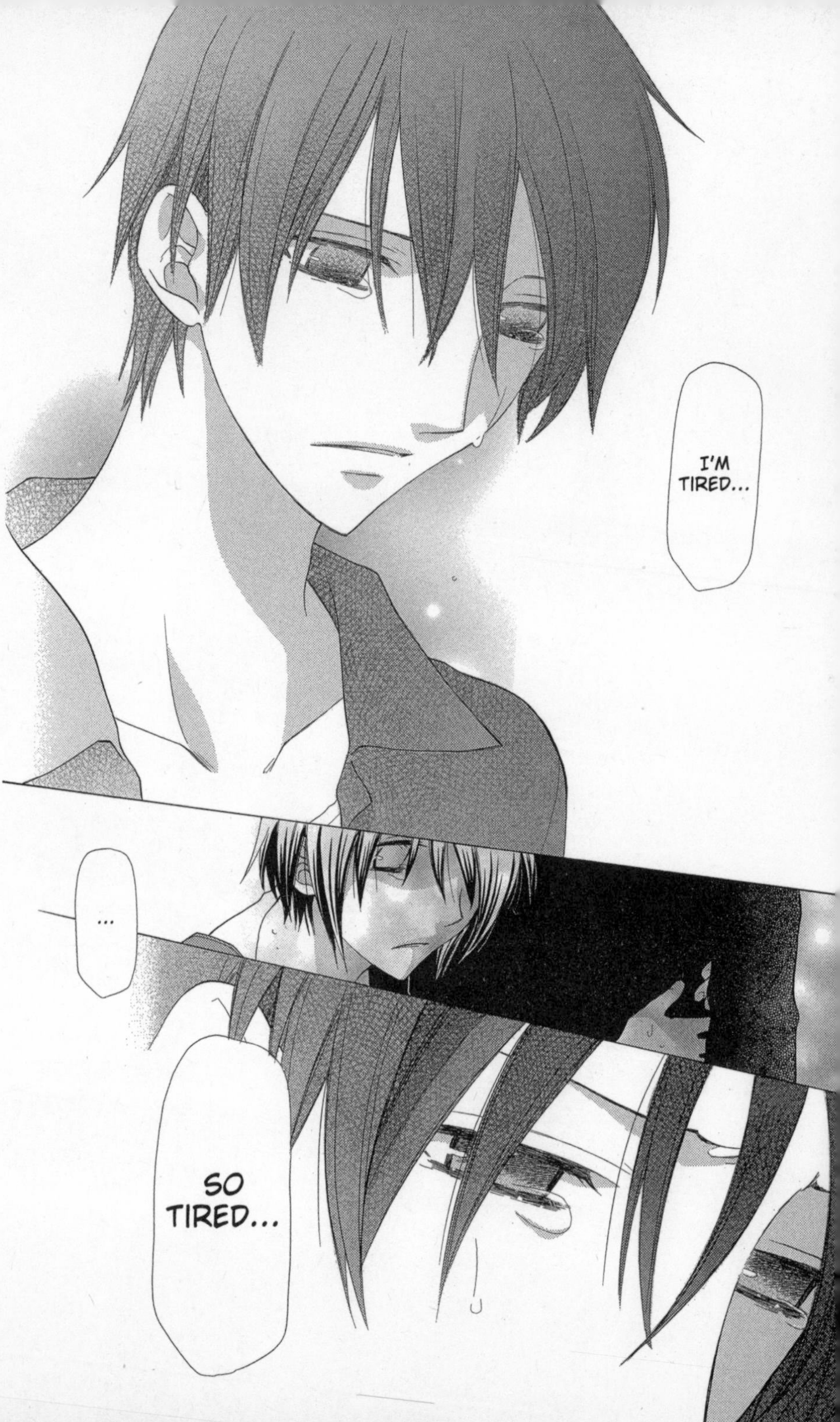
I'M TIRED...
...
SO TIRED...

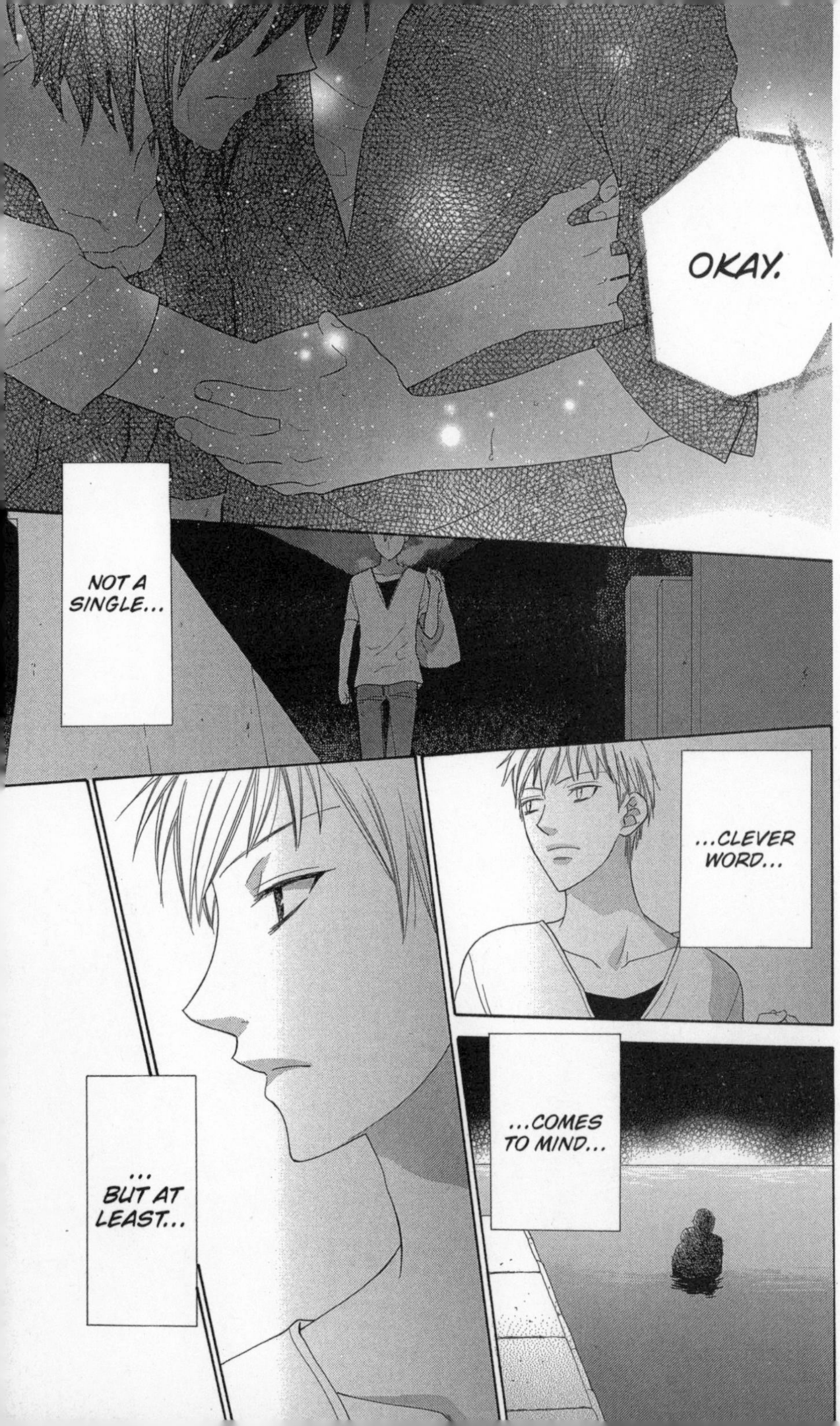
OKAY.
NOT A SINGLE...
...CLEVER WORD...
...COMES TO MIND...
...BUT AT LEAST...

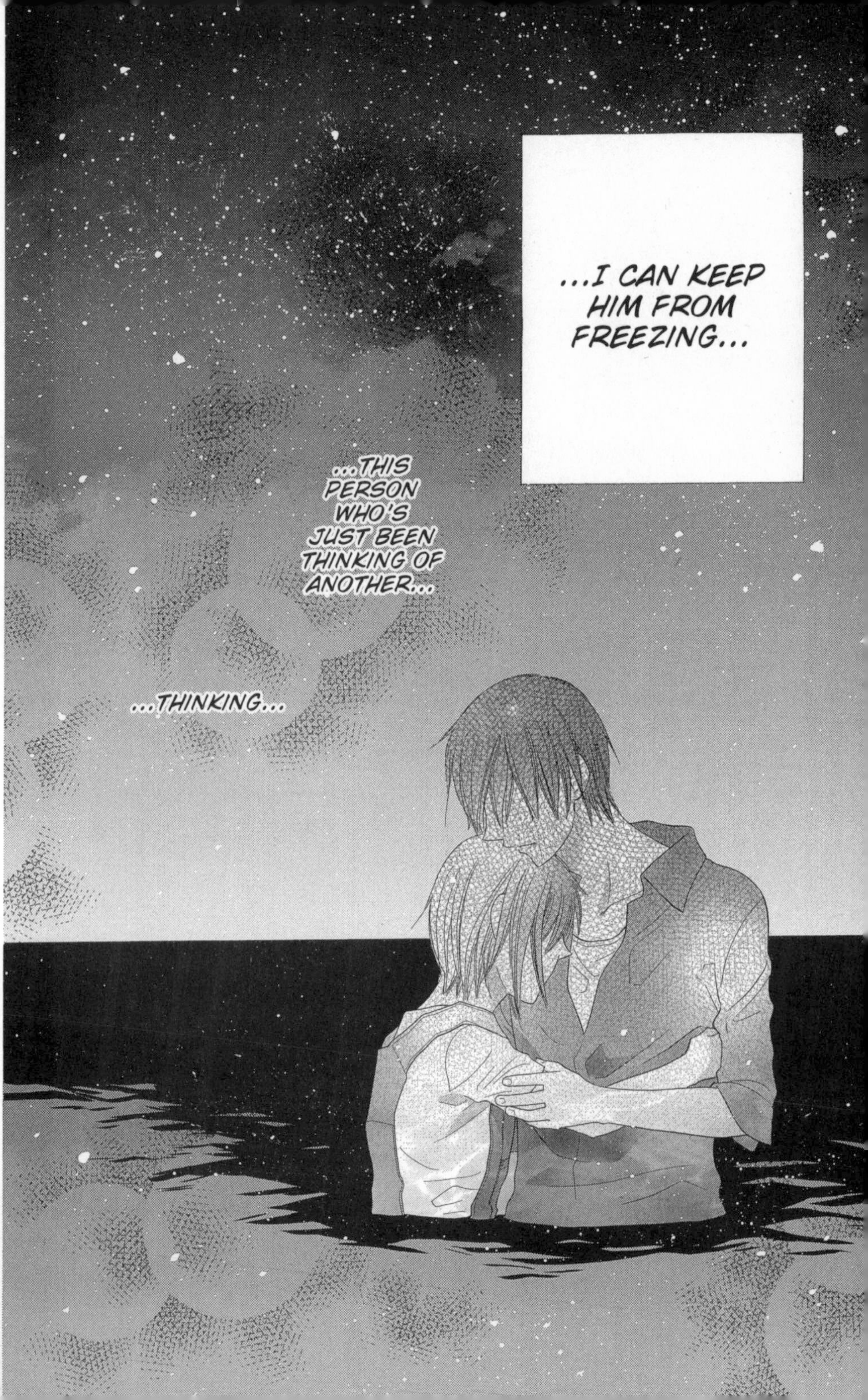
...I CAN KEEP HIM FROM FREEZING...
...THIS PERSON WHO'S JUST BEEN THINKING OF ANOTHER...
...THINKING...

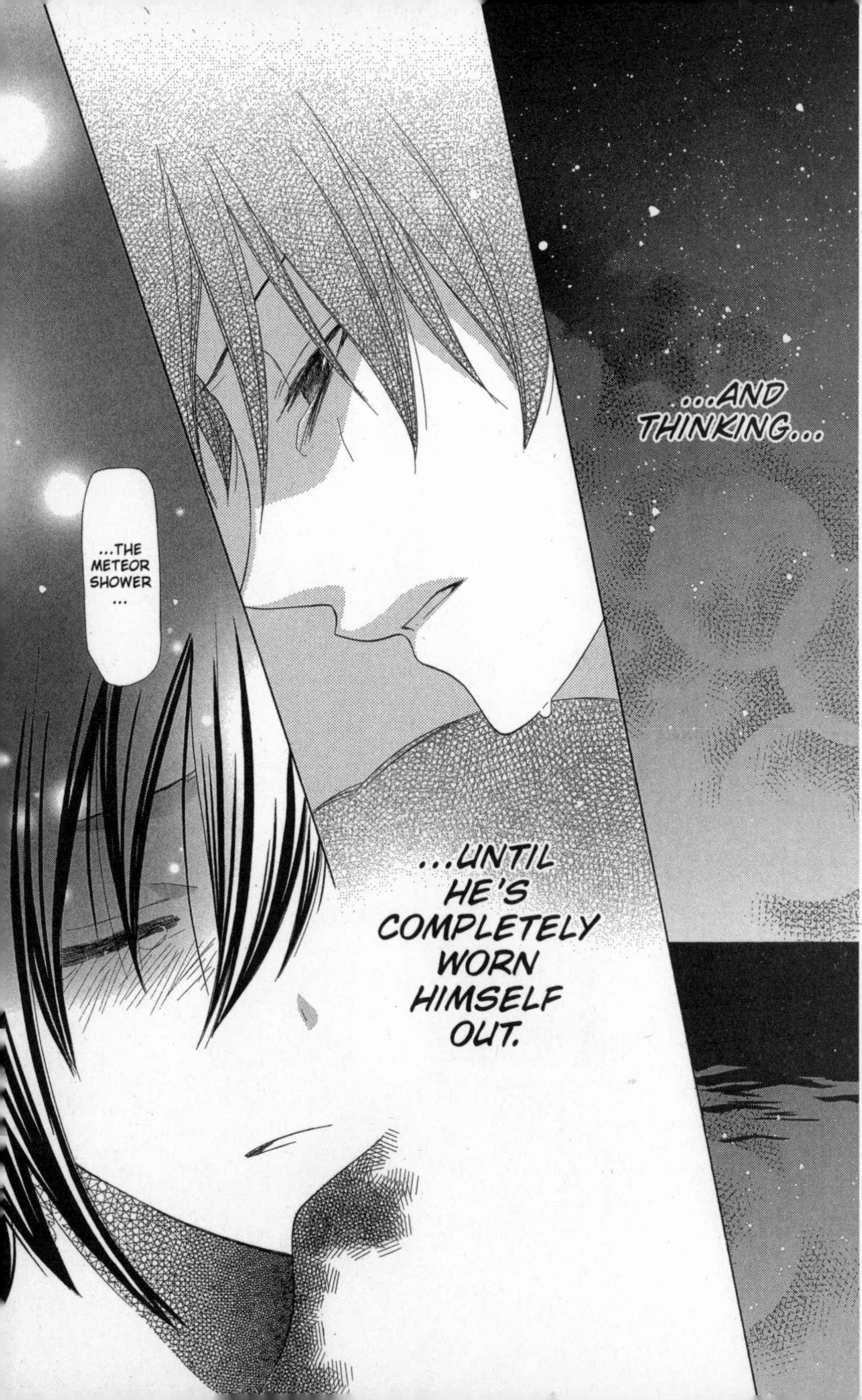
...AND THINKING...
...UNTIL HE'S COMPLETELY WORN HIMSELF OUT.
...THE METEOR SHOWER ...

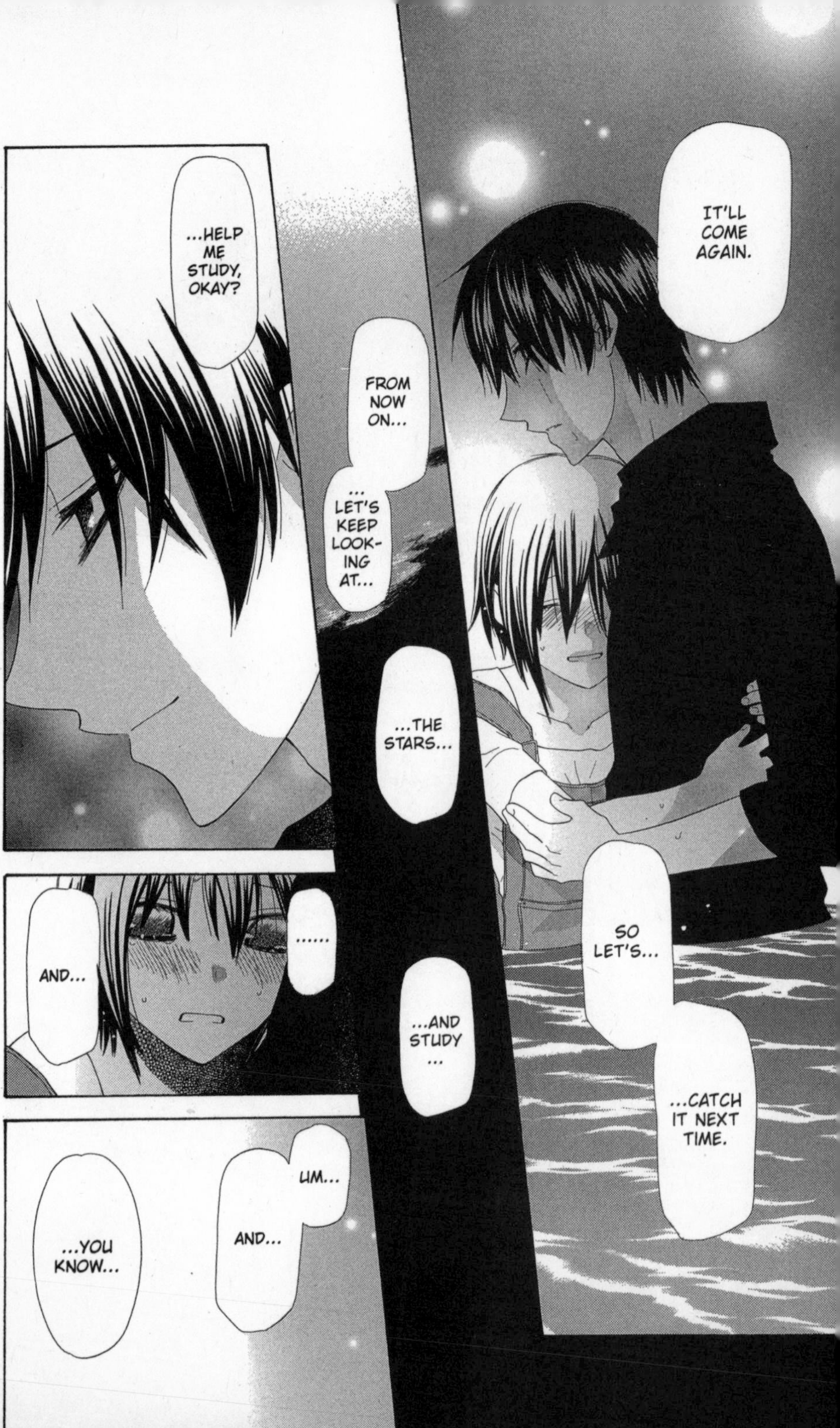
IT'LL COME AGAIN.
SO LET'S...
...CATCH IT NEXT TIME.
FROM NOW ON...
...LET'S KEEP LOOKING-ING AT...
...THE STARS...
...AND STUDY...
...HELP ME STUDY, OKAY?
......
AND...
UM...
AND...
...YOU KNOW...

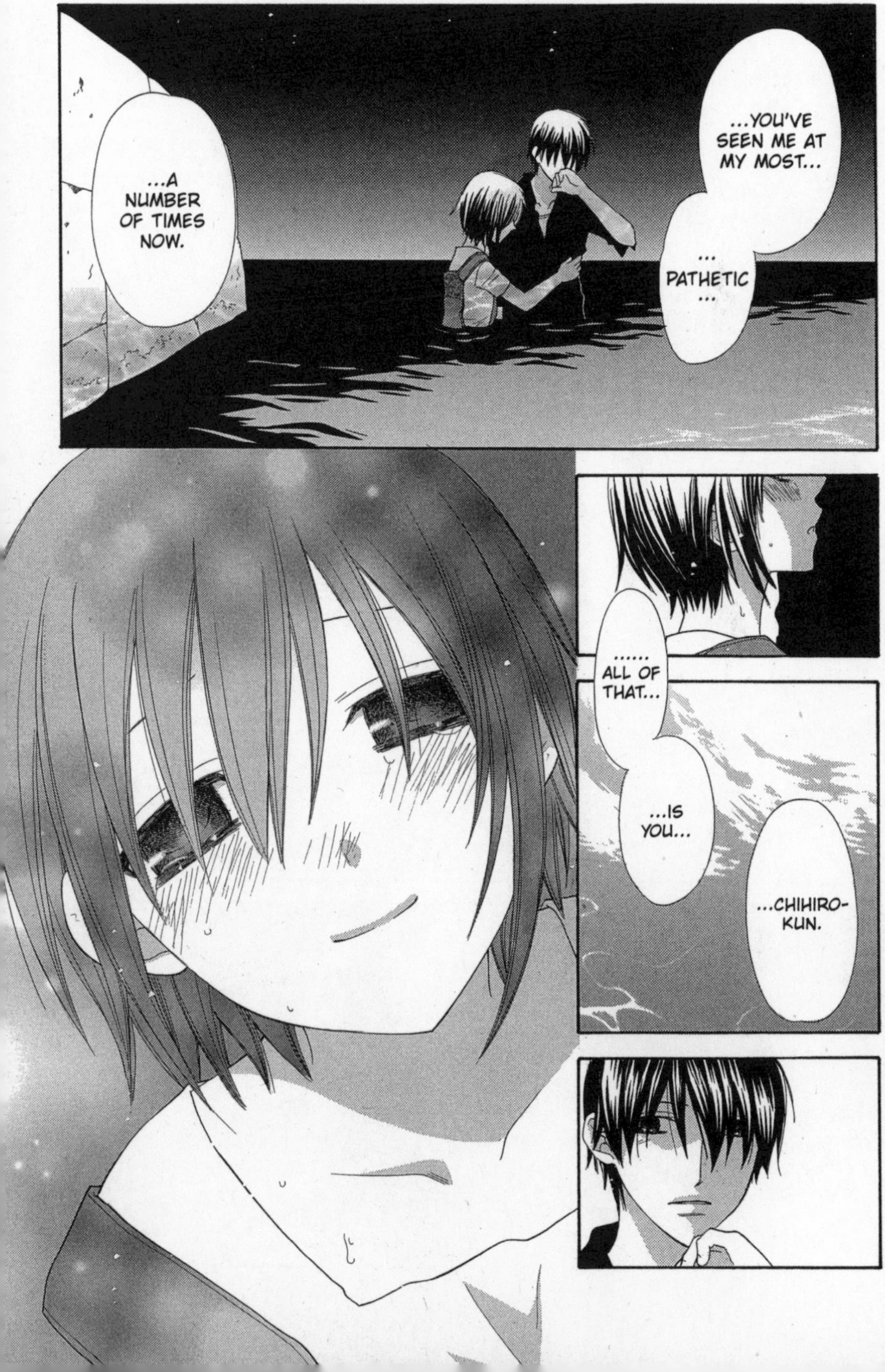
...YOU'VE SEEN ME AT MY MOST...
...PATHETIC...
...A NUMBER OF TIMES NOW.
......ALL OF THAT...
...IS YOU...
...CHIHIRO-KUN.

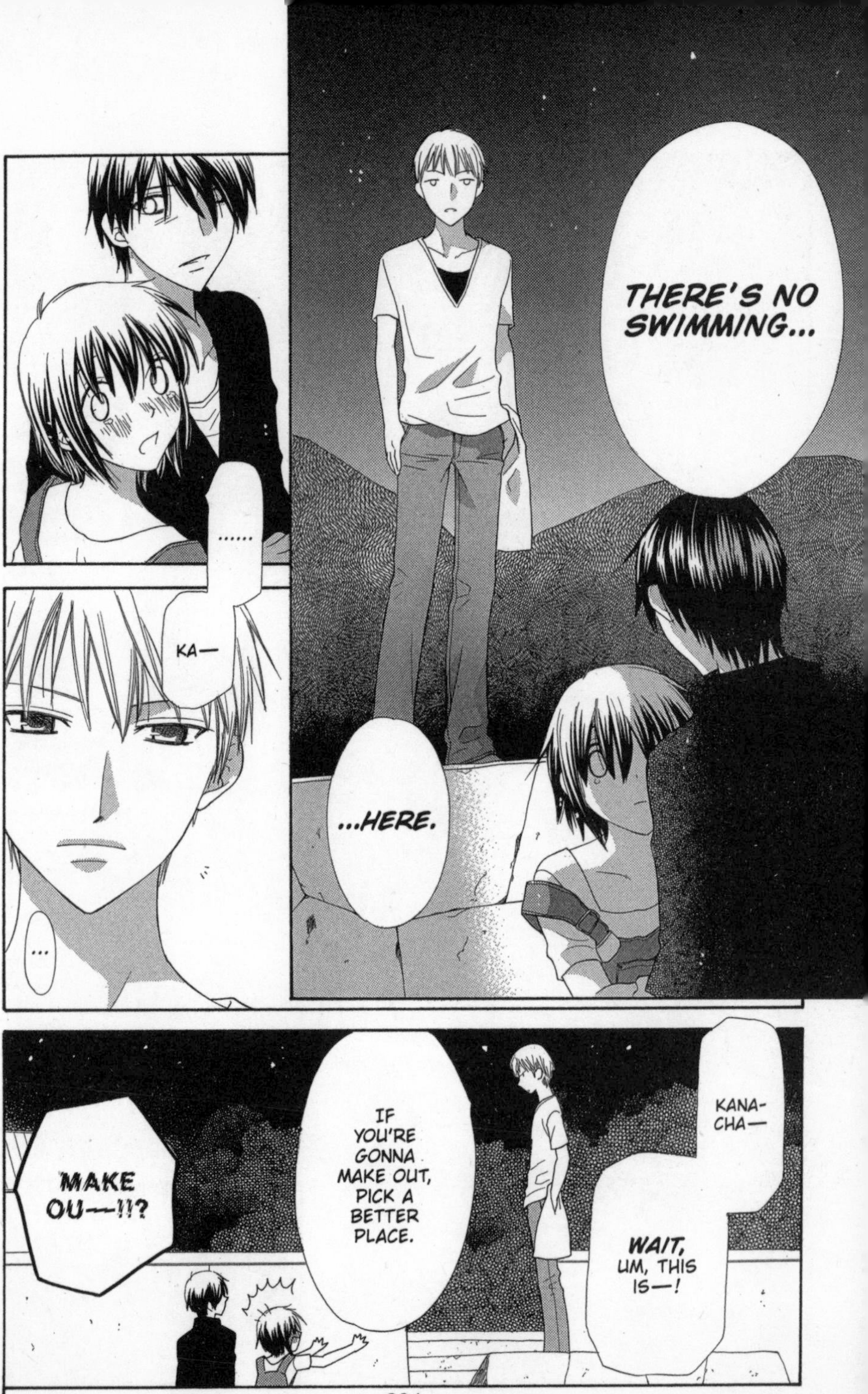
THERE'S NO SWIMMING...
...HERE.
......
KA—
...
KANA-CHA—
WAIT, UM, THIS IS—!
IF YOU'RE GONNA MAKE OUT, PICK A BETTER PLACE.
MAKE OU—!!?

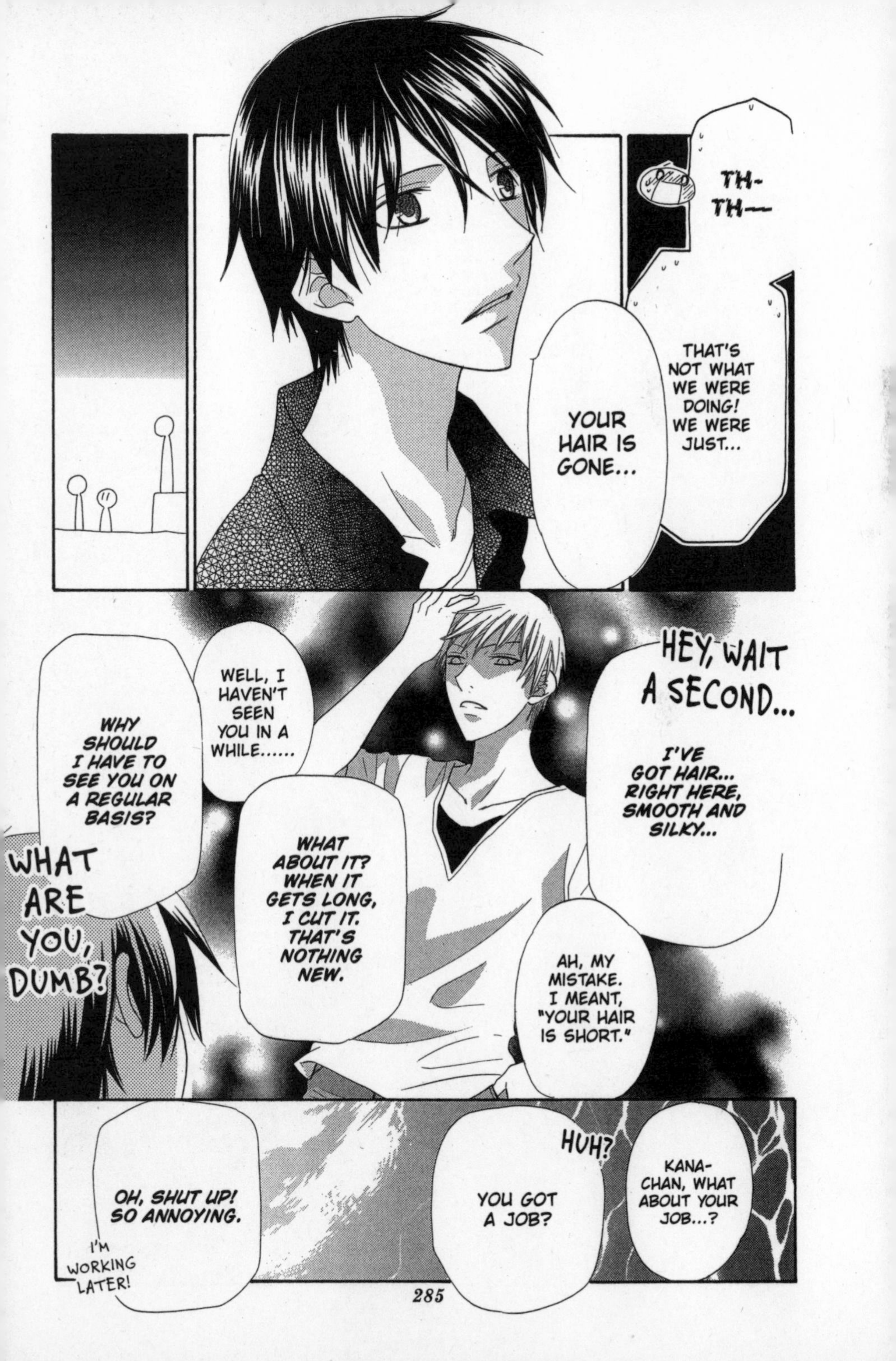
TH- TH—
THAT'S NOT WHAT WE WERE DOING! WE WERE JUST...
YOUR HAIR IS GONE...
HEY, WAIT A SECOND...
I'VE GOT HAIR... RIGHT HERE, SMOOTH AND SILKY...
AH, MY MISTAKE. I MEANT, "YOUR HAIR IS SHORT."
WELL, I HAVEN'T SEEN YOU IN A WHILE......
WHAT ABOUT IT? WHEN IT GETS LONG, I CUT IT. THAT'S NOTHING NEW.
WHY SHOULD I HAVE TO SEE YOU ON A REGULAR BASIS?
WHAT ARE YOU, DUMB?
KANA-CHAN, WHAT ABOUT YOUR JOB...?
HUH?
YOU GOT A JOB?
OH, SHUT UP! SO ANNOYING.
I'M WORKING LATER!

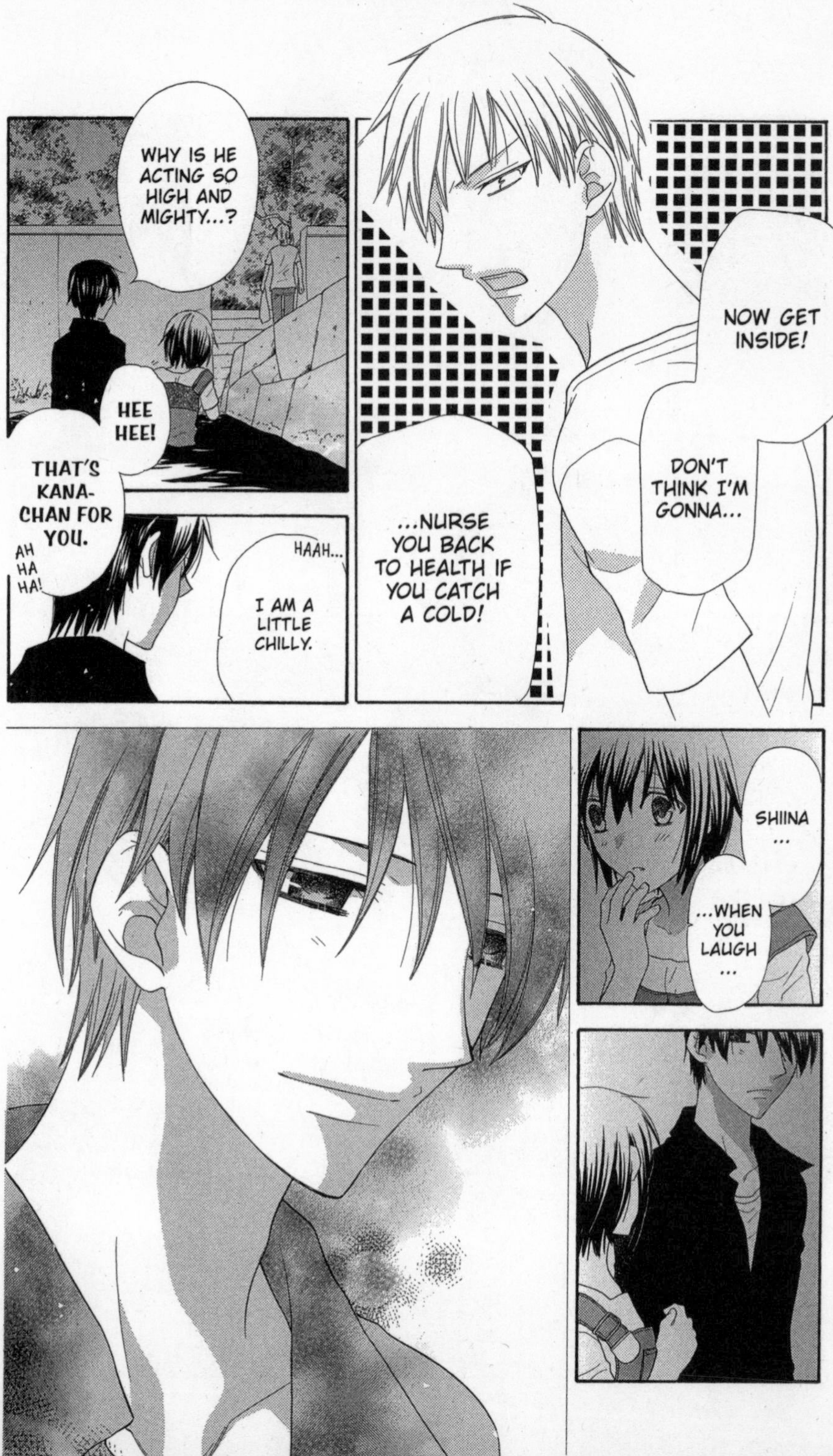
NOW GET INSIDE!
DON'T THINK I'M GONNA...
...NURSE YOU BACK TO HEALTH IF YOU CATCH A COLD!
WHY IS HE ACTING SO HIGH AND MIGHTY...?
HEE HEE!
THAT'S KANA-CHAN FOR YOU.
AH HA HA!
HAAH...
I AM A LITTLE CHILLY.
SHIINA ...
...WHEN YOU LAUGH ...

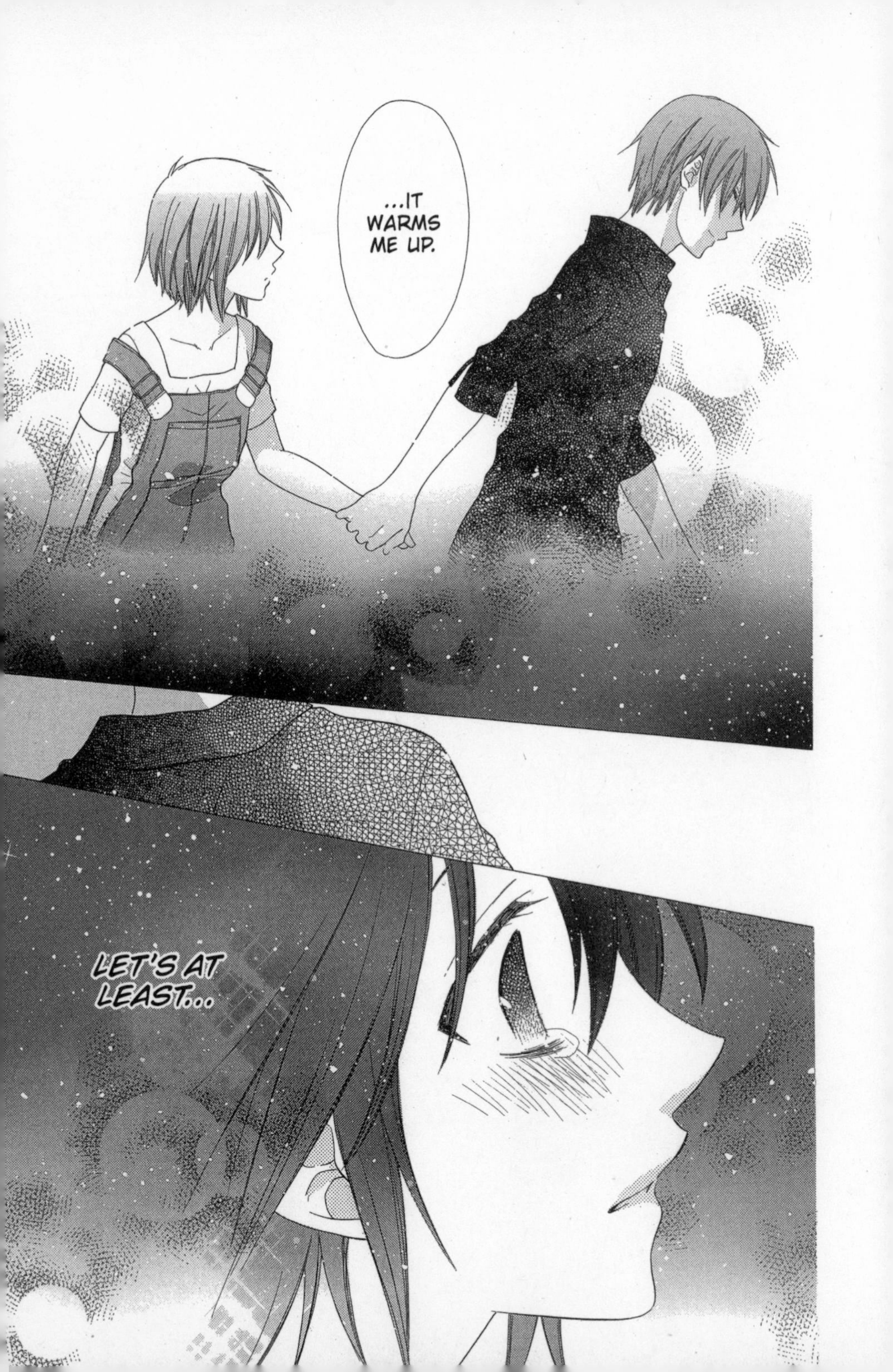
...IT WARMS ME UP.
LET'S AT LEAST...

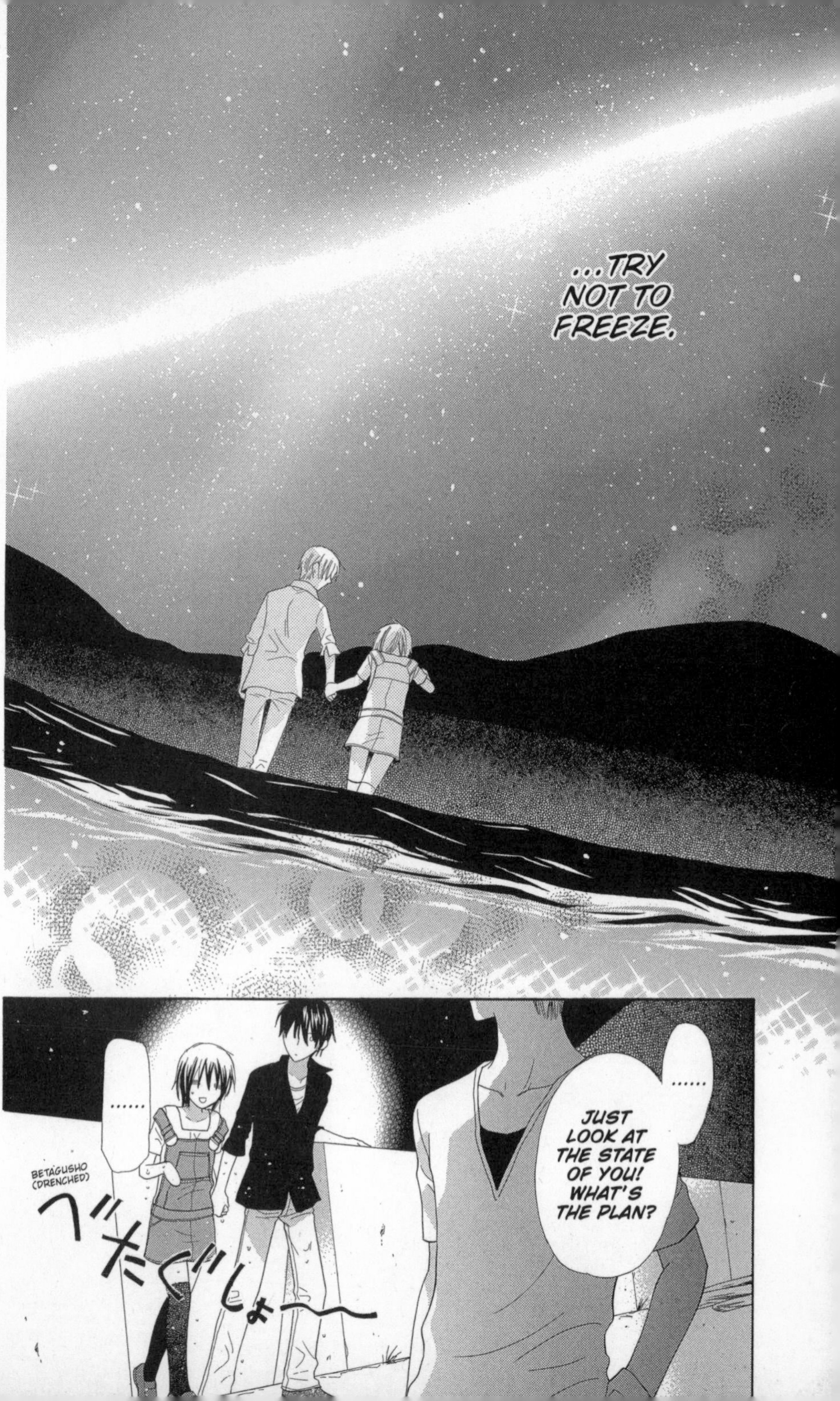
...TRY NOT TO FREEZE.
......
JUST LOOK AT THE STATE OF YOU! WHAT'S THE PLAN?
......
BETAGUSHO (DRENCHED)
べたぐしょ〜〜

Chapter 33

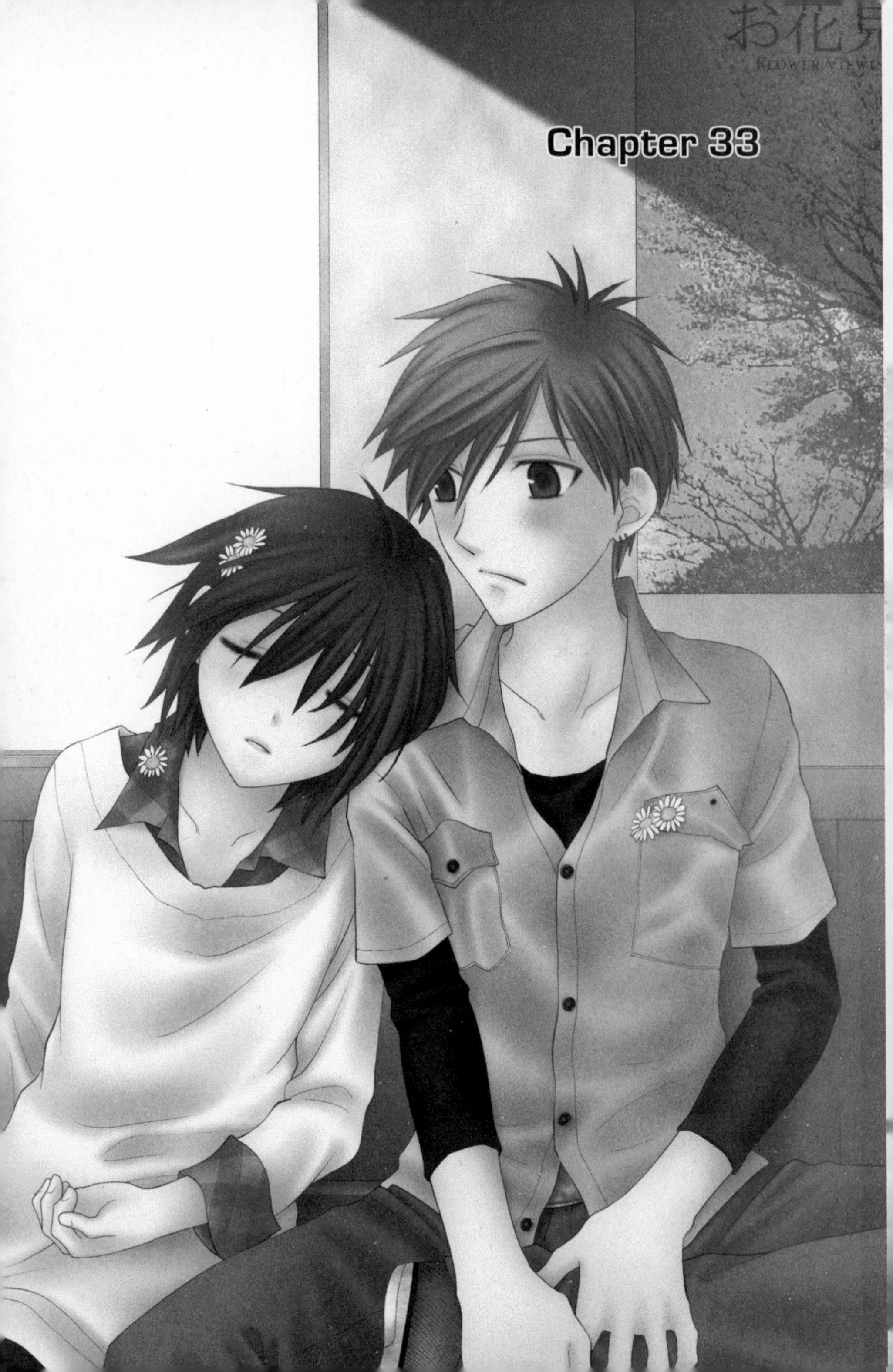

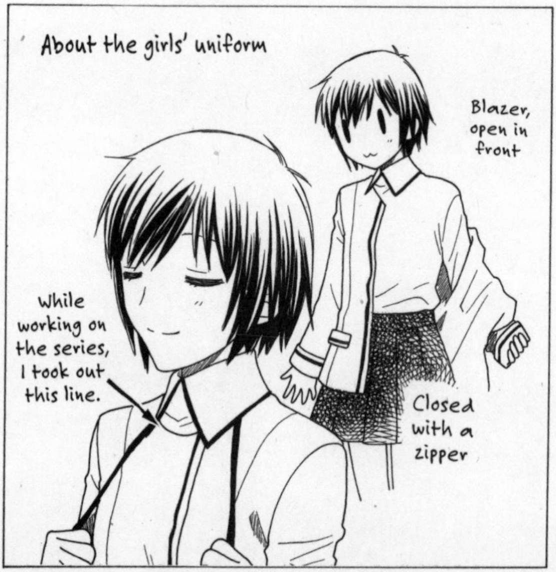
About the girls' uniform
Blazer, open in front
Closed with a zipper
While working on the series, I took out this line.

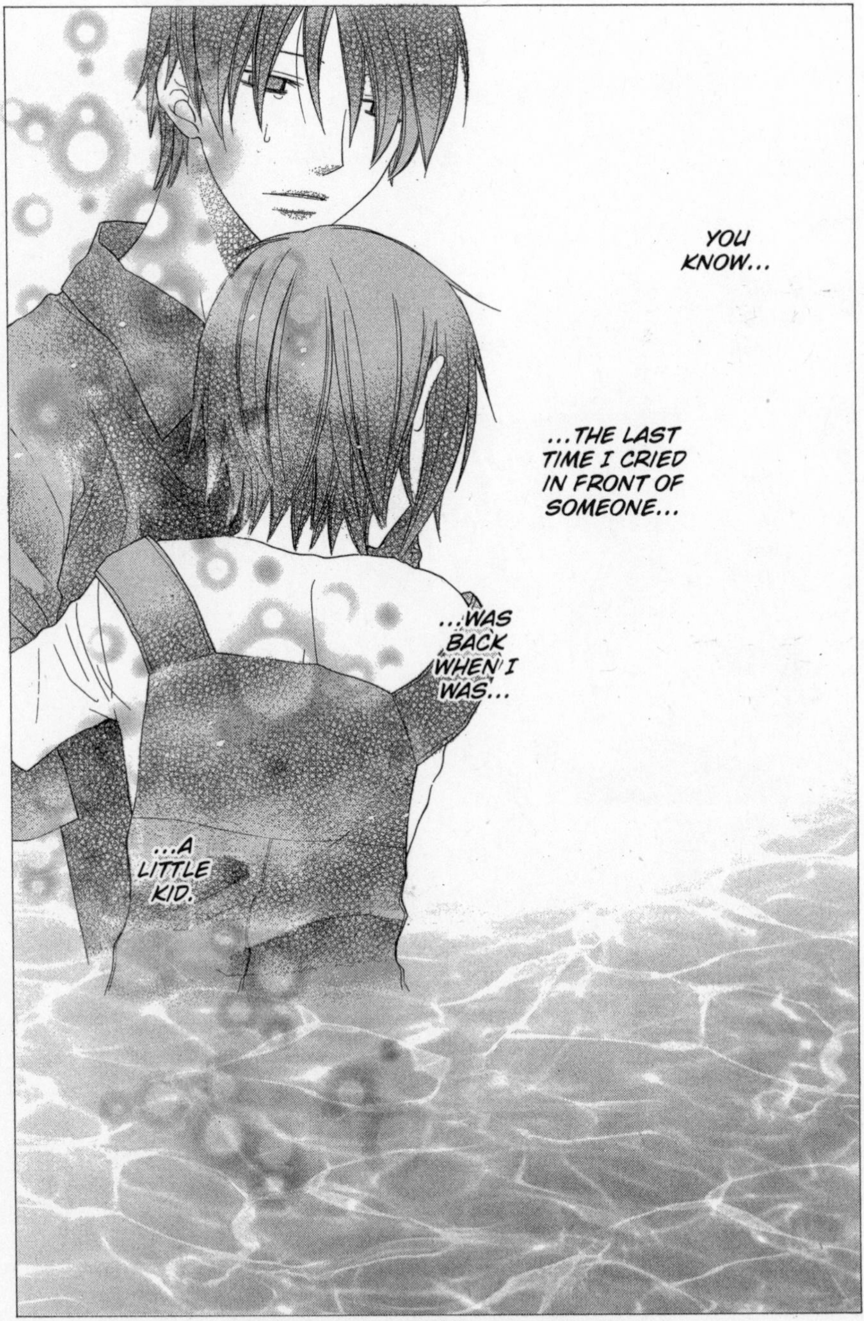
YOU KNOW...
...THE LAST TIME I CRIED IN FRONT OF SOMEONE...
...WAS BACK WHEN I WAS...
...A LITTLE KID.

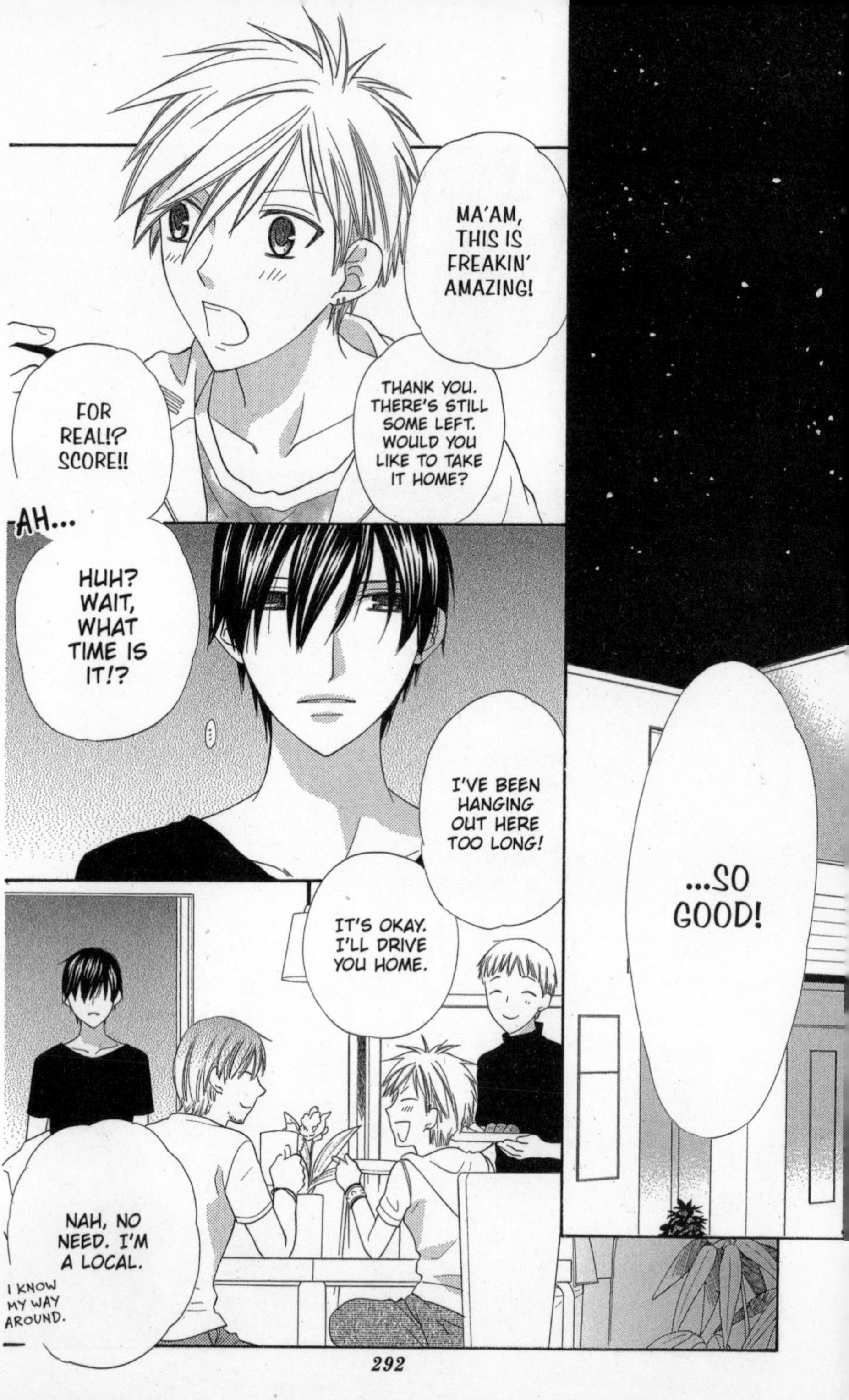
...SO GOOD!
MA'AM, THIS IS FREAKIN' AMAZING!
THANK YOU. THERE'S STILL SOME LEFT. WOULD YOU LIKE TO TAKE IT HOME?
FOR REAL!? SCORE!!
-AH...
HUH? WAIT, WHAT TIME IS IT!?
I'VE BEEN HANGING OUT HERE TOO LONG!
IT'S OKAY. I'LL DRIVE YOU HOME.
NAH, NO NEED. I'M A LOCAL.
I KNOW MY WAY AROUND.

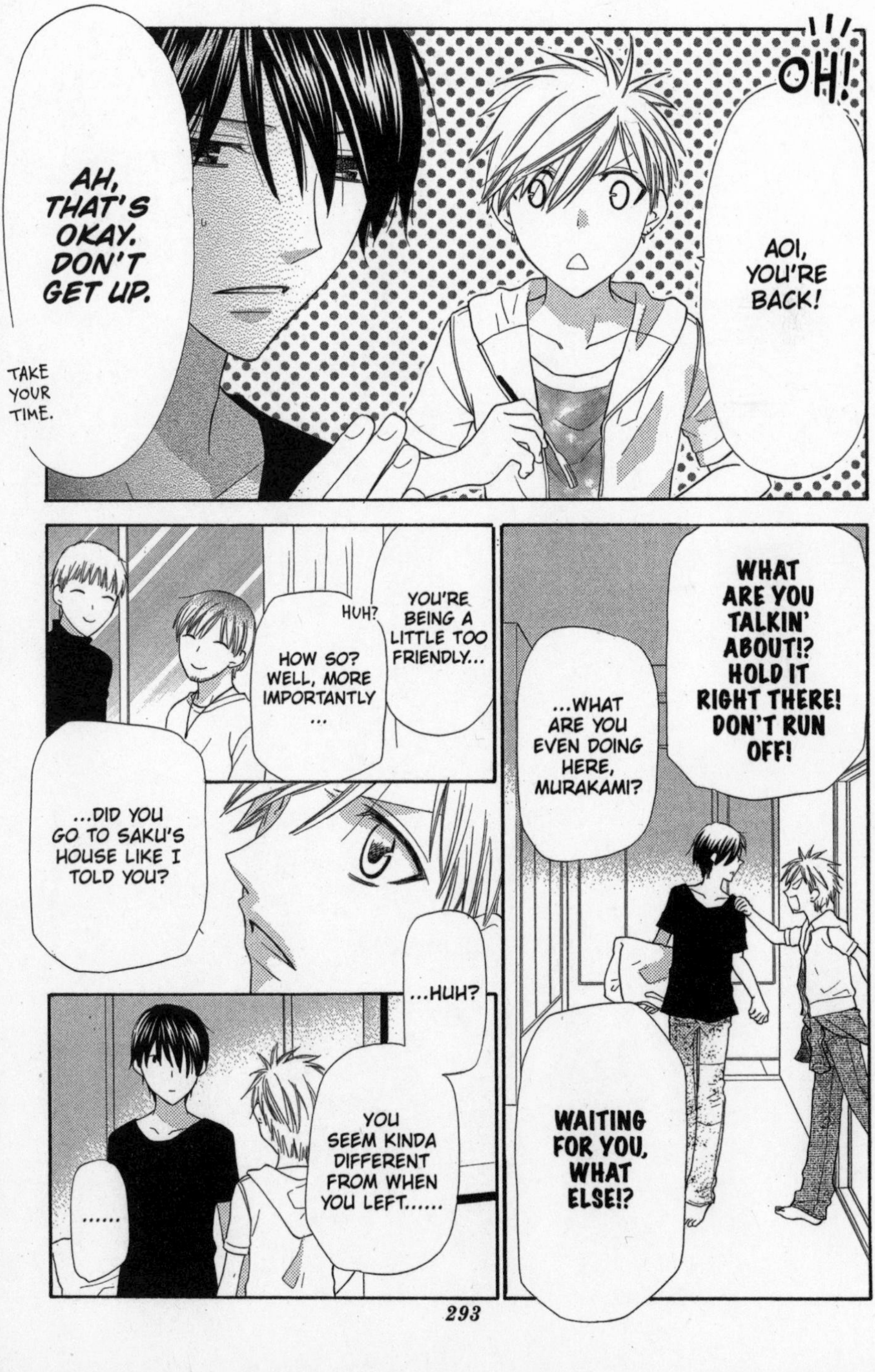
OH!
AOI, YOU'RE BACK!
AH, THAT'S OKAY. DON'T GET UP.
TAKE YOUR TIME.
WHAT ARE YOU TALKIN' ABOUT!? HOLD IT RIGHT THERE! DON'T RUN OFF!
...WHAT ARE YOU EVEN DOING HERE, MURAKAMI?
WAITING FOR YOU, WHAT ELSE!?
YOU'RE BEING A LITTLE TOO FRIENDLY...
HUH?
HOW SO? WELL, MORE IMPORTANTLY ...
...DID YOU GO TO SAKU'S HOUSE LIKE I TOLD YOU?
...HUH?
YOU SEEM KINDA DIFFERENT FROM WHEN YOU LEFT......
......

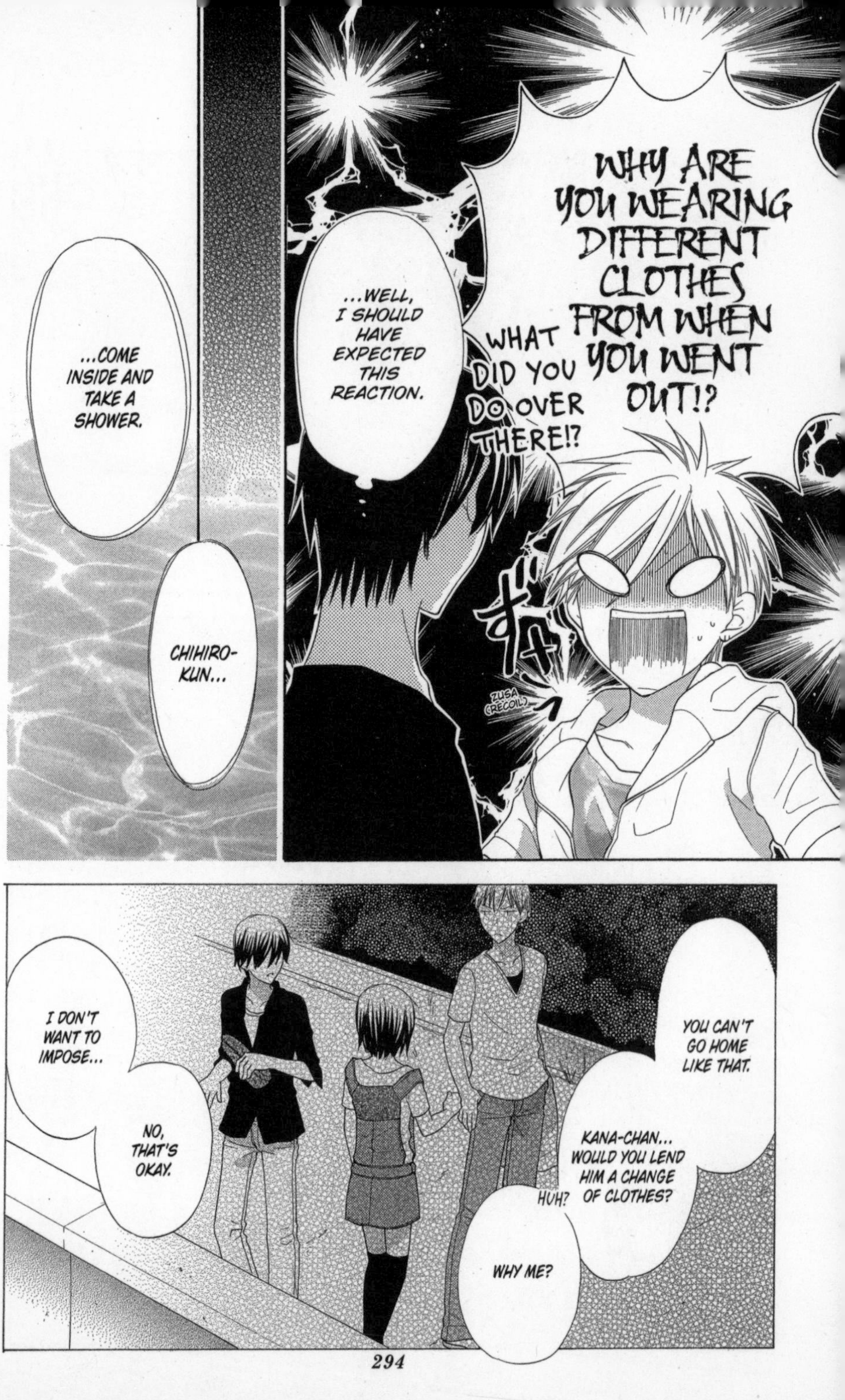
WHY ARE YOU WEARING DIFFERENT CLOTHES FROM WHEN YOU WENT OUT!?
WHAT DID YOU DO OVER THERE!?
...WELL, I SHOULD HAVE EXPECTED THIS REACTION.
ZUSA (RECOIL)
...COME INSIDE AND TAKE A SHOWER.
CHIHIRO-KUN...
YOU CAN'T GO HOME LIKE THAT.
KANA-CHAN... WOULD YOU LEND HIM A CHANGE OF CLOTHES?
HUH?
WHY ME?
I DON'T WANT TO IMPOSE...
NO, THAT'S OKAY.

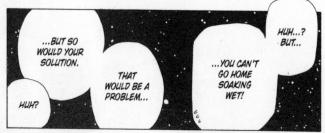

HUH...? BUT...
...YOU CAN'T GO HOME SOAKING WET!
THAT WOULD BE A PROBLEM...
...BUT SO WOULD YOUR SOLUTION.
HUH?
...I KIND OF...
...FEEL LIKE AN IDIOT FOR BEING BOTHERED BY IT, BUT...
?
WHAT'S THIS...?
ARE YOU SAYING YOU WON'T WEAR CLOTHES THAT I'VE WORN BEFORE......?
KANADE-SAN, YOU'RE A GUY, SO I'M SURE YOU CAN SYMPATHIZE WITH MY RELUCTANCE...
THE MORE WE TALK ABOUT IT, THE DUMBER I FEEL...

Out of all the characters in Twinkle Stars, the tallest is Yuuto. The next tallest is Kana-chan.

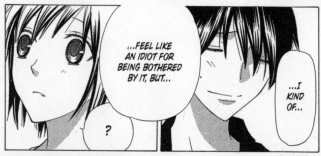

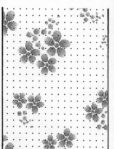

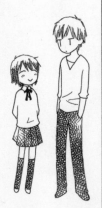

Sakuya is the shortest.

I haven't decided on their exact heights.

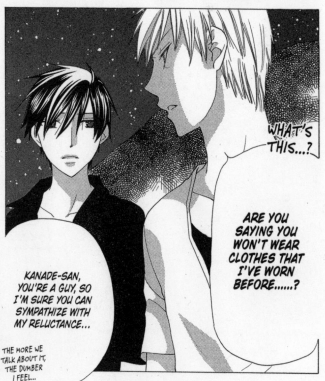

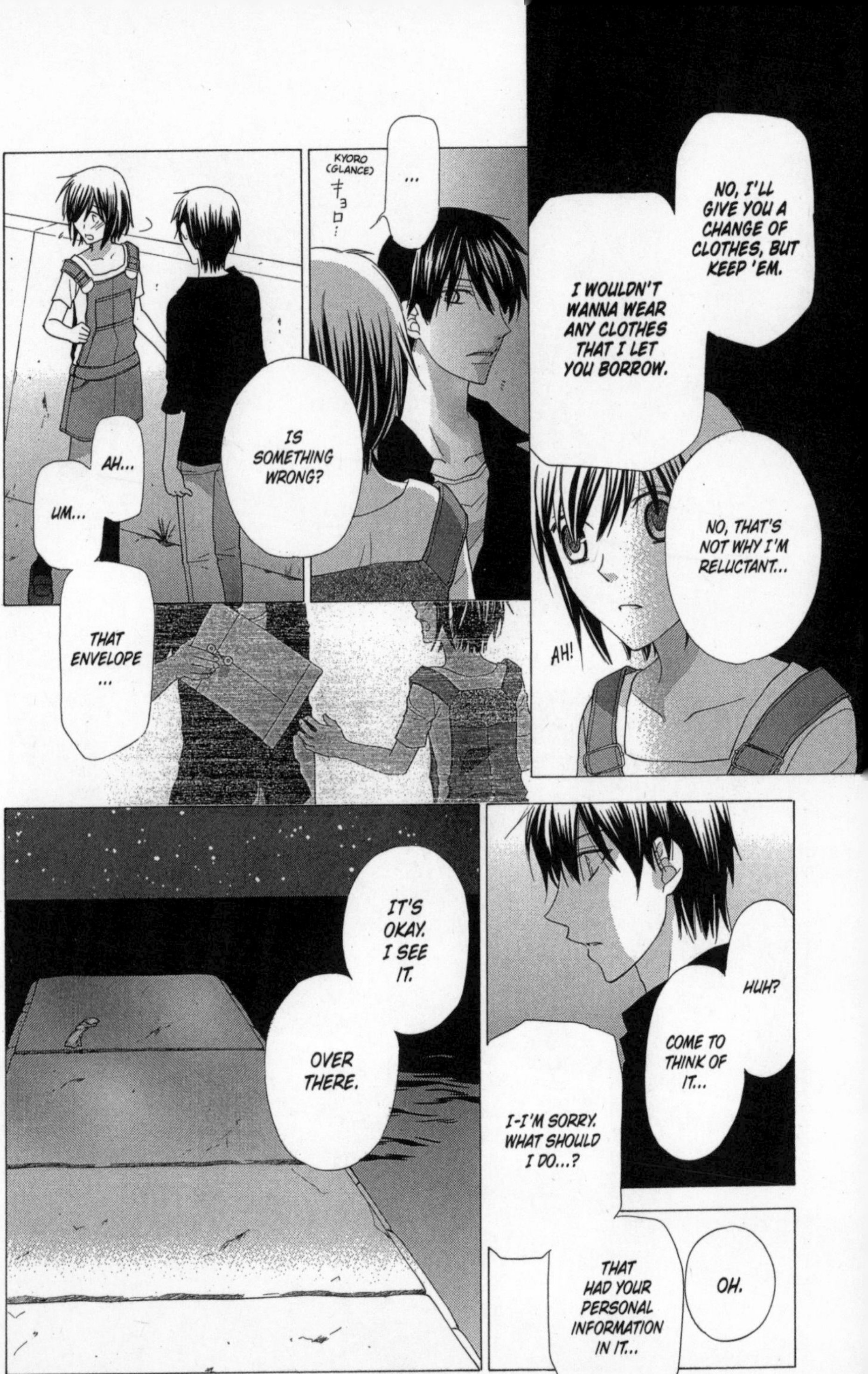
NO, I'LL GIVE YOU A CHANGE OF CLOTHES, BUT KEEP 'EM.
I WOULDN'T WANNA WEAR ANY CLOTHES THAT I LET YOU BORROW.
NO, THAT'S NOT WHY I'M RELUCTANT...
AH!
...
KYORO (GLANCE)
キョロ…
IS SOMETHING WRONG?
AH...
UM...
THAT ENVELOPE ...
HUH?
COME TO THINK OF IT...
THAT HAD YOUR PERSONAL INFORMATION IN IT...
OH.
I-I'M SORRY. WHAT SHOULD I DO...?
IT'S OKAY. I SEE IT.
OVER THERE.

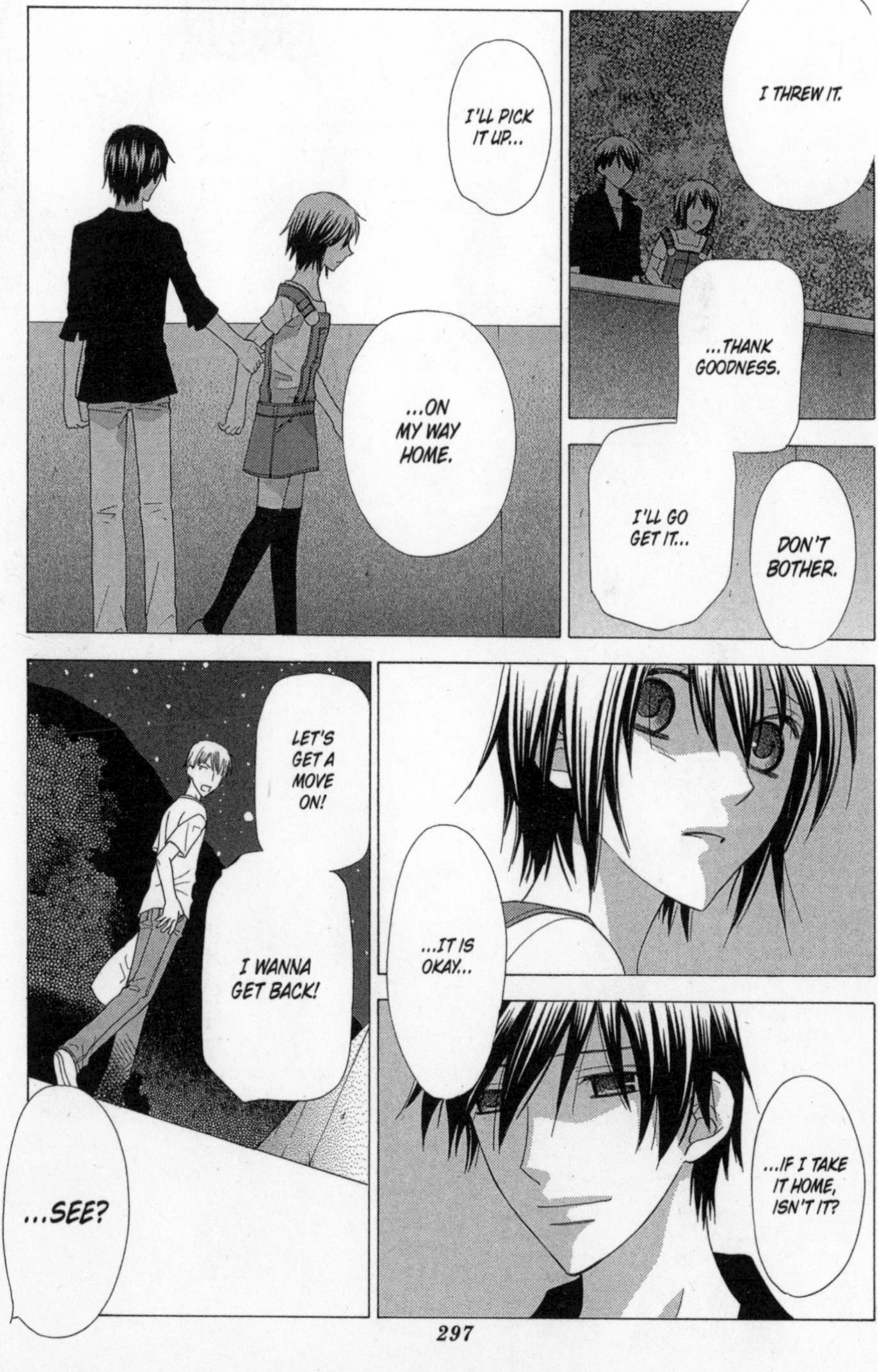

I THREW IT.
...THANK GOODNESS.
I'LL GO GET IT...
DON'T BOTHER.
I'LL PICK IT UP...
...ON MY WAY HOME.
...IT IS OKAY...
...IF I TAKE IT HOME, ISN'T IT?
LET'S GET A MOVE ON!
I WANNA GET BACK!
...SEE?

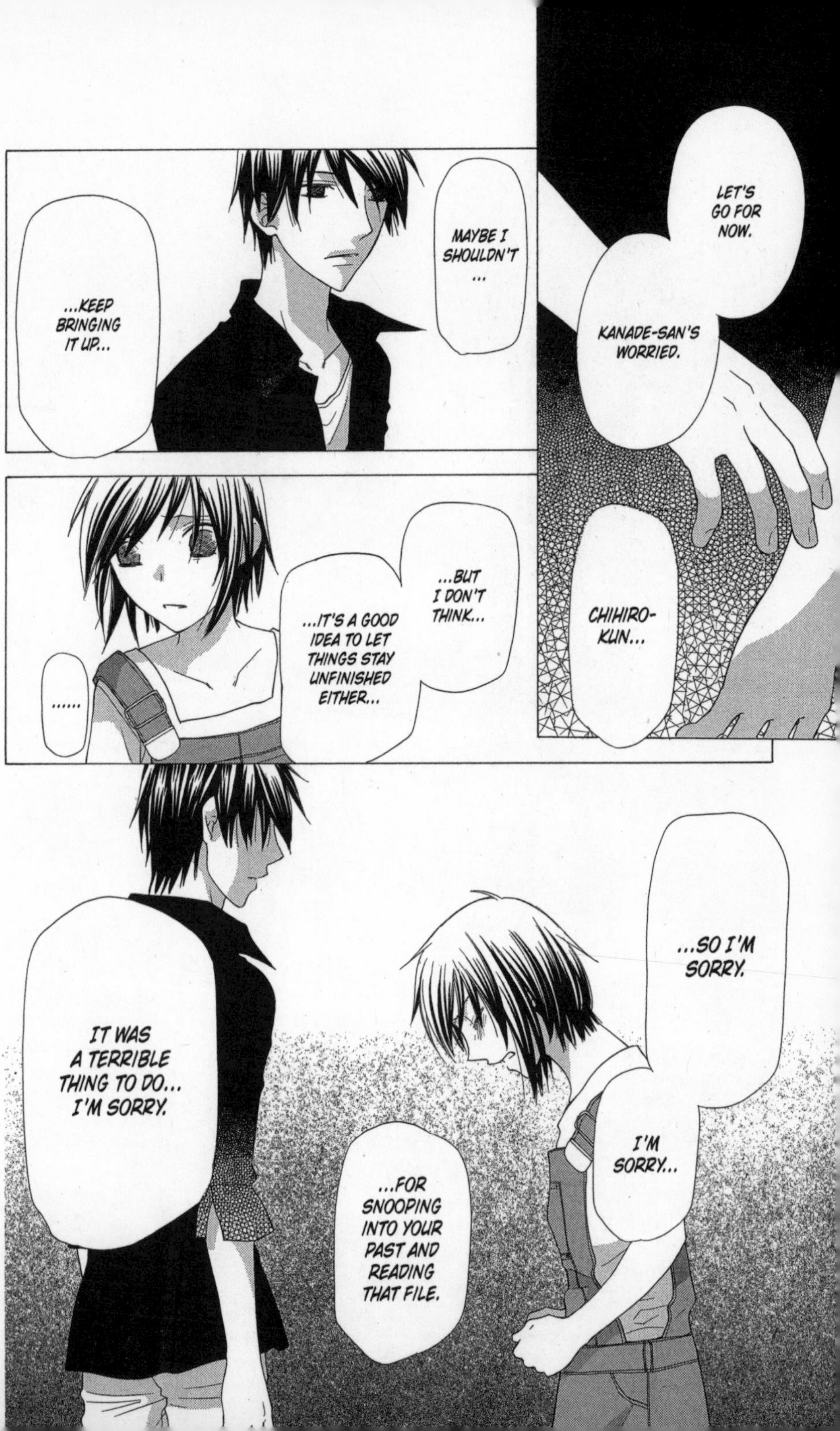
LET'S GO FOR NOW.
KANADE-SAN'S WORRIED.
CHIHIRO-KUN...
MAYBE I SHOULDN'T ...
...KEEP BRINGING IT UP...
...BUT I DON'T THINK...
...IT'S A GOOD IDEA TO LET THINGS STAY UNFINISHED EITHER...
......
...SO I'M SORRY.
I'M SORRY...
...FOR SNOOPING INTO YOUR PAST AND READING THAT FILE.
IT WAS A TERRIBLE THING TO DO... I'M SORRY.

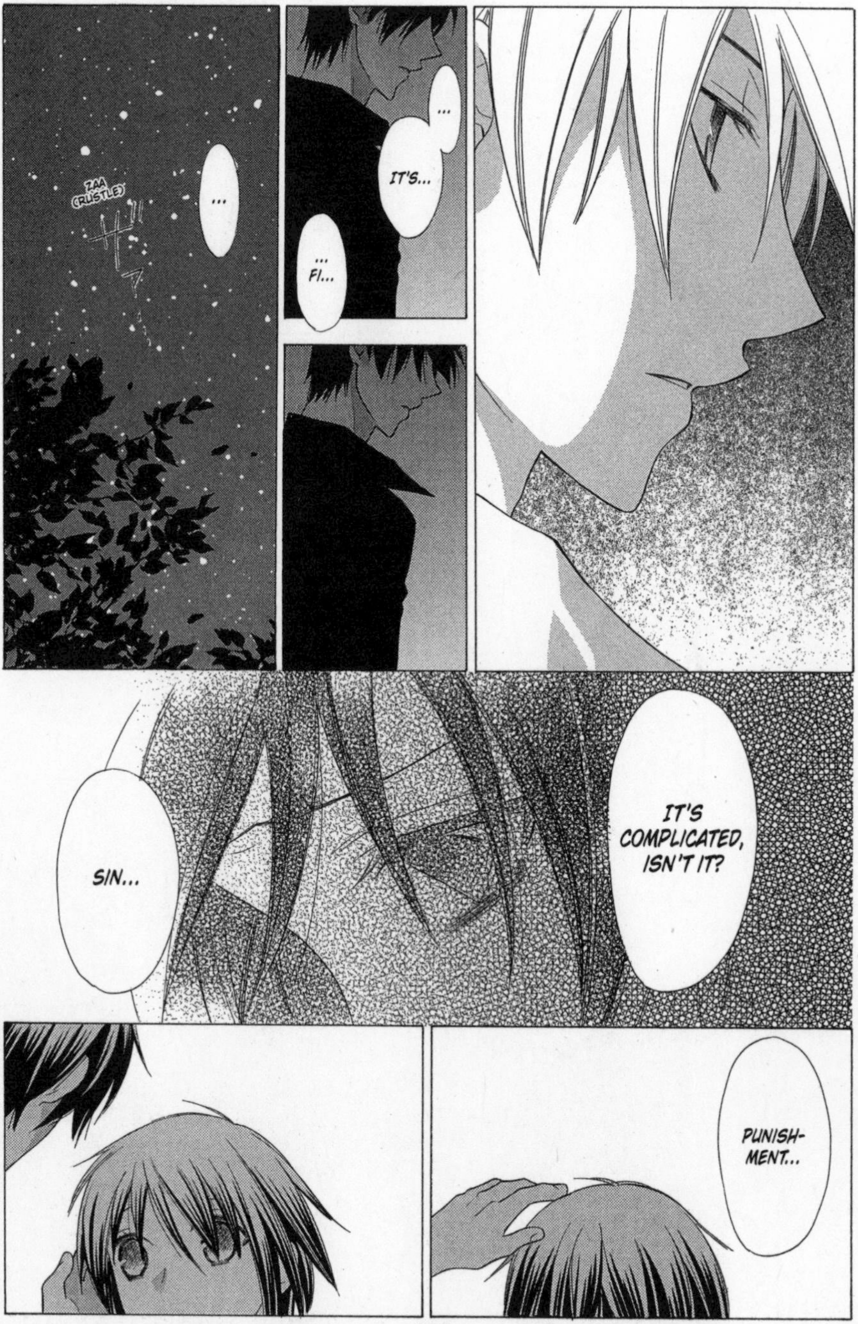
...
IT'S...
... FI...
...
ZAA (RUSTLE)
IT'S COMPLICATED, ISN'T IT?
SIN...
PUNISHMENT...

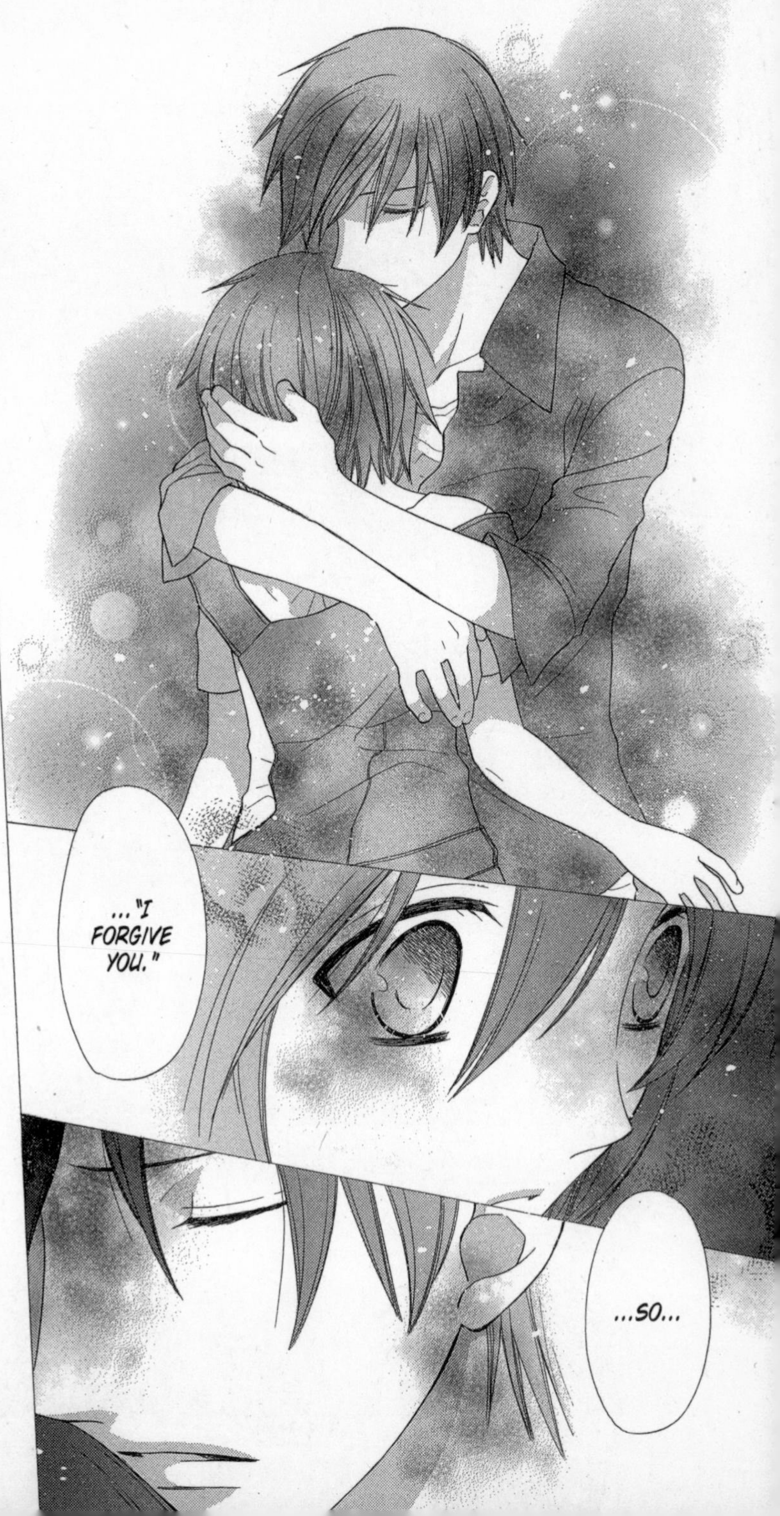
..."I FORGIVE YOU."
...SO...

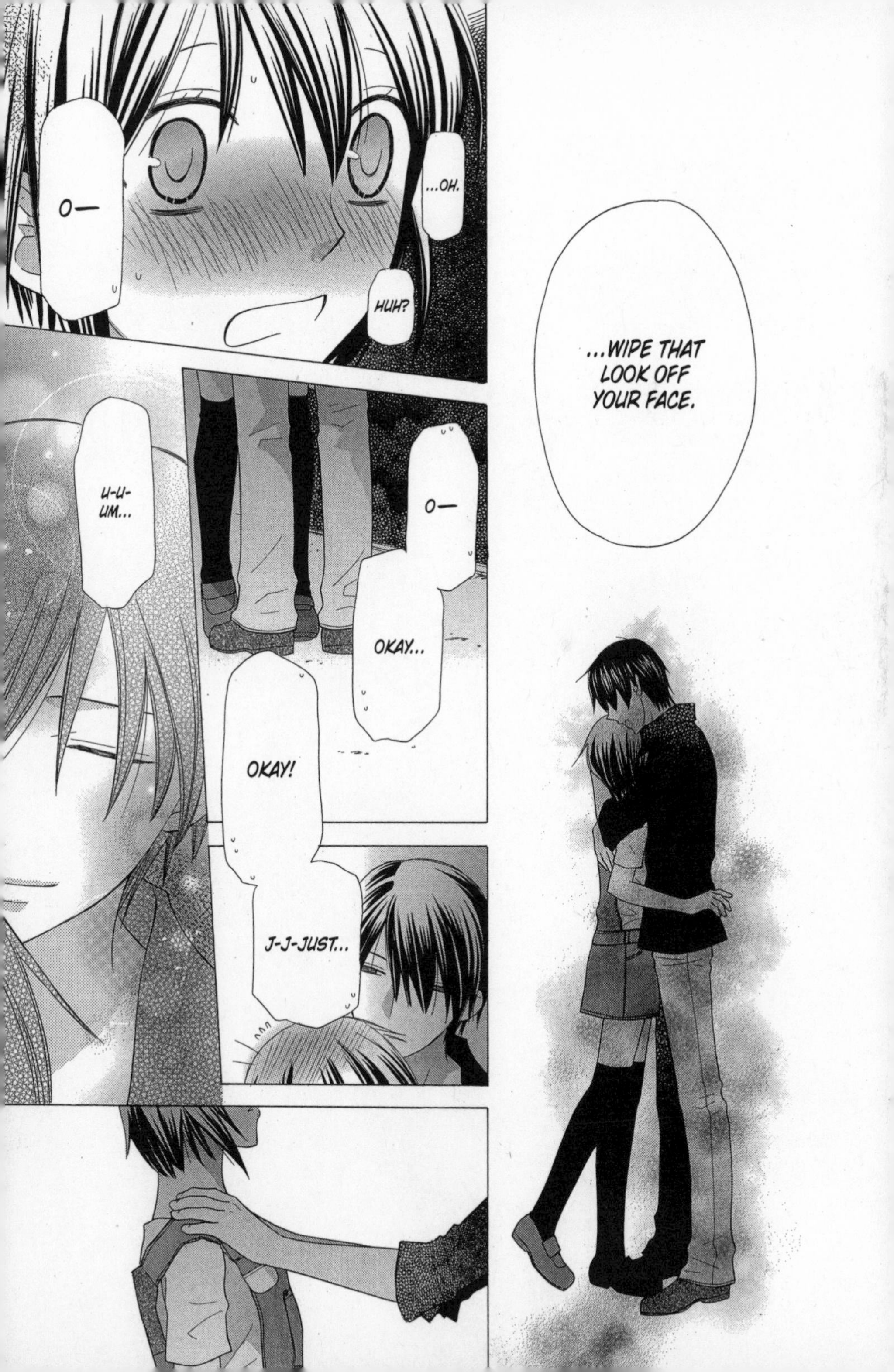
...WIPE THAT LOOK OFF YOUR FACE.
...OH.
HUH?
O—
O—
OKAY...
OKAY!
U-U-UM...
J-J-JUST...

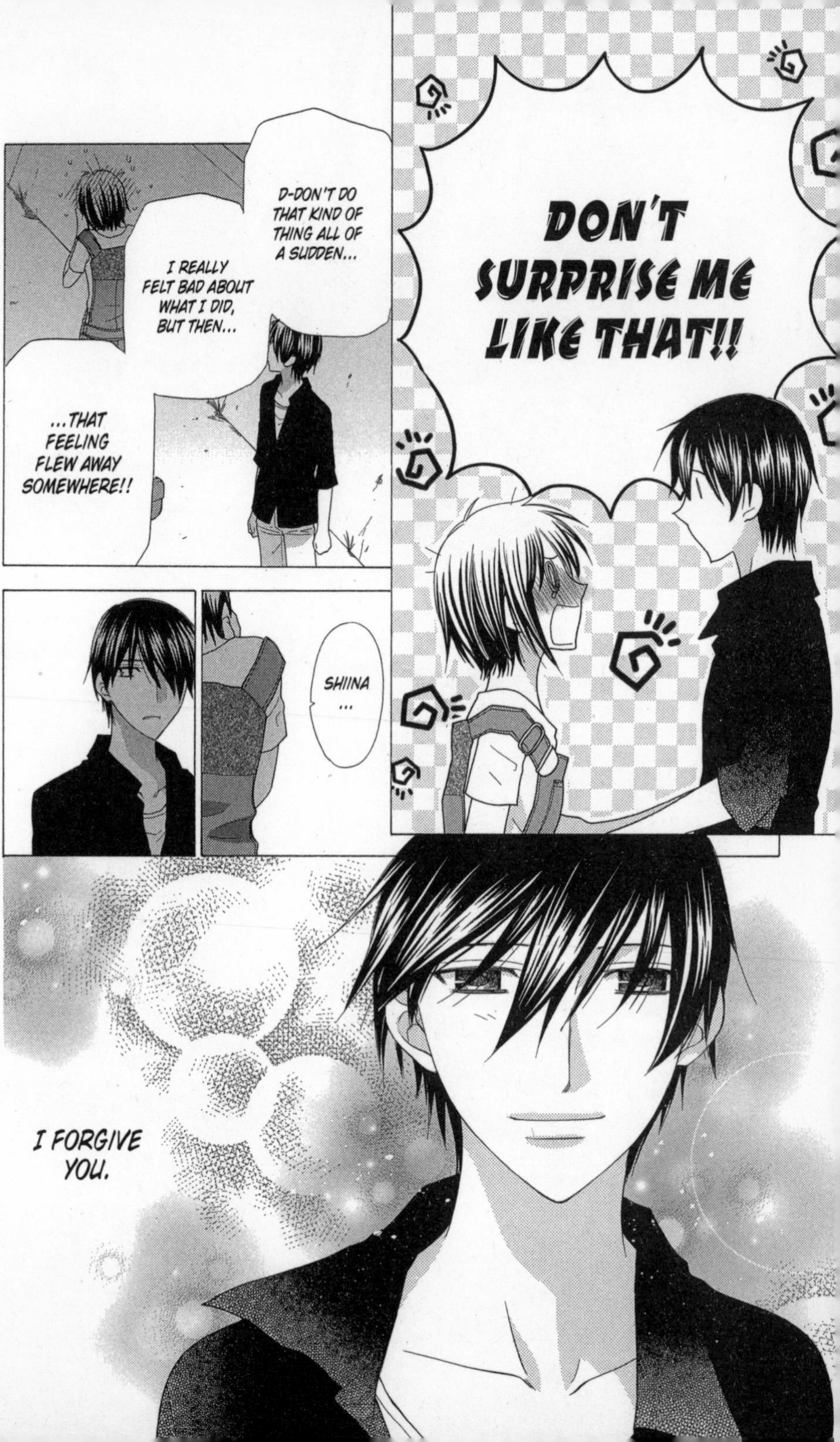
DON'T SURPRISE ME LIKE THAT!!
D-DON'T DO THAT KIND OF THING ALL OF A SUDDEN...
I REALLY FELT BAD ABOUT WHAT I DID, BUT THEN...
...THAT FEELING FLEW AWAY SOMEWHERE!!
SHIINA...
I FORGIVE YOU.

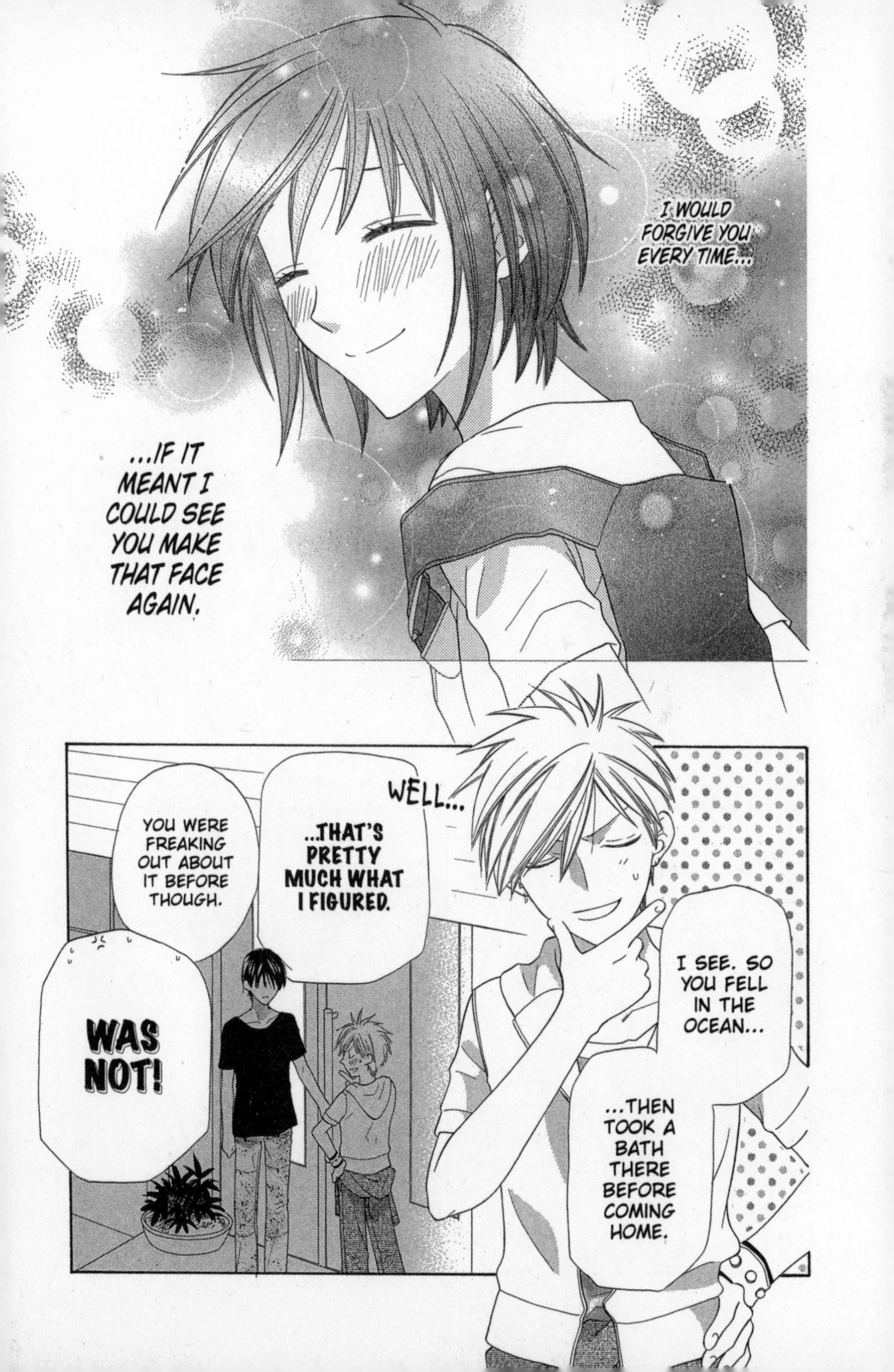
I WOULD FORGIVE YOU EVERY TIME...
...IF IT MEANT I COULD SEE YOU MAKE THAT FACE AGAIN.
I SEE. SO YOU FELL IN THE OCEAN...
...THEN TOOK A BATH THERE BEFORE COMING HOME.
WELL...
...THAT'S PRETTY MUCH WHAT I FIGURED.
YOU WERE FREAKING OUT ABOUT IT BEFORE THOUGH.
WAS NOT!

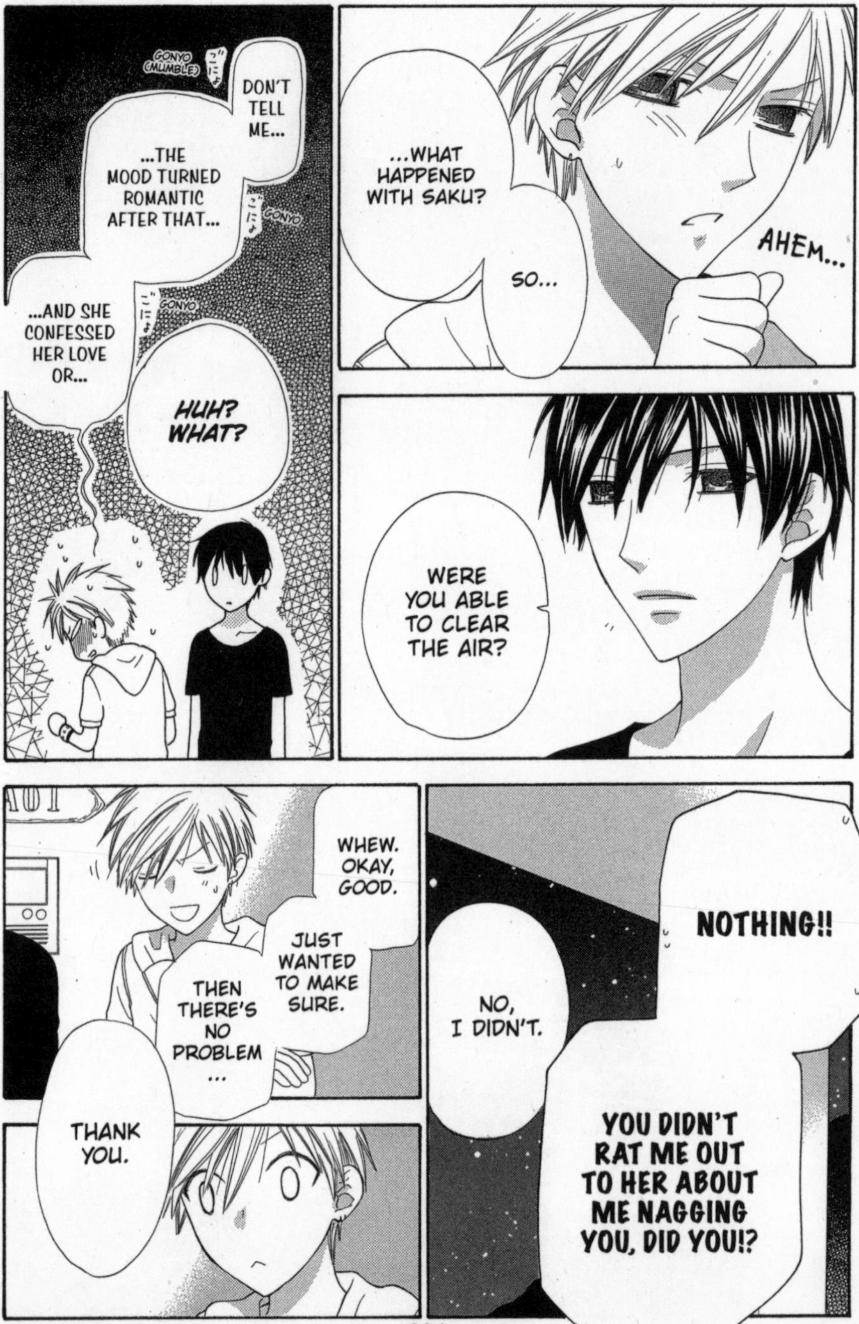
AHEM...
SO...
...WHAT HAPPENED WITH SAKU?
WERE YOU ABLE TO CLEAR THE AIR?
GONYO (MUMBLE)
DON'T TELL ME...
...THE MOOD TURNED ROMANTIC AFTER THAT...
GONYO
GONYO
...AND SHE CONFESSED HER LOVE OR...
HUH? WHAT?
NOTHING!!
YOU DIDN'T RAT ME OUT TO HER ABOUT ME NAGGING YOU, DID YOU!?
NO, I DIDN'T.
WHEW. OKAY, GOOD.
JUST WANTED TO MAKE SURE.
THEN THERE'S NO PROBLEM ...
THANK YOU.

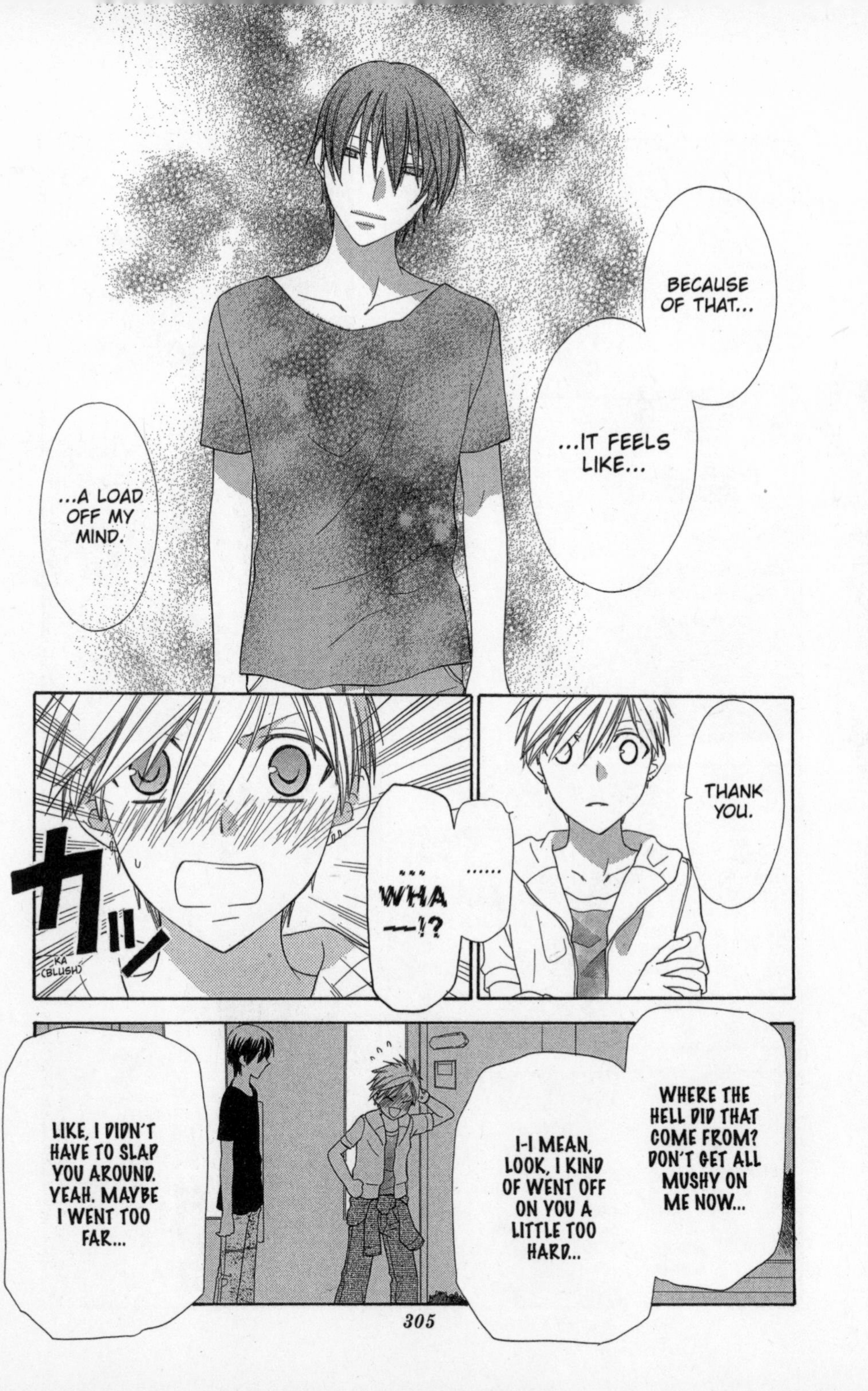
BECAUSE OF THAT...
...IT FEELS LIKE...
...A LOAD OFF MY MIND.
THANK YOU.
......
...WHA—!?
カッ
KA (BLUSH)
WHERE THE HELL DID THAT COME FROM? DON'T GET ALL MUSHY ON ME NOW...
I-I MEAN, LOOK, I KIND OF WENT OFF ON YOU A LITTLE TOO HARD...
LIKE, I DIDN'T HAVE TO SLAP YOU AROUND. YEAH. MAYBE I WENT TOO FAR...

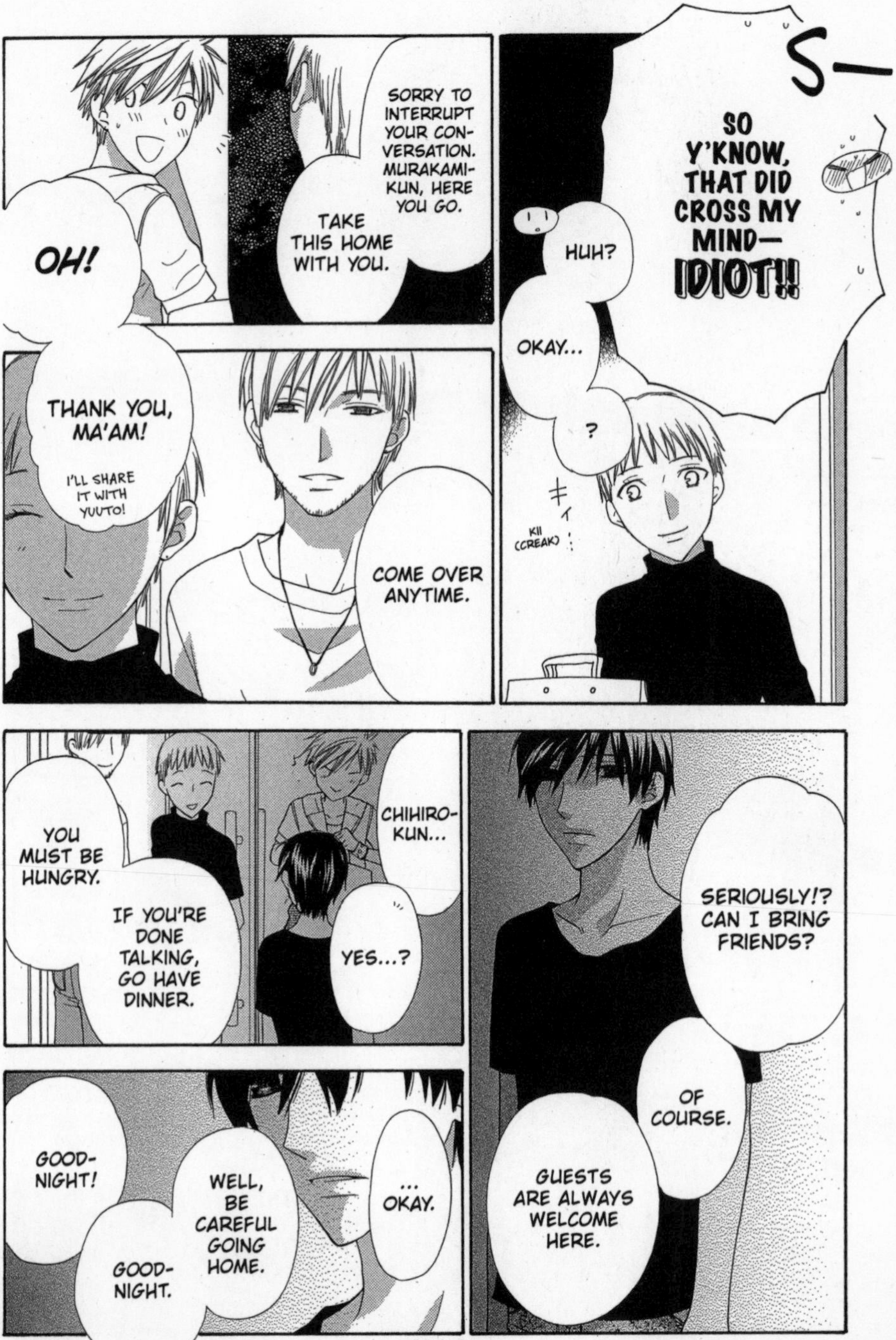
S—
SO Y'KNOW, THAT DID CROSS MY MIND— IDIOT!!
HUH?
OKAY...
?
KII (CREAK)
SORRY TO INTERRUPT YOUR CON- VERSATION. MURAKAMI- KUN, HERE YOU GO.
TAKE THIS HOME WITH YOU.
OH!
THANK YOU, MA'AM!
I'LL SHARE IT WITH YUUTO!
COME OVER ANYTIME.
SERIOUSLY!? CAN I BRING FRIENDS?
OF COURSE.
GUESTS ARE ALWAYS WELCOME HERE.
CHIHIRO- KUN...
YES...?
YOU MUST BE HUNGRY.
IF YOU'RE DONE TALKING, GO HAVE DINNER.
... OKAY.
WELL, BE CAREFUL GOING HOME.
GOOD- NIGHT!
GOOD- NIGHT.

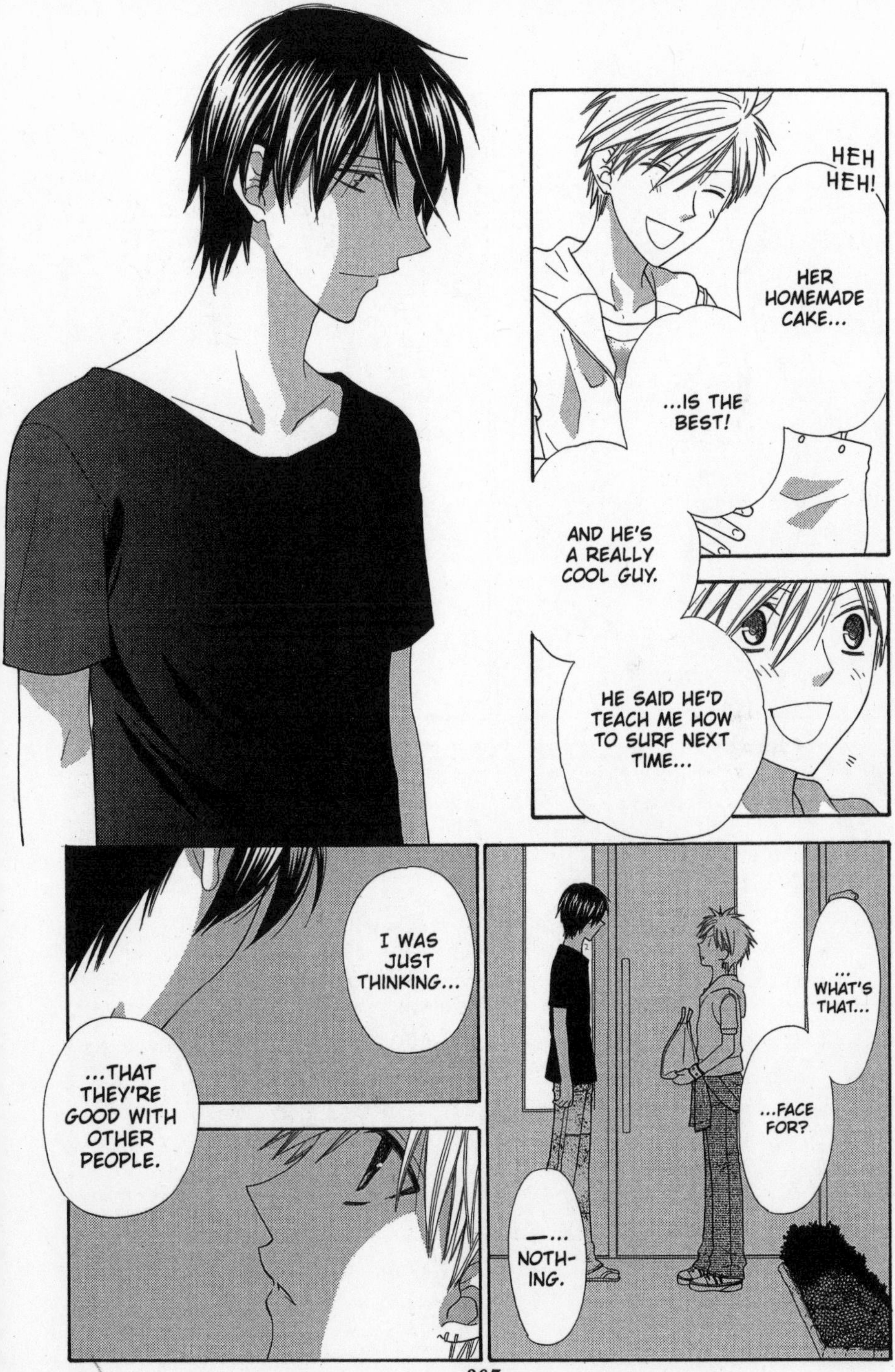
HEH HEH!
HER HOMEMADE CAKE...
...IS THE BEST!
AND HE'S A REALLY COOL GUY.
HE SAID HE'D TEACH ME HOW TO SURF NEXT TIME...
... WHAT'S THAT...
...FACE FOR?
—... NOTH-ING.
I WAS JUST THINKING...
...THAT THEY'RE GOOD WITH OTHER PEOPLE.

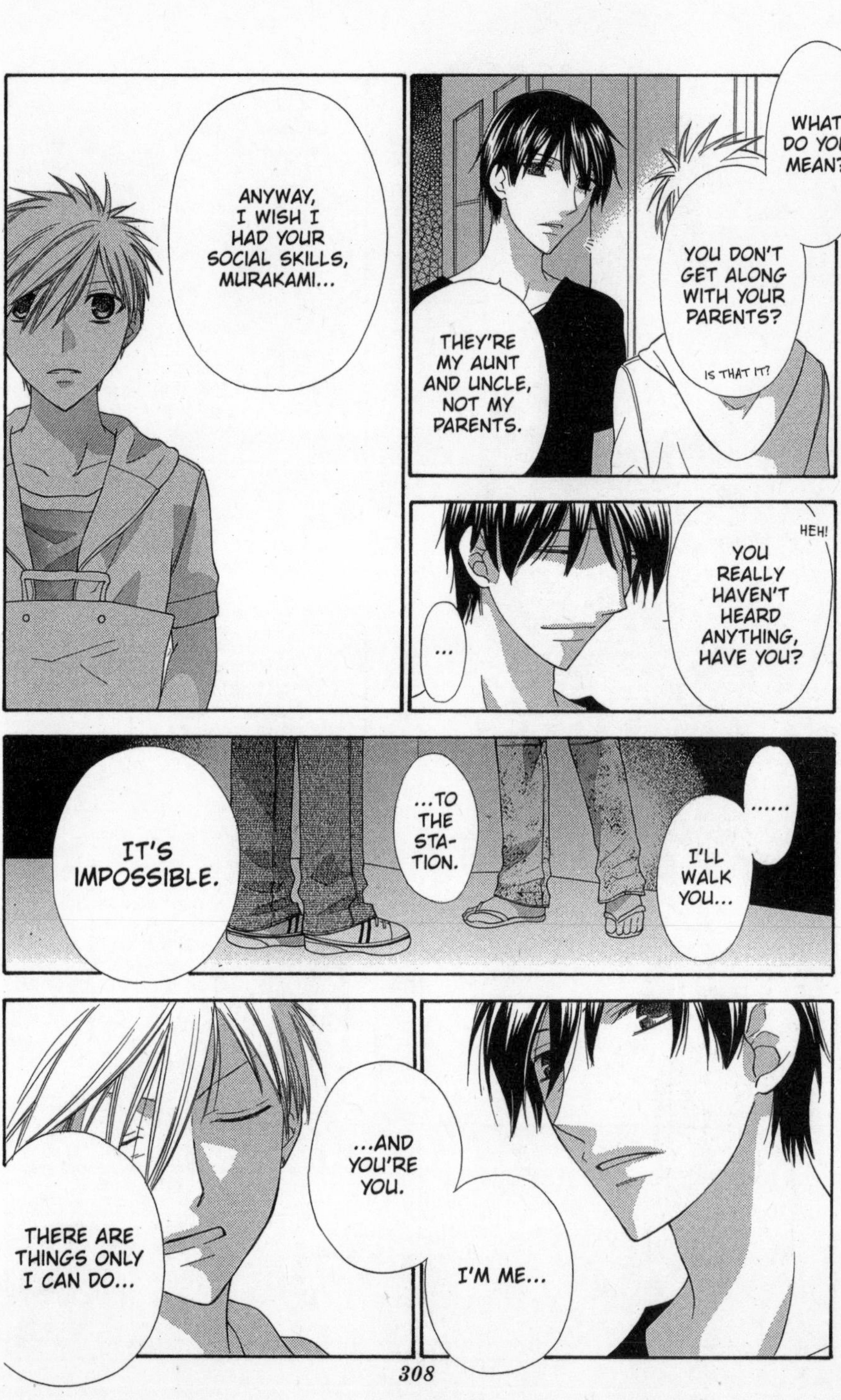
WHAT DO YOU MEAN?
YOU DON'T GET ALONG WITH YOUR PARENTS?
IS THAT IT?
THEY'RE MY AUNT AND UNCLE, NOT MY PARENTS.
HEH!
YOU REALLY HAVEN'T HEARD ANYTHING, HAVE YOU?
...
ANYWAY, I WISH I HAD YOUR SOCIAL SKILLS, MURAKAMI...
......
I'LL WALK YOU...
...TO THE STATION.
IT'S IMPOSSIBLE.
I'M ME...
...AND YOU'RE YOU.
THERE ARE THINGS ONLY I CAN DO...

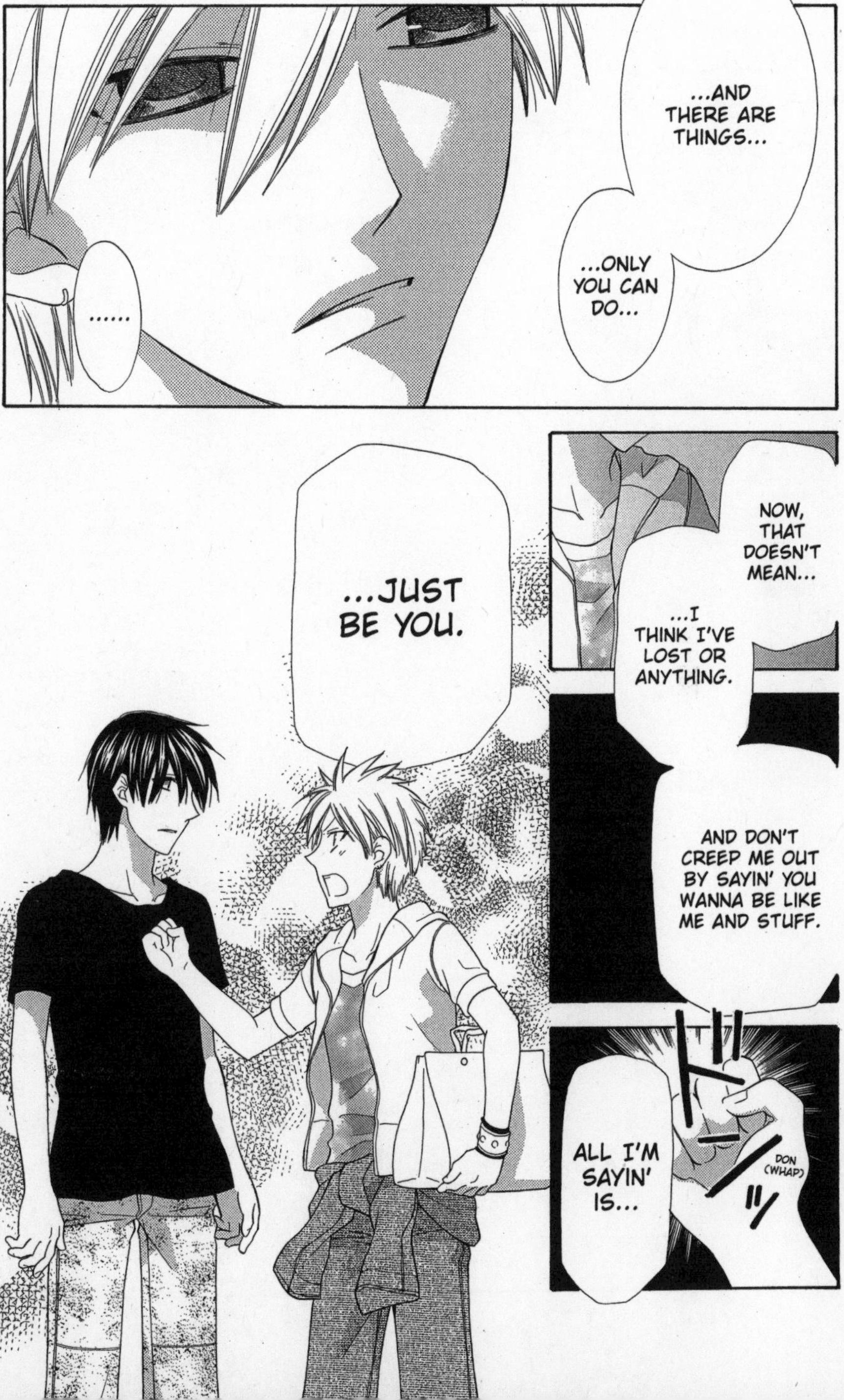
...AND THERE ARE THINGS...
...ONLY YOU CAN DO...
......
NOW, THAT DOESN'T MEAN...
...I THINK I'VE LOST OR ANYTHING.
AND DON'T CREEP ME OUT BY SAYIN' YOU WANNA BE LIKE ME AND STUFF.
DON (WHAP)
ALL I'M SAYIN' IS...
...JUST BE YOU.

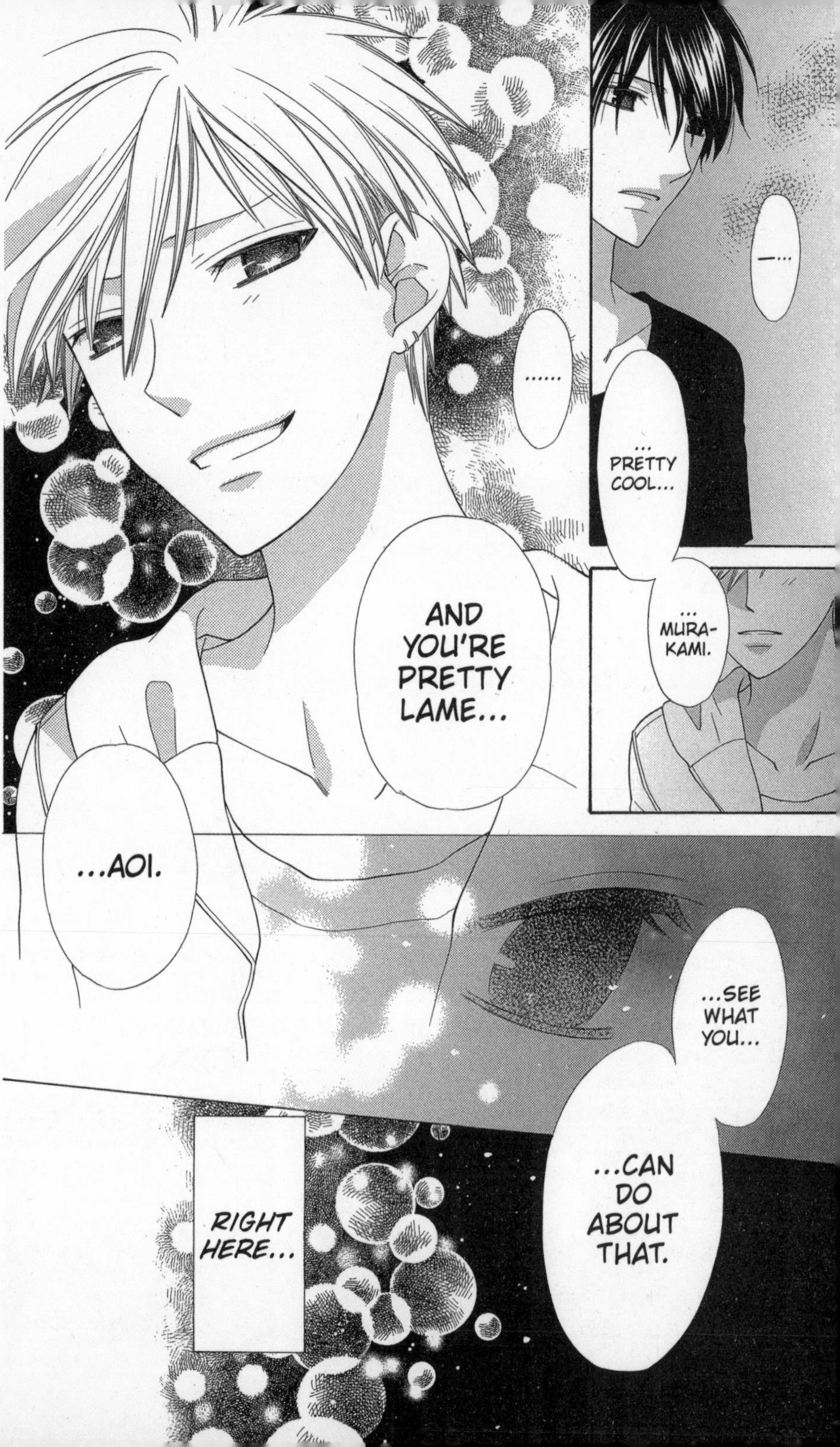
—...
... PRETTY COOL...
... MURA-KAMI.
......
AND YOU'RE PRETTY LAME...
...AOI.
...SEE WHAT YOU...
...CAN DO ABOUT THAT.
RIGHT HERE...

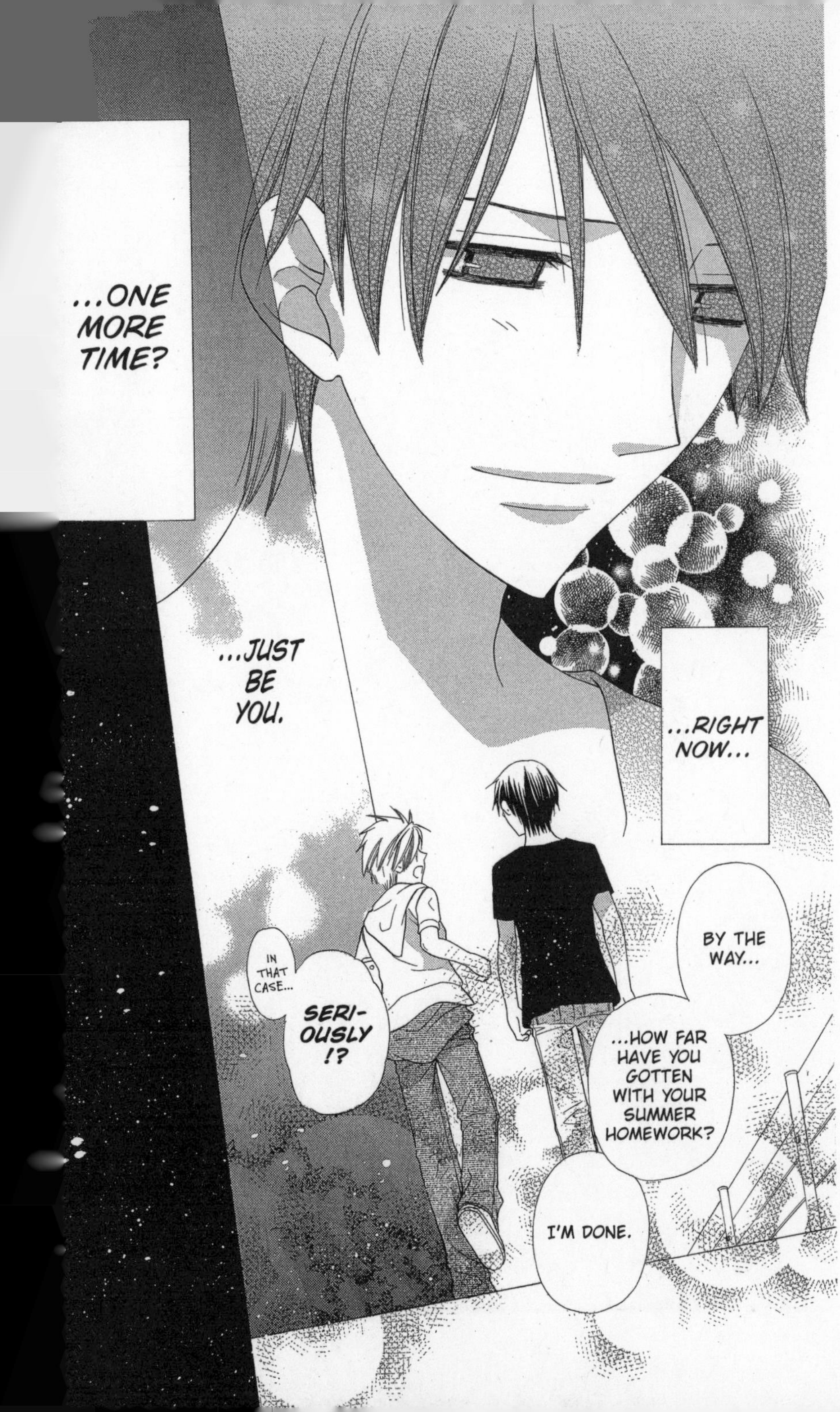
...ONE MORE TIME?
...RIGHT NOW...
...JUST BE YOU.
BY THE WAY...
...HOW FAR HAVE YOU GOTTEN WITH YOUR SUMMER HOMEWORK?
I'M DONE.
SERIOUSLY!?
IN THAT CASE...

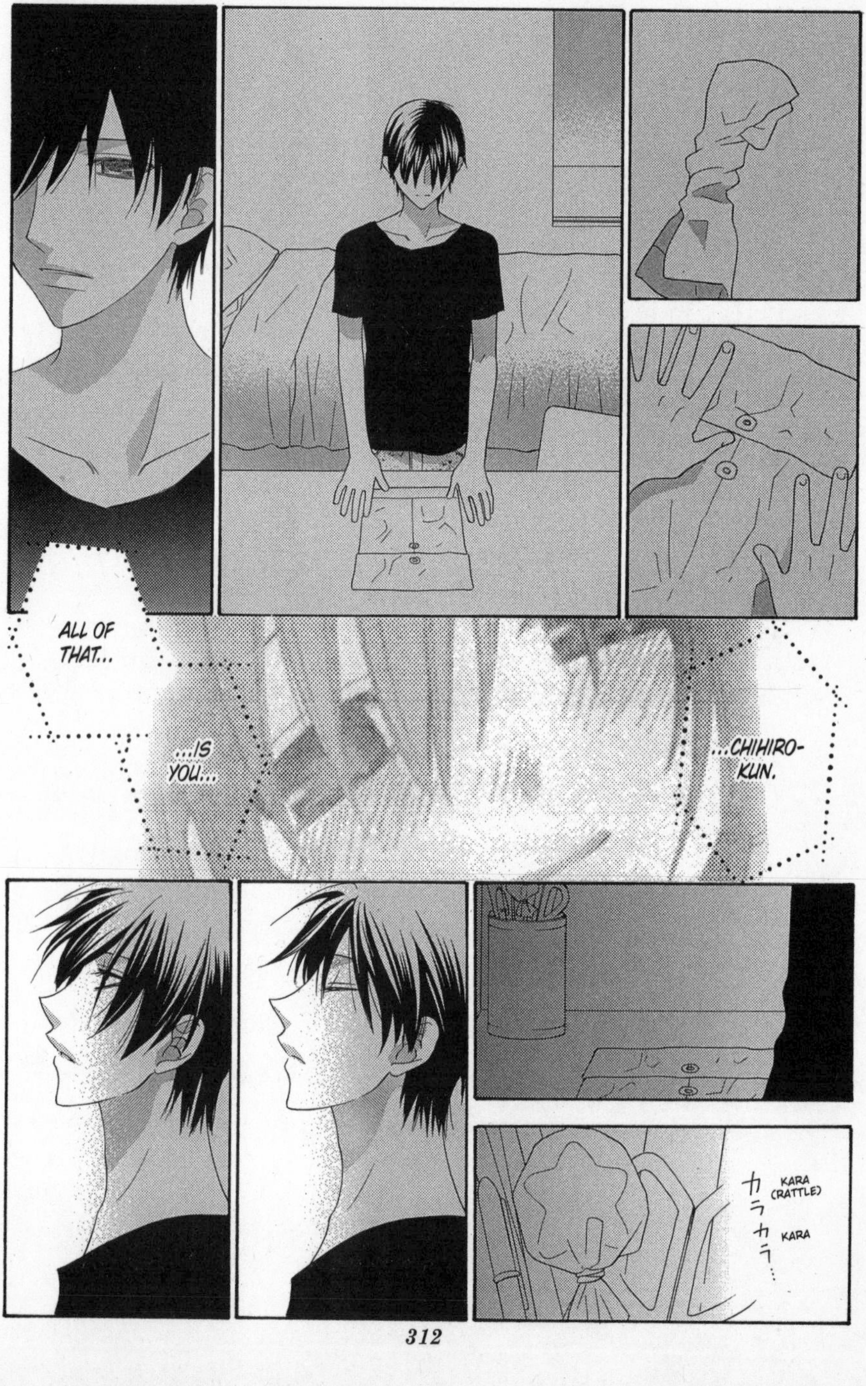
ALL OF THAT...
...IS YOU...
...CHIHIRO-KUN.
カラ
KARA (RATTLE)
カラ…
KARA

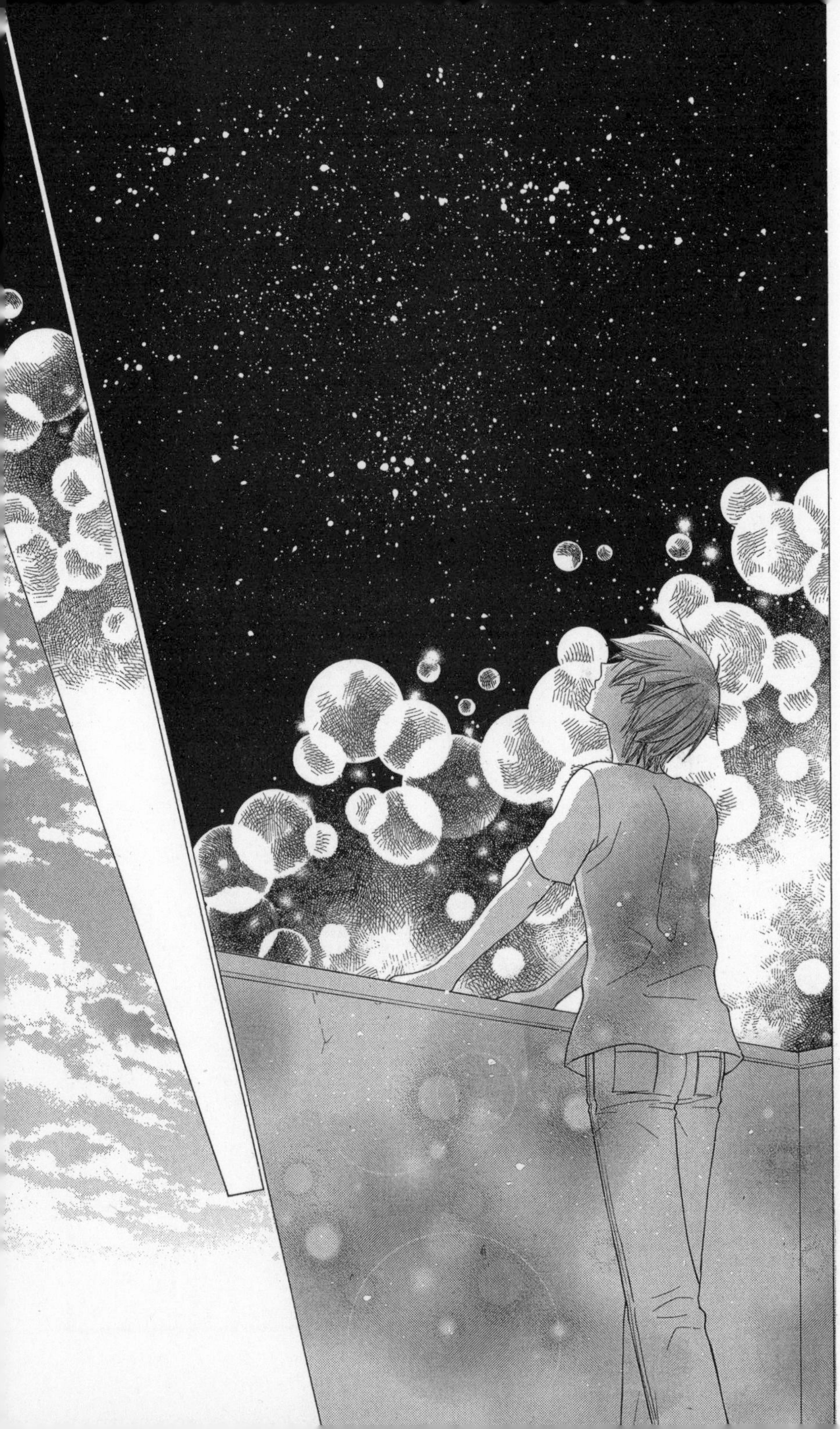

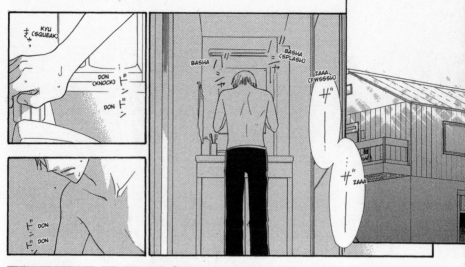

KYU
(SQUEAK)

BASHA
(SPLASH)

BASHA
(SPLASH)

ZAAA
(FWSSSH)

DON
(KNOCK)

DON

DON

DON

...
ZAAA

DON

DON

DON

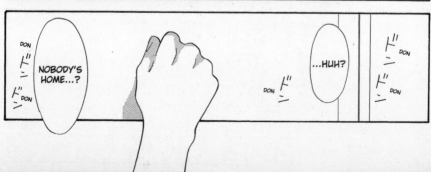

DON

DON

DON

NOBODY'S
HOME...?

...HUH?

DON

DON

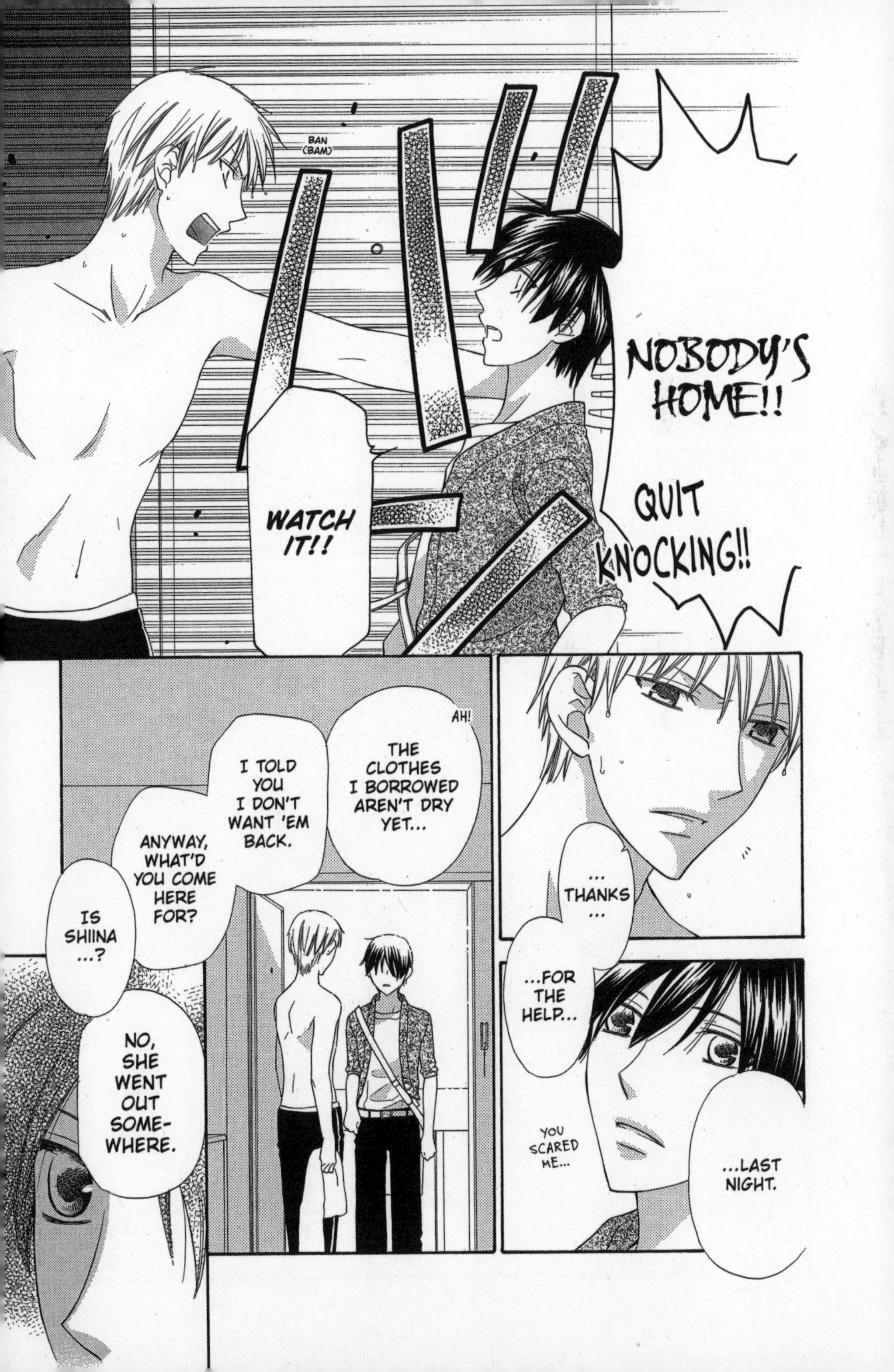
NOBODY'S HOME!!
QUIT KNOCKING!!
BAN (BAM)
WATCH IT!!
... THANKS ...
...FOR THE HELP...
...LAST NIGHT.
YOU SCARED ME...
AH!
THE CLOTHES I BORROWED AREN'T DRY YET...
I TOLD YOU I DON'T WANT 'EM BACK.
ANYWAY, WHAT'D YOU COME HERE FOR?
IS SHIINA ...?
NO, SHE WENT OUT SOME-WHERE.

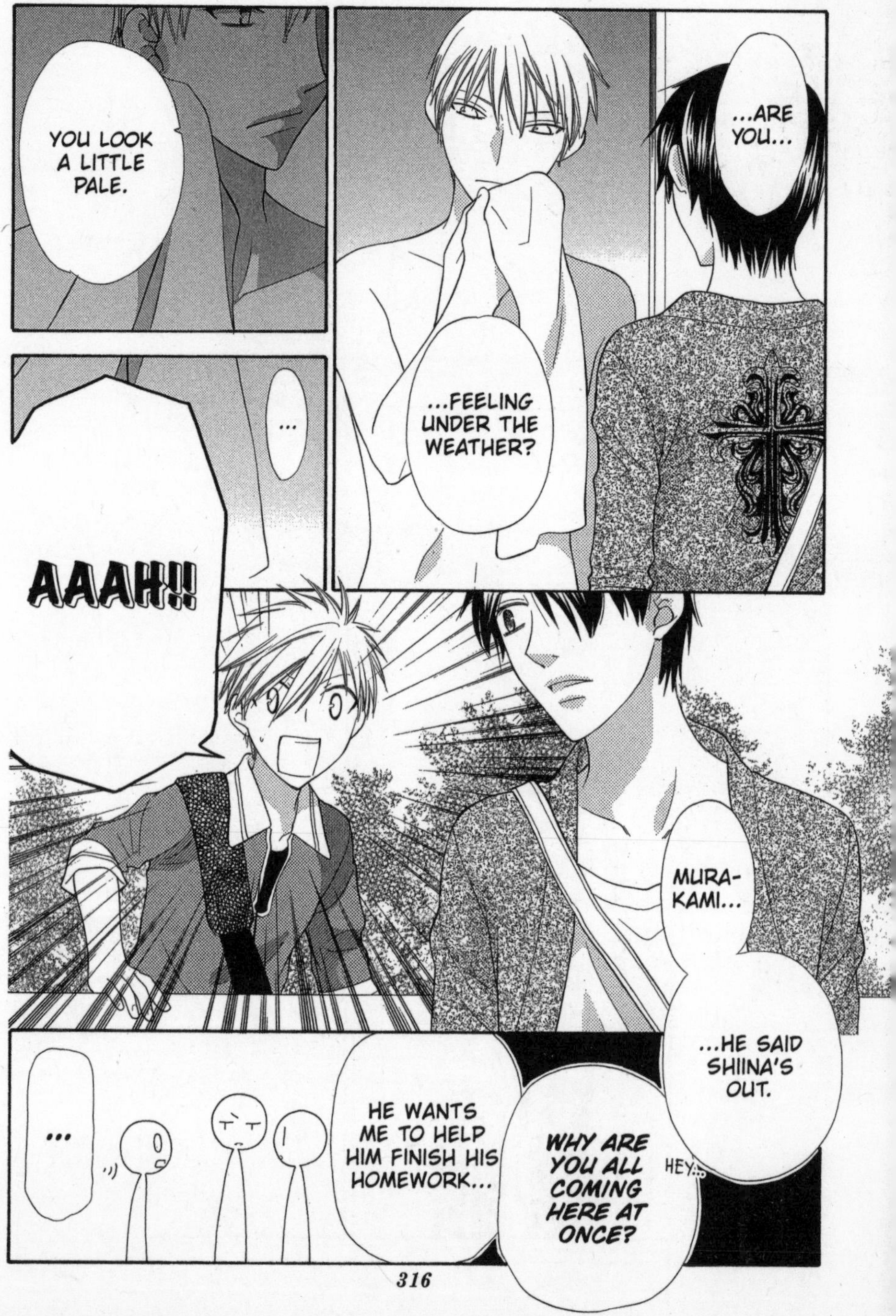
...ARE YOU...
...FEELING UNDER THE WEATHER?
YOU LOOK A LITTLE PALE.
...
AAAH!!
MURA-KAMI...
...HE SAID SHIINA'S OUT.
HEY...
WHY ARE YOU ALL COMING HERE AT ONCE?
HE WANTS ME TO HELP HIM FINISH HIS HOMEWORK...
...

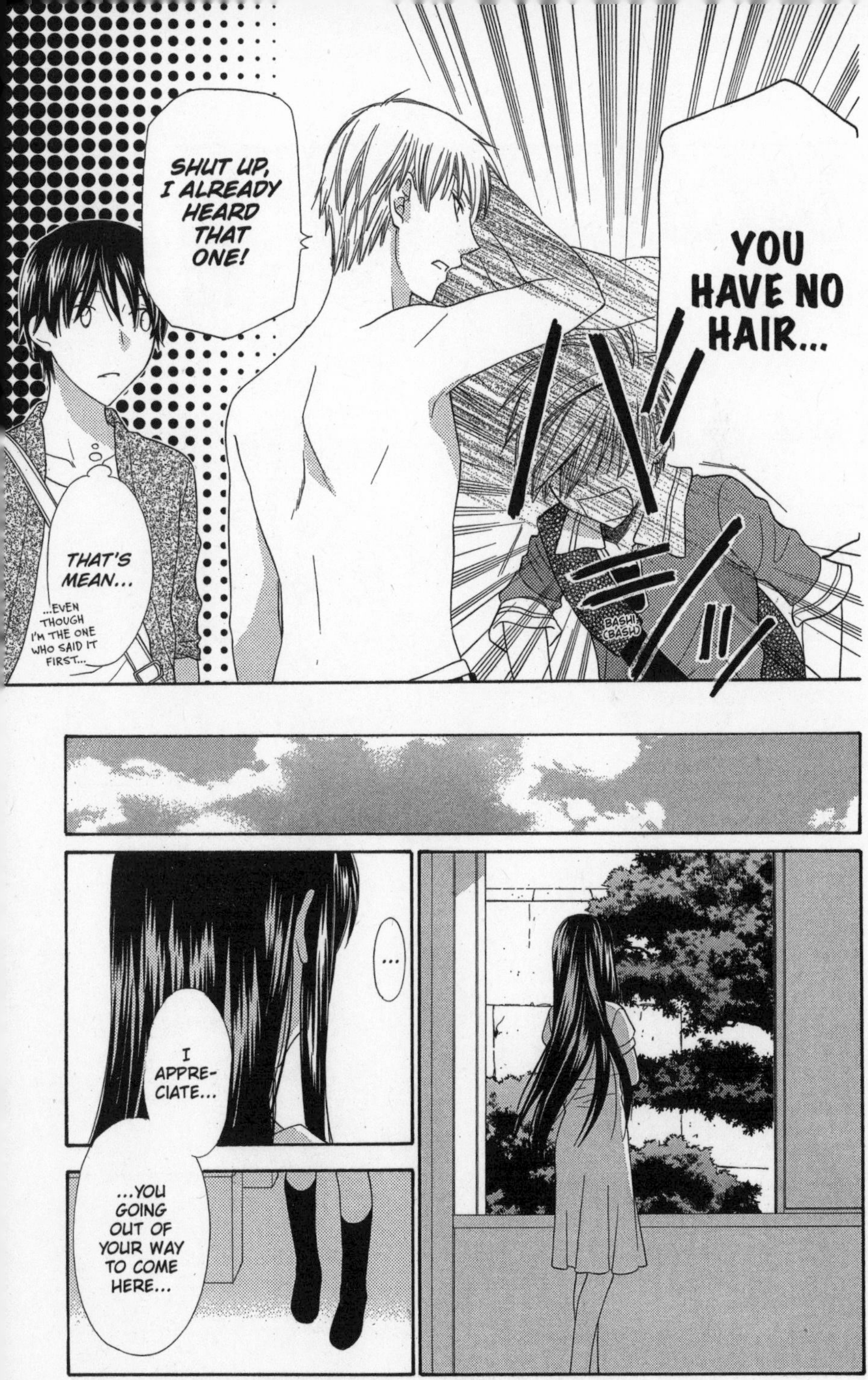
YOU HAVE NO HAIR...
BASHI (BASH)
SHUT UP, I ALREADY HEARD THAT ONE!
THAT'S MEAN...
...EVEN THOUGH I'M THE ONE WHO SAID IT FIRST...
...
I APPRECIATE...
...YOU GOING OUT OF YOUR WAY TO COME HERE...

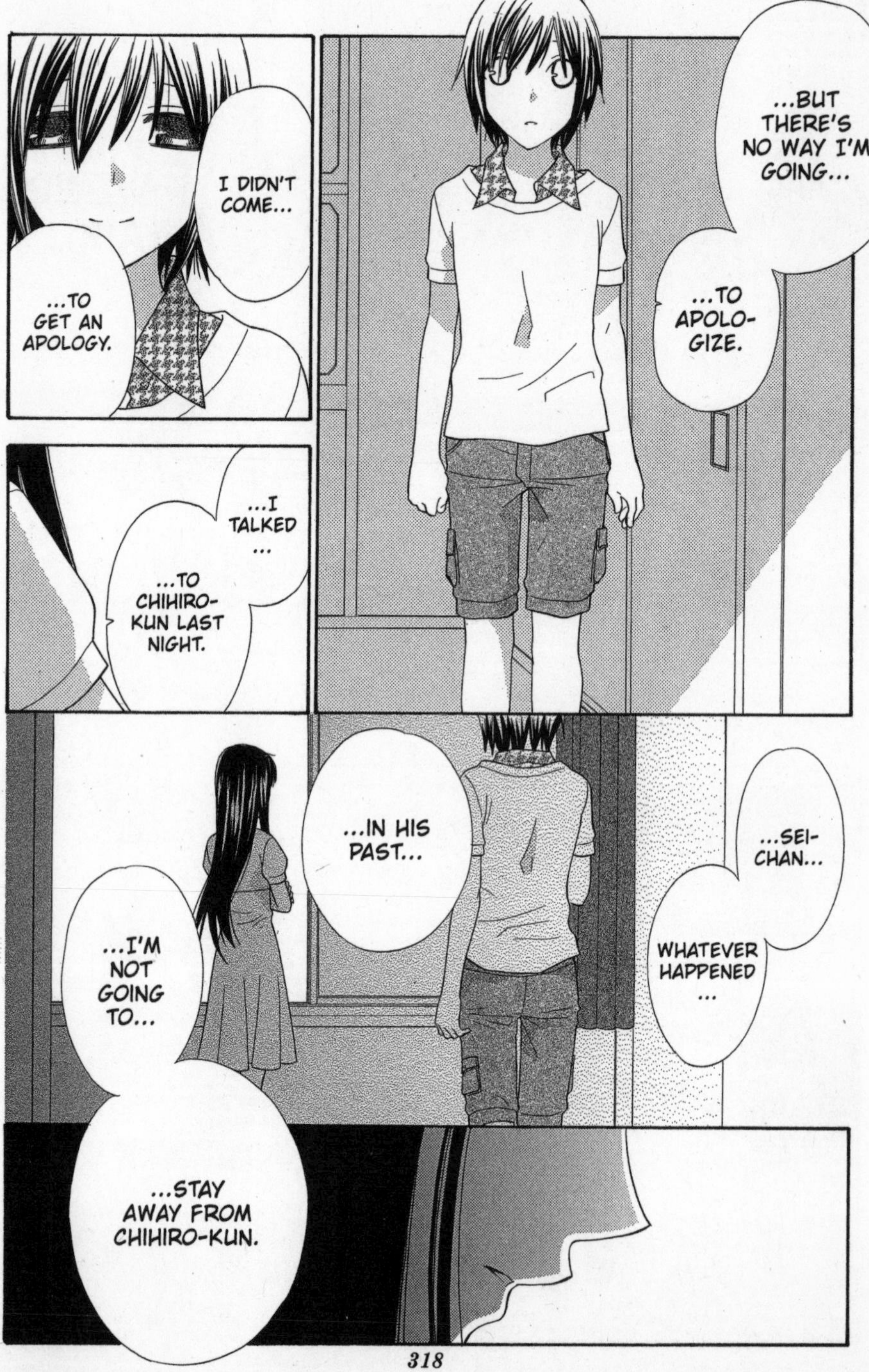
...BUT THERE'S NO WAY I'M GOING...
...TO APOLOGIZE.
I DIDN'T COME...
...TO GET AN APOLOGY.
...I TALKED...
...TO CHIHIRO-KUN LAST NIGHT.
...SEI-CHAN...
WHATEVER HAPPENED...
...IN HIS PAST...
...I'M NOT GOING TO...
...STAY AWAY FROM CHIHIRO-KUN.

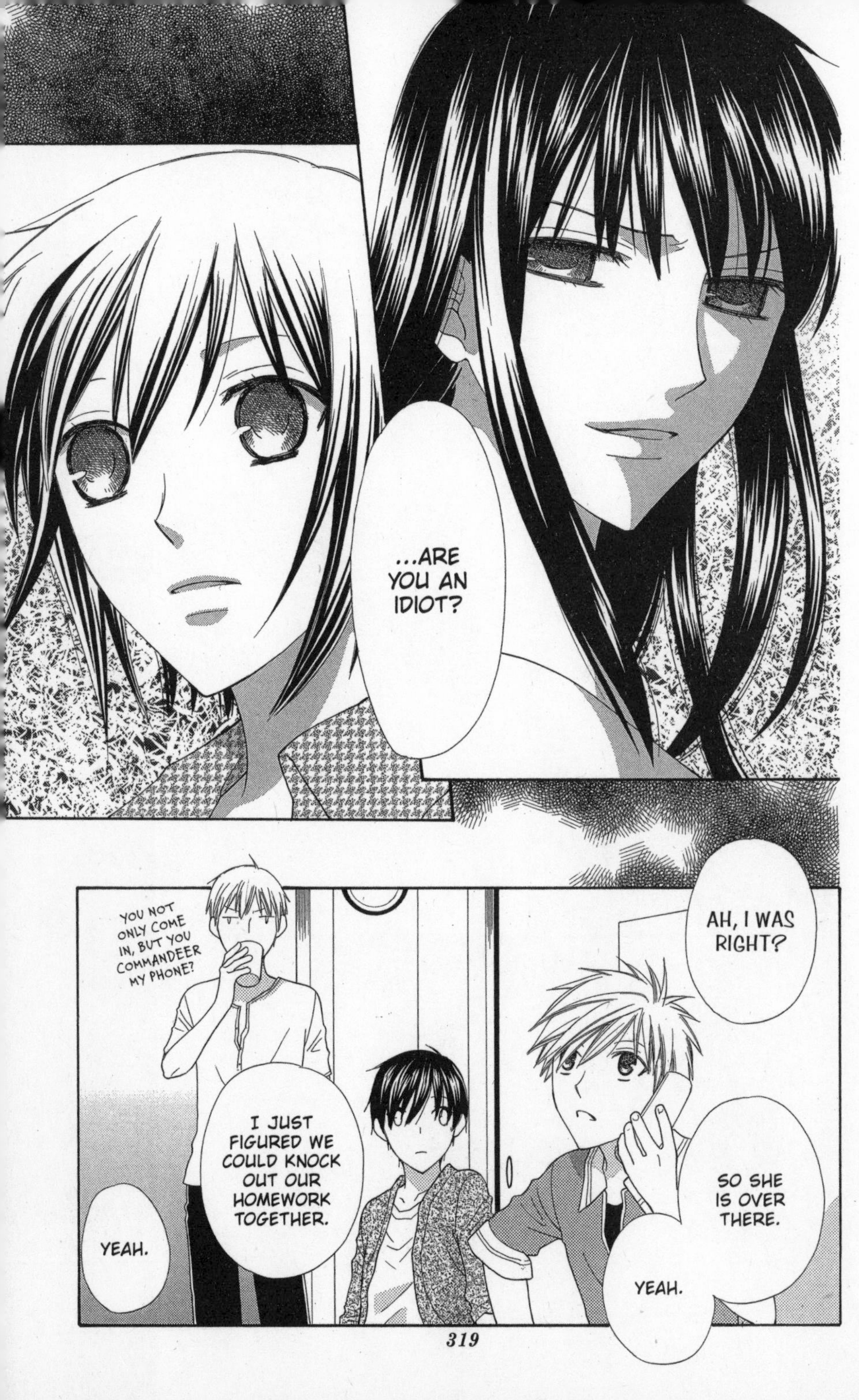
...ARE YOU AN IDIOT?
AH, I WAS RIGHT?
SO SHE IS OVER THERE.
YEAH.
YOU NOT ONLY COME IN, BUT YOU COMMANDEER MY PHONE?
I JUST FIGURED WE COULD KNOCK OUT OUR HOMEWORK TOGETHER.
YEAH.

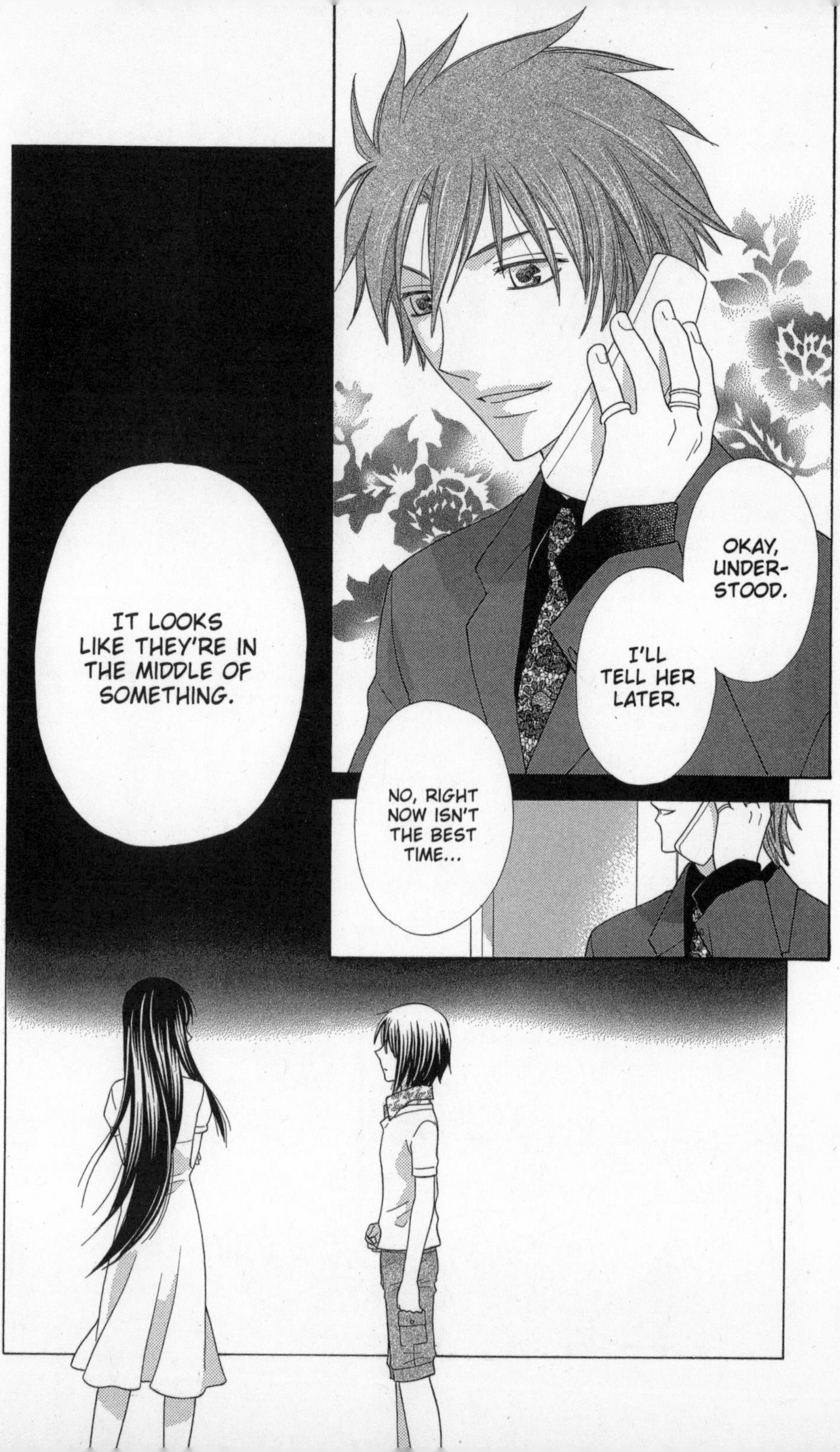
OKAY, UNDER-STOOD.
I'LL TELL HER LATER.
NO, RIGHT NOW ISN'T THE BEST TIME...
IT LOOKS LIKE THEY'RE IN THE MIDDLE OF SOMETHING.

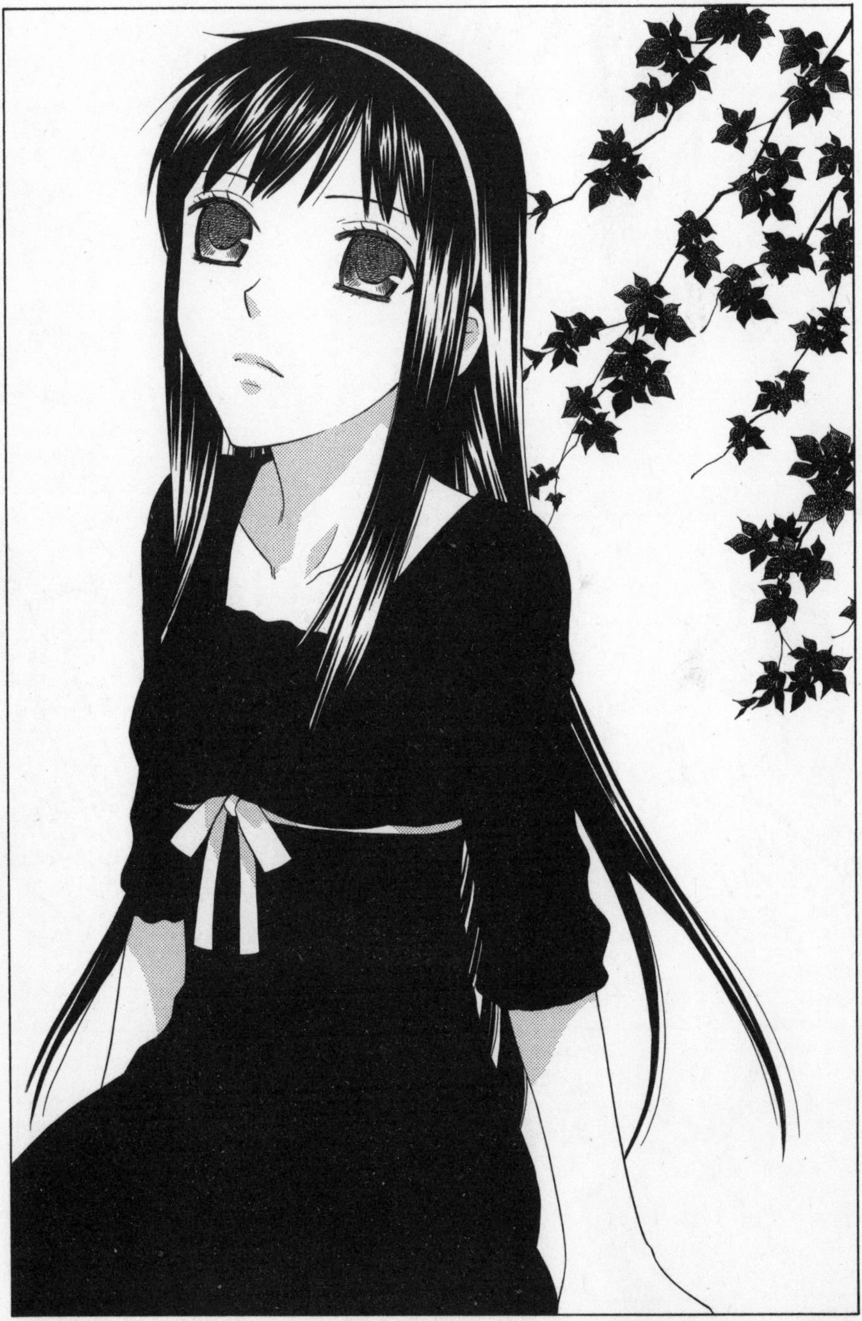

Chapter 34

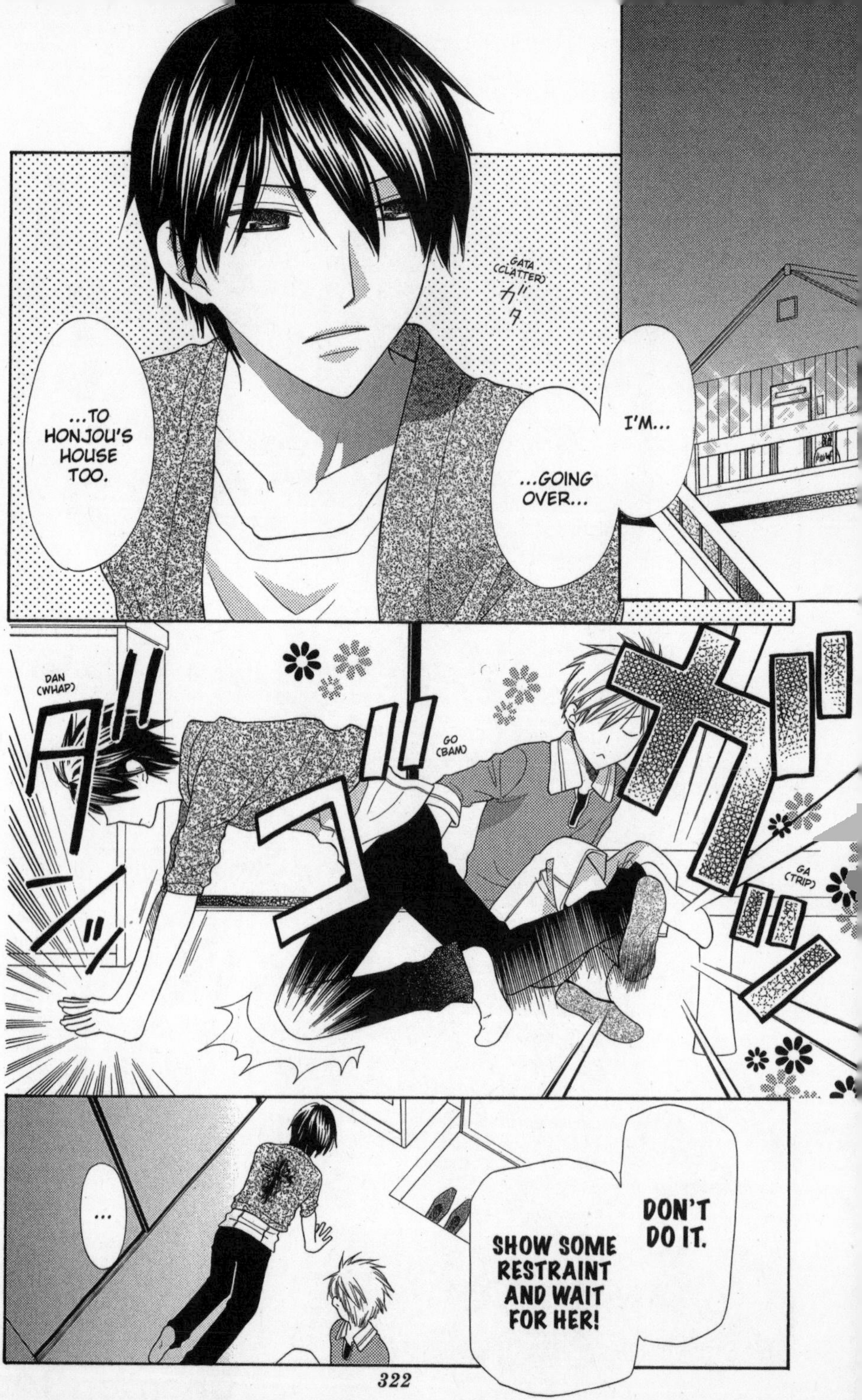
I'M... ...GOING OVER...
GATA (CLATTER)
...TO HONJOU'S HOUSE TOO.
GA (TRIP)
GO (BAM)
DAN (WHAP)
DON'T DO IT. SHOW SOME RESTRAINT AND WAIT FOR HER!
...

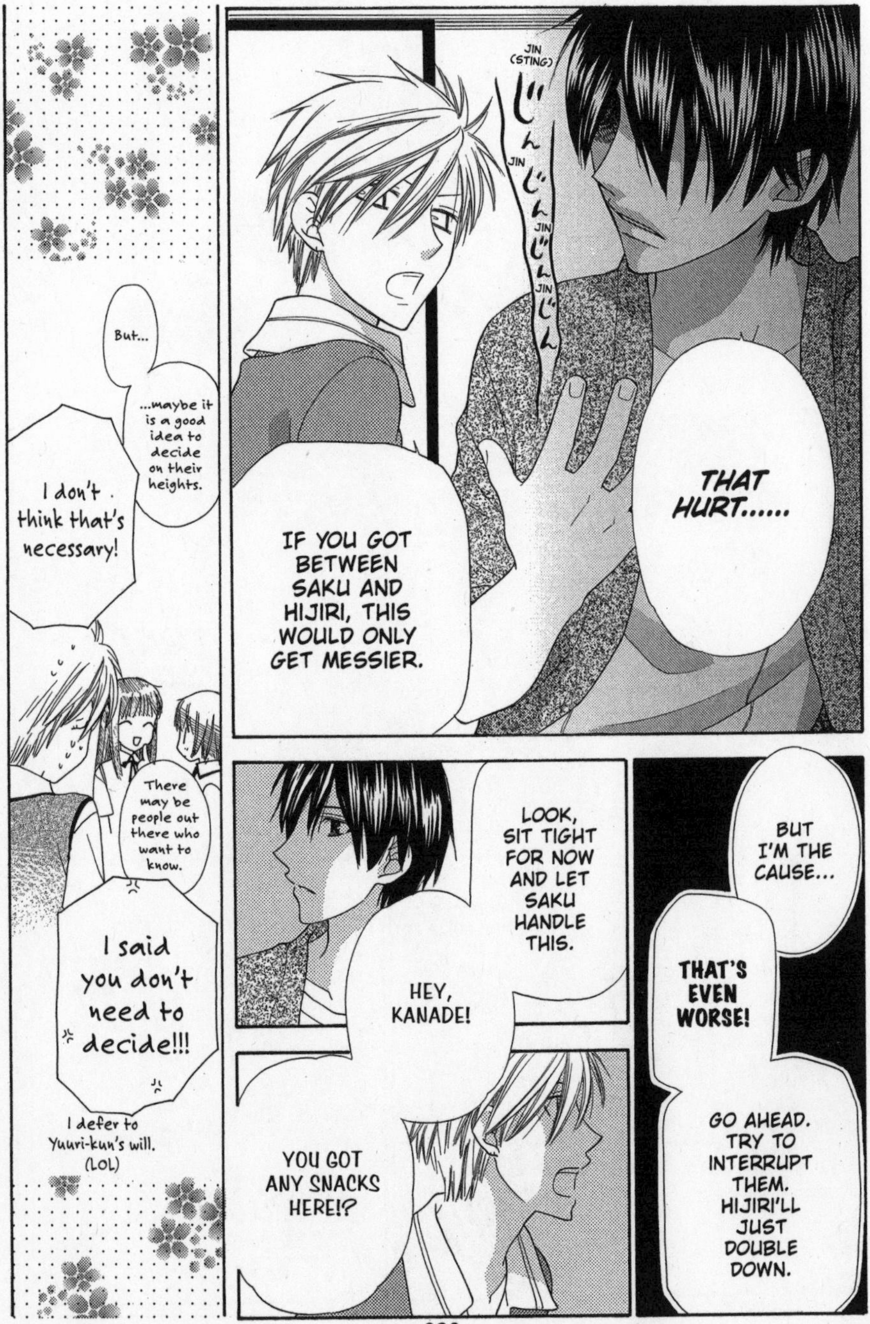
JIN (STING)
じん
JIN
じん
JIN
じん
JIN
じん
THAT HURT......
IF YOU GOT BETWEEN SAKU AND HIJIRI, THIS WOULD ONLY GET MESSIER.
BUT I'M THE CAUSE...
THAT'S EVEN WORSE!
GO AHEAD. TRY TO INTERRUPT THEM. HIJIRI'LL JUST DOUBLE DOWN.
LOOK, SIT TIGHT FOR NOW AND LET SAKU HANDLE THIS.
HEY, KANADE!
YOU GOT ANY SNACKS HERE!?
But...
...maybe it is a good idea to decide on their heights.
I don't think that's necessary!
There may be people out there who want to know.
I said you don't need to decide!!!
I defer to Yuuri-kun's will. (LOL)

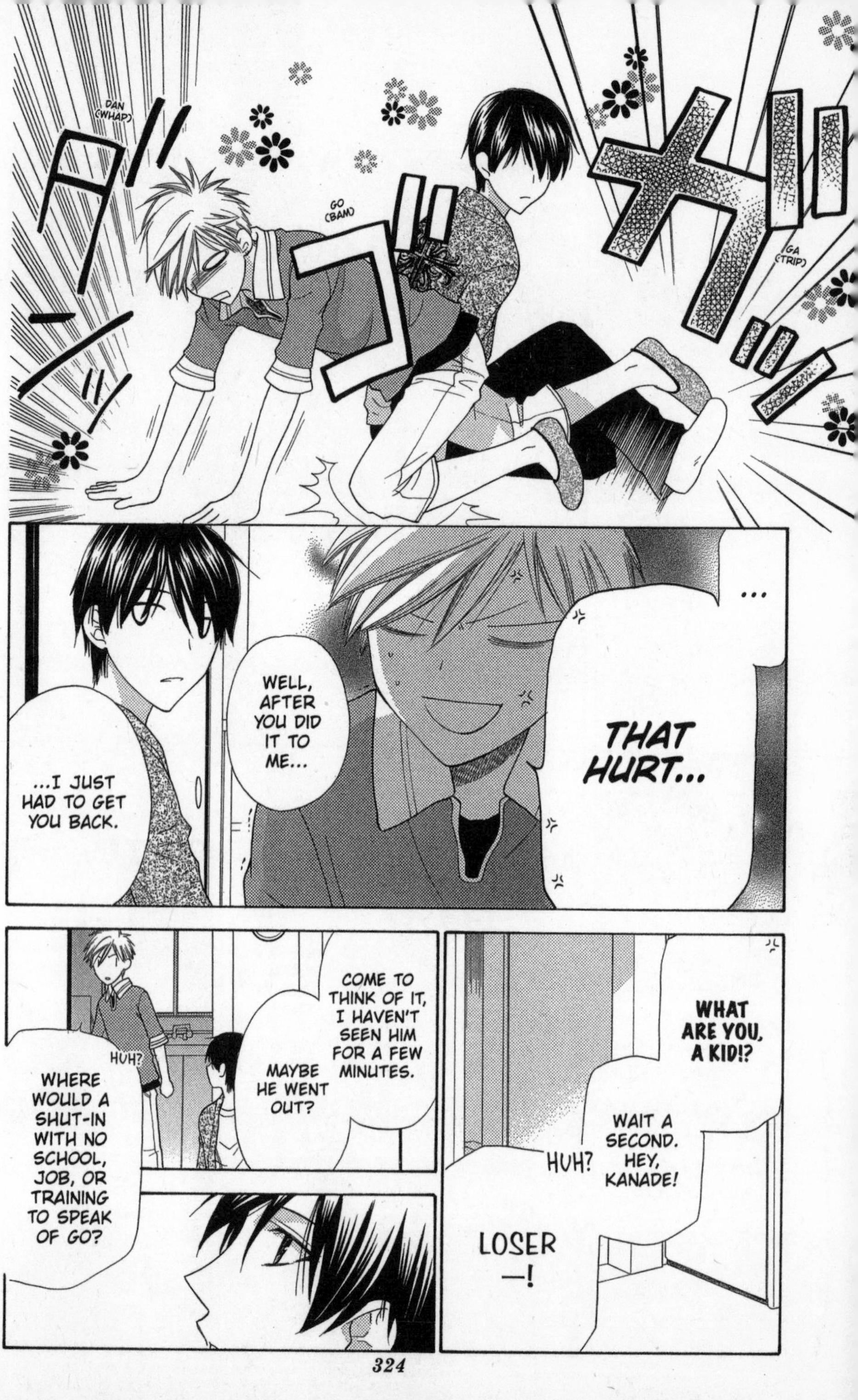
GA (TRIP)
GO (BAM)
DAN (WHAP)
...
THAT HURT...
WELL, AFTER YOU DID IT TO ME...
...I JUST HAD TO GET YOU BACK.
WHAT ARE YOU, A KID!?
WAIT A SECOND. HEY, KANADE!
HUH?
LOSER —!
COME TO THINK OF IT, I HAVEN'T SEEN HIM FOR A FEW MINUTES.
MAYBE HE WENT OUT?
HUH?
WHERE WOULD A SHUT-IN WITH NO SCHOOL, JOB, OR TRAINING TO SPEAK OF GO?

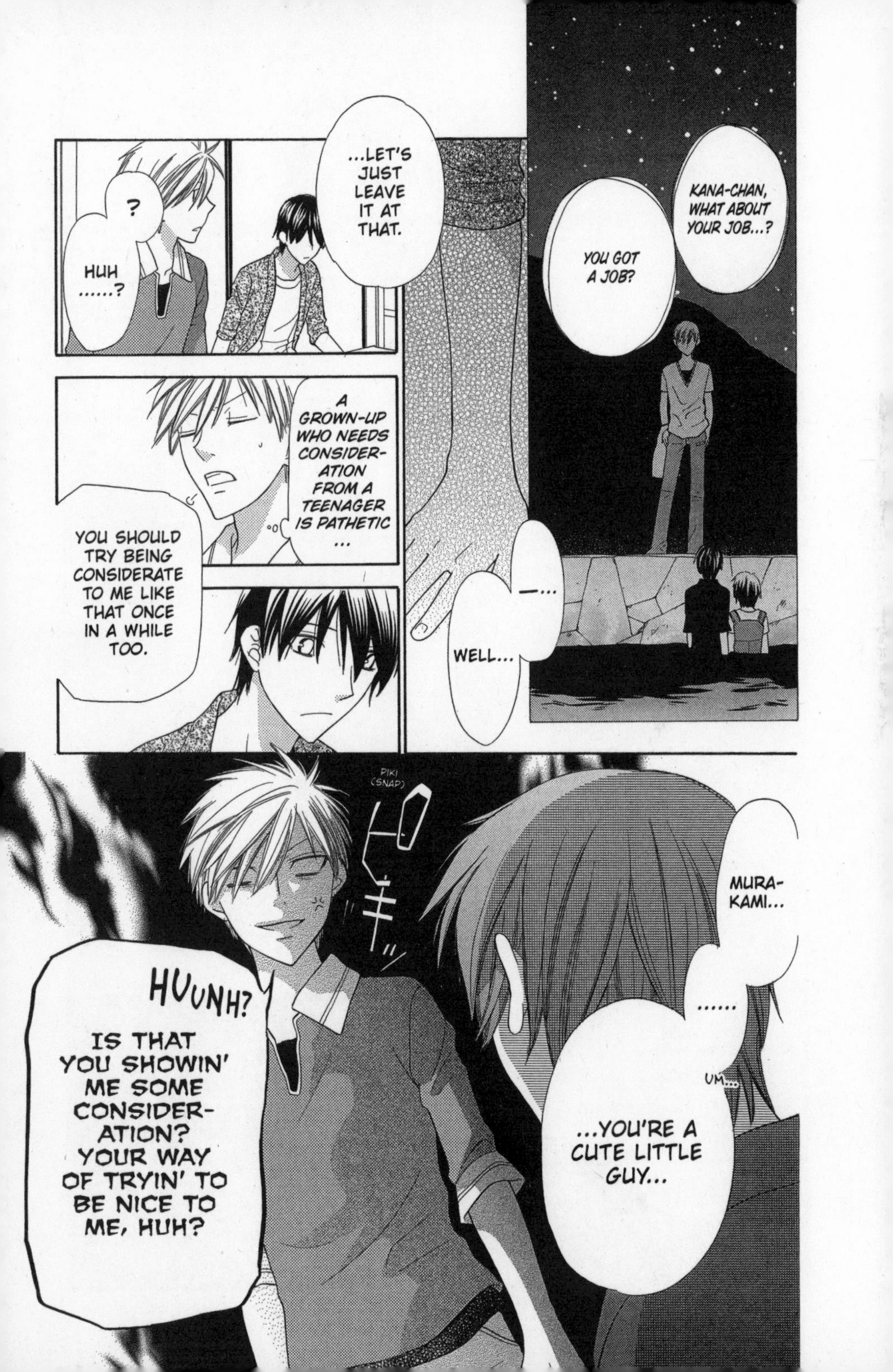

KANA-CHAN, WHAT ABOUT YOUR JOB...?
YOU GOT A JOB?
—...
WELL...
...LET'S JUST LEAVE IT AT THAT.
?
HUH ......?
A GROWN-UP WHO NEEDS CONSIDER-ATION FROM A TEENAGER IS PATHETIC ...
YOU SHOULD TRY BEING CONSIDERATE TO ME LIKE THAT ONCE IN A WHILE TOO.
MURA-KAMI...
......
UM...
...YOU'RE A CUTE LITTLE GUY...
PIKI (SNAP)
HUUNH?
IS THAT YOU SHOWIN' ME SOME CONSIDER-ATION? YOUR WAY OF TRYIN' TO BE NICE TO ME, HUH?

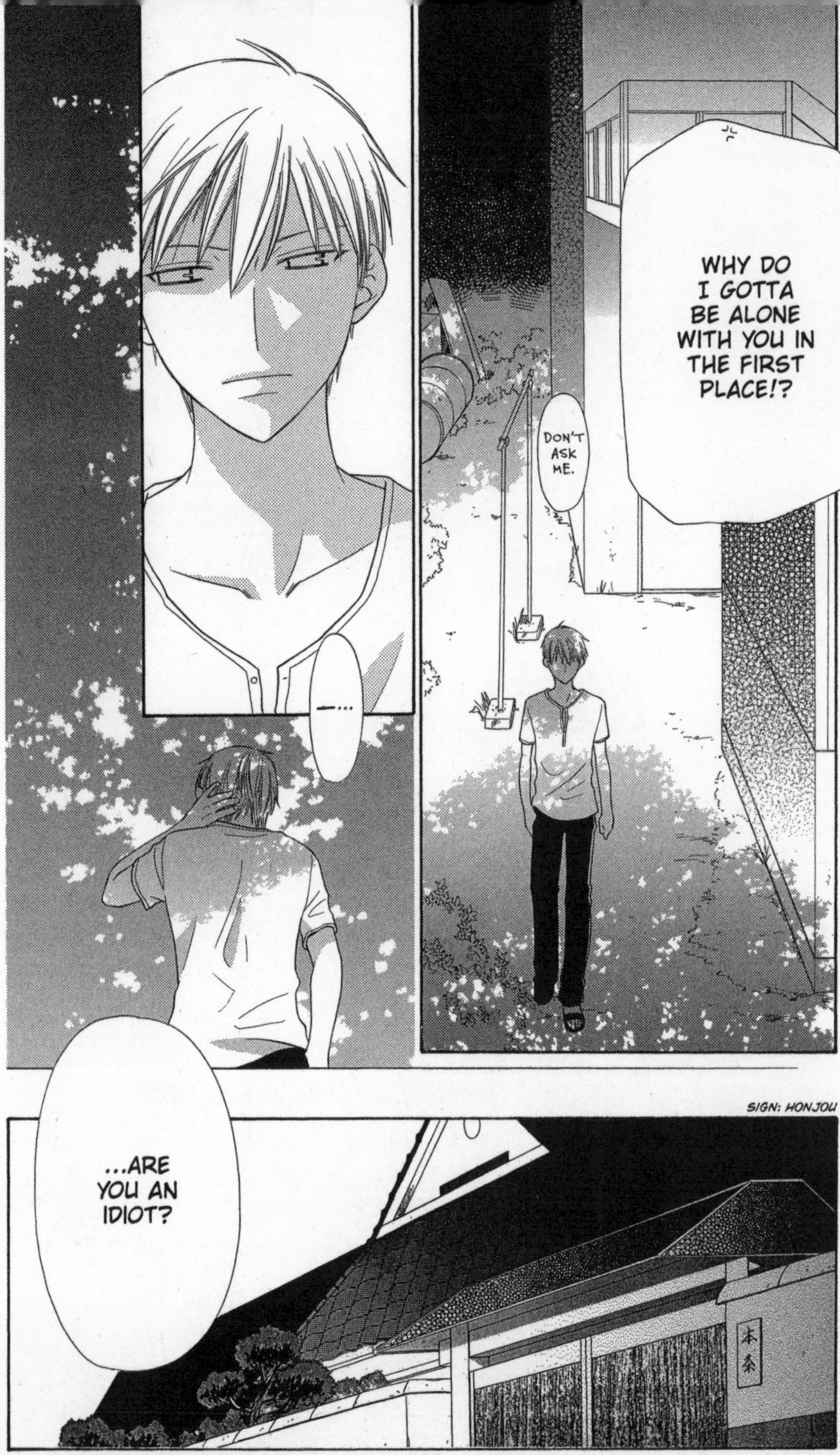

WHY DO I GOTTA BE ALONE WITH YOU IN THE FIRST PLACE!?
DON'T ASK ME.
—...
...ARE YOU AN IDIOT?
SIGN: HONJOU
本条

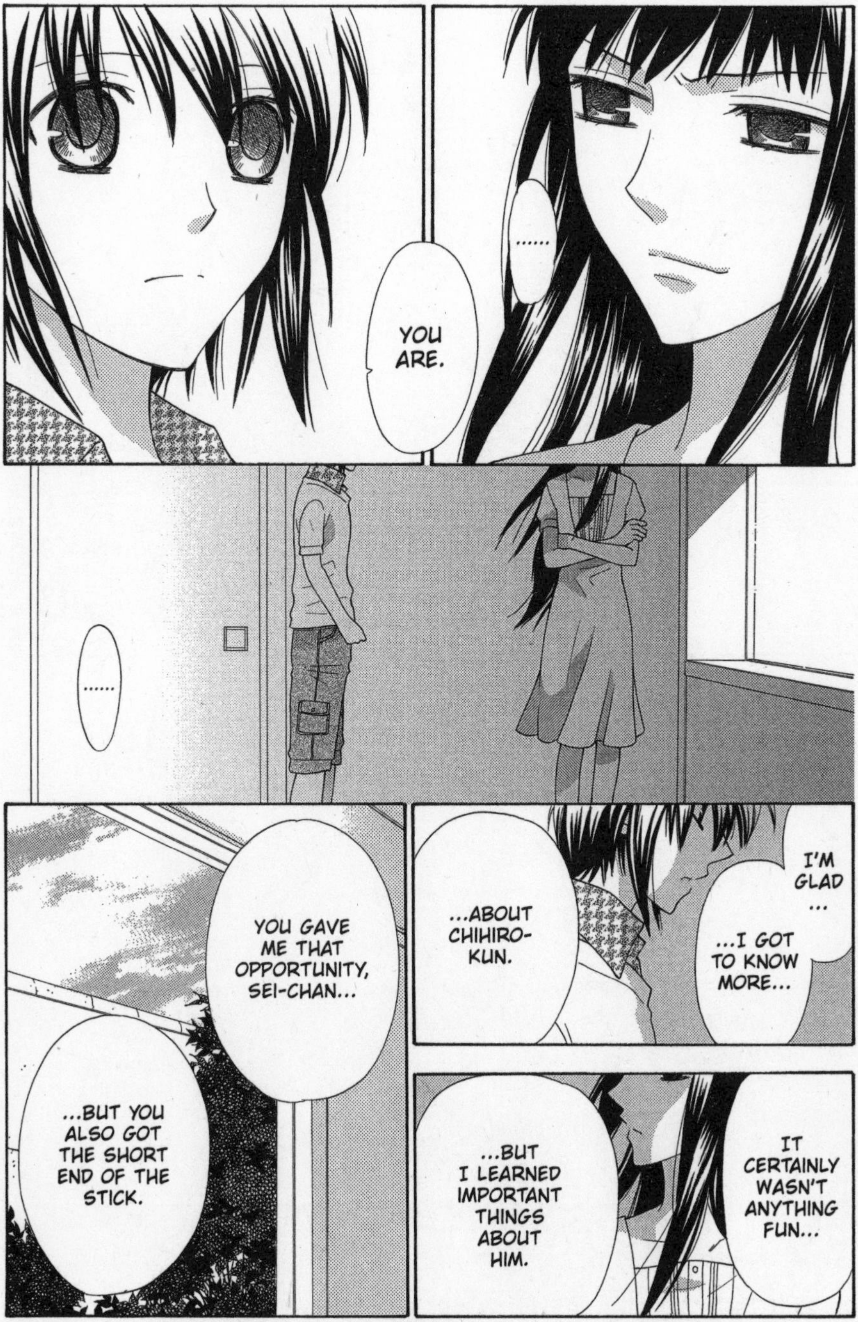

......
YOU ARE.
......
I'M GLAD...
...I GOT TO KNOW MORE...
...ABOUT CHIHIRO-KUN.
IT CERTAINLY WASN'T ANYTHING FUN...
...BUT I LEARNED IMPORTANT THINGS ABOUT HIM.
YOU GAVE ME THAT OPPORTUNITY, SEI-CHAN...
...BUT YOU ALSO GOT THE SHORT END OF THE STICK.

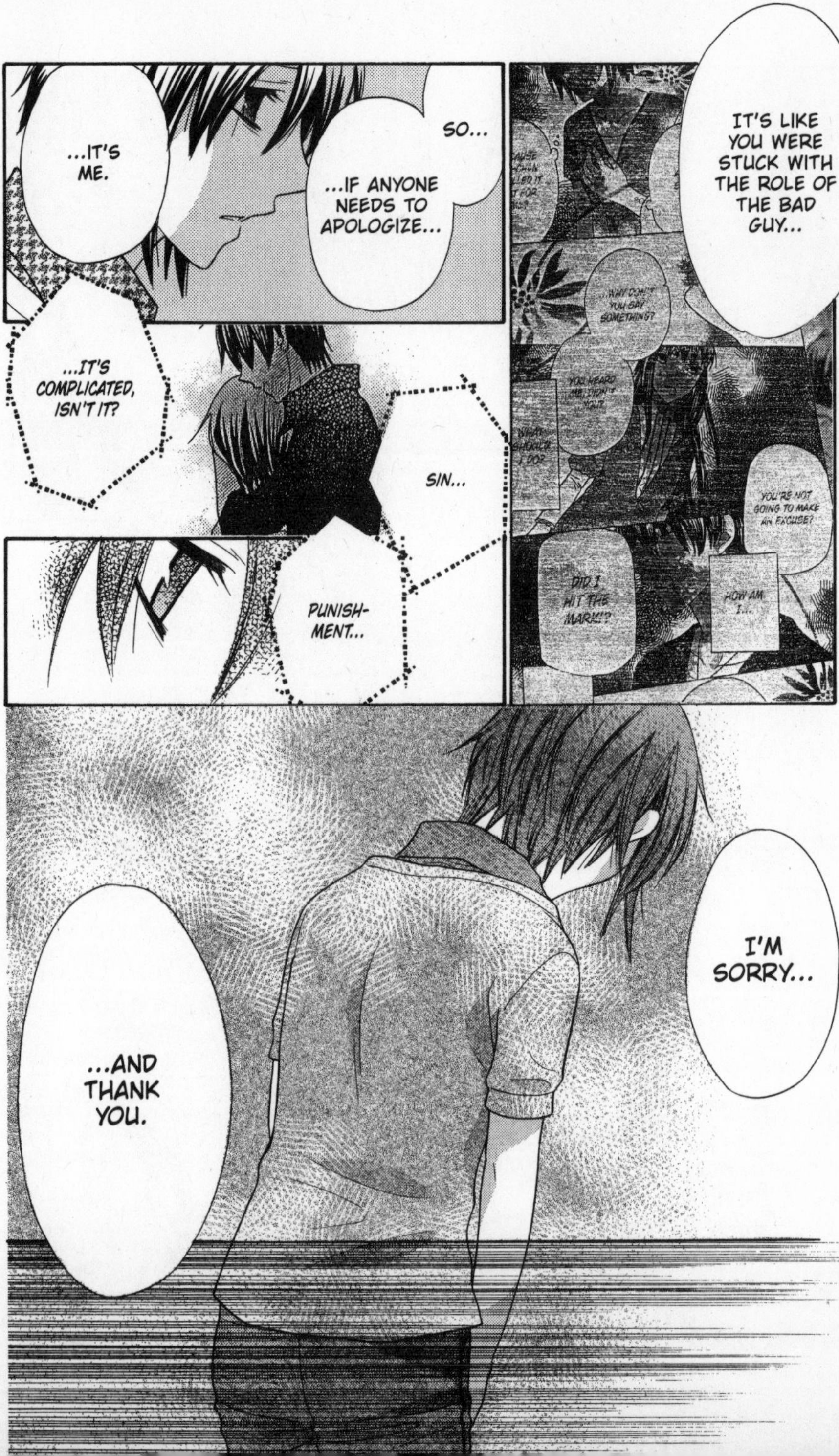
IT'S LIKE YOU WERE STUCK WITH THE ROLE OF THE BAD GUY...
...WHY DON'T YOU SAY SOMETHING?
YOU HEARD ME, DIDN'T YOU?
WHAT SHOULD I DO?
YOU'RE NOT GOING TO MAKE AN EXCUSE?
HOW AM I...
DID I HIT THE MARK!?
SO...
...IF ANYONE NEEDS TO APOLOGIZE...
...IT'S ME.
SIN...
...IT'S COMPLICATED, ISN'T IT?
PUNISH-MENT...
I'M SORRY...
...AND THANK YOU.

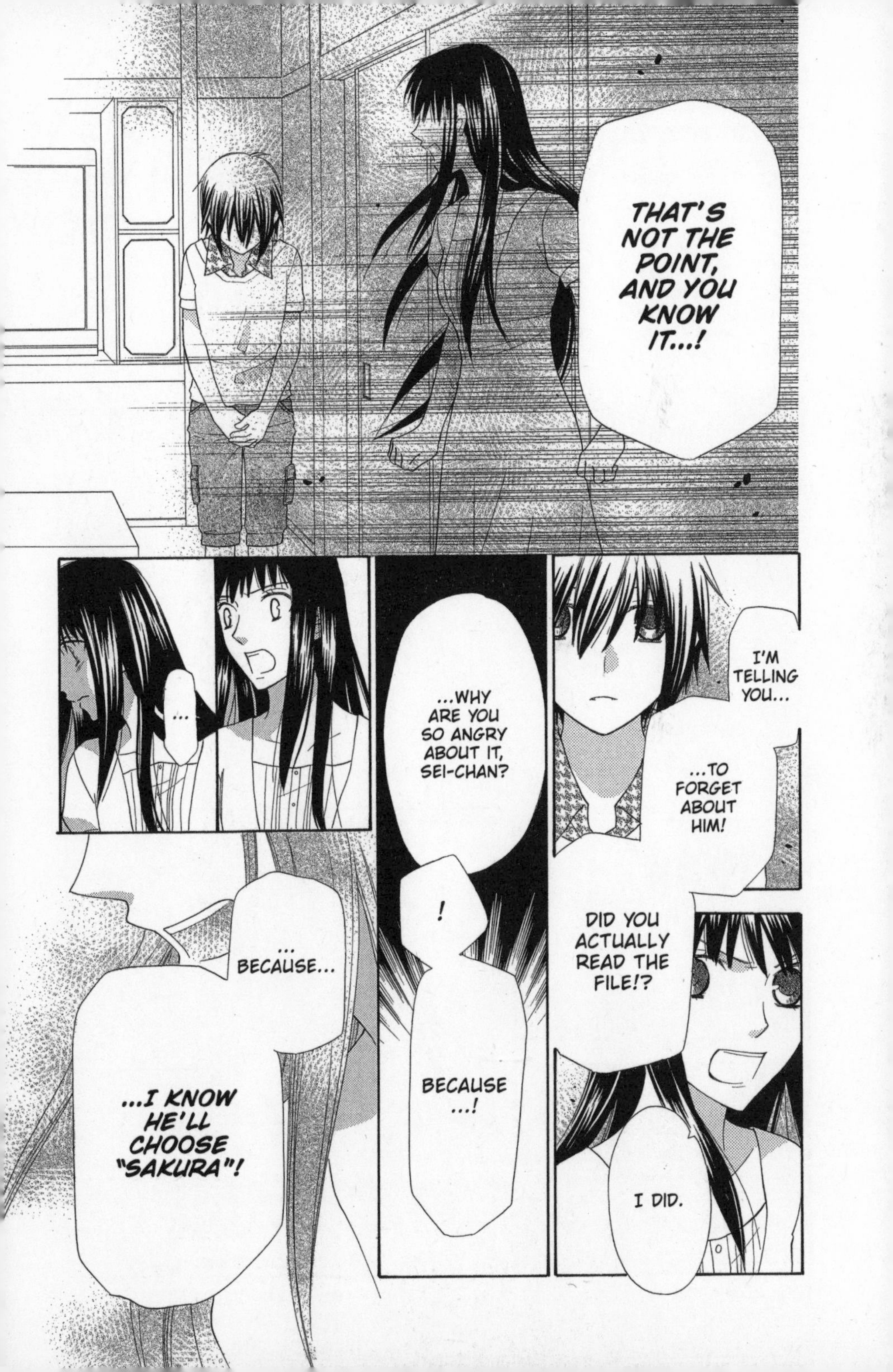
THAT'S NOT THE POINT, AND YOU KNOW IT...!
I'M TELLING YOU...
...TO FORGET ABOUT HIM!
DID YOU ACTUALLY READ THE FILE!?
I DID.
...WHY ARE YOU SO ANGRY ABOUT IT, SEI-CHAN?
!
BECAUSE ...!
...
... BECAUSE...
...I KNOW HE'LL CHOOSE "SAKURA"!

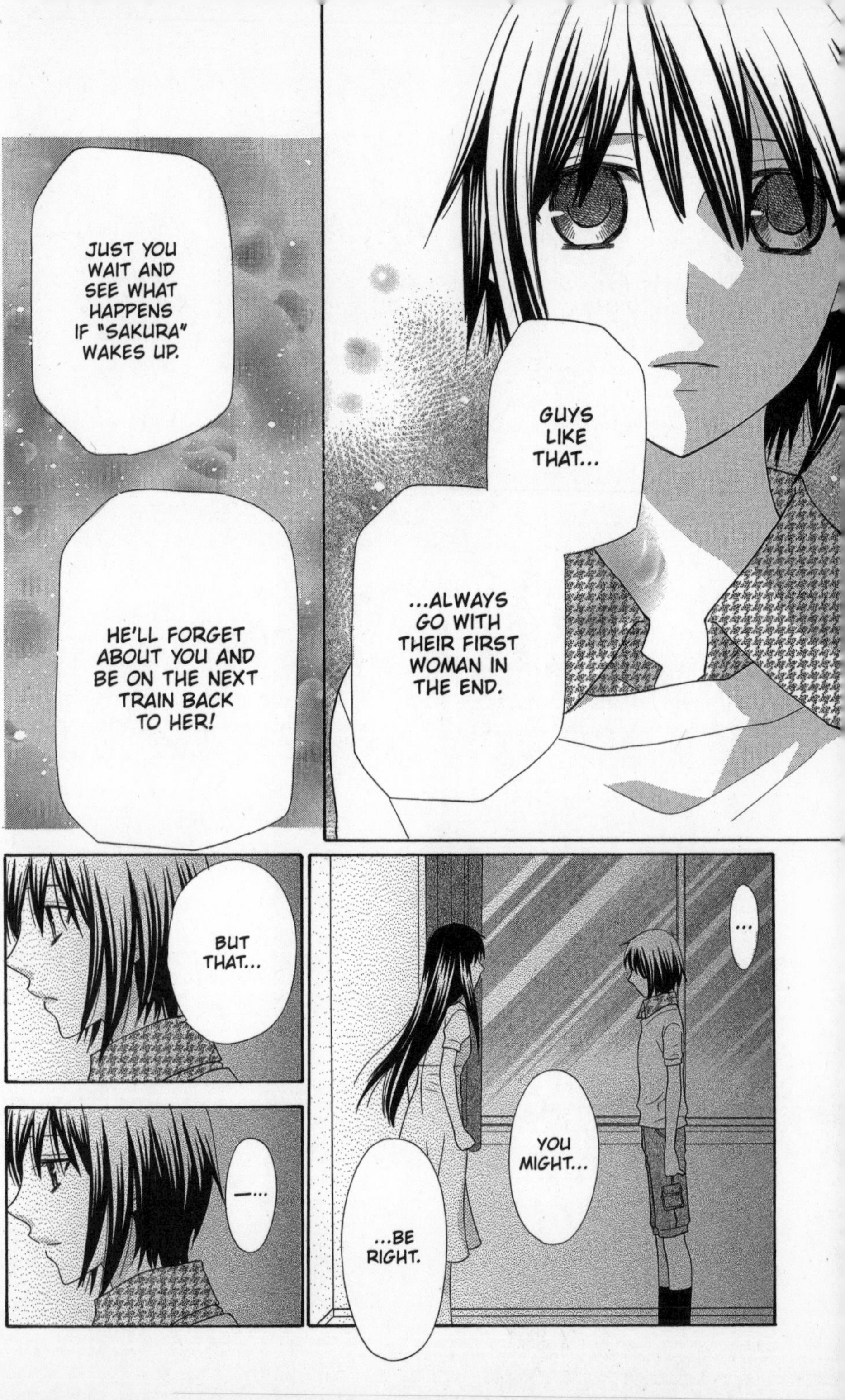
GUYS LIKE THAT...
...ALWAYS GO WITH THEIR FIRST WOMAN IN THE END.
JUST YOU WAIT AND SEE WHAT HAPPENS IF "SAKURA" WAKES UP.
HE'LL FORGET ABOUT YOU AND BE ON THE NEXT TRAIN BACK TO HER!
...
YOU MIGHT...
...BE RIGHT.
BUT THAT...
—...

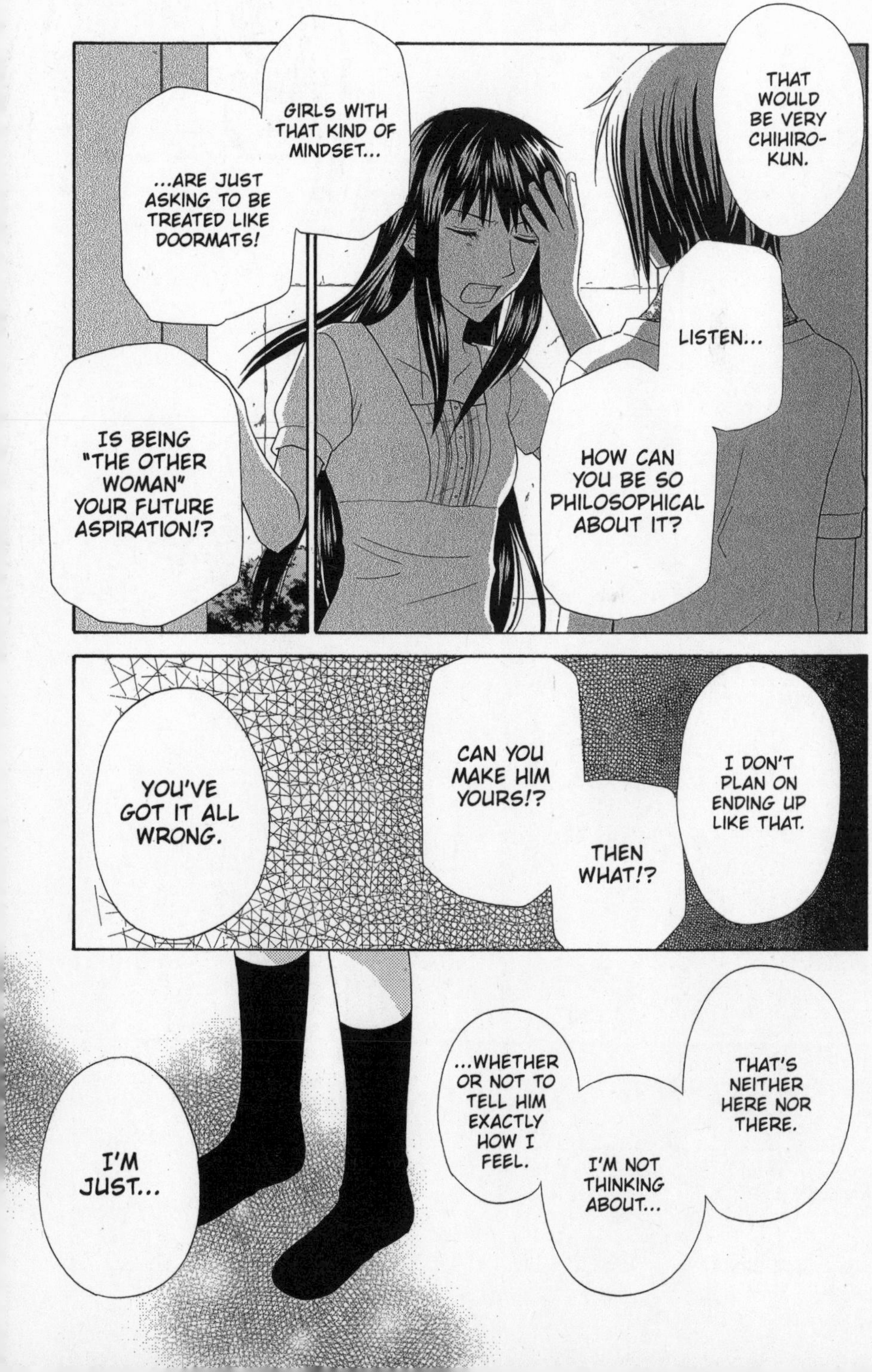
THAT WOULD BE VERY CHIHIRO-KUN.
LISTEN...
HOW CAN YOU BE SO PHILOSOPHICAL ABOUT IT?
GIRLS WITH THAT KIND OF MINDSET...
...ARE JUST ASKING TO BE TREATED LIKE DOORMATS!
IS BEING "THE OTHER WOMAN" YOUR FUTURE ASPIRATION!?
I DON'T PLAN ON ENDING UP LIKE THAT.
THEN WHAT!?
CAN YOU MAKE HIM YOURS!?
YOU'VE GOT IT ALL WRONG.
THAT'S NEITHER HERE NOR THERE.
I'M NOT THINKING ABOUT...
...WHETHER OR NOT TO TELL HIM EXACTLY HOW I FEEL.
I'M JUST...

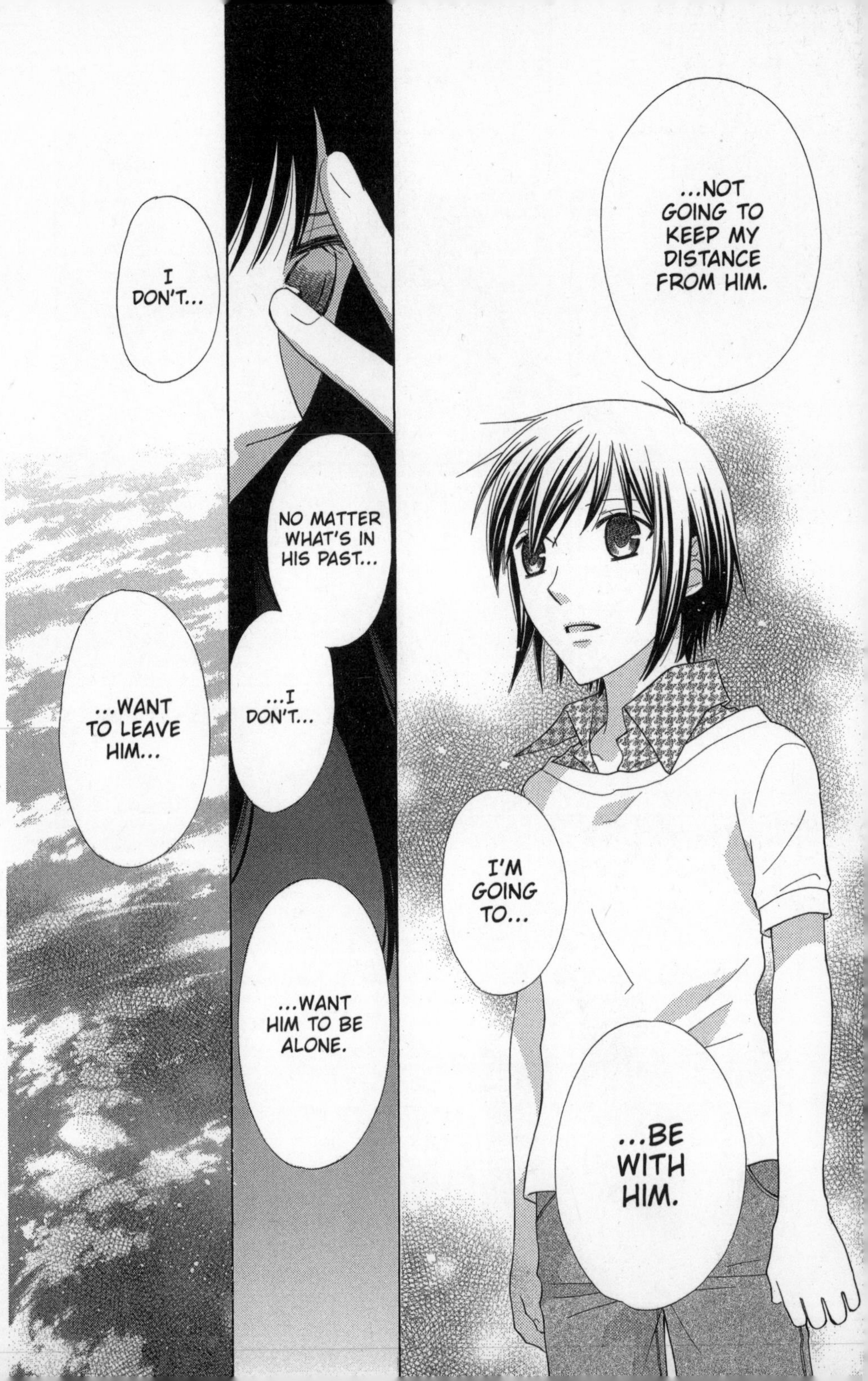

...NOT GOING TO KEEP MY DISTANCE FROM HIM.
I'M GOING TO...
...BE WITH HIM.
NO MATTER WHAT'S IN HIS PAST...
...I DON'T...
...WANT HIM TO BE ALONE.
I DON'T...
...WANT TO LEAVE HIM...

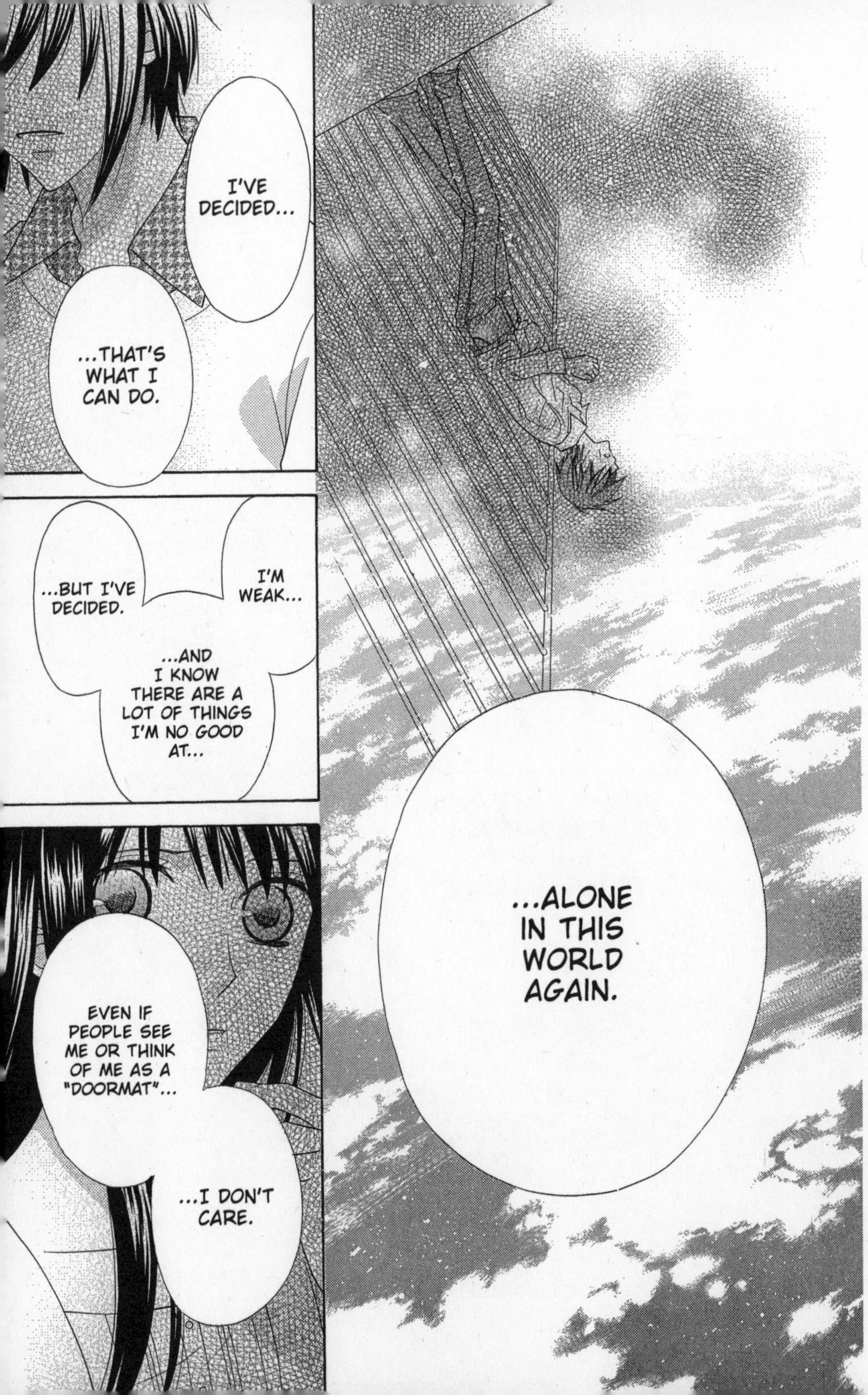
...ALONE IN THIS WORLD AGAIN.
I'VE DECIDED...
...THAT'S WHAT I CAN DO.
I'M WEAK...
...AND I KNOW THERE ARE A LOT OF THINGS I'M NO GOOD AT...
...BUT I'VE DECIDED.
EVEN IF PEOPLE SEE ME OR THINK OF ME AS A "DOORMAT"...
...I DON'T CARE.

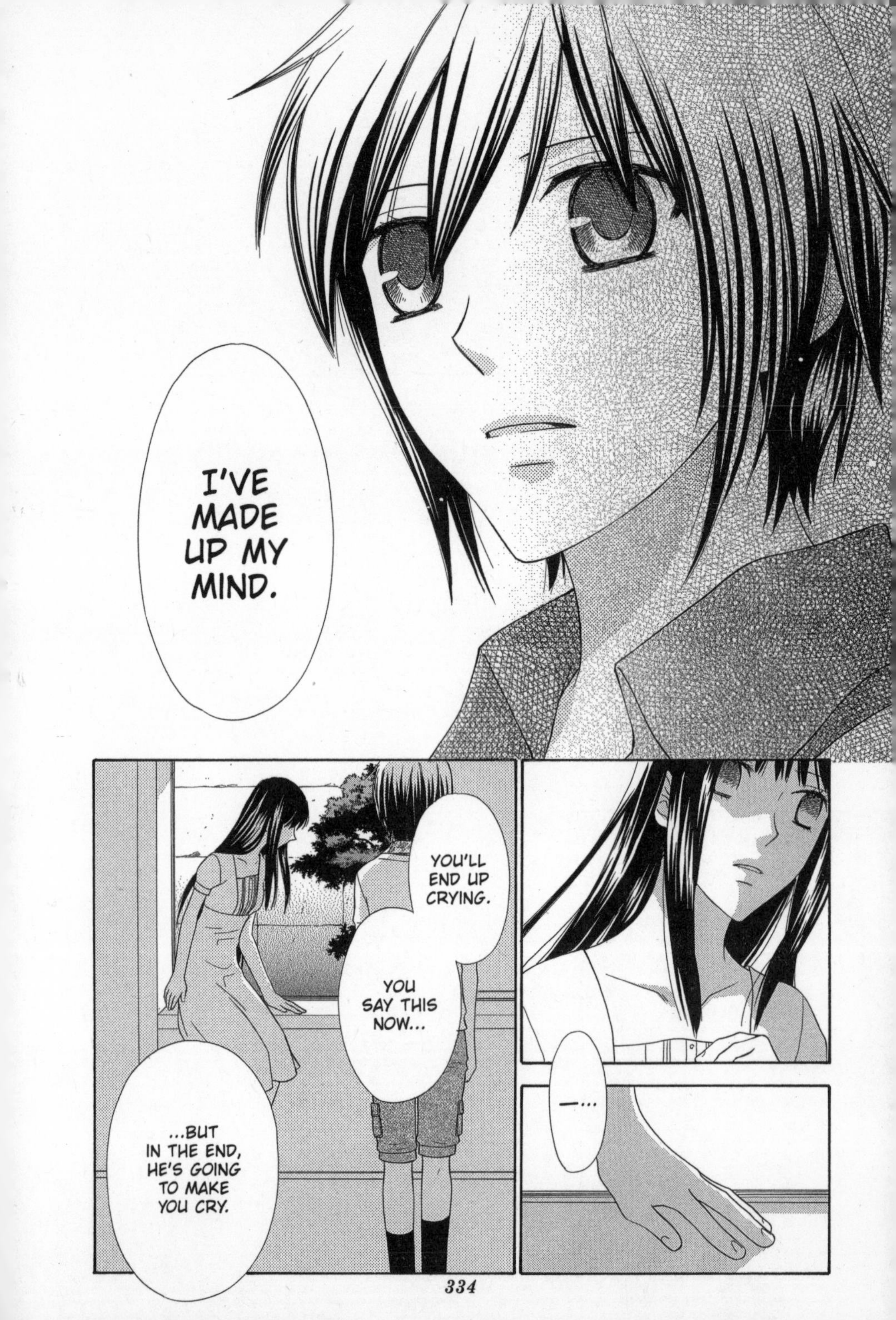
I'VE MADE UP MY MIND.
—...
YOU'LL END UP CRYING.
YOU SAY THIS NOW...
...BUT IN THE END, HE'S GOING TO MAKE YOU CRY.

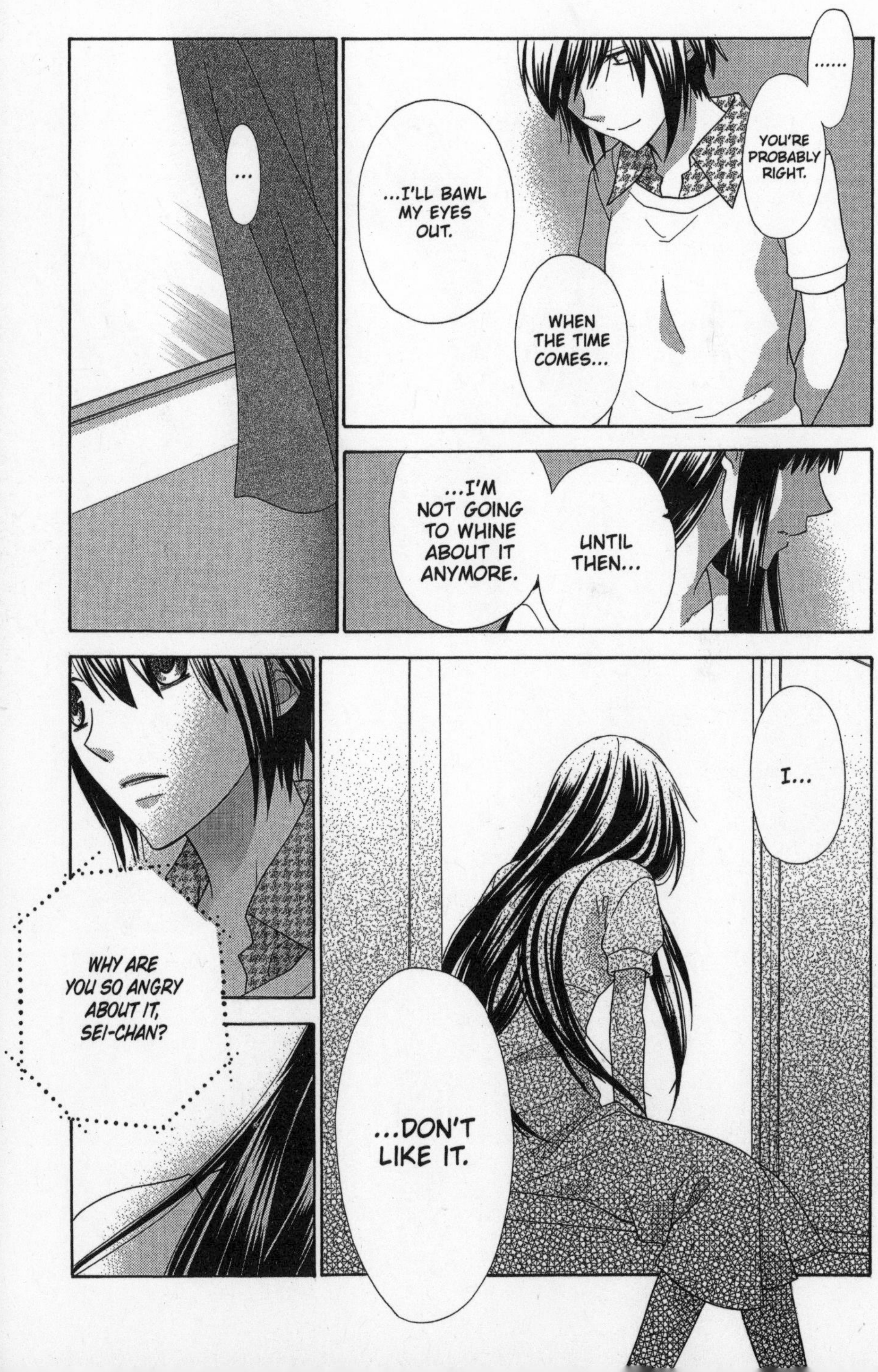
......
YOU'RE PROBABLY RIGHT.
WHEN THE TIME COMES...
...I'LL BAWL MY EYES OUT.
UNTIL THEN...
...I'M NOT GOING TO WHINE ABOUT IT ANYMORE.
...
I...
...DON'T LIKE IT.
WHY ARE YOU SO ANGRY ABOUT IT, SEI-CHAN?

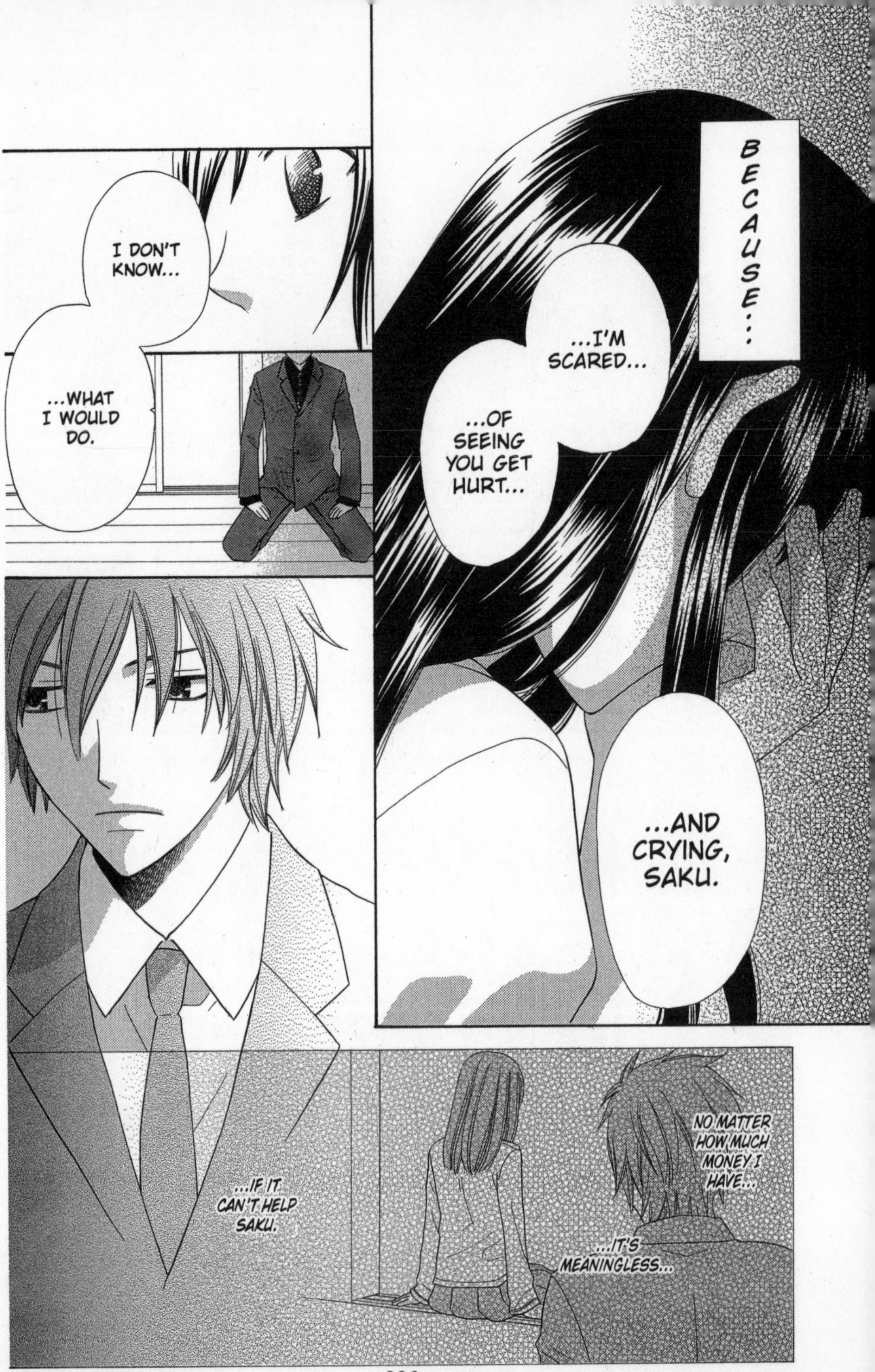
BECAUSE...
...I'M SCARED...
...OF SEEING YOU GET HURT...
...AND CRYING, SAKU.
I DON'T KNOW...
...WHAT I WOULD DO.
NO MATTER HOW MUCH MONEY I HAVE...
...IT'S MEANINGLESS...
...IF IT CAN'T HELP SAKU.

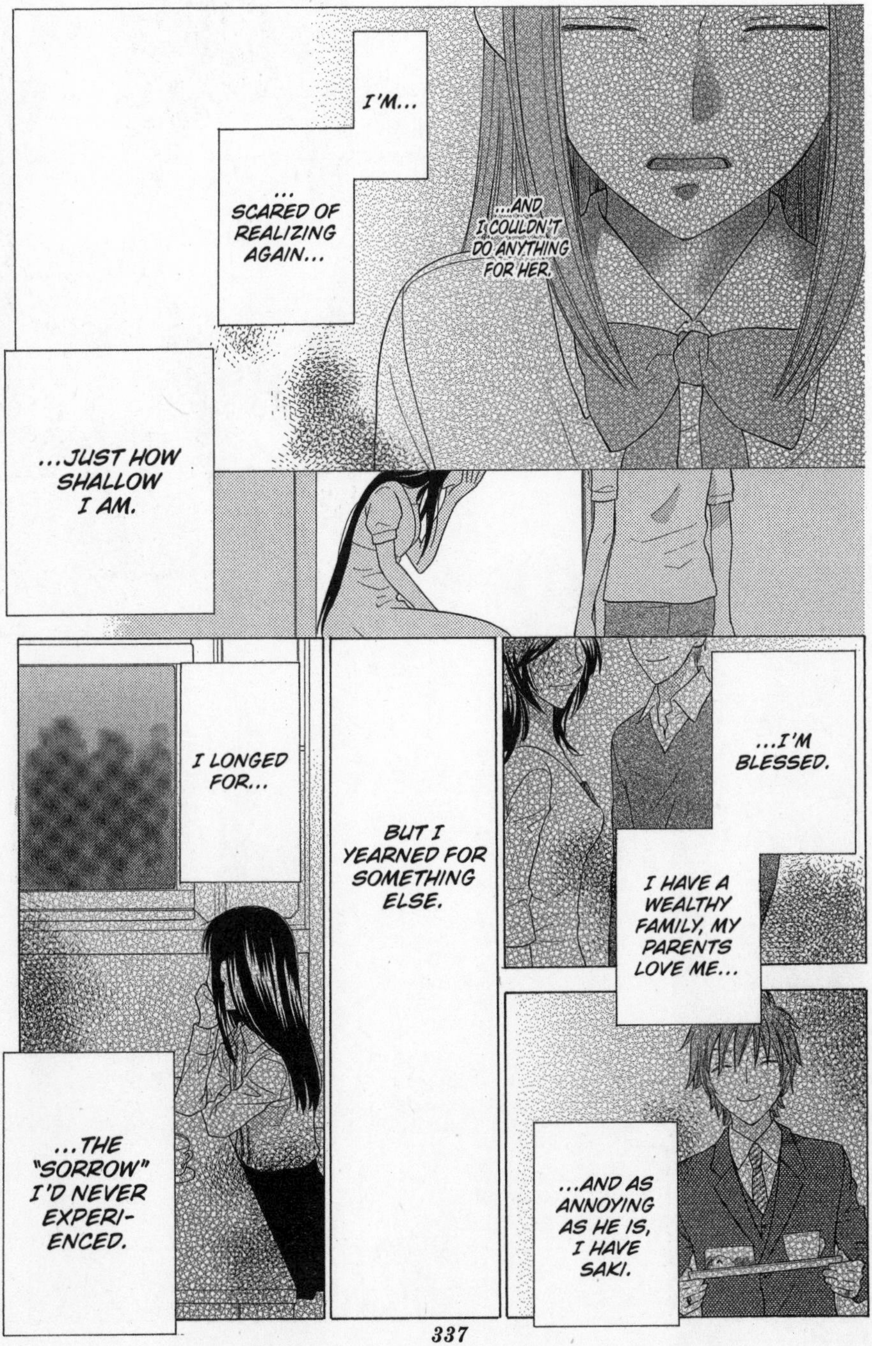
...AND I COULDN'T DO ANYTHING FOR HER.
I'M...
...SCARED OF REALIZING AGAIN...
...JUST HOW SHALLOW I AM.
...I'M BLESSED.
I HAVE A WEALTHY FAMILY, MY PARENTS LOVE ME...
...AND AS ANNOYING AS HE IS, I HAVE SAKI.
BUT I YEARNED FOR SOMETHING ELSE.
I LONGED FOR...
...THE "SORROW" I'D NEVER EXPERI-ENCED.

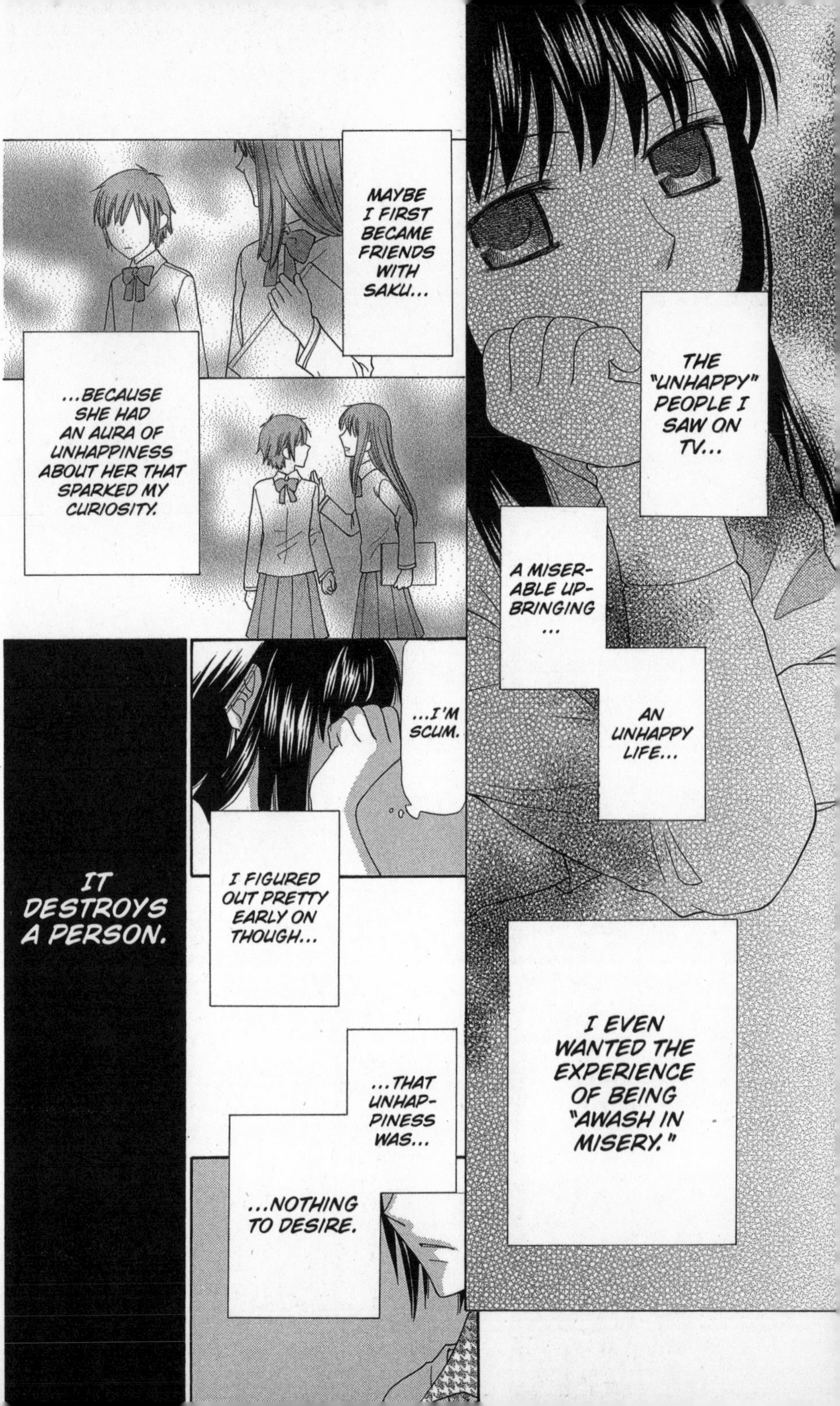
THE "UNHAPPY" PEOPLE I SAW ON TV...
A MISER-ABLE UP-BRINGING...
AN UNHAPPY LIFE...
I EVEN WANTED THE EXPERIENCE OF BEING "AWASH IN MISERY."
MAYBE I FIRST BECAME FRIENDS WITH SAKU...
...BECAUSE SHE HAD AN AURA OF UNHAPPINESS ABOUT HER THAT SPARKED MY CURIOSITY.
...I'M SCUM.
I FIGURED OUT PRETTY EARLY ON THOUGH...
...THAT UNHAP-PINESS WAS...
...NOTHING TO DESIRE.
IT DESTROYS A PERSON.

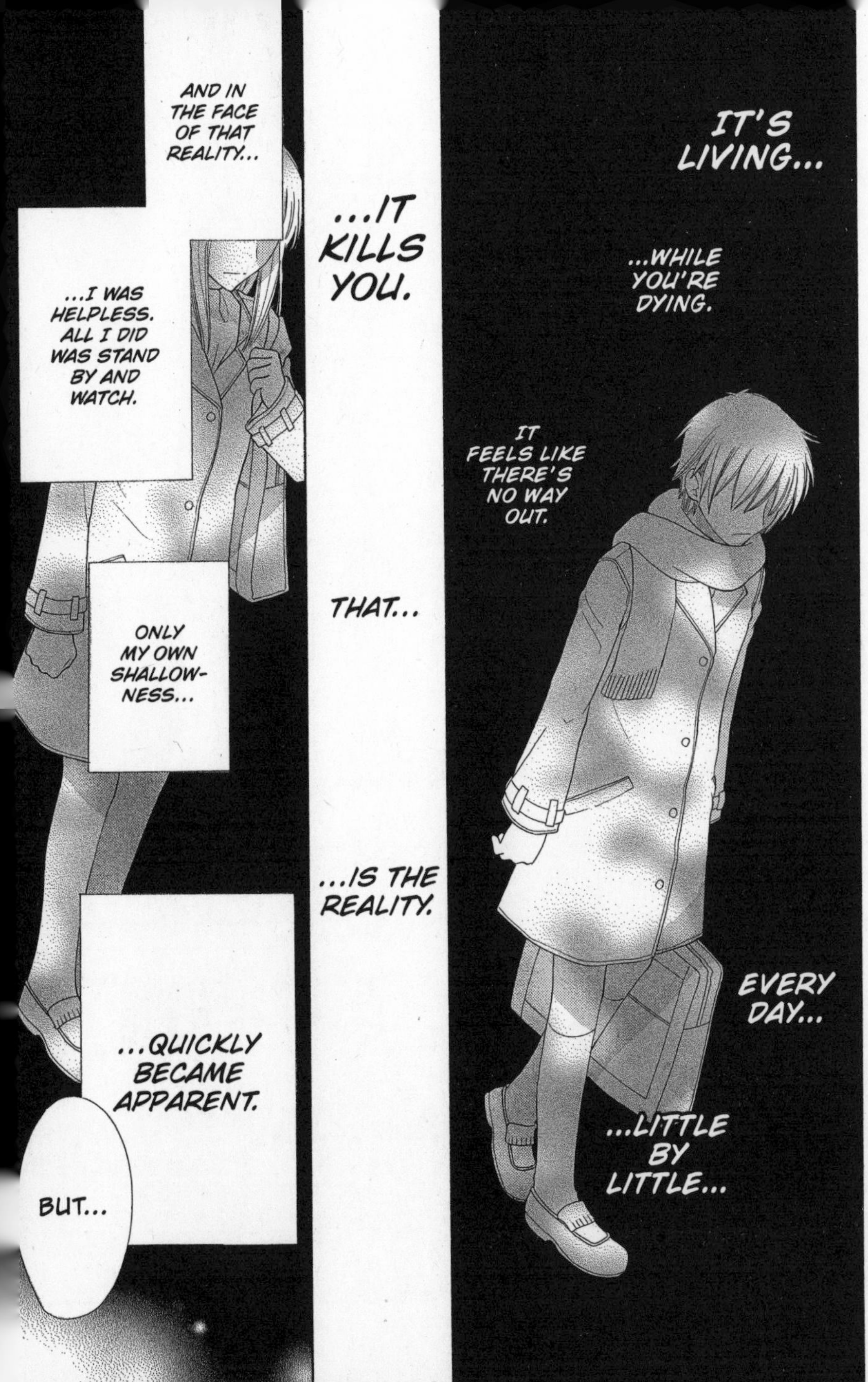
IT'S LIVING...
...WHILE YOU'RE DYING.
IT FEELS LIKE THERE'S NO WAY OUT.
EVERY DAY...
...LITTLE BY LITTLE...
...IT KILLS YOU.
THAT...
...IS THE REALITY.
AND IN THE FACE OF THAT REALITY...
...I WAS HELPLESS. ALL I DID WAS STAND BY AND WATCH.
ONLY MY OWN SHALLOWNESS...
...QUICKLY BECAME APPARENT.
BUT...

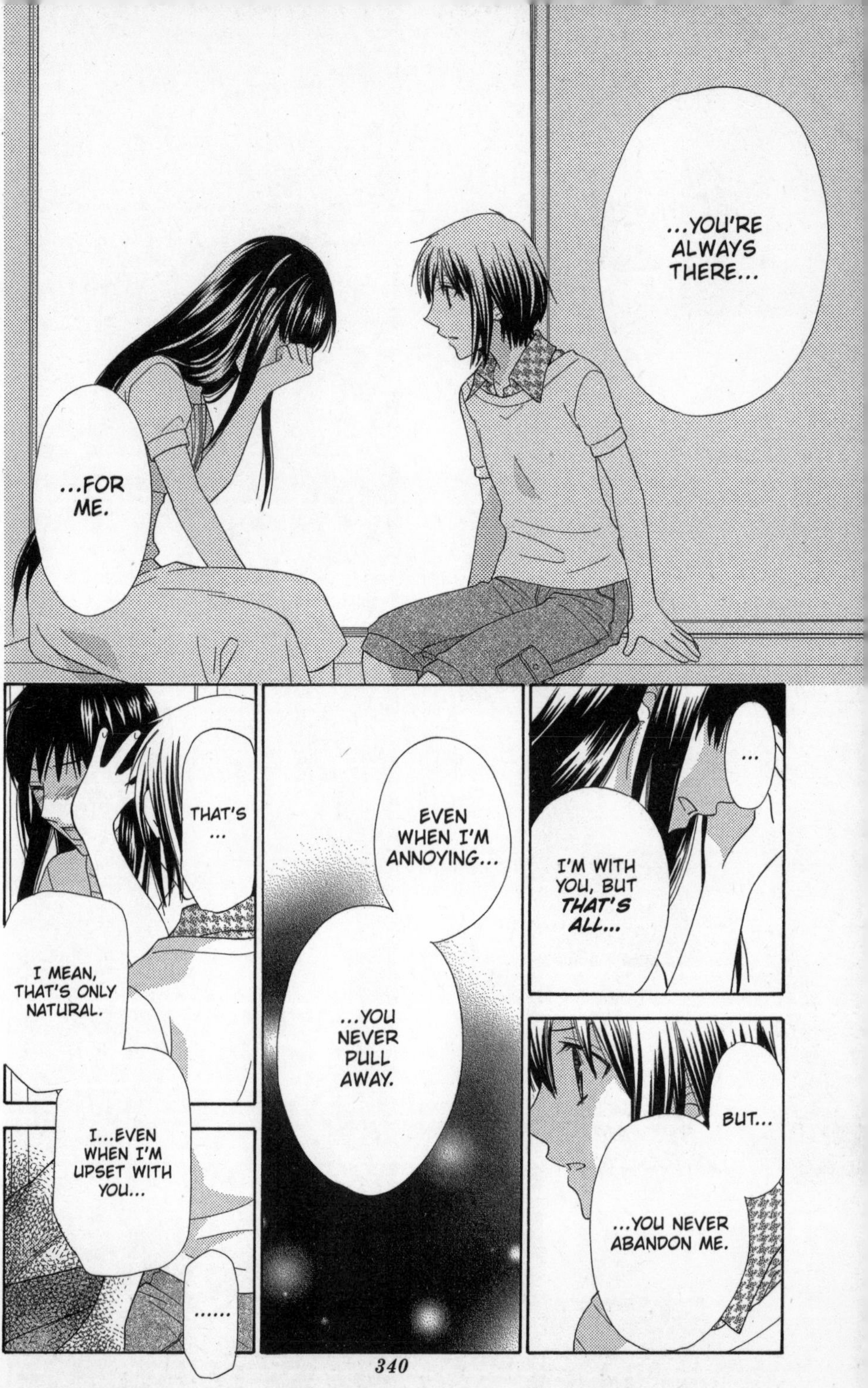
...YOU'RE ALWAYS THERE...
...FOR ME.
...
I'M WITH YOU, BUT *THAT'S ALL*...
BUT...
...YOU NEVER ABANDON ME.
EVEN WHEN I'M ANNOYING...
...YOU NEVER PULL AWAY.
THAT'S ...
I MEAN, THAT'S ONLY NATURAL.
I...EVEN WHEN I'M UPSET WITH YOU...
......

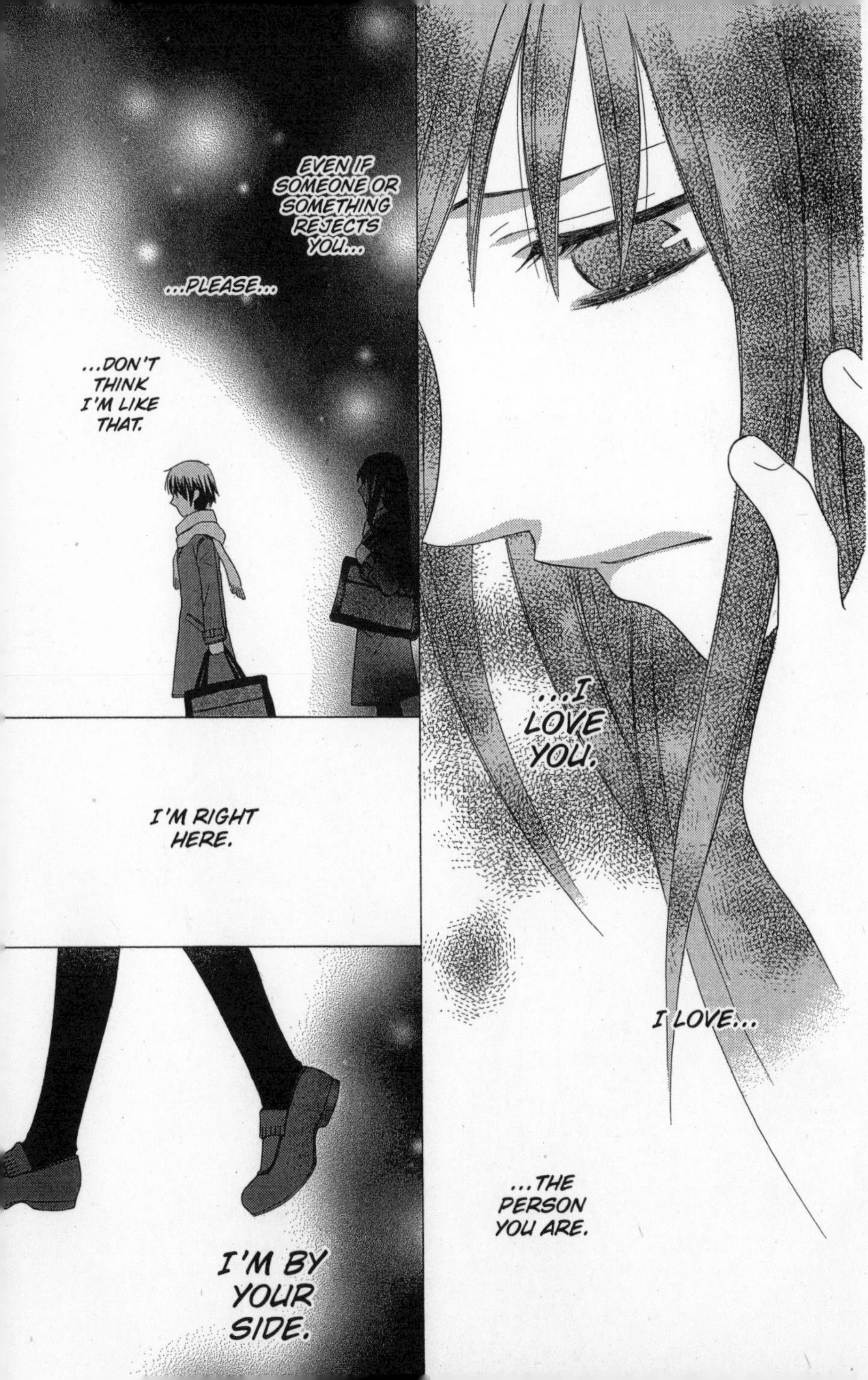
...I LOVE YOU.
I LOVE...
...THE PERSON YOU ARE.
EVEN IF SOMEONE OR SOMETHING REJECTS YOU...
...PLEASE...
...DON'T THINK I'M LIKE THAT.
I'M RIGHT HERE.
I'M BY YOUR SIDE.

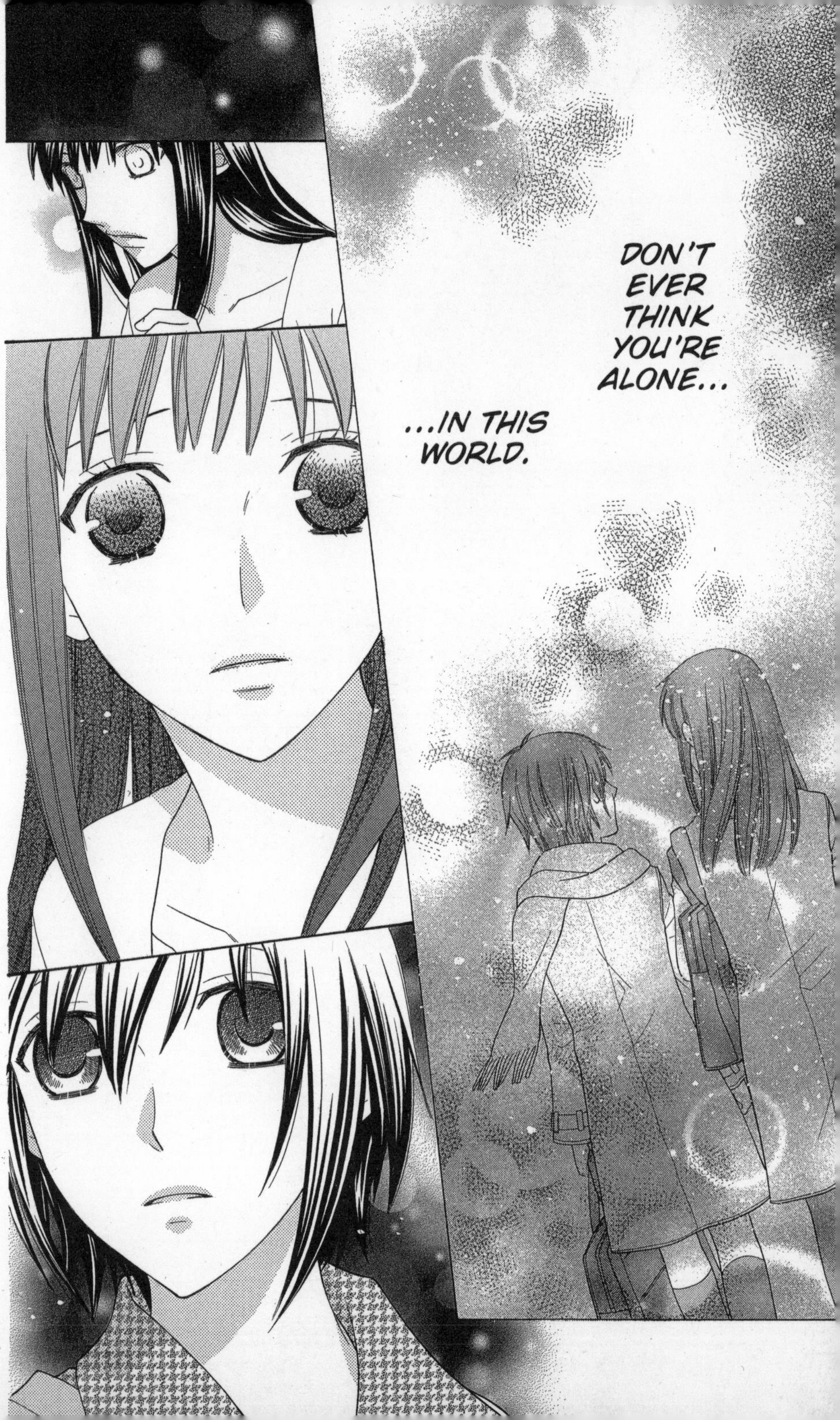
DON'T EVER THINK YOU'RE ALONE...
...IN THIS WORLD.

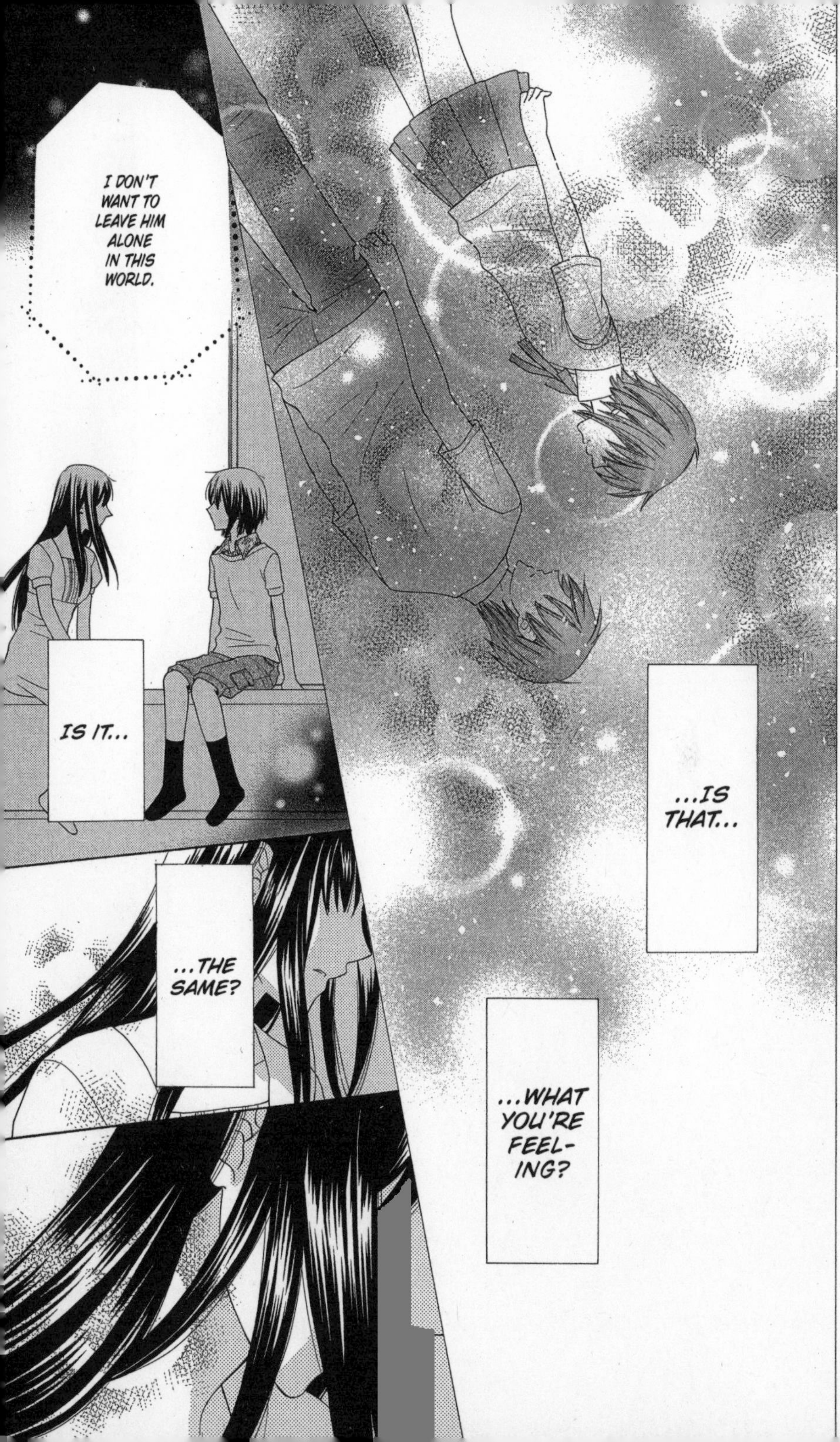
I DON'T WANT TO LEAVE HIM ALONE IN THIS WORLD.
...IS THAT...
...WHAT YOU'RE FEEL-ING?
IS IT...
...THE SAME?

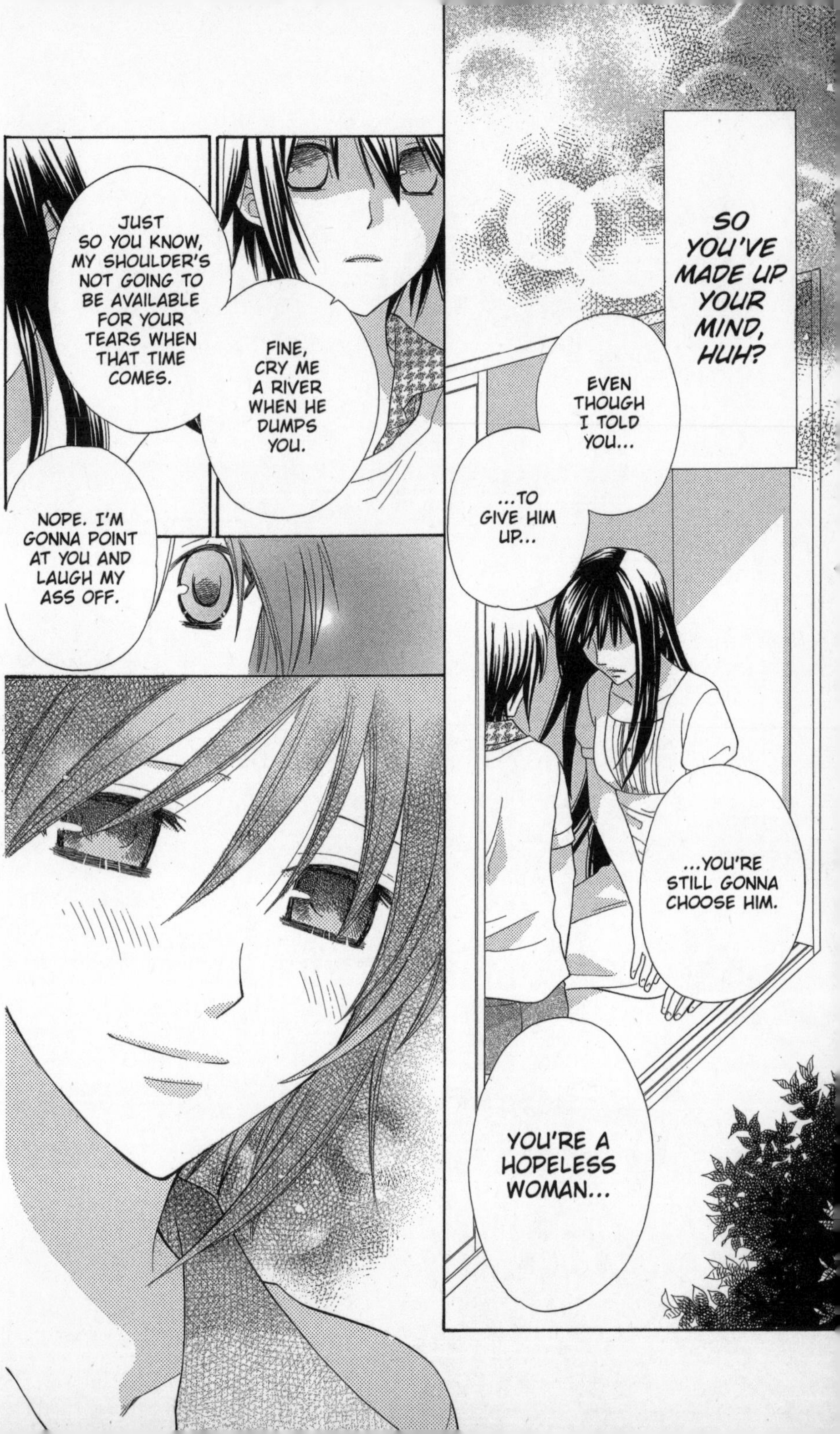
SO YOU'VE MADE UP YOUR MIND, HUH?
EVEN THOUGH I TOLD YOU...
...TO GIVE HIM UP...
...YOU'RE STILL GONNA CHOOSE HIM.
YOU'RE A HOPELESS WOMAN...
FINE, CRY ME A RIVER WHEN HE DUMPS YOU.
JUST SO YOU KNOW, MY SHOULDER'S NOT GOING TO BE AVAILABLE FOR YOUR TEARS WHEN THAT TIME COMES.
NOPE. I'M GONNA POINT AT YOU AND LAUGH MY ASS OFF.

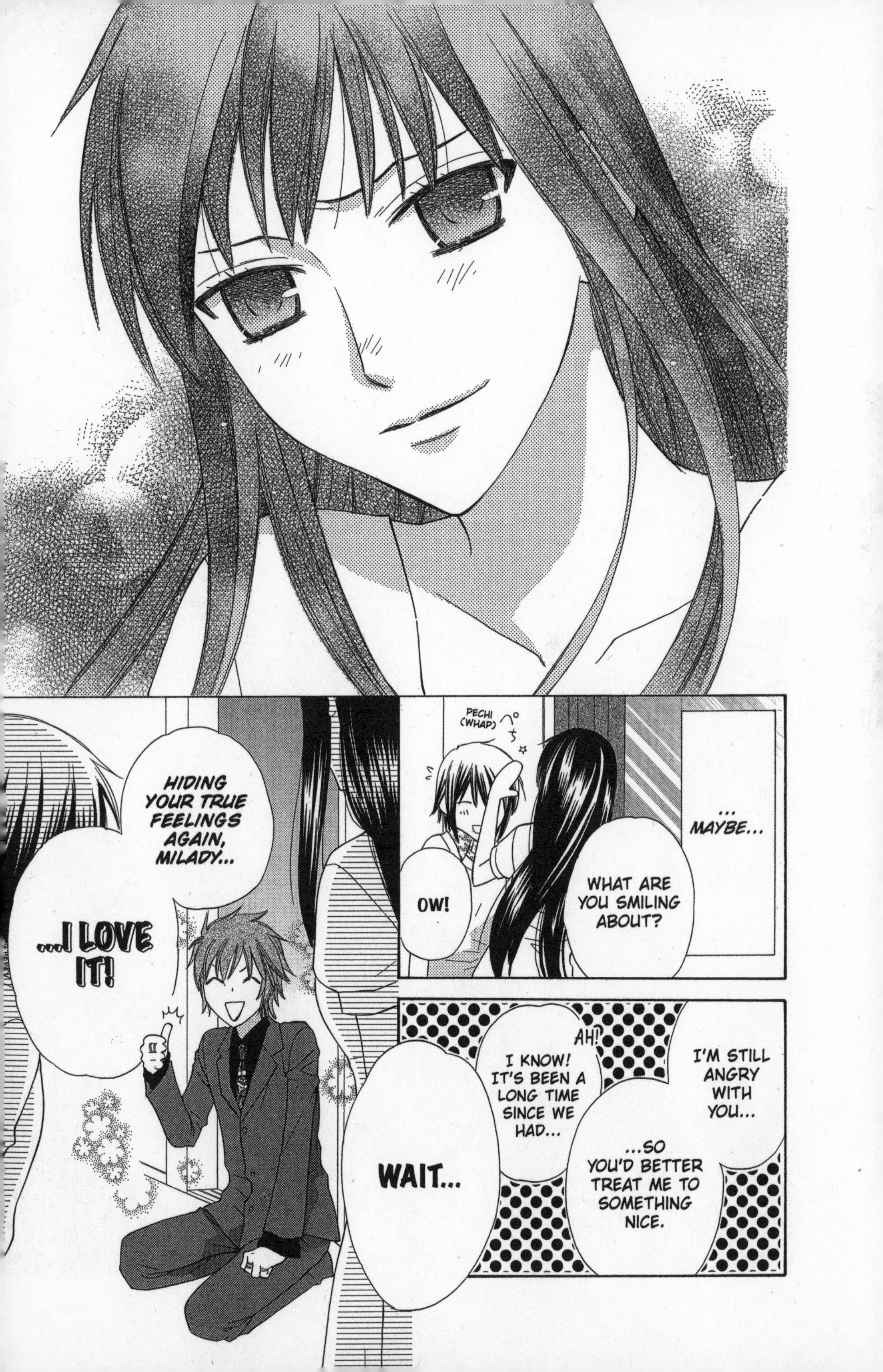
...MAYBE...
WHAT ARE YOU SMILING ABOUT?
PECHI (WHAP)
OW!
I'M STILL ANGRY WITH YOU...
...SO YOU'D BETTER TREAT ME TO SOMETHING NICE.
AH!
I KNOW! IT'S BEEN A LONG TIME SINCE WE HAD...
WAIT...
HIDING YOUR TRUE FEELINGS AGAIN, MILADY...
...I LOVE IT!

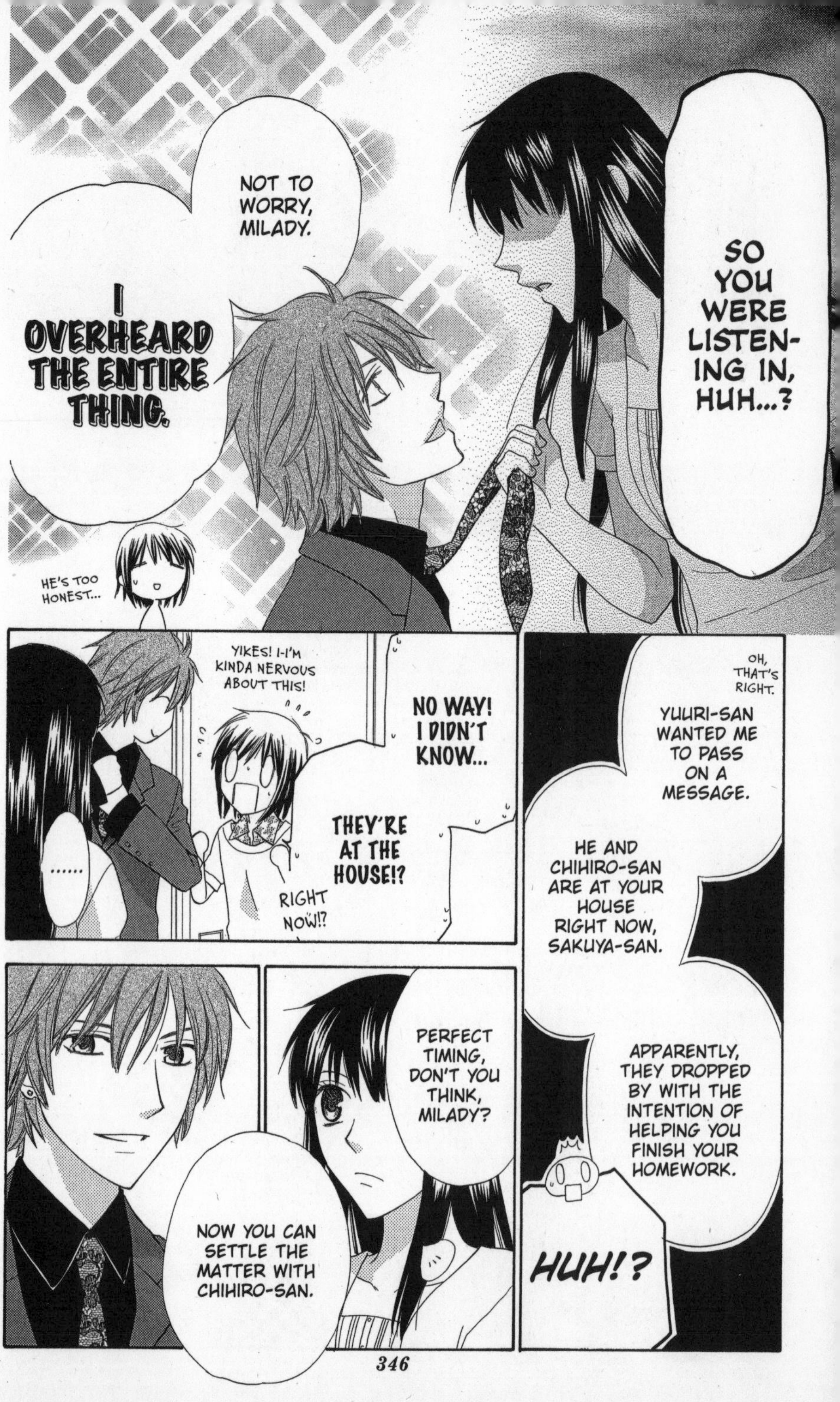
SO YOU WERE LISTENING IN, HUH...?
NOT TO WORRY, MILADY.
I OVERHEARD THE ENTIRE THING.
HE'S TOO HONEST...
OH, THAT'S RIGHT.
YUURI-SAN WANTED ME TO PASS ON A MESSAGE.
HE AND CHIHIRO-SAN ARE AT YOUR HOUSE RIGHT NOW, SAKUYA-SAN.
APPARENTLY, THEY DROPPED BY WITH THE INTENTION OF HELPING YOU FINISH YOUR HOMEWORK.
HUH!?
NO WAY! I DIDN'T KNOW...
THEY'RE AT THE HOUSE!?
RIGHT NOW!?
YIKES! I-I'M KINDA NERVOUS ABOUT THIS!
......
PERFECT TIMING, DON'T YOU THINK, MILADY?
NOW YOU CAN SETTLE THE MATTER WITH CHIHIRO-SAN.

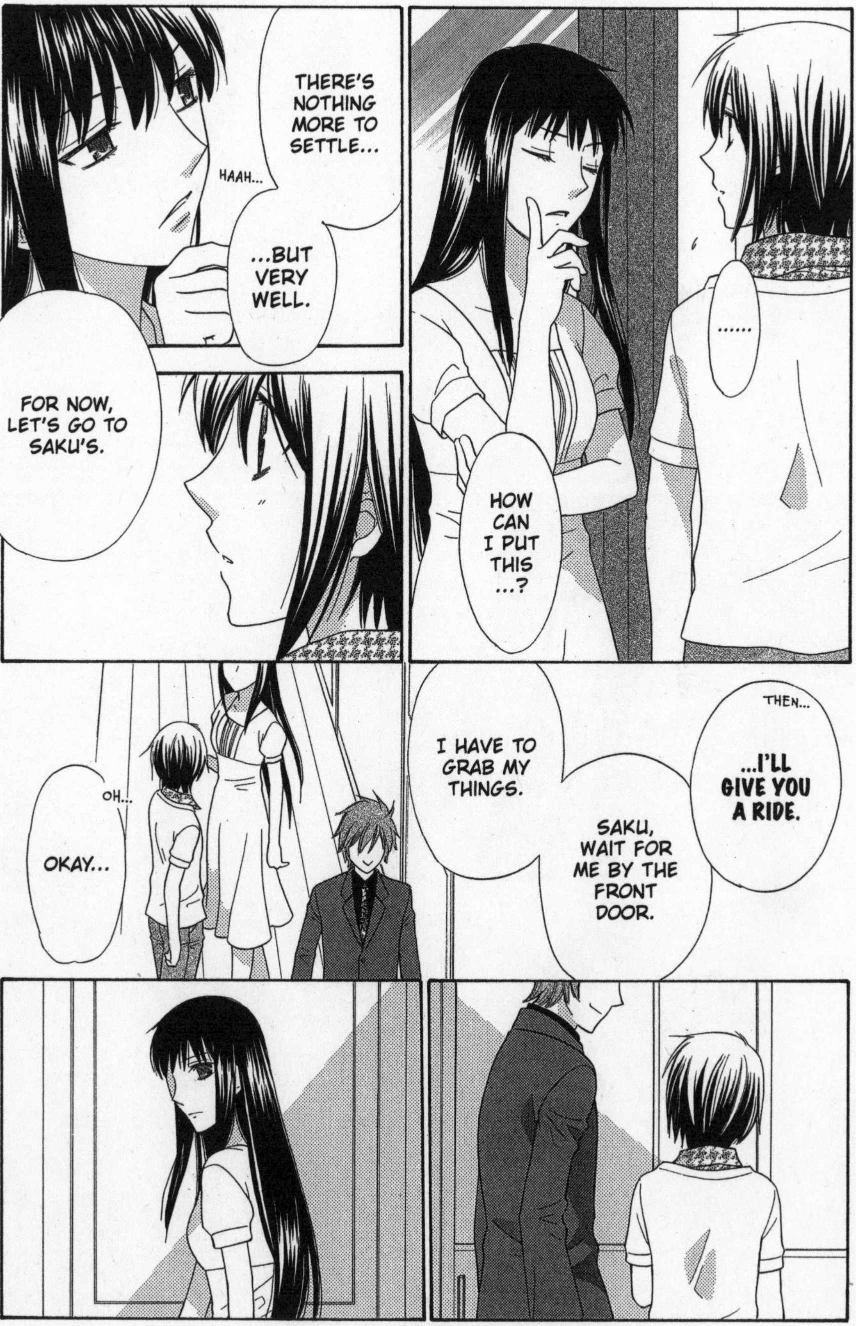
......
HOW CAN I PUT THIS ...?
THERE'S NOTHING MORE TO SETTLE...
HAAH...
...BUT VERY WELL.
FOR NOW, LET'S GO TO SAKU'S.
THEN...
...I'LL GIVE YOU A RIDE.
I HAVE TO GRAB MY THINGS.
SAKU, WAIT FOR ME BY THE FRONT DOOR.
OH...
OKAY...

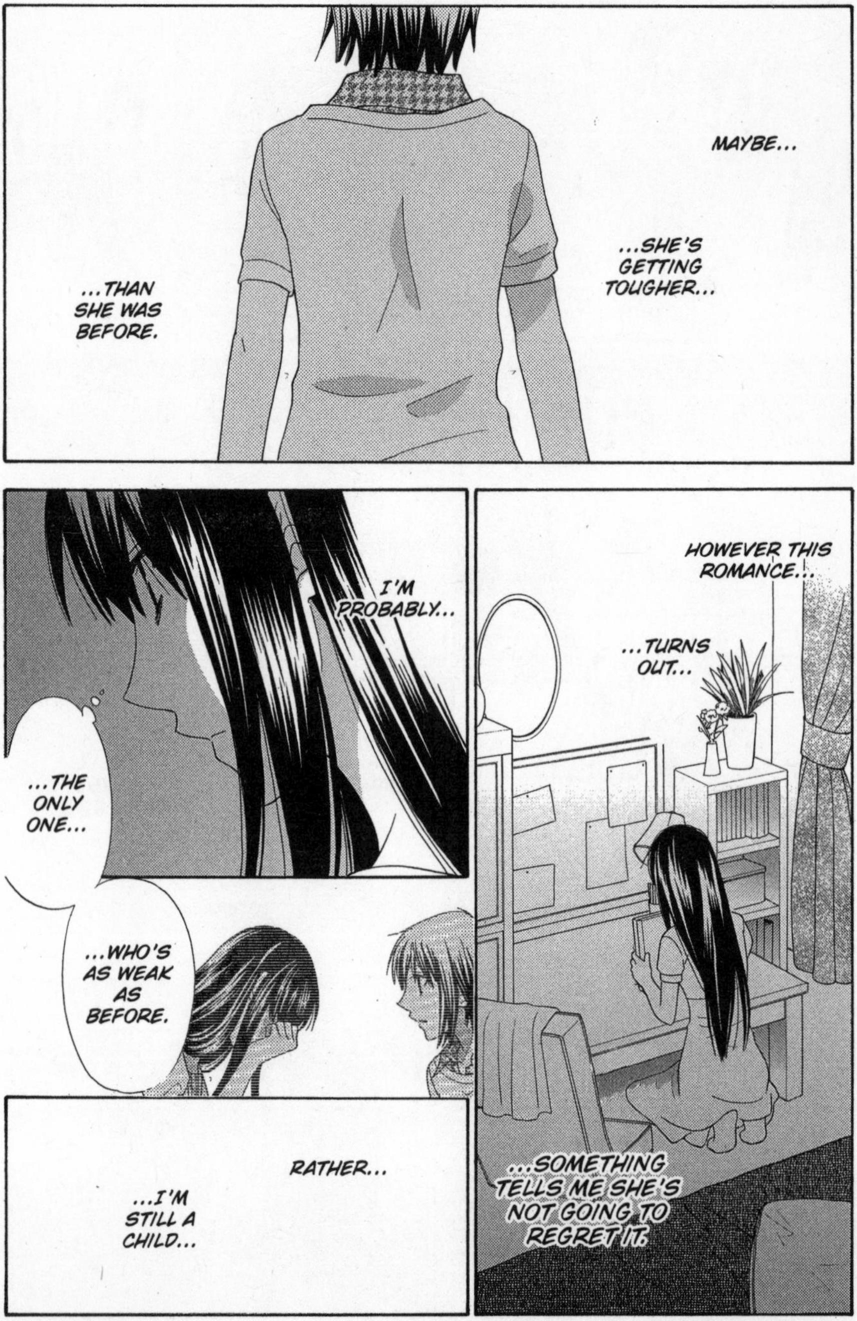
MAYBE...
...SHE'S GETTING TOUGHER...
...THAN SHE WAS BEFORE.
HOWEVER THIS ROMANCE...
...TURNS OUT...
...SOMETHING TELLS ME SHE'S NOT GOING TO REGRET IT.
I'M PROBABLY...
...THE ONLY ONE...
...WHO'S AS WEAK AS BEFORE.
RATHER...
...I'M STILL A CHILD...

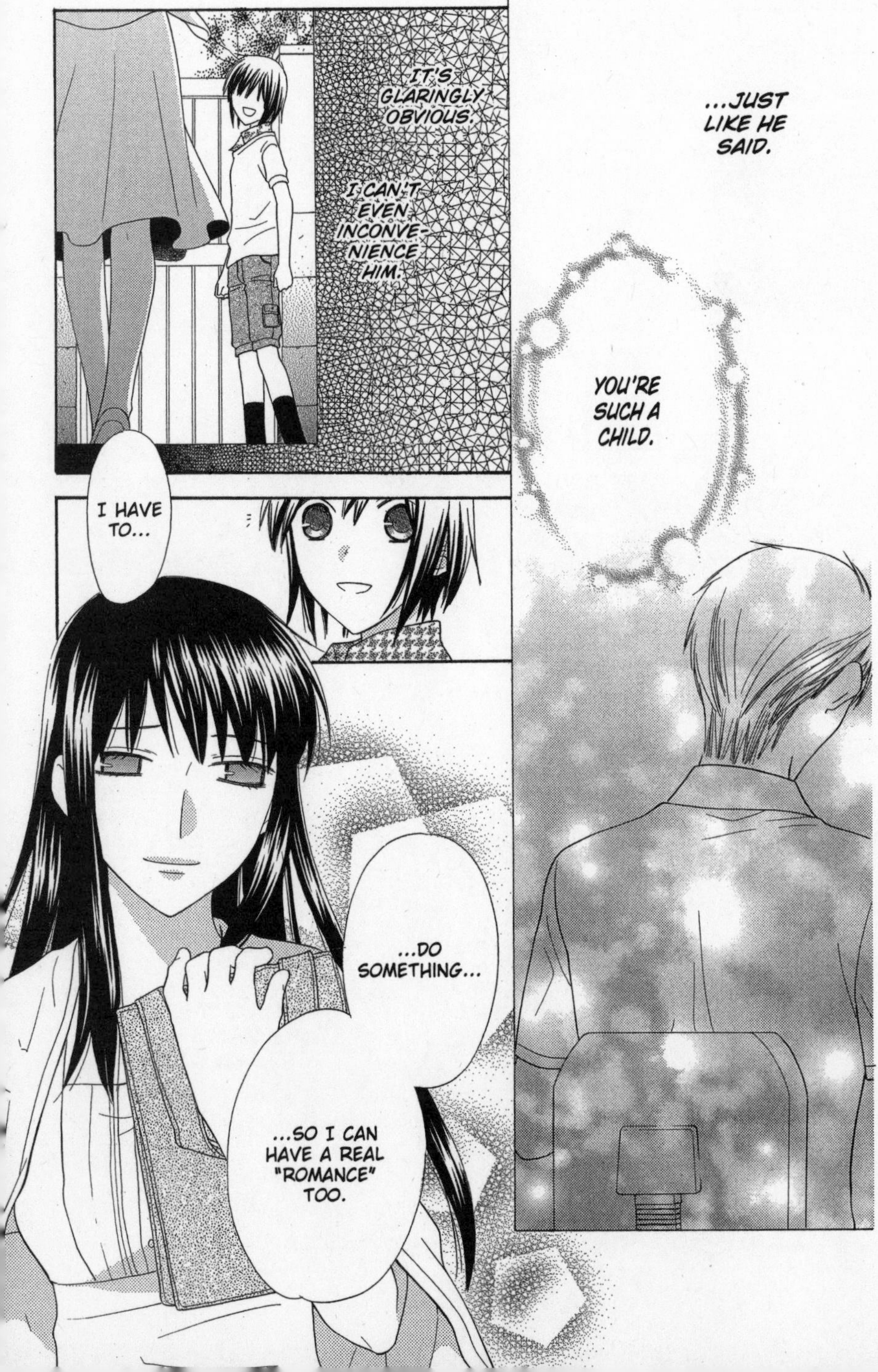
...JUST LIKE HE SAID.
YOU'RE SUCH A CHILD.
IT'S GLARINGLY OBVIOUS.
I CAN'T EVEN INCONVENIENCE HIM.
I HAVE TO...
...DO SOMETHING...
...SO I CAN HAVE A REAL "ROMANCE" TOO.

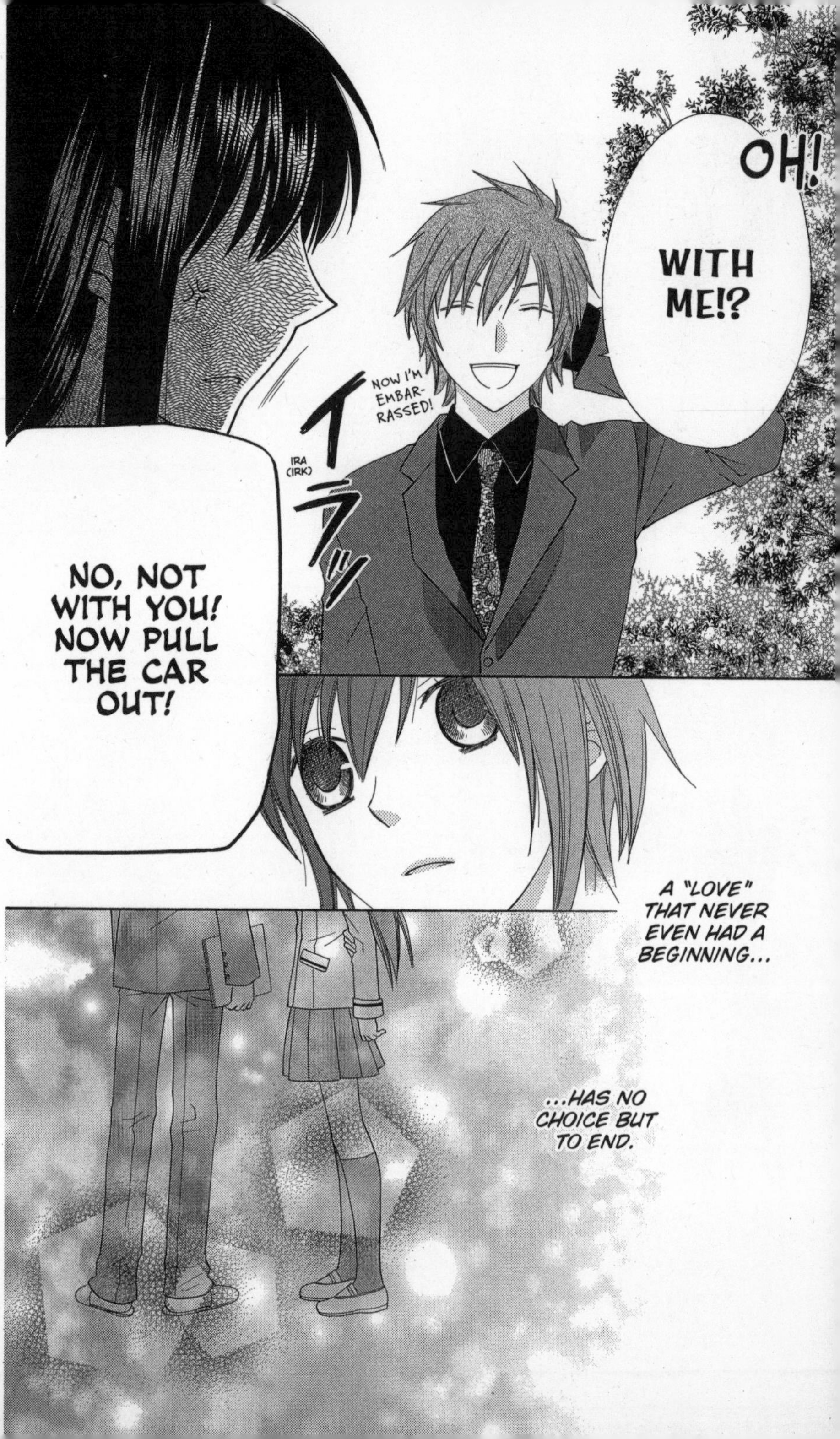
OH!
WITH ME!?
NOW I'M EMBARRASSED!
イラッ
IRA (IRK)
NO, NOT WITH YOU! NOW PULL THE CAR OUT!
A "LOVE" THAT NEVER EVEN HAD A BEGINNING...
...HAS NO CHOICE BUT TO END.

Chapter 35

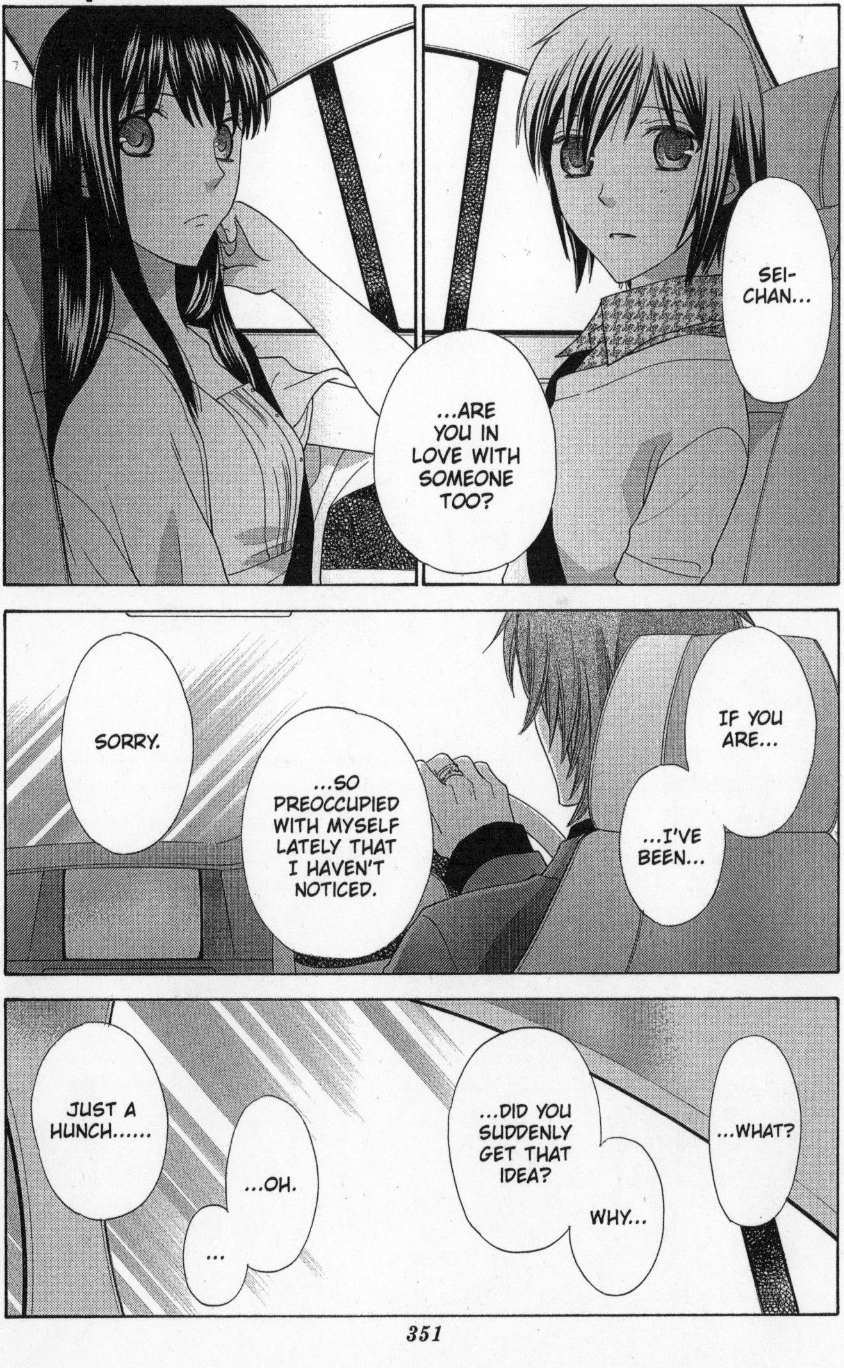
SEI-CHAN...
...ARE YOU IN LOVE WITH SOMEONE TOO?
IF YOU ARE...
...I'VE BEEN...
...SO PREOCCUPIED WITH MYSELF LATELY THAT I HAVEN'T NOTICED.
SORRY.
...WHAT?
WHY...
...DID YOU SUDDENLY GET THAT IDEA?
...OH.
...
JUST A HUNCH......

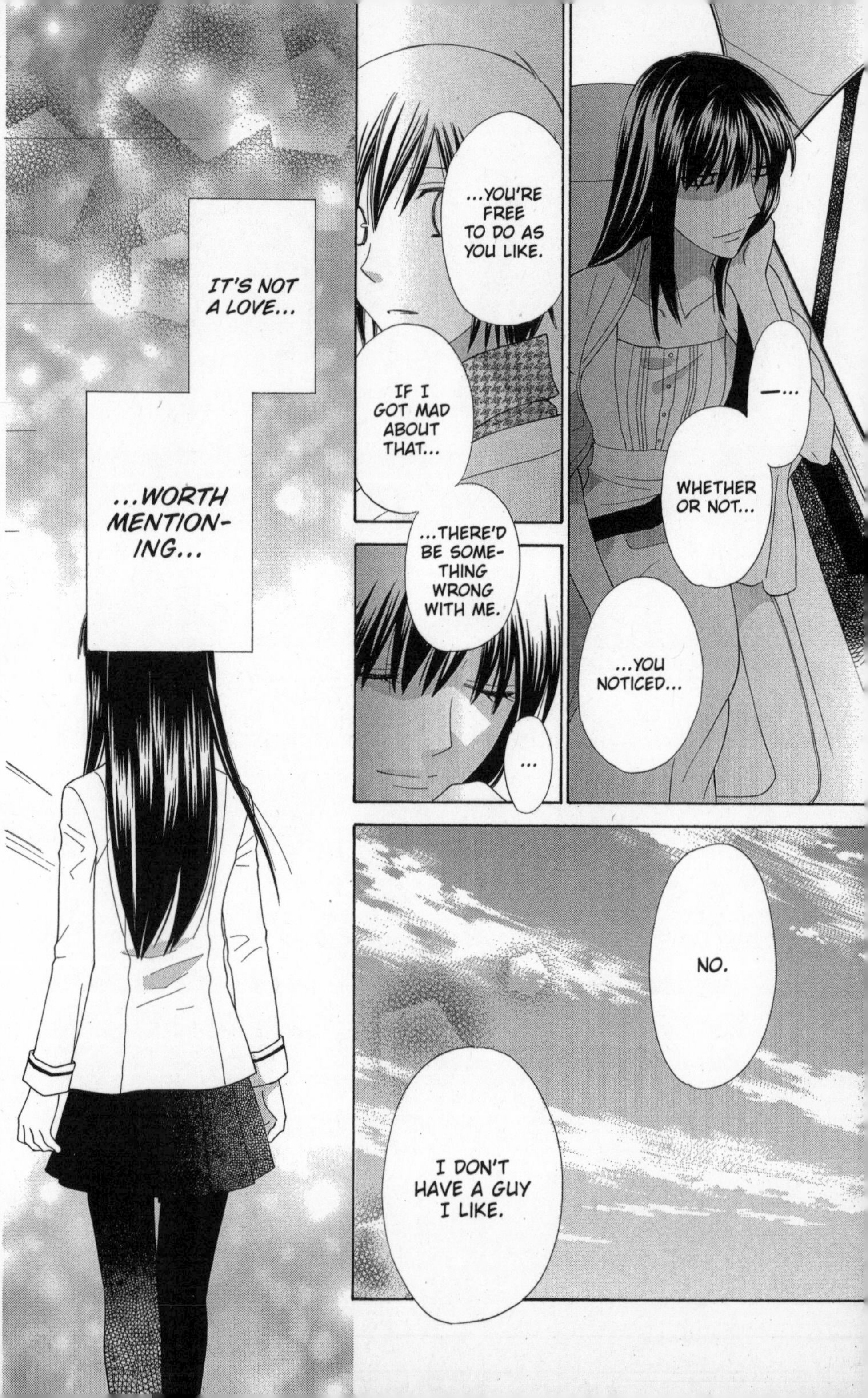
—...
WHETHER OR NOT...
...YOU NOTICED...
...YOU'RE FREE TO DO AS YOU LIKE.
IF I GOT MAD ABOUT THAT...
...THERE'D BE SOME-THING WRONG WITH ME.
...
NO.
I DON'T HAVE A GUY I LIKE.
IT'S NOT A LOVE...
...WORTH MENTION-ING...

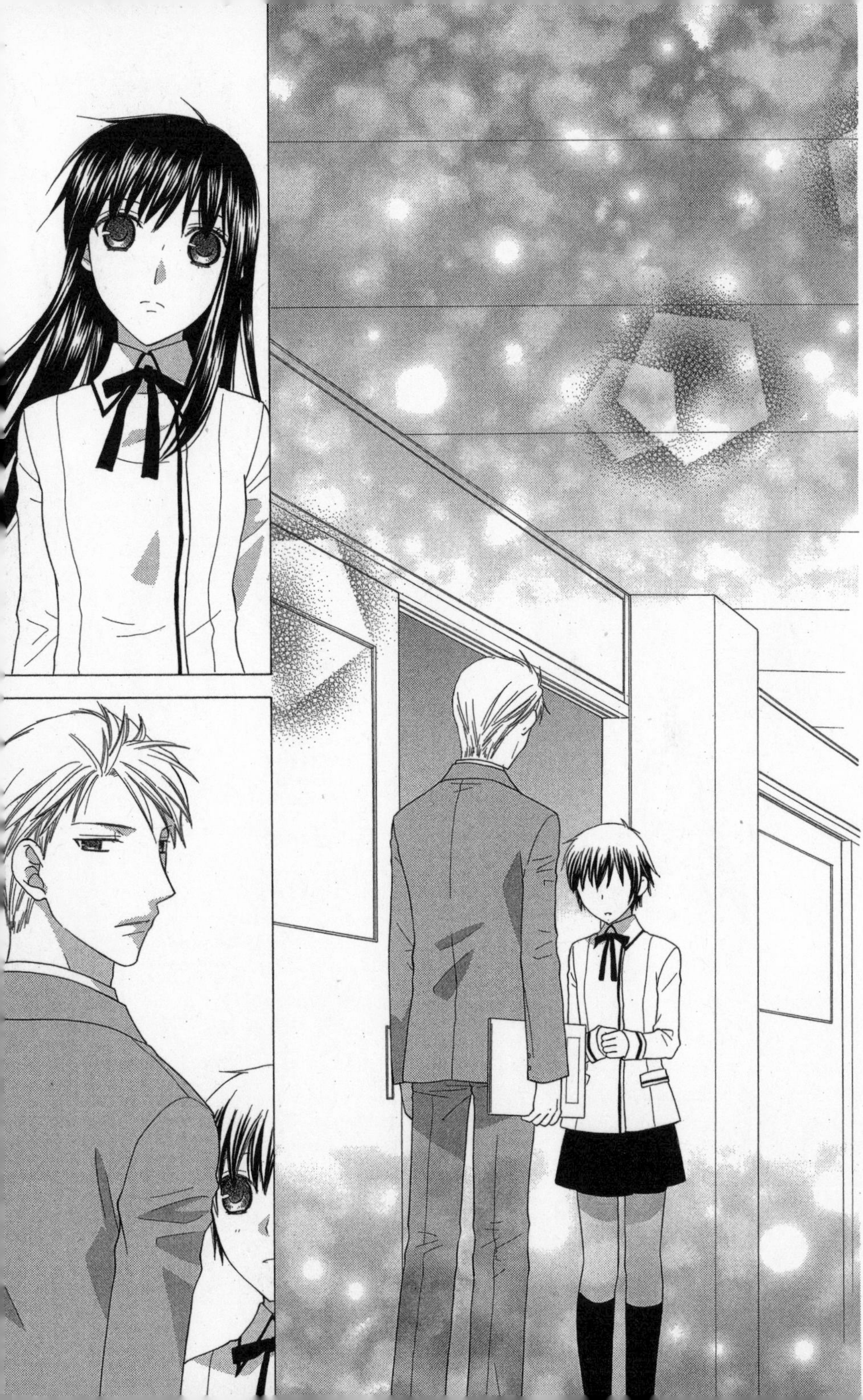

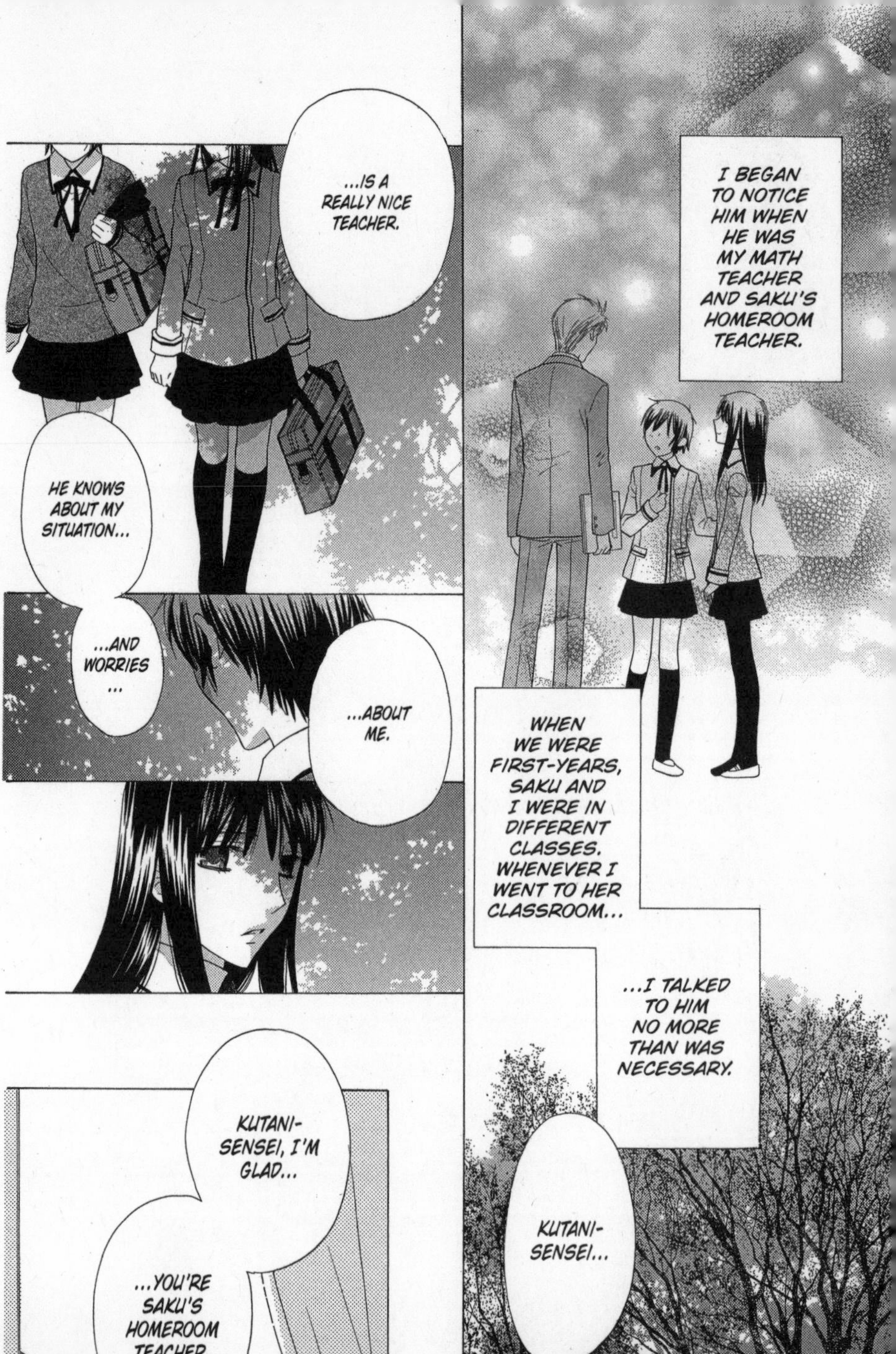
I BEGAN TO NOTICE HIM WHEN HE WAS MY MATH TEACHER AND SAKU'S HOMEROOM TEACHER.
WHEN WE WERE FIRST-YEARS, SAKU AND I WERE IN DIFFERENT CLASSES. WHENEVER I WENT TO HER CLASSROOM...
...I TALKED TO HIM NO MORE THAN WAS NECESSARY.
KUTANI-SENSEI...
...IS A REALLY NICE TEACHER.
HE KNOWS ABOUT MY SITUATION...
...AND WORRIES...
...ABOUT ME.
KUTANI-SENSEI, I'M GLAD...
...YOU'RE SAKU'S HOMEROOM TEACHER.

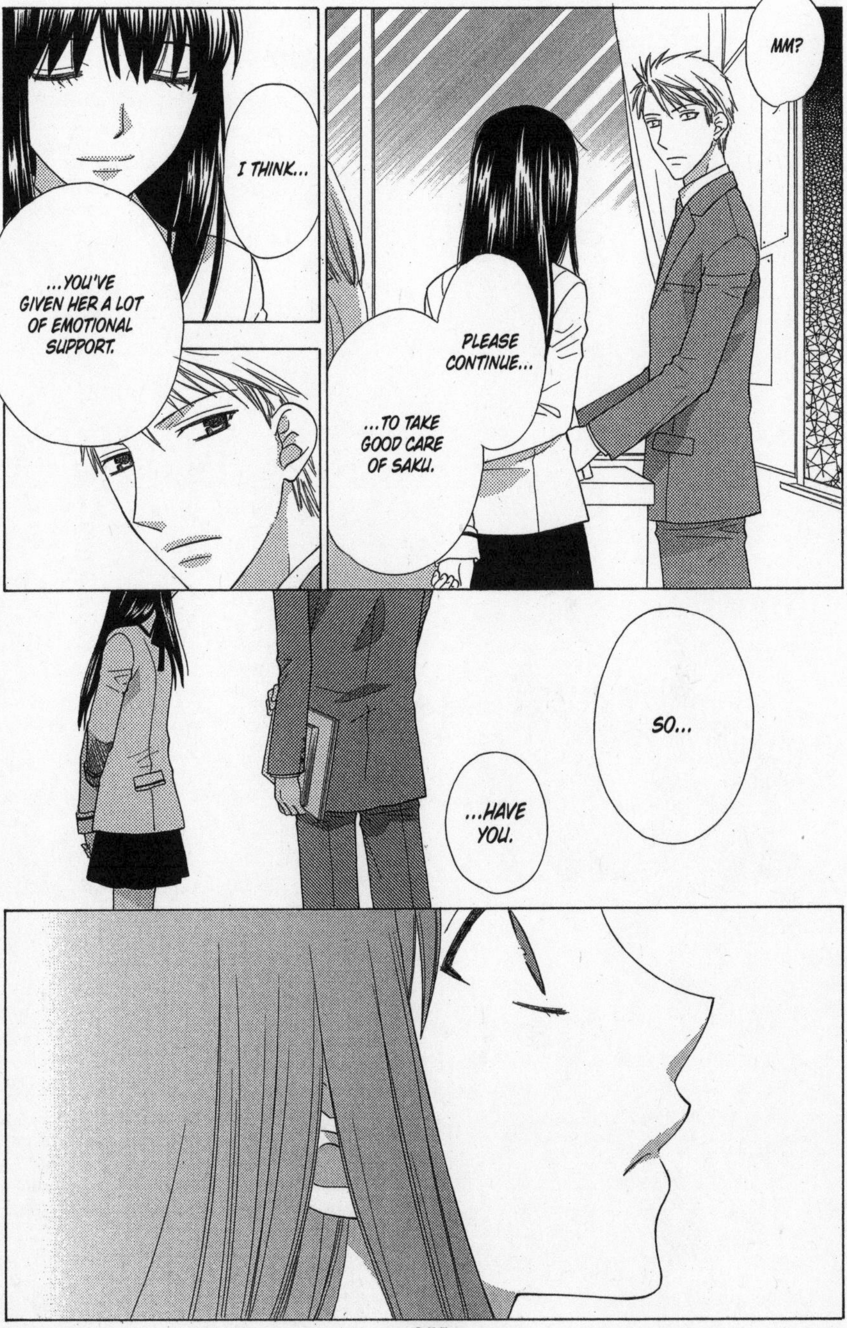
MM?
PLEASE CONTINUE...
...TO TAKE GOOD CARE OF SAKU.
I THINK...
...YOU'VE GIVEN HER A LOT OF EMOTIONAL SUPPORT.
SO...
...HAVE YOU.

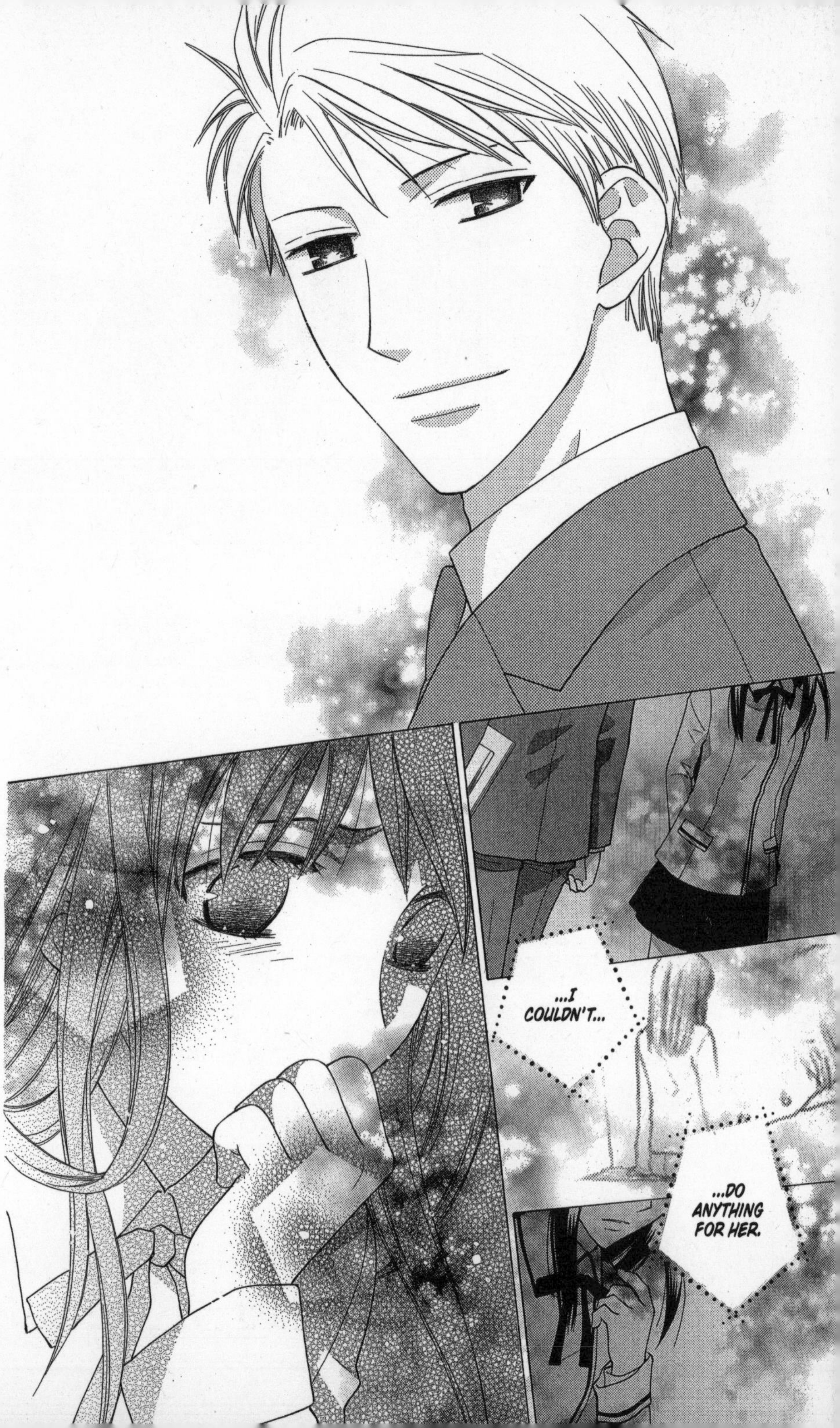
...I COULDN'T...
...DO ANYTHING FOR HER.

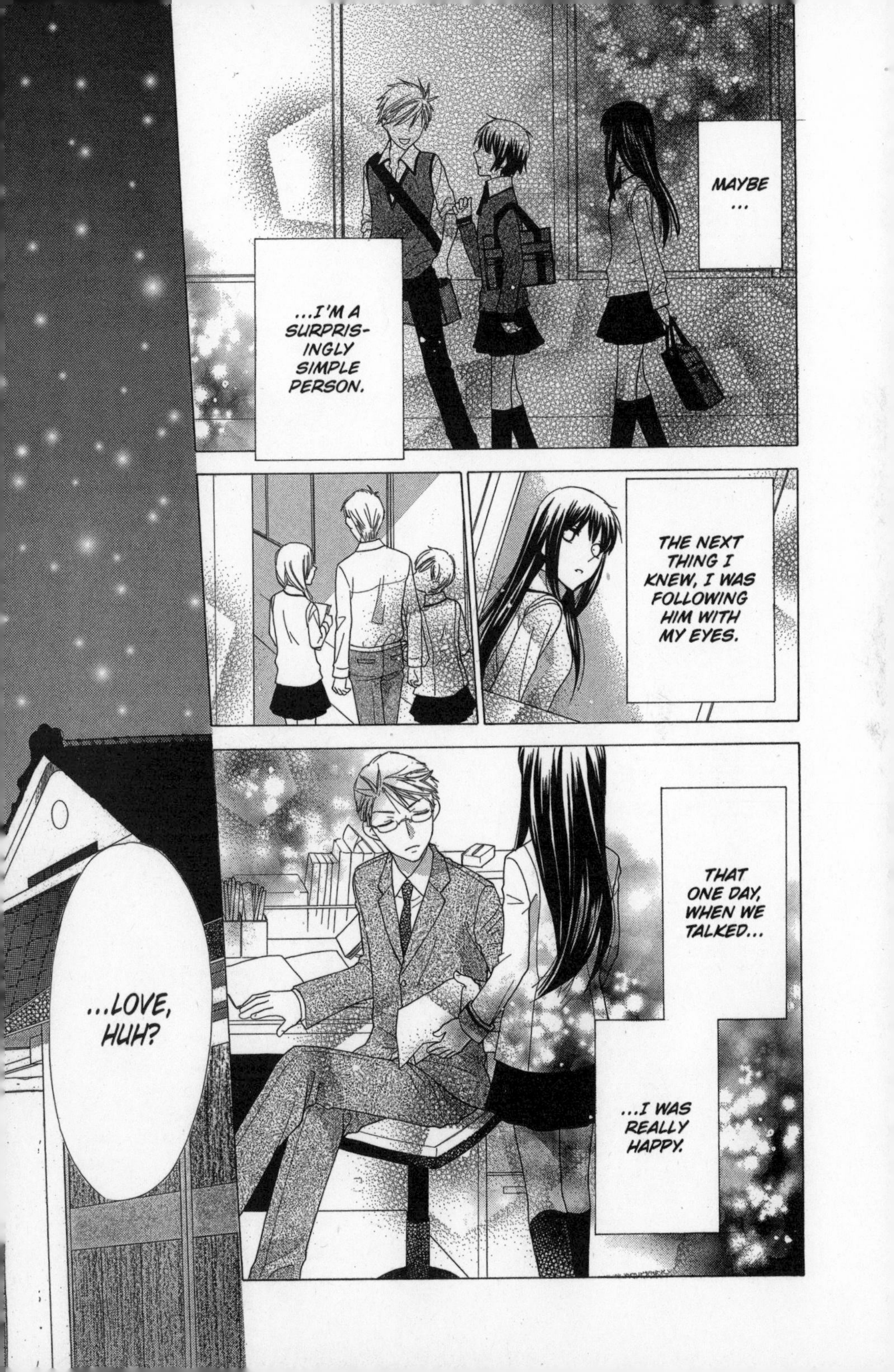

MAYBE ...
...I'M A SURPRIS-INGLY SIMPLE PERSON.
THE NEXT THING I KNEW, I WAS FOLLOWING HIM WITH MY EYES.
THAT ONE DAY, WHEN WE TALKED...
...I WAS REALLY HAPPY.
...LOVE, HUH?

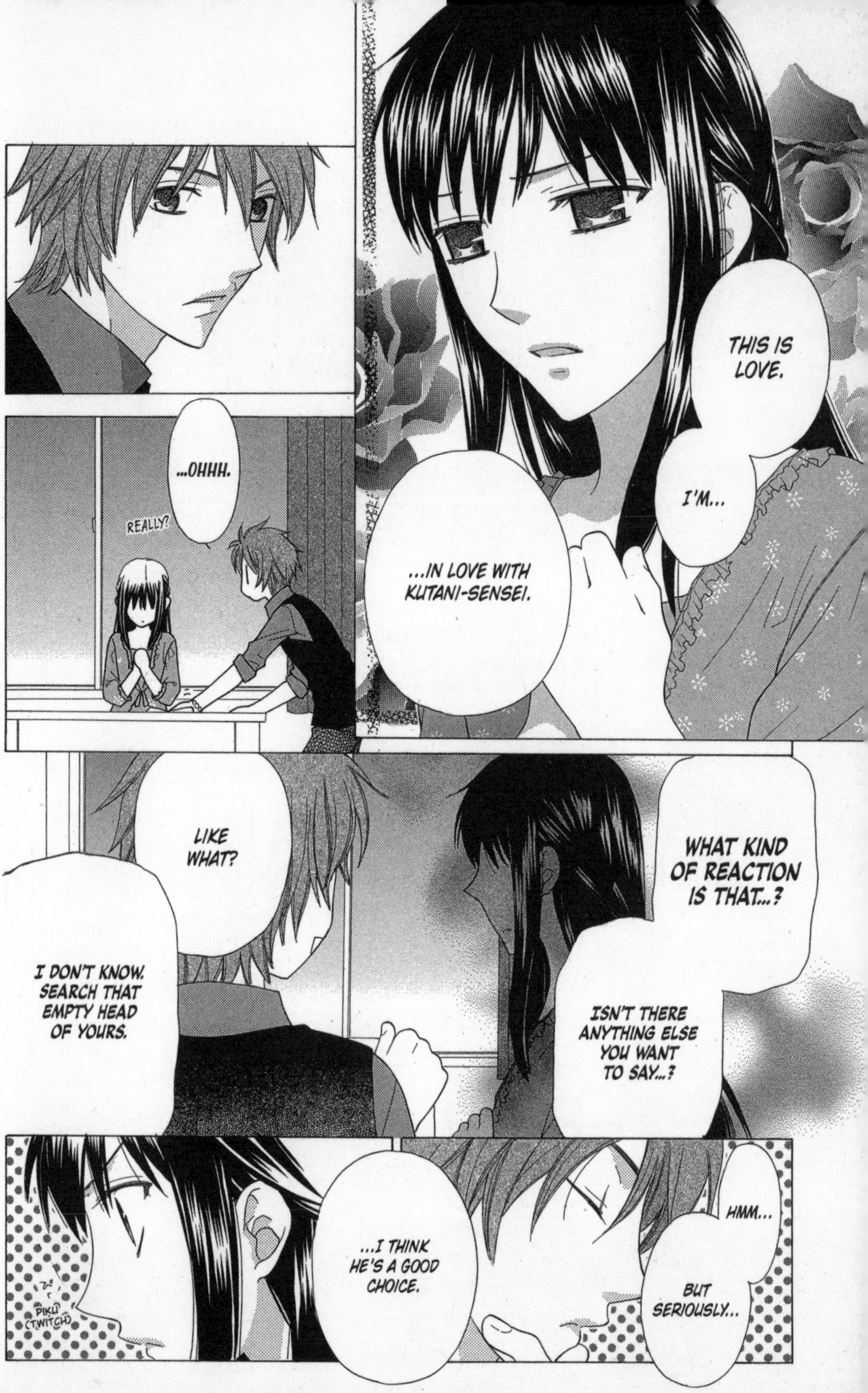
THIS IS LOVE.
I'M...
...IN LOVE WITH KUTANI-SENSEI.
...OHHH.
REALLY?
WHAT KIND OF REACTION IS THAT...?
ISN'T THERE ANYTHING ELSE YOU WANT TO SAY...?
LIKE WHAT?
I DON'T KNOW. SEARCH THAT EMPTY HEAD OF YOURS.
HMM...
BUT SERIOUSLY...
...I THINK HE'S A GOOD CHOICE.
PIKU (TWITCH)

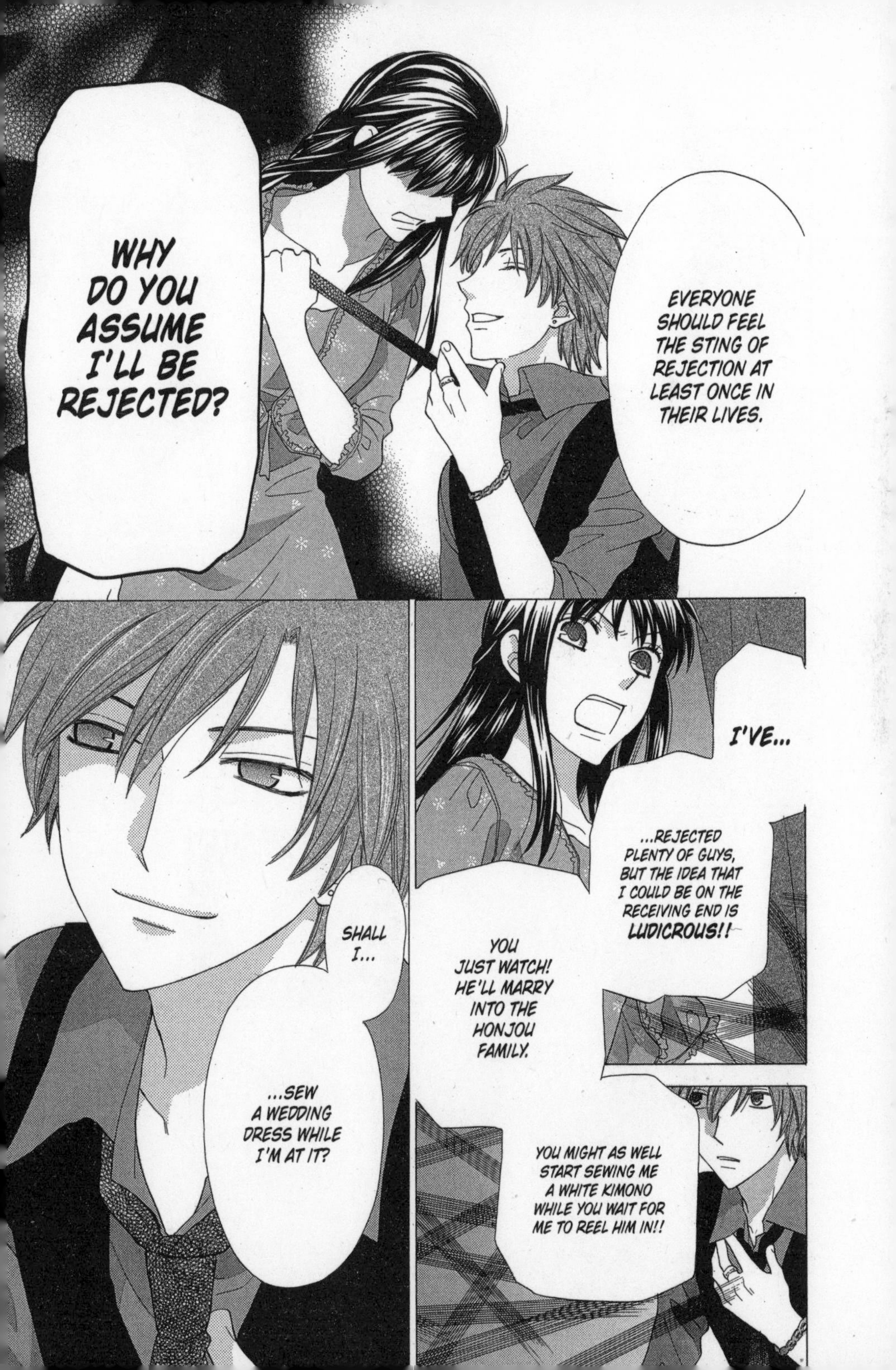
EVERYONE SHOULD FEEL THE STING OF REJECTION AT LEAST ONCE IN THEIR LIVES.
WHY DO YOU ASSUME I'LL BE REJECTED?
I'VE...
...REJECTED PLENTY OF GUYS, BUT THE IDEA THAT I COULD BE ON THE RECEIVING END IS LUDICROUS!!
YOU JUST WATCH! HE'LL MARRY INTO THE HONJOU FAMILY.
YOU MIGHT AS WELL START SEWING ME A WHITE KIMONO WHILE YOU WAIT FOR ME TO REEL HIM IN!!
SHALL I...
...SEW A WEDDING DRESS WHILE I'M AT IT?

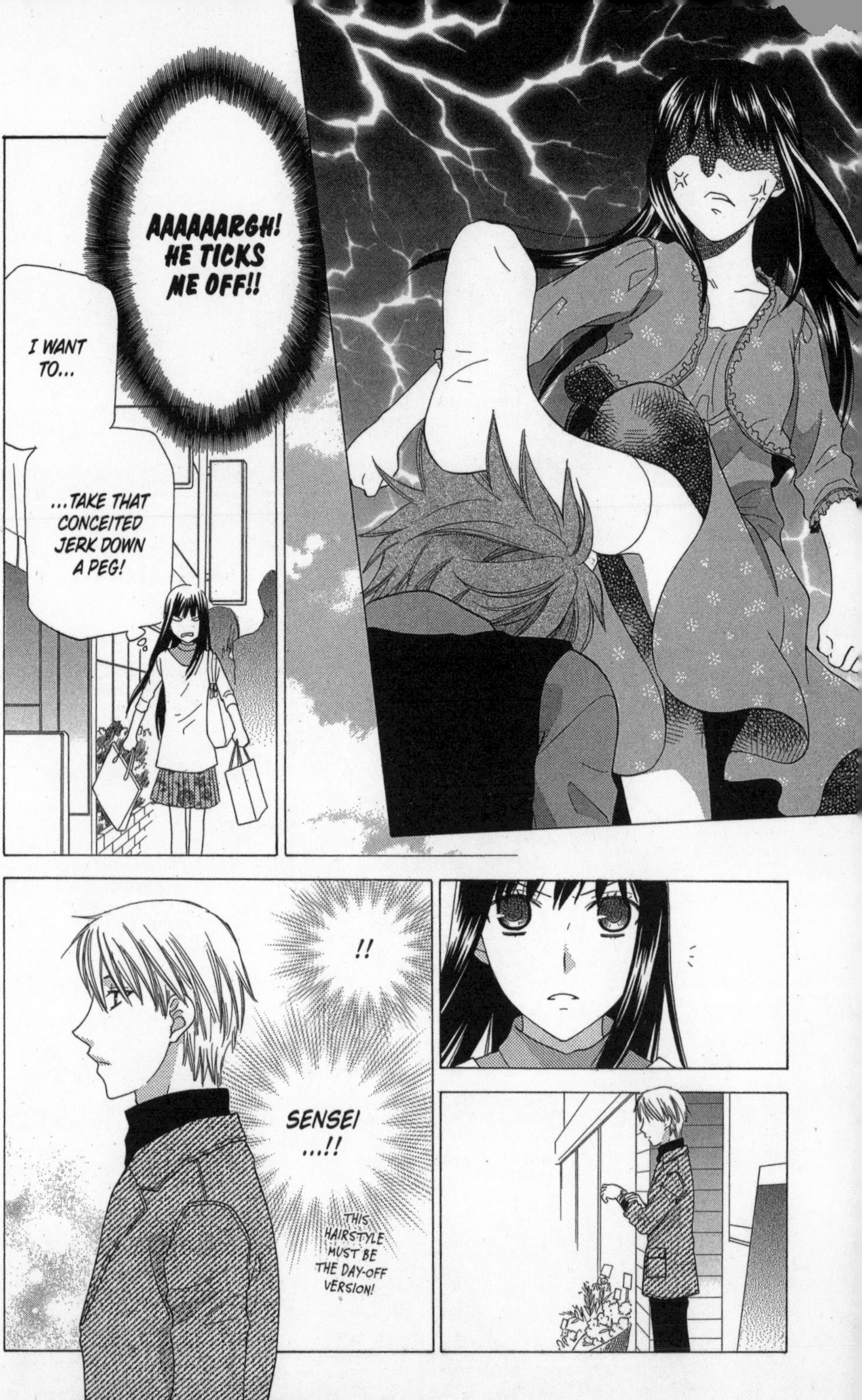
AAAAAARGH! HE TICKS ME OFF!!
I WANT TO...
...TAKE THAT CONCEITED JERK DOWN A PEG!
!!
SENSEI ...!!
THIS HAIRSTYLE MUST BE THE DAY-OFF VERSION!

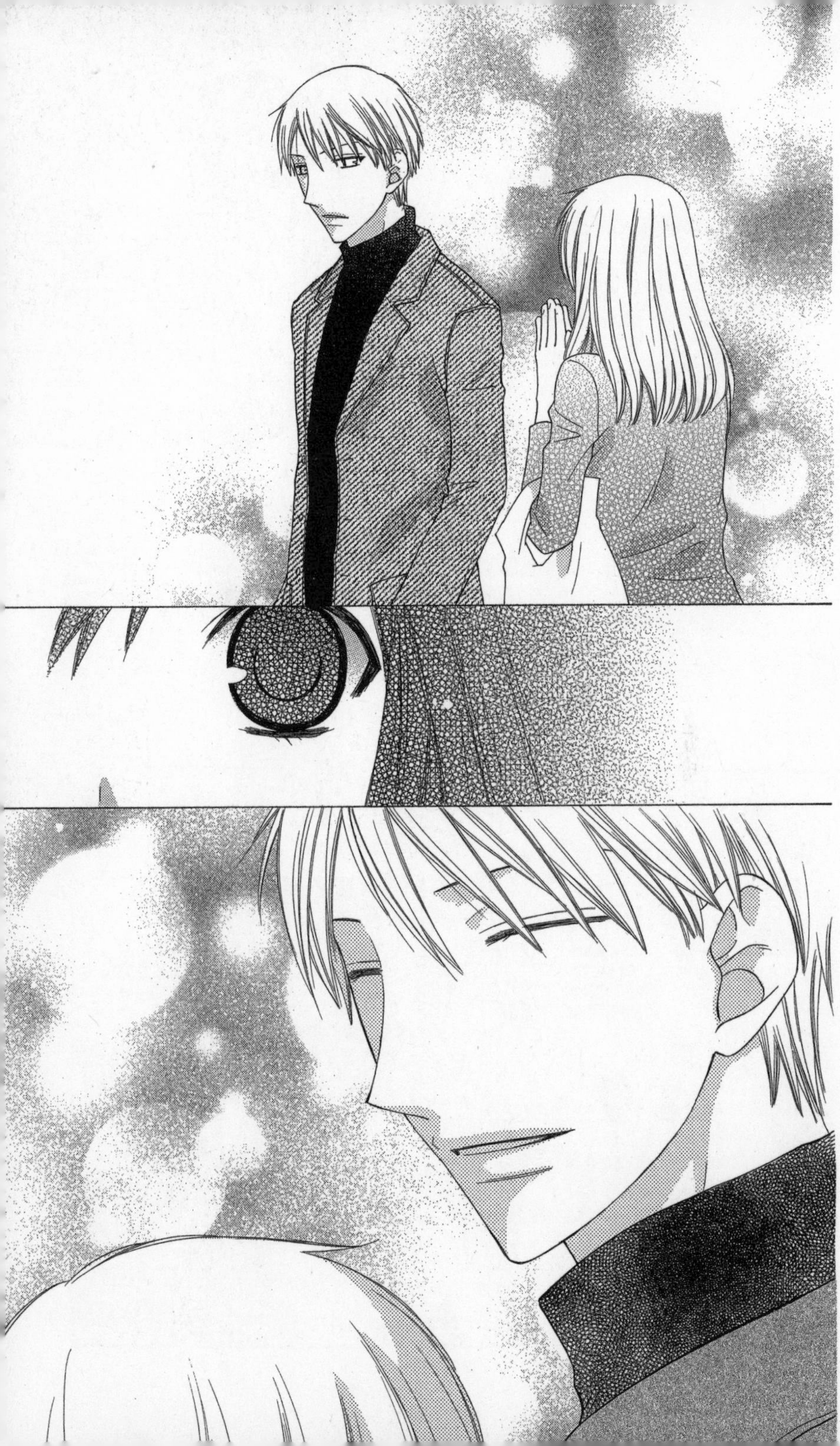

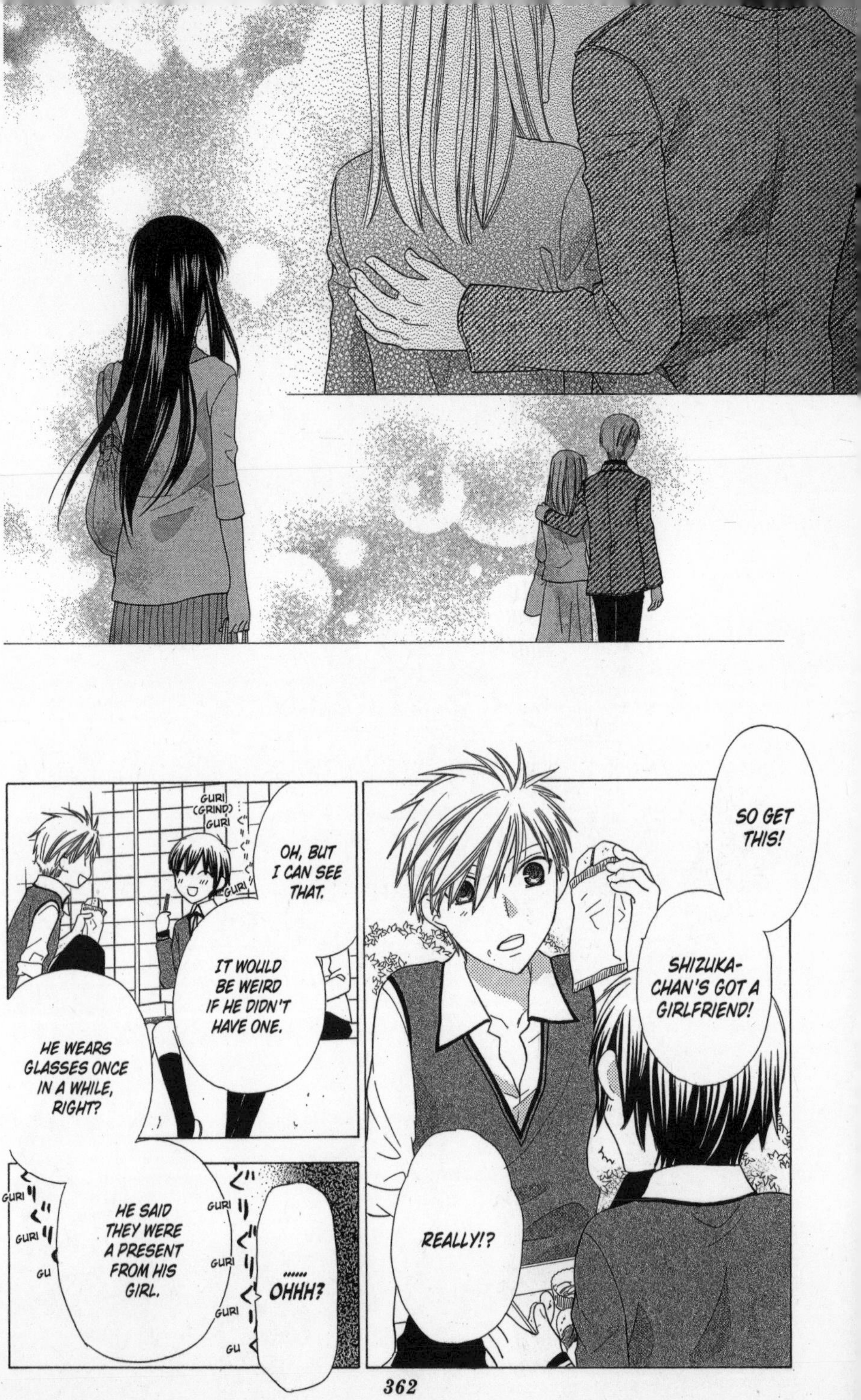
SO GET THIS!
SHIZUKA-CHAN'S GOT A GIRLFRIEND!
REALLY!?
GURI (GRIND) GURI
GURI
OH, BUT I CAN SEE THAT.
IT WOULD BE WEIRD IF HE DIDN'T HAVE ONE.
HE WEARS GLASSES ONCE IN A WHILE, RIGHT?
GURI GURI GU
HE SAID THEY WERE A PRESENT FROM HIS GIRL.
GURI GURI GURI GU
......OHHH?

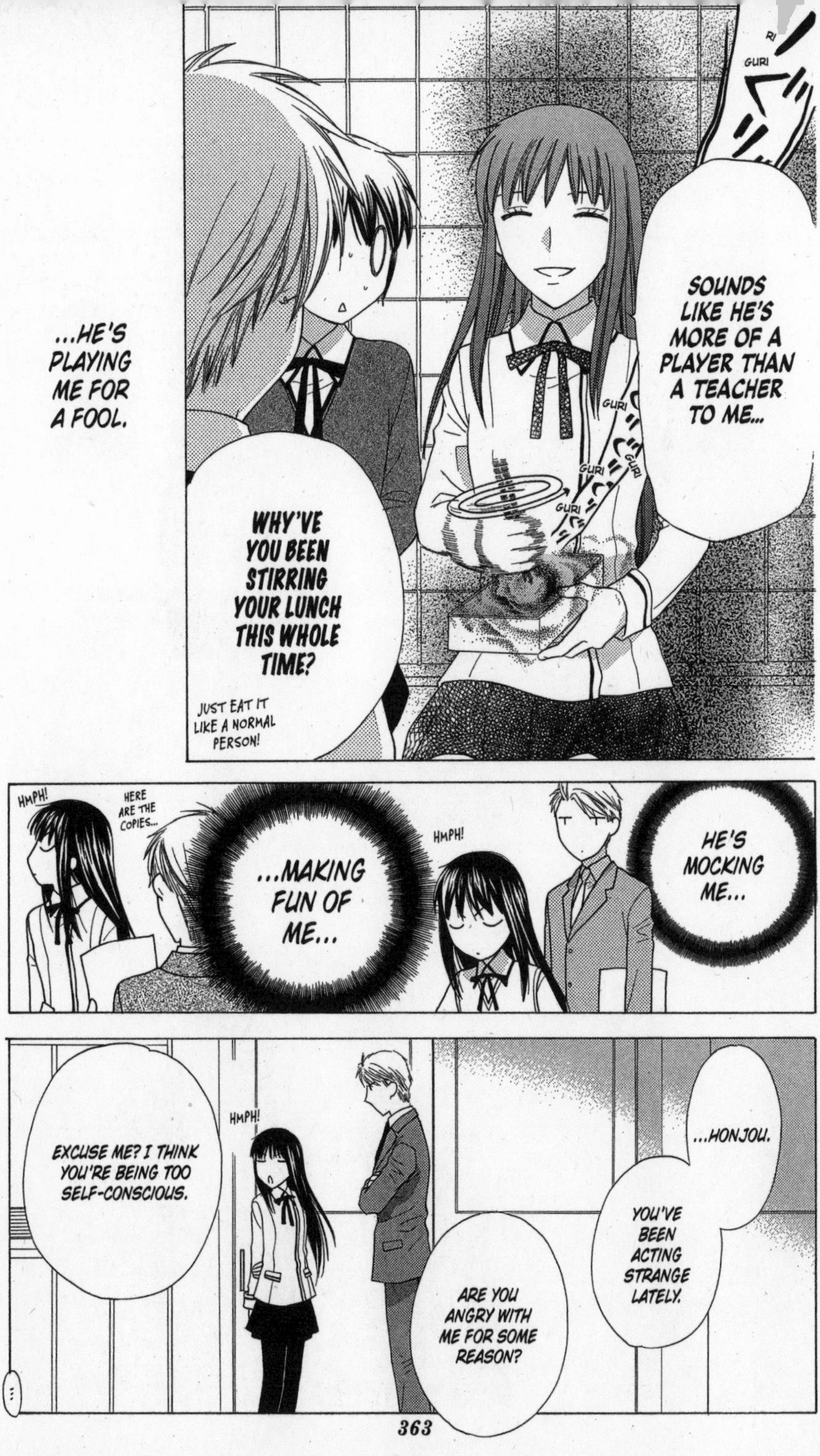
RI
GURI
SOUNDS LIKE HE'S MORE OF A PLAYER THAN A TEACHER TO ME...
GURI
GURI
GURI
GURI
WHY'VE YOU BEEN STIRRING YOUR LUNCH THIS WHOLE TIME?
JUST EAT IT LIKE A NORMAL PERSON!
...HE'S PLAYING ME FOR A FOOL.
HE'S MOCKING ME...
HMPH!
...MAKING FUN OF ME...
HERE ARE THE COPIES...
HMPH!
...HONJOU.
YOU'VE BEEN ACTING STRANGE LATELY.
ARE YOU ANGRY WITH ME FOR SOME REASON?
HMPH!
EXCUSE ME? I THINK YOU'RE BEING TOO SELF-CONSCIOUS.
...

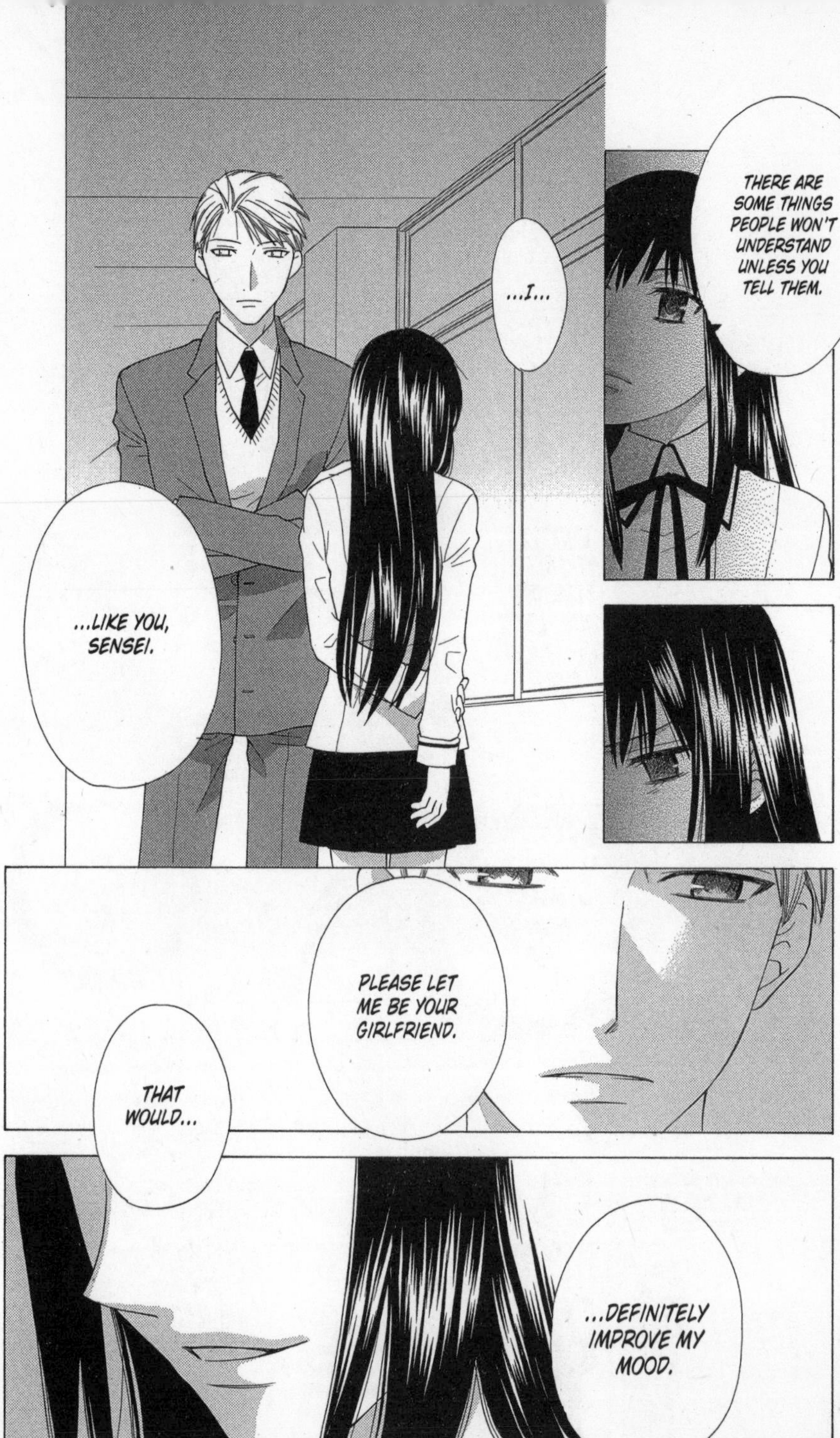
THERE ARE SOME THINGS PEOPLE WON'T UNDERSTAND UNLESS YOU TELL THEM.
...I...
...LIKE YOU, SENSEI.
PLEASE LET ME BE YOUR GIRLFRIEND.
THAT WOULD...
...DEFINITELY IMPROVE MY MOOD.

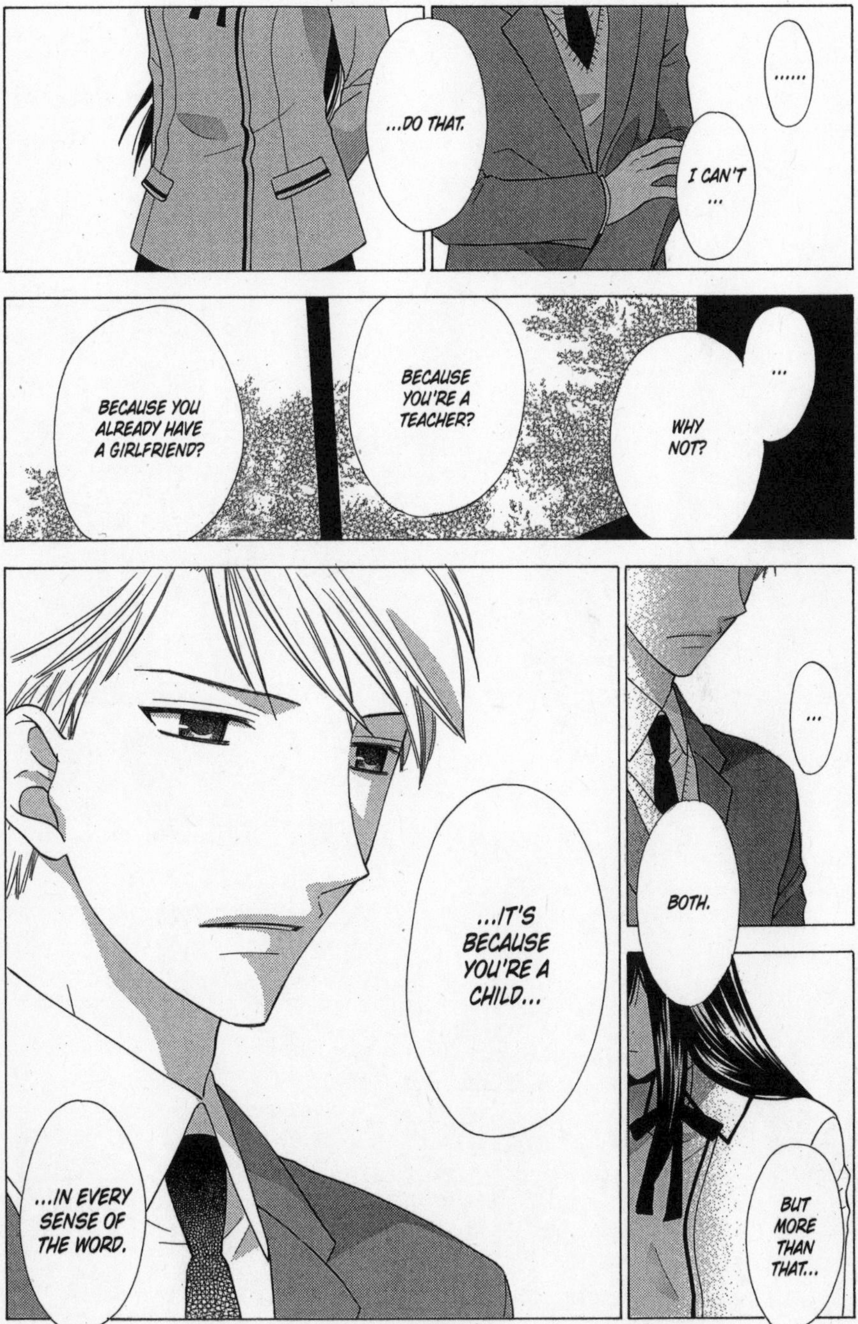
......
I CAN'T ...
...DO THAT.
...
WHY NOT?
BECAUSE YOU'RE A TEACHER?
BECAUSE YOU ALREADY HAVE A GIRLFRIEND?
...
BOTH.
BUT MORE THAN THAT...
...IT'S BECAUSE YOU'RE A CHILD...
...IN EVERY SENSE OF THE WORD.

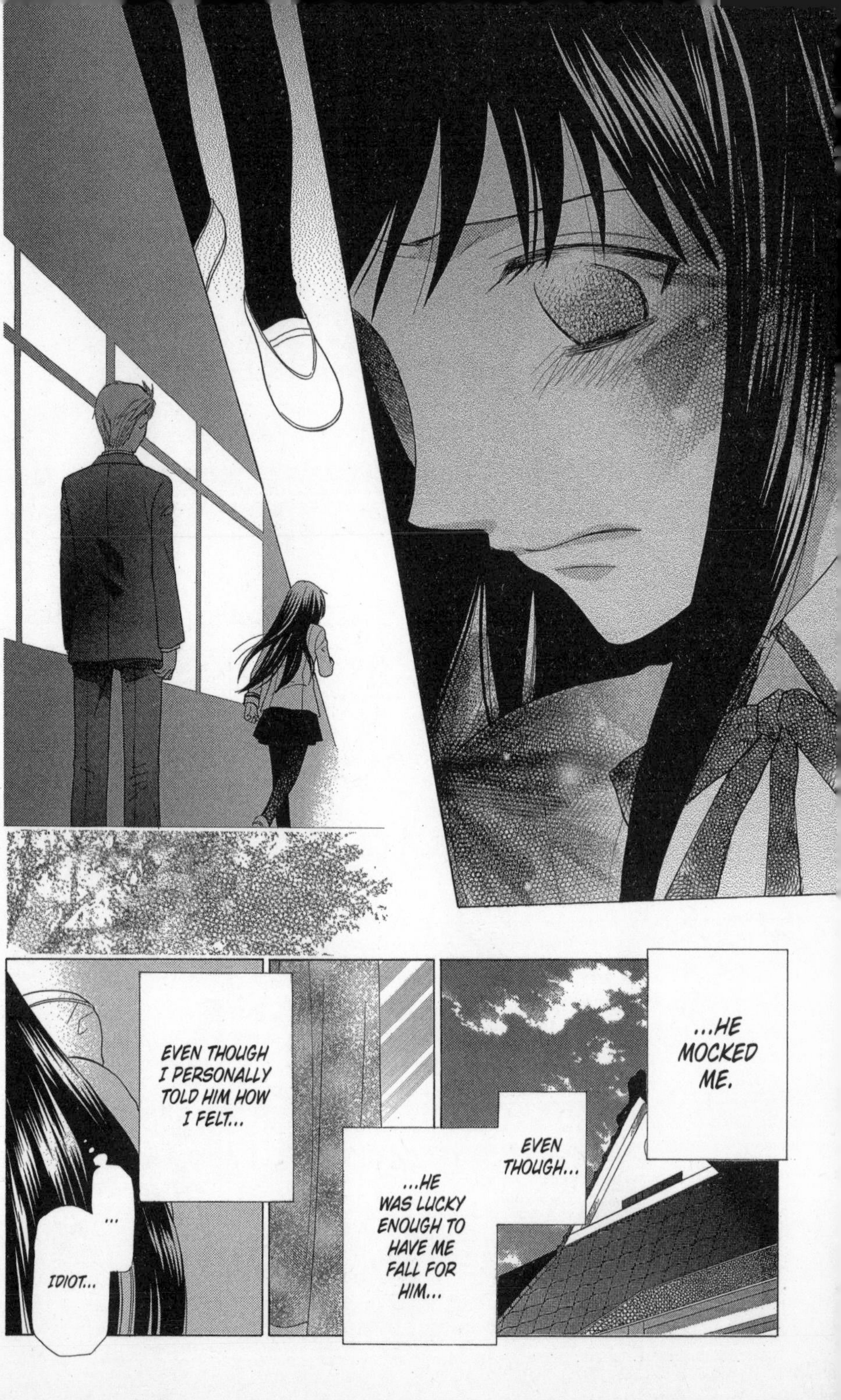
...HE MOCKED ME.
EVEN THOUGH...
...HE WAS LUCKY ENOUGH TO HAVE ME FALL FOR HIM...
EVEN THOUGH I PERSONALLY TOLD HIM HOW I FELT...
...
IDIOT...

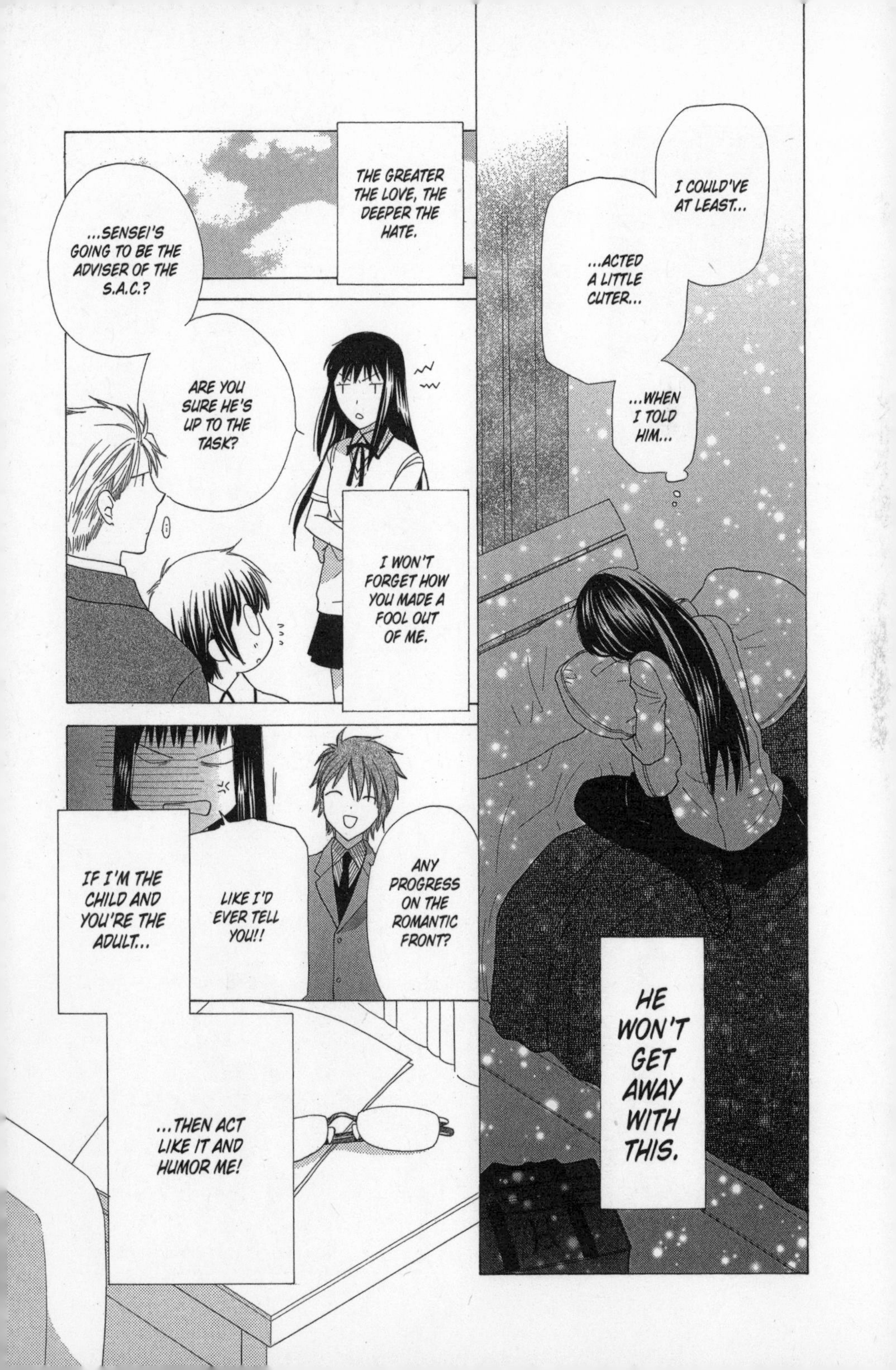

I COULD'VE AT LEAST...
...ACTED A LITTLE CUTER...
...WHEN I TOLD HIM...
HE WON'T GET AWAY WITH THIS.
THE GREATER THE LOVE, THE DEEPER THE HATE.
...SENSEI'S GOING TO BE THE ADVISER OF THE S.A.C.?
ARE YOU SURE HE'S UP TO THE TASK?
I WON'T FORGET HOW YOU MADE A FOOL OUT OF ME.
ANY PROGRESS ON THE ROMANTIC FRONT?
LIKE I'D EVER TELL YOU!!
IF I'M THE CHILD AND YOU'RE THE ADULT...
...THEN ACT LIKE IT AND HUMOR ME!

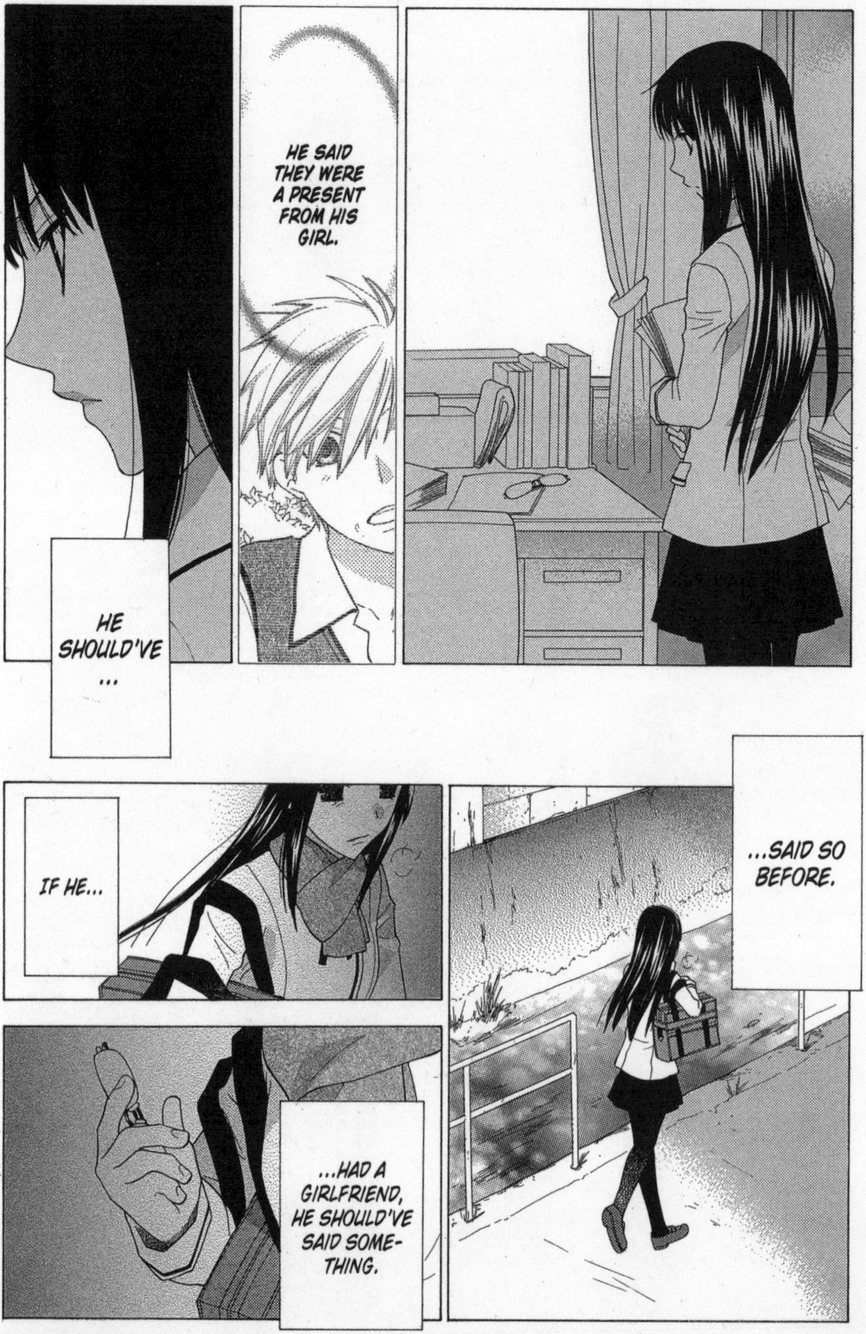
HE SAID THEY WERE A PRESENT FROM HIS GIRL.
HE SHOULD'VE ...
...SAID SO BEFORE.
IF HE...
...HAD A GIRLFRIEND, HE SHOULD'VE SAID SOME-THING.

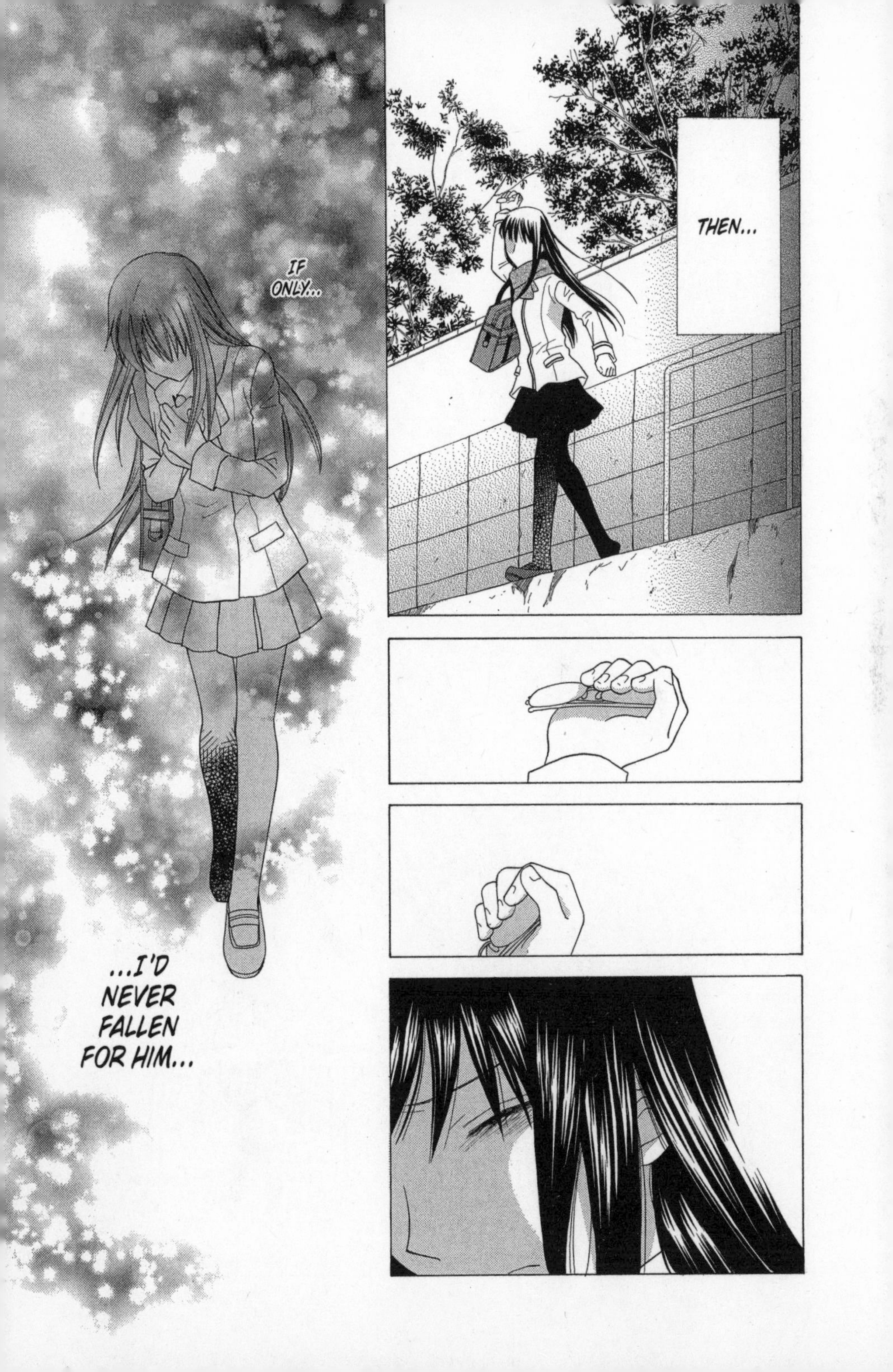
THEN...
IF ONLY...
...I'D NEVER FALLEN FOR HIM...

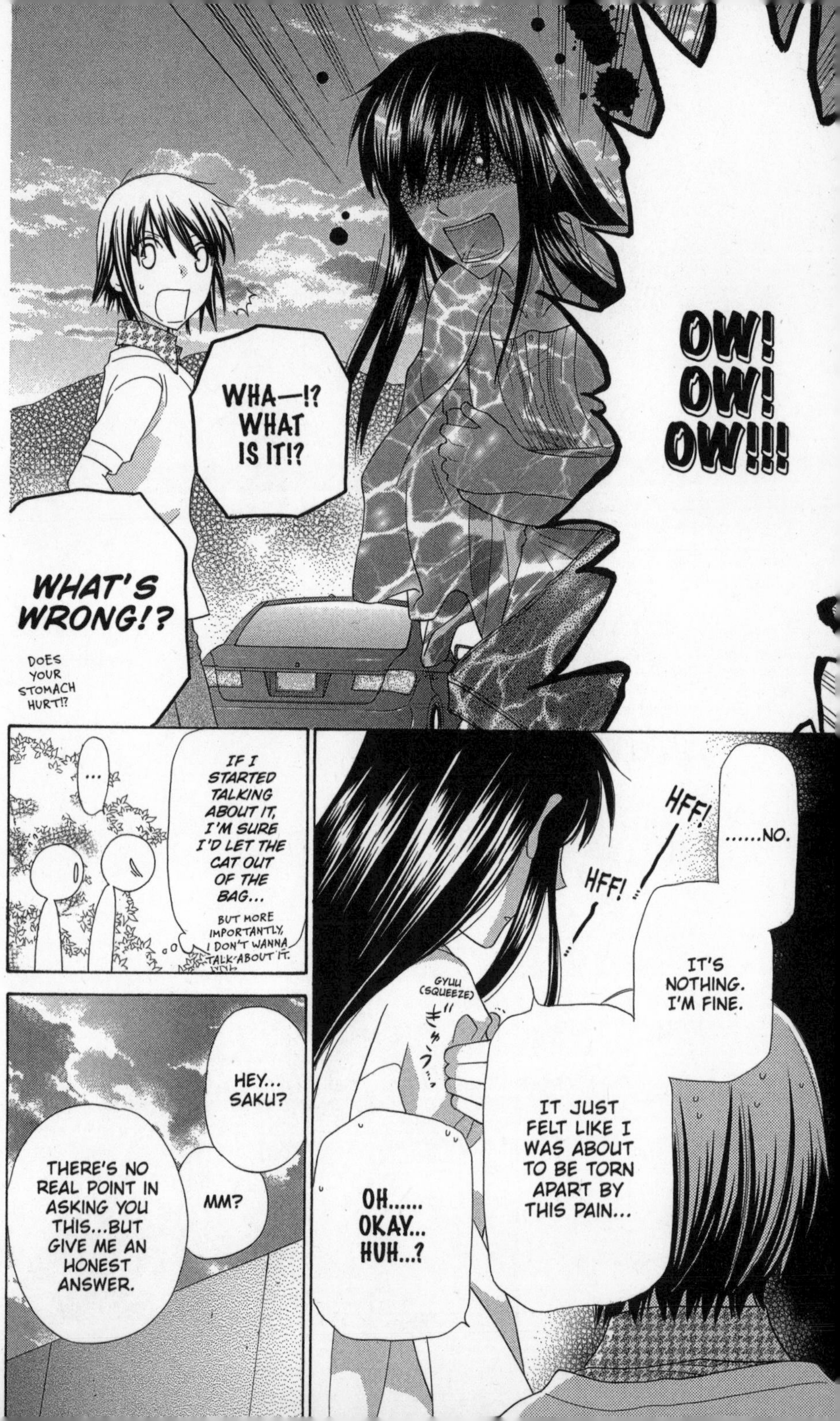
OW! OW! OW!!!
WHA—!? WHAT IS IT!?
WHAT'S WRONG!?
DOES YOUR STOMACH HURT!?
HFF!
HFF!
......NO.
IT'S NOTHING. I'M FINE.
GYUU (SQUEEZE)
IT JUST FELT LIKE I WAS ABOUT TO BE TORN APART BY THIS PAIN...
OH...... OKAY... HUH...?
IF I STARTED TALKING ABOUT IT, I'M SURE I'D LET THE CAT OUT OF THE BAG...
BUT MORE IMPORTANTLY, I DON'T WANNA TALK ABOUT IT.
...
HEY... SAKU?
MM?
THERE'S NO REAL POINT IN ASKING YOU THIS...BUT GIVE ME AN HONEST ANSWER.

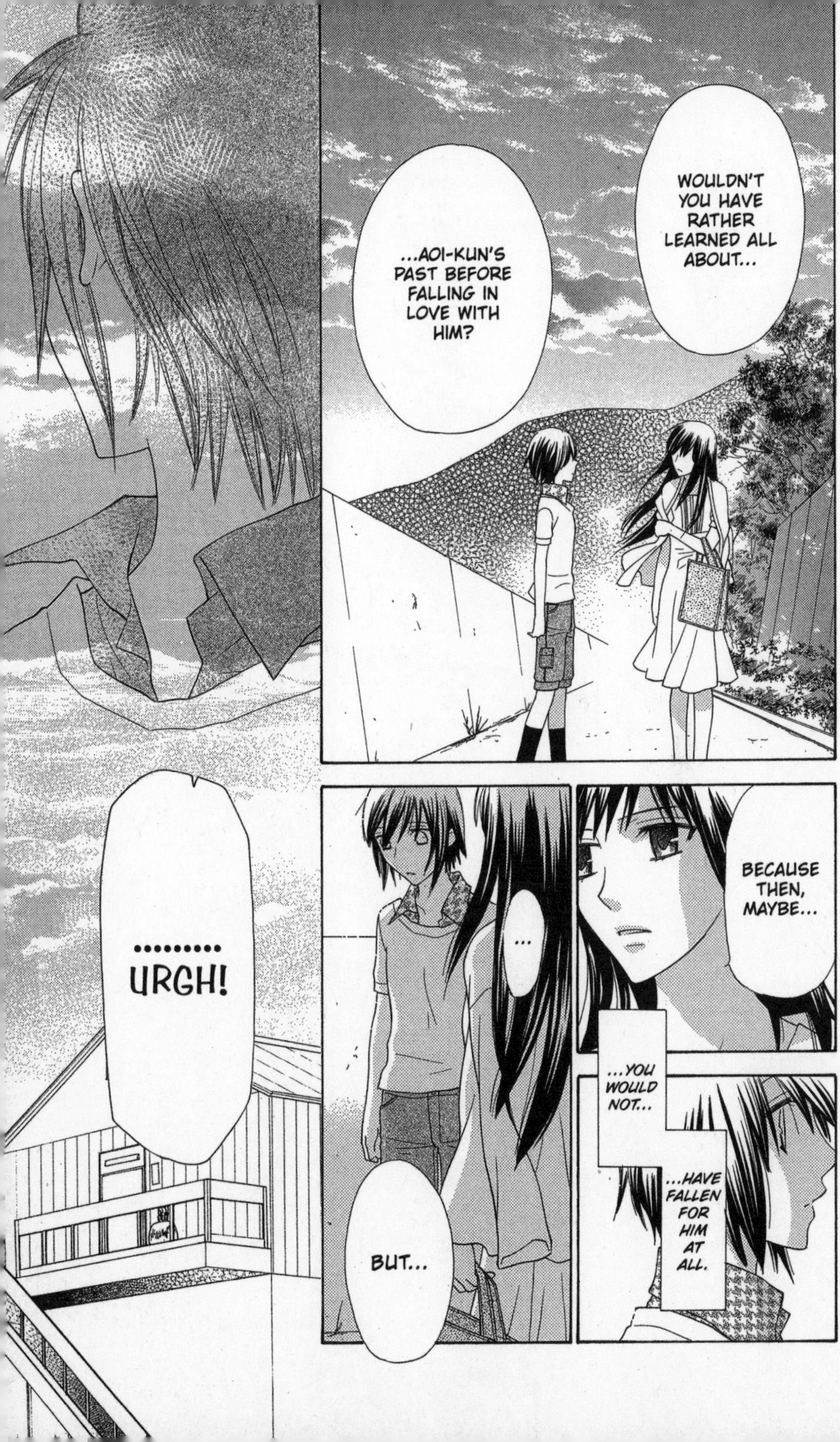
WOULDN'T YOU HAVE RATHER LEARNED ALL ABOUT...
...AOI-KUN'S PAST BEFORE FALLING IN LOVE WITH HIM?
BECAUSE THEN, MAYBE...
...YOU WOULD NOT...
...HAVE FALLEN FOR HIM AT ALL.
...
BUT...
....
URGH!

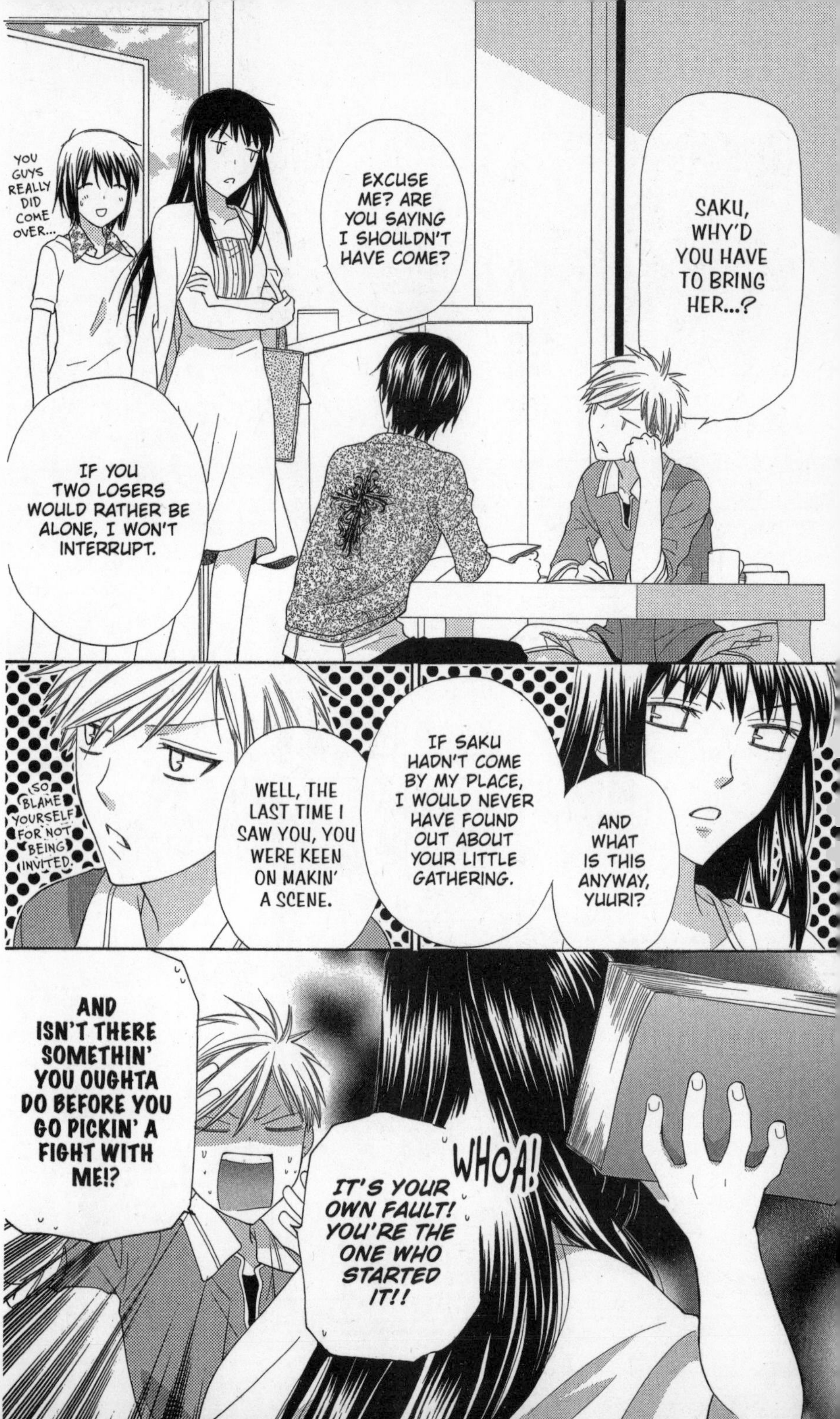
SAKU, WHY'D YOU HAVE TO BRING HER...?
EXCUSE ME? ARE YOU SAYING I SHOULDN'T HAVE COME?
YOU GUYS REALLY DID COME OVER...
IF YOU TWO LOSERS WOULD RATHER BE ALONE, I WON'T INTERRUPT.
AND WHAT IS THIS ANYWAY, YUURI?
IF SAKU HADN'T COME BY MY PLACE, I WOULD NEVER HAVE FOUND OUT ABOUT YOUR LITTLE GATHERING.
WELL, THE LAST TIME I SAW YOU, YOU WERE KEEN ON MAKIN' A SCENE.
SO BLAME YOURSELF FOR NOT BEING INVITED.
WHOA!
IT'S YOUR OWN FAULT! YOU'RE THE ONE WHO STARTED IT!!
AND ISN'T THERE SOMETHIN' YOU OUGHTA DO BEFORE YOU GO PICKIN' A FIGHT WITH ME!?

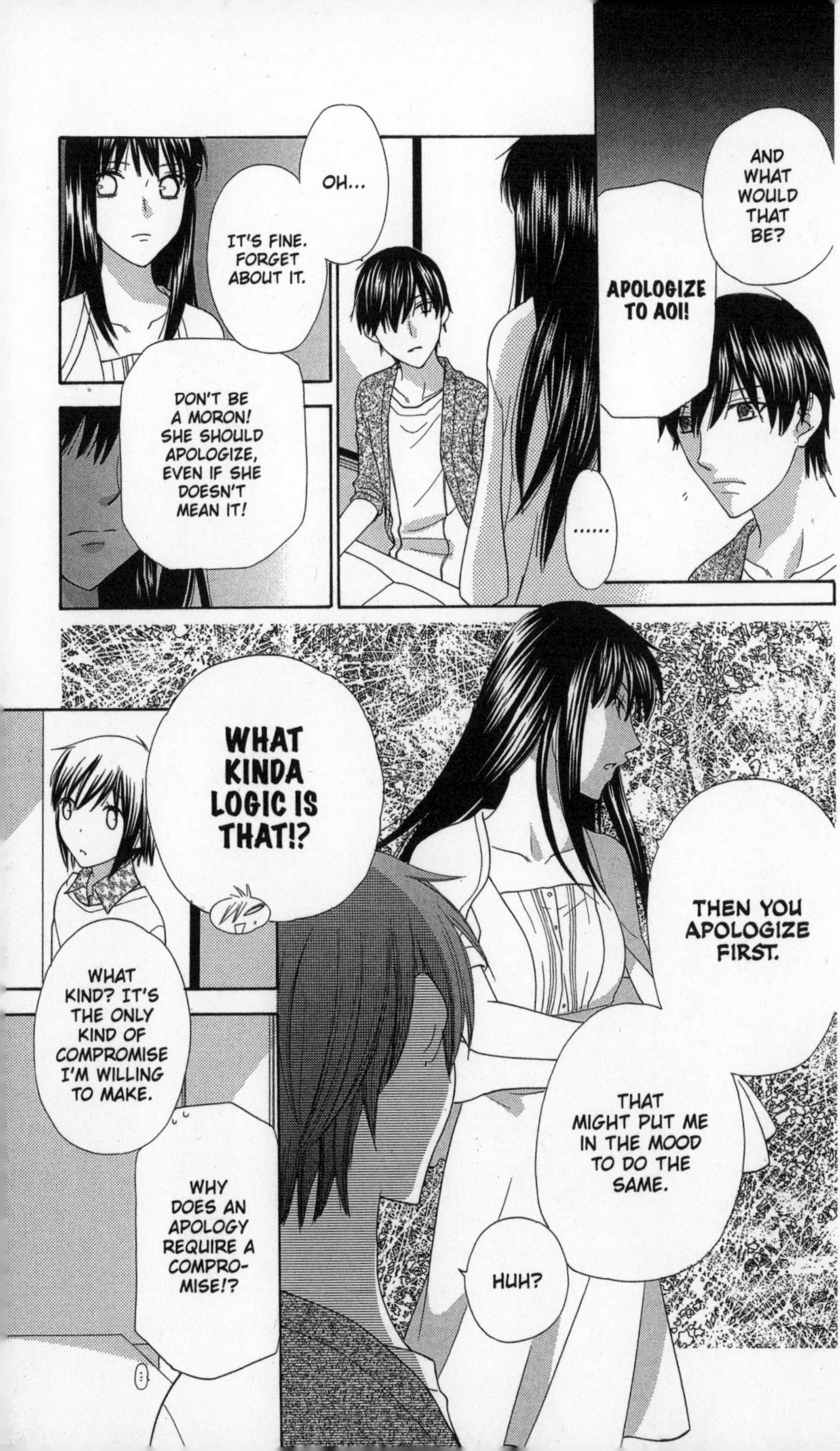

AND WHAT WOULD THAT BE?
APOLOGIZE TO AOI!
......
OH...
IT'S FINE. FORGET ABOUT IT.
DON'T BE A MORON! SHE SHOULD APOLOGIZE, EVEN IF SHE DOESN'T MEAN IT!
THEN YOU APOLOGIZE FIRST.
THAT MIGHT PUT ME IN THE MOOD TO DO THE SAME.
HUH?
WHAT KINDA LOGIC IS THAT!?
WHAT KIND? IT'S THE ONLY KIND OF COMPROMISE I'M WILLING TO MAKE.
WHY DOES AN APOLOGY REQUIRE A COMPROMISE!?
...

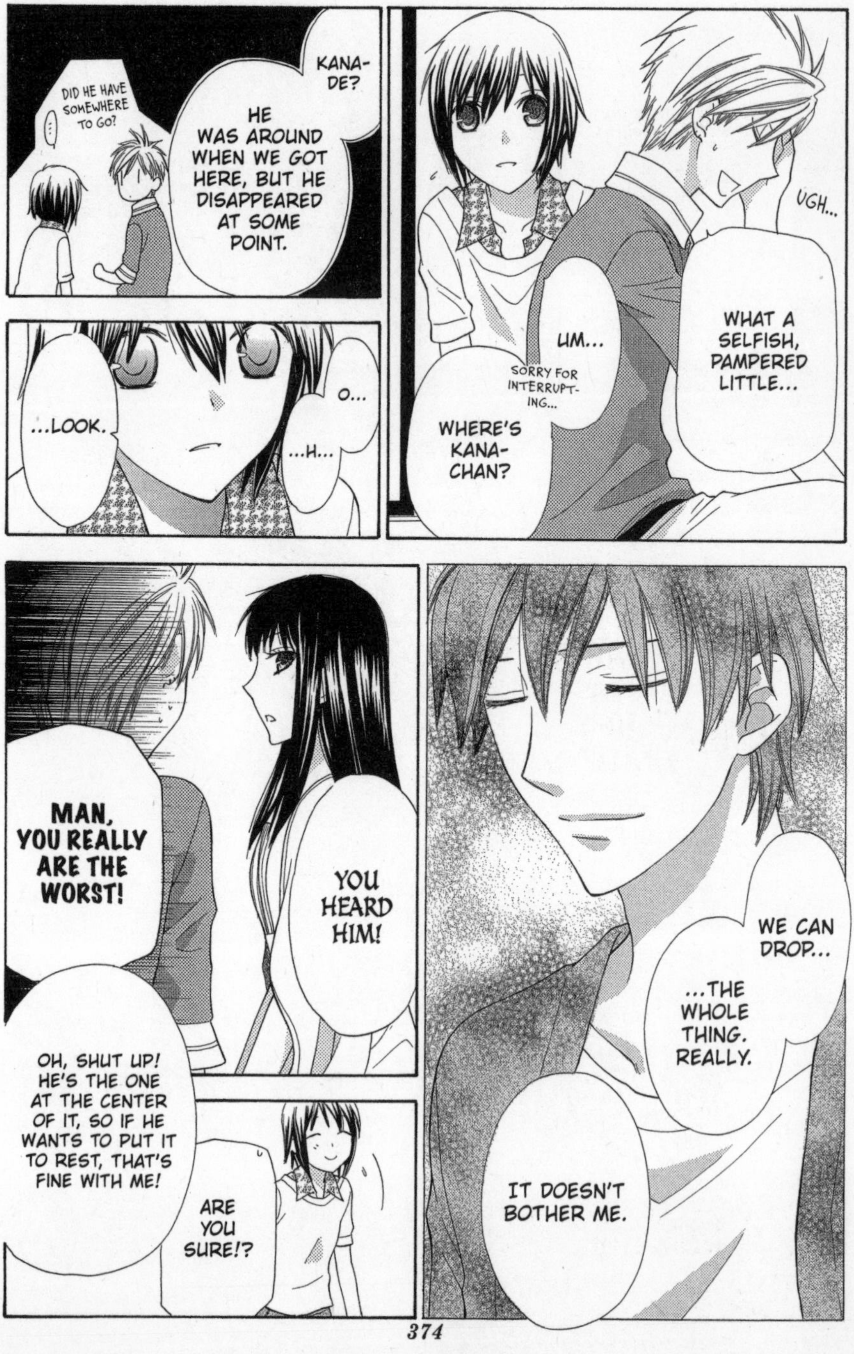
UGH...
WHAT A SELFISH, PAMPERED LITTLE...
UM...
SORRY FOR INTERRUPTING...
WHERE'S KANA-CHAN?
KANA-DE?
HE WAS AROUND WHEN WE GOT HERE, BUT HE DISAPPEARED AT SOME POINT.
DID HE HAVE SOMEWHERE TO GO?
...
O...
...H...
...LOOK.
WE CAN DROP...
...THE WHOLE THING. REALLY.
IT DOESN'T BOTHER ME.
YOU HEARD HIM!
MAN, YOU REALLY ARE THE WORST!
ARE YOU SURE!?
OH, SHUT UP! HE'S THE ONE AT THE CENTER OF IT, SO IF HE WANTS TO PUT IT TO REST, THAT'S FINE WITH ME!

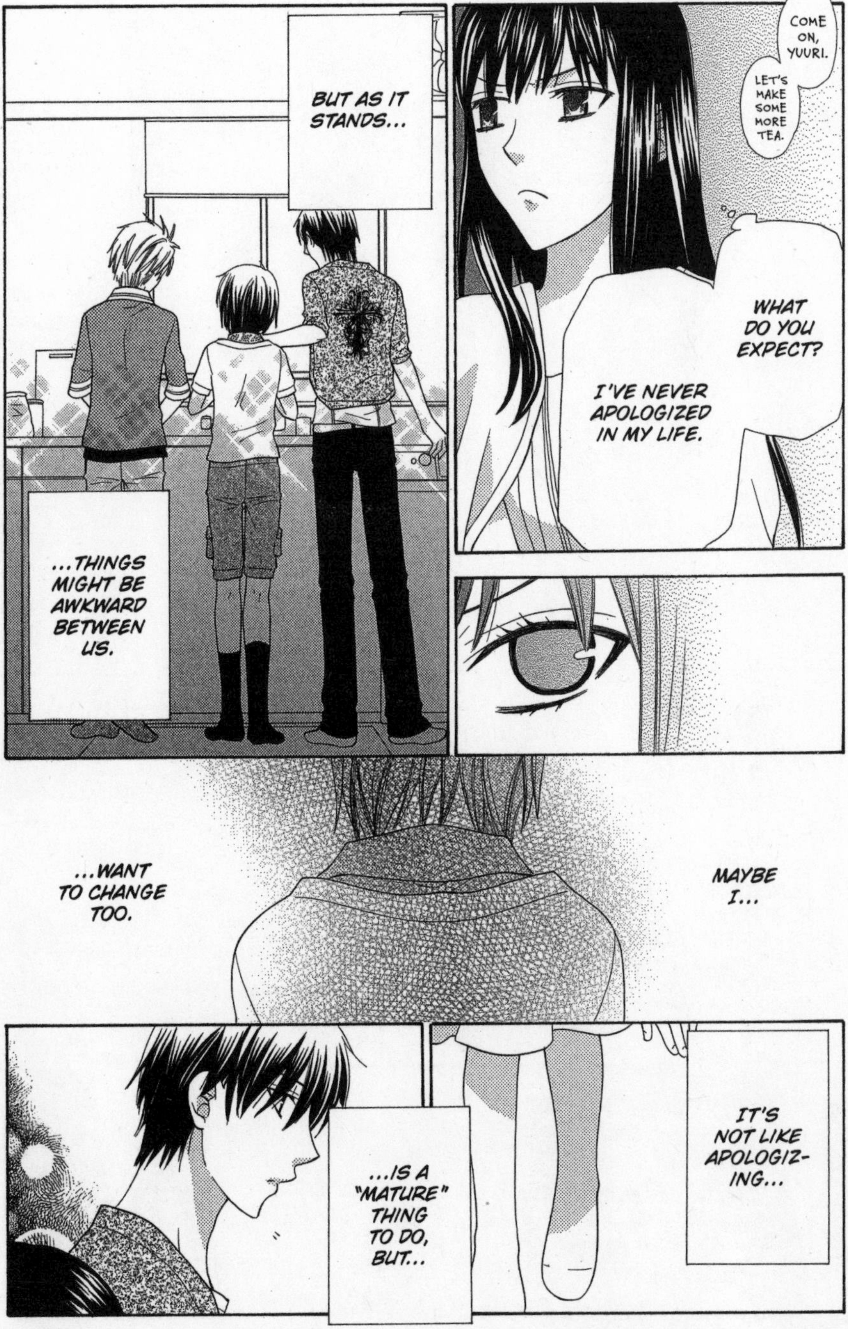
COME ON, YUURI.
LET'S MAKE SOME MORE TEA.
WHAT DO YOU EXPECT?
I'VE NEVER APOLOGIZED IN MY LIFE.
BUT AS IT STANDS...
...THINGS MIGHT BE AWKWARD BETWEEN US.
MAYBE I...
...WANT TO CHANGE TOO.
IT'S NOT LIKE APOLOGIZ-ING...
...IS A "MATURE" THING TO DO, BUT...

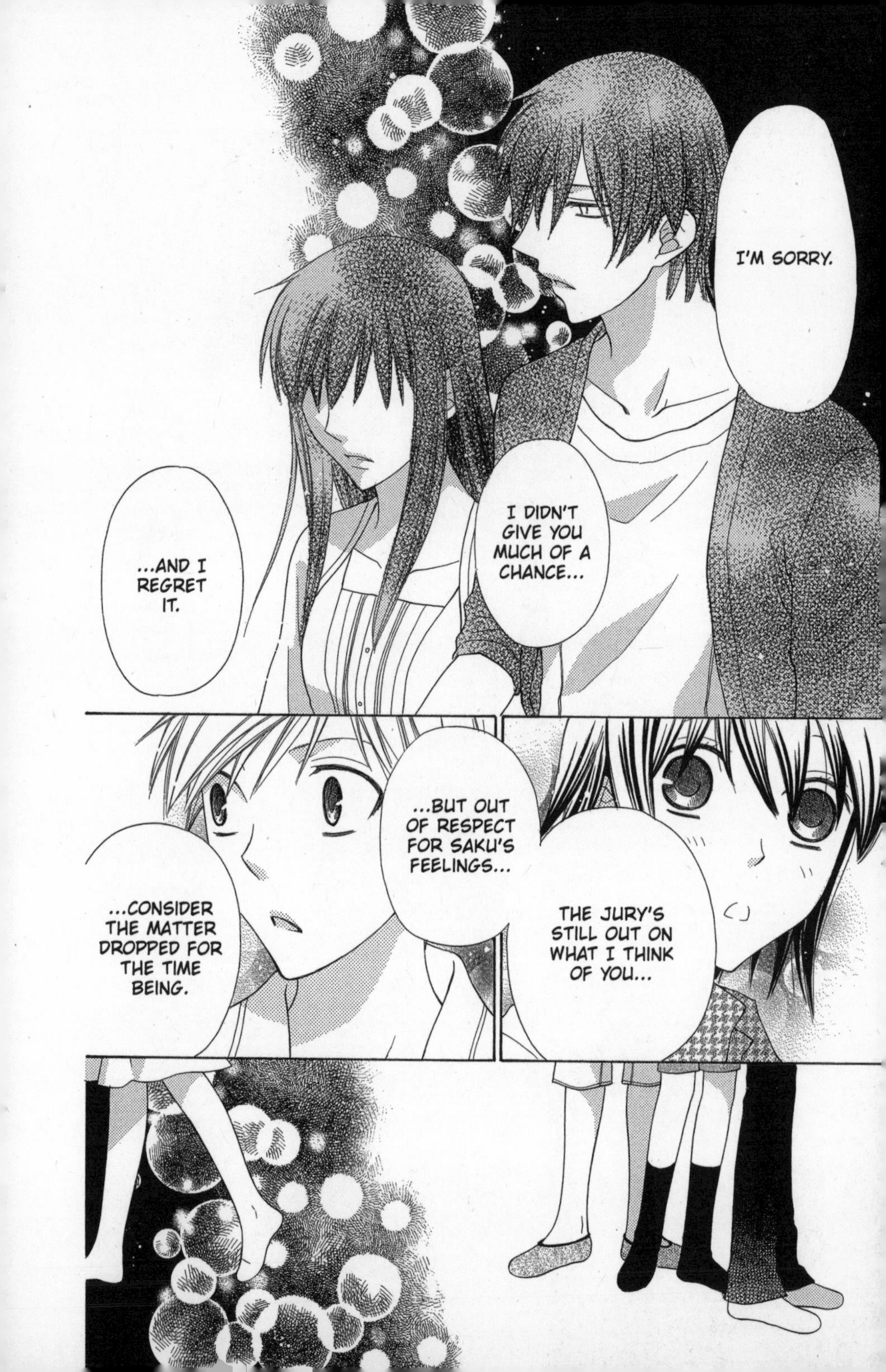
I'M SORRY.
I DIDN'T GIVE YOU MUCH OF A CHANCE...
...AND I REGRET IT.
THE JURY'S STILL OUT ON WHAT I THINK OF YOU...
...BUT OUT OF RESPECT FOR SAKU'S FEELINGS...
...CONSIDER THE MATTER DROPPED FOR THE TIME BEING.

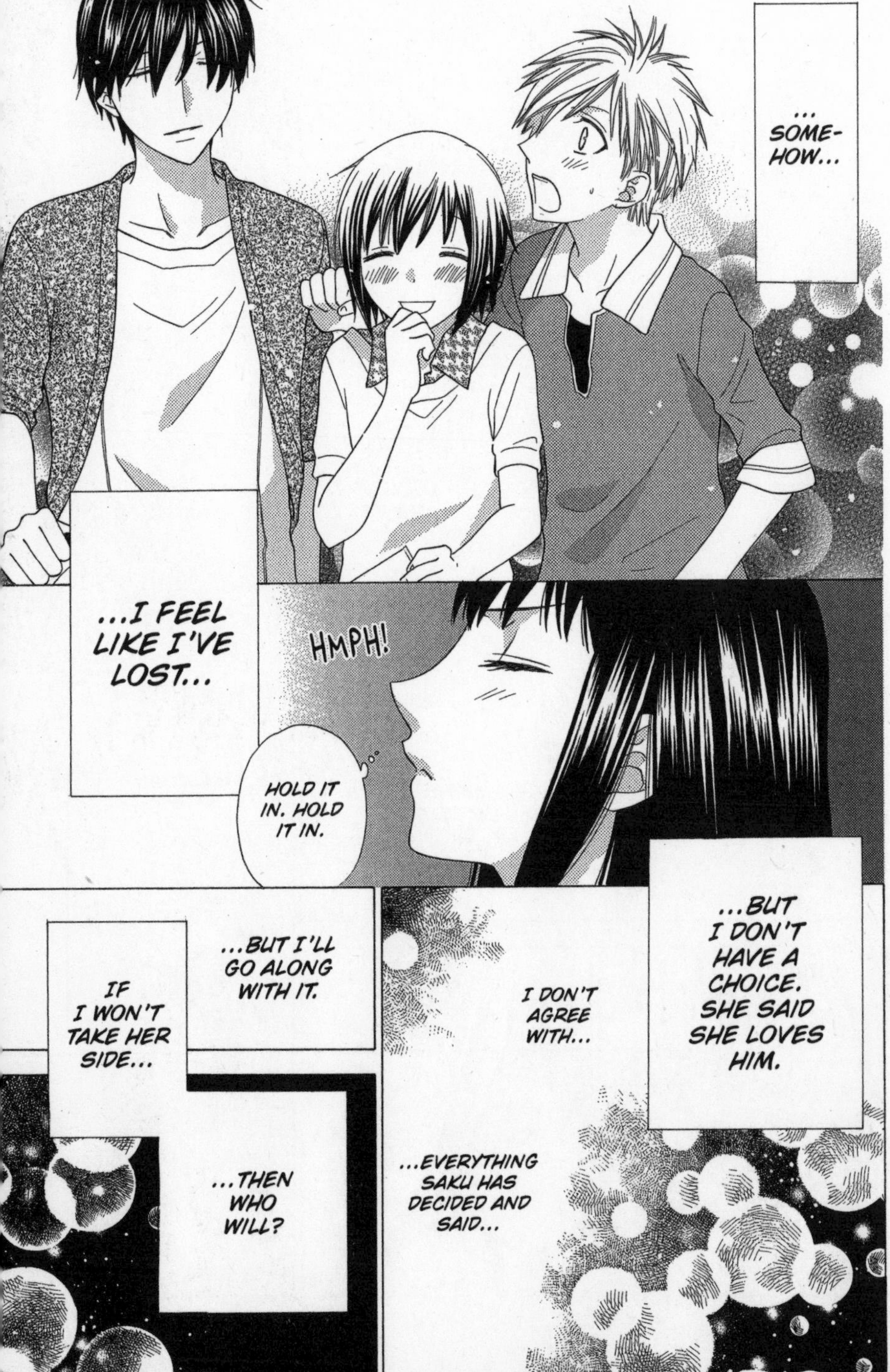
...SOME-HOW...
...I FEEL LIKE I'VE LOST...
HMPH!
HOLD IT IN. HOLD IT IN.
...BUT I DON'T HAVE A CHOICE. SHE SAID SHE LOVES HIM.
I DON'T AGREE WITH...
...EVERYTHING SAKU HAS DECIDED AND SAID...
...BUT I'LL GO ALONG WITH IT.
IF I WON'T TAKE HER SIDE...
...THEN WHO WILL?

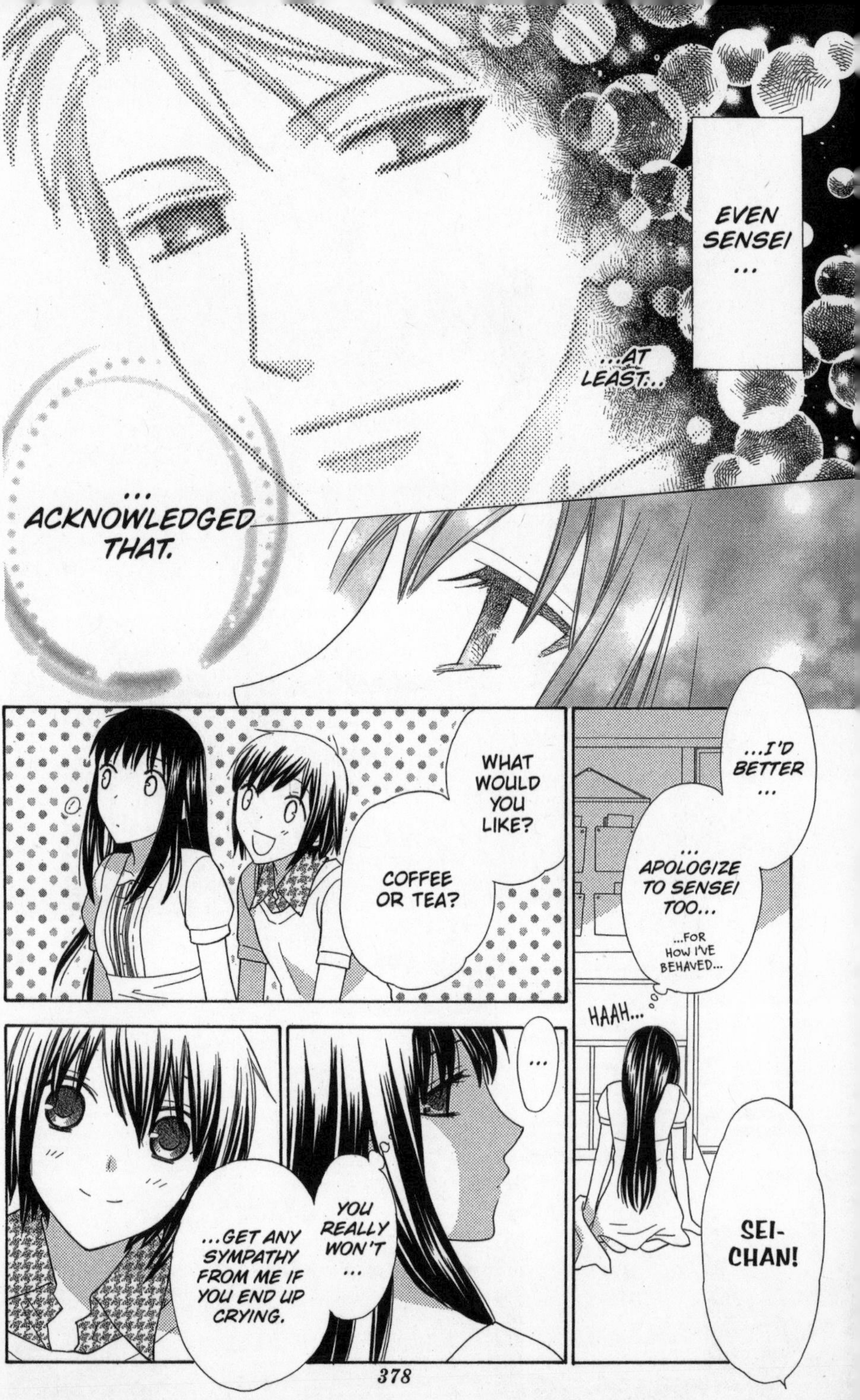
EVEN SENSEI ...
...AT LEAST...
... ACKNOWLEDGED THAT.
...I'D BETTER ...
... APOLOGIZE TO SENSEI TOO...
...FOR HOW I'VE BEHAVED...
HAAH...
SEI-CHAN!
WHAT WOULD YOU LIKE?
COFFEE OR TEA?
...
YOU REALLY WON'T ...
...GET ANY SYMPATHY FROM ME IF YOU END UP CRYING.

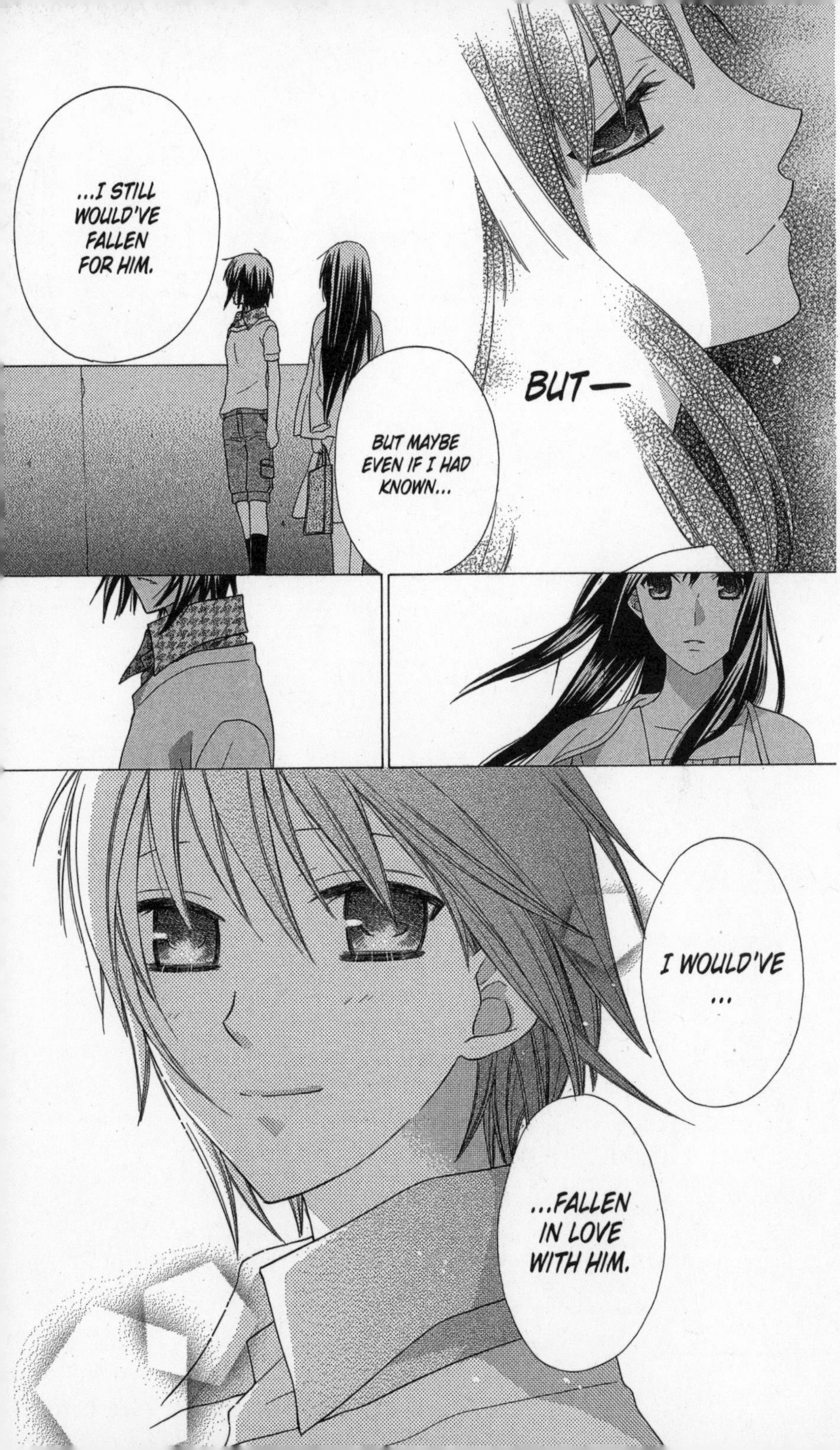
BUT—
BUT MAYBE EVEN IF I HAD KNOWN...
...I STILL WOULD'VE FALLEN FOR HIM.
I WOULD'VE ...
...FALLEN IN LOVE WITH HIM.

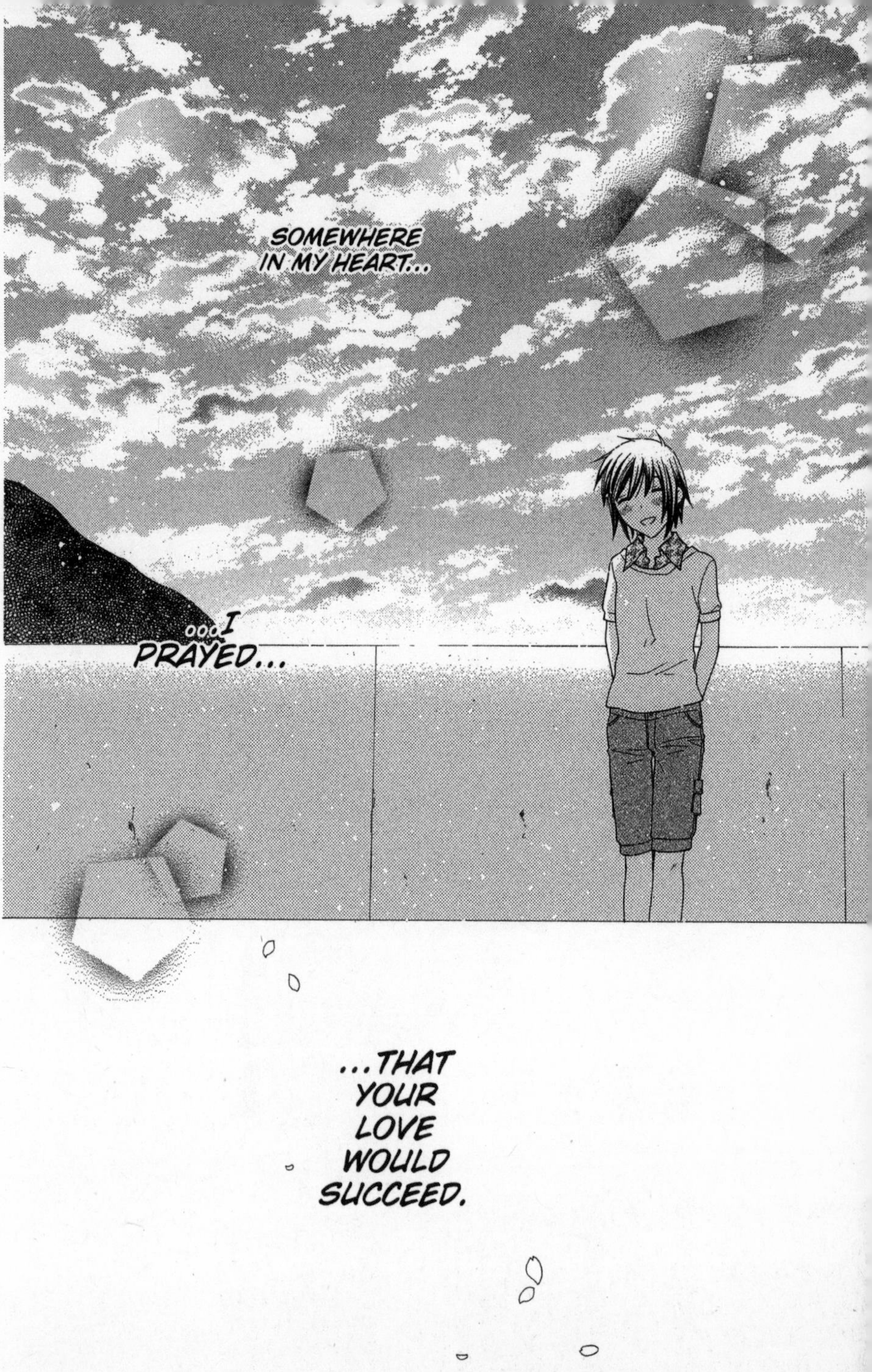
SOMEWHERE IN MY HEART...
...I PRAYED...
...THAT YOUR LOVE WOULD SUCCEED.

Twinkle Stars 3: The End

Feelings of Gratitude

Harada-sama Araki-sama
Mother My editor

Everyone who supports me
and reads this series

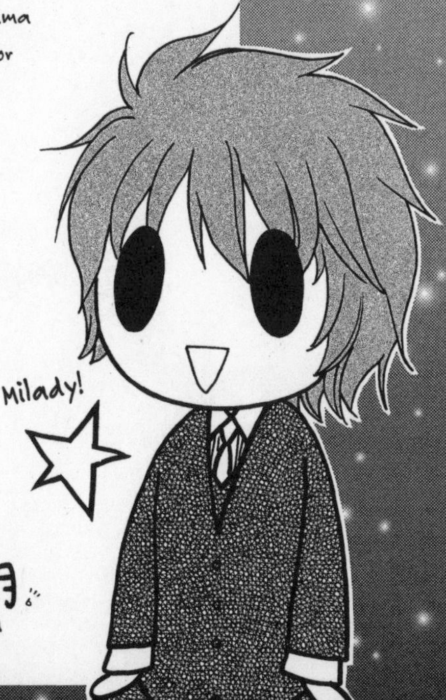
Milady!

高屋 奈月
Natsuki Takaya

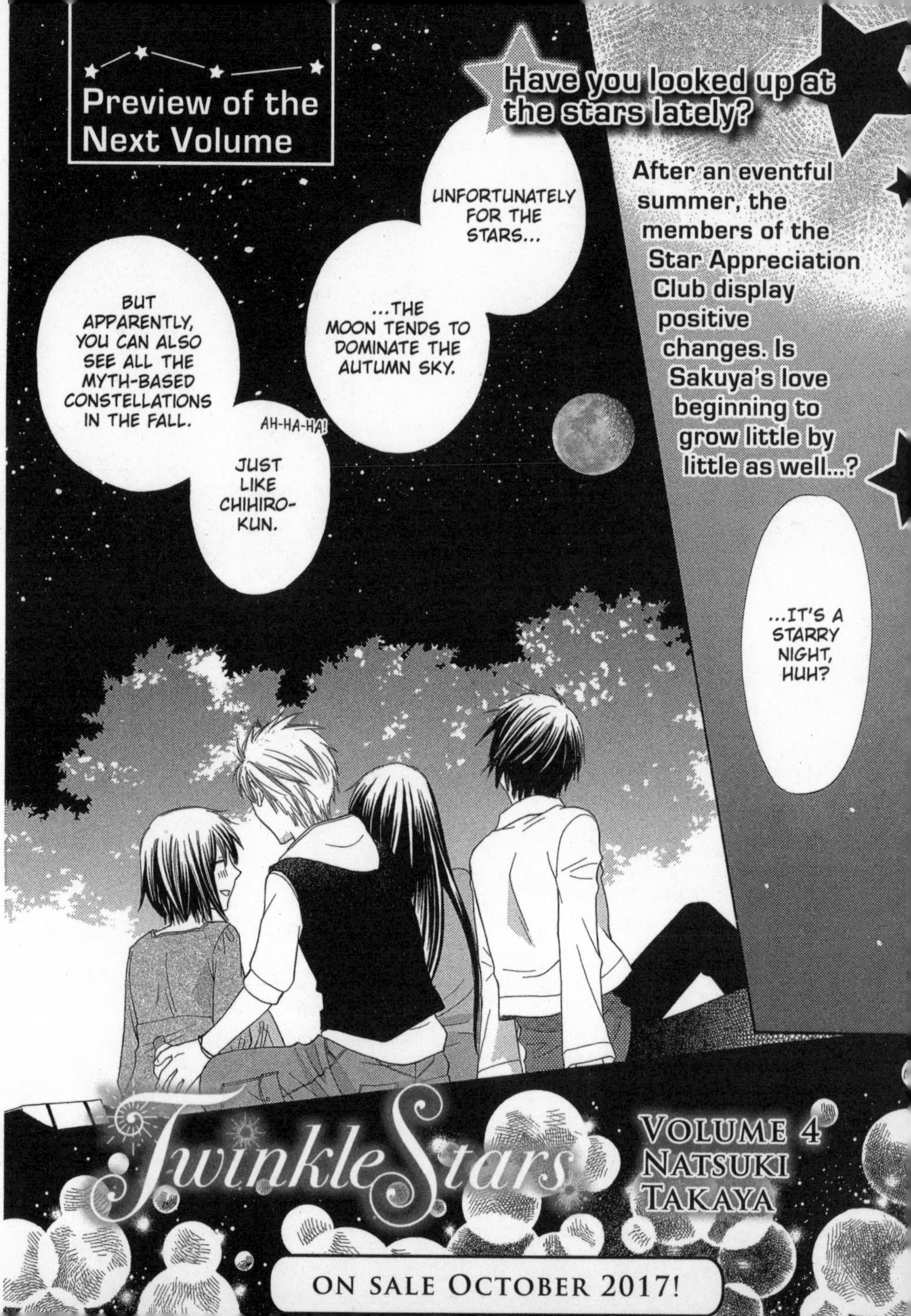
Preview of the Next Volume
Have you looked up at the stars lately?
After an eventful summer, the members of the Star Appreciation Club display positive changes. Is Sakuya's love beginning to grow little by little as well...?
...IT'S A STARRY NIGHT, HUH?
UNFORTUNATELY FOR THE STARS...
...THE MOON TENDS TO DOMINATE THE AUTUMN SKY.
BUT APPARENTLY, YOU CAN ALSO SEE ALL THE MYTH-BASED CONSTELLATIONS IN THE FALL.
AH-HA-HA!
JUST LIKE CHIHIRO-KUN.
Twinkle Stars
VOLUME 4
NATSUKI TAKAYA
ON SALE OCTOBER 2017!

TRANSLATION NOTES

COMMON HONORIFICS

no honorific: Indicates familiarity or closeness; if used without permission or reason, addressing someone in this manner would constitute an insult.

-san: The Japanese equivalent of Mr./Mrs./Miss. If a situation calls for politeness, this is the fail-safe honorific.

-sama: Conveys great respect; may also indicate that the social status of the speaker is lower than that of the addressee.

-kun: Used most often when referring to boys, this indicates affection or familiarity. Occasionally used by older men among their peers, but it may also be used by anyone referring to a person of lower standing.

-chan: An affectionate honorific indicating familiarity used mostly in reference to girls; also used in reference to cute persons or animals of either gender.

Names

As with the main character in *Fruits Basket*, many of the characters in *Twinkle Stars* have names that play around with gender. "Sakuya" and "Yuuri" are gender-neutral names, while "Kanade," "Chihiro," and "Shizuka" (all men) have typically feminine names. Saku's best friend, Hijiri Honjou, has the masculine nickname "Sei."

Page 20

Amezaiku: Traditional candy sculpture made from heat-softened sugar and starch taffy. Usually crafted into colorful animal shapes by the artisan's own hands and specialty tools.

Page 114

"You and Sakura are in the same boat.": Sakura often refers to herself in the third person, a common character trait that usually gives the sense that a character is somewhat childish and/or spoiled. Young Japanese children do often refer to themselves in this way, but it usually tapers off by middle school, as it is frowned upon (as being childish) by parents and teachers. In manga and anime, however, it's much more common and is typically used by cute, young women.

Page 131

"When I die...I want it to be under this cherry blossom tree.": When reading the original line in Japanese, it's not hard to guess where Sakura got her name from—the Japanese word for "cherry blossom tree."

Page 359

White kimono: Traditional garb worn by the bride in a Japanese wedding ceremony. In many cases, the bride then switches to a Western-style white wedding dress for the reception.

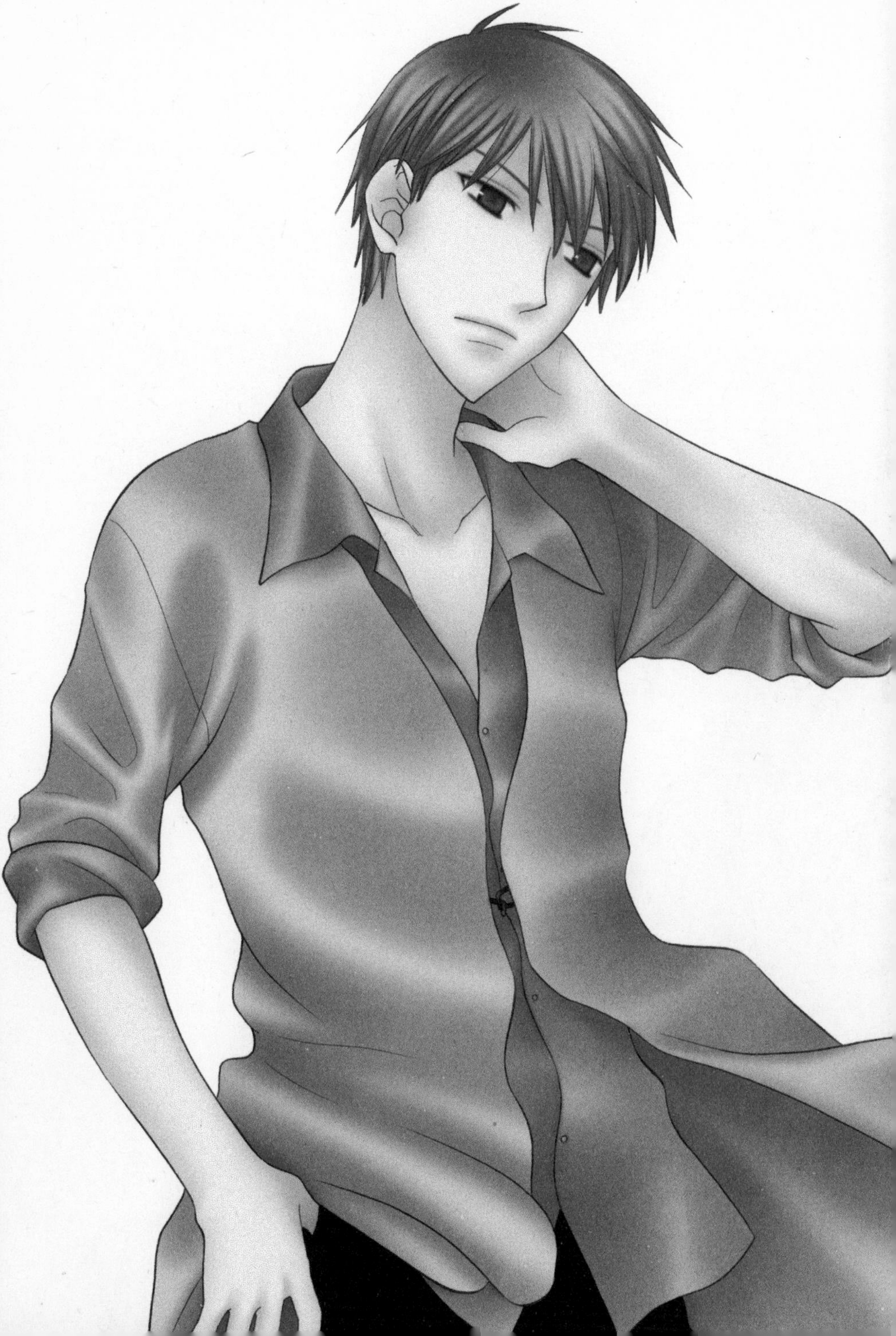

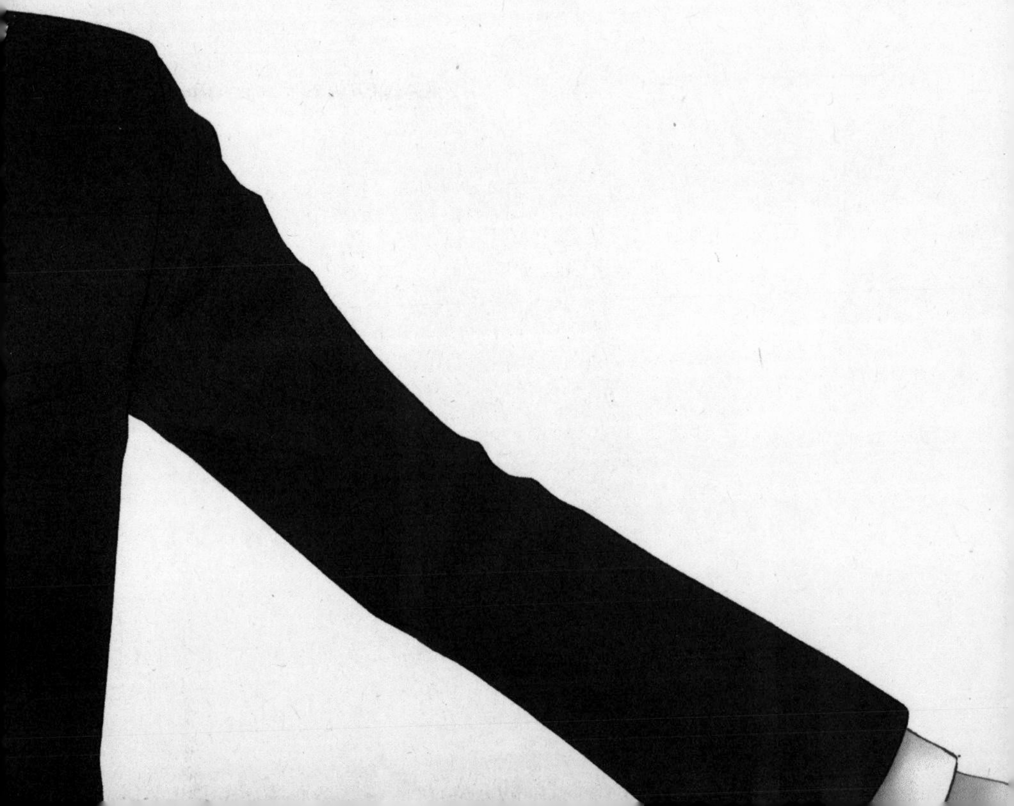

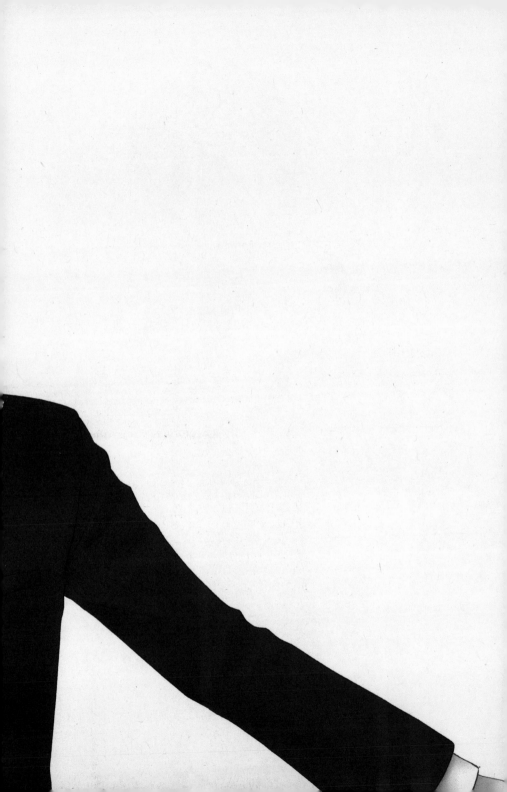

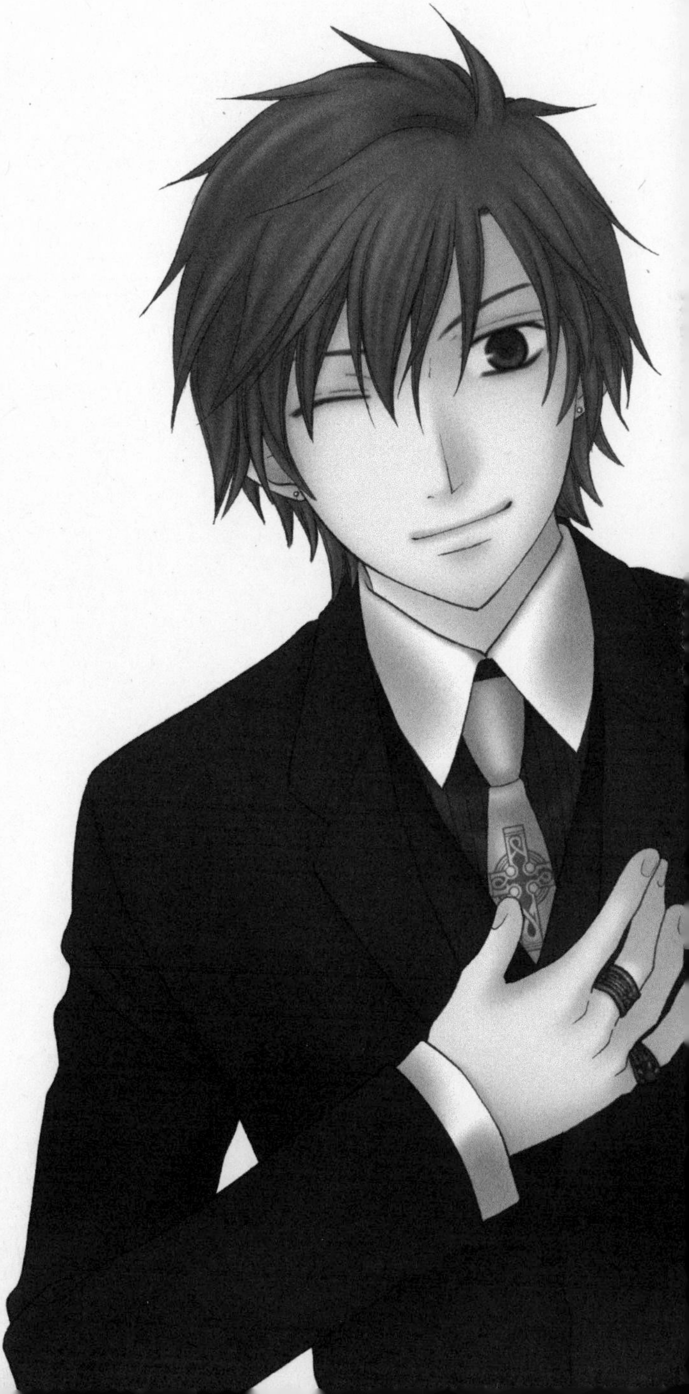

TwinkleStars

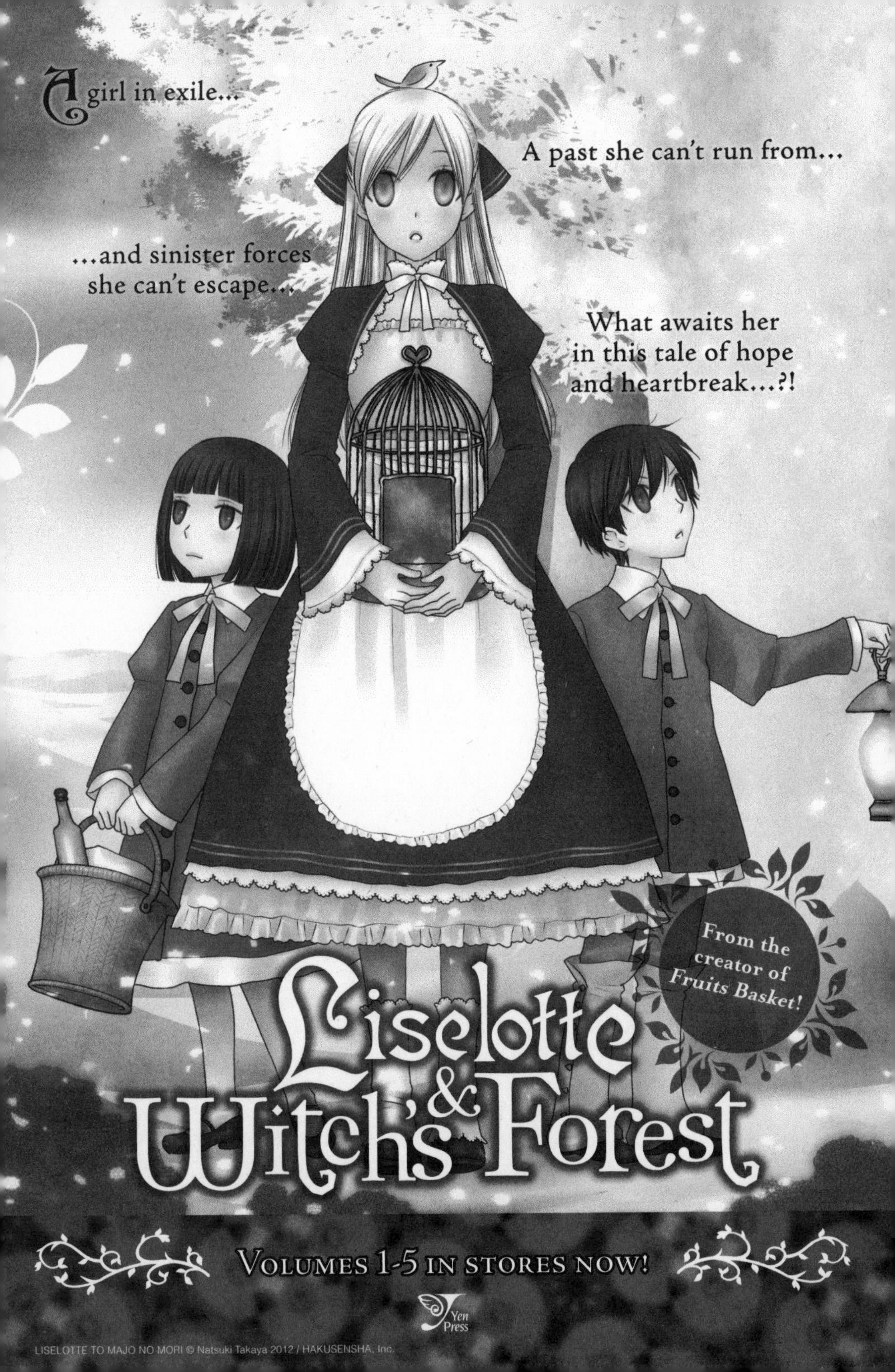
A girl in exile...
A past she can't run from...
...and sinister forces
she can't escape...
What awaits her
in this tale of hope
and heartbreak...?!
From the creator of Fruits Basket!
Liselotte & Witch's Forest
VOLUMES 1-5 IN STORES NOW!
Yen Press
LISELOTTE TO MAJO NO MORI © Natsuki Takaya 2012 / HAKUSENSHA, Inc.

Natsuki Takaya

Translation: Sheldon Drzka ★ Lettering: Lys Blakeslee, Katie Blakeslee

HOSHI WA UTAU, Vol 5, 6 by Natsuki Takaya
© Natsuki Takaya 2009
All rights reserved.
First published in Japan in 2009 by HAKUSENSHA, Inc., Tokyo.
English language translation rights in U.S.A., Canada and U.K. arranged with
HAKUSENSHA, Inc., Tokyo through Tuttle-Mori Agency, Inc., Tokyo.

English translation © 2017 by Yen Press, LLC

Yen Press
1290 Avenue of the Americas
New York, NY 10104

Visit us at yenpress.com
facebook.com/yenpress
twitter.com/yenpress
yenpress.tumblr.com
instagram.com/yenpress

First Yen Press Edition: July 2017

Yen Press is an imprint of Yen Press, LLC.
The Yen Press name and logo are trademarks of Yen Press, LLC.

Library of Congress Control Number: 2016946117

ISBNs: 978-0-316-36095-1 (paperback)
978-0-316-36099-9 (ebook)

10 9 8 7 6 5 4 3 2 1

BVG

Printed in the United States of America